Teaching Reader

C000083129

"A book of this kind is *long* overdue. . . . It is a *giant* contribution to the field. With its emphasis on a socioliterate approach to reading and literacy, it nicely captures the prevailing view of academic literacy instruction. Its extremely skillful and well-developed balancing act between theory and practice allows it to appeal to a wide variety of readers. Pre- and in-service teachers, in particular, will benefit immensely."

Alan Hirvela, The Ohio State University

"A compendium like this that addresses reading issues at a variety of levels and in a variety of ways is most welcome. . . . Congratulations on excellent work, a fabulous partnership, and on moving us all forward in our thinking about reading issues!"

Vaidehi Ramanathan, University of California, Davis

A comprehensive manual for pre- and in-service ESL and EFL educators, this frontline text balances insights from current reading theory and research with highly practical, field-tested strategies for teaching and assessing L2 reading in secondary and post-secondary contexts.

John S. Hedgcock is Professor of Applied Linguistics at the Monterey Institute of International Studies.

Dana R. Ferris is Associate Professor in the University Writing Program at the University of California, Davis.

Teaching Readers of English
Students, Texts, and Contexts

John S. Hedgcock
Monterey Institute of International Studies

Dana R. Ferris
University of California, Davis

Routledge
Taylor & Francis Group

NEW YORK AND LONDON

First published 2009
by Routledge
711 Third Avenue, New York, NY 10017

Simultaneously published in the UK
by Routledge
2 Park Square, Milton Park, Abingdon, Oxon, OX14 4RN

Routledge is an imprint of the Taylor & Francis Group, an informa business

Transferred to Digital Printing 2011

© 2009 Routledge, Taylor and Francis

Typeset in Minion by
Swales & Willis Ltd, Exeter, Devon

Library of Congress Cataloging in Publication Data
A catalog record has been requested for this book

British Library Cataloguing in Publication Data
A catalogue record for this book is available from the British Library

ISBN 10: 0–415–99964–2 (hbk)
ISBN 10: 0–8058–6347–8 (pbk)
ISBN 10: 0–203–88026–9 (ebk)

ISBN 13: 978–0–415–99964–9 (hbk)
ISBN 13: 978–0–8058–6347–5 (pbk)
ISBN 13: 978–0–203–88026–5 (ebk)

Brief Contents

Contents

Preface

This book presents approaches to the teaching of second language (L2) readers in the context of current theoretical perspectives on L2 literacy processes, practices, and readers. *Teaching Readers of English* is designed as a comprehensive teacher-preparation book, as well as a resource for in-service teachers and L2 literacy researchers. The volume focuses on preparing instructors who work with L2 and multilingual readers at the secondary, post-secondary, and adult levels. *Teaching Readers of English* likewise examines vocabulary development, both as a tool for facilitating effective reading and as a language-learning goal in itself. We have attempted to craft the book to appeal to several distinct audiences:

- Teacher educators and graduate students in TESOL preparation programs;
- In-service ESL and EFL instructors currently engaged in teaching reading and related literacy skills;
- Pre-service teachers of secondary English and their instructors;
- In-service teachers of secondary English;
- Researchers involved in describing L2 literacy and investigating L2 reading pedagogy.

Teaching Readers of English addresses the needs of the first four groups by providing overviews of research related to L2 reading, as well as numerous opportunities to reflect on, develop, and practice the teaching skills needed for effective ESL and EFL literacy instruction. We hope that researchers in the field will also benefit from our syntheses and analyses of the literature on various topics in L2 literacy education. Preview and post-reading review questions in each chapter are designed to stimulate readers' thinking about the material presented. Application Activities at the end of each chapter provide hands–on practice for pre- and in-service teachers, as well as resources for teacher educators. Because of this book's dual emphasis on theory and practice in L2 literacy instruction, it would serve as an appropriate primary or supplementary text in courses focusing on L2 reading theory, as well as practical courses that address literacy instruction.

As a discipline, L2 reading is still viewed by some as an emergent field. Consequently, few resources have been produced to help pre- and in-service L2 educators to become experts in a discipline that is becoming recognized as a profession in its own right. Therefore, one of our primary goals in *Teaching Readers of English* is to furnish readers with a synthesis of theory and practice in a rapidly evolving community of scholars and professionals. We have consistently and intentionally focused on providing apprentice teachers with practice activities, such as reader background surveys, text analyses, and instructional planning tasks that can be used to develop the complex skills entailed in teaching L2 reading. Although all topics of discussion are firmly grounded in reviews of relevant research, a feature that we feel distinguishes this volume from others is its array of hands-on, practical examples, materials, and tasks. By synthesizing theory and research in accessible terms, we have endeavored to craft chapter content and exercises in ways that enable readers to appreciate the relevance of the field's knowledge base to their current and future classroom settings and student readers.

Overview of the Book

We have sequenced the book's chapters to move from general themes to specific pedagogical concerns. Situated in a broad literacy framework, Chapter 1 presents an overview of reading theory and pedagogical models that have influenced and shaped approaches to L2 literacy instruction. It also presents a comparative discussion of writing systems, culminating with a discussion of the dynamic interactions of skills and strategies that comprise L2 reading. Most importantly, Chapter 1 introduces an argument that we pursue throughout the volume; that is, whereas certain literacy processes transcend linguistic and cultural boundaries, unique characteristics and challenges set L2 reading apart from L1 reading. We embrace the view that teaching learners to read successfully in an L2 such as English requires thought, analysis, and attention.

Chapters 2 and 3 focus respectively on the two most important elements of the interactive process known as reading: readers and texts. In Chapter 2, we discuss and define more precisely what characterizes an L2 reader, acknowledging the growing complexity of the term and the diversity of the student audience. Chapter 2 examines numerous background variables that influence literacy development, including the unique characteristics of individual readers. Chapter 3 provides a definition and in-depth analysis of the structural properties of text, with a specific focus on challenges faced by readers in their encounters with (L1 and) L2 texts and with English texts in particular. Chapter 3 concludes with a practical discussion of the linguistic components of texts, suggesting that teachers in some contexts may wish to present direct lessons targeting these features. In all of these chapters, we aim to present a perspective on L2 reading instruction that is firmly grounded in the precept that literacies are socially constructed.

Based on the socioliterate premises outlined especially in Chapters 1 and 2, Chapter 4 addresses fundamental concerns related to the teaching of any L2 literacy course: needs assessment, syllabus design, materials selection, and lesson planning. Chapter 5 (intensive reading) and Chapter 6 (extensive reading) present detailed examinations of the two major curricular approaches to teaching L2 reading. The remaining chapters then focus on specific topics of persistent interest to L2 literacy educators: the use of literature in L2 reading instruction (Chapter 7), vocabulary learning and teaching (Chapter 8), and approaches to reading assessment (Chapter 9).

Although the organization of individual chapters varies according to topic, all contain the following components:

- *Questions for Reflection.* These pre-reading questions invite readers to consider their prior experiences as students and readers and to anticipate how these insights might inform their professional beliefs and teaching practices;
- *Further Reading and Resources.* A concise list at the end of each chapter provides a quick overview of the print and online sources cited, as well as other outlets of relevant information;
- *Figures and Tables.* These textual illustrations provide sample authentic activities, lesson plans, sample texts, and so on, which teachers can use and adapt in their own instructional practice;
- *Reflection and Review.* These follow-up questions ask readers to examine and evaluate the theoretical information and practical suggestions introduced in the main text;
- *Application Activities.* Application Activities follow each Reflection and Review section, presenting a range of hands-on practical exercises. Tasks include collecting data from novice readers, text analysis, evaluating real-world reading materials, developing lesson plans, designing classroom activities, and executing and evaluating classroom tasks and assessments. Several chapters also include *Appendices* that contain sample texts and instructional materials.

As readers, writers, researchers, teachers, and teacher educators, we find the field of L2 literacy development (which entails both reading and writing) to offer many challenges and rewards. It was our classroom experience working with multilingual readers and with L2 teachers that initially ignited our interest in compiling a book that would help teachers develop both professional knowledge and confidence as teachers of reading. We hope that this book will provide its readers with accurate information, meaningful insights, and practical ideas for classroom teaching. It is also our hope that *Teaching Readers of English* will convey our enthusiasm and passion for this rapidly evolving and engaging field of intellectual inquiry and professional practice.

John's Acknowledgments

Thanks are due to the Monterey Institute for my Fall semester 2007 sabbatical leave, which I dedicated to exploring the L2 reading literature anew and to writing early draft material. I owe special thanks to the M.A. students in my Spring 2008 ED 562 (Teaching Reading) course, who diligently read the draft version of the book, responded thoughtfully and substantially to the material, and reminded me how enjoyable it can be to look at teaching in novel ways. Their hard work, enthusiasm for reading, and passion for teaching were infectious and energizing. As always, I am also indebted to the Library staff at the Monterey Institute, who not only supply me continually with volumes of books and articles, but who also cheerfully grant me more special privileges than I deserve.

Like Dana, I would like to credit an early source of inspiration for me, Professor Stephen Krashen, whose teaching and research drew me to literacy studies when I was a graduate student. Finally, I offer my profound thanks to Simon Hsu for his perpetual reassurance, moral support, and good cheer through the ups and downs of the writing process.

Dana's Acknowledgments

I am grateful to my graduate students and former colleagues at California State University, Sacramento who have helped me to develop and pilot materials used in this book. In particular, I would like to thank the CSUS M.A. students in my Spring 2008 English 215A (ESL Reading/Vocabulary) course, who patiently worked with the draft version of this book, responded enthusiastically, and gave great suggestions. As always, I am thankful for the opportunity to have my thinking and practice informed and challenged by these individuals. I am also grateful for the sabbatical leave I received from my former institution, CSUS, for the Spring 2007 semester, which allowed me extended time for this project.

Working on this book has also made me again appreciative of the contributions of two of my graduate school professors—Stephen Krashen and the late David Eskey of the University of Southern California—not only to the field of L2 reading research but also to the formation of my own knowledge base and philosophies on the subject. Both were excellent teachers and mentors, and I am indebted to them for their work, their example, and the ways they encouraged me as a student.

On a personal level, I would like to extend my love and gratitude to my husband, Randy Ferris, my daughters, Laura and Melissa Ferris, and my faithful yellow Labrador retriever, Winnie the Pooch, who was a great companion and thoughtful sounding board during my sabbatical!

Joint Acknowledgments

Our work on this project would have been much less rewarding and enjoyable without the gentle guidance and persistent encouragement of our outstanding editor, Naomi Silverman. Her expertise and unfailingly insightful advice assisted us in innumerable ways as our ideas evolved and as the collaborative writing process unfolded. Despite her sometimes crushing workload, Naomi managed to help us out whenever we needed her input. We offer our profound thanks for her confidence in us and for her many contributions to this book's evolution. In addition, we deeply appreciate the incisive and exceptionally useful feedback on earlier versions provided by Barbara Birch, Alan Hirvela, and Vaidehi Ramanathan. Finally, we are grateful for the diligent work of Meeta Pendharkar and Alfred Symons at Routledge, and of Richard Willis, who saw the project through its final stages of development.

John Hedgcock
Dana Ferris

Credits

- Figure 1.3 is derived and adapted from a drawing in Bernhardt (1991b), *Reading development in a second language: Theoretical, empirical, and classroom perspectives* (p. 15), originally published by Ablex.
- Figure 1.4 is adapted from Birch (2007), *English L2 reading: Getting to the bottom* (2nd ed., p. 3). Figure 4.4 is adapted from Ferris and Hedgcock (2005), *Teaching ESL composition: Purpose, process, and practice* (2nd ed., p. 100). Figures 1.4 and 4.4 are used with permission from Taylor and Francis.
- Figure 1.6 originally appeared in Bernhardt (2005), "Progress and procrastination in second language reading" (*Annual Review of Applied Linguistics, 25*, pp. 133–150). Figure 8.1 was adapted from a similar figure in Nation (2001), *Learning vocabulary in another language*. We thank Cambridge University Press for its policy concerning reproduction and adaptation of these resources.
- The "Second Chances—If Only We Could Start Again" selection by Brahm in Appendix 3.1 originally appeared in the *Sacramento Bee* in 2001; the text appears here with permission.
- Sarton's (1974) essay, "The Rewards of Living a Solitary Life" (Appendix 5.1), first appeared in the *New York Times*, as did the Greenhouse (2003) essay, "Going for the look—but risking discrimination" (Appendix 5.2); both selections are used with permission.
- Figure 9.2 is based on and adapted from Urquhart and Weir (1998), *Reading in a second language: Process, product, and practice* (Addison Wesley Longman).

- Figure 9.11 is a slightly altered rubric from Groeber (2007), *Designing and using rubrics for reading and language arts, K-6* (p. 23). This figure appears with permission from Corwin Press.

Chapter 1
Fundamentals of L1 and L2 Literacy
Reading and Learning to Read

Questions for Reflection

- Do you have any recollection of learning to read at home or at school in your primary language or in a second/foreign language? If so, what were those processes like? How were they similar or different across languages?
- How is text-based communication similar to and distinct from speech-based communication? How is *learning* to read and write distinct from acquiring speech and listening skills? Why?
- What are some of the principal challenges that you associate with reading certain kinds of text? What are the main obstacles that novice readers face in *learning* to read?
- Why do you think it is important for novice ESL and EFL teachers to become acquainted with the principles and practices of *reading* instruction (in contrast to other skills, such as speaking, listening, writing, or grammar)?

The high premium that many people place on literacy skills, including those necessary for performing well in school and in the workplace, emerges largely from the degree to which educated adults depend on text-based and digital resources for learning and communication. When educated people think about how and why literacy is important, few question the fundamental notion that reading is a crucial building block, if not the chief cornerstone, of success at school, at work, and in society (Feiler, 2007; Gee, 2008; McCarty, 2005). In primary education around the globe, one of the first things children do at school is participate in literacy lessons and "learn to read." Of course, "the developmental transformations that mark the way to reading expertise begin in infancy, not in school" (Wolf, 2007, p. 223).

In many parts of the world, primary-level teachers receive specialized education and training in teaching children to read, sometimes in two or more languages. As children advance toward adolescence, they may undergo sustained literacy instruction designed to enhance their reading comprehension, fluency, and efficiency. Formal "reading" courses taper off as children progress toward and beyond secondary school—except, perhaps, for foreign or second language instruction. Many language teachers assume that teaching and learning a foreign or second language (L2)[1] depends on reading skills. In fact, they may devote considerable time and effort to promoting L2 reading skills among their students, often under the assumption that learners already have a developed system of literate knowledge and skill in their primary language(s) (L1s).

In contrast, teachers in disciplines such as science and mathematics, social studies, and the arts may need to assume that their pupils or students already know "how to read." Such educators may not provide much, if any, explicit instruction in the mechanics of processing texts. Similarly, many teachers of writing at both the secondary and tertiary levels often assume that students know "how to read" (or at least that students have been *taught* to read). Paradoxically, while formal education, professional activities, and use of the Web depend on reading efficacy, many educators find themselves under-equipped to help their students develop their reading skills when students need instructional intervention. In other words, we may not recognize the complexity of reading because, as proficient readers, we often take reading ability for granted, assuming that reading processes are automatic.

It is easy to overlook the complexity of reading processes, as many of us do not have to think much about how we read. After all, you are able to read and understand the words on this page because you have somehow "learned to read" English and have successfully automatized your ability to decode alphabetic symbols and interpret meaning from text. Precisely how you achieved this level of skill, however, is still not fully understood (Smith, 2004; Wolf, 2007). Our experiences as students, language teachers, and teacher educators have led us to a profound appreciation of the complexity of the reading process and for the fact that, for many novice readers—whether working in L1 or L2—reading processes are far from automatic. We have also come to recognize the sometimes overwhelming challenges of *teaching reading* to language learners. Reading, learning to read, and teaching reading are neither easy nor effortless.

In this chapter, we consider fundamental aspects of the reading process that make it a complex social and cognitive operation involving readers, writers, texts, contexts, and purposes. We will introduce contemporary principles of literacy and literacy development to familiarize readers with definitions of key constructs in the interrelated fields of literacy studies, L1 and L2 reading research, and pedagogy. Our aim is to help readers develop a working knowledge of key issues, insights, and controversies in L2 literacy education by presenting an overview of key theories, models, and metaphors. Our chief focus is on the literacy development of multilingual learners in secondary and postsecondary educational settings.[2] Naturally, we refer to research on L1 literacy development among children, which has richly informed agendas for L2 literacy research and instruction. In the first part of this chapter, we consider contemporary views of literacy as a socio-psychological construct that frames reading development and processes among L1 and L2 learners. By comparing research and theory associated with prevailing processing metaphors, we explore instructional issues of particular relevance to the teaching of L2 reading. These issues include the uniqueness of L2 reading processes, interactions between L1 and L2 literacy, and the importance of strategies-based instruction in promoting L2 literacy.

The Nature of Literacy and Literacies

Before examining the mechanics of reading, we must situate reading processes and instruction with respect to the sociocultural and educational contexts where reading skills are valued. As Urquhart and Weir (1998) noted, "the teacher of reading is in the business of attempting to improve literacy" (p. 1). Although reading skill is central to any definition of literacy, L2 educators should understand that literacy entails not only cognitive abilities (Bernhardt, 1991a, 1991b), but also knowledge of sociocultural structures and ideologies (Cope & Kalantzis, 2000; Cummins, Brown, & Sayers, 2007; Gee, 1991, 2003; Goldenberg, Rueda, & August, 2006; Lewis, Enciso, & Moje, 2007; Pérez, 2004b, 2004d; Robinson, McKenna, & Wedman, 2007). Literacy, after all, is "a part of the highest human impulse to think and rethink experience in place" (Brandt, 1990, p. 1).

We can refer to *reading* and *writing* as literate processes, and we frequently use the term *literacy* as a countable noun when describing skills, knowledge, practices, and beliefs allied with specific disciplines and discourse communities (e.g., *academic literacy, workplace literacy, computer literacy, financial literacy,* and so forth). Across disciplines, wrote Barton (2007), "the term **literacy** has become a code word for more complex views of what is involved in reading and writing" (p. 5). A literate person can therefore become "competent and knowledgeable in specialized areas" (Barton, 2007, p. 19). Literacies are multiple, overlapping, and diverse: "People have different literacies which they make use of, associate with different domains of life. These differences are increased across different cultures or historical periods" (Barton, 2007, p. 37). Eagleton and Dobler (2007), for example, insisted that "current definitions of literacy must include digital texts such as those found on the Web" (p. 28).

Contemporary conceptions of literacy do not characterize literacy merely as a cluster of isolated processing skills. Scribner and Cole (1981) framed literacy as a system of socially organized *literacy practices*. This view led to an "emerging theory of literacy-as-social-practice" (Reder & Davila, 2005, p. 172), now widely known as the New Literacy Studies (NLS) (Barton & Hamilton, 1998; Street, 1984, 1995). As a socioculturally organized system, literacy consists of much more than an individual's ability to work with print-based media. Reading and writing may be the most visible or tangible processes in literacy development, but literacy practices go beyond reading and writing alone (Eagleton & Dobler, 2007; Kern, 2000; Purcell-Gates, 2007). Literacy practices refer to "common patterns in using reading and writing in a particular situation. People bring their cultural knowledge to an activity" (Barton, 2007, p. 36).

In an NLS view, literacy is more than a skill or ability that people "acquire"—it is something that people *do* in the course of everyday life. We can refer to what people do with their knowledge of literate practices as *literacy events*. Heath (1982) defined a *literacy event* as "any occasion in which a piece of writing is integral to the nature of the participants' interactions and their interpretative processes" (p. 93). Barton's (2007) synthesis of the complementary relationship between *literacy practices* and *literacy events* illustrates the inherently social nature of literacy:

> Together events and practices are the two basic units of analysis of the social activity of literacy. Literate events are the particular activities where literacy has a role; they may be regular repeated activities. Literacy practices are the general cultural ways of utilizing literacy which people draw upon in a literacy event. [I]n the example . . . of a man discussing the contents of the local paper with a friend, the two of them sitting in the living room planning a letter to the newspaper is a literacy event. In deciding who does what, where and when it is done, along with the associated ways of talking and the ways of writing, the two participants make use of their literacy practices. (p. 37)

Literacy is further understood in terms of the individual's relationship to literate communities and institutions (e.g., fellow readers and writers, teachers, employers, school, online networks, and so on). Scholars such as Freire (1968), Gee (1988, 1996), and Street (1984) have proposed that literacy can privilege some people while excluding others, as societies and discourse communities use literacy to enforce social controls and maintain hierarchies. The NLS approach assumes (1) that *context* is fundamental to any understanding of literacy and its development (Barton, 2007; Barton & Tusting, 2005; Collins & Blot, 2003) and (2) that literate and oral practices overlap and interact (Finnegan, 1988; Goody, 1987; Olson & Torrance, 1991; Stubbs, 1980; Tarone & Bigelow, 2005).

Because it is grounded in social context, NLS research offers implications for how we might view reading processes, reading development, and reading pedagogy. As already suggested, one insight that departs from conventional notions is that literacy consists of much more than reading and writing (Czerniewska, 1992; Kern, 2000; Purcell-Gates, 2007; Purcell-Gates, Jacobson, & Degener, 2008; Smith, 2004, 2007). Literacy practices and literacy events are not limited to libraries and schools. "Literacy development is a process that begins early in childhood, long before children attend school, and involves many different skills and experiences" (Lesaux, Koda, Siegel, & Shanahan, 2006a, p. 77). Although L2 reading teachers may be confined to the classroom in their encounters with learners, literacy education should not be limited to promoting school-based literacies alone (Freire & Macedo, 1987; Gee, 2000; Kalantzis & Cope, 2000). After all, literacy is "rooted in people's intimate everyday experiences with text" (Reder & Davila, 2005, p. 173). These daily experiences can range from the most mundane (e.g., scribbling a grocery list, dashing off a quick e-mail message, checking MapQuest for driving directions) to those with high-stakes consequences (e.g., composing a college admissions essay or crafting a letter of resignation).

Classrooms, of course, are unquestionably key sites for cultivating school and non-school literacies (Pérez, 2004a). Students must develop literate skills that will enable them to succeed in school, although some of these skills may never be part of the curriculum (Alvermann, Hinchman, Moore, Phelps, & Waff, 2006; Bloome, Carter, Christina, Otto, & Shuart-Faris, 2005; Gee, 1996, 2005; Kutz, 1997; Pérez, 2004c). In other words, surviving and thriving in school require much more than developing literacy in the traditional sense: Learners must also develop new behaviors and attitudes while cultivating social alliances. Novice readers must learn "a set of complex role relationships, general cognitive techniques, ways of approaching problems, different genres of talk and interaction, and an intricate set of values concerned with communication, interaction, and society as a whole" (Wertsch, 1985, pp. 35–36).

Literate practices and literacy events of all sorts involve interaction and social activity around written texts, which are the products of a kind of technology—writing itself (Bazerman, 2007; Grabe & Kaplan, 1996; Olson, 1994; Olson & Cole, 2006; Ong, 1982; Wolf, 2007).[3] As such, writing is a value-laden cultural form, "a social product whose shape and influence depend upon prior political and ideological factors" (Gee, 1996, p. 58). Because "the immediate social context determines the use and nature of texts" (Reder & Davila, 2005, p. 175), texts and their uses are inherently tied to power at some level: "[L]iteracy can be seen as doing the work of discourse and power/knowledge" (Morgan & Ramanathan, 2005, p. 151). In this view, literacy and literacy development are never neutral, as literate activity involves learners, teachers, and many others (Gee, 2002). Moreover, "all literacy events carry ideological meanings" (Reder & Davila, 2005, p. 178), although we may not be aware of these meanings in the learning or teaching process. Nonetheless, L2 literacy educators can benefit from cultivating a critical awareness of how "literacy practices provide the textual means by which dominant values and identities (e.g., avid consumers, obedient workers, patriotic citizens) are normalized and, at times, resisted" (Morgan & Ramanathan, 2005, pp. 152–153).[4]

Such critical perspectives, informed by NLS research and theory, are valuable for reading teachers: They remind us that literacy practices and literacy events pervade culture and everyday life. Literacy emerges as a kind of knowledge and skill base, as well as a socialization process (John-Steiner & Meehan, 2000). Describing early literacy development, Smith (1988) argued that children become successful readers "only if they are admitted into a community of written language users," which he called the "literacy club" (p. 2). Before they can read or write a single word, children become members of a *literacy club* similar to the community of oral language users into which infants are inducted at birth. "The procedures are the same, and the benefits are the same—admission to the club rapidly results in becoming like established members in spoken language, in literacy, and in many other ways as well" (Smith, 1988, p. 2).

Unique conditions affect adolescents and adults acquiring L2 literacy, yet the principle that literacy is socially embedded unquestionably applies to developing literacy in an additional language. Kern (2000) defined L2 literacy as "the use of socially-, historically-, and culturally-situated practices of creating and interpreting meaning through texts" (p. 16). Being literate in another language requires a critical knowledge of how textual conventions and contexts of use shape one another. And because literacy is purpose-sensitive, it is dynamic "across and within discourse communities and cultures. It draws on a wide range of cognitive abilities, on knowledge of written and spoken language, on knowledge of genres, and on cultural knowledge" (Kern, 2000, p. 16).

These dynamic aspects of literacy must include *digital literacy* (sometimes called *cyberliteracy* or *electronic literacy*), which we associate with "technology-mediated textual, communicative, and informational practices" (Ingraham, Levy, McKenna, & Roberts, 2007, p. 162). Literacy and reading in the 21st century must be characterized in terms of "an ecology that includes broad-based access to many different media" (Mackey, 2007, p. 13). These media include television and film, as well as digital audio and video files that can be stored and retrieved at will on a computer or other device in a range of formats (Eagleton & Dobler, 2007; Gee, 2003; Hawisher, 2004; Kapitzke & Bruce, 2006; Olson & Cole, 2006). Laptop computers, MP3 players, iPods, handheld devices, and mobile telephones make print and non-print sources available almost anywhere. The social milieu in much of the world is saturated with digital media. In fact, "very few Western young people come to print texts without a vast background of exposure to texts in many other media" (Mackey, 2007, p. 13). We must expect L1 and L2 students in many settings to know how to navigate websites and electronic texts, view artwork and photographs, listen to audio recordings, and watch live action, video, and animations, all with impressive facility (McKenna, Labbo, Kieffer, & Reinking, 2006; McKenna, Labbo, Reinking, & Zucker, 2008; Thorne & Black, 2007; Valmont, 2002).

Moore (2001) estimated that more than 80% of the data available in the world is "born digital, not on paper, fiche, charts, films, or maps" (p. 28). That proportion has unquestionably risen above 80%, and the availability of computers in school settings has also increased. Parsad and Jones (2005) reported that, as of 2003, nearly 100% of U.S. schools had Internet access, 93% of classrooms were wired, and the mean ratio of learners to wired computers was about 4.4 to 1. Access to wired computers in schools with high minority enrollments and in economically disadvantaged neighborhoods unfortunately drops below these averages (DeBell & Chapman, 2003; Parsad & Jones, 2005; Wells & Lewis, 2005); only about 16% of the world's population currently use the Internet (de Argaez, 2006). Nonetheless, as a consequence of increasingly widespread Internet access and the proliferation of laptop and desktop computers with CD-ROM and DVD capabilities, many of today's students "can instantaneously access more information delivered in multiple formats than at any other time in the history of education" (Valmont, 2002, p. 92). For this growing learner population, "literacy in a polysymbolic environment" includes expertise in decoding and encoding print-based media, as well as "interpreting and constructing in visual and other symbolic worlds" (Valmont, 2002, p. 92). More specifically, digital literacy entails not only producing written and oral messages, but also generating and interpreting sounds, images, graphics, videos, animations, and movements (Cummins et al., 2007; Eagleton & Dobler, 2007).

In the remainder of this chapter, we explore L1 and L2 reading and reading development from a sociocognitive perspective. We believe that L2 reading teachers can best serve their students by viewing the learning and teaching of reading as much more than skill-oriented practice (Lee & Smagorinsky, 2000; Meyer & Manning, 2007). We must engage students "in real literacy events," which Kern (2000) explicitly distinguished from "just rehearsing reading and writing skills." To develop L2 literacy, students must "learn not only about vocabulary and grammar but also about discourse and the processes by which it is created" (p. 17). To synthesize salient insights from research and theory in NLS and related fields, we propose the following global principles, which we can apply to our work as literacy educators:

- Literacy is a cognitive and a social activity, which we can describe in terms of *literacy practices*, which are played out during *literacy events*.
- Literacies are multiple and associated with different participants, purposes, social relations, settings, institutions, and "domains of life" that support literate knowledge (Barton, 2007, p. 37).
- Literacy events reference socially constructed symbol systems that facilitate communication, create meaning, and represent the world. These systems require users to understand, adopt, and even reshape conventions (genres, discourse structure, grammar, vocabulary, spelling).
- As symbolic systems that draw on writing and speech, literacies enable us to represent and cognize about ourselves, others, and our world (Kern, 2000).

- Literacy requires problem-solving. Reading and writing "involve figuring out relationships" among words, larger units of meaning, and "between texts and real or imagined worlds" (Kern, 2000, p. 17).
- Literacy entails knowledge of language and the ability to use it, as well as cultural understanding, belief systems, attitudes, ideals, and values that "guide our actions" in literate communities (Barton, 2007, p. 45).
- Literacy events shape us and our literacy practices as we engage in literacy events over our lifetimes. "Literacy has a history," which defines individuals as well as literate communities (Barton, 2007, p. 47).
- Literacy in the industrialized world "means gaining competent control of representational forms in a variety of media and learning how those forms best combine in a variety of genres and discourse" (Warschauer, 1999, p. 177).

Working with Writing Systems

As a defining function of literacy, reading is a chief focus of this chapter. Before reviewing models of L1 and L2 reading, we will consider factors that set reading apart from other skill areas. First, however, we would like to stress that language proficiency and literacy should be viewed as interdependent. In outlining their model of how children develop language skills, language awareness, and literacy, Ravid and Tolchinsky (2002) asserted that "the reciprocal character of speech and writing in a literate community makes [language and literacy] a synergistic system where certain features (e.g., basic syntax) originate in the spoken input" (p. 430). Meanwhile, features such as complex syntax and specialized vocabulary "originate in the written input. Together . . . they form a 'virtual loop' where speech and writing constantly feed and modify each other" (p. 430). Because written language—whether in print or hypertext form—exhibits properties that are distinct from speech (Biber, 1988, 1995; Wolf, 2007) and because texts may predetermine the range of meanings that they express, "spoken language and written language can rarely be the same" (Smith, 2004, p. 42).

As a tool that "increases human control of communication and knowledge," writing "uses a written symbol to represent a unit of language and not an object, event, or emotion directly" (Birch, 2007, p. 15). Writing practices and conventions are always deeply "socially contextualized," unlike oral language, which entails a comparably "universal set of cognitive skills" (Grabe & Kaplan, 1996, p. 17). Whereas oral language emerges among virtually all human populations, scripts and writing systems are always (and only) transmitted by and within certain cultures—but not by or within *all* cultures. Learning and using a writing system, though reliant on linguistic competence, thus requires specialized knowledge and skills that may not be as "natural" as acquiring speech (Bialystok, 2001; Lee, 2000; Taylor & Olson, 1995; Wolf, 2007).[5] This special expertise entails using graphical elements (written symbols) to mediate thought and language (itself a symbolic system). Three elements distinguish written language: "script, sound, and meaning" (Hoosain, 1995, p. 131). The ability to understand or create a written text may allow people to *re-present* or recreate a spoken message (in the case of phoneme- and syllable-based writing systems). Alternatively, knowing a writing system may enable people to re-present or recreate a message with little or no reference to sounds (in the case of logographic writing systems). Figure 1.1 presents a very partial comparative list of writing system categories used by speakers, readers, and writers of selected modern languages.

Although a careful study of the world's writing systems is not practical here, it is useful for L2 reading teachers to recognize the diverse properties exhibited by writing systems. Scripts derive from a range of linguistic and non-linguistic units, such as meaning, syllables, phonemes (sounds), phonemic and phonetic features (e.g., voicing, tone), and combinations thereof. L2 students may know a writing system that differs significantly from that of the target language, though teachers should not assume that knowing a different writing system necessarily inhibits L2 reading development (Akamatsu, 2003; Cook & Bassetti, 2005; Dressler & Kamil, 2006; Koda, 1993, 1995). At the same time, they should not presuppose that mastery of an L1 writing system is necessarily transferable to a developing L2 writing system (Bialystok, 2001; Koda, 2005; Mori, 1998).

A few basic features and contrasts are worth noting as we consider how writing systems themselves might influence reading, writing, and thinking. For example, *logographic* systems—unlike the phoneme-based system used by speakers of English and other European languages—rely on *graphs* (symbols) that represent words or even concepts. Arabic numerals, mathematical symbols, and other non-phonemic *logograms* (e.g., @, #, %, ¢, $, £, €, ¶, and so on) do not actually have speech equivalents: They cannot be pronounced, but they have names (e.g., the "at" sign or commercial "at," the pound sign, and so on). These logograms can be used by readers and writers of any language.

Chinese characters, the basis for Japanese *kanji* and Korean *hanzza*, represent a widely-used logographic system thought to contain about 60,000 forms that should perhaps be called *sinograms* (Birch, 2007). The term *sinogram* is more accurate, as over 80% of the symbols in the Chinese lexicon are made up of a *radical* or *signific* (one of about 200 root symbols that represent an element of meaning such as a word), plus a phonetic complement, which signals how the word can be pronounced. Many sinograms indicate approximate meanings and pronunciations, requiring readers to "guess or memorize the appropriate sound of the phonetic complement" and "associate the [graph] with a word that they already know" (Mair, 1996, p. 201). Phonetic complements can be variably pronounced, and many sinograms can represent multiple meanings but a single sound. Chinese script also lacks grammatical clues such as markers for tense, aspect, and so forth. Consequently, novice readers of Chinese must learn to link spoken syllables and words with sinograms that express a particular meaning (Birch, 2007; Leong, 1995; Li, Gaffiney, & Packard, 2002).

CATEGORY		LANGUAGE	SCRIPT NAME	REGION OF USE	SAMPLE TRANSCRIPTION
Logographic		Chinese	Sinograms	China, Taiwan	Pǔtōnghuà ("common speech") 普通话 (Simplified Chinese) 普通話 (Traditional Chinese)
		Japanese	kanji	Japan	Kanji — 漢字
		Korean	hanzza (hancha)	N. Korea, S. Korea	Hanja — 漢文教育用基礎漢字
		—	Arabic numerals	World	1, 2, 3, 4 ...
		—	Mathematical functions	World	+, −, ÷, ±, =, ∓, <, >, ∞, etc.
Syllabic	Syllabary	Japanese	kana	Japan	Hiragana — 平仮名 Katakana — 片仮名, カタカナ, or かたかな
		Tamil	Tamil syllabary	S. India, Sri Lanka, Singapore	Tamil — தமிழ்
		Cherokee (Tsalagi)	Cherokee syllabary	N. Carolina, Oklahoma	Tsalagi — tsa-la-gi/chaw la gee
Phonemic/phonetic	Alphabetic-syllabary	Korean	hangul	N. Korea, S. Korea	Hangeul — 한국어
		Thai	Thai alphabet	Thailand, Midway Islands, Singapore	Thai — ภาษาไทย
	Consonantal alphabet	Arabic	Arabic	Middle East, N. Africa	عربي
		Farsi (Persian)	Arabic	Iran	Farsi — فارسی
		Hebrew	Hebrew	Israel	Ivrit — עברית
	Alphabetic-transparent	Spanish	Roman	Latin America, Spain	Español
		Russian	Cyrillic	Russia, E. Europe	Russkiy yazyk — русский язык
		Modern Greek	Greek	Greece	Ελληνικά
	Alphabetic-opaque	English	Roman	N. America, Europe, S. Asia, Australia, and elsewhere	English
		French	Roman	France, E. Canada, W. Africa, French Polynesia	Français

FIGURE 1.1. Comparison of Selected Writing Systems. Adapted from Birch (2007, p. 16).

Experts estimate that a reader of Chinese needs an inventory of about 6,600 sinograms to grasp most text types; in order to read a scholarly or literary text, one needs an inventory of about 30,000 symbols (Mair, 1996)! Clearly, Chinese writing places high demands on memory. At the same time, although some spoken dialects of Chinese (e.g., Mandarin, Taiwanese Mandarin, Cantonese, Shanxi) may be mutually unintelligible, literate speakers of these varieties can communicate in writing using the same set of characters, many of which may have changed little since their introduction four millennia ago. For a literate Chinese speaker learning English, some aspects of reading English texts may seem relatively easy, while processes such as word analysis might require developing novel skills and strategies (Leong, 1995; Venezky, 1995).

Similar adjustments may be required for literate speakers of languages with *syllabic* or hybrid (syllabic and alphabetic) scripts, but for different reasons. Logographic and sinographic symbols represent concepts, things, and words; syllabic scripts represent sounds and sound clusters. Some syllabic systems (e.g., Mesopotamian, Egyptian, Korean *hangul*) evolved from logographic systems and still bear logographic traces. Others (e.g., Japanese *kana* and the Cherokee and Tamil syllabaries) were devised to associate a single symbol with a consonant-vowel (CV) or consonant-vowel-consonant (CVC) sequence; these syllabic units have natural beats and rhythms. Like the alphabetic graphs (letters) in a phonemic system, syllabic graphs are essentially indivisible: Each symbol represents "a unified whole" that cannot be dissected into discrete consonants and vowels (Birch, 2007, p. 19). The 47-symbol Japanese *kana* comprises two subsystems: *Katakana* graphs allow for transcription of foreign borrowings, whereas *hiragana* express grammatical functions. By themselves, *kana* graphs enable readers and writers of Japanese to represent any speech form. This feature may account for why Japanese schoolchildren appear to learn *kana* symbols at a very early age (Morton & Sasanuma, 1984; Steinberg, 1995). As Figure 1.1 indicates, Japanese texts are written using *katakana* and *hiragana* graphs, in combination with Chinese-derived *kanji* logographs. Literacy in Japanese thus requires a specialized mastery of three interrelated writing systems that activate a range of memory, recognition, decoding, and interpretation skills (Koda, 1995; Mori, 1998).

Japanese is not unique in drawing on two or more scripts in its writing system. Korean and Thai writing systems, for example, involve a combination of syllabic and alphabetic features. In the same way that Chinese script is not completely logographic in nature, syllabic writing systems can also include alphabetic elements. Alphabetic systems are based on the *alphabetic principle*, which holds that an arbitrary symbol (graph or letter) can signify a single sound (consonant or vowel) and that these symbols can be arranged in a sequence to form a word (Birch, 2007; Byrne, 1998). With minor adjustments (e.g., the use of diacritical marks such as accents [ˆ], umlauts [¨], tildes [~], cedillas [̧], and so on), a single alphabet containing a surprisingly small number of alphabetic symbols can potentially be used to write any language, although some alphabets are designed to capture the phonological and phonemic features of particular languages or language groups. The Roman (Latin) alphabet is used to transcribe in English, German, Spanish, and many other languages; the Cyrillic alphabet is used to transcribe Russian, Ukranian, Bulgarian, and numerous Slavic languages; the Greek alphabet is used by speakers of Greek. Inherently tied to speech as they are, alphabets require readers to know the spoken language. In other words, to read a text written in an alphabetic *orthography* (spelling system) such as English, German, Russian, or Greek, one must be able to relate spoken words to written words, and vice versa. In contrast, one could conceivably develop literacy in Chinese without developing speaking and listening skills (although Chinese can be transcribed alphabetically using a system known as *pinyin*).

Alphabetic systems, of course, involve diverse representation systems, as phoneme–grapheme (sound–symbol) correspondence varies considerably across orthographies (Daniels & Bright, 1996). This variation can naturally pose challenges for novice L1 and L2 readers (Aro, 2006; Birch, 2007; Grabe & Stoller, 2002; Hudson, 2007; Malatesha Joshi & Aaron, 2006; Pérez, 2004e; Tabaski, Sabatini, Massaro, & Calfee, 2005). Alphabetic systems that represent consonants and vowels can be classified as *transparent, opaque,* or somewhere in between—depending on how closely they adhere to the one-to-one alphabetic principle. For example, some linguists consider the orthographic systems of Korean (which uses *hangul* script), Serbian (which uses the Cyrillic alphabet), as well as Finnish and Turkish (which use the Roman alphabet) to be transparent because their close sound–symbol correspondence enables readers to "sound out" words easily. The orthographies of Greek, Italian, and Spanish (which use the Greek and Roman alphabets, respectively) are thought to be a little less transparent; German and Swedish (written in Roman script) reflect even less phonological regularity.

Continuing this comparison, French and Danish (which are also transcribed in the Roman alphabet) are considered less transparent (more opaque) than German and Swedish. English orthography is yet more opaque than French and Danish orthography, as readers of English cannot rely on one-to-one phoneme–grapheme mappings when it comes to pronunciation (Grabe & Stoller, 2002; Koda, 1999). Phonological irregularity requires learners to master both the predictable sound-symbol correspondences and the irregular features, which must be stored as part of the reader's lexical knowledge base (vocabulary) (see Chapter 8). Even more opaque on the continuum are the consonantal orthographies of Arabic, Hebrew, and Aramaic, which require readers to insert vowels, mainly with diacritical markers. Although the 28 consonant graphemes of Standard Arabic generally match one-to-one with corresponding consonants (and a small subset of vowels), the absence or near-absence of vowels can lead to considerable ambiguity, as readers may have to guess a word's grammatical function from the syntactic context (Bauer, 1996; Birch, 2007). On the transparency continuum, logographic systems such as Chinese script, Japanese *kanji*, and Korean *hanzza* are considered to be highly opaque, for the reasons discussed above.

This continuum is informed by research on the Orthographic Depth Hypothesis (ODH), which proposes that regular, or *shallow*, orthographies such as Serbian and Spanish encourage readers to analyze words phonologically (i.e., at the intraword level) (Defior, Cary, & Martos, 2002; Katz & Frost, 1992). In contrast, the ODH maintains that phonologically irregular, or *deep*, orthographies such as English and French require readers to rely less on intraword analysis than on lexical information unique to individual words (Grabe & Stoller, 2002; Koda, 1999, 2007b; Wolf, 2007). The research implications of the ODH are potentially wide-ranging. We now know, for example, that readers process words differently in their encounters with different orthographies (Geva & Siegel, 2000; Harris & Hatano, 1999; Muljani, Koda, & Moates, 1998). Thus, we might reasonably predict that L2 readers "tend to use some L1 processing when they try to read the L2, although the tendency influences beginning L2 reading more than advanced L2 reading." Nonetheless, the influence of L1 literacy on L2 reading development "is an issue that will not be easily resolved on general grounds (because there are endless L1s and L2s to compare)" (Grabe & Stoller, 2002, p. 49). Although questions concerning how L1 orthographic knowledge influences L2 reading remain, we agree with Grabe and Stoller (2002), who pointed out that "understanding more about a student's L1 literacy skills and orthography may help explain possible difficulties in word recognition, fluency, and reading rate" (p. 49).

Reading Processes: Fundamentals

Our survey of the dimensions of literacy emphasized the interaction between the social and cognitive functions of literate knowledge and practices. In reviewing the unique properties of writing as a culturally-transmitted communication system, we likewise touched on the roles that writing systems play in the learning and teaching of reading. We now turn our attention to reading as both a cognitive process and as a defining function of literacy. We would urge readers to view reading against a sociocultural backdrop that considers not only the global and local contexts where reading instruction takes place, but also readers' many purposes for reading (Barton, 2007; Pérez, 2004b, 2004d; Pressley, Billman, Perry, Reffitt, & Reynolds, 2007; Purcell-Gates et al., 2008).

About 1.5 billion people can read or have learned to read (Hudson, 2007; Wolf, 2007), leading us to wonder just how such an impressive number of persons can overcome the heady challenges of mastering a writing system. Theory, research, instructional practice, and educational policy have contributed to current accounts of what it means to "read," how novices become readers, and how educators can guide students toward functional literacy. These are key themes of this book, and the remainder of this chapter will explore efforts to define the reading process before reviewing influential conceptualizations of reading and reading development. Rather than working our way through a catalogue of formal theories or models, we will review these conceptualizations in terms of how they relate to three guiding metaphors, known as bottom-up, top-down, and interactive approaches (see Figure 1.2). In considering how research findings compare and contrast, we will concentrate on capturing the unique demands placed on the L2 reader, as well as reading skills and strategies thought to be teachable.

Before examining theoretical insights into reading processes, we would like to explain why a theoretically grounded approach is indispensable in teaching L2 reading. Our own practice as L2 literacy educators has been richly informed by advances in reading research, and we agree with Bernhardt's (2005) premise that "a theory is only as good as its practical application" (p. 142). We urge teachers to draw on the research base in formulating their own theories and in decision-making about curricula, materials, instruction, and assessment (Auerbach & Paxton, 1997; Meyer & Manning, 2007). Our experience as teachers and teacher educators supports Grabe's (2004) observation that "doing what works" can inhibit progress and effective teaching. Practitioner knowledge is not always open to competition from new ideas other than fashions and bandwagons, and "it is easily abused when teaching practices become fossilized or politicized" (p. 60). Grabe therefore urged teachers to search for reliable evidence that might support a particular instructional model in order to "minimize some of the negative consequences of informal practitioner lore." To be effective teachers, we should aim for "a merging of practitioner knowledge and persuasive research support" (p. 60).

We should further recall that, like literacy itself, formal theories and research-based models are always sociohistorically embedded, as well as limited with respect to their potential application in local classroom contexts. Similarly, the implications of any empirical study depend on the characteristics of the setting, participants, tasks, materials, and time frame of the research, making comparisons across studies difficult (Barnett, 1989; Hudson, 2007). Thus, we should take a cautious approach to "translating" any theory or empirical conclusion into classroom practice. Moreover, our survey of dominant models and metaphors is necessarily informed by L1 research, which has in many respects led the way in shaping L2 reading research (Eskey, 2005; Hudson, 2007). L2 insights "often converge with the L1 reading research literature," permitting us to draw "major implications from L1 research findings in general, and especially from research on instructional issues" (Grabe, 2004, p. 45). In addition, "far more research has been carried out on reading in L1 contexts" (Grabe & Stoller, 2002, p. 10). Unquestionably, L1–L2 distinctions must be recognized, as we argue below (see Figure 1.3 and related discussion). Nonetheless, "L1 and L2 reading abilities are similar enough in terms of cognitive processing skills that L2 researchers and practitioners can draw on—but not accept wholesale—L1 instructional research when it seems appropriate to do so" (Grabe, 2004, p. 58). With judicious adaptation, "many, if not most, of the effective instructional practices in L1 settings will also be effective in L2 settings" (Grabe, 2004, p. 59).

Describing and Defining Reading Processes

Scholars "have been concerned with the process of reading for thousands of years," and although extensive research has been conducted, we still lack a "clearly stated, empirically supported, and theoretically unassailable definition" (Bernhardt, 1991b, p. 5). To ground our discussion of guiding metaphors in reading research, we present a varied list of definitions, with a view toward representing the complexity of evolving conceptualizations of the reading process.

- "Understanding a written text means extracting the required information from it as efficiently as possible" (Grellet, 1981, p. 3).
- Reading means "dealing with **language messages in written or printed form**" (Urquhart & Weir, 1998, p. 14, emphasis in original).
- Reading means reconstructing "a reasonable spoken message from a printed text, and making meaning responses to the reconstructed message that . . . parallel [responses] to the spoken message" (Carroll, 1964, p. 62).
- "Reading is a neuronally and intellectually circuitous act, enriched as much by the unpredictable indirections of a reader's inferences and thoughts, as by the direct message to the eye from the text" (Wolf, 2007, p. 16).
- Reading is "a complex, multifaceted pursuit requiring the continuous deployment and integration of multiple operations . . . [A]dept reading is a constellation of interfaced capabilities, ranging from mechanical mappings to more sophisticated conceptual manipulations, such as reasoning and inferencing" (Koda, 2004, p. 227).
- "**Reading** can go from the mechanical uttering of the newsreader to the innumerable levels of interpreting any text. In the sense of understanding meanings, reading has always been applied to a wide range of phenomena, including the reading of barometers, tea-leaves and facial expressions" (Barton, 2007, p. 18).
- Reading is no different from "any other kind of thought, except that with reading, thought is engendered by a written text. Reading might be defined as thought stimulated and directed by written language" (Smith, 2004, p. 27).
- For the billion or more people with Internet access and the emerging generation of "digital natives," reading is synonymous with "reading the Web" (Boardman, 2004; Wolf, 2007)—"intelligently finding, evaluating, and making use of a great variety of sources of information" (Warschauer, 1999, p. 158).
- "Reading on the Web is similar to reading in print, but when viewed

from both cueing systems and transactional perspectives, it is clear that Web reading is more complex than print reading" (Eagleton & Dobler, 2007, p. 28).

The definitions advanced by Grellet (1981) and Urquhart and Weir (1998) straightforwardly assert that reading entails constructing meaning from written text. Carroll (1964) explicitly associates reading with the reconstruction of a spoken message. These definitions are not uncontroversial, as "simple" definitions of reading may overlook the fact that reading typically occurs in a rich sociocultural environment. The definitions proposed by Wolf (2007) and Koda (2004) focus more directly on the cognitive and neurological operations involved in reading. In line with our discussion of literacy and literacies, Barton (2007) offers a broad definition of reading that goes beyond mediation around a text. Smith (2004, 2007), meanwhile, stresses the cognitive dimension of reading, asserting that reading and thought are inseparable.

Warschauer's (1999) definition encompasses cognition and meaning-making, as well as the complex operations required to work effectively with hypertext and other digital media. Eagleton and Dobler (2007) stress that automatic comprehension of print-based and electronic media requires the same "foundational skills" (decoding, fluency, and vocabulary). At the same time, reading in a digital medium is dynamic and decidedly non-linear. When reading *hypertext*, for instance, "click on a word and you might see or hear its definition—or both. Click on a name, and a picture of a person . . . might appear." Readers using hypertext "have choices about which, if any, links they want . . . to access . . . Readers become 'authors' when they have control over reading materials. The nonlinear nature of hypertext challenges traditional ideas about reading" (Valmont, 2002, p. 94).

In the survey of reading metaphors that follows, we argue that the complexity of reading defies simple definitions and that diverse characterizations of reading may be complementary. We further concur with Hudson (2007), who articulated three assumptions that can help us make sense of competing models. The first of these is that "reading is meaning based" (Hudson, 2007, p. 28). Second, we should assume that "the active reader provides a lot of the information necessary to comprehend any text" (Hudson, 2007, p. 28). Third, *reading* is not synonymous with *learning to read* or with *teaching reading*. To clarify this distinction, Hudson (2007) emphasized that reading is *not* "(1) the reinforcement of oral skills; (2) grammatical or discourse analysis; (3) the acquisition of new vocabulary; (4) translation practice; (5) answering comprehension questions; (6) practice to improve reading ability"—although these strategies may play a productive role in acquiring reading skills (pp. 28–29) (see Chapters 3, 5, and 8).

With these assumptions in mind, we can compare L1 and L2 reading models, which we have organized around three familiar categories or metaphors:

bottom-up views, *top-down* views, and *interactive* (or integrative) views, which we classify in Figure 1.2. A historic view of reading that we do not examine closely is one that we might call cumulative or additive. In such a view, novice readers accumulate reading skills and strategies, somehow stacking them up in their heads until they become proficient users of these functions. Contemporary theorists reject such a simple account of reading development, as literacy research overwhelmingly demonstrates that "knowledge sources are not additive, but rather operate synchronically, interactively, and synergistically" (Bernhardt, 2005, p. 140). This premise coincides with reading models aligned with interactive views, which enjoy currency among leading researchers (e.g., August & Shanahan, 2006a; Bernhardt, 2005; Eskey, 2005; Farris, Fuhler, & Walther, 2004; Grabe & Stoller, 2002; Hudson, 2007; Konold, Juel, McKinnon, & Deffes, 2003; Rumelhart, 1977; Weaver, 2002). Few experts are strong adherents of "polar" (bottom-up and top-down) views, and teachers have the most to gain from the insights of research that embraces an interactive, integrated approach. Nonetheless, we believe it is instructive to acquaint teachers with contributions of the polar approaches, which have unquestionably led to a fuller understanding of the complex layers of knowledge and skill that underlie reading proficiency.

We intentionally refer to bottom-up, top-down, and interactive categories as metaphors, rather than as models or theories, as the latter "represent metaphorical generalisations that stem from comprehension research" from the 1970s to the present (Grabe & Stoller, 2002, p. 31). Terms such as "bottom-up," "top-down," and "interactive" refer to conceptualizations, rather than to coherent, testable *theories*. Researchers such as Bernhardt (2005) view such classifications in historical terms, but these categories provide useful tools for comparing divergent yet complementary methods of characterizing reading processes and their development. In the following sections, we explore these three metaphors in reference to the global observations presented in Figure 1.2, bearing in mind that a bottom-up/top-down dichotomy is misleading. By highlighting the complementary features of each, we will emphasize the relevance of what Grabe and Stoller (2002) described as "modified interactive models," which will help us to reconcile incompatible claims.

Bottom-up Views of Reading and Reading Development

As Figure 1.2 indicates, bottom-up accounts imply that reading is initiated at the "bottom" level of text structure, from discrete, visual units such as graphemes, morphemes, and words. To construct meaning from a text, the reader works her way "upward" to larger-level units such as phrases, sentences, paragraphs, and chunks of written discourse (see Figure 1.4). This bottom-up processing operation is analyzable as a "mechanical pattern in which the reader creates a piece-by-piece mental translation of the information in the text"—typically with little reference to background knowledge. In a strict bottom-up view, readers linearly process "each word letter-by-letter, each sentence word-by-word and each text

	Bottom-up views	Top-down views	Interactive and integrated views
Orientation and Conceptual Framework	▪ Driven mainly by textual elements: Readers construct mental translation of text piece by piece ▪ Discrete and primarily linear: Grapheme → (Phoneme) → Meaning	▪ Driven mainly by reader goals and expectations ▪ Holistic ▪ Proposition- and discourse-oriented ▪ Socioculturally situated	▪ Readers draw simultaneously on bottom-up and top-down operations to capture meaning ▪ Higher-level and lower-level reading processes influence one another ▪ May be socioculturally situated ▪ Compensatory and multidimensional
Aims	▪ Account for how readers construct meaningful messages from discrete (structural) elements that underlie text	▪ Explain (a) how readers construct meaning by bringing prior knowledge (schemata) to the act of reading and (b) how readers use multiple textual cues to understand text-based messages	▪ Explain how bottom-up and top-down processes interact with and complement one another
Focal areas	▪ Emphasis on how readers read ▪ Emphasis on lower-order subskills	▪ What readers comprehend ▪ Higher-order subskills ▪ Efficiency of linguistic over graphemic information	▪ What readers comprehend ▪ Why readers read ▪ How readers read ▪ Interaction of higher- and lower-order subskills
Reader Processes	▪ Decode print letter-by-letter, word-by-word, clause-by-clause; reconstruct spoken messages from print ▪ Controlled processing → Automatic processing ▪ Word recognition → Comprehension → Re-association	▪ Guess meaning based on textual cues and schematic knowledge ▪ Predict, sample, confirm, and correct meanings derived from text ▪ Decoding involves: (a) Grapheme → Meaning or (b) Grapheme → Phoneme → Meaning	▪ Develop inferences with the aid of schemata, strategies, and discrete structural knowledge
Key areas of Knowledge	▪ Graphology, phonemics, phonology, morphology, the lexicon, grammar	▪ Schemata ▪ Syntax ▪ Lexico-semantics	▪ All areas listed at left, configured bidirectionally
Role of Memory	▪ Important: To free up space in working memory, readers must automatize component skills	▪ Important: Readers have a limited capacity for text processing	▪ Important: Readers rely on recall to construct meaning representations
Readers	▪ Readers are autonomous (if not isolated) ▪ Readers viewed as mental processors	▪ Readers belong to literate communities ▪ Readers are motivated, active, and selective ▪ Readers read with expectations	▪ Readers develop and activate reading skills both autonomously and in collaboration with fellow readers ▪ Reader motivation, decision-making, and expectations affect integration of top-down and bottom-up skills
Instructional Parallels	▪ Phonics-based instruction	▪ Whole Language instruction	▪ Content- and genre-based instruction, LSP, EAP, ESP

FIGURE 1.2. Comparative Matrix of Metaphors for Reading Processes and Development.

sentence-by-sentence" (Grabe & Stoller, 2002, p. 32), proceeding "in a fixed order, from sensory input to comprehension and appropriate response" (Hudson, 2007, p. 33). A further feature of bottom-up models is an association between lexical meaning (represented in morphemes and words) and phonemic and phonological form (the sounds of words and their parts) (Birch, 2007; Weaver, 2002).

A strong proponent of a bottom-up account of reading, Gough (1972) asserted that "we . . . read letter by letter." Citing evidence that we read "serially from left to right," Gough claimed that readers recognize symbols (e.g., letters) almost instantaneously, then converting them into phonemic equivalents (p. 335). This position claimed close phoneme–grapheme correspondences: "[T]he contents of the character register [alphabet] are somehow transposed into abstract phonemic representations" (Gough, 1972, p. 338). Phonemic representations enable readers to search the mental lexicon; following word recognition, readers comprehend words and ultimately sentences, which mysteriously become available for further processing by an undefined cognitive processor. Hudson (2007) described this processor as "psychologically divine" (p. 35). Readers are next thought to re-associate linguistic data with speech output. Clearly, Gough's bottom-up model suffers from several weaknesses, including its equation of reading with speech, its narrow focus on "sentences" (rather than propositions or texts), and its reliance on ill-defined (and untestable) processing mechanisms.

LaBerge and Samuels (1974) proposed a more well-developed bottom-up processing model accounting for how readers' understanding of textual components influence processing operations (Bernhardt, 1991b; Hudson, 2007). A chief focus of the LaBerge and Samuels (1974) model is how readers *automatize* reading skills. To achieve automaticity, readers initially practice macro-level processing skills such as grapheme identification in a controlled, deliberate way. With practice, processing skills gradually become automatic, thereby relieving demands on working memory (Anderson, 1995; Nuttall, 1982; Schunk, 2000). Attention and memory are crucial in this perspective, which assumes that readers can only manage several processing subtasks at once if no single task requires more attention than the other tasks. Automatized processes are thought to entail two levels of decoding and text comprehension that operate simultaneously and efficiently. LaBerge and Samuels (1974) compared fluent reading to ball handling in basketball. Ball handling, a macro-level skill, requires players to manage multiple subskills (e.g., dribbling, passing, catching, and so forth) all at once. Like a skilled reader, a successful player handles ball handling automatically—without much forethought or conscious effort. If the macro-level skill is automatic, then the subskills and the interdependencies among them have also become automatic (Carpenter, Miyake, & Just, 1994; Donin, Graves, & Goyette, 2004; Kuhn & Rasinski, 2007).

The LaBerge and Samuels (1974) model involves perceiving print information, which is "then sent to various locations in the brain for processing" (Bernhardt, 1991b, p. 7). In line with Gough (1972), LaBerge and Samuels (1974) held that readers associate the visual representation of spelling patterns, words, phrases, and sentences with phonological memory and then with semantic memory, as in the following schematic:

GRAPHEME → PHONEME → SEMANTIC REPRESENTATION (MEANING)

This operation results in automatic processing of print "over multiple experiences" (Hudson, 2007, p. 36). Unlike Gough, LaBerge and Samuels distinguished four interdependent memory resources (visual, phonological, semantic, and episodic), focusing on "characteristics of print as the essence of the process it attempts to describe" (Bernhardt, 1991b, p. 7). With its emphasis on increasing automaticity, the model explains reading development in terms of freeing up cognitive resources (chiefly, memory) for text comprehension. In addition, LaBerge and Samuels (1974) allowed for the activation of background (schematic) knowledge in interpreting strings such as *The President's press conference was can___ed*, although their account of reading is predominantly linear (Samuels & Kamil, 1984). Bernstein (1991b) noted that LaBerge and Samuels do not satisfactorily account for meaning: Their model "projects the image that perception is the key factor and that what is understood is not terribly important" (p. 7). Perception and phonological awareness unquestionably play a crucial role in learning to read and in executing many reading tasks (Kucer & Silva, 2006; Stahl & Murray, 1994; Stanovich, Cunningham, & Cramer, 1984). Nevertheless, this exclusively bottom-up view neglects other vital functions, knowledge sources, motivations, attitudes, and purposes associated with effective reading (Grabe & Stoller, 2002; Matthewson, 1994; Verhoeven & Snow, 2000).

A third influential bottom-up model is that of Just and Carpenter (1980, 1987), who characterized text as the most essential component of reading comprehension. Whereas Gough (1972) and LaBerge and Samuels (1974) implicitly viewed text as consisting of strings of individual words, Just and Carpenter characterized text in much richer discursive terms, including complex, interrelated features such as *cohesion* and *coherence*. Cohesion refers to surface-level forms in a text that "signal relationships . . . between sentences or clausal units" (Grabe & Kaplan, 1996, p. 55). In brief, cohesive features mark "the syntactic or semantic connectivity of linguistic forms" such as connectives (e.g., *because, although,* and so on) (Crystal, 2003, p. 81). Coherence refers more broadly to the underlying, macro-level connections among propositions across a text. Although reliant on cohesion, coherence is established by textual organization and "congruence with the reader's background knowledge," among other things (Hudson, 2007, p. 173). Because it recognizes these complex textual features, the Just and Carpenter (1980) model stressed that reading comprehension is non-linear and that readers take actively select passages for processing. In this view, what a reader has already read influences what she will read next and how she will interpret it. Just and Carpenter likewise posited a cognitive feedback process in which the meanings that a reader constructs from latter passages inform (re-)interpretations of earlier passages (Bernhardt, 1991b). Unlike the bottom-up approaches reviewed above, the Just and Carpenter model does not assume the need for phonological encoding or decoding.

As Figure 1.2 suggests, bottom-up approaches and their historical antecedents have tended to reinforce a traditional, encoding/decoding framework, which Sperber and Wilson (1988) schematized as follows:

MESSAGE → ENCODER → CHANNEL → DECODER → MESSAGE

Early bottom-up views (e.g., Gough, 1972) would insist on conversion (encoding) of graphemic sequences into a phonological (vocal) form, which the reader then decodes into a semantic message. This strong view, "entrenched in much Western thought" (Hudson, 2007, p. 28), has at times strongly influenced reading instruction. The most notable, if not notorious, method allied with extreme bottom-up models is *phonics*, defined by Strickland (1998) as "instruction in the sound-letter relationship used in reading and writing" (p. 5). In the heyday of phonics instruction during the 1960s and 1970s, *analytic phonics* was commonly practiced in U.S. schools. Analytic phonics instruction begins "by teaching children some words and then helping [them] to 'analyze' those words and learn phonics rules and generalizations based on those words" (Cunningham, 2000, p. 184). This approach, often embodied in *basal reader* series, entailed a fixed pattern of instruction and a graded syllabus (Goodman, Shannon, Freeman, & Murphy, 1988; National Reading Panel, 2000).

In analytic phonics lessons, the teacher might introduce a letter-sound correspondence in context (e.g., the lax, or "short" vowel [I] in *hit, big, little,* and *middle*), and then lead drill-like exercises to reinforce grapheme–phoneme associations. Auditory exercises might require learners to produce target phonemes or graphemes via oral reading practice. In subsequent tasks, students might identify the target letter or sound as it occurs in carefully constructed word lists. A lesson might then feature worksheets requiring students to transcribe words containing the target phoneme or grapheme. Written exercises might entail fill-in-the-blank exercises focusing on words containing the target letter or cluster and exemplifying typical orthographic patterns (Beck, 2006; Cunningham, 2000; Farris et al., 2004; Stahl, Duffy-Hester, & Dougherty Stahl, 1998; Weaver, 2002).

Synthetic phonics instruction similarly teaches individual graphemes and letter clusters. This method demonstrates how to form letter combinations to construct words. As in analytic phonics, letters and sounds are explicitly introduced and exemplified via representative word sets. Exercises lead students through a process of blending sounds to form words in isolation. Students read these words chorally and in small groups. Instruction then shifts to reading a "decodable" text (often a story) purposefully composed with a high proportion of words exemplifying the target letter or sound (Stahl et al., 1998). Such highly-controlled texts are the hallmark of basal readers, which often build on phoneme–grapheme correspondences by linking phonics to meaning and by embedding letter-, syllable-, and word-based study in literate contexts (Farris et al., 2004). Spelling-based approaches feature word study exercises such as sorting words by their first letter or by grammatical category (Rasinski & Padak, 2001). In "making words" models, students manipulate sets of six to eight letters to form words, with the goal of using the letters in a set to construct a single word (Cunningham & Hall, 1994). In word-making lessons, the teacher leads students in sorting words according to their spelling patterns and then using these words in reading and writing activities. A final example of a synthetic phonics approach is known as analogy-based phonics: Children are taught that "if you know how to read and spell *cat*, you can also read and spell *bat*, *rat*, *hat*, *sat*, and other rhyming words" (Cunningham, 2000, p. 184). These analogic sets are sometimes called *phonograms*.

In L2 reading instruction, strong forms of bottom-up approaches are perhaps rarely practiced, as many L2 educators have come to reject fundamental bottom-up principles. Top-down and interactionist proponents point out that bottom-up views over-emphasize discrete units such as graphemes, phonemes, syllables, and words—often to the exclusion of a systematic focus on meaningful, authentic *texts*. Nonetheless, theorists such as Just and Carpenter (1987) considered aspects of discourse structure, as well as readers' formal and content knowledge in their model. A further shortcoming of extreme bottom-up approaches, which assume reading to be an encoding–decoding operation (Sperber & Wilson, 1986), is that they focus chiefly on individual reader processes, rather than on readers as novice members of a literate community or on the social nature of reading (Eskey, 2005; Lee, 2000; Smith, 1988, 2004, 2007) (cf. Figure 1.2). These objections have been partly addressed by researchers and practitioners who have identified common ground between bottom-up and top-down approaches.

L1 reading experts have argued that bottom-up practices such as phonics-based instruction can be embedded in meaningful contexts, purposefully leading readers to global comprehension (rather than focusing on individual, automatized information-processing skills) (Block & Pressley, 2007; Dahl, 2000; Dahl & Scharer, 2000; Ehri, 2004; Eskey, 2005; Farris et al., 2004; Freeman & Freeman, 2000; Stahl et al., 1998; Weaver, 2002). In its position statement on L2 literacy instruction, the International Reading Association (IRA) (2007) denounced "the 'reading wars'—the pitting of phonics against literature in literacy instruction, as if the two were incompatible." The IRA similarly called for "curriculum development that effectively integrates phonics into the reading program." Birch (2007) and others (e.g., Bernhardt, 1991b, 2005; Eskey, 2005; Freeman & Freeman, 2000; Grabe & Stoller, 2002; Hudson, 2007) have likewise noted that bottom-up practices play a vital role in productive L2 reading instruction. Certain elements of bottom-up instruction (e.g., in sound–spelling decoding, alphabetic encoding, word knowledge, syntactic processing, and so forth), in fact, may be essential to developing L2 literacy (Barnett, 1986; Koda, 2004; Stanovich & Stanovich, 1999).

Top-down Views of Reading and Reading Development

Top-down approaches to understanding reading and reading development contrast with bottom-up views in several crucial respects, as Figure 1.2 indicates. Nonetheless, we should emphasize that the bottom-up/top-down contrast is not dichotomous and that these descriptors are best viewed as useful metaphors that help us to compare diverse yet overlapping methods. A salient feature that distinguishes top-down from bottom-up approaches is that the former "assume that reading is primarily directed by reader goals and expectations" (Grabe & Stoller, 2002, p. 32). Readers initiate the reading process with expectations about texts and the information that texts present. In engaging with texts, readers sample information to determine which expectations were accurate, modifying expectations that don't match text content. In sampling, effective readers direct their eyes to the passages most apt to contain the information they seek. Although we do not fully understand *how* readers formulate such expectations, we hypothesize that "these expectations might be created by a general monitoring mechanism (i.e., an executive control processor)" (Grabe & Stoller, 2002, p. 32).

Reading as a guessing game. Goodman (1968) referred to this top-down view of reading as a *psycholinguistic guessing game* in which readers deploy grammatical and lexical knowledge to depend less and less on the linear decoding of graphemes and (re)encoding of graphemes into phonemes. Emphasizing the "cognitive efficiency involved in a reliance on existing syntactic and semantic knowledge" (Hudson, 2007, p. 37), Goodman's top-down model favored direct interaction between print and meaning, as this simple schematic shows:

GRAPHEME → MEANING

Goodman nonetheless acknowledged that text decoding could entail three sequential components, one of which is phonemic or phonological:

GRAPHEME → PHONEME → MEANING

Regardless of whether reading entails or requires phonological encoding or decoding, Goodman (1968) stressed that reading "is exceedingly complex." To appreciate this complexity, we must recognize how oral and written language interact to make communication possible. In addition, "we must consider the special characteristics of written language and special uses of written language. We must consider the characteristics and abilities of the reader [that] are prerequisite to effective reading" (Goodman, 1968, p. 15).

For Goodman, constructing meaning from text necessitates four interdependent procedures: *predicting* content and text structure, *sampling* material, *confirming* predictions, and *correcting* inaccurate or incomplete predictions (Hudson, 2007). These procedures assume a purposeful reader who activates diverse knowledge sources (e.g., content, vocabulary, linguistic and rhetorical structure) and skill sets (e.g., word recognition, sentence and discourse processing, cognitive and metacognitive strategies) while reading. Goodman's guessing game model maintains that readers do not need to perceive or identify all textual features to become efficient; it values "the cognitive economy of linguistic information over graphemic information" (Hudson, 2007, p. 37). Efficient readers select the minimum cues necessary to make accurate guesses (Nuttall, 2005). For Goodman (1976), reading depends on "partial use of . . . minimal language cues selected from perceptual input on the basis of the reader's expectation." As readers process partial information from a text, "tentative decisions are made to be confirmed, rejected, or refined as reading progresses" (p. 498).

We should note that leading reading researchers (e.g., Gough & Wren, 1999; Pressley, 1998; Stanovich & Stanovich, 1999) have dismissed Goodman's guessing game model, claiming that effective readers seldom engage in guessing. Good readers, according to Grabe and Stoller (2002), "guess much less than poor readers" (p. 72). Along with Goodman, Smith (1988, 2004, 2007) and others have nonetheless argued in favor of top-down approaches, emphasizing that the human memory and visual system limit the amount of information that can be processed, stored, and retrieved. Top-down supporters claim that these limitations make it impossible for discrete, bottom-up processes such as those listed in Figure 1.2 to work efficiently in the wide range of literacy events that readers may encounter. Smith (2004) practically dismissed bottom-up perception in arguing that "all learning and comprehension is interpretation, understanding an event from its context (or putting the event into a context)." All reading, he wrote, "is interpretation, making sense of print. You don't worry about specific letters or even words when you read, any more than you care particularly about headlights and tires when you identify a car" (p. 3). Although such perspectives place a premium on developing macro-level literacy skills, "top-down views highlight the potential interaction of all processes (lower- and higher-level processes) . . . under the general control of a central monitor" (Grabe & Stoller, 2002, p. 32).

Goodman and others have often cited evidence from *reader miscue analysis* to support top-down approaches to reading instruction. Goodman (1965) introduced the term "miscue analysis" to represent how readers make sense of graphemic cues in print. Miscue analysis tracks and scrutinizes the errors made by readers while reading aloud (Brown, Goodman, & Marek, 1996; Goodman & Burke, 1972; Goodman, Watson, & Burke, 2005). Consider, for instance, the following printed text with a novice reader's oral errors superimposed and signaled with editing marks:

Marko (1)   *door (2)*   ∅ *(3)*
When Mariko opened the drawer, she noticed ~~that~~ the box was

          ∅ *(4)*
missing. What ~~had~~ happened to it? Had Roberto taken it to

a (5)   *worrying (6)*
the beach house without telling her? Now she was worried.
‿‿‿   ‿‿‿‿‿‿‿‿

                          car (7)   *house (8)*
Maybe she should borrow Lina's van and drive to the beach‿
                                              ‿‿‿

now to find Roberto.

The eight miscues represent error types that can be classified in several ways. Some cues are visual in that the spoken word may resemble the word in the text, as in miscues (1) and (6). Semantic cues involve words or phrases that express meanings similar to those in the text, as in miscues (2) and (7): A *door* and a *drawer* can both be opened, and a *car* and a *van* can both be driven. Samples (2) and (7) may also represent syntactic miscues, as *door* and *drawer* are both nouns that collocate with the verb forms in the adjacent text. The omissions reflected in miscues (3) and (4) are also syntactic in nature. Modern English grammar allows the conjunction *that* in (3) to be deleted. The omission of the auxiliary *had* in (4) is grammatically allowable but changes discourse meaning, as *had* expresses a more remote time frame (past perfect, as opposed to past simple in the miscue). The substitution of the indefinite article *a* for the definite article *the* in miscue (5) might be labeled as syntactic: *A* is grammatical, but it is not pragmatically acceptable (the context suggests that *the beach house* is known to the narrator, Mariko, and the reader). Miscue (6), which replaces the past participle *worried* with the present participle *worrying* is also grammatically possible, but the substitution changes the meaning of the original. Finally, the insertion of *house* in miscue (8) might be visual, syntactic, or both: The collocation *beach house* is certainly allowable (syntactic) and appears in close proximity in the third sentence (visual). In working with L2 readers, we may clearly need an additional category to account for miscues resulting from interlingual transfer, as we suggest below.

Miscues occur when the expected response (i.e., what appears on the page) and the observed response (miscue) do not match (Farris et al., 2004; Weaver, 2002). By analyzing, classifying, and tallying miscues, teachers and researchers can generate profiles of readers' error patterns, which presumably reflect how readers make sense of print messages and convert them from symbol to meaning (Goodman, 1965).[6] Miscues such as those examined above reflect a novice reader's reasonable—and, importantly, well-informed—predictions and sampling processes. This method assumes first that miscues are systematic and second that unanticipated responses (miscues) result from the same reading process as do expected responses (accurate oral reading of textual cues) (Brown et al., 1996). Miscue analysis research consistently suggests that reading errors parallel the syntactic and semantic context of any single lexical item (word or phrase). In

L1 literacy education, miscue analysis ignited great interest in teaching reading strategies, as well as fervor for using this method in reading assessment. As experts such as Weaver (2002) and Wixson (1979) have cautioned, miscue analysis results should be interpreted carefully, as the method does not account for text difficulty, reader proficiency, or differences in learning style.

In considering miscue analysis and what it reveals about reading processes, we might question where the knowledge that enables readers to predict, guess, and construct meaning comes from. In both top-down and interactive views, such knowledge is frequently represented as *schematic* knowledge, which we explore at some length in Chapter 2. Briefly, *schema* describes what a learner knows about a topic, a text, and its functions. *Schemata* (the plural form of *schema*) consist of mental frameworks that emerge from prior experience. *Schema theory* holds that expectations and assumptions "are externally constructed and impose external constraints on the ways in which we understand messages" (Schiffrin, 1994, p. 104). Text comprehension can thus depend on schemata, which help us make sense of new facts, text types, formal patterns, and practices (Rumelhart, 1980).

Whole Language instruction. Our account of top-down approaches would be incomplete without a discussion of the *Whole Language* (WL) movement, perhaps the most noteworthy instructional manifestation of top-down views. Inextricably associated with the work of Goodman (1986, 1996),[7] WL gets its name from the principle that the whole (e.g., of a text, a learner's knowledge base) is always greater than the sum of its parts (Fountas & Hannigan, 1989). It is "the whole that gives meaning to it parts" (Shrum & Glisan, 2005, p. 193). WL instruction constitutes not only an array of educational approaches but also a philosophy of L1 and L2 literacy education (Freeman & Freeman, 1992, 2002; Weaver, 2002).

The WL movement values process, with "comprehension of the whole story . . . stressed over breaking words down into pieces" (Farris et al., 2004, p. 66). WL approaches are frequently associated with constructionist views of learning and education, in which learners develop knowledge and skill from firsthand experience by "constructing" and expanding their knowledge base.

WL, wrote Goodman (1986), "is firmly supported by four humanistic-scientific pillars. It has a strong theory of learning, a theory of language, a basic view of teaching and the role of teachers, and a language-centered view of the curriculum" (p. 26). A hallmark of the WL curriculum is the use of "real, relevant materials," often consisting of children's, adolescent, and adult literature (Morrow & Gambrell, 2000). Further, learners "are given choices as to what they . . . read or discuss" (Farris et al., 2004, p. 66).

WL instruction ignited considerable controversy in the 1980s and 1990s in the US, with critics charging that WL neglected or ignored the need to teach bottom-up skills such as phoneme–grapheme correspondence, phonemic awareness, word recognition, word analysis, and so on (see Figure 1.2). Many WL critics and skeptics, often strong proponents of phonics-based instruction, have attributed declining reading scores in U.S. schools and the "literacy crisis" to WL curricula and instruction (American Federation of Teachers, 1999; Anderson, Hiebert,

Scott, & Wilkinson, 1985; McCardle & Chhabra, 2004; National Reading Panel, 2000; Snow, 2004; Snow, Burns, & Griffin, 1998). Ehri (2004) and Sweet (2004) presented contemporary critiques of the WL movement and WL-inspired instruction. A chief criticism of WL is that research evidence favors bottom-up, phonics-based instruction and that novice readers simply do not "sample and confirm," as top-down theorists claim (Just & Carpenter, 1987). Some critiques have also invoked ideological, political, and even religious arguments, and it is likely that some condemnations of WL reflect hyperbolic claims, misguided reasoning, and a degree of misunderstanding of WL precepts and practices. Stephen Krashen's (1999) book *Three Arguments Against Whole Language and Why They Are Wrong* succinctly challenged key claims against WL theory and practice. Krashen (2004), McQuillan (1998), Rigg (1991), Smith (2004, 2007), Smith and Elley (1997), and Weaver (2002) further counterbalanced more strident objections to WL and related top-down models of literacy education, arguing that WL instruction can take many forms and that WL approaches by no means exclude such bottom-up practices as developing phonemic awareness (Flippo, 2001; Graves & Graves, 2003; Weaver, 1998, 2002).

The ongoing and sometimes bitter dispute between WL proponents and phonics advocates appears to have diminished in recent years—or perhaps the level of acrimony has simply declined. Over a decade ago, Smith and Elley (1997) observed that "the last word has clearly not been spoken in the debate surrounding the relative merits of phonic-based and [WL] methods." Most teachers, they noted, "attempt to avoid the extreme positions and artificial constraints of many . . . experimental studies . . ." (p. 148). Smith (2004) later asserted that WL "has been sidelined rather than vanquished" (p. ix), despite Pearson's (2000) announcement of WL's demise. WL and schema-theoretic views may have been over-applied (Bernhardt, 2005), and the attention of L1 and L2 experts has shifted toward interactive approaches to reading instruction. We nonetheless uphold the fundamental principles of the WL movement, which do not preclude the judicious deployment of bottom-up and integrated practices, as indicated in subsequent chapters. We support Pressley's (2002) approach to "balanced teaching" and concur with the IRA's (2007) rejection of "exaggerated . . . claims that blame student failure on inattention to phonics" and of the "reading wars," which misleadingly oppose bottom-up to top-down views of literacy.

Interactive and Integrated Views of Reading and Reading Development

We do not believe that bottom-up and top-down views of reading are dichotomously related, nor do we view sharp distinctions as particularly useful for L2 reading teachers: As Hudson (2007) observed, ". . . both the strict bottom-up and top-down models are too naïve and simplistic" (p. 34). We would also reiterate that the profession has "few adherents to the strong form of either polar approach" (Hudson, 2007, p. 3). In fact, a systematic pairing of top-down and bottom-up practices may serve teachers and learners best (Dahl, 2000; Farris et al., 2004; Freeman & Freeman, 2000; Kucer & Silva, 2006; Robinson et al., 2000; Weaver, 2002). After all, L2 reading is "a diverse, complicated, and frustrating landscape to traverse, let alone explain or predict" (Bernhardt, 2000, p. 791). An interactive view of reading and learning to read enables us to draw from the strengths of bottom-up and top-down paradigms while keeping in mind the multiple practices, processes, and participants involved in literacy education (see Figure 1.2).

The schematic drawing in Figure 1.3, inspired by Bernhardt's (1991b) reader-based, sociocognitive view, reminds us that L2 reading involves five indispensable components: the literate context, the text, the reader (and her purposes for reading), text processing operations, and the reader's reconstructed message. This simple drawing partly captures the interaction metaphor introduced in Figure 1.2. The schematic sketched in Figure 1.4, adapted from Birch (2007) and informed

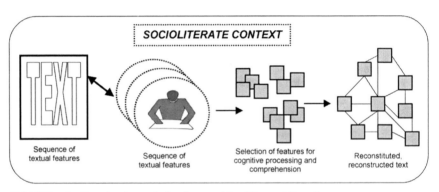

FIGURE 1.3. Reader-based, Sociocognitive View of Reading.
Adapted from Bernhardt (1991b, p. 15, Figure 1.7).

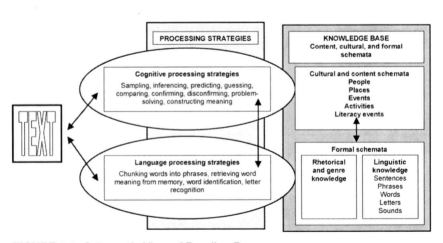

FIGURE 1.4. Schematic View of Reading Processes.
Adapted from Birch (2007, p. 3, Figure 1.1) and Carr et al. (1990, p. 8).

by component skills models (e.g., Carr, Brown, Vavrus, & Evans, 1990), aims to capture dimensions of the interaction metaphor by specifying both top-down and bottom-up components of text processing operations.

Before examining reading models aligned with the interactive metaphor, we should acknowledge the pitfalls of adopting the compromise position implied by interactive approaches. Grabe and Stoller (2002) asserted that L1 and L2 reading literature often assumes that "one can take useful ideas from a bottom-up perspective and combine them with key ideas from a top-down view" (p. 33). This reasoning "leads to a self-contradictory model," as the essential components of bottom-up processing (i.e., efficient automatic processing in working memory) "are incompatible with strong top-down controls on reading comprehension" (Grabe & Stoller, 2002, p. 33). As Figure 1.4 suggests, top-down operations are deployed mainly for higher-level processing. To reconcile such contradictions, Grabe and Stoller (2002) proposed *modified interactive models*, which account for the automatic processes that the reader carries out "primarily in a bottom-up manner with little interference from other processing levels or knowledge resources" (p. 33). For example, a reader may recognize words by perceiving information from graphemes, phoneme–grapheme correspondences, and spelling. At the same time, efficient word recognition may not require contextual or schematic knowledge: Activating schematic resources can be time-consuming, although readers certainly may draw on context for operations such as disambiguating word meaning. Furthermore, Hudson (1993, 2007) cautioned that the interactive metaphor can be restrictive: "The interaction appears to be other than top-down interacting with bottom-up, at least for readers at all but the lowest ability" (Hudson, 2007, p. 103).

Interactive and integrated models that avoid inappropriate coalescing of bottom-up and top-down theories tend to focus on how readers simultaneously activate multiple knowledge sources (e.g., graphology, orthography, vocabulary, syntax, schemata, and so on). For example, the *Interactive Compensatory Model* outlined by Stanovich (1980, 1986, 1991, 2000) assumes that an underdeveloped skill area or knowledge source brings about compensatory reliance on another more automatized skill area. The Stanovich model holds that readers eventually develop effective reading processes and that emergent processes frequently interact. It further maintains that automatic processes (e.g., grapheme and word recognition) can operate independently and that reading difficulties precipitate interaction among subskills and compensatory processing. A compensatory model describes "how knowledge sources assist or take over for other knowledge sources that are inadequate or nonexistent—i.e., what they use to compensate for deficiencies" (Bernhardt, 2005, p. 140). For instance, a reader who encounters a novel word and lacks knowledge of its meaning may compensate for that knowledge gap by using the linguistic context to generate inferences about the word's meaning. In contrast to many top-down approaches, which presuppose that less-skilled readers seldom use higher-level processes, Stanovich's compensatory model predicts that less-skilled readers deploy both high- and low-level strategies to overcome reading difficulties. The compensatory model likewise accounts for individual differences in reading development and attainment.

A second interactive model of reading, associated with *connectionist* theories of language acquisition, claims that mental operations take place in parallel, rather than serial, fashion (McClelland, Rumelhart, & Hinton, 1986). Also known as the *parallel distributed processing* (PDP) framework, connectionism assumes that serial cognitive processing would take too much time and that a faulty step in the operation would short-circuit the entire comprehension process (Rumelhart, Smolensky, McClelland, & Hinton, 1986). In a connectionist view, cognitive processing refers to how "patterns of activation are formed over [neuron-like] units through their excitatory and inhibitory interactions" (McClelland & Rumelhert, 1985, p. 159). Sometimes described as a word recognition model of reading and language learning (Plaut, McClelland, Seidenberg, & Patterson, 1996), connectionist theories of reading posit text processing as an intelligent system that can operate without explicit rules (Bernhardt, 2005; Koda, 2004).

Rather than acting on the basis of rules, our cognitive systems organize information and learn from exposure to input sources, including text and other media formats. Connectionist accounts are described as bottom-up in nature (Grabe & Stoller, 2002), but recent PDP-oriented research has stressed that the human information-processing system activates many interdependent units (sometimes called *nodes*) that formulate hypotheses based on probabilities (Ellis, 2003). Connectionist views appeal to advocates of interactive models, as they account for how graphic, syntactic, semantic, and schematic influences interact while explaining the computational aspects of reading (Hudson, 2007). In reading, the cognitive system anticipates that any grapheme, word, sentence, or discourse unit might appear on the basis of information that has already undergone processing: Multiple associations over time help individuals build sets of probabilities. Consider how a reader might select the missing grapheme <*t*> in the phrase, *the threa___ of climate change*, in an article on global warming: Cultural and content schemata, as well as orthographic and vocabulary knowledge, will enable her to disambiguate by eliminating <*d*> as the missing letter in *threat*. A connectionist account would explain how the reader's cognitive system considers multiple options from different levels of knowledge at the same time.

Verbal Efficiency Theory (VET), a third interactive model that continues to enjoy currency, characterizes learning to read in terms of "incrementing a store of graphemically accessible words" (Perfetti, 1991, p. 33). VET, like the LaBerge and Samuels (1974) model, holds that the efficiency of local (text-level) processes restricts comprehension (Perfetti, 1985, 1988). The model reflects bottom-up properties, including the premise that interaction is confined to graphemic features, graphemes, phonemes, and word-level units such as bound and free morphemes. Perfetti's (1991) *restricted-interaction model* ". . . allows no influences from outside lexical data structures, no importation of knowledge, expectancies, and beliefs. Skilled word recognition is context-free" (p. 34). This restriction might lead us to classify Perfetti's framework as bottom-up. However, Perfetti specified *local text processes* and *text-modeling processes* as interactive and integrative. Local text processes require readers to retrieve the meanings associated with a word and then select the meaning that best fits the "local" context in which the word appears. As she reads, the reader combines words into propositions, which she integrates with the propositions available in working memory. How long and how well this material is stored in memory depends partly on the text's cohesion and coherence. An interactive dimension of VET is that the reader is thought to combine concept and schematic knowledge with textual propositions in the text modeling process. In other words, in building a "model" of the text, the reader constructs a representation of its meaning by filling gaps in her understanding with schematic knowledge. Perfetti (1988) argued that efficient modeling processes depend on automatic semantic, orthographic, and phonetic skills; in line with Stanovich's (1980, 2000) compensatory model, such efficiency enables skilled readers to devote attentional resources to new material (cf. Recht & Leslie, 1988).

A fourth interactive approach, that of Rayner and Pollatsek (1989), is similar to VET in that it is grounded in a bottom-up, information-processing perspective, although it is informed mainly by the physiological aspects of human vision. Rayner and Pollatsek focus on the relationship between eye movement and fixation time, on the one hand, and long-term and working memory structures, on the other. This model assumes that eye fixation triggers a reader's lexical access, with access proceeding directly from textual processing or indirectly through phoneme–grapheme correspondences. Eye movement and lexical access proceed serially, with the reader fixing her gaze on subsequent words, and so on. As she retrieves meaning, the reader attaches it to a text representation that she constructs in working memory, a procedure similar to that proposed by Perfetti (1991).

What gives this framework an interactive dimension is what occurs in working memory, where Rayner and Pollatsek (1989) claim an inner speech mechanism constructs a literal, semantic, and syntactic representation of the text. The reader's ability to parse words, phrases, and sentences on the page rapidly permits her to detect inconsistencies in a way that is perhaps comparable to the inferencing, confirmation, disconfirmation, and decision-making operations described in Goodman's (1986) guessing game model. On encountering an inconsistency or "don't understand" message, the reader redirects her eye movement to the relevant text and then consults working memory to generate a new interpretation (Rayner & Pollatsek, 1989). A weak point of the Rayner and Pollatsek model is that it posits reading as a serial process. On the other hand, it not only assumes a top-down/bottom-up interaction, but also aims to explain comprehension and interpretation by using observable, measurable phenomena such as eye movement and fixation (Hudson, 2007).

Comprehension-as-construction, the fifth and final interactive model that we examine, focuses on how readers and authors negotiate meaning through text. Pearson and Tierney (1984) proposed a *composing* model of reading, which reflects the schema-theoretic principle that understanding text entails the construction of meaning (Tierney & Pearson, 1983). The Pearson and Tierney (1984) model assumes that readers participate actively in literacy events who *compose* meaning as they read, rather than merely reciting or "processing" text for the sole purpose of "comprehension." The thoughtful reader, according to Pearson and Tierney (1984), "reads as if she were a writer composing a text for yet another reader who lives within her" (p. 144)—not unlike Smith's (1983) concept of "reading like a writer." Comprehension-as-construction proposes that readers approach texts assuming that authors provide enough clues about text meaning to allow readers to reconstruct the intended message (Hudson, 2007).

Pierson and Tierney designated four simultaneous roles for the reader. As a *planner*, the reader identifies goals, activates schematic knowledge, and decides on how she will identify with the text (if at all). As a *composer*, she searches for coherence and fills textual gaps—as readers do in a schema-theoretic view. As *editor*, the reader appraises her interpretations of the text, assessing its coherence and meaningfulness. Finally, as a *monitor*, the reader acts as planner, composer, and editor, determining which of these functions predominate at a given moment in the reading process, rather like an executive processor (Grabe & Stoller, 2002). Asserting multiple roles for the reader is congruent with cognitive process theories claiming that writers move back and forth between reader and writer perspectives in the writing process (Flower & Hayes, 1981). Comprehension-as-construction also shares features in common with *reader response theory*, which focuses on the reader's subjective responses to text, intellectual growth, and self-expression (Hirvela, 1996, 2004; Iser, 1978; Langer, 1992).

Our survey of bottom-up, top-down, and interactive views of L1 and L2 reading is far from comprehensive. Despite a remarkable accumulation of research, "we actually know relatively little about how people become good L2 readers" (Grabe & Stoller, 2002, p. 2). At the same time, we hope that our comparison of models allied with these three metaphors points toward common insights that support an interactive or integrated perspective. Bernhardt (2005) recently called for a view of L2 reading "based on the interrelationships of languages, on the impact of linguistic and literacy knowledge, and on principles of learning" (p. 137). Regrettably, we lack a single coherent theory that would explain L2 reading and how it is learned. Nonetheless, researchers and teachers can appreciate the value of avoiding strong versions of bottom-up and top-down views while recognizing that naïve interactive approaches can overlook contradictory predictions (Grabe & Stoller, 2002; Hudson, 2007).

Understanding L2 Reading Processes

We begin this section on the unique aspects of L2 reading processes with a reminder that, to this point, we have drawn rather liberally on L1 and L2 literacy studies and reading research. We believe that L2 educators have much to gain from the achievements and expertise of L1 literacy specialists. In addition, as Grabe (2004) pointed out, whereas L2 reading research and instruction have much to gain from L1 research and its implications, it is inappropriate to adopt

L1-based conclusions on a "wholesale" or uncritical basis. L1–L2 parallels provide substantial evidence that "many, if not most . . . effective instructional practices in L1 settings will also be effective in L2 settings (with reasonable adaptations)" (Grabe, 2004, p. 59), although we do not presuppose that L1 and L2 readers engage in cognitive processing in the same ways. Figure 1.5, which informs the discussion below, summarizes key linguistic, psycholinguistic, experiential, individual, and sociocultural factors that distinguish L2 reading processes and development patterns.

The Linguistic Threshold Hypothesis

Many L2 learners and teachers can affirm that "reading proficiency in an L2 does not develop as completely or as 'easily' as it apparently does" in one's L1 (Grabe & Stoller, 2002, p. 2). As noted earlier, divergent writing systems and orthographies partly account for the unique difficulties of acquiring L2 literacy, as do learner differences such as age, the onset of bilingualism and biliteracy, positive and negative interlingual transfer, and factors related to L1 and L2 literacy instruction (Bernhardt & Kamil, 1995; Bialystok, 2001; Dressler & Kamil, 2006; Koda, 2005). We also know that learning to read in an L2 setting differs significantly from learning to read in an L1 setting. Because of general L2 proficiency, orthography, fluency, processing abilities, and L1 transfer (or inhibition), "L2 reading can be a

	Unique Features of L2 Reading Processes and Development
Linguistic Threshold	A minimum level (threshold) of general L2 proficiency may be required to develop functional L2 reading skills; L1 reading processes may rely on naturally emerging knowledge of vocabulary, grammar, discourse, genres, and so on
Metalinguistic and Cognitive Awareness	L2 reading may rely on greater metalinguistic and metacognitive awareness than does L1 reading, which depends less on explicit linguistic knowledge
Print environment	L2 reading may take place in environments with low exposure to L2 print sources and few opportunities to practice L2 reading; L1 reading often takes place in settings where readers have ready access to reading materials
Role of Multiple Linguistic Systems	L2 reading processes may involve access to two or more languages and orthographies, which may interact in complex ways (e.g., positive and negative interlingual transfer), whereas L1 reading involves no such pre-existing symbolic system and involves no potential for negative interlingual transfer
Age and Maturation	Acquisition of L2 reading skills may begin in childhood, adolescence, or adulthood, often simultaneously with the acquisition of L2 speaking, listening, writing, and grammar skills; L1 literacy development typically begins in childhood, during or after L1 oral and aural skills emerge
Completeness	L2 reading may be (or is perceived to be) more cognitively and metacognitively challenging than L1 reading; L2 reading development may therefore be less "complete" than L1 reading development for some learners

FIGURE 1.5. Differences between L1 and L2 Reading Processes and Development Patterns.
Sources: Grabe and Stoller (2002), Hudson (2007), Koda (2004).

distinct cognitive activity (particularly for older L2 students and EFL students)" (Grabe, 2004, pp. 58–59). The following section introduces constructs that set L2 reading apart from L1 reading—namely, the linguistic threshold hypothesis and cross-linguistic transfer. Chapter 2, which focuses on the unique characteristics of L2 readers, explores implications of these and other constructs for L2 literacy instruction.

The notion of a *linguistic threshold*, introduced by Cummins (1976), holds that bilingual learners must attain a "threshold level of L2 competence" to achieve balanced bilingual proficiency. As Figure 1.5 indicates, the *linguistic threshold hypothesis* as it applies to L2 reading holds that L2 readers must first reach a "threshold" level of general L2 knowledge and skill before they can be expected to make substantial progress as L2 readers. Alderson (1984) brought this proposition into focus by asking whether L2 reading difficulties were more strongly influenced by L2 skill (or lack thereof) than by (L1) literacy (Bernhardt, 2000; Bialystok, 2001; Pichette, Segalowitz, & Connors, 2003). Empirical studies have, indeed, demonstrated that L2 learners with well-developed L1 literacy skills are only able to apply those reading skills in the L2 if their global L2 proficiency is sufficiently developed (Clarke, 1979, 1980; Cziko, 1978). An insufficient L2 proficiency level "short-circuits" L2 reading development (Goodman, 1988).

As Cummins (1976) and (Kern, 2000) cautioned, we should not conceive of such a threshold as invariable or absolute. Rather, the threshold may vary from learner to learner as a function of cross-linguistic differences, the frequency of L2 use, the communicative demands placed on the learner, the nature of reading tasks, and so on (Koda, 2007b; Koda & Zehler, 2007). It is undeniable that L1 reading ability, L2 proficiency, and L2 reading skills share a complex, dynamic relationship, but research appears to converge on a few notable trends. In a survey of empirical studies, Hudson (2007) concluded that "second language proficiency plays a greater role than does first language reading ability" (p. 73), despite earlier claims by Carrell (1991) and others (e.g., Yorio, 1971) that L1 reading ability is a stronger predictor of L2 reading attainment. The predominance of L2 competence is most pronounced at lower L2 proficiency levels, in line with *Verbal Efficiency Theory* (VET) (Perfetti, 1985, 1988, 1991), which predicts that low-proficiency L2 learners have automatized only a small number of text processing operations. Hudson (2007) further suggested that the L2 threshold may operate "on a sliding scale" (p. 67): L2 proficiency more robustly influences L2 reading at lower levels of proficiency and reading skill, whereas L1 reading ability interacts more strongly with L2 reading among higher-level readers.[8]

Evidence favoring a linguistic threshold is consistent and substantial, but we would not wish to suggest that such a threshold is universal or stable, even within a single L2 population. In a review of threshold studies involving a range of L1 groups, L2s, literacy levels, and demographic factors, Bernhardt (2005, p. 137) calculated the following proportional contributions to L2 reading measures:

| L1 Reading skill | 14–21% |
| L2 Linguistic knowledge | 30% |

Though impressive, these cumulative results account for only 50% of the variance in L2 reading performance, leaving half of the variance unexplained. Bernhardt (2005) suggested that comprehension strategies, reader interest, reader engagement, content knowledge, and motivation might collectively address this wide gap, as illustrated in her compensatory model of L2 reading (see Figure 1.6). Despite the complex factors underlying the unexplained variance in Bernhardt's compensatory model, the likelihood of a linguistic threshold influencing L2 reading development suggests useful instructional implications, which we explore in Chapter 2. In the final sections of this chapter, we survey global and local components that comprise L2 reading, as well as strategies known to promote the process.

Components of L2 Reading: Skills and Subskills

In defining literacy and reading processes earlier in this chapter, we referred to reading as a *skill* and as a *process*. Harris and Hodges (1981) concisely defined *skill*

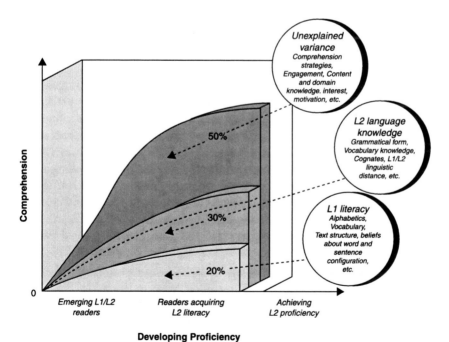

FIGURE 1.6. Compensatory Model of Second Language Reading.
Source: Bernhardt (2005, p. 140).

as "an acquired ability to perform well; proficiency" (p. 298); Alexander and Jetton (2000) described skills as "essential academic habits" (p. 296). Although these commonsense views enjoy wide currency, L1 and L2 literacy educators may wish to view reading skill not as a unitary competence, but rather as an "acquired ability" that comprises interrelated yet separable (and arguably teachable) sub-skills. According to Grabe and Stoller (2002), reading skills "represent linguistic processing abilities that are relatively automatic in their use and their combinations (e.g., word recognition, syntactic processing)" (p. 15). Goodman (1967, 1969, 1986) and Smith (2004) would object to the premise that reading can be broken down into component skills: Top-down perspectives assume that language and literacy are learned as a whole through communication (see Figure 1.2). A component-skills perspective, in contrast, posits reading as "a complex, multidimensional operation." In this view, reading can "be dissected into a series of theoretically distinct procedures, each requiring a wide range of skills" (Koda, 2004, p. 229). We believe that integrative approaches are congruent with a component-skills perspective, which provides reading teachers with valuable instructional tools (Carr & Levy, 1990). Notably, comparisons of multiple influences of component skills can provide educators with clues for identifying readers' strengths and deficiencies, providing insights into component skills that instruction might productively target (see Chapters 4 and 5).

Proctor and Dutta (1995) proposed a useful componential view in which reading skill is "goal directed," "highly integrated and well organized," "acquired through practice and training," and gradually automatized (p. 18). In line with Bernhardt's (2005) compensatory view, Proctor and Dutta (1995) held that "cognitive demands are reduced as skill is acquired" and that reading can be analyzed in terms of its perceptual, motor, and cognitive operations (p. 18). Hudson (2007) similarly observed that research has consistently identified four reading skill categories: (1) decoding (word attack) skills; (2) comprehension skills; (3) fluency skills; and (4) critical reading skills. Although these four skill categories might be separable at the descriptive level, they are functionally interdependent in an interactive perspective, as illustrated in Figures 1.7–1.9. What we refer to as *reading comprehension* by definition requires decoding ability, as Figure 1.4 implies. Successful comprehension may also necessitate fluency and critical reading skills, depending on the text in question, its relative difficulty, the context for reading, and the reader's goals (Rasinski, Blachowicz, & Lems, 2006; Shanahan, 2006). An instance where speed and critical reading, in addition to decoding and comprehension, are indispensable would be the case of a student taking the Test of English as a Foreign Language (TOEFL), Scholastic Aptitude Test (SAT), or Graduate Record Exam (GRE).

We would therefore caution educators against viewing *reading skill* as synonymous with *reading comprehension*. Comprehension can be viewed as a component of the broader category of reading skill, and the relationships between the two must be understood (Koda, 2004; Nuttall, 2005). We also recognize that literacy instruction may involve tension between holistic, top-down principles and bottom-up, component-skills precepts. Given our evolving understanding of the complexity of L1 and L2 reading, we would suggest that such tension is inevitable and even useful. When expert readers read, the high-level skills that enable them to read successfully may defy "dissection." Novice readers, in contrast, may not yet have developed the ability to integrate and deploy multiple skills so efficiently, as Bernhardt's compensatory model (Figure 1.6) implies. Hudson (2007) proposed that, once novice learners "have moved past . . . very early recognition skills, they can be presented with more complex literacy tasks in order to push them into engaging more of the reading skills that affect comprehension." However, research consistently shows that "it is not likely to be productive to isolate . . . skills . . . and focus on them until they are learned" (p. 292). Middle ground can perhaps be found in the recognition that component skills operate most effectively in clusters when readers engage in purposeful, meaningful reading tasks that embed strategic and metastrategic practice.

Before enumerating reading skills, we should clarify the essence of reading comprehension and to distinguish it as a subcategory of skill. When a proficient reader reads fluently, reading for comprehension necessitates "very rapid and automatic processing of words, strong skills in forming a general meaning representation of main ideas, and efficient coordination of many processes under very limited time constraints" (Grabe & Stoller, 2002, p. 14). Comprehension may thus be more complex than we think, requiring the deployment of interrelated subskills such as fluency, efficiency, and speed, which we can theoretically measure (see Chapter 9).[9] It is important to recognize, however, that speed and comprehension are quite different (Brenitz, 2006; Haynes & Carr, 1990; Shanahan, 2006). Referring to Carver's (1997, 2000) research on levels of text understanding among L1 readers, Koda (2004) observed that, as processing demands increase, reading rate decreases. College-level readers can scan moderately challenging academic texts at a rate of about 600 words per minute (wpm), but when asked to memorize text material, their average speed drops to 138 wpm. Although comprehension can go hand in hand with speed, the demands of the reading task and the reader's purpose for reading may favor one over the other.

In exploring expert sources on reading skills, we may encounter numerous lists and taxonomies, which abound in the literature, making it difficult for teachers and materials developers to settle on a single inventory of (sub)skills to target (Brown & Haynes, 1985). In a synthesis of reading skills research, Rosenshine (1980) observed that findings converged on the seven subskill areas listed in Figure 1.7, which break down the four broad skill categories introduced above into more specific functions.

Many expert sources subdivide these subskills into extremely detailed lists containing 30 or more component functions, as did Munby (1978), whose taxonomy was designed to guide teachers and materials developers in setting goals for L2 literacy instruction.[10] Figure 1.8, inspired by Gordon's (1982) skill descriptors for novice L1 readers and adapted for more advanced readers,

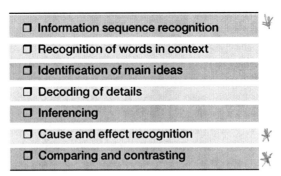

FIGURE 1.7. Reading Subskills.
Source: Rosenshine (1980).

exemplifies the level of detail achieved by researchers and theorists. Similar inventories present hierarchies of lower- to higher-order (sub)skills, analogous to Bloom's (1956) well-known processing taxonomy. Figure 1.9, based on a three-level model, represents one such hierarchy.

Figure 1.9 identifies a skills continuum ranging from lower-level, bottom-up functions (e.g., decoding) to higher-level operations (e.g., scanning, comparing), which entail interactive processes (see Figure 1.2). Skills hierarchies should not be interpreted in an *a priori* fashion, as the field has not reached consensus on what constitutes higher- or lower-order skills, which are relative and subject to the influence of the context for reading (Alderson, 1990; Alderson & Lukmani, 1989; Hudson, 1993). Skills hierarchies can be extremely useful in developing curricula and constructing syllabi, but they should never be used wholesale as prescriptions for instructional design (see Chapter 4). Moreover, subskills may overlap within and across categories, frequently functioning interdependently. In line with Bernhardt's compensatory model (Figure 1.6), readers deploy more skills and do so more efficiently as their reading proficiency evolves. Finally, we should recall that L1 and L2 research consistently fails to support "strictly hierarchically ordered reading skills" (Hudson, 2007, p. 103).

L2 Reading Strategies

Despite the absence of a single, comprehensive taxonomy of L1 and L2 reading skills and expert consensus on a reading skills hierarchy, teachers have much to gain from decades of reading skills research. Such research insights help us to understand the complexity of reading, identify goals, plan instruction, and construct tools for assessing performance and progress. A consequence of skills-oriented research involves the identification of reading *strategies*, which many contemporary reading experts believe to be learnable and teachable. We dedicate the bulk of our attention to reading strategies in Chapters 3, 5, and 8, where we recommend methods for integrating strategy instruction and practice

Reading Skills Development

Name letters	Recognize contractions	Use a dictionary pronunciation key
Identify consonants and vowels	Divide words	Define high-frequency words
Read words on sight	Recognize synonyms, antonyms, and homonyms	Decode compound words
Recognize "silent" letters	Draw on and develop a rich working vocabulary	Use context clues to understand meaning
Recognize rhyming words	Understand polysemy (multiple meanings)	Recognize multiple phoneme–grapheme correspondences (e.g., "hard" and "soft" c)
Identify word roots and affixes (prefixes and suffixes, plural markers)	Recognize blends and consonant and vowel digraphs (e.g., ch, ee)	

Reading Comprehension Development

Categorize words and information	Modify incorrect predictions	Understand and use figurative language
Sequence words and information	Recognize and repair miscomprehension	Understand literary and academic forms
Follow directions	Integrate text information with existing schematic knowledge	Evaluate characters, narrators, authors
Read for information at a rapid speed	Identify tone or emotion in a text	Evaluate narrative settings
Retell a story	Generate inferences	Draw factual conclusions
Identify key words	Judge reliability of source	Distinguish fact from fiction and opinion
Identify main ideas	Compare and contrast	Recognize purposes for reading
Summarize	Judge propositional content	Shift purposes for reading as needed
Predict outcomes	Deploy strategies to monitor comprehension	Read critically

Reading, Research, and Study Skills

Alphabetize	Use tables of contents, indexes, and glossaries efficiently	Use text-based, visual, and interactive electronic resources to collect and compile information: apply QUEST model (Question, Understand resources, Evaluate, Synthesize, Transform)
Cross-reference	Understand and synthesize information from various sources	
Use dictionary efficiently	Classify books and online sources by genre category	
Use encyclopedia efficiently	Use atlases, maps, graphs effectively	

FIGURE 1.8. Three Sets of Reading Competencies for Readers of English.
Sources: Block and Pressley (2008), Eagleton and Dobler (2007), Gordon (1982), Grabe and Stoller (2001, 2002).

LEVEL 1	LEVEL 2	LEVEL 3
Decode print	Identify graphemes, syllables, words, word boundaries, phrases	Scan, fixate, anticipate, classify, test, match, verify hypotheses
Make sense of print	Assign meaning to words, phrases, and sentences	Anticipate grammatical and semantic categories, match and verify hypotheses
Question print-based messages	Identify discrepancies among divergent messages and between text content and what is known	Retrieve information from long-term memory, compare, make inferences

FIGURE 1.9. Three-Level Descriptions of Reading Skills.
Sources: Hudson (2007), Koda (2004); Lunzer, Waite, and Dolan (1979); Nuttall (2005).

into the teaching of reading. Before concluding this chapter, we would like to clarify the relationship between skills and strategies. Skills "refer to information-processing techniques that are automatic" and "are applied to a text unconsciously." In contrast, strategies consist of "actions selected deliberately to achieve particular goals" (Paris, Wasik, & Turner, 1996, p. 611). Strategies are "deliberate, goal/problem-oriented, and reader-initiated/congrolled" (Koda, 2004, p. 205). Although definitions of skills and strategies sometimes blur, the distinctions highlighted by Paris et al. and Koda are important. For Rubin (1987), reading strategies consist of "operations, steps, plans, routines used by . . . learners to facilitate the obtaining, storage, retrieval, and use of information" (p. 19), a definition consistent with the definitions advanced by Anderson (1991, 1999), Chamot and El-Dinary (1999), Cohen (1996), and numerous others.

Chamot and O'Malley (1994a) proposed three strategic categories, commonly referenced in the literature, which are useful as we explore strategy-oriented instruction. According to Chamot and O'Malley (1994b), *cognitive strategies* entail strategies that enable readers to complete cognitive tasks during reading (e.g., inferencing, word analysis). *Metacognitive strategies*, in contrast, regulate cognitive processing, as when readers monitor comprehension or correct inaccurate predictions. Meanwhile, *social and affective strategies* permit learners to interact cooperatively with peers and teachers during reading tasks. Socioaffective strategies might include seeking the meaning of unfamiliar words from a peer or confirming a prediction with a teacher. As in the case of reading subskills, strategy taxonomies abound (see Anderson, 1991; Chamot & O'Malley, 1994a; Cohen, 1998; Foster, 2005; Koda, 2004; Mokhtari & Sheorey, 2008). Space limitations prevent us from reproducing detailed inventories here, but Figure 1.10 provides a useful sampling of reading strategy types that exemplify the categories proposed by Chamot and O'Malley (1994b) (also see Appendix 4.1).

Strategy instruction has ignited widespread interest in L2 instruction, including L2 literacy education. A leading reason is that, with sufficient practice and contextualization, strategies can "become generated and applied automatically as

☐ Specify a purpose for reading
☐ Plan a reading process
☐ Preview the text
☐ Predict text contents
☐ Verify predictions
☐ Generate questions about the text
☐ Locate answers to questions
☐ Compare text to existing schemata
☐ Summarize textual information
☐ Generate inferences
☐ Notice and analyze text structure
☐ Re-read
☐ Use discourse markers to understand textual relationships
☐ Check comprehension accuracy
☐ Track reading difficulties
☐ Repair comprehension failures
☐ Critique a text or point of view
☐ Reflect on and discuss what has been learned

FIGURE 1.10. Sample Reading Strategies.
Adapted from Grabe and Stoller (2002).

skills." Conversely, "an emerging skill can become a strategy when . . . used intentionally" (Paris et al., 1991, p. 611). Educational advantages of explicit strategy instruction in academic contexts include the following:

1. Strategies permit readers to organize and assess textual material;
2. Cultivating reading strategies enhances attentional resources, memory, communication, and learning processes;
3. Readers can select strategies and individualize their strategy repertoires;
4. Strategic reading activates metacognition and motivation;
5. Reading strategies are teachable through direct instruction;
6. Strategic reading can improve not only language and literacy skills, but also disciplinary knowledge. (Paris et al., 1991)

Empirical evidence consistently favors cognitive and metacognitive strategy training (see Dressler & Kamil, 2006; Farris et al., 2004; Grabe & Stoller, 2002; Hudson, 2007; Israel, Collins Block, Bauserman, & Kinnucan-Welsch, 2005; Koda, 2004;

Mokhtari & Sheorey, 2008; National Reading Panel, 2000; Trabasso & Bouchard, 2002; Weaver, 2002). We should acknowledge that critics such as Macaro (2006) have argued that strategic instruction and practice may not influence L2 competence and performance as extensively as many believe. In subsequent chapters, we explore practical implications for maximizing strategic tools in the teaching of L2 reading.

Chapter Summary

We have endeavored to acquaint readers with perspectives on processes and development patterns in L1 and L2 reading and to situate these perspectives in a socioculturally-informed literacy framework. Although our principal focus in this book involves understanding *reading* and outlining best practices for effective L2 reading instruction, we believe that reading instruction can be truly effective only when learners and teachers connect reading and learning to read with the contexts and purposes for reading. We surveyed models of reading and their implications for L2 literacy instruction by associating them with bottom-up, top-down, and interactive (integrative) metaphors, which we view as useful descriptive tools (rather than as distinct categories). Recognizing the limitations of interactive approaches, which may naïvely imply compatibility between bottom-up and top-down views (Hudson, 2007), we suggested that "modified interactive models" (Grabe & Stoller, 2002) may offer the most productive means of making sense of a sometimes dizzying research landscape.

Our exploration of reading skills, subskills, and strategies similarly touched on the key targets of L2 reading research and instruction. Research in these domains may likewise offer disparate or inconclusive findings, yet we find a remarkably high degree of convergence on several global insights. Grabe (2004) proposed the following ten implications for the teaching of L2 reading, which we develop in greater detail in the remaining chapters of this book:

Research Implications for Reading Instruction

1. Ensure word recognition fluency (Chapters 3, 9).
2. Emphasize vocabulary learning and create a vocabulary-rich environment (Chapter 9).
3. Activate background (schematic) knowledge in appropriate ways (Chapters 2–9).
4. Ensure effective language knowledge and general comprehension skills (Chapters 3–5, 9).
5. Teach text structures and discourse organization (Chapters 3–5, 7).

6. Promote the strategic reader rather than teach individual strategies (Chapters 3–5, 8, 9).
7. Build reading fluency and reading rate; aim for reading efficiency (Chapters 4–9).
8. Promote extensive reading (Chapter 6).
9. Develop students' intrinsic motivation for reading (Chapters 2–4, 6, 7).
10. Plan and implement a coherent curriculum for student learning (Chapters 3, 4, 7–9). (Adapted from Grabe, 2004, p. 46)

These principles are not designed to prescribe a "universal curriculum" (Grabe, 2004), but rather to offer practical guidelines for designing and implementing L2 literacy instruction. Methods of teaching reading, wrote Grabe (2004), "need to vary in important ways for L2 learners depending on context, learner needs, and language proficiency levels" (p. 45). Moreover, as we will see in subsequent chapters, "any instructional setting and any group of curriculum developers must determine priorities based on student needs, institutional expectations, and resource constraints" (Grabe, 2004, p. 46).

Further Reading and Resources

We recommend the sources listed below for further reading on key issues introduced in this chapter. Bibliographic information for published sources can be found in the References section at the end of the book. Relevant URLs are also provided, but we caution readers that these tend to change.

Handbooks and state-of-the-art reviews of L1 and L2 reading research
August & Shanahan (2006a, 2007); Eskey (2005); Flurkey, Paulson, & Goodman (2007); Kamil (2008); Kamil (2008); Kamil et al. (2000); National Reading Panel (2000); National Reading Panel (2000); Perfetti (2003); Pressley et al. (2007); Stahl and Hayes (1997); Sullivan (2002); Willis (2007)
Reading, human evolution, and the brain
Manguel (1996); Wolf (2007)
Comprehensive sources on L2 reading processes and development
Grabe and Stoller (2002); Hudson (2007); Koda (2004, 2007a); Koda & Zehler (2007); Urquhart & Weir (1998)
Literacy studies
Barton (2007); Barton & Hamilton (1998); Blanton (1998); Comings, Garner, & Smith (2007); Edelsky (2006); Gee (1996); Goodman & Martens (2007); Purcell-Gates (2007); Purcell-Gates et al. (2008); Reder & Davila (2005); Rivera & Huerta-Macias (2007); Street (1984, 1995); Wray & Medwell (2007)

Writing systems (Omniglot website)
http://www.omniglot.com/
L1 literacy, reading, and language arts
Dozier (2006); Farris et al. (2004); Gambrell, Morrow, & Pressley (2007); Glasgow & Farrell (2007); Keene (2008);); Lapp, Flood, Brock, & Fisher (2007); Lapp, Flood, & Farnan (2007); Lundy (2007); Rasinski et al. (2006); Smith (2004, 2006, 2007); Sturtevant et al. (2006); Weaver (2002)
L2 reading research
Bernhardt (1991b, 2000, 2005); Carrell, Devine, & Eskey (1988); Grabe (2004); Sullivan (2002)
L2 reading instruction
Aebersold & Field (1997); Fitzgerald & Graves (2004); Grabe (2004); Mokhtari & Sheorey (2008); Nuttall (2005)
Digital literacies and technology-enhanced L1 and L2 literacy instruction
Cummins, Brown, and Sayers, 2007; Eagleton & Dobler (2007); Kress (2002); Mackey (2007); McKenna et al. (2006, 2008). Murray & McPherson (2005); Thorne & Black (2007); Valmont (2002)
L2 reading journals
Reading in a Foreign Language (http://nflrc.hawaii.edu/rfl/)
International Reading Association (IRA) website
http://www.ira.org/
Center for Applied Linguistics (CAL) literacy education website
http://www.cal.org/topics/le/
National Council of Teachers of English (NCTE) elementary and secondary ESL instruction websites
http://www.ncte.org/collections/elemell
http://www.ncte.org/collections/secell
Teachers of English to Speakers of Other Languages (TESOL) website
http://www.tesol.org/
Reading process models website
http://io.uwinnipeg.ca/~hkatz/fridge/cogread/cogread.html
National Institute for Literacy
http://www.nifl.gov/
National Institute for Literacy Special Collections
http://www.nifl.gov/lincs/collections/policy/resource.html

Reflection and Review

1. Identify and discuss reasons for framing reading, learning to read, and reading instruction in the context of literacy and literacies.
2. How is a *literacy practice* distinct from a *literacy event*? How does each construct help us define and understand the other? How might these con-

structs guide us in planning literacy courses, selecting materials, delivering instruction, and assessing students?

3. How can L2 reading instructors benefit from familiarizing themselves with the world's writing systems and knowing about how orthographies differ?

4. In what ways could the concept of orthographic transparency (or opacity) as reflected in the Orthographic Depth Hypothesis be important for L2 readers and L2 reading teachers?

5. Evaluate the definitions of reading presented on pp. 15–16. Which definitions align with your current views of L1 and L2 reading? Which do you find to be the most accurate and complete? Why?

6. In classifying models of reading, why is it important to view descriptors such as top-down, bottom-up, and interactive as metaphors, rather than as theories? Why do you think there is such a profusion of perspectives on reading? What do you think this variety says about our understanding of what it means to become a skilled L1 or L2 reader?

7. Considering the contributions of noted scholars (e.g., Bernhardt, Goodman, LaBerge & Samuels, Pierson & Tierney, Smith, Stanovich), compare the strengths and weaknesses of bottom-up, top-down, and interactive/integrated perspectives on reading. Of the models reviewed in this chapter, which approaches most persuasively account for L1 and L2 reading development? Which models are most informative for L2 reading instruction? Why?

8. Discuss the consequences of viewing contrasting perspectives on reading processes and development as complementary and of combining selected elements of competing models.

9. According to the literature surveyed in this chapter, what are the respective roles of schematic knowledge, L2 proficiency, metalinguistic knowledge, and L1 reading capabilities in the development of L2 literacy? How might your understanding of these factors influence your theory of L2 reading and your practice as a literacy educator?

10. How are reading strategies distinct from skills, and why is this distinction important for curriculum designers, teachers, and assessors?

Application Activities

Application Activity 1.1
Exploring Beliefs and Myths about Reading and Reading Development

Based on your prior knowledge, experience, and understanding of this chapter, indicate agreement (A), disagreement (D), or uncertainty (U) about the statements below. Edit statements to reflect your viewpoint more accurately. Discuss your responses with a peer, justifying your position with relevant evidence.

Belief Statements	A	D	U
1. Reading is the most critical skill needed for academic success.			
2. Reading comprehension depends on the decoding of sound–symbol correspondences.			
3. Reading is a purely cognitive skill whose complexity is not yet completely understood.			
4. Reading processes involve the sequential identification of letters, words, and larger units of discourse.			
5. As a universal cognitive process, reading is minimally affected by local and cultural influences.			
6. Background (schematic) knowledge is more important than grammatical or lexical knowledge in comprehending written text.			
7. The choice of reading materials for a literacy course should based on the strategies to be practiced and the skills to be mastered.			
8. As readers read, they guess about meaning using minimal language cues, which they select based on their expectations.			
9. L1 readers are not fully conscious of coherence devices when they read; therefore, L2 readers don't need to worry about them.			
10. A reading course should optimally feature only materials that are immediately relevant to learners' needs and interests.			
11. To maximize instruction, academic reading courses should focus chiefly on genres and texts from students' fields of study.			
12. Readings used for instructional purposes should be authentic and unsimplified (i.e., not "treated" or "simplified").			
13. Novice L2 readers need explicit instruction focusing on formal rules (e.g., phonics, spelling, word formation, grammar, discourse) to develop reading proficiency.			
14. Because scientific and other academic genres are the least culture-bound, such materials cause L2 students fewer comprehension difficulties than do non-academic materials.			

Application Activity 1.2
Position Statement on L2 Reading Instruction

Imagine that you are applying for positions as an L2 literacy teacher. Your application must include a statement of your position on the teaching and learning of L2 literacy. Based on this chapter's survey of reading models and metaphors, your responses to the prompts in Application Activity 1.1, as well as some further reading of your own (see Further Reading and Resources), compose a 250- to 500-word position statement on L2 literacy learning and teaching.

Application Activity 1.3
Reflection on Schema Knowledge and Activation

Anderson and Pearson (1984) predicted the following outcomes of schema activation during the reading process:

- New knowledge interacting with existing knowledge produces comprehension.
- Readers recall information from novel texts that align with their existing schemata, but they may overlook or rationalize details and meanings that fail to match current knowledge.
- Advance organizers improve readers' comprehension.
- When texts suggest new concepts to readers, this novel material engages readers in problem-solving and meaning-making, leading to comprehension.

In a two- to three-page reflective discussion, consider the implications of these aspects of schema activation for learning to read and for teaching (L1 or L2) reading. Review your own experience with content, cultural, and formal schemata. How have you used these knowledge sources to read and learn? Consider how your schematic knowledge has changed (or not changed) in response to the material presented in this chapter.

Application Activity 1.4
Exploring the Role of Schematic Knowledge in Text Comprehension

Reading researchers (e.g., Birch, 2007) have argued that it is nearly impossible for readers to construct meaning exclusively on the basis of textual input, as no text can contain all the information necessary for complete comprehension. Some experts (e.g., Carrell, 1988b, 1988c) have maintained that L2 readers may rely too heavily on text-based processes, thereby neglecting bottom-up skills and strategies (e.g., decoding, word analysis, and so forth). Based on the literature on schema theory reviewed in this chapter and at least one of the primary sources mentioned, compose a two- to three-page argument explaining your agreement or disagreement with the claim that texts cannot by themselves contain enough information for readers to comprehend them. How can texts and genres very in this regard? Use text samples to justify your position.

Application Activity 1.5
Matching Skills and Subskills to Texts

Select a brief, self-contained text from a book, magazine, newspaper, or online source. Based on the reading metaphors, skills, and strategies presented in this chapter, identify the skills and subskills that readers would need to comprehend the text sample successfully. Prepare a two- to three-page written discussion, noting why the (sub)skills you identified would be especially relevant for a particular L2 reader or reader population.

Application Activity 1.6
Exploring L2 Literacy Policy, Research, and Practice

In their executive summary of a comprehensive review of L2 literacy research in the US, August and Shanahan (2006b) concluded that "instruction that provides substantial coverage in the key components of reading—identified by the National Reading Panel (2000) as phonemic awareness, phonics, fluency, vocabulary, and text comprehension—has clear benefits for language-minority students." Such conclusions are designed to shape educational policy, which can significantly influence teachers and students. Consequently, it can be valuable for L2 reading teachers to acquaint themselves with governmental policies, public opinion, and research trends that can affect curriculum and assessment.

Review a sampling of current policy documents and position statements on L2 literacy education (see Further Reading and Resources for Web links to the IRA, CAL, NCTE, TESOL, or another relevant professional organization). You may also wish to consult policy documents published by your educational institution, school district, education department, or ministry of education. Prepare a summary of two or three such documents, comparing their recommendations and mandates. What theoretical and ideological positions do they reference and embrace (or reject)? Why? Evaluate these positions in light of your own experience as a reader and what you have learned from this chapter.

Chapter 2
L2 Reading
Focus on the Reader

Questions for Reflection

- What are some your earliest memories of reading (home, school, and so on)? In what ways (if any) do you think those early experiences have shaped your current reading practices and attitudes toward reading?
- If you have had significant exposure to reading in a second language, how have those experiences been similar to or different from reading in your primary language?
- If you were preparing to teach an L2 reading course (or a course serving L2 readers), what information would be helpful to have about the students before planning the syllabus, selecting texts, and preparing lessons?

As discussed in Chapter 1, reading is a complex interaction of cognitive processes and strategies (used by the reader) and various types of information (contained in the text). Earlier models of reading instruction have tended to focus primarily either on *bottom-up processes* (for decoding and comprehending the text) or *top-down skills* (for activating the background knowledge and prediction strategies of the reader). As we noted, an over-emphasis on either side of the interaction overlooks important aspects of the reading process and risks leaving some students behind (Lipson, 1983; Reynolds, Taylor, Steffensen, Shirey, & Anderson, 1982).

In this chapter and the next we examine these issues further. First, we focus on the *reader*, especially the L2 reader, in an effort to understand how readers' prior knowledge and individual characteristics impact their interaction with a particular text—and how these interactions can vary across readers. In the next chapter, we will look at the notion of "text" itself, its component parts, and the challenges they present to L2 readers in particular.

An individual reader brings a number of different things into the reading process, including *purposes* for reading (e.g., for survival, information/learning, or pleasure), *background* (the influences of family, school, and culture or subculture of origin), *attitudes* toward reading and literacy in general (which may be shaped both by purpose and background), and *prior knowledge* (linguistic, content, and rhetorical) related to the information in the text. In addition, readers bring *individual differences* in personality, *learning styles and strategies, reading strategies,* and life experience. Thus, a group of readers encountering the same text at the same point in time (e.g., in a class or a book group) will not have identical experiences with reading the text or the same reactions to or interpretations of it. Even the same reader interacting with the same text at different points in her life will experience it differently because the reader herself has changed over time.

In this chapter, we look more carefully at these *reader-based variables* in the reading process, discuss challenges specific to L2 readers, and address the practical implications of these variables for *needs assessment, course design, text selection,* and *classroom instruction.* We examine these implications in further detail in Chapters 3–5.

Who Are L2 Readers?

Children learning to read in their L1 have the advantage of years of oral language exposure that have helped them to develop a vocabulary of thousands of words, mastery of the phonological system, and strongly developed intuitions about L1 morphology and syntax. College students who have always been educated in their L1s have 12 or more years of literacy experience and exposure in that language. In contrast, L2 readers began in acquiring their target language later, have less acquired knowledge of it, and have had less experience with (and exposure to) L2 texts. Although L1 literacy skills, if they exist, appear to transfer to and facilitate L2 reading, they also can cause confusion due to cross-linguistic differences (Birch, 2007; Genesee & Geva, 2006; Koda, 2004; see Chapters 1 and 3).

The academic literacy demands of upper-secondary and postsecondary education are challenging (Scarcella, 2003; Spack, 1997), and even many L1 students are not adequately prepared to meet these standards and need remedial coursework in reading and/or writing when they begin college. These expectations are typically more daunting for L2 readers, who do not have an equivalent linguistic foundation to that of L1 peers. L2 readers may never have read much at all in the L2, and their prior L2 education may not have helped them to develop basic academic reading skills and strategies.

Before discussing the knowledge that all readers possess and its sources and influences, it is important to articulate more precisely what we mean by an "L2 reader" and/or an "L2 learner." As we stated in the introduction to this volume, the primary student audience on which we focus involves students in upper-secondary and postsecondary contexts whose primary or home language was not the target language or present language of instruction (e.g., English in the US). However, within this broad definition are at least four distinct *student audiences* who may be found in a variety of different instructional settings.

International (Visa) Students

Until quite recently, the most visible and "traditional" ESL population consisted of students pursuing an education in an English-speaking country or at an English-medium institution. In curriculum development, course design, and materials construction, certain assumptions are made about *international students*:

- They are well educated and fully literate in their L1s.
- They tend to be from relatively affluent, even privileged backgrounds.
- Their L2 education in their home countries has been traditional (i.e., grammar-based rather than communicative) with limited opportunities for extended reading and writing practice and even fewer for listening and speaking development.
- They are at least somewhat unfamiliar with the L2 culture and educational system and may experience various degrees and stages of culture shock.
- They plan to return to their home countries after completing their studies.

Of course, any teacher who has worked with international students is well aware of the tremendous variation across students with regard to those assumptions. Furthermore, we observe great differences according to students' home countries, languages, and cultures—and even wider variation when it comes to individual differences, which we explore below. However, our point here is that the list outlined above represents *assumptions* that many educators make in approaching this particular student audience. The related implications of these assumptions for teaching L2 readers who are international students include the following:

- They are capable, experienced L1 readers, so at least some of that literacy experience can/will transfer to the L2 task.
- They may never have read more than a page or two at a time in the L2, so they will need encouragement and motivation to build reading speed and fluency and extensive reading habits (at least for L2).
- In selecting texts and tasks, teachers will need to be sensitive to those students' relative unfamiliarity with L2 culture.

EFL Students

EFL (English as a Foreign Language) students differ from international ESL students in that they are *not* pursuing their education in an L2–medium institution or cultural milieu. In other words, they are analogous to English-speaking high school or college students who study French, Spanish, and so forth, as a "foreign" language, either to fulfill graduation requirements or as a major field of study. L2 instructors encountering EFL students in their home cultures can make many of the same assumptions listed above for international students, but three notable differences distinguish them. First, obviously students in their home countries do not experience culture shock. Second, their motivations and interests may not be identical to those of international students. The latter group, knowing that they will not only have to complete their English course requirements but *all* of their academic work in the L2, may be more intrinsically motivated to improve their L2 skills. For reading teachers, these circumstances may mean, for example, that international students may be more open and responsive to suggestions about extensive L2 reading outside of the class. Third, EFL students may not have the same resources outside of class to develop their L2 skills (e.g., interaction with native speakers, L2 television and radio, unlimited print resources in the L2). Consequently, their language development in general may unfold more slowly, and teachers must be more creative in providing students with opportunities to be exposed to the language in general and to L2 text in particular (Brown, 2007b).

Immigrant Students

Over the past 25 years, English-language programs have been impacted by a growing number of ESL students who came to their new country as *adolescent or adult immigrants*, either as legal permanent residents ("green card" holders in the US) or as undocumented residents. Many of these immigrants are refugees from war-affected countries, fleeing religious or political persecution, or seeking improved economic opportunities. These immigrants are different from international students in almost every way imaginable: About the only area of overlap is the fact that their home language (L1) was not English. These students may or may not be well educated or literate in their L1s, often living in poverty and dependent upon public assistance. In addition, immigrant learners may have experienced trauma in their home countries or during their immigration, and their L2 education may have been informal or disrupted by life events. Teachers of these L2 readers should not assume strong language or literacy skills (in either L1 or L2), but they should also realize that the "immigrant" audience is extremely diverse. For example, whereas some students may be poor and undereducated, others may have been highly educated professionals back in their home countries. Like international students, they may lack cultural and academic knowledge that would help them read L2 texts, but unlike the former group, immigrant students may be unable to respond effectively to tasks that ask them to compare their home culture with the L2 culture, as their experience of the "home" culture may have been interrupted or even traumatic (McKay & Wong, 2000; Olsen, 1997).

Generation 1.5 Students

A more recently emerging group of learners are so-called *Generation 1.5 students* (Harklau, Losey, & Siegal, 1999; Rumbaut & Ima, 1978).[1] The children of first-generation immigrants, Generation 1.5 students either arrived in the new country at an early age or were born there. Although they are typically native-born or naturalized citizens of their parents' new country, they fall into the "L2" population because their primary/home language was their parents' L1, not English (or another L2). They usually have received all or most of their education in the L2, may or may not be literate at all in the L1, and may be well assimilated into the L2 culture—in contrast to the other groups. Still, they face challenges that account for the "1.5" label: they are caught between languages and cultures. They had a later start in the L2 compared with monolingual native English speakers but have not fully acquired the L1, in the sense that they may lack the advanced language and literacy skills one gains as one moves through the educational system. They have been raised in an L2 setting but often feel strong ties to the L1 culture.

It has been challenging for educational systems to know exactly how to serve Generation 1.5 learners. At early ages, they may have been placed in bilingual or ESL programs, depending on the resources available in local school systems. By middle school, many likely were mainstreamed into regular courses, but their relatively undeveloped language and literacy skills may have caused them to fall below grade level in their academic subjects. Many Generation 1.5 students fall further and further behind, often dropping out before finishing high school. Those learners who persevere into advanced secondary and postsecondary instruction are often shocked to be placed into remedial courses and even counseled into "ESL" courses, a designation they thought they had left behind years before. Their college instructors are often similarly surprised to discover that Generation 1.5 students, whose oral proficiency appears native-like and who seem as assimilated as other native-born students, still produce non-native features in their writing and speech, struggle with comprehension of academic texts and lecture material, and lack a well-developed academic vocabulary.[2]

It is ironic that Generation 1.5 learners may be more "at risk" academically than their international counterparts, despite their much greater exposure to the L2 over the years. It seems that strong L1 literacy skills (and a consistent educational experience) may well be a better predictor of a student's ability to succeed at more advanced academic levels than extensive naturalistic but hit-or-miss "exposure" to the L2 over time (Bosher & Rowekamp, 1998; Leki, 2007; Leki, Cumming, & Silva, 2006). Again, of course, we observe wide variation within categories and across individual students. There are many success stories of Generation 1.5 learners to accompany the tales of struggling students and drop-outs. In fact, it can be dangerous to make public policy or educational decisions based on these broad generalizations. Nonetheless, as a starting point for individual teachers, it is helpful to know that "L2 readers" are not all the same and that "one size does not fit all" in setting goals, selecting texts, and designing reading instruction. Figure 2.1 briefly summarizes these distinctions across L2 student audiences.

Language Skill or Knowledge Area	International/EFL	Immigrant	Generation 1.5
Formal Knowledge about L2	Yes	In some cases	No
Listening/Speaking Skills	Weak (but varies cross-culturally)	Adequate listening and conversation skills, pronunciation weaknesses	Appear fluent and confident in aural/oral skills
L1 Academic Literacy Skills	Strong	Varies considerably	Weak or none
L2 Academic Reading Skills	Strong foundation, limited experience	Varies depending upon educational profile	Weak
L2 Writing Skills	Adequate, with some areas of weakness	Weak	Stronger than immigrant group

FIGURE 2.1. Academic Language and Literacy Development Across Different L2 Student Audiences.
Adapted from Ferris (2009).

Implications of Multiple Student Audiences for Reading Instruction

For a variety of educational and sociocultural reasons, nearly all L2 students struggle with academic reading tasks at two foundational levels: (1) the amount of unknown or unfamiliar vocabulary in academic texts, which may include general vocabulary, academic vocabulary, and discipline-specific vocabulary; and (2) the amount of reading required, which is often far beyond their prior educational experiences in any language, but especially in L2 (cf. Grabe, 2004; see Chapters 1 and 8).

As already noted, international students are usually fully literate in their L1s and have had formal instruction in L2. They thus have transferable reading skills and experience as well as a solid foundation in the grammar and vocabulary of the L2 to bring to L2 academic reading. In contrast, international students may also have had few opportunities to read extensively in the L2. Finally, because international students have relatively limited familiarity with the L2 culture, certain elements of texts and tasks may be unfamiliar to them (see Chapters 3 and 5 for further discussion of this point).

Later-arriving immigrants may or may not be fully literate in their L1s, depending on their educational pathways and immigration circumstances. In addition, because they have only been acquiring English for a few years and in most cases their L2 was developed through "ear learning" (Reid, 1998), a strong foundation in the L2 cannot be assumed, either. As a result, they may struggle with academic reading at the college level on a variety of levels, possessing neither the literacy nor language skills adequate for the task.

Generation 1.5 students may likewise struggle with academic reading. Most do not have fully developed L1 literacy skills to transfer to L2 reading. Some spent their high school years in remedial or ESL classes, which in many cases did not provide challenging enough academic reading opportunities (Harklau, 1994; Hartman & Tarone, 1999; Leki, 1999). Thus, the nature and substance of their English language and literacy education has not always been equivalent to that of monolingual native English speakers. For example, whereas their "mainstream" peers may have studied canonical literary texts in their secondary English courses, they may have read simpler texts. That said, Generation 1.5 students have some advantages in that their strong oral foundation will help them to approach L2 texts with more confidence and more highly developed intuitions about the language and to understand classroom presentations that may provide helpful background information. At the same time, they likely will need instruction and practice in various types of intensive reading skills to which they may not previously have been exposed.

L2 Reading in Non-academic Settings

Finally, before moving on from this overview, we should acknowledge that L2 reading instruction may also occur in *non-academic settings* such as adult education or vocational programs designed to teach basic survival skills. Although L2 students in these settings most typically are from the "recent immigrant" group, international students and Generation 1.5 learners are also served by such institutions. As noted by Bell and Burnaby (1984), L2 students in these settings may be completely illiterate or nonliterate in any language or may be only functionally literate in their L1s. Alternatively, they may be highly literate in their L1s but nonliterate in the L2 or may have no experience with the orthography of the L2 (e.g., Chinese speakers learning to read English using the Roman alphabet) (Birch, 2007; Hilles & Sutton, 2001). The immediate goals of reading instruction will most likely be quite different in adult education or vocational courses, focusing on practical literacy skills. However, as reading is an important aspect of long-term language development, teachers should also expose students to enjoyable reading experiences/texts as soon/as much as possible. In addition, students in many adult education programs may aspire to further academic work at the two- or four-year college level. Moreover, teachers need to be aware of these differing levels of literacy skill and knowledge that may co-exist in the same class, even when students' oral L2 proficiency level appears equivalent. For instance, although not all students need to learn the Roman alphabet and sound–symbol correspondences, some of them might.

In short, information about students' prior L1/L2 experiences with language and literacy is critical to understanding the student audience(s) present in a classroom or program in order to conduct the needs analysis required for course design (see Chapter 4). The following list summarizes variables that could be included in a student intake form or background questionnaire (also see Application Activities 2.1 and 2.2).

- ☐ Birthplace (student's or parents');
- ☐ Visa, immigration, or citizenship status;
- ☐ Educational context(s) (in L1 or L2 setting or both);
- ☐ Schooling in English;
- ☐ English language instruction (when and where);
- ☐ Self-reported language use (Do students read and write in both L1 and L2? Which language do they use most frequently or consider their "best" or "primary" language?);
- ☐ Other information about educational history (e.g., TOEFL or IELTS results, GPA, high school diploma) (for sample instruments, see Ferris [2009]; Goen, Porter, Swanson, & van Dommelen [2002]; Reid [1998]).

What a Reader Knows

With these broadly based group distinctions in mind, we turn to our discussion of what a reader knows or brings to the reading process. Consideration of student schemata (see Chapter 1) is important in selecting texts and especially in class-room instruction, and it should be immediately apparent that schemata differ-ences across readers are both very significant and especially salient when readers have differing cultural and linguistic backgrounds.

Influences of Family and Society

A primary source of background knowledge and schema formation in reading is the home/family environment. For example, were readers raised in a home in which reading was explicitly valued? Did they see their parents reading for pleasure, entertainment, and information? Did parents read to them and with them? Were books, magazines, and newspapers readily available, and did parents and other relatives or caregivers encourage them to read? What attitudes were expressed toward reading—were children praised for reading, or were they told to put down the book and go out and play, do chores, or socialize with others?

Even within the same culture, family attitudes and practices with regard to reading can vary dramatically. One family may take weekly trips to the library, while their neighbors have televisions in every room. Some parents may enjoy reading and/or understand its importance and offer incentives to children for summer reading; others may consider it odd or lazy or antisocial and ridicule family members who spend time reading silently for pleasure.

Some of these differing attitudes and practices in homes may well be rooted in socioeconomic and educational disparities, but they are often culturally influ-enced as well. In Heath's (1983) landmark study, *Ways with words*, she describes the literacy practices and attitudes within three distinct communities or sub-cultures in the southeastern United States, finding differences across groups that had effects on children's knowledge and expectations about reading when they entered school. For example, in one community (nicknamed "Trackton" by Heath), there was a strong oral tradition, and children were given approval for being good storytellers—even to escape responsibility or punishment. When Trackton children went to school, they were sometimes branded as "liars" when they responded "creatively" to their teachers.

Family and community attitudes vary cross-culturally, as well (Barton, 2007; Gee, 2008; Kutz, 1997; Smith, 2004; Street, 1995). In many societies, reading is a social and practical activity but not one undertaken in isolation or for entertainment—parents might read newspapers to find community information and instructions or recipes to carry out everyday activities. If they immigrate to the United States, some parents might be confused by the common elementary school homework assignment to read a self-selected text for 20 minutes each night or by the classroom practice known as sustained silent reading—it might cause them to lose respect for teachers for "wasting" their children's time.

School Influences

Children's views of and attitudes toward reading can be influenced both positively and negatively by school-based reading experiences (Huss, 1995). A teacher of beginning readers in school needs to be aware of the types of literacy experience children have had during the preschool years. If a child attaches little value to literacy and has little opportunity or encouragement to read at home, the teacher can help by reading aloud to children (to show them how pleasurable reading can be), by engaging in activities to show them the usefulness of reading (e.g., cooking or assembling a model), by making interesting and appropriate reading materials available, and by giving students the opportunity to discuss and enjoy books together. Many children who were not encouraged to read at home have been "hooked on books" by a caring and creative teacher (Day & Bamford, 1998; Krashen, 2004).

On the other hand, school reading experiences can counteract positive reading models at home if "reading" consists entirely of mechanical worksheets, difficult phonics exercises, artificial texts with strictly controlled vocabulary and syntax, or force-fed lists of vocabulary and spelling words. At best, students in these courses may conclude that reading is only fun at home; at worst, they may decide that all reading is difficult and unpleasant. The teacher of adults will thus do well to probe students' backgrounds as to both family and school experiences with reading, a process that produces insights about students' attitudes and skills (see Chapter 4).

It is also important to observe that reading skills in general have declined even in highly literate and educated societies such as the US. The typical pattern is for children to *learn to read* between kindergarten and Grade 3; beyond that, they *read to learn*, which among other things means that most teachers beyond early primary grades do not see "teaching" students to read as part of their job description, nor would they know where or how to begin doing so (see Chapter 1). Although schools often provide reading specialists who offer pull-out instruction to students struggling with literacy, supplemented by a burgeoning business in private after-school tutoring or learning centers that teach remedial reading and study skills, far too many young adults finish high school and enter college with below-average literacy skills, especially academic reading skills.

School-based reading variables are even more complex to consider when discussing L2 readers. If adult L2 readers have been educated in another culture, they will also be influenced by the literacy views embodied by that educational system. For instance, in some countries, "reading" consists of intense line-by-line analysis, memorization, and recitation (Aebersold & Field, 1997; Birch, 2007; Koda, 2004). Of necessity, texts are "digested" in much smaller amounts; for instance, students might intensively study a short passage rather than reading several hundred pages for overall meaning. Furthermore, students from some cultures may not have been encouraged to question or think critically about published texts; thus, the types of questioning and analysis encouraged in Western educational settings may be new to them and even make them quite uncomfortable (Atkinson, 1999). In addition, L2 readers educated as minority language students in the US have a different set of challenges to face. Their early reading experiences may have been in L1 (either at home or in a school-based bilingual or dual-immersion program) or in L2 (in an immersion program, a pull-out ESL program, or a mainstream classroom). Because their primary or home language was not English, they did not have the same oral language basis for English literacy that L1 English students do.

The above discussion is not intended to aim criticism at any particular educational system, though there doubtless are legitimate concerns to be raised. Rather, it is to point out that school-based influences on reading can vary dramatically depending on students' backgrounds, and this variation is likely to be much more extreme across L2 readers. Teachers of L2 readers thus need to find out as much as they can about their students' prior educational experiences, especially as they pertain to reading in L1 and/or L2.

Types of Reader Schemata

As already noted, readers bring different subtypes of schemata to the task of reading a particular text. First are *linguistic schemata,* which are formal in nature. As a written record of language, a text can include sounds and symbols, morphemes, words, phrases and sentences, and markers of cohesion and reference within and among sentences (see Chapters 1 and 3 for a more detailed discussion). Linguistic schemata provide the most basic threshold for beginning to read a text. Put simply, one cannot read in a language that one does not know, even if the reader is an expert on the content of the text—even, hypothetically, if the text is a transliteration of a text the reader authored!

We have observed that beginning readers have the advantage of years of exposure to the oral language in which they are learning to read. To put these facts into perspective, by age 6 most children have built a vocabulary of thousands of words, have mastered all of the phonemes in their L1, and have an advanced grasp of its morphology and syntax. It would take an L2 learner years of classroom study or naturalistic exposure to the L2 to attain that threshold of linguistic competence (Nation, 2001; see also Chapter 8). In fact, most older L2 readers begin to grapple with L2 texts far sooner than that because they are in school or work settings requiring them to engage in literacy tasks (Brown, 2007a). As discussed in detail in Chapter 3, gaps in various types of linguistic schemata can cause comprehension breakdowns for L2 readers. Further, within a particular program or even a single classroom, students' relative levels of L2 proficiency will influence their ability to benefit from and cope with L2 texts and reading instruction (Alderson, 1984; Carrell, 1983a, 1983b, 1983c, 1984a, 1984b, 1984c;

Clapham, 1996; Keshavarz, Atai, & Ahmadi, 2007; Koh, 1985; Lee, 1986; Peretz & Shoham, 1990). We discuss the issue of L2 proficiency in reading course design in Chapter 4.

A second type of schemata to consider are *formal schemata*, knowledge about specific ways in which various text types may be organized. Young children who have stories read to them develop story schemata (or scripts). For instance, they learn that narratives are typically presented in chronological order, that there is often a problem–solution sequence, and that specific characters are important in each story. They acquire all of this knowledge about narratives without ever listening to a lecture on "the elements of fiction"; rather, they simply gather the information through exposure to stories. As students gain life experience and are exposed to various genres, they acquire other types of formal textual schemata as well, including, for instance, how recipes, newspaper columns, academic essays, research papers, and lab reports are structured (Smith, 1988, 2004). One of the authors remembers taking several constitutional law courses as part of an undergraduate minor in political science and learning how to read primary documents (U.S. Supreme Court opinions) for the first time. The process was difficult at first but became easier as students learned through repeated exposure how most judicial documents are structured and where to look for the most important information, such as the actual holding (decision), fact patterns, and reasoning based on prior case law.

Research suggests that knowledge of text macrostructure or formal schemata can be highly facilitative to readers in general, although some L2 readers may also have gaps in formal schemata. These problems derive from two primary sources. First, L2 readers with relatively limited experience in reading (whether in L1 or L2) may have had less exposure to different genres and thus may not have acquired formal schemata to the degree that some of their peers have. Second, some L2 readers may have extensive reading experience in their L1s but not much in their L2. Some formal schemata may transfer cross-linguistically or cross-culturally (such as story schemata), whereas other text-type conventions may vary between the L1 and L2. For example, in U.S. argumentative essays, writers are expected to expose their own stance on the issue under discussion and to present arguments and evidence to support that stance (Connor, 1996, 2002, 2003, 2005; Connor, Nagelhout, & Rozycki, 2008; Leki, 1991; Matsuda, 1997, 2001; Scollon, 1997). However, in other rhetorical traditions, argumentation is designed simply to lay out the issues for the readers' consideration, rather than persuade them to the author's particular point of view (see Hinds, 1987). Because students may have developed different formal schemata, it may be helpful or necessary for teachers to assist them in discerning text macrostructure (Brantmeier, 2005; Fecteau, 1999; Hudson, 2007). Chapters 3 and 5 present specific suggestions along these lines.

A final important construct in reading comprehension involves *content schemata*, the reader's prior knowledge of the ideas in a particular text. Content schemata are important for all readers, but specific aspects of content knowledge may be particularly problematic for L2 readers (Carrell & Eisterhold, 1983). Especially in the case of L2 readers reared and educated in certain cultural environments (the international/EFL/immigrant groups discussed earlier), certain kinds of cultural information represented in texts can cause *comprehension gaps.* For example, biblical references found in canonical Western texts (e.g., Milton's *Paradise Lost*) may cause confusion to students unfamiliar with those religious and cultural traditions. At a more basic level, a reference to a "Get out of Jail Free" card used in the American board game Monopoly (see Brahm's "Second Chances" [2001], discussed in Chapters 3 and 7) might raise questions for an L2 reader. Carrell and Eisterhold (1983) provide an example of a text which refers to freeways as "expensive parking lots" (p. 563). Teachers need to be aware of gaps in students' content schemata that may make specific texts challenging, particularly for their L2 students, and think of ways to develop schemata where they are lacking (see Chapter 5 for specific suggestions).

What the L2 Reader Knows: Final Thoughts

In a landmark essay, Eskey (1986) discussed the challenges faced by L2 readers in terms of a two-part *gap* model, consisting of the *comprehension gap* and the *confidence gap.* Eskey subdivided the comprehension gap into several different components (linguistic, pragmatic, and cultural); we discussed these issues earlier in this section and will address them further in Chapter 3. However, before we move on, it is helpful to describe the confidence gap, which is directly related to the comprehension gap and the factors of which it is composed. Eskey (1986) noted that even highly competent L1 readers may lack confidence when faced with L2 texts and that this lack of confidence may short-circuit effective L1 reading strategies (Clarke, 1980) and lead to unsuccessful L2 reading behaviors. Such behaviors, according to Eskey, may include inefficient reading strategies (e.g., reading too slowly, reading word-for-word), misuse of dictionaries (either overuse or underuse; see Chapter 8), and avoidance of L2 reading (thus depriving the L2 student both of important reading practice and exposure to L2 text for second language acquisition; see Chapter 6).

It is helpful and important for L2 reading teachers to be aware of these confidence issues for at least two reasons. First, knowledge of affective factors confronting their students may help teachers—who themselves are likely confident and enthusiastic readers of the target language—develop empathy for and patience with their students' anxieties about and even resistance to reading. Second, awareness of the ways in which a lack of confidence can undermine students' reading behaviors can help teachers to design reading exercises (e.g., timed reading to improve speed), strategy training activities (e.g., effective dictionary use), and assignments (e.g., extensive reading requirements) that may directly address students' less successful L2 reading practices. Practical suggestions along these lines are provided in Chapters 3, 5, and 6.

Individual Differences among L2 Readers

This chapter has examined the different audiences of L2 readers, the various influences that form readers' background knowledge (schemata), the ways in which L2 readers' knowledge and experiences may be different from those of monolingual native speakers, and learner attitudes toward reading. However, in addition to discussing L2 readers in general and specific subgroups of L2 readers, it is important to recall that these subgroups are made up of individual students. There are specific ways in which student readers are unique and vary even from others in the same class with similar cultural or demographic profiles. The study of individual differences in second language acquisition (SLA) is a substantial subtopic that is far beyond the scope of this chapter or even this volume.[3] Thus, in this section, we focus on three reader-based issues that seem especially important in relation to L2 reading: motivation, learning styles, and learner strategies.

Motivation

As with individual differences, *learner motivation* has been an important issue in education in general and language learning in particular. Early L2 researchers further discussed motivation by subdividing the construct into dichotomies such as *intrinsic* versus *extrinsic motivation* (Brown, 2007a, 2007b; Deci, 1975; Dörnyei, 1998; Dörnyei & Csizér, 1998) and *integrative* versus *instrumental motivation* (e.g., Brown, 2007a, 2007b; Gardner & Lambert, 1972; Gardner & MacIntyre, 1991). The former refers to the *source* of motivation (from within oneself, in contrast to being imposed by others), whereas the latter identifies different *reasons* or *orientations* for pursuing L2 knowledge (to understand and participate in L2 discourses and cultural practices for pragmatic reasons such as employment). Although SLA research suggests that either integrative or instrumental motivation (or orientation) can bring about successful L2 behaviors, most scholars agree that intrinsic motivation, which can express itself either integratively or instrumentally, is more powerful than extrinsic factors (Brown, 2007a).

In most classroom settings, it is reasonable to assume that most students are instrumentally oriented (i.e., studying the L2 primarily for practical reasons). It is thus important for teachers to promote and facilitate the development of intrinsic motivation—in other words, to persuade and demonstrate to students that through their own effort they can achieve excellence and autonomy in pursuit of their self-selected goals (Brown, 2007a; Dörnyei & Csizér, 1998). In the case of reading instruction, cultivating intrinsic motivation can take many forms. For example, if teachers persuade their students that extensive reading offers long-term benefits for their language acquisition, they can provide extrinsic motivation by engaging students in extensive reading as part of a course (see Chapter 6). Students will consequently discover for themselves that reading is beneficial and enjoyable, adopting the habit of reading extensively in the L2 after the course ends (i.e., become intrinsically motivated to do so).

Beyond the general issues of students' orientations toward learning and the sources of motivation are specific questions related to *purposes for reading* and *student interests.* Although the latter two factors are related, they are not identical. Helping student readers understand and establish purposes for reading a particular text is an important step in the pre-reading phase (see Chapter 5). Such understanding helps students adjust their reading styles appropriately. For instance, it can help to address the "confidence gap" mentioned earlier if students understand that their approach to reading several hundred pages of a textbook for an undergraduate course can and should be distinct from the intensive reading of a much shorter text, such as a journal article. If students grasp that they can read longer passages for general understanding rather than specific mastery of every single detail, it may help them to read those longer assignments more quickly and to feel less overwhelmed by the task. Although the purpose(s) for assigned reading are usually determined by the teacher (though they need not always be), when students select their own reading, their reading styles vary according to their purposes (or motivations) for reading a particular text.

As an illustration, imagine reading a magazine that you enjoy but under two different circumstances. In the first, you encounter the text in a dentist's waiting room, knowing that you perhaps have five to ten minutes before being called in for your appointment. Given that your reading time is limited, you might scan the cover or the table of contents to find the most interesting article and then skim the article quickly so that you can finish it.[4] In the second situation, you purchase the magazine at an airport newsstand prior to boarding a long flight. Because you have plenty of time not only to read one interesting article but the entire magazine, your approach might be quite different—a leisurely cover-to-cover perusal of the publication. In fact, you would be motivated to read more slowly in order to make the magazine "last" so that you can pass the time during the flight. The point of this discussion is that, in the same way more general motivations for learning/reading may interact among students in a classroom, purposes for reading specific texts will vary according to the text, the context, and the individual reader—and these differences affect how people read and how successful and enjoyable those reading experiences are. As teachers become aware of these differences, they can help students address the confidence gap and develop effective reading strategies for various genres and texts.

A related but distinct issue pertains to student interest in particular texts and topics. Fundamentally, it should be obvious that students benefit more from— and engage more deeply in—reading texts containing material that interests them. The term "interest," however, has several different shades of meaning in this discussion. In its most general sense, individuals have divergent interests or passions or hobbies or avocations, such as photography, fashion, music, sports, or politics. The proliferation of magazines, Web-based materials, and even cable television channels on almost any topic imaginable attests not only to the wide range of interests that people possess, but also the seemingly infinite sources of information and/or entertainment available pertaining to those topics. Awareness of this general range of interests can help teachers choose topics and texts for assigned classroom reading and to build a classroom library or reading list for student-selected extensive reading.

While considering students' general interests is valuable, teachers must realize that reader "interest" may vary depending on external circumstances. For instance, students may be only marginally "interested" in the course content of their required political science course but extremely interested in getting a good grade in that course. As Hudson (2007) observed,

> [a]ttitude toward reading may also be modified by a change in goals by the reader. For example, if a reader is presented with a topic that is not particularly of interest to her or him, it might be assumed that the intention to read would be slight. However, if the reader knew that a comprehension examination was going to follow the reading, the goal may shift from understanding the uninteresting content to doing well in an examination. (p. 54)

In short, general motivation, specific purpose, and individual interest frequently can and do converge in academic reading tasks. Survey research demonstrates that reader attitudes "do not show positive correlations between topic interest and comprehension" (Hudson, 2007, p. 54). The shifting sands of "interest," as described above, may help to explain this rather counterintuitive finding.

Finally, students may well discover an interest in a new topic introduced to them through carefully selected texts and well executed classroom activities to support the reading of those texts. They may also find new interests through extensive reading activities (e.g., through self-selected reading or through class-mates' sharing materials they enjoyed) or through research projects on self-selected topics. Learning to appreciate the complexity and appeal of new topics and even new disciplines is, after all, one of the goals and positive outcomes of the educational process. This is to say that, although individual student interests should be considered during course design and text selection processes, teachers should not feel completely constrained by them either (see Chapter 4). As a practical matter, it is nearly impossible to please everyone. At the same time, teachers should not be insensitive to the interests and knowledge base of a par-ticular student audience, nor should they assume that what interests them will also appeal to the students. For example, an article from *Money* magazine on various retirement savings vehicles might be extremely interesting to a middle-aged teacher but far less so to college freshmen!

Learning Styles

Educators and psychologists have examined cognitive and *learning styles* for some decades (e.g., Ausubel, 1968; Ausubel & Robinson, 1969; Cassidy, 2004; Hill, 1972). L2 researchers have further examined links between specific learning styles and SLA as well as the interaction of individual styles and cultural norms (e.g., Brown, 2007a; Cohen, 1998; Ehrman, 1996; Ehrman & Oxford, 1990, 1995; Reid, 1987, 1995). Learning styles have been defined as "a general predisposition . . . toward processing information in a particular way" (Skehan, 1991, p. 288) and have been posited to be the result of intertwined cognitive, affective, and personality traits (Brown, 2007a; Keefe, 1979). Space does not permit a full discussion of learning styles, either in general or with regard to SLA. In this section, we focus on two specific learning style dichotomies that appear to be especially relevant to reading: (1) *global* and *analytical* styles; and (2) *verbal* and *auditory* styles (including the subcategories of *visual-verbal* and *visual-nonverbal* styles).

Global and analytical learning styles. A salient contrast among learners is that between *analytical learners*—students who focus carefully on details and who move precisely and systematically through the learning process—and *global learners*, who process information in a more holistic (top-down) way, often getting the gist of the input without necessarily paying much attention to specific details (Cassidy, 2004; Ehrman & Oxford, 1990, 1995). As an everyday illustration, one of the authors is an extremely global learner with a life partner who is very analytical. In fact, this author is so global that s/he has been known to go to the video rental store (or, these days, the Internet) and rent a movie that s/he has already seen, having no memory of having watched it before! (On the positive side, for this global learner it is like seeing the movie for the first time. This same author happily re-reads favorite books, as well.) In contrast, the author's partner would not only remember having seen the movie but could quite easily recount every significant detail and even some minor ones.

Several other overlapping learning, cognitive, and personality style categories reflect this global–analytic contrast, such as *field independence* and *field dependence*, *left-* or *right-brain dominance*, *tolerance* or *intolerance of ambiguity*, and the *Sensor* (detail-oriented) or *Intuitive* (systems thinker) continuum on the Myers-Briggs Type Indicator (Brown, 2007a, 2007b; Ehrman & Oxford, 1990; Myers & McCaulley, 1985, Reid, 1995). Field independence is defined as the "ability to perceive a particular relevant item or factor in a 'field' of distracting items" (Brown, 2007a, p. 382). In contrast, those who are field-dependent find that "the parts embedded in the field are not easily perceived, although that total field is perceived more clearly as a unified whole" (Brown, 2007a, p. 381). Those who are field-independent have an easier time with activities such as finding "Waldo" in the *Where's Waldo* children's activity books or with quickly scanning large portions of text to find specific items (e.g., a classified advertisement in a newspaper, a definition in a dictionary, or a telephone number in a directory). Individuals who are tolerant of ambiguity more easily process and adapt to information that runs counter to their existing knowledge structures or is internally contradictory. For learning or reading in English, ambiguity tolerance is helpful when a learner encounters irregular or exceptional morphological or syntactic forms or multiple meanings of the same lexical item (Brown, 2007a; Chapelle & Green, 1992; Chapelle & Roberts, 1986).

Although the definitions of these labels are not identical, there is enough similarity among them that individuals may display characteristics that pattern together to comprise a global or analytical profile (see Figure 2.2). It is important to note, however, that these descriptions represent continua rather than strict dichotomies. Moreover, students/readers can and should make adjustments to their preferred styles when circumstances require such adaptation.

It is easy to see how analytical or global tendencies can affect one's reading processes. Analytical readers may be able to answer specific questions about characters, plot, facts, and details, yet they may fail to grasp the overall meaning or message of a text. They see the trees, but not the forest. In contrast, global learners may develop an overall sense of a passage but may need access to the actual text to identify specific details. In other words, analytical learners may be drawn more to bottom-up approaches to reading, whereas top-down approaches may better suit global learners (see Chapter 1).

Teachers should use their knowledge about global and analytical learning styles and their effects on reading in two ways. First, they should acknowledge that they will have both types of learners in every classroom: They must remember that these learning styles tend to pattern along a continuum rather than being a strict dichotomy. In other words, although some students may be extremely analytical and others extremely global, many others may fall somewhere between the ends of the spectrum. Thus, teachers should facilitate balanced, nuanced forms of reading experiences that meet the needs of individual learners regardless of cognitive style. For example, analytical L2 learners might be perfectly happy with a tightly structured syllabus that moves them systematically through various reading skills using worksheets or software programs with exercises and quizzes that have right and wrong answers. However, such an approach would be tedious and frustrating to global learners—and, considering the big picture, would not fully meet the needs of analytical learners, either, as such rigid structure leaves little room for the interpretation, inferencing, or critical analysis of texts that students need to undertake at higher academic levels. On the other hand, a top-down,

Characteristic	Analytical Learner	Global Learner
Field independence	Yes	No
Brain hemisphere dominance	Left	Right
Tolerance of ambiguity	No	Yes
Myers-Briggs Indicator: Sensor (S) or Intuitive (N)	S	N

FIGURE 2.2. Prototypes of Global and Analytical Learners.

globally oriented reading course might leave analytical learners wondering what they have accomplished and might fail to help global learners understand that attention to text-specific detail is often necessary. We hope that the discussion in Chapter 1 established that reading is a complex endeavor involving simultaneous top-down and bottom-up processing. This discussion of varying student learning styles provides further support for a balanced approach to reading instruction.

Second, understanding differences between analytical and global learning styles should convince teachers of the importance of explaining to students that different reading tasks involve different purposes and therefore call for diverse styles of reading. If one is reading an instruction manual or a tax form, one had better be analytical (i.e., systematic and attentive to detail). In contrast, if one has 300 pages of assigned reading for a history course or a Victorian novel to finish, one needs to take a global approach (or may never graduate).

To identify and evaluate students' needs, strengths, and weaknesses with regard to global or analytical learning/reading styles, teachers can administer questionnaires or interview students. For example, a student who says she reads a great deal in L1 and L2 may be a more global learner; a student who says she reads slowly or frequently looks up words in the dictionary may be analytical. Teachers can also evaluate students using informal or formal assessment tools (see Chapters 4 and 9). For instance, teachers can, ask students to read a short passage at an appropriate difficulty level and then take it away after five or ten minutes, followed by response to specific detail and main idea questions. How students cope with the different questions will give teachers insights about where they fall on the global or analytical scale. Teachers can also ask students questions orally during class discussions. Once teachers have identified potential strengths and problem areas, they may wish to discuss them with students by means of a written assessment, a one-to-one conference, or a class discussion of styles and strategies. Assessments and feedback can be followed up with class or individualized activities that help students to focus on the trees or the forest, as necessary and applicable.

Visual and Auditory Learners. A second learning style contrast that appears to have particular applicability to reading instruction is the distinction between *visual* learners—those who process information best through what they see—and *auditory* learners, whose primary mode of processing is through their ears. Several quick everyday questions can help students to identify their primary mode of input-processing. For example, teachers can ask how many students prefer to receive the news or other information through reading it in a newspaper or on online versus hearing it on television or the radio. They can also be asked whether they would prefer to receive classroom instructions about an assignment or activity in written form or explained orally by the teacher. Obviously, a reading course, which focuses on the printed word, will appeal most to visual learners. The challenge for the teacher, then, is to assist the auditory types with the reading process, which can be approached in several practical ways:

- **Reading aloud** to students, whether for pleasure or as they follow along with a (relatively short) printed text;
- Using **audiobooks** (CDs, podcasts, or analog recordings) and **video** to supplement the reading of literature and other works;
- Encouraging students to **discuss** what they have read through class discussions, reading groups, oral reports, and so on.

Another distinction within the visual processing mode is the difference between *visual-verbal* and *visual-nonverbal* learners (Felder & Henriques, 1995; Mayer & Massa, 2003; Sinatra, 1986). Those who have visual-verbal preferences process input better when words are the primary vehicle of communication; visual-nonverbal learners benefit from other types of visual information such as maps, graphs, charts, and pictures. Again, an everyday illustration of this is to ask students how they prefer to receive directions to a new address. Would they prefer to find the location on a map, or would they cope better with step-by-step verbal directions ("Turn left on J Street, go one mile and turn left at the light on Folsom Boulevard," and so forth)?

Teachers can help the visual-nonverbal learners to cope with mostly verbal texts in several ways:

- Selecting texts that contain pictures, graphics, or subheadings (still verbal but removed from the mass of verbiage in the main body of the text);
- Using graphic organizers (see Chapter 5, 7, and 9 for examples) to help students to pull out important information from visual-verbal texts and process it in a nonverbal (or less verbal) form that may assist overall comprehension.

In courses that focus on reading for academic or discipline-specific purposes, visual-verbal learners can benefit from instruction and assistance in correct interpretation of nonverbal information in a text (e.g., how to read bar graphs) and in using nonverbal information in addition to verbal information to understand the message conveyed in a particular text.

Finally, regarding L2 readers in particular, it is important to note that students who are literate in an L1 with a different orthography may have had different experiences processing written texts than those who are monolingual readers of English. For example, students who became literate in a logographic writing system (e.g., sinograms) have learned to recognize and interpret visual cues (or radicals) to identify the meaning of individual characters (see Chapters 1 and 3). In contrast, those who became literate by means of an alphabetic system such as English have learned to associate symbols with sounds. This difference means that, regardless of individual preferences for auditory or visual learning, students have been conditioned by their early reading experiences to attend primarily to specific graphological features. In short, individual differences among readers may interact with cross-linguistic distinctions in courses that include L2 readers (Birch, 2007; Koda, 2004; Reid, 1987, 1995).

As noted above, learning styles represent a substantial area of inquiry. In the interest of thoroughness in our discussion of "the reader" in this chapter, we have attempted to highlight selected issues that could specifically affect the teaching of L2 readers. Although it can be helpful for teachers to understand these factors and, where possible and necessary, to adjust instruction accordingly, it is also helpful to remember that learning style preferences are not set in stone and that most readers adjust to varying circumstances.

As an illustration, one of the authors is an extremely visual (verbal) learner, to the point that s/he can barely read a map or interpret a graph and has difficulty processing information such as a phone number or the spelling of a word delivered orally. However, when this author was a college undergraduate at a large public university, s/he was required to take a number of large lecture courses held in enormous lecture halls seating 500 or more students. This was long before the advent of PowerPoint presentations and other commonly used visual aids. Consequently, this exceedingly visual learner had to adapt to an auditory presentation style. Although these were never the author's favorite courses, s/he did succeed in learning the information and earning good grades in them. This is to say that, as Brown (2007a) put it: "Perhaps an 'intelligent' and 'successful' person is one who is 'bicognitive'—one who can manipulate both ends of a style continuum" (p. 120). Teachers must not only consider their own presentation and instructional styles but also help students to recognize their own preferences and strengths and make adjustments in less-than-optimal learning contexts for their individual styles.

Learner Strategies

The construct of learning strategies and its implications for reading were introduced in Chapter 1. Most L2 reading experts, including Grabe (2004), agree that understanding and teaching effective *reading strategies* is extremely important. Arguably the primary goal of an L2 reading course is not to cover specific texts but rather to assist students in developing and improving reading skills that will help them throughout their academic, professional, and personal lives, not to mention facilitating overall second language acquisition. Grabe and Stoller (2002) made a helpful distinction between "teaching reading strategies" and developing *strategic readers*, noting that isolated strategy instruction seldom transfers to students' subsequent reading experiences beyond the L2 literacy course. Rather, they observed that "the goal of reading instruction is not to teach individual reading strategies but rather to develop strategic readers, a development process that requires intensive instructional efforts over a considerable period of time" (pp. 81–82). Figure 1.10 provides one helpful list of strategies used by effective readers. Similar lists exist are available in the L2 reading literature (Aebersold & Field, 1997; Brown, 2007b; Hudson, 2007; Scarcella & Oxford, 1992).

As this discussion of reading strategies pertains to our focus on L2 readers, we would offer three observations. First, in the same way that successful writers may use different approaches (distinct from those of other good writers and even across varying types of writing tasks), individual readers use a variety of strategies. Both of the authors, for instance, are avid highlighters of professional and informational texts, buy highlighters in bulk, and never go anywhere without one. This approach to interacting with texts (and reviewing texts already read) is successful for us but irritating to our friends and colleagues who borrow our books and find the highlighting distracting. As already noted, L2 readers may be successful L1 readers who need to transfer those strategies to L2 texts or to adjust them because of cross-linguistic transfer difficulties. Further, they may be inexperienced or unsuccessful readers of any kind of L1 or L2 text, or somewhere between those two extremes. This is another reason for which learning about students' prior reading experiences and their unconscious, "default" reading strategies is important for teachers as they design courses, select texts, and plan classroom instruction (see Chapters 4 and 5).

Second, the range of background experiences discussed above, especially in different groups or audiences of L2 students, may have resulted in the inculcation of certain reading strategies and the (implicit) discouragement of others. For example, Figure 1.10 identifies "Critiqu[ing] a text or point of view" as a beneficial reading strategy, but students from some cultural traditions may never have been asked or allowed to give their own opinion or analysis of a published author's text (Aebersold & Field, 1997; Atkinson, 1999). English-speaking teachers of L2 readers should be careful not to assume that students already understand how to apply certain strategies to their reading.

A final implication of reading strategy research for a systematic focus on the reader is that classroom strategy instruction—or the development of strategic readers—should at its core be an individualized process. Such instruction may include personalized initial assessment of strategy knowledge and use, instruction that accommodates students' most salient needs, and assessments that evaluate not only students' strategy use in classroom exercises but also their subsequent reading experiences. Grabe and Stoller (2002) offered several suggestions for L2 literacy teachers providing strategy instruction:

- integrate strategy use and discussions about strategy use into every lesson;
- introduce strategy use;
- model strategies overtly through verbalizing;
- raise student awareness of different strategies;
- guide students in reflecting on strategy uses;
- discuss using strategies to understand difficult texts;
- provide students with opportunities to read a lot; and
- engage in tasks that require strategic reading. (pp. 84–85)

To this helpful list we might add creating an individualized strategy development plan for each student at the beginning of the course and asking students to track their learning and usage of strategies in a log or class notebook. We further recommend requiring students to reflect on how strategy instruction helped them in intensive and extensive reading tasks, and building into the course assessment plan an appraisal of each student's progress in understanding and utilizing specific strategies previously identified as goals for him/her (or, as appropriate, for the entire class). This personalized process is analogous to suggestions we have made elsewhere about individualized error treatment plans for student writers (Ferris, 2002; Ferris & Hedgcock, 2005) and student-directed vocabulary development (see Chapter 8). Our point here is that a generalized list of reading strategies to cover in a course syllabus will only be useful insofar as it is (a) responsive to the teacher's understanding of the needs of the class as a whole (see Chapter 4); and (b) considers individual students' backgrounds, learning styles, and prior strategy use, whether successful or ineffective.

Focus on the Reader: Implications

Our discussion has highlighted several different but interrelated subtopics: (1) different subgroup or audience profiles of what we call L2 readers; (2) the various influences of family, school, and society that comprise an individual reader's background knowledge as she approaches L2 reading in general and specific texts; and (3) individual differences in motivation, learning styles, and learner strategies that may influence student behaviors, practices, and responses to reading instruction. Understanding these intersecting reader dimensions point toward practical implications for the teacher of L2 readers.

Needs Assessment and Course Goals

We discuss course design and its components of needs analysis and goal-setting in detail in Chapter 4. A substantial and extensive understanding of the reader-based issues in this chapter should be a major factor in course planning, as should institutional and curricular issues that might constrain how courses are designed and taught. This assertion might seem self-evident, but in our observation, few teachers take the time to discover the general characteristics of the student audience(s) in their classes, let alone the specific backgrounds, interests, and abilities of the individual students. Rather, most teachers rely on an assigned textbook to set the priorities for and deliver literacy instruction. In other words, they may allow a textbook author or publisher, who cannot possibly know the needs of a particular audience, to make crucial instructional decisions. Teachers may further assume, based on their own experience and intuitions, that they already know what a class of students needs (Grabe, 2004). If nothing else, we hope that the ideas presented in this chapter have convinced readers that learning about their student audience—before a course commences, once it begins, and as it progresses—is critically important in both designing and delivering effective L2 literacy instruction (see Chapters 4 and 9).

Text Selection

We have emphasized that teachers should develop a sense of student character-istics and to inquire into student interests as they select texts for their courses (whether they are ordering textbooks for students to purchase, choosing indi-vidual texts for classroom lessons, or developing a reading list or library for extensive reading assignments). Although generalizations such as "avoid L2 texts with antiquated language or with a heavy regional 'accent' " might be useful advice as a starting point, the teacher should ask detailed questions about students before making final decisions about which texts to adopt or reject. Where feasible, it is desirable to allow students some choice and input about what they will or will not read (especially for extensive reading components of a course) so that they will be motivated, comfortable, and confident as they engage in reading L2 texts. However, teachers should not discard from consideration a text that might have unfamiliar content or language if that text might help address course goals and student needs. Rather, awareness of student background knowledge and experi-ence should inform teachers as they prepare to use materials for instructional purposes (see Chapters 3–5 and 7 for further discussion of this point).

Classroom Instruction

As already noted, understanding students' background knowledge as it pertains to a text being considered might affect pre-reading activities and instruction (e.g., topic-specific vocabulary that might be unfamiliar to international students, cultural or historical information that might be unknown to some). This under-standing should affect choices about various types of vocabulary instruction and development (see Chapters 3, 5, and 8). Awareness of student learning styles and strategies—in general, that most/all classes will include learners with a range of styles, and in particular, individual students' strengths and weaknesses with strategy (non)use—will also help teachers in designing a syllabus, planning lessons, and delivering instruction in ways that appeal to a range of learners. Consideration of students' knowledge, experience, interests, and needs should also help the teacher in designing classroom assessment and post-reading extension activities (see Chapters 5, 7, and 9 for examples). In short, consideration of the reader should influence L2 literacy instruction at every conceivable level and stage.

Chapter Summary

We began this chapter by observing that reading is an interaction between the knowledge and experiences of an individual reader and the characteristics of a given text (to be discussed at length in Chapter 3). This chapter focused on the *reader*, first by defining and examining the various L2 student audiences teachers might encounter (and the possible practical implications of those differences), then by looking at the various influences that shape readers' attitudes toward literacy and the background knowledge they bring to the interaction with a text, and finally by examining several components (motivation, learning styles, learner strategies) of individual differences across students, emphasizing these components as they pertain to reading in particular (rather than a comprehensive focus on learning or second language acquisition). Briefly, we examined the following issues:

- L2 readers may include *international students, students in EFL settings, resident immigrants, Generation 1.5 students, and students in nonacademic settings.* Each subgroup will have different experiences of—and orientations toward—literacy; these distinctions have specific implications for literacy instruction.
- When readers interact with a text, a number of background variables related to *family, school, and societal* experiences influence not only their prior knowledge about that text (schemata) but also their attitudes toward reading in general. These influences are especially relevant in the case of L2 readers.
- Within a given group of learners, we observe individual differences with regard to *motivation* (why they are studying/reading; general and specific purposes for reading; interests), *learning styles* (analytical or global; auditory or visual [verbal or nonverbal], and *learning/reading strategies* (successful or unsuccessful, conditioned [or not] by prior L1 reading experiences and/or the characteristics of the L1 and its written form). Where feasible and appropriate, teachers should design courses with these individual differences in mind.

> ■   These interacting L2 reader characteristics should inform and guide teachers in *needs assessment, course design, text selection,* and *classroom instruction.*

A focus on the reader, as we have examined it here, is an important but often neglected aspect of L2 literacy instruction. The discussion in this chapter should remind us that there is (or should be) no universal approach to teaching L2 readers (Grabe, 2004). Although the types of careful investigation of student characteristics suggested before and during a literacy course are time-consuming, they are also indispensable and may well be the difference between a successful or unsuccessful learning experience for L2 readers and their instructors.

Further Reading and Resources

Below is a list of selected sources and materials referred to in this chapter. Where applicable, URLs are provided, though we caution readers that these tend to change. Bibliographic information for published sources can be found in the References section at the end of the book.

Sources on Generation 1.5 learners
  CATESOL Journal special issue (Goen et al., 2002); Harklau, Losey, & Siegal (1999); *The Reading Matrix* (2004); Roberge, Siegal, & Harklau (2008)
Classic early sources on L2 readers
  Carrell & Eisterhold (1983); Clarke (1980); Eskey (1986)
Landmark study on background influences on literacy
  Heath (1983)
Motivation & L2 learners
  Gardner & Lambert (1972); Gardner & MacIntyre (1991); Dörnyei (1998); Dörnyei & Csizér (1998)
Learning styles in L2 instruction
  Chapelle & Green (1992); Chapelle & Roberts (1986); Cohen (1998); Ehrman (1996); Ehrman & Oxford (1990, 1995); Reid (1987, 1995)
Lists of strategies of (un)successful L2 readers
  Aebersold & Field (1997); Brown (2007a); Grabe & Stoller (2002); Hudson (2007); Scarcella & Oxford (1992)
Sample reader/student background surveys
  Brown (2007b); Ferris (2009); Ferris & Hedgcock (2005); Goen et al. (2002); Reid (1998, 2006)
Free online survey design instrument
  www.surveymonkey.com

Reflection and Review

1. What are the implications of the different "audiences" of L2 readers (i.e., international students, Generation 1.5, and so on) for course design and instruction? If two or more of these subgroups were in the same ESL literacy course, what might be the challenges and possible adjustments for teachers?
2. One point made in the section about readers' backgrounds is that life experiences and influences may affect students' attitudes toward reading (in any language). What might some of those attitudes be, and how might they affect literacy instruction?
3. What reader background factors are particularly relevant or problematic for L2 readers? If you were teaching a course that served both monolingual English speakers and L2 readers, how might this awareness influence your instructional practices and choices?
4. Review the discussion of motivation and how it affects L2 reading. What motivational factors are beyond the teacher's control or influence, and what can a teacher do to enhance student motivation?
5. Are you an analytical or global learner? A visual or auditory learner? Can you identify strengths and problems resulting from your style preferences and your effectiveness as a reader? How might such awareness affect you as a teacher? What might you need to do or learn to teach learners whose styles are distinct from your own?
6. This chapter recommended an individualized approach to reading strategy instruction (or developing *strategic* readers). What do you think about this suggestion? Does it seem feasible, or do you feel that such an approach is perhaps unnecessary or too cumbersome for a teacher to undertake?

Application Activities

Application Activity 2.1
Brainstorming and Listing Reader-Based Information for Course Planning

Imagine that you are about to teach a new L2 reading course. Brainstorm three lists:

a. Background information that it would be helpful to obtain about your students before beginning to plan your course;
b. Ways in which you could elicit this information, both before the course starts and once it is underway;
c. How your teaching and planning might respond to the information you collect.

If you are completing this activity in a classroom setting, compare and contrast your lists with those of your classmates and instructor.

Application Activity 2.2
Surveying Reader(s) about their Backgrounds

Identify an L2 reader (or group/class of readers) with whom you might be interested in working.

a. Considering the ideas presented in this chapter, design an interview protocol or questionnaire (for an individual reader) or a survey (for a group of readers) that would investigate student demographics, background knowledge and experiences, motivational factors, and learning styles and strategies (for strategies, consult Figures 1.10 and 4.2).

b. Conduct the interview or administer your survey. For an entire class of respondents, you may wish to use an online survey design and collection instrument such as www.surveymonkey.com.

c. In a written report or oral presentation, analyze your findings, considering the following questions:

- If you were going to tutor this student or teach this group, what learner background information will affect how you will work with them?
- What did you learn about learner attitudes toward reading and interests? How might this knowledge affect your text selection and other instructional choices?
- What did you learn about learner styles and strategies, and what are the implications of that information for how you would work with them? Based on knowledge of their strategy use, what goals might you set?

Application Activity 2.3
Working with an L2 Reader

Identify an L2 reader and work with her for several tutoring sessions. Complete the following activities, synthesizing your findings in a written or oral report:

a. Find out about the reader's background, interests, and so forth, using the ideas suggested in this chapter, in Application Activity 2.2, or in Chapter 4.

b. Assess the reader's abilities by completing a miscue analysis (see Chapter 1), by having her read a text and respond to comprehension, interpretation, and analysis questions, and by attempting to place her on at least two different L2 proficiency scales (see Chapters 1, 4, and 9).

c. Based on your interview and assessment, select a short text that would be interesting and appropriate for the student and identify two to three reading strategies that you would like to help the student develop by working intensively with this text.

d. Over a couple of tutoring sessions, work through the text with the student and specifically on your target strategies. Design several formal or informal procedures to assess the student's progress.

e. Analyze what you have learned about understanding and working with L2 readers by moving through this tutoring sequence. Speculate about whether your efforts will help the student read more effectively in the future. What student-, text-, and tutor-based variables might predict success (or lack thereof) in the case of this reader and tutoring process?

Application Activity 2.4
Analyzing a Text to Identify Possible Schemata Gaps

For this activity, consider one of the texts included in the Appendices to Chapters 3, 5, or 7. Examine the text considering the following questions and report your findings in writing or in a class presentation.

a. **Background knowledge:** What historical, cultural, and legal information might be useful to students before they read the text?

b. **Vocabulary:** What words or phrases are potentially problematic in this text? Consider specialized or academic vocabulary and idiomatic expressions that might be unfamiliar. See Chapters 3 and 8 for vocabulary analysis tools.

c. How might you provide (or help students find) background information that could assist them in understanding this text?

d. Which words or phrases you might gloss or preteach for the students?

e. For what audiences or groups of students might this text be appropriate or inappropriate? Why do you think so?

Chapter 3
L2 Reading
Focus on the Text

Questions for Reflection

- Think about L2 reading you may have done. What are aspects of the *text itself* that you found most challenging? If you were in a language course, what did your teacher do (or could your teacher have done) to help you grapple with the demands of the text(s) you read?
- As you think about English and English-language texts, what elements of English text might be particularly challenging to an L2 reader? If you are an English L2 reader, what have you found most challenging about reading in English, compared with your L1 and other L2s you may have learned?
- Appendix 3.1 contains a short first-person essay by a high school senior named Joshua Brahm entitled "Second Chances—If Only We Could Start Again," which was published in 2001 in the *Sacramento Bee*. Before reading this chapter, take time to look over this text, noting elements that might be problematic for an English L2 reader. Retain these notes for reconsideration or discussion after reading this chapter.

As discussed in Chapter 1, approaches to teaching reading in general and L2 reading in particular have seesawed between parts-centered and meaning-based extremes. The contributions of psycholinguistic "top-down," Whole Language, and interactionist orientations toward reading in recent decades have been considerable and important, as they have emphasized an understanding of the *reader*—their background knowledge, experiences, personalities, and motivations and how they interact with a particular text—and an appreciation for reading whole texts for meaning and even enjoyment.

Nonetheless, the prevalence of top-down views of reading in some circles has caused a decrease in attention to "bottom-up" (or text-focused) aspects of reading and to helping students to grapple with the information contained in texts. As we have noted, this trend can sometimes be counterproductive (see Chapter 1). For L2 readers, in particular, an over-emphasis on top-down strategies is especially problematic, as L2 readers are far more likely than their L1 counterparts to have linguistic gaps that may cause them to struggle with or misread texts (Birch, 2007; Eskey, 1986; Grabe & Stoller, 2002; Hudson, 2007; Koda, 2004). In this chapter, we therefore focus on the "bottom-up" side of the reading interaction, looking first at what constitutes a *text* and what types of information are encoded in texts. We then examine features of texts in general and dimensions of English-language texts that pose specific challenges for L2 readers, concluding with practical recommendations for text selection and text-based skills instruction.

What Is a Text?

A variety of definitions of text have been advanced by reading theorists, linguists, and specialists in text analysis. One general definition of a *text* is "a verbal record of a communicative act" (Wallace, 1993, p. 6). Under this definition, a text could either be written or a transcribed version of speech. A similar definition offered by Wallace is "the physical manifestations of language," which include not only orthographic symbols such as letters of the alphabet or characters but also non-verbal elements such as capitalization, punctuation, paragraphing, and format. To these basic definitions we can add this one: a sample of written language that has a unified meaning (Grabe & Kaplan, 1996). This latter definition highlights the notion that the definition of *text* goes beyond a collection of random words or sentences, even if they are formatted to appear visually cohesive (e.g., in the form of a paragraph).

Text analysts have attempted to define textual elements and explain how they interact to form a unified whole that conveys meaning. One model proposed by Kintsch (1994, 1998), Kinstch and van Dijk (1978), and Kintsch and van Dijk and Kintsch (1983) divides text into <u>*microstructure*</u> and <u>*macrostructure*</u>. The microstructure consists of individual text-based *propositions*, whereas the macrostructure organizes them into summary statements that capture the main theme of a text. Another model, described by Meyer (1975) and Meyer and Rice (1982, 1984), utilizes the term "idea unit" rather than proposition and emphasizes how idea units are related to one another in a text (e.g., through cause-and-effect, problem/solution, description, and comparison). Although the models differ with respect to details, what the two lines of research on text structure have in common are: (1) an understanding that texts comprise both smaller, discrete pieces of text as well as an overall theme or meaning; (2) an awareness of the implicit and explicit ways in which smaller textual elements are connected to one another and to the meaning of the text as a whole; and (3) evidence that readers are better able to grasp and recall macrostructure and themes than individual propositions or idea units.

In addition to larger, more general notions of text, individual readers must grapple with multiple types of information encoded in texts. These include *orthography* (writing/spelling system used), *words*, *morphosyntactic information*, *cohesive ties*, and *text structure*. As already noted, textual information also includes typographic information such as capitalization, punctuation, and paragraphing (see Chapter 1). For each of these elements, we will discuss the challenges they present for L2 readers of English.

Orthography

By definition, a text is rendered into some sort of written form. As discussed in Chapter 1 (see also Birch, 2007), orthographies can be divided roughly into three categories: *logographic* (e.g., Chinese, Japanese *kanji*), *syllabic* (e.g., Japanese *kana*, Korean *hangul*), and *alphabetic* (e.g., Arabic, English, Russian, Greek). Understanding these three general categories goes well beyond awareness that each uses different types of symbols. Rather, the organizing principle of each is different from the others. Most L2 reading teachers understand that beginning-level students who are literate and educated in an orthography different from that of the target L2 need to learn the basics of that orthography (a Chinese ESL student must learn the Roman alphabet). However, teachers probably underestimate the difficulty of this endeavor in at least two ways. First, learning a new orthography is not simply a matter of learning to draw and recognize a different set of symbols: Depending on the distance between the L1 and L2 systems, the L2 reader may have to learn an entirely new way of processing visual information, as predicted by the Orthographic Depth Hypothesis (see Chapter 1). For instance, if L1 Chinese readers are exposed to an L2 alphabetic system, they have to adjust to the concept that alphabetic symbols represent sounds, not meanings. In other words, they must understand and apply the alphabetic principle. They may attempt to approach reading in English by memorizing entire words rather than decoding them using phoneme–grapheme correspondences, an approach consistent with their L1 processing experience but one that would be only partially successful in reading English.

Second, teachers may underestimate L2 reading difficulties among students whose L1 is transcribed in the same script or orthography. For instance, L1 Spanish readers may find it difficult to decode English, with its opaque orthography. Students from many different language backgrounds may struggle with the English vowel system, which tends to be larger and more complex than in most other languages (see Chapter 1). In short, L2 literacy instructors need to know: (1) if their students are literate in their L1; (2) if so, what orthographies are represented by those L1s; (3) the challenges or difficulties those L1 writing systems might present for L2 readers; and (4) how to present basic information about the L2 orthography and how to help students develop L2-appropriate processing strategies that might be different from those used to read L1 script.

Words

Whether an orthographic system is alphabetic, logographic, syllabic, or some combination of those, the *word* is the most basic unit of a written text. For readers, words present several distinct but related challenges. First, research is clear that fluent, independent readers have developed a large recognition vocabulary (see Chapter 8). That is, successful readers have a large inventory of words that they know on sight from memory; they do not have to decode or break words into morphemes or syllables to comprehend their meaning (Grabe, 1991, 2004; Grabe & Stoller, 2001, 2002; Laufer, 1998; Koda, 2004; Nation, 2001). "Individual words are critical building blocks in text-meaning construction, and *efficiency in converting graphic symbols into sound, or meaning, information is indispensable for comprehension*" (Koda, 2004, p. 29, emphasis added). Thus, for L1 or L2 readers, a prerequisite for successful reading is an adequate sight vocabulary. Second, word *recognition* is obviously not enough: Readers must also have an adequate and accurate knowledge of word *meanings*. This is a complex matter for English reading, as the English lexicon contains many words that express similar meanings (*synonymy*). Conversely, multiple meanings can be associated with single word in English (*polysemy*) (see Chapter 8 for definitions and examples). A reader therefore must not only recognize a word on sight but also understand (or be able to infer) its particular localized, contextual meaning. Third, L2 readers must grapple not only with words themselves and their range of meanings in the L2, but also ways in which words' denotations and connotations (reference, social, and affective meanings) are similar to or different from corresponding L1 lexical item(s) in their L1. These cross-linguistic contrasts add a layer of complexity that monolingual L1 readers do not encounter (Koda, 2004). We will discuss and illustrate each of these issues in turn. Chapter 8 provides an in-depth discussion of vocabulary development in L2 reading.

Word recognition. There has been some controversy in reading research about the specific processes used by readers to identify words while reading. For instance, it was postulated that readers only "sampled" enough of the words in a text (or graphemes in a word) to construct meaning using top-down prediction strategies: The reader first generates a preliminary hypothesis about the written message, "then *selects the fewest, most productive cues necessary to confirm or reject that expectation. This is a sampling process* in which the reader takes advantage of his knowledge of vocabulary, syntax, discourse, and the 'real world' " (Clarke &

Silberstein, 1979, p. 49, emphases added). However, as discussed in Chapter 1, subsequent research has indicated that the notion of "sampling" is problematic in several respects (Birch, 2007; Carrell, 1983a, 1983b; Hudson, 2007; Koda, 2004). First, to the degree that sampling occurs at all, it involves proficient, experienced readers of a particular language, not novice readers, and certainly not readers at lower L2 proficiency levels. Thus, if teachers adopt the "sampling" argument, they may neglect important bottom-up processing skills in their instruction. Second, it is not entirely clear whether the "sampling" hypothesis is accurate: Contradicting the claims of top-down proponents, recent research demonstrates that "most text words are thoroughly processed during reading . . . deficient word recognition is directly linked to poor comprehension" (Koda, 2004, p. 30). Although these processes may have become more automated and unconscious among experienced readers, that does not mean they are not still occurring (Birch, 2007; Koda, 2004). Third, as noted in Chapter 1, encouraging readers to "guess" at or "sample" texts may promote strategies more appropriate for some reading processes (light pleasure reading) than others (textbooks or instructions for setting up a gas barbecue grill) (Birch, 2007).

For L2 readers who are literate in their L1s, L2 word recognition may be even more complex due to interlingual differences in orthography and L1-based processing strategies (see Carrell, Pharis, & Liberto, 1989; Dressler & Kamil, 2006; Genesee, Geva, Dressler, & Kamil, 2006; Wang & Koda, 2005; Wang, Koda, & Perfetti, 2003). For instance, readers of logographic systems such as Chinese are accustomed to detecting visual cues (*radicals*) in individual characters that represent the character's meaning (semantic radicals) and pronunciation (phonetic radicals). Such strategies may be helpful in reading English words that have common, recognizable morphemes (e.g., *unhappiness*) or that can be easily sounded out using individual symbols or onset-rime patterns (e.g., *cat*). These strategies are less useful with words that do not have transparent morphology or spelling (e.g., *thorough*). L1 readers of non-Roman-alphabetic languages (e.g., Hebrew, Arabic) may learn to focus heavily on consonants for decoding and have trouble distinguishing similar-looking words that differ only in their vowels (e.g., *bat, bet, but, beat*). Even readers of other Roman-alphabetic languages (e.g., Spanish) must adjust to the fact that English is less phonetically transparent than their L1 and that straightforward decoding strategies that work well in Spanish will have to be supplemented in English with other contextual knowledge to identify words that do not have one-to-one sound–symbol correspondences.[1]

Birch (2007) observed that some L2 readers come into an ESL class without adequate knowledge of the graphs (alphabet) used in English texts. Teachers often assume this prior knowledge and do not spend time presenting it or teaching decoding skills. Further, similar to young English-speaking children who learn to "sing" the alphabet and to identify letters by name but who are, in fact, years away from actual reading, L2 readers may have learned the Roman alphabet but cannot "identify graphs quickly and effortlessly as they are reading" (Birch, 2007, p. 83). Given the well-established importance of word recognition for effective reading and comprehension, it may be extremely important for teachers to present grapheme-to-phoneme (letter-to-sound) relationships systematically and to provide opportunities for students to practice rapid identification through word recognition exercises.

Word meaning. As previously noted, synonymy and polysemy, particularly in English, make semantic knowledge extremely complex. Learning a lexical item and recognizing it in print is not a one-time event, as words typically have more than one meaning, and readers must select the correct interpretation in a given text (see Chapter 8). Examples abound in English, but we will provide just one here. The verb *tell* can be used transitively (*tell a story*) or intransitively (*tell me about your trip*), but its core (reference) meanings include: to "utter, give an account, or give a command" (compiled from several definitions in www.dictionary.com). The word's connotations (social and affective meanings) can be positive ("Would you like me to *tell* you a story?") or negative ("*Tell* him to stop that right now!"). However, the word can be used in slang form as a noun: A *tell* in poker, as viewers of a 2006 James Bond film learned, means a clue, such as a twitch or a hand gesture, that another player unintentionally gives when he or she is pretending to have excellent cards. A seemingly unrelated noun form of *tell* is a bank employee known as a *teller*, an employee who helps customers complete transactions such as deposits and withdrawals. The connection between the primary verb form *tell* and the noun *teller* was exploited in a recent newspaper advertisement for a bank: "We want to be listeners, not *tellers.*" An English reader encountering the word *tell* (or *teller*) in a text must sort through this variety of syntactic information (transitive, intransitive), positive and negative connotations, idiomatic collocations (*tell* a lie, rather than **speak a lie* or **say a lie*), and alternate noun forms.

Later in this book (Chapters 5, 6, and 8), we discuss approaches to vocabulary learning and instruction, but for this discussion we will simply observe that word knowledge is crucial for reading, that acquiring such knowledge is a long-term process, and that selecting appropriate word meanings in a specific text is a complex endeavor. In fact, as noted by Koda (2004), it is so complex that beyond a basic vocabulary of several thousand high-frequency words that should be explicitly and systematically presented to learners (see Chapter 8), the only realistic way for L2 readers to acquire this extensive and sophisticated lexical knowledge is through repeated and varied exposure to vocabulary items through extensive reading (see Chapters 6 and 8).

Cross-linguistic word knowledge. An obvious difference between L1 and L2 readers is that L2 readers have acquired tens of thousands of words in their L1s. This prior knowledge may at times be beneficial and at others inhibitory, but its existence certainly changes the interaction between reader and text (Dressler & Kamil, 2006; Genesee, Geva, Dressler, & Kamil, 2006). Knowledge of shared cognates between a reader's L1 and L2 can be an advantage in comprehending L2 texts. On the other hand, divergent lexical patterns across languages may cause confusion. For example, Spanish has two distinct verbs, *conocer* and *saber,* whose

English equivalent is "to know." *Conocer* refers to being familiar with someone or something (e.g., "I've known Bob for 20 years"). *Saber* refers to possessing knowledge (e.g., "I know how to read"). A Spanish-speaking learner of English might initially be confused by the use of "know" for these distinct interpretations, but it is arguably easier to substitute one L2 word for two L1 words than vice versa (the task of the English L1 reader tackling Spanish). Regardless, the experience of L2 readers will always be informed by their L1 lexical knowledge, even when they are highly proficient in the L2: The L2 lexicon "integrates the established semantic content of their L1 equivalents, rather than creating new semantic specifications of its own ... the activation of the L1 is automatic, and therefore cannot be consciously controlled by the learner during L2 lexical processing" (Koda, 2004, p. 67). There does not appear to be anything that the learner or teacher can do to *prevent* the L1 lexicon from affecting L2 vocabulary acquisition and reading comprehension, but it is important to understand that knowledge of word meaning in a text is not only affected by the complexities of the L2 but also by prior L1 acquisition.

Morphosyntactic Information

In addition to individual words, a text is composed of both *morphological* information within words and the *syntactic* information that makes phrases and sentences intelligible. Readers use this grammatical information during text processing. For example, readers of English encountering a word preceded by *a* or *the* and ending with *–(e)s* can recognize that word as a noun, even if the word itself is unfamiliar. The effects of regular patterns in morphology and syntax can be demonstrated by examining a text containing *nonce* (nonsense) words, such as the following stanza from Lewis Carroll's *Jabberwocky*:

> 'Twas brillig, and the slithy toves
> Did gyre and gimble in the wabe;
> All mimsy were the borogoves,
> And the mome raths outgrabe.

L1 and L2 readers with metalinguistic knowledge of English should be able to answer the following questions fairly easily:

1.   In what tense or time frame is the action, and how do you know? (past, because of past tense forms such as *was, did*, and *were*)
2.   To what grammatical category does *slithy* belong? (adjective, because it comes between a definite article and a plural noun *toves*)
3.   To what grammatical category does *outgrabe* belong, and what else do we know about it? (verb because it follows a subject noun phrase,

the mome raths; it is an irregular past tense form of the verb because the time frame of the stanza is past tense and is nor marked by a regular *–ed* ending).

Morphosyntactic information can be an important tool in reading. For instance, to the degree that readers of English are aware of inflectional morphemes (e.g., plural and tense markers), common derivational morphemes (e.g., *–ness* converting adjectives to nouns, or *–al* converting nouns to adjectives), and basic word order patterns (subject–verb–complement; adjective–noun), they have additional tools to analyze unfamiliar words and to construct meaning from phrases and sentences. It is also important to observe the distinction between implicit and explicit metalinguistic knowledge. For example, readers may have sufficient knowledge to answer our questions about "Jabberwocky" without being able to articulate the formal rules contained in the parenthetical explanations.

Morphosyntactic knowledge and textual information can be highly facilitative to readers of particular languages, but such knowledge can present distinct challenges for L2 readers. Typological research reveals wide cross-linguistic variation in morphology (Birch, 2007; Comrie, 1981, 1989; Croft, 2003; Song, 2001). That is, languages differ substantially both in how many morphemes a word can contain and in the degree to which those morphemes can be separated from one another in word analysis. Evidence suggests that morphological differences across languages affect how readers process words and that L1 reading experience may cause L2 learners to overlook or ignore important L2 morphological cues, thus short-circuiting helpful "intraword analysis" skills that can enhance word- and sentence-level comprehension (Koda, 2004; Lesaux, with Koda, Siegel, & Shanahan, 2006; Schmitt & Meara, 1997; Taft & Zhu, 1995). For example, Chinese has primarily an *isolating* morphology, meaning that words typically consist of a single morpheme or of compounds easily analyzed into distinct morphemes. In contrast, English morphology relies on complex processes such as derivation and inflection, meaning that a single word can comprise many morphemes. It has been suggested that "Chinese learners of English reading do not process the grammatical information from derivational and inflectional morphology, or that they do not process it efficiently and automatically" (Birch, 2007, p. 138).

Under Comrie's (1981) scheme, English has an extremely complex morphological system. Some words consist of single morphemes (*cat*), others consist of easily analyzable morphemes (e.g., *unhappily, laptop*), whereas others include several different types of morphological information (*ate*, which contains the root verb *eat* + an irregular past tense marking), and others have many inseparable morphemes with foreign roots (e.g., *pneumonia, leukemia*). The wide variety of word types in English might increase the cognitive load for ESL/EFL readers "whose languages contain predominantly one type of word and who therefore might be unused to the other types. The problems might reside in their knowledge base (mental lexicon and semantic memory) or their processing strategies" (Birch, 2007, p. 135).

Arguably the most straightforward aspect of English morphology is the inflectional system, consisting of only eight specific morphemes: the plural and possessive markers on nouns (*boys, boy's*), the present, past, perfect, and progressive markers on verbs (*walks, walked, (have) walked, walking*), and the comparative and superlative inflections on adjectives (*smarter, smartest*). These morphemes commonly occur in English texts, and certainly it is important for L2 readers to understand and recognize them. English inflectional morphology also includes many alternate forms of these morphological functions, such as irregular plurals or zero plurals on nouns (e.g., *women, sheep, furniture*), prohibition against inflecting certain nouns for possessive (e.g., *the TV's volume* is too loud), irregular or zero tense markings on verbs (e.g., *went, put*) and constraints on inflecting certain adjectives for comparative or superlative (e.g., *beautifuller, *intelligentest*). There are also useful derivational prefixes and suffixes in English (*un–, –er, –al, –ness,* and so on), yet they are not always used systematically. Thus, it is important for teachers to be aware not only that their students might be hampered by different L1-based processing strategies but also that English morphology is complex and far from simple to teach or to learn.

As for syntactic structures, it has been argued that in some texts, longer sentences are actually easier to comprehend because they contain explicit intrasentential connectors or because they involve elaboration, such as an explanation of a term or concept earlier in the sentence (Biber, 1988; Davison, Wilson, & Herman, 1985; Hudson, 2007). Such syntactic maneuvers, wrote Koda (2004), "reflect the speaker's or writer's conscious effort to signal the logical connections between clauses. It seems reasonable, therefore, to conclude that neither syntactic complexity nor sentence length can automatically be linked with comprehension difficulty" (p. 97). That said, it may also be that less proficient L2 readers cannot benefit from sentence connectors or elaboration structures to the degree that fluent L1 readers can: Perhaps the "shorter is better" argument might hold for at least some L2 readers (Koda, 2004, p. 109).

It has also been suggested by SLA researchers and L2 reading researchers alike that certain syntactic structures are more basic and therefore easier for beginning readers to process. For example, because the passive voice construction in English deviates from canonical Subject-Verb-Object (SVO) word order found in most English sentences (at least where logical subject vs. grammatical subject is concerned), passive constructions may be harder for English L2 readers still in earlier stages of language development. Similar suggestions have been made about relative clauses (e.g., *The teacher **that the parents and students all hated** was transferred to a different school*), especially those embedded within subject noun phrases, thus creating more distance between the subject and the main verb), about structural ambiguity (e.g., *The magician tapped the man with the cane*), and about deletion and substitution (e.g., *Joe did his laundry and I did mine, too*). Along these lines, an earlier study by Cohen, Glasman, Rosenbaum-Cohen,

Ferrara, and Fine (1979) suggested that syntactically "heavy" constructions such as very long subject noun phrases made academic texts more difficult for Israeli ESL university students.

Research on the effects of syntactic constructions and cross-linguistic differences (syntactic distance between L1 and L2) on L2 reading comprehension has been relatively scarce. Considering the interacting factors involved in text processing, which include background knowledge about the content, lexico-semantic knowledge, understanding of cohesive devices and text structures, and metalinguistic awareness, it is no doubt far too simplistic to posit that a text will be too difficult, too easy, or just right for L2 readers based on sentence length or the presence or absence of other syntactic elements such as those mentioned above. However, it is also likely that varying degrees of L2 proficiency in general and L2 reading skills in particular will make syntactic issues more relevant for some students than others.[2] Thus, in text selection, syntactic complexity should be one of several factors considered by teachers in determining whether a particular text is appropriate for students (or whether additional support or explanation will be needed as students read the text) (Charrow, 1988; Ulijn & Strother, 1990). We will return to text analysis and selection later in this chapter; here we elaborate further on how word and sentence features factor into the important and widely used construct of *readability*.

Readability: Definitions, elements, and calculations. Readability can be measured in terms of quantifiable linguistic and textual factors, including word and sentence length (Carrell, 1987b), as well as word frequency and familiarity (Chall, 1958; Elley, 1969; Klare, 1963; Nation, 2001). Measures of readability commonly used in L1 reading research and instruction include the Flesch-Kincaid Reading Ease (RE) Formula and the Flesch-Kincaid Grade Level Formula. The following version of the Flesch-Kincaid formula, simplified by Carrell (1987b), focuses on the easily measurable features of word and sentence length:

$$\text{Flesch-Kincaid RE} = 0.4 \, (\text{ASL}) + 12 \, (\text{ASW}) - 16$$

ASL = Average sentence length: number of words ÷ number of sentences
ASW = Average number of syllables per word: number of syllables ÷ number of words

Using the Flesch-Kincaid Formula, a text's readability is calculated by determining average sentence length (ASL, expressed in terms of words per sentence) and average word length (ASW, expressed in terms of syllables per word). The Flesch-Kincaid RE score is easy for teachers, parents, and librarians to use because the value converts to a U.S. grade school level (the Flesch-Kincaid Level). For example, the following paragraph, which we will consider as a self-contained text, contains 219 words, eight sentences, and a total of 477 syllables. Its Flesch-Kincaid RE score is 12.0, the equivalent of a 12th-grade text.

The related Flesch RE Formula is perhaps less commonly used but generates a value that offers teachers and materials developers a rough index of surface features that might affect reader comprehension. Using the same ASL and ASW values as the Flesch-Kincaid RE Formula, the Flesch RE Formula reads as follows:

$$\text{Flesch RE} = 206.835 - 1.015\ (\text{ASL}) - 84.6\ (\text{ASW})$$

Applying the Flesch RE Formula to the paragraph you are reading, we would generate a Flesch RE score of 50.0 on a scale of 0 to 100. Higher scores reflect easier reading; lower scores reflect more difficult reading. Average Flesch RE scores generally fall in a range between 6 and 70. A text with a Flesch score of 90 to 100 is thought to be easily comprehended by a Grade 5 reader; a text with a Flesch score of 60 to 70 is thought to be easily processed by a Grade 8 or 9 reader. A college graduate should reasonably interpret texts scoring in the 0 to 30 range. As a further point of reference, *Time* magazine generally scores in the low 50s on the Flesch scale; *Reader's Digest* articles score around 65. In contrast, academic journals predictably achieve much lower readability scores in the high 20s and low 30s; legal documents often achieve scores in the teens or lower.

Although both the Flesch RE Formula and Flesch-Kincaid Grade Level Formula are perhaps among the most frequently used readability indices for English-language texts, researchers have developed dozens of readability formulæ over the past several decades (Klare, 1974–1975; Weaver & Kintsch, 1991), including the Fry Readability Formula (Fry, 1977), which is widely used because of how easily it can be applied manually. Computer software makes calculating readability scores very easy for teachers and materials developers, provided texts are available in digital form. Not only are readability calculators widely available at little or no cost via the Web (see Further Reading and Resources), word processing software is frequently bundled with a readability indexing tool. Microsoft Word for both PC and Mac platforms, for example, generates both Flesch RE and Flesch-Kincaid Grade Level scores as part of the application's grammar and spell-check functions, which also report features such as word count, number of passive sentence strings, and so forth.

Teachers who use readability formulæ and calculators should, of course, do so with the understanding that quantitatively-based measures such as Flesch, Flesch-Kincaid, and Fry are based on surface-level textual properties, most of which are confined to the sentence level. Such tools cannot sensitively analyze discourse-level properties such as coherence, cohesion, propositional density, and so on (Britton & Gulgoz, 1991; Carrell, 1987b; Grabe, 1997; Hudson, 2007; Kintsch, 1994; Miller & Kintsch, 1980). For example, any text can achieve a high Flesch RE score but lack cohesion and coherence, thus compromising a competent reader's ability to make sense of it. We would further caution L2 reading teachers that most such formulæ are not designed with the L2 reader in mind. Furthermore, readability is a complex construct that involves not only the observable characteristics of a text, but also the aptitude, knowledge, experience, skill, efficiency, and motivation that the *reader* brings to the text and to the reading task (Carrell, 1987a, 1987b; Kintsch, 1988, 1994, 1998), as well as to the *situation* for reading (Kintsch, Welsch, Schmalhofer, & Zimny, 1990) (see Chapters 1 and 2).

Text Cohesion

Beyond individual words and sentences are the explicit ways in which a writer ties ideas together within and among sentences. These include specific connectives, which may be temporal (e.g., *before, after*), additive (e.g., *in addition, further*), causal (e.g., *because, consequently, therefore*), or adversative (e.g., *however, nonetheless, on the other hand*) (Halliday & Hasan, 1976; Hudson, 2007; Irwin, 1986; Koda, 2004). Other types of explicit clue include relevance indicators (e.g., *it is important to note, to reiterate*), summary indicators (e.g., *in conclusion, in sum*), and enumerators (e.g., *first, second, finally*) (Koda, 2004; Lorch, 1989). Relationships between ideas can also be signalled through various types of reference, including full or partial repetition of key words and phrases, synonyms for key words and phrases, and pronoun reference (Halliday & Hasan, 1976). Such references can be *anaphoric*, referring back to something/someone already stated in the text (e.g., *My dog **Bruce** is so dumb that **he** can't find **his** way home when **he** gets out of the yard*) or *cataphoric*, referring to something or someone about to be introduced (e.g., *Knowing that **she** would be going home from college soon, **Laura** saved all **her** laundry for **her** mother to do*).

Certain types of cohesion tend to occur more frequently in some genres and text types than in others. For instance, the explicit connectors are found more in written than in spoken texts and in academic texts than in literary or journalistic texts (Biber, 1988, 2006; Hyland, 2004a, 2004b). Further, relationships among ideas are also signaled by the author through the ordering of sentences within paragraphs, through the ordering of paragraphs and sections within the text as a whole, by section dividers (e.g., titles, subheadings, and so on) and by other typographic features (e.g., bolding, centering, or underlining text). Authors intend these features to be helpful to readers and to make their ideas and text structure transparent. A reader's ability to recognize and interpret these cohesive ties as a road map to understanding the text as a whole is critical (Hudson, 2007). Because the types of cohesive ties available vary across languages, it can be very important for teachers to consider them in text selection and perhaps to design lessons aimed at helping students to understand the most common types and to recognize their utility in the text materials being studied.

Typography

As already noted, written texts may contains nonverbal elements not found in speech and potentially helpful (or confusing) to a reader. These include text formatting (paragraphing, indentation, spacing, bolding, italicizing), punctuation, and capitalization. Recognition of basic punctuation marks (a period and a question mark) can help readers who may be unclear on the syntactic rules governing what constitutes a "sentence" or how to form questions properly—the terminal punctuation and initial capitalization can quickly help them to identify the sentence type without needing a sophisticated analysis, and repeated exposure to those sentence types through reading will help them to internalize the syntactic patterns. Because paragraphs tend to separate idea units in prose texts, understanding what a new paragraph looks like (through indenting and spacing) provides visual cues to the author's text divisions and relationships among ideas. Because these conventions vary cross-linguistically, it can be important for inexperienced L2 readers to recognize what they mean and their utility for overall text comprehension.

Special considerations for digital texts. As discussed in Chapter 1, an understanding of texts must also include those in computer-generated formats (Eagleton & Dobler, 2007; Moore, 2001; Withrow, 2004). In addition to print versions of books, magazines, newspapers, and so forth, we must also understand that today's "texts" and "reading" may not only be generated digitally but entirely processed in that format, as well. Thus, when we mention the typographical features outlined above, in digital formats we must add graphics, audio, video, hyperlinks to other websites, and so forth (Valmont, 2002). Researchers are in the early stages of understanding how the processing of digital texts is similar to or different from hard-copy texts, yet 21st-century teachers and their students must make themselves aware of the options, the enhancements, and the possible risks or pitfalls (e.g., readers being distracted by all the "extras," breaking their concentration by jumping to a new website, having more limited or different comprehension strategies because less text can be viewed on a screen than on a printed page, and so on) (Mackey, 2007). For students whose computer and Internet experiences have been more limited, it may be beneficial to discuss with students how to approach digital texts (Eagleton & Dobler, 2007).

Text Structure

Beyond the specific words, sentences, and other marks on a page is the underlying *structure* governing a particular text type. For instance, as everyday readers, we learn that recipes typically begin with a list of ingredients followed by sequential steps to follow to prepare the dish. We learn that newspaper headlines tend to be economical (only a few words to capture the gist of the article), and that news stories on the front page of the newspaper are supposed to report facts objectively, whereas opinion columns and editorials provide more analysis and personal opinions about current events. We learn that stories tend to be organized chronologically and to contain a plot, characters, setting, conflict, and theme (Smith, 1988, 2004). Thus, part of the information contained in a text includes its text type or genre, as well as the global organizational pattern(s) it represents. Readers may pick up such patterns unconsciously and automatically through repeated exposure and without explicit instruction (though such instruction may be useful and even necessary for *writing*). We discuss strategies for helping L2 readers discern and analyze text structure in Chapters 5 and 7.

Further, L2 readers who are literate in their L1s and who have experience reading L1 texts may have been exposed to differing rhetorical patterns (Connor, 1996; Eggington, 1987; Hinds, 1987; Hirvela, 2004; Hudson, 2007; Kaplan, 1966; Koda, 2004; Soter, 1988). L2 reading studies have found that students' awareness of top-down text structures improved their recall and comprehension of texts (e.g., Carrell, 1984a; Hyon, 2001, 2002). However, studies of the impact of instruction on text structure on L2 reading comprehension have yielded mixed and inconclusive findings; both content familiarity and L2 proficiency also appeared to be influential variables. Although conscious awareness of global features of different text types may again be more critical for L2 writing than L2 reading, teachers should again take text structure issues (especially as they vary cross-linguistically) into consideration in their text selection and in designing instruction (see Chapter 5 for suggestions for examining text structure as part of an intensive reading lesson).

Text Information: Summary

We have looked at numerous elements and information types included in what we call a text. These ranged from the script in which the text is written to word- and sentence-level information to cohesive ties to global text structure. We could examine these issues at a much more technical and theoretical level than we have attempted here (for detailed treatments, see Birch, 2007; Hudson, 2007; Koda, 2004). Our goal in this section was to introduce them briefly and to discuss what may be challenging or problematic about these various elements for L2 readers in general, and, at points, for English L2 readers in particular.

This discussion is important, given several decades of emphasis on top-down reading instruction during which practitioners assumed that a combination of reader background knowledge and sustained exposure to text through extensive reading would make all readers, whether L1 or L2, able to grapple successfully with almost any text (e.g., Day & Bamford, 1998; Dupuy, Tse, & Cook, 1996; Krashen, 2004; Smith, 2004). Such a view underestimates the complexity of the reading process, the differences across text types and purposes for reading them, and the importance of the information within a text itself. As they select texts, plan instruction, assist students, and assess progress, teachers must be aware of textual elements that can challenge or inhibit L2 readers. Such considerations and discussions may feel overly technical and dry at times, but they are nonetheless necessary. We turn in the next sections to the practical implications of our focus on the text—first, in discussing how teachers can use this information in evaluating and selecting texts for students to read, and second to discussing specific ways in which teachers can help L2 readers build their bottom-up knowledge and processing skills.

Focus on the Text: Implications for Text Selection

In Chapter 2, we discussed how awareness of student background knowledge (including L2 proficiency) and interests can inform text selection for classroom use. In this section, we look at how a careful examination of the text features listed in Figure 3.1 can help teachers select appropriate materials for a particular group of students. We discuss broader issues regarding text selection in the syllabus design process in Chapter 4.

Selecting and Analyzing Texts for Intensive Reading Instruction

In planning a lesson or series of lessons, a teacher may work with a specific text for several days or even weeks (see Chapter 5). Thus, careful analysis of that text is extremely important for the success of that lesson sequence in students' ongoing literacy development. We cannot stress this enough: Text selection is *critical* to the effectiveness of intensive reading lessons. Teachers should thus consider a variety of issues before committing their own and students' time and energy to a specific text. These issues include the ones already discussed above as well as the student/reader variables described in Chapter 2; they should also include the following text-based variables.

Length. For individual readings, teachers need to find a balance between texts that are too daunting for the students' reading experience and proficiency level and texts that do not challenge students adequately (Seymour & Walsh, 2006). Many students have very limited experience with reading in the L2; if they are in academic settings, they must learn to cover substantial amounts of material for general education and major courses, depending on the discipline. L2 reading teachers need to find ways to push students further in their reading without overwhelming or discouraging them. In addition to considering students' L2 proficiency and prior reading experience, teachers need to consider how the text selections fit into the overall course syllabus (see Chapters 4 and 7). If a text is

---

- ❏ Text length (both individual texts and course readers)
- ❏ "Extra-textual" characteristics (e.g., vocabulary glosses, pictures, headings, special text formatting; audio, video, graphics, and hyperlinks in digital texts)
- ❏ Vocabulary (proportion of unfamiliar content-specific, general, and academic words; frequency of occurrence; helpfulness of surrounding contexts)
- ❏ Morphology (inflectional and derivational morphemes that could assist readers with sentence processing and word analysis)
- ❏ Syntax (sentence length/complexity, sentence types, "advanced" structures such as passive constructions, relative clauses, and so on)
- ❏ Explicit cohesive devices such as connectives and referential ties
- ❏ Text macrostructure: logical ordering of ideas, transparency of logical relations, and overall discourse structure

FIGURE 3.1. Bottom-Up Text Selection Considerations.

lengthy, how will teachers approach assigning and teaching it over a period of days or weeks so that students have a successful and positive experience with it?

Visual information and comprehension aids. In looking at text materials, teachers might also consider whether additional visual information (both verbal and non-verbal) might assist students as they read the selections in the text. For example, does the material provide glosses (definitions) for key words and phrases provided, as well as infrequent or unusual words? Are glosses provided at the beginning or end of readings, in the back of a book, or in the margins? Does the selection provide photos or other illustrations? Does the text provide helpful titles and subheadings? Are formatting and typographical conventions such as boldface type, italics, and underscoring utilized effectively? If it is a digital text, are there audio, video, and graphic elements that might help the students as they read it?[3] Although these factors are not necessarily make-or-break aspects of text selection, they can help teachers assess the relative merits of competing texts they might be considering.

Vocabulary. Earlier research suggested that a text with about 5% of unfamiliar vocabulary was at about the right level for students, but more recent estimates place the number closer to 2% (Hudson, 2007; Koda, 2004; Nation, 2001; see Chapter 8). Although "vocabulary knowledge" can be difficult to assess (what does it mean to "know a word" for the purposes of reading?), it is clear that teachers should take vocabulary difficulty under serious advisement in text selection. The issue is further complicated by the fact that a text may include different types of potentially problematic vocabulary, including content-specific specialized vocabulary, more general vocabulary, idiomatic, and cultural-specific items—any or all of which may pose problems for L2 learners, depending on their prior L2 knowledge (see Chapter 8).

Consider the data sample in Figure 3.2, taken from Folse (2004). This short text, designed specifically for language instruction, addresses what seems to be a

---

The Price of Baseball: Colorado Rockies Give In to Hickey's Contract Demands

The **Colorado Rockies** completed *a deal* with the **Chicago White Sox** for **second baseman** Jonathan Hickey early yesterday morning, according to the *Chicago Tribune.*

The **Rockies** agreed to <u>ship</u> their **star pitcher** to **Seattle** in *a rather complex deal* that also gave **two minor leaguers** as well as **$8 million** to the Chicago team. Sources familiar with the *on-again, off-again contract negotiations* confirmed that **Rockies** owner Kevin Lewis had spent weeks trying to resolve the issues of Hickey's contract <u>perks,</u> including the use of a chartered jet for the **four-time All-Star** and his wife.

Hickey agreed to *waive his no-trade clause* after the **Rockies** secured jet service under the terms of his *staggering seven-year, $125 million contract* and addressed *a clause* that grants him **high-priced seats at games.** As usual in these **trades,** team physicians must still *exchange medical data* before the *commissioner's office can approve the trade.*

bold = topic-specific (baseball) vocabulary
italics = potentially problematic general vocabulary
<u>underline</u> = idiomatic vocabulary

FIGURE 3.2. Vocabulary Difficulty—Sample Text.
Source: Folse (2004, p. 31).

familiar topic, baseball. The selection is not especially syntactically complex. However, closer examination reveals that this short selection presents a number of potential problems with regard to vocabulary.[4] For example, students may be familiar with the *Colorado Rockies* as a mountain range but not as a major-league baseball team. They may also not know that Seattle has a team; thus, the reference to the Rockies *shipping* their star pitcher to Seattle (naming the city but not the team) may not make sense. We also notice other topic-specific items as well, such as *second baseman, minor leaguers, All-Star,* and *commissioner's office.* More general vocabulary that may be unfamiliar might include the reference to the *exchange* of *medical data* (meaning that before the trade can be completed, the team doctors must verify that the players involved are not injured) and other business-, trade-, and deal-related vocabulary. Students may be familiar with "deals" being made in business settings but unaware that in professional sports players can be traded from one team to another and that other considerations, such as cash, game tickets, private jets, and *no-trade clauses* may factor into such transactions. Finally, the selection contains several idiomatic expressions: *ship* (which usually applies to packages, not people), *star* (meaning the best or most famous player on a team), and *perks* (a vernacular shortening of *perquisites,* extra benefits added to a player's contract in addition to his salary).

Teachers cannot put every text they are considering under such microscopic scrutiny, but this example demonstrates that there may be more to consider with regard to unfamiliar vocabulary in a text than we might realize. When evaluating a text for classroom use, teachers should ask themselves what vocabulary may be unfamiliar (remembering the different categories discussed above), whether the text as a whole is transparent and accessible enough to compensate for possible vocabulary difficulties, and what adjustments may need to be made to the text itself or during instruction to help students grapple with unfamiliar items as they read (see Chapter 8).

Several corpus-based, computerized approaches can help teachers with this analysis. One example is the Vocabulary Profiler (VP) found in www.lextutor.ca. This free and easy-to-use tool allows teachers to enter texts (either by pasting them or uploading them) for analysis. An example of the output (based on the baseball text in Figure 3.2) is shown in Figure 3.3. This table shows that about 70% of the words in the text are from the K1/K2 lists (general service lists of the first one and two thousand [K1–K2] most frequent words in English texts), 11.6% are from the *Academic Word List* (AWL) (Coxhead, 2000), and 18% are "off-list" words (i.e., not part of a research corpus). Further output (shown online but not in Figure 3.3) indicates that the text has a low type–token ratio, meaning that most of the words in the text occur only once. This basic statistical information suggests that the text may, in fact, be too difficult lexically for many L2 readers, as nearly 30% of the words are likely to be unfamiliar, and no words occur frequently enough in the text to assist students with sorting out their meanings.[5]

However, the picture is a bit more complex than that. The VP also provides a color-coded picture of which words in the text fall into each category. For

Families	Types	Tokens	Percent
K1 words (1–1000):	65	108	69.68%
Function:	...	...	(36.13%)
Content:	...	...	(33.55%)
K2 words (1001–2000):	1	1	0.65%
1k+2k		...	(70.33%)
AWL words (academic):	14	14	11.61%
Off-list words:	?	20	18.06%
			100%

FIGURE 3.3. Vocabulary Profiler Output for Baseball Text.
Retrieved May 3, 2007 from http://www.lextutor.ca/vp/eng/output.pl?

instance, we discover that all of the city, team, and player names are in the "off-list" category, as are most of the baseball-specific and idiomatic expressions. Most of the business-related vocabulary (i.e., *contract, confirmed, clause,* and *medical data*) comes from the AWL. Beyond simple percentages, this profile gives teachers a clearer picture of the nature of potential difficulties. Proper nouns and even baseball terminology may not be too difficult for students, but some of the AWL and idiomatic words might well be. Although the VP and other tools like it should not be the sole source of teacher decision-making about a text, it can both provide an objective analysis of the vocabulary and even call to teachers' attention potentially problematic lexical items.

Further, these items should not be considered in isolation in the text selection process. Whether a lexical item will be problematic for readers also depends on the helpfulness of the context in which it occurs—the text as a whole, the specific sentence, and the surrounding sentences. Contexts can be very helpful, neutral, or even misleading (Folse, 2004). In determining whether vocabulary is too difficult and which words or phrases might be problematic, teachers should also assess whether students will be able to analyze them in the immediate context without additional assistance or with much struggle as they read. Taking again the baseball text example in Figure 3.2, if students have ever observed or played baseball, they are likely to know what a *second baseman* is—thus allowing them to guess in the first sentence that the *Colorado Rockies* and *Chicago White Sox* are the names of baseball teams, even if they are completely unfamiliar with major league baseball. Further, the capitalization of the team names and the player's name, together with students' likely awareness of *Colorado* and *Chicago* as place names will help students to guess at what may be transpiring in the sentence and then in the text as a whole. Similarly, they may know what a *deal* is in business if not in professional sports, so that they can extend that background knowledge to the term in the first sentence.

Morphology and syntax. Morphology bridges the word- and sentence-level features to consider in text selection. For instance, in examining potentially difficult vocabulary, teachers might note whether an unfamiliar lexical item exhibits recognizable derivational morphology that could help students analyze or guess the word's meaning (or which could be the basis of a classroom lesson on using morphological cues to learn and understand new words). At the sentence level, teachers might note whether inflectional and derivational morphology could help students identify grammatical relationships (such as plural or verb tense markers) or to process the function of a word within a sentence (e.g., a derivational suffix that signals a particular grammatical category, such as *–ness*, which derives a noun from an adjective, as in *kind* → kindness).

Probably the more salient issue in text selection is syntactic complexity. The teacher might look at overall sentence length and type (simple, compound, complex) and might also notice more difficult syntactic constructions such as passive constructions, relative clauses, subordination, subjunctives, verb phrases with modal auxiliaries, and so forth. Teachers should not simply look for texts with short, choppy sentences, and although helping students grapple with authentic text is important, if a text is full of long, difficult, complex sentences, it might be frustrating and difficult for students, especially if it also contains a high percentage of unfamiliar vocabulary and content. However, the occasional challenging sentence in a text should not in and of itself be a deterrent in text selection. The "Second Chances" text in Appendix 3.1 is a good example (also see Questions for Reflection at the beginning of this chapter and in Application Activities 3.1 and 3.2). The text has a lot to recommend it: It has a universal, accessible theme (getting a second chance when one has made mistakes), it is written by a young adult, the vocabulary overall is not too challenging, and most of the sentences are fairly short and uncomplicated. However, the opening sequence, reprinted below, has several challenging syntactic elements.

> Have you ever thought, "If I could start life over again from the beginning, what would I do differently?" . . .
> If I could just wake up and find myself in the hospital where I was born, in the body of a newborn but with the brain of someone who has already tried life for 17 years, I know there are a lot of things I would do differently. (Brahm, 2001)

First, the excerpt contains two occurrences of the subjunctive mood (statements contrary to fact): "If I could . . . I would . . . ." The passage also contains a "quotation" (punctuated as one) that is actually a hypothetical internal dialogue, rather than something said aloud. Finally, the text contains the relative clause, "someone *who has already tried life* for 17 years . . ." These syntactic features perhaps should not overshadow the other strengths of the text, but it is worth noting that they might cause some initial confusion for students, especially as they occur at the very outset of the text. Considering our earlier discussion of readability, we should acknowledge that this passage receives a Flesch RE score of 67.1 and a Flesch-Kincaid grade-level score of 12, making the passage more challenging than we might initially believe.

Cohesive devices and text structure. Another aspect of a text worth considering is whether its logical relations are transparent to readers. Does the text include explicit connecting words and phrases that can help to serve as a road map for student comprehension? Are key words and phrases explained, defined, repeated, or paraphrased? Are pronoun referents clear? It has been claimed that logical connectors add to a text's readability (Celce-Murcia & Olshtain, 2000; Halliday & Hasan, 1976; Irwin, 1986; Roller, 1990). The "Second Chances" text contains relatively few of them, whereas a chapter from an academic textbook or a journal article may have many. In the absence of explicit logical connectors, the teacher should also consider whether the sequencing of sentences and paragraphs makes the author's intent and train of thought clear to the reader. Certain text types, such as literary selections, may require more effort on the part of the reader than others (see Chapter 7), and if the teacher decides to use a text that is relatively less transparent in its structure, the students may need more help putting the pieces together (e.g., with graphic organizers; see Chapters 5 and 7).

Text Selection Issues: Summary

As we conclude this section, we would like to clarify two points, possibly in tension with each other. First, we regard careful, thoughtful text selection as *absolutely essential* to successful reading instruction and experiences (Aebersold & Field, 1997; Hirvela, 2004; Shrum & Glisan, 2005; Silberstein, 1994). This principle includes texts that a class as a whole will study together in intensive reading lessons (Chapter 5), self-selected materials for extensive reading (Chapter 6), and the specific case of literary texts (Chapter 7). Beyond awareness of reader background knowledge and interest (Chapter 2), text selection should take specific characteristics of the actual text into consideration. We have suggested specific ways in which teachers can examine texts and even teach students to examine them for self-selected reading.

At the same time, text selection is perhaps more of an art than a science. The various text characteristics we have discussed—length, vocabulary, context, morphology, syntax, cohesion, and text structure—are all important, yet they interact in different ways depending on the text, the students, and the goals of instruction (both course and lesson). For instance, a text with a relatively high proportion of unfamiliar vocabulary may still be used successfully if, for instance, students already have substantil prior knowledge about the topic or if teachers wish to challenge students and offer practice with inferencing. Moreover, if a text has an appealing, accessible theme, and the teacher's primary goal for selecting it is to give students ideas to write about in a composition, the fact that it has challenging syntax or few explicit cohesive devices may not be especially relevant or problematic. Finally, if text analysis reveals potentially problematic aspects, these features may guide the teacher to provide further instructional support, rather than lead her to reject the text. This is to say that, although teachers should carefully analyze texts, a range of interacting variables can and should help teachers determine whether and how a particular text (or book) is appropriate for their students.

Focus on the Text: Building Bottom-Up Skills and Strategies

We have so far examined components of written texts, ways in which those elements may be challenging for L2 readers, and implications of that awareness for text selection. Before we leave our focus on the text, we will close by highlighting specific implications of this discussion for classroom instruction. In what ways can teachers help students to grapple not only with texts examined in the reading class but also to learn skills and strategies transferable to literacy events outside the classroom? It is to this "bottom-up" side of the reading interaction that we now turn.

Before going further, we should reiterate that we subscribe to an interactive view of the reading process (see Chapter 1). Activating and developing students' schemata, encouraging prediction and guessing, and reading for meaning are all critical components of reading instruction and student success. Early in our careers, we found that many of the ESL reading texts available were bottom-up, skills-based curricula that included little, if any, actual reading. Often, instructional "texts" consisted of short, contrived excerpts designed to practice word recognition, skimming, scanning, and so forth. We do not advocate a return to those days. Nonetheless, as reading instructors have enthusiastically embraced top-down approaches to reading—which are, after all, more interesting and fun and less technical than some of the topics we have covered in this chapter—there has been a swing away from recognizing problems L2 readers may have with texts and helping students to build their text-based comprehension skills (Birch, 2007; Eskey, 1986; Hudson, 2007; Koda, 2004; Urquhart & Weir, 1998). This shift is problematic for students at all levels, but it is particularly unfortunate for those at lower levels of L2 proficiency and those who have limited literacy experience in any language.

Bottom-Up Skills: Approaches and Activities

The degree to which the specific suggestions that follow are appropriate will vary according to the students' L1 background, prior literacy experience, L2 proficiency, and the goals and constraints of a particular teacher and course. For instance, a teacher who meets her students six hours per week can prioritize time, activities, and skills differently than one who only meets a class two hours per week. Some bottom-up skills and strategies to consider are summarized in Figure 3.4 and are discussed in detail below.

Orthography. If students are at low L2 proficiency levels but literate in L1, it is worth considering whether they need formal instruction in the L2 writing system (Birch, 2007; Grabe & Kaplan, 1996; Grabe & Stoller, 2002; Parry, 1996). If

1. **Orthography:** letter/symbol recognition; L2 sound–symbol correspondences

2. **Words:** Automatic recognition skills, vocabulary knowledge (most frequent 2,000 words; word analysis skills; dictionary skills; vocabulary-in-context skills)

3. **Morphemes:** Understanding of the eight inflectional morphemes (and exceptions); common affixes used to derive new words

4. **Sentences:** Basic sentence patterns (SVO, simple, compound, complex); complex constructions such as passive voice, modals, relative clauses, subjunctives, conditionals, infrequent verb tense/aspect combinations

5. **Cohesion:** Recognizing connective words and phrases; understanding different forms of reference

6. **Coherence and text structure:** Common orders in different text types (e.g., story structure, expository essay structure, comparison-and-contrast options, and so on)

7. **Typographical elements:** Punctuation, capitalization, and text formatting (including digital features, if applicable)

FIGURE 3.4. Bottom-Up Skills and Strategies for Classroom Instruction.

they are English L2 students and have become literate in a non-alphabetic system, they must first know the Roman alphabet and its typographical conventions (capital and lower-case letters, names of letters, and the sound(s) associated with each grapheme). Learners must also understand that we read words fundamentally by using a phonemic approach (i.e., matching symbols with sounds to decode or identify words and then matching these forms with meanings) rather than looking at a symbol or set of symbols and memorizing its meanings. L1 readers of non-Roman alphabets likely understand phonemic processing but need to learn the Roman alphabet. Readers whose L1 orthographies rely on the Roman alphabet must simply learn how the alphabet is used differently across the two orthographies (e.g., that English may contain relatively more distinct vowel and diverse spellings for them; that the differences between vowels tend to be more precise and meaningful than in many other languages) (Grabe & Kaplan, 1996; Smith, 2004). ESL and EFL readers must also learn that, because of the diverse historical origins of the English lexicon, Modern English orthography exhibits many irregularities and peculiarities and that simple decoding will not always suffice for word identification. Our students, for instance, have been confounded by differences between "police" and "polite," which differ in spelling by only one letter but which are pronounced quite differently.

Word identification. As previously noted, fluent readers develop *automaticity*, the ability to recognize or identify many words rapidly, which reduces short-term memory load and improves comprehension. Automaticity develops principally through word knowledge and repeated exposure to written text (see Chapter 8). An L1 English speaker learning to read has already heard the word *the* hundreds of thousands of times in a few short years of life and develops an understanding of its highly complex pragmatic functions. *The* is one of the most frequent words in English, yet it is initially challenging for novice L1 readers because it cannot be easily sounded out. However, English-speaking children quickly learn to recognize it, commit it to memory, and maintain that knowledge by encountering the word over and over again in print.

In contrast, ESL and EFL readers usually do not have the same advantage of a well-developed oral vocabulary: Typically, they are building their L2 vocabularies at the same time as they are attempting to develop L2 reading skills. Thus, they must simultaneously *learn* the new words in English and learn to *recognize* them in print (Nation, 2001; Schmitt, 2000). That said, the fact that learners may already be literate and can match newly learned words to print equivalents helps them to learn L2 vocabulary more quickly because they have both oral/aural and visual modes of processing on which to draw. In contrast, children learn to comprehend and use oral language years before beginning to read (see Chapter 1). Although building a basic L2 vocabulary and providing a great deal of reading practice are the best ways to develop learner automaticity (Birch, 2007; Flavell, Miller, & Miller, 2002; Hudson, 2007; Koda, 2004), some students may find it helpful also to complete timed word recognition exercises and timed-reading activities. Such tasks cannot by themselves develop student fluency and automaticity, but they can help students understand that reading more quickly in the L2 is not only possible but beneficial. As confidence-builders, timed reading programs are especially helpful if used consistently (e.g., a few minutes at the beginning of each class period, or several times a week) and if students track their progress in speed and accuracy (through responding to a few comprehension questions immediately after reading) (see Birch [2007, pp. 176–177], Fry [1977], and Jensen [1986, pp. 107–114] for steps toward implementing reading rate development programs; see Figure 3.5 for a brief synopsis).

Vocabulary knowledge. We discuss vocabulary acquisition, vocabulary learning strategies, and approaches to vocabulary instruction in Chapter 8. For this discussion of bottom-up text-based processing, we will simply make the following observations:

First, L2 readers need a basic *threshold inventory* of words that they understand

☐ Select texts that are brief (400–800 words), comprehensible, and accessible.

☐ Decide on a timing system and explain it clearly to students.

☐ Show students how to maintain reading rate (words per minute; accuracy) charts.

☐ Use timed reading consistently (every day or several times per week).

☐ Encourage students to measure their own progress, not compete against classmates.

FIGURE 3.5. Guidelines for Timed Reading Programs.

and can recognize in print (see Chapter 8). Second, word meanings can be so complex, variable, idiosyncratic, and text-specific that teachers and students need to understand that the only realistic way to develop advanced vocabulary knowledge is through repeated exposure to words in diverse contexts (i.e., through extensive reading in the L2—see Chapter 6). Third, students need to understand that a word they know in one context may mean something different (and be subject to different register constraints) in others. Figure 3.6 shows a lesson sequence designed not only to help students to interpret "staggering" in the baseball text in Figure 3.2 but also to reinforce the principle that words can convey divergent meanings in different texts and to practice dictionary use skills.

Morphemes. Despite the morphological complexity of Modern English, it can be helpful to present basic morphological concepts to students to help them grapple with texts. First, they can learn the eight inflectional morphemes, be introduced to a few of their exceptions, and analyze how those morphemes function in a typical page of text (as in Appendix 3.2). Second, such *word attack* tasks can introduce learners to frequent and productive derivational affixes, leading them to understand how morphological functions can enable them to recognize and analyze new words. Figure 3.7 provides a chart of basic inflectional and derivational morphemes that can be presented (also see Application Activity 8.8).

Syntax. Without turning a reading course into a grammar course, teachers might want to introduce basic sentence patterns and some of the more difficult constructions found in texts, such as the passive voice, relative clauses, and so forth. The point of a brief introduction is not to prepare learners to pass a grammar test or even to produce these constructions in writing, but rather to develop their awareness of how syntax conveys information and provides clues to text meaning. For example, if students read in the newspaper that a prominent politician said, "Mistakes were made," they can recognize that the passive voice was used and that it can be a syntactic mechanism to avoid personal responsibility (contrast with "I made mistakes"). Examples of reading-focused lessons that highlight syntactic issues are included in Chapter 5.

Cohesion and Reference. As already noted, it can be extremely helpful for reading comprehension to ensure that L2 readers recognize and understand cohesive devices and reference markers. Figure 3.8 provides list of features to present and a brief text-based lesson sequence highlighting several items.

Text Structure. Students educated and literate in other languages may benefit from becoming aware of typical text organization patterns in the L2. To the degree that they can recognize and interpret common patterns, formal schemata that can facilitate overall comprehension are built. Figure 3.9 presents a sample activity illustrating common pattern of classification and description (also see Chapters 5 and 7).

Typography. Students new to reading in L2 may benefit from brief presentations on capitalization conventions (which vary across languages), on the role and function of the frequent punctuation marks, and on how text is positioned

1. The online dictionary www.dictionary.com provides these definitions for *stagger:*
   a. to walk, move, or stand unsteadily;
   b. to falter or begin to give way, as in an argument or fight;
   c. to waver or begin to doubt, as in purpose or opinion; hesitate: *After staggering momentarily, he recognized that he had to make a decision;*
   d. to cause to reel, totter, or become unsteady: *This load would stagger an elephant;*
   e. to shock; render helpless with amazement or the like; astonish: *The vastness of outer space staggers the mind;*
   f. to cause to waver or falter: *The news staggered her belief in the triumph of justice;*
   g. to arrange in a zigzag order or manner on either side of a center: *The captain staggered the troops along the road;*
   h. to arrange otherwise than at the same time, esp. in a series of alternating or continually overlapping intervals: *They planned to stagger lunch hours so that the cafeteria would not be rushed;*
   i. *Aeronautics.* to arrange (the wings of a biplane or the like) so that the entering edge of an upper wing is either in advance of or behind that of a corresponding lower wing.
2. Note that the primary (first) definition of "stagger" is "to walk, move, or stand unsteadily." Consider the following examples:
   a. The man *staggered* home after having five beers at the bar.
   b. Students often *stagger* under the heavy weight of their backpacks.
3. Now look again at how "stagger" is used in the "baseball" text: ". . . his *staggering* seven-year, $125 million contract . . ." Is "staggering" being used as a verb? Do you think the meaning here is the same as in the primary definition and the two examples above? Explain.
4. Which of the nine definitions given above appears closest to the way "staggering" is used in this text? Why do you think so? Using the definition you have selected, see if you can write a paraphrase of the sentence. (**Note:** A possible paraphrase might be "His seven-year, $125 million contract is astonishing," but other variations are possible.)
5. Now see if you can write a new sentence (not related to the baseball text) in which you use "staggering" as it is used in the text. (**For example:** "My staggering success on the vocabulary quiz encouraged me to study just as hard for the next one.")
6. Pick several other words from the text that are new to you or used in unfamiliar ways. Try to define them, check the dictionary definitions, and compare/match the dictionary information to the text.
7. What have you learned from this exercise about the different ways words can be used? What strategies can you use when you encounter new words or usages in texts you are reading?

FIGURE 3.6. Understanding Vocabulary in Context Student Exercise.*
* This exercise assumes students have read the "Price of Baseball" text in Figure 3.2.

Inflectional Morphemes	
General Categories	Examples
Nouns *–s (plural)* *–'s (possessive)*	*The books were on the table.* *The boy's book was on the floor.*
Verbs *–s (third person singular present tense)* *–ed (regular past tense)* *–ed (regular past participle)* *–ing (present participle)*	*She walks home every day.* *She walked home yesterday.* *She has walked home every day this week.* *She is walking home right now.*
Adjectives *–er (comparative form)* *–er (superlative form)*	*Cats are smarter than dogs.* *My cat is the smartest of all.*
Derivational Morphemes	
Prefixes	Suffixes
Beginning *dis–, pre–, re–, un–*	*–er, –able, –ible, –ful, –less, –ness, –y*
Intermediate *anti–, co–, de–, en–, fore–, il–, im–,in–, ir–,* *inter–, non–, over–, post–, semi–, sub–,* *super–*	*–age, –al, –an, –ant, –ent, –ese, –est, –ic, –ive,* *–like, –ment, –or, –some, –th, –ward*
Advanced *ad–, circum–, contra–, counter–, ex–, extra–,* *out–, sur–*	*–ance, –hood, –ism, –ity, –ize, –osis, –ship*

FIGURE 3.7. Common Derivational and Inflectional Morphemes.
Adapted from Birch (2007).

on a page, including margins, text direction, spacing, and paragraph indentation. A summary of basic features in English writing that could be presented is provided in Figure 3.10. Several of these features may appear more particular to teaching writing skills than reading skills, but it is important for students to understand that typographical conventions convey information about the text, that these conventions can vary cross-linguistically, and that punctuation cues facilitate comprehension. For example, common nouns are capitalized in German but not in English. In Spanish, questions are indicated by punctuation marks at both the beginning and the end of the sentence. In contrast, English orthography involves only sentence-final punctuation.

Summary: Textual Elements and Bottom-Up Instruction

Readers of this final section may feel some discomfort at points: It may be necessary at elementary L2 levels to teach the alphabet and phonemic correspondences, and although it seems obvious that vocabulary work is important for readers, building students' knowledge of morphology, syntax, and cohesion might seem

1. Teach or review common cohesive devices (see Chart A below), giving students practice in finding examples in a published text that they have already read.
2. For a text you are currently working on, instruct students to complete Chart B (provide examples from the text to start them off), using Chart A as a reference.
3. Point out that for reading, the recognition of cohesive devices provides a "road map" to the author's main ideas. At the sentential level, cohesion markers can help them infer the meanings unfamiliar lexical items and deconstruct long, complex sentences.

Chart A: Common Cohesive Devices

Cohesion Types	Examples
Reference Forms	
Definite article (*the*)	*the book*
Pronouns (*it, the, them*)	*They are serious problems.*
Demonstrative pronouns and determiners (*this, that, these, those*)	*This is unusual.* *These students are very talented.*
Comparative forms (*such a; such; another; other*)	*Such a response was unexpected.* *Another factor was age at arrival.*
Coordinating conjunctions (*and, but, yet, so*)	*We tried to see the exhibit, but we could not get tickets.*
Sentence adverbs (*however, therefore, furthermore, in addition*, and so on)	*However, there is still a problem to be solved.*
Lexical Forms	
Partial repetition (*two good students* → the students)	*Two men were at the bus stop. These men looked angry that the bus was late.*
Exact repetition (*she looks*)	*She looks happy. She looks successful. She looks exactly like the Abercrombie and Fitch models.*
Synonym (*stupid/dumb*)	*My dog Bruce was sweet but stupid. He was so dumb that he couldn't find his way home.*
Classifier (*issue, concern, problem, suggestion*, and so on)	*Alcohol abuse is a huge problem among college students. One solution might be required alcohol awareness workshops for new students.*
Subordinating conjunctions/subordinate clauses	*Although many parents and educators are concerned about students' alcohol abuse, so far no one has developed a successful solution.*

Chart B: Cohesion Analysis Chart

Instructions to students

Refer to the specific paragraphs in the text* that are listed in the first column of the chart. Using "Common cohesive devices" (Chart A), complete the following analysis chart.

Paragraph (¶) number	¶-initial Phrase Connecting Ideas to Previous ¶	Cohesion Type(s)	¶ Topic (Read first few sentences; paraphrase in your own words)
. . . .	. . . .	. . . .	. . . .
. . . .	. . . .	. . . .	. . . .
. . . .	. . . .	. . . .	. . . .
. . . .	. . . .	. . . .	. . . .

Instructions to teachers

This lesson sequence could draw on published texts or sample student texts. In a writing sequence, it also could be used for peer review or self-analysis for revision. The first time you use this activity, identify specific paragraphs for analysis. Depending on the text, some paragraphs may illustrate the point better than others. If the analysis activity is repeated with a different text later, ask students to identify specific paragraphs that illustrate the use of cohesion well.

FIGURE 3.8. Understanding and Recognizing Text Cohesion.
Adapted from Frodesen and Eyring (2007.)*

* This activity and the charts were inspired by a workshop given by Jan Frodesen of UC Santa Barbara at UC Berkeley on October 27, 2007. We have adapted the materials somewhat, but the concept is hers.

1. Look at paragraphs 5–28. What "varieties of friendship" does Viorst introduce? Complete the chart below. The first one has been done for you.

Categories and ¶ Numbers	Brief Description
Convenience friends (5–8)	People we see in our everyday lives, such as neighbors or parents of your children's classmates. You may help each other, but it is not a deep or close friendship.
. . . .	. . . .
. . . .	. . . .
. . . .	. . . .
. . . .	. . . .
. . . .	. . . .
. . . .	. . . .

2. Now look at the introduction (paragraphs 1–4) and conclusion (paragraphs 29–31). What is their purpose, and how do the seven categories described by Viorst relate to the points she makes in the beginning and ending paragraphs?
3. Considering the essay as a whole, what would you say Viorst's main point is? See if you can state it in one sentence. How do the different parts of the essay help you to understand the meaning of the entire text?

FIGURE 3.9. Analyzing Text Structure.*

* This activity is based on the text by Judith Viorst described in Appendix 3.2.

1. Margins (top, bottom, left, right)
2. Writing left to right
3. Writing to the end of the line before advancing to the next line
4. Paragraph indentation
5. Capitalization: first word of sentence, proper nouns, pronoun
6. End-of-sentence punctuation (period, question mark, exclamation)
7. Placement of punctuation (next to the word it follows, never by itself at the beginning of a line)
8. Internal punctuation (comma, semicolon, colon, quotation mark) and its functions in conveying text meaning (e.g., a colon introduces a list or a closely related idea; quotation marks surround dialogue, and so on)
9. The apostrophe and its functions
10. The use of bold, italics, and underline to convey emphasis or importance
11. The use of hyperlinks in a digital text as a cross-referencing tool
12. Italics to indicate the foreign origins of a word

FIGURE 3.10. Basic Typographical Features Sample Listing.

beyond the scope of what most reading teachers expect (or want) to accomplish. Nonetheless, we include these points here in the interest of thoroughness. If we wish to understand what makes text processing and comprehension difficult for L2 readers, we must examine *all* interacting elements of texts, not just the obvious ones (topic, content, vocabulary, and text structure). Any and all of these components, from the alphabet to subordinating conjunctions to pronoun reference, may challenge students as they encounter texts. Teachers may be surprised to discover that even relatively "advanced" L2 readers may still experience comprehension breakdowns related to one or more of these bottom-up textual elements. To reiterate, L2 readers undertake a challenge that is quite distinct from that faced by L1 readers, who already have a large oral vocabulary and proficient knowledge of morphology, syntax, logical relations, and text structure before they even begin to read. In short, L2 readers experience linguistic gaps that go well beyond orthography and basic vocabulary. We do our students a disservice if we are not aware of these components ourselves as we analyze and select texts and as we teach reading.

Chapter Summary

This chapter has introduced the following principles:

- A *text* is a written act of communication that expresses a unified message.
- Texts include a variety of elements, including orthography, lexical items, morphemes and sentences, cohesive elements, and text structure. They also include graphological information such as punctuation, capitalization, and formatting.
- All of these elements of texts may present challenges for L2 readers due to cross-linguistic factors (differences between L1 and L2) and still-evolving L2 proficiency.
- Teachers should look carefully and analytically at textual features as they select texts and prepare them for classroom reading instruction.
- Depending on student needs and abilities, teachers should also consider presentations and lessons to help students develop bottom-up processing skills and understand how various textual elements interact to create meaning.

We would not maintain that a reading course should become an introductory linguistics course. However, we recommend that teachers consider what their students know and do not know about the linguistic structure of the L2. Where necessary, instruction should provide this basic knowledge, as well as the practice students need in order to use that knowledge to comprehend texts.

Further Reading and Resources

The list below refers to key sources and materials referred to in this chapter. Where applicable, URLs are provided, though we caution readers that these tend to change. Complete bibliographic information can be found in the References section at the end of the book.

Sources on bottom-up approaches to L2 reading
  Birch (2007); Dubin, Eskey, & Grabe (1986)
Detailed information on cross-linguistic processing in L2 reading
  Koda (2004, Chapters 3, 5, & 6)
Sources on the "linguistic threshold" for L2 reading and on the "short-circuit" hypothesis
  Clarke (1980); Cummins (1979, 1981)
Sources on challenges of English vocabulary learning
  Birch (2007); Folse (2004); Nation (2001)
Vocabulary Profiler (for assessing vocabulary difficulty in a text)
  www.lextutor.ca/vp
Academic Word List (AWL) highlighter (highlights words from AWL words in uploaded text)
  http://www.nottingham.ac.uk/~alzsh3/acvocab/awlhighlighter.htm
Readability sources and calculators
  Carrell (1987b); Fry (1977)
Readability calculator
  http://www.standards-schmandards.com/exhibits/rix/
VOA websites (audio files and printed texts/transcripts)
  http://www.voanews.com/specialenglish/index.cfm
NPR websites (audio files and printed texts/transcripts)
  http://www.npr.org
BBC Learning English website (multiple audiovisual and print resources)
  http://www.bbc.co.uk/worldservice/learningenglish/

Reflection and Review

1. The first part of this chapter defined the notion of text and identified the different specific components of texts. Which ideas were new or surprising to you?

2. This chapter argued that cross-linguistic factors (specifically L1–L2 differences) are crucial to understanding challenges faced by L2 readers when they encounter L2. Do you agree with this position, or do you believe (a) that once you can read in one language, you can read in another, or (b) that L2

knowledge and proficiency, not L1 knowledge, makes L2 reading difficult (or some L2 readers more successful than others)?

3. Prior to reading this chapter, had you ever looked at a text with this degree of technical precision or specificity—one that you were assigned to read as a student or that you were going to ask students to read? What are the advantages of learning what to look for and how to do so? What are potential drawbacks or pitfalls?

4. The last section of this chapter suggested that, if students lack basic L2 knowledge (e.g., about the alphabet, morphosyntactic patterns, cohesive devices, and so on), teachers should consider presenting those concepts explicitly so that students learn to recognize them in texts. When, and to what degree, might such "technical" lessons be appropriate in an L2 reading class? When might they be unnecessary? What would you as a teacher need to know or review in order to provide such information effectively?

5. What are the benefits of providing bottom-up processing instruction and practice to L2 readers? What are the potential dangers or drawbacks of spending class time on these issues? How should a teacher keep such concerns from overshadowing other course goals—and from turning the course from a *reading* course to a course *about reading*?

Application Activities

Application Activity 3.1
Evaluating a Sample Text

In the Questions for Reflection at the beginning of this chapter, you looked at a short text entitled "Second Chances—If Only We Could Start Again," taking notes on aspects of the text that you thought might pose difficulties for L2 readers. Now that you have read about the different types of text information and how it can be challenging for L2 students, look again at the text and your notes. What might be challenging about:

a. Specific words that students might not recognize because they are not particularly common in English?
b. Words that students will likely recognize but whose meanings they may not understand in this particular discursive context?
c. Unusual or challenging morphology or syntax?
d. The sequence of idea units and the connections among them?
e. The organizational structure of the text as a whole?

Prepare a brief written or oral summary of your findings, discussing your findings with your peers and instructor.

Application Activity 3.2
"Second Chances"—Vocabulary Profiler Analysis

Complete the steps below and respond to the questions.

a. Go to www.lextutor.ca/vp and click on "VP English" (upper left of screen).
b. Type or scan the "Second Chances" text in Appendix 3.1 and paste it into the window of the VP screen. Then click "submit window."
c. You should see an analysis with a table similar to Figure 3.3 on the left, a type–token analysis on the left, and a color-coded profile of the text below the tables.
d. Analyze the results. What percentage of the words are in the K1/K2 categories? AWL and off-list? Review the type–token analysis. Are words repeated, or do they tend to be used only once?
e. Look at the specific words (color-coded) from each category. Looking in particular at the AWL and off-list categories, are any of those words similar to the ones you identified in your own previous analysis of this text (see Questions for Reflection at the beginning of the chapter and Application Activity 3.1)? Were there other words that you didn't notice as being potentially unfamiliar?
f. A word's appearance in the AWL or off-list category doesn't necessarily mean that it will be difficult for L2 students. Are there words in this text that are *not* on the K1/K2 list that you nonetheless think will be relatively easy for students to read?
g. A word's appearance in the K1/K2 list does not necessarily mean it might not pose problems for L2 readers in this particular text. What K1/K2 words in "Second Chances" are used atypically and might confuse students?
h. The helpfulness of the surrounding context (the text as a whole, the sentence in which a word appears, and the sentences immediately around it) can help determine whether unfamiliar vocabulary will be difficult for readers. Review the items that you identified in questions e. and f. as potentially difficult for students. Examine those items in the text. Will the local or global contexts provide enough clues for students to read those words without difficulty?
i. Considering your responses to questions e–h, list five to ten words from the text that you might pre-teach, gloss, or feature in post-reading vocabulary work. Remember that the primary goal at this stage is *text comprehension* rather than *long-term vocabulary development* (see Chapters 5 and 8).

Application Activity 3.3
Text Analysis

a. Imagine that you are selecting texts for a cohort of learners familiar to you (e.g., a class you have observed or are teaching, a student you are tutoring).

Obtain two text samples currently being used with those students—two readings from a textbook or elsewhere, or two excerpts from a longer work (e.g., a novel).

b.   For each text, complete the text analysis worksheet below.

c.   Orally or in writing, respond to these questions. Do you think the texts are appropriate for the students? Why or why not? If you were using them for teaching, what textual features might be difficult for these students, and how would you approach helping the students as you teach these texts?

Text Analysis Worksheet

Complete one for each text.

1.   Skim the text to capture its content. Do you think it would appeal to its target audience (i.e., the students in the class you are considering)? Why or why not?

2.   Considering the L2 literacy and proficiency level(s) of the class, do you think the text is too long, too short, or about right? Explain your thinking.

3.   Look only at the first two to three paragraphs (or 100 words or so) of the text. What morphosyntactic and cohesive features do you notice? Consider:

   ▪   Inflectional and derivational morphology: what explicit morphological cues help establish grammatical relations and word meanings?

   ▪   Syntactic complexity: sentence length; relative number of simple, compound, and complex sentences; features such as prepositional phrases, passive constructions, introductory adverbials, relative clauses, indirect speech, and so forth.

   ▪   Explicit cohesion markers: pronoun reference, repetition, synonyms, connectives, and so on.

   ▪   Other clues to text flow, such as paragraphing and punctuation, graphics, and so forth.

   Which of these features might help an emerging L2 reader in text comprehension? Which could potentially prove challenging or confusing? Explain.

4.   Type or scan at least 250 words of the text. Then go to www.lextutor.ca and click on "vocabprofile." Complete the chart below.

Percentages	Potentially Difficult Words from K2 and AWL Sections (Select 5–10)	Off-List Words that May Require Explanation (Select up to 10)
K1 words:	1.	
K2 words:	2.	
AWL words:	3.	
Off-list words:	4.	
	5.	
	6.	
	7.	
	8.	
	9.	
	10.	

5. For each K2, AWL, or off-list item that you listed in step 4, do you think the surrounding context makes the meaning of the word or phrase clear? Complete the chart below.

Word or Phrase	Context Helpful? (Yes/No/Maybe)

6. Considering the same passage that you typed or scanned for step 4, use one of the computer- or Web-based tools discussed in this chapter to calculate readability scores.

7. Now that you have closely analyzed this text, do you believe that it would be appropriate for the student audience you identified? What adjustments would you make to the text itself or to your instruction to make it a successful and effective choice? Explain your thinking.

Application Activity 3.4
Developing Bottom-Up Classroom Presentations

Consider a class or group of students with whose needs and abilities you are familiar. Pick one or two of the "bottom-up" text features discussed in the last section of this chapter and illustrated in Figures 3.4 to 3.10 (e.g., pronoun reference, consonant sound–symbol correspondences, inflectional morphology) and develop a brief classroom presentation in which you:

a.   Explain the structure or feature to the students, providing examples;
b.   Produce a practice activity in which the students can identify naturally occurring instances of that feature in an authentic text.

Choose a text or use one included in the appendices of this book. See Appendix 3.2 for a mini-lesson model. If you complete this activity as a class assignment, share your ideas with a group of peers and solicit their feedback. Reflect on and discuss the steps you took (e.g., consulting a grammar reference) to develop your presentation and the (print and digital) resources you found helpful.

Appendix 3.1

Second Chances—If Only We Could Start Again

Joshua Brahm (*Sacramento Bee*, 2001)

Have you ever thought, "If I could start life over again from the beginning, what would I do differently?"

I have, and it can be a pretty depressing subject. Yet I still think about it sometimes, generally after I've made a big mistake and hurt someone's feelings.

If I could just wake up and find myself in the hospital where I was born, in the body of a newborn but with the brain of someone who has already tried life for 17 years, I know there are a lot of things I would do differently.

When I was younger, I lied to my parents a lot to get out of trouble. It was really stupid, but I did it and it took my parents a long time to trust me again.

I joined the band at my church when I was 12, and got really stuck up about it. I thought I was pretty cool to be doing something other kids couldn't do. I later learned that once you nurture pride in your heart, it takes a long time to "clean it out." It took me four years.

I've made other mistakes, too. I'll look back and think, "I should have been nicer to my brother then, or obeyed my parents better." Those mistakes have brought painful consequences.

Unfortunately, I've come to realize a painful but surprisingly obvious fact of life: We don't get a second chance. Isn't that simple? Once we make a mistake, that's it. No extra tries, bonus chances, or Get Out of Jail Free cards.

That realization is particularly painful after I blow it big time. You can do things to make it up, like sincerely apologizing when you hurt someone's feelings. But you can't completely take it back.

Am I just reminding you of a hard fact? It depends on your perspective. For people who are a bit melancholy (like me), it could be taken like that. Yet to someone who looks at life positively, it could be a message of hope.

If we could take that wisdom of knowing that we only get one shot at life, maybe we would think twice about doing something wrong. And if everyone tried to live life more carefully, can you imagine the effect that would have on the world?

It's something to think about.

Appendix 3.2
Sample Mini-lesson on Morphology

Note: This exercise is based on Judith Viorst's essay, "Friends, Good Friends—and Such Good Friends" (see Spack [1998a]; also accessible online at http://www.deil.uiuc.edu/eslservice/units/introtopw/activity2.htm). This lesson plan assumes that students have already read the essay for general comprehension and vocabulary. The explanation starts at a fairly basic level but is intended for intermediate to advanced L2 readers to help them understand how a basic morphological feature (pluralization) is represented in an authentic text.

Explanation

Nouns (words that name a person, place, thing, event, or idea) in English are marked with a **plural** ending when there is "more than one" in the sentence. For instance, in the sentences:

1. **Two boys** sat on the bench.
2. **The boys** sat on the bench.
    the word *boys* in both refers to "more than one." In sentence 1, it refers to exactly two boys. In sentence 2, we do not know how many boys there are, but we know that there is more than one. How do we know? In sentence 1, the word *two* tells us. But in both sentences, the word *boy* is marked with an -*s* to tell us that it is **plural.** Contrast this with sentence 3:
3. **The boy** sat on the bench.
    Regular plural endings. In sentence 3, we know that there is only *one* boy because there is no plural marker (-s) on the noun *boy*. The most common plural ending in English is -*s*. Look at paragraph one of Viorst's essay:

Women are **friends**, I once would have said, when they totally love and support and trust each other, and bare to each other the **secrets** of their soul, and run–no **questions** asked–to help each other, and tell harsh **truths** to each other (no, you can't wear that dress unless you lose ten **pounds** first) when harsh **truths** must be told.

Nouns with irregular plurals. Notice that a number of the nouns (marked in bold) have plural endings. This is a very common marker in English texts. However, plurals can be much more complex. Take the very first word of the paragraph, *women.* It is also plural, even though it is not marked with an -*s.*

Nouns with no plurals. Also, nouns are sometimes not made plural. Look now at paragraphs 2 and 3 of the essay. Find the regular plural nouns (the ones that are marked with -*s*). Then find other nouns which are not marked with -*s.* Why aren't those nouns marked for plural?

Nouns that sometimes are plural and sometimes are not. The same noun can be made plural in some sentences but not in others. As an example, think of the noun *truth.* We are told as children that it is important to "tell the truth," and it is said that "The truth shall set you free." In both of those sentences, truth is not marked for plural. But in paragraph 1, Viorst twice uses *truth* as a plural (*harsh truths*).

Now look at the several uses of the word *friendship* in paragraph 3. Why is it plural in some cases but not in the final one? How do you explain the presence or absence of plural markings in the examples of *truth* and *friendship* in this text?

Can you think of other examples of nouns that (a) are made plural without adding -*s*; (b) are not made plural; or (c) are sometimes made plural and sometimes not? Look through the rest of Viorst's essay to find other examples from these categories and complete the chart below. There is one example for each category to get you started.

Noun Plural Category	Examples from the Text (Paragraph Number)
Nouns with "s" plural	*friends* (1)
Nouns with other plural	*women* (1)
Nouns with no plural	*affection* (2)
Nouns that sometimes are marked for plural and sometimes are not	*friendship* (3)

Chapter 4
Syllabus Design and Instructional Planning for the L2 Reading Course

---

Questions for Reflection

- Have you been asked to express your educational needs or expectations in any of your secondary or postsecondary courses? Were your needs and expectations satisfactorily met?
- Reflecting on your experience as a student, think about syllabi presented in the courses you have taken. In what ways were these course outlines and syllabi helpful or not helpful to you? What components do you think are essential and especially useful in a course outline?
- How do you think the aims and structure of a literacy course should accommodate students' sociocultural backgrounds, literacy histories, and future literacy needs?
- In what respects is planning an L2 literacy or reading course distinct from planning a course in a different discipline or content area? Why?
- In your experience as a learner, what aspects of textbooks and instructional materials have you found valuable to your learning? What components have you found to be unhelpful or informative? Why?
- If you have worked as a teacher, identify characteristics that you value most highly in a course book or materials package. What distinguishes a good textbook from a poor one?
- What do you believe to be the fundamental elements of a successful

literacy lesson? What tasks or activities should such a lesson feature, and why? How should lesson components be sequenced, and what literacy skills should be featured?

- If you have had experience as a classroom teacher, how has systematic lesson planning guided your instruction and promoted student learning? Why?
- Based on your experience as a classroom learner or as a teacher (if applicable), craft a list of essential characteristics of a purposeful, productive, and engaging literacy task.

Earlier in this book, we introduced theoretical foundations of prevailing practices in literacy education, exploring the unique demands placed on L2 readers and the properties of L2 text that make learning to read in an L2 a significant challenge. In this chapter, we aim to outline operational principles for planning ESL and EFL literacy courses and propose flexible tools for planning classroom instruction leading to effective knowledge- and skill-building. This chapter will elaborate on core precepts examined in Chapters 1–3, with a view toward demonstrating how teachers might apply these precepts in executing their responsibilities as course designers, lesson planners, materials developers, and assessors. This chapter concentrates chiefly on the day-to-day tasks of L2 literacy educators, namely, learner needs assessment, syllabus construction, instructional planning, materials development, and task design.

Before addressing these vital processes, however, we would like to review core research-based principles and insights that shape our procedural recommendations. We introduced the first such principle at the close of Chapter 1: "Plan and implement a coherent curriculum"—a commonsense but challenging goal articulated by Grabe (2004, p. 46). Achieving coherence in a curriculum, of course, requires specifying instructional aims, as well as "the identification and development of appropriate content" (Stoller, 2004, p. 267). Although coherence implies systematic planning, it does not necessarily imply a fixed or rigid approach. In fact, instruction needs "to vary in important ways for L2 learners depending on context, learner needs, and language proficiency levels" (Grabe, 2004, p. 45). Reading instruction must not only accommodate context and learner characteristics; it must also strike an appropriate balance between bottom-up and top-down skills (see Chapter 1). In their review of Carver's (1997) innovative research, Grabe and Stoller (2002) concluded that reading instruction and assessment should target comprehension abilities, reading rate, and fluency. They further observed that "reading abilities involve comprehension of extended text under some time pressure to read fluently," noting that reading rate, fluency, and quantity of reading are all central to cultivating comprehension (Grabe & Stoller, 2002, p. 123). Along with maintaining balance in the L2 reading curriculum, surveys of research and practice consistently reveal the necessity for L2 literacy instruction to "provide appropriate guidance and support for learners' efforts," a principle that Kern (2000) described as "teaching reading as design" (p. 129). To that end, we propose a systematic appraisal of students' L1 and L2 literacy backgrounds, as well as their real and perceived needs in terms of reading skills and strategies. Equipped with an understanding of learner skills and expectations, teachers can sensitively undertake the crucial work of planning courses and lessons.

Needs Assessment: Understanding Learner Needs and Institutional Expectations

Needs assessment, or needs analysis, can be described in global terms as those activities "involved in gathering information that will serve as the basis for developing a curriculum that will meet the learning needs of a particular group of students" (Brown, 1995, p. 35). Specifically, the needs assessment (NA) process entails "procedures for identifying and validating needs, and establishing priorities among them" (Pratt, 1980, p. 79). These procedures should be viewed as integral to the teaching, learning, and evaluation cycle, rather than as something that we do only prior to teaching (Bailey, 1998; Berwick, 1989; Brindley, 1989; Brown, 1995; Nunan, 1988, 1989, 2001; Richards, 2001). Graves (2000) defined NA as a dynamic function of teaching, "an ongoing process of gathering information about students' needs and preferences, interpreting the information, and then making course decisions based on the interpretation in order to meet the needs" (p. 98). NA further entails conversation among stakeholders (teachers, learners, parents, administrators) about the teaching-learning process (Walker, 2003). Finally, we embrace the precept that continuous NA assumes that "learning is not simply a matter of learners absorbing pre-selected knowledge the teacher gives them, but is a process in which learners—and others—can and should participate" (Graves, 2000, p. 98).

Before examining nuts-and-bolts aspects of NA, it is useful to specify the meanings of key elements of the NA process. Clearly, learner *needs* are the gravitational center of NA, but we recommend viewing needs in discriminating terms. Berwick (1989), for example, distinguished *felt needs* (those that students actually have) from *perceived needs*, which reflect the way that teachers and other stakeholders *perceive* learner needs. Similarly, *target needs* refer to what learners need to acquire and why; in contrast, *learning needs* refer to those relating to student motivation and how they expect to learn (Hutchinson & Waters, 1987). Teachers and course developers often find that reconciling these needs categories is complex, as learner populations are diverse, and their needs may not fully coincide with how educators envision those needs. In her definition of NA, Graves (2000) also referred to students' *preferences*, a variable that is often conflated with what Berwick (1989) called felt needs.

To avoid confusion created by these fuzzy constructs, we recommend maintaining a distinction between students' "actual" *needs* and students' *perceived needs* or *beliefs*, as the latter are often cover terms for *preferences*. Genuine learner needs might best be viewed as variables that can be measured through some reasonably objective, consistent tool or standard. For instance, an EAP student with intermediate-level L2 reading skills who needs advanced proficiency in order to meet a university's admissions requirements has a true *need* to develop advanced-level reading skills. In contrast, this same student may *perceive* her needs somewhat differently, perhaps characterizing her L2 reading skills as better than intermediate. In other words, her perceived needs may reflect *beliefs* that do not fully match objectively measured *needs*. *Need* and *perceived need* in this instance are not synonymous. Learner *preferences* can further complicate the range of variables at play in NA, although we can minimize confusion by viewing preferences as preferences (not as needs!). Our hypothetical EAP student, for example, has needs and perceived needs; she may simultaneously exhibit preferences, such as a strong desire to improve her L2 reading skills by reading comic books and entertainment magazines or a predilection for reading instruction that emphasizes top-down over bottom-up skills. Needs, perceived needs, and preferences must all be taken into account in the NA process, but we should view these three categories as potentially divergent and independent of one another.

As suggested in Chapter 2, teaching reading to ESL and EFL learners requires specialized expertise. We therefore need a systematic method of inquiring into the diverse backgrounds, schemata, skills, actual and perceived needs, and preferences that students bring to the L2 literacy course (Ferris & Hedgcock, 2005; Johns & Price-Machado, 2001; Snow, Griffin, & Burns, 2007). Graves (2000) proposed a clear, cyclical NA model that "involves . . . decisions, actions, and reflections" to be undertaken by the teacher. Figure 4.1 illustrates this cycle. Although space constraints prevent us from elaborating on each of these stages, ample resources presenting in-depth treatments of all phases of the NA process are readily available (see Further Reading and Resources).

In line with the principle that NA "needs to be understood as something that teachers can see and do as part of teaching" (Graves, 2000, p. 99), the following sections introduce tools for determining useful data sources, collecting and synthesizing information, and interpreting these findings for instructional planning. Some of these data (e.g., institution type, students' target disciplines, their immigration status) are obvious to teachers and require no formal collection steps. However, information concerning learners' demographic backgrounds, language proficiency, and educational achievement may be available only by eliciting data directly from students or from institutional authorities. Although frameworks for conducting effective NA in L2 contexts abound (e.g., Brown, 1995; Burnaby, 1989; Dudley-Evans & St. John, 1998; Graves, 2000; Munby, 1978; Nunan, 2001; Reid, 1995), we concentrate here on tools that are easy to adapt and construct, practical to administer, and simple to analyze in the classroom context.

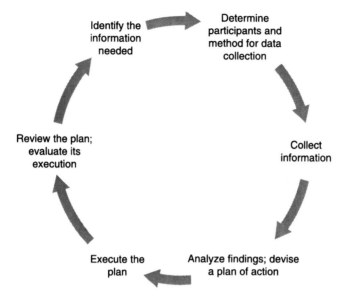

FIGURE 4.1. The Needs Assessment Cycle.
Based on Graves (2000, p. 100).

These tools include written and Web-based questionnaires, informal interviews, and ongoing observation, among other options. Rather than presenting an "off-the-rack" survey or interview format, we offer the categories and variables listed in Figure 4.2 as components to consider in devising NA instruments tailored to local contexts, institutions, and students' literacy profiles. A number of the categories in Figure 4.2 intersect and even overlap. For instance, students' expressed interests may dovetail with their reasons for pursuing an L2 literacy course and will likely influence their attitudes toward a course and its content. In the following discussion, we therefore consider factors that cluster thematically, rather than addressing each of the items presented in Figure 4.2.

Demographic Profile

As explained in Chapter 2, understanding the demographic profile of any learner population enables teachers and materials developers to know who their students are and to determine other variables to examine in the NA process. Information concerning age will clearly determine the literacy skills that a course should feature, the goals that might undergird the syllabus, as well as the genres and text sources to be used as content. Students' prior educational and professional background must also be considered, as these variables can point to an appropriate starting point for L2 literacy instruction. Length of formal instruction and the nature of prior training can provide a rough index of students' readiness; such information can tell us something about students' experiences as language

1. **Student demographics**
   - Age
   - Gender
   - Educational experience
   - Work background and career aspirations
   - Nationality
   - Ethnic background
   - Primary language(s)
   - Immigration status (if applicable)
   - Family background
2. **Students' level of L2 proficiency and knowledge**
   - Measured proficiency in reading, listening, speaking, writing, and grammar
   - L2 vocabulary size
3. **Students' L1 and L2 literacy skills**
   - Literate experience and knowledge in home (L1) culture(s), including school-based and other literacies
   - Literate experience and knowledge in target (L2) culture, including school-based and other literacies
4. **Students' intercultural and cross-linguistic knowledge**
   - Prior experience in the L2 and other sociocultural environments
   - Familiarity with sociocultural and pragmatic dimensions of the L2
   - Awareness of cross-linguistic similarities and differences, especially those affecting literacy
5. **Students' interests**
   - General topics and issues of interest to students
   - Personal experiences and areas of interest
   - Educational/professional experiences and areas of interest
6. **Students' preferred learning styles and strategies**
   - Expectations concerning teaching and assessment methods
   - Preferred methods and strategies for learning
   - Preferences (and dispreferences) for collaborative learning
7. **Students' attitudes and motivational profiles**
   - Attitudes toward themselves as learners
   - Attitudes toward fellow learners
   - Attitudes toward the teacher
   - Attitudes toward formal instruction
   - Attitudes toward the target language (L2), its user communities, and its literate practices
8. **Students' and others' learning aims**
   - Reasons for enrolling in an L2 literacy course
   - Short- and long-term goals as L2 readers and writers
   - Expectations concerning course outcomes
9. **Target context(s)**
   - Situations where students will engage in literacy events beyond the classroom
   - Topics about which students will read and write in their fields of study and careers
   - Disciplinary or professional settings where students will use L2 text and speech
10. **Literacy skills and strategies needed for academic, professional, and vocational tasks**
    - Purposes for which students will read and produce L2 texts
    - Level of need for understanding and giving directions
    - Level of need for seeking and sharing information in print-based and digital media
    - Communicative functions, genres, and registers typical in students' target disciplines, professions, and literate communities

FIGURE 4.2. Variables to Consider in the NA Cycle.
Sources: Brown (1995); Ferris and Hedgcock (2005); Graves (2000); Munby (1978); Seymour and Walsh (2006).

learners, readers, writers, note-takers, discussion participants, test-takers, and so on. Knowledge of students' nationalities, ethnicities, and L1 backgrounds can similarly provide a picture of the homogeneity of a particular population (as is usually the case in EFL instruction) or of its national and linguistic heterogeneity (as is often the case in ESL settings). Chapters 1–3 pointed out that such background information can provide valuable clues about learners' formal, content, and cultural schemata.

We include immigration status as an important NA component, as this variable can tell us a great deal about students' literacy histories and needs, a point discussed at length in Chapter 2. Clearly, immigration status is not relevant in most EFL settings where the student population is homogeneous in terms of its ethnic, national, and linguistic composition and where English is truly a *foreign* language (and likely not a medium of instruction). In contrast, immigration status in ESL settings can certainly distinguish one learner population from another. In Chapter 2, we pointed out that educators in North American contexts distinguish recent immigrants from learners who are second- and even third-generation immigrants. For such learners, English is not, in fact, a "second" language. These Generation 1.5 students may exhibit unique language and literacy profiles, having been educated predominantly or exclusively in English (Ferris, 2009; Harklau et al., 1999; Roberge et al., 2008; Seymour & Walsh, 2006). Educators at the secondary and postsecondary levels have discovered that Generation 1.5 learners require literacy instruction specifically tailored to their educational histories and literacy needs, which might include enhanced training in academic reading and writing.

A final demographic variable that is frequently overlooked relates to learners' family backgrounds and status as so-called *traditional* or *nontraditional* students in higher education contexts. Traditional students tend to be younger and may have experienced few if any interruptions in their progress through secondary school and into postsecondary education. In contrast, nontraditional (or *returning*) students may have experienced one or more interruptions in their educational careers. These interruptions can involve long periods of employment, in addition to time devoted to caring for children, elderly family members, and so forth. Nontraditional students may reinitiate their formal studies while remaining employed and may simultaneously manage personal, financial, and family commitments at the same time. Representing a range of age groups, nontraditional students may face circumstances that can have a direct influence on their participation, motivation, confidence, and performance in the classroom. Nontraditional students may enroll in adult school or college for compelling personal and economic reasons, such as no longer having young children at home and a desire to pursue employment outside the home. Because nontraditional students may understandably require special guidance in adjusting to the demands of formal education, teachers should anticipate the linguistic, academic, and sociocultural challenges faced by such students so that instruction can sensitively accommodate their needs (Seymour & Walsh, 2006).

L2 Proficiency and Literate Background

Measures of students' L2 proficiency as well as their L1 and L2 literacy skills provide us with vital information about the purposes, content, and sequence of L2 reading instruction (Benesch, 1996; Fang & Schleppegrell, 2008; Graves, 2000; Johns, 1997, 2003). Irrespective of their L1 literacy, adolescent and adult L2 readers may draw on at least two bases of knowledge in building their L2 proficiency: L1 knowledge and emergent L2 knowledge. Many EFL and ESL learners are fully multilingual, capable of functioning in several languages (see Chapters 1 and 2). In Chapter 1, our examination of the linguistic threshold hypothesis revealed that general L2 proficiency is likely the strongest predictor of success in developing L2 literacy. In fact, L2 proficiency appears to be a stronger influence on L2 reading ability than even L1 literacy skills (Bernhardt, 2005; Hudson, 2007). Similarly, language testing research (Alderson, 1993; Droop & Verhoeven, 2003; Pike, 1979) has revealed "surprisingly strong relations" between L2 grammatical knowledge and reading skill (Grabe, 2004, p. 51).

These conclusions, of course, do not preclude the potential for positive transfer of L1 knowledge and literacy skills to L2 literacy development. Carson, Carrell, Silberstein, Kroll, and Kuehn (1990), for example, argued that we must consider L2 proficiency, as well as "the possibility of interaction of first language literacy skills" with the development of L2 proficiency and literacy (p. 248). A systematic NA must therefore describe not only overall L2 proficiency (which entails speaking, listening, reading, and writing skills), but also skill areas such as grammatical awareness, pragmatic competence, and so forth (Ferris, 1998). In other words, the NA process must somehow profile students' communicative competence, which comprises (1) grammatical competence, (2) discourse competence, (3) sociolinguistic competence, and (4) strategic competence (Canale, 1983; Canale & Swain, 1980). Finally, as argued in Chapters 1, 2, 8, and 9, we must likewise assess the size of students' active L2 vocabularies, as research evidence overwhelmingly demonstrates that "a large vocabulary can facilitate reading comprehension" (Hudson, 2007, p. 227). This array of information is indispensable in making informed decisions "about the kinds of texts to use, which skills to develop, which elements . . . to emphasize, and so on" (Graves, 2000, p. 103).

Student Interests

The principle that teachers and course developers should carefully target learners' interests in selecting materials and delivering instruction is almost axiomatic in communicative language teaching (CLT) and most contemporary approaches to language and literacy education (Brown, H. D., 2007b; Brown, J. D., 1995; Csizér & Dörnyei, 2005; Dörnyei, 2001, 2002; Kumaravadivelu, 2003, 2006; Nuttall, 2005). "Everyone agrees that students are likely to read more if they are interested in the topics of their assigned readings" (Grabe & Stoller, 2002, p. 239). Nonetheless, a word about tracking student interests and purposes is in order. Not only can this information enable the teacher to orient course content to students' experience and expectations, it can also provide insight into unfamiliar topical and disciplinary material that might appeal to students and stimulate their interest in new content (Dörnyei, 2001). Seymour and Walsh (2006) listed several ways in which student interests can influence macro-level planning and day-to-day instruction:

- the topics selected for reading assignments;
- the latitude allowed students in selecting materials and the degree of guidance they require;
- the effort required to enhance student motivation to read and build confidence in their literacy skills;
- the range of reading strategies to be taught, practiced, and assessed.

No L2 reading syllabus, of course, can possibly appeal to *all* students' interests and expectations all of the time. Attempting to fulfill everyone's topical expectations is simply impractical and may, indeed, be detrimental. In many EFL and ESL contexts, for example, "reading topics are determined largely by textbook chapters and mandated curricula" (Grabe & Stoller, 2002, pp. 239–240). Selecting materials according to students' reported interests is unquestionably worthwhile, whether we are devising a syllabus from scratch or supplementing a prescribed syllabus. Nonetheless, we would discourage teachers from allowing student interests to serve as the sole driver of a syllabus or curriculum. All skilled readers naturally encounter unfamiliar texts on unfamiliar topics that necessitate the use of diverse skills and strategies, as noted in Chapters 1–3. Knowledgeable teachers and materials developers are well equipped to identify and select topics and texts that, while perhaps not instantly appealing to all learners, reflect students' true *needs*—current and future.

Student Preferences, Strategies, and Styles

A final but essential component of needs assessment includes surveying students' predispositions toward classroom instruction and independent learning (Ferris & Hedgcock, 2005). Useful and informative questions about learners' preferences include those posed by Graves (2000): "How do the learners expect to be taught and tested? How do they prefer to learn? How well do they work in groups? What role do they expect the teacher to take? What roles do they expect to take?" (p. 103). As indicated elsewhere in this book (see Chapters 1, 3, 5, and 8), research on learner strategies and styles persuasively demonstrates how these personal and dynamic variables affect learning in the classroom and elsewhere (Cohen, 1998). Reading research suggests systematic ways in which teachers can diagnose students' styles and preferences, raise awareness of productive reading strategies, and facilitate the cultivation of new and more varied strategies (Gambrell et al., 2007; Hudson, 2007; Koda, 2004; Nuttall, 2005; Verhoeven & Snow, 2000).

Designing and Administering NA Instruments

Appendix 4.1 presents a sample NA questionnaire designed to collect demographic details, proficiency information, learner preferences, and related literacy needs data extracted from Figure 4.2. The survey addresses aspects of learners' predispositions and perceptions that are subject to change over time and that may be best measured in the classroom context. Inspired by similar instruments available in the literature on L2 instructional design and literacy education (e.g., Brown, 1995; Cohen, 1998; Grabe & Stoller, 2002; Graves, 2000; Heilman, Blair, & Rupley, 2002; Reid, 1995), our Appendix 4.1 questionnaire was constructed by a team of instructors teaching a high-level, academic ESL course in a university-based Intensive English Program (IEP). Students completed this comprehensive survey online before the first day of classes, after placement into the course. Major components of the survey could be adapted for administration via other Web-based tools such as Survey Monkey (http://www.surveymonkey.com/). The instrument could easily be administered using paper and pencil before or during the first class meeting. We present this instrument as a model that might serve as a template for readers; we would encourage teachers to design data collection tools geared specifically for their institutions and students. We would also note that, owing to the survey's length, teachers might select just a few sections or administer parts of the questionnaire in smaller installments.

Our Appendix 4.1 survey represents features that reflect both the educational context and the designers' familiarity with the learner population. For example, the prompts are crafted for nonimmigrant students with limited experience in English-medium classrooms. Items invite students to report their perceived expertise as readers and writers of English, as well as their strategy repertoires, literacy experiences and attitudes, genre and content preferences, and classroom work styles. After collating frequencies and qualitative responses, the instructors used the responses to address reading strategies explicitly in the course and to plan the syllabus to accommodate identified needs and preferences. Survey responses not only guided instructors' long- and short-term planning, but also provided data on which students later reflected as an index of their progress in the course (notably in the Literacy Portfolio—see Appendix 4.2). Twice during the term and once at the end of the course, instructors informally solicited student opinions about their progress and satisfaction with their learning, referring to their initial reactions to the survey. Near the end of the term, the instructors designed a reflective assignment in which students compared their initial perceptions to their cumulative achievements as developing readers and identified reading goals for their next term. Students included these reflections in their end-of-term Literacy Portfolios (Appendix 4.2).

Periodic collection of self-reported data through formal and informal means enables teachers to understand their students' real and perceived literacy needs, in addition to their work patterns, study habits, task-type preferences, and so on. In addition to surveys, Brown (1995) and Graves (2000) suggested deploying various instrument types, including performance and proficiency tests, institutional records, interviews, conferences, class meetings, and observations of students' classroom behavior (e.g., during pair and group work). Instruments used to assess learner needs and expectations should be both practical and responsive to the educational context. In some settings, teachers might collect rich learner data by conducting interviews guided by prompts similar to those in a reliable questionnaire. Along similar lines, we should emphasize that the administration of a pre-course survey, no matter how thorough, does *not* in itself constitute needs assessment. Responsible NA is by definition an ongoing process that supports macro-level processes (i.e., curriculum and syllabus design), in addition to micro-level processes such as constructing lessons, learning tasks, assignments, and assessment tools (see Figure 4.1). Effective teaching weaves ongoing NA processes throughout a course, enabling teachers to deliver instruction that capitalizes on students' strengths, overcomes their weaknesses, and avoids dispreferred task types (Ferris & Hedgcock, 2005; Richards, 2001; Willis & Willis, 2007).

Establishing Goals and Objectives for Teaching and Learning

Systematic data on student readers and their literacy backgrounds should provide sufficient raw material to identify long- and short-term aims for a course. The global learning targets around which instructional programs and syllabi are designed are often called *goals*, "the main purposes and intended outcomes of your course" (Graves, 2000, p. 75). Shrum and Glisan (2005) noted that goals are "often stated in broad terms" (p. 67). *Objectives*, meanwhile, consist of "statements about how the goals will be achieved" (Graves, 2000, p. 76). Objectives should characterize "what the learner will be able to do . . . as a result of instruction, defined in terms of observable behavior" (Shrum & Glisan, 2005, p. 67). In working our way through objectives, we break goals "into learnable and teachable units. By achieving . . . objectives, the goal will be reached" (Graves, 2000, p. 76). The formulation of goals and objectives is thus an integrated, reciprocal task: Goals shape and frame objectives, while the step-by-step achievement of objectives should lead to the fulfillment of goals. Furthermore, goals should systematically guide—and be guided by—the assessments used to appraise student achievement and proficiency (see Chapter 9).

To illustrate the distinction between goals and objectives, as well as the interdependent relationship between them, Graves (2000) provided the following summary of literacy aims for an advanced-level course:

Goal

Students will be able to utilize the skills of reading and writing for the purposes of: socializing, providing and obtaining information, expressing personal feelings and opinions, persuading others to adopt a course of action, in the targeted topic areas.

Objectives

Students will be able to:

- Read and comprehend materials written for native speakers when the topic and language are familiar;
- Read simple materials independently, but may have to guess at meanings of longer or more complex material;
- Write short notes, uncomplicated personal and business letters, brief journals, and short reports;
- Write brief analyses of more complex content when given the opportunity for organization and advance preparation, though errors may occur more frequently. (Graves, 2000, pp. 242–243)

Whereas these objectives are intended to guide reading instruction and assessment over the course of a semester or academic year, they derive directly from the statement of macro-level literacy goals. By necessity, goal statements identify broad skill areas and performance categories, as we see in the following English Language Literacy outcomes from the *National TESOL Standards* for Grades 9–12 students:

The students will:

ELL2-D. Develop reading comprehension

- Use basic reading skills;
- Acquire and apply new vocabulary to reading;
- Distinguish between fact and opinion;
- Predict outcomes of various reading selections;
- Read a variety of written materials.

(*National TESOL Standards, English Language Arts—ESL: English Language Literacy 2*, available: http://www.gisd.k12.nm.us/standards/esl/9-12tesol_gisd.html–ESL4)

These macro-level ESL literacy goals are broad, whereas the following English-for-content outcomes reflect specific performative goals. These aims not only reflect reading subskills associated with *learning to read* but also reference academic functions associated with *reading to learn* (Grabe & Stoller, 2002):

The students will:

EFC-E. Comprehend reading materials

- Read a variety of Math, Science, and Social Studies materials
- Predict outcomes of various reading selections
- Use new English vocabulary
- Distinguish between fact and opinion
- Demonstrate basic reading skills
- Scan material for relevant information

(*National TESOL Standards, English Language Arts—ESL: English for Content*, available: http://www.gisd.k12.nm.us/standards/esl/9-12tesol_gisd.html#ESL5)

Notably, these goal and objective statements spell out expectations for learner performance, a common though not uncontroversial practice. For example, White (1988) argued that "the pre-specification of outcomes inherent in behavioral objectives may be seen as conflicting with the essential speculative nature of the education process" (p. 30).[1] Nonetheless, we concur with curriculum design experts (Brown, 1995; Graves, 2000; Mager, 1962; Shrum & Glisan, 2005) who stress the advantages of specifying performance outcomes, conditions for learning, and measurement criteria. A primary benefit of articulating goals and objectives is that the process specifies what stakeholders expect of students in terms of performance. In addition, detailing the skills that students will develop and how they will display those skills may avoid the common pitfall of teachers expressing goals and objectives from the viewpoint of what and how they will *teach* (rather than what and how students will *learn*). "Clear goals help to make teaching purposeful because what you do in class is related to your overall purpose. Goals and objectives provide a basis for making choices about what to teach and how" (Graves, 2000, p. 79). Specific performance characteristics enable the teacher to monitor learner progress as reflected in observable outcomes. Unambiguous aims statements make goals and objectives comprehensible not only to teachers and students, but also to other stakeholders, such as fellow instructors, administrators, and parents.

Curriculum theory usefully classifies goals and objectives in diverse, practical ways that illuminate the value of designing literacy instruction in a framework that respects the diversity of L2 students while recognizing the need for a system of accountability. We present the following survey of classification schemes to help teachers understand that instructional aims are multidimensional and dynamic: Goals and objectives "evolve as a function of the changing needs of . . . students as their skills develop" (Ferris & Hedgcock, 2005, p. 88). Genesee and Upshur (1996) proposed a five-category framework designed to help teachers evaluate teaching and learning in a single skill area such as reading:

- **Language goals** specify linguistic skill outcomes, which might likewise include specific L2 reading goals, such as mastering bottom-up and top-down skills;
- **Strategic goals** describe strategies that students will develop and use;
- **Socioaffective goals** target attitudinal and behavioral changes that will result from instruction;
- **Philosophical goals** promote the cultivation of values and beliefs to enhance learning;
- **Method or process goals** identify language and literacy activities in which learners will engage.

Stern's (1992) goal-setting scheme, expanded to address both language and literacy development, includes categories similar to those of Genesee and Upshur (1996) while specifying potential learning outcomes in somewhat greater detail:

- **Proficiency goals** describe what students will be able to do with their language and literacy skills (e.g., comprehend and interpret texts efficiently);
- **Cognitive goals** entail explicit knowledge and learning about language and literacy (e.g., grammar, vocabulary), as well as about culture (e.g., pragmatics);
- **Affective goals** relate to developing favorable attitudes toward the L2, its users, and its literate practices;
- **Transfer goals** include skills for transferring knowledge and strategies acquired in the classroom to literacy events outside the classroom.

Graves's (2000) own scheme, called the KASA framework, similarly identifies four categories but differentiates knowledge, awareness, and skill:

- **Knowledge goals** "address what students will know and understand," including "knowledge about language and about culture and society";
- **Awareness goals** "address what students need to be aware of when learning a language" and its literacies, including self-awareness, meta-linguistic understanding, and knowledge of which strategies work best for particular functions;
- **Skills goals** "address what students can do with the language," including reading and writing, as well as "the functions and tasks one accomplishes through language";
- **Attitude goals** concern "the affective and values-based dimensions of learning," such as learners' feelings and their views of the L2 and its communities of users. (Graves, 2000, p. 83)

These frameworks for identifying learning goals show that instructional aims need not be "cast in cement" (Graves, 2000). Indeed, it might be more appropriate to view a goal or objective statement as "an informed guess at what you hope to accomplish given what you know about your context, your students' needs, your beliefs about how people learn, and about your experience with the particular content" (Graves, 2000, p. 93). We concur with Graves and others who maintain that formalized goals and objectives should be subject to adjustment as needed. After all, formalized aims "are most effective when a variety of types are used and when the level of specificity for different objectives is allowed to diverge" (Brown, 1995, p. 95). Explicitly presenting instructional goals and objectives in syllabi and assignments permits teachers to:

- transform learner needs into teaching points that can be sequentially organized;
- identify target skills and strategies that underlie instructional points;
- determine the degree of specificity for teaching activities in the syllabus;
- deploy teaching materials that accommodate learner needs and expectations;
- devise a plan for assessing learner performance and progress;
- evaluate teaching effectiveness. (Farris et al., 2004; Ferris & Hedgcock, 2005; Graves, 2000)

We embrace a flexible approach to identifying, stating, and implementing goals and objectives, which should respond to the findings of a careful NA process. Nonetheless, we recognize that many literacy educators and curriculum designers must adhere to *a priori* aims and standards established by governmental authorities. As Shrum and Glisan (2005) observed, "a recent paradigm shift in curricular and daily lesson planning results from an increasing focus on standards-based goals and integrated language instruction" (p. 67). This observation refers to the strong trend in the US and Canada toward government-legislated instructional standards in K–12 education and beyond, as well as standardized tests mandated by federal and regional authorities. In the US, for example, the No Child Left Behind Act (NCLBA) of 2001 has precipitated the implementation of student and teacher performance standards, along with widespread deployment of high-stakes performance and proficiency tests. Such legislation has understandably met with criticism and resistance from educators and professional organizations, a number of whom have asserted that NCLBA mandates have been under- or unfunded, resulting in poorly designed standards and assessments (Allington, 2006; Pressley et al., 2007).

Efforts to standardize educational goals and to develop nationally and internationally recognized benchmarks and assessments are gaining momentum around the globe. Ministries of education in European Union states, for example, are attempting to construct a uniform system specifying language and literacy goals, currently formalized in working documents such as the *Common European Framework of Reference for Languages: Learning, Teaching, Assessment* (CEFR). A careful discussion of standards-based education is beyond the scope of this book, but we readily acknowledge that many L2 literacy educators must design and deliver instruction according to mandated prescriptions. With that reality in mind, we recommend that teachers familiarize themselves with the standards in place in their contexts. We further suggest reviewing literacy standards and assessments developed and validated by credible professional organizations such as ACTFL, IRA, NCTE, and TESOL (see Further Reading and Resources section at the end of this chapter). Such comprehensive standards enable teachers not only to gear their teaching and assessment practices to normative expectations in the field but also to maintain a balanced focus on strategies and skills. Ideally, goals and objectives should take shape in response to learner needs as revealed in the NA process.

Developing an L2 Literacy Syllabus: Design Principles

Effective NA procedures should lead to the identification and articulation of explicit, achievable, and measurable instructional aims, which should undergird a course syllabus, a vital document consisting of two fundamental components. The first of these involves a contractual agreement between instructor and students that specifies course outcomes and how they will be achieved (Ferris & Hedgcock, 2005; Kroll, 2001). Because the instructor and students are bound by policies and practices outlined in the syllabus, "it is important that these conform to [institutional] policies and produce a fair, productive setting for teaching and learning" (Seymour & Walsh, 2006, p. 14). The second essential component involves a framework that lays out a sequence of units, lessons, texts, classroom procedures, and assessments (Gordon, 1982; Graves, 2000; Nuttall, 2005; Richards, 2001). This sequence must meet students at their current level of reading proficiency, leading them progressively (though not necessarily linearly) through increasingly challenging literacy events and toward a broader range of strategies and skills.

Prior to introducing course planning mechanics, we would like to remind readers of key insights introduced in previous chapters. Chapter 1 reviews ten core principles adapted from Grabe (2004), several of which are particularly relevant to the task of syllabus construction:

- Activate background (schematic) knowledge in appropriate ways;
- Ensure effective language knowledge and comprehension skills;
- Teach text structures and discourse organization;
- Promote the strategic reader rather than teach individual strategies;
- Build reading fluency and reading rate—aim for reading efficiency;
- Develop students' intrinsic motivation for reading;
- Plan and implement a coherent curriculum for student learning.

Koda's (2004) reminders pertaining to systematic reading instruction are also instructive in planning an L2 reading course: "[T]raining must emphasize skills causally related to reading performance; the target skills must allow modifications arising from practice; and the trainees must be developmentally ready for incorporating the target skills in their reading processes" (p. 263).

Satisfying these principles and conditions is a tall order for even the most seasoned teacher. Fortunately, informed by accurate NA results, we can fulfill multiple expectations by taking methodical steps toward selecting materials, sequencing instruction, and devising strategically oriented, skill-building tasks and assignments (Willis & Willis, 2007). In Figure 4.3, we present a checklist designed to assist teachers in providing learners with information needed about course aims, content, performance expectations, policies, assignments, and so on. Although not exhaustive, Figure 4.3 can likewise serve as an advance organizer for our discussion of syllabus design. To exemplify how we might put these principles into practice, Appendix 4.2 presents a sample syllabus for the same university-based ESL course referenced in Appendix 4.1.

Crafting the Course Description

Explicit course goals and the subsidiary learning objectives leading to those goals should supply teachers with organizing principles for crafting a workable course description and outline. As the checklist in Figure 4.3 suggests, we believe that a crucial function of a course description is to pre-reveal expected course outcomes. We have argued elsewhere that we must understand how planning

1. Practical Information
- ❏ Course name, number, meeting times, location, and Web address (if applicable)
- ❏ Instructor's name and contact information (office location, consultation hours, campus telephone number, and e-mail address)
- ❏ Prerequisites and related requirements

2. Course Goals and Primary Content
- ❏ Course goals and objectives
- ❏ Course content, as well as aspects of literacy and the reading process to be practiced and assessed
- ❏ Description of what constitutes progress toward the achievement of course aims (see item 7)
- ❏ Quantity and scope of reading material to be covered in class activities and outside assignments

3. Reading Materials
- ❏ Bibliographic information for all text sources, as well as details about their availability
- ❏ List of reading assignments, their sequence, page ranges, and deadlines

4. Reading Assignments
- ❏ Number and description of reading assignments (e.g., genre, length, and so on)
- ❏ Description of which assignments will involve independent work, peer collaboration, teacher intervention, and so forth
- ❏ Indication of how many and which assignments will be timed
- ❏ Description of requirements concerning form and presentation of assignments (e.g., length, text and electronic file formatting, electronic file submission procedures, and so forth)
- ❏ Policies governing late work, revised assignments, collaboration, and so on

5. Instructional Processes and Procedures
- ❏ Description of how class time will be allocated (e.g., balance of reading practice, collaborative tasks, class discussions, lecture, quizzes and tests, and so forth)
- ❏ Expectations concerning student preparedness and participation in classroom and online discussions, group tasks, and so on

6. Performance Requirements and Policies
- ❏ Summary of compulsory assignments and their deadlines
- ❏ Description of assessment criteria, including how student work will be evaluated
- ❏ Explanation of policies concerning attendance, participation, missed assignments, classroom conduct, and so on

7. Assessment Procedures
- ❏ Description of assessment criteria and how they will be applied
- ❏ Account of how final course grades are weighted (if applicable) and calculated
- ❏ Justification of assessment and marking procedures

8. Course Schedule or Timetable
- ❏ If practicable, a week-by-week or session-by-session calendar of dates, themes, events, reading assignments, and deadlines (considerable flexibility is often required with course timetables to accommodate inevitable changes, delays, and negotiated syllabi)

FIGURE 4.3. Syllabus Checklist.
Sources: Ferris and Hedgcock (2005); Seymour and Walsh (2006).

decisions will help learners meet course objectives (Ferris & Hedgcock, 2005). The sample syllabus in Appendix 4.2 briefly states that the chief course goal is to "develop [students'] reading . . . skills and strategies using a range of academic and non-academic materials." The description then lists seven learning objectives presented in *SWBAT* (Students Will Be Able To . . .) form (Aebersold & Field, 1997). Students may not read or pay attention to these details unless the teacher calls attention to them, but we find that highlighting expected outcomes can be a valuable teaching and learning strategy at the beginning of a term and as a course unfolds. An explicit discussion of literacy aims may acquaint students with your educational philosophy, and "a well-organized course description will inspire students with confidence that the course will be equally thoughtful and organized" (Seymour & Walsh, 2006, p. 14).

Constructing the Course Outline

Organizing a coherent sequence of reading materials, classroom activities, and assignments can pose challenges for both novice and experienced instructors. To address these challenges, Graves (2000, p. 125) proposed a five-component model for sequencing courses. These components consist of overlapping processes, which we paraphrase as follows:

1. Determining the course's organizing principle(s);
2. Identifying units or modules based on the organizing principle(s);
3. Sequencing units or modules;
4. Determining the language, literacy, content, and skills for each unit;
5. Organizing content and skills within and across units.

This scheme is not a simple recipe for preparing a workable course outline, as "the way that you conceptualize content and set goals and objectives depends on your teaching (and learning) experience" (Graves, 2000, p. 127). Nonetheless, course content can be systematically broken down into smaller, more manageable units. Course content, target skills, and student tasks can be meaningfully organized by theme, skill area, function, or any combination of these. For example, in the sample syllabus supplied in Appendix 4.2, the course outline tracks the thematic organization of the core textbook (Smith & Mare, 2004). To some degree reflecting a content-based approach to L2 reading instruction (Crandall, 1995; Genesee, 1998; Nunan, 2001; Snow & Brinton, 1997; Stoller, 2004), our sample course outline presents a linear sequence of interrelated reading selections keyed to topics such as "Society: school and family." The unit sequence and internal unit structure offer a chronological scaffold that reflects both a semester-long overview and a week-by-week timetable. Within thematic units, the outline specifies learning tasks and assessments, spaced at regular intervals and serving as intermediate targets. These are points at which the teacher should monitor the progress of students' reading skills, reading comprehension, research, and study skills (see Chapter 1, especially Figures 1.7–1.9). Though minimally detailed, the outline in Appendix 4.2 provides teacher and students with a road map for a 15-week semester, explicitly signaling important benchmarks along the way (i.e., unit and chapter boundaries, unit tests, steps toward compiling the final portfolio), as well as end-of-term activities designed to integrate new skills and knowledge (i.e., the literacy portfolio and final unit test).

A syllabus, no matter how systematic the course description and outline, cannot do the work of ensuring that target learning objectives are met. Although a syllabus is an indispensable teaching tool and a valuable organizing apparatus for students, the teacher must ensure that the sequence of materials and tasks provides multiple opportunities for students to practice, enhance, and assess their reading skills and strategies cyclically (cf. Chapter 9). In our sample syllabus (Appendix 4.2), for example, the outline offers a calendar of events, but it does not actually show how students will practice and test target reading skills and strategies iteratively through (and within) units, reading selections, exercises, and assessments. The fact that numerous occasions for top-down and bottom-up skills practice are interwoven throughout the course is largely implicit. By working our way through meaningful content that poses progressively greater cognitive challenges, we can hope to draw on students' current schematic knowledge, build new schemata, and consequently improve their reading efficiency.

The content sequence in a course outline should serve as a cyclical framework for practicing strategies and subskills, progressively leading students to master reading functions corresponding to higher levels of proficiency (see Figures 1.8 and 1.9, as well as Chapters 2 and 3). Course content should serve as both the means and message for cultivating effective reading knowledge and skill (Block & Pressley, 2007; Carlo, 2008; Johnson & Swain, 1997; Leaver & Stryker, 1989; Met, 1999; Pally, 2000; Pica, 2002; Smagorinsky, 2008; Stoller, 2004). This sequence should begin with students' current level of L2 reading proficiency clearly in mind; in other words, target texts for an L2 literacy course should be carefully *graded*, in line with views of working within and beyond the *zone of proximal development* (ZPD), the distance between one's current developmental state and the next stage of cognitive functioning (Vygotsky, 1986).

Numerous experts (e.g., Nation, 2001) have championed the use of graded reading materials (e.g., basal readers) to develop students' reading speed, fluency, and strategic skills. At the same time, we should reiterate that recent evidence contradicts the common view that text length, genre, and structural complexity should closely match students' proficiency level (Gascoigne, 2002; Maxim, 2002). In fact, we should *not* restrict ourselves to assigning novice L2 readers short texts dealing with concrete information, nor should we be compelled to select "simplified" texts for novice and intermediate readers (Young, 1993, 1999; see Chapter 3). Grading text materials in a course or unit may actually inhibit the development of readers' abilities to interpret authentic texts and process diverse genres (Allen, Bernhardt, Berry, & Demel, 1988; Shrum & Glisan, 2005). Rather, "students should be given the opportunity to use the information in the text, grammar, vocabulary, and discourse markers that connect ideas and help with comprehension" (Shrum & Glisan, 2005, p. 175). To ensure broad exposure, text complexity or difficulty should not rigidly determine how a literacy syllabus is graded.

We conclude our discussion of syllabus design by offering practical recommendations for approaching the nuts and bolts of planning a course from scratch or updating an existing course. First, we encourage teachers to refer explicitly to course aims as a means of justifying planning decisions. Second, we recommend planning the course outline with an academic calendar showing the exact number of class meetings and holidays. In this way, we know exactly how many classroom (and online) hours are available for instruction. To simplify the process of organizing a course, we encourage teachers to model their outlines on the basis of a well-designed syllabus, which may do a fine job of providing structure for a course. As Graves (2000) pointed out, "it may be possible to reshape the syllabus, depending on the institutional givens" (p. 127). We would caution that, whereas some textbooks are organized with meticulous care and may provide workable sequences of instruction, using a textbook's table of contents as a surrogate for a course outline is not advised (see Chapter 3). An excellent textbook can ease a teacher's planning responsibilities, but it can never be a substitute for a syllabus that integratively addresses student needs, course goals, and institutional standards (Airasian & Russell, 2008).

Third, we would remind teachers that, because no timeline should be etched in stone, "a ruthless sense of realism must go into planning [a] course" (Tarvers, 1993, p. 42). To build in flexibility, we recommend setting aside one or two sessions per term as "flex" (flexible) periods, if possible. A free session now and then can provide useful padding for reading tasks that overflow, lessons that take longer than planned, and unexpected cancellations. If the course proceeds as anticipated, the extra time can be a wonderful gift that can be used profitably for further reading practice, student–teacher conferences, free voluntary reading (FVR), or sustained silent reading (SSR) (see Chapter 6.) Fourth, it can be useful to allow generous time gaps between reading assignments and exercises to accommodate slower readers and the likelihood that some students may occasionally need time to re-read certain texts. We have found that even experienced literacy teachers tend to over-plan by including too much material in their syllabi.[2] Avoiding the temptation to cover more material than is necessary not only reduces pressure on students but also builds in time for the teacher to respond to student writing and mark assignments, thereby ensuring timely return of student work. Finally, in line with our advice to plan flexibly, we remind teachers that it is sometimes necessary (and beneficial) to modify course content after a term gets underway. For example, we may wish to supplement a reading selection with a more current text, make a substitution, eliminate a text that students find too difficult, or adjust an assignment deadline. Although clear goals and systematically sequenced texts and tasks are essential to delivering a purposeful course, so is the need to view a course outline as an outline—not as a rigid prescription for day-to-day planning and teaching.

Selecting and Working with Textbooks

A crucial task that goes hand in hand with designing a syllabus and organizing a course outline involves selecting appropriate materials, which may involve a published textbook, a set of authentic materials not originally intended for educational purposes, or a combination of the two. Chapter 3 explores the linguistic and rhetorical aspects of L2 texts and suggests methods for integrating authentic and pedagogical texts into the L2 literacy curriculum. Chapters 5–7 further address instructional strategies for working with various text types to promote L2 students' reading fluency, accuracy, efficiency, and strategies. Congruent with the material presented in Chapters 2 and 5, we urge readers to supplement textbooks with authentic texts accompanied by thoughtfully constructed pre-, while-, and post-reading tasks (Block & Pressley, 2007; Crandall, 1995; Eskey, 2005; Graves & Graves, 2003; Weaver, 2002; Willis & Willis, 2007). In this section, we examine the matter of textbook selection and adoption, partly because textbooks pervade educational systems throughout the world. In fact, textbooks often constitute the backbone for courses and entire curricula. As Graves (2000) acknowledged, many educators "are required to use textbooks, a majority of teachers don't have the time or resources to prepare their own materials, and so textbooks are a necessity" (p. 173). We recognize this reality and encourage teachers to become discriminating users and critics of published textbooks.

As we turn our attention to principles for evaluating and using textbooks effectively, we will summarize arguments for and against designing literacy courses around published sources:

Benefits of Using a Textbook

- A textbook can offer a useful linear and hierarchical framework, particularly if the book's content and apparatus are keyed to the teacher's goals and student profile. A well-designed textbook can facilitate instructional planning.
- When adopted by a program or institution, a textbook can serve as a common reference point in delivering a curriculum, thereby ensuring uniformity. A common textbook or series can ensure that a course or curriculum adheres to established goals within and across course levels. It can likewise give students and teachers a sense of continuity.
- A textbook can give students a sense of predictability, as well as a tool for understanding what will be expected of them in the reading course.
- A high-quality textbook provides reading material, activities, and projects that offer numerous instructional options. Some textbooks and series provide further instructional aids, such as teachers' guides, slides, video materials, software, companion websites, and even Web-based tutorial assistance.
- Along with teaching ancillaries, some publishers bundle with their textbooks assessment packages, which may include quizzes, tests, assignments, and scoring guides.

Drawbacks of Relying on a Textbook

- A textbook's content and apparatus might not match a course or student proficiency levels. A textbook that is too difficult may discourage students and pose problems for the teacher; a textbook that does not challenge students will fail to develop their L2 literacy skills.
- The approach, content, and apparatus of a textbook may not suit the interests, needs, or expectations of a particular learner cohort. A textbook's combination of task types may be poorly suited to a student population (e.g., too many or too few vocabulary-focused activities, critical reading tasks that are too narrow or too open-ended).
- Published textbooks may focus too much or too little on narrow dimensions of reading and literacy. Some textbooks emphasize top-down skills almost to the exclusion of bottom-up competencies; others may neglect broader literacy skills in favor of discrete, bottom-up skills.
- Reading selections, exercises, activities, and visual enhancements may be inauthentic, unappealing, or too tightly controlled (graded) for length and lexical complexity, leading to boredom and low motivation on the part of students.[3]
- Textbooks often contain source material that quickly loses currency and relevance (e.g., journalistic texts).
- Some textbooks rigidly follow a mechanical, linear order, making it difficult to deviate from the prescribed sequence. Similarly, a textbook may prescribe a syllabus that is too ambitious.

We encourage teachers to approach textbook selection with realistic expectations and a critical eye. Evaluating and selecting materials for a course can be intimidating, partly because of the overwhelming number of published sources available for teaching L2 reading. Consequently, we propose the following general questions to help teachers make quick preliminary decisions about which textbooks might merit careful review and about those that might be readily eliminated from further consideration:

Does the textbook . . .

- Cover topics, genres, and literacy skills targeted in your course?
- Present suitable samples of the genres and text types that you want students to read, analyze, interpret, critique, and reproduce?
- Contain clear, well-constructed activities, tasks, and projects that will help students develop L2 literacy skills targeted in the objectives?

- Provide an adequate number of useful, productive, provocative, and socioculturally appropriate discussion topics, classroom activities, and reading assignments?
- Present information, explanations, procedures, strategies, and supplemental sources that will help you present new material, skill incentives, and reading strategies to your students effectively?
- Appeal to you in terms of its approach, organization, completeness, visual features, and practicality? (Adapted from Ferris & Hedgcock, 2005)

We have found it helpful to review these questions from the point of view of our students: A negative response may clearly signal that a textbook isn't eligible for inclusion on your short list.

The Textbook Evaluation Checklist in Appendix 4.3 is designed to help teachers evaluate and compare textbooks that make their initial cut, a process that should be keyed to explicit, consistent criteria. We constructed this tool to facilitate teachers' decision-making processes and to present a systematic set of features to consider in reviewing published sources. We encourage readers to consult comparable textbook evaluation tools (e.g., Brown, H. D., 2007b; Brown, J. D., 1995; Byrd, 2001; Epstein & Ormiston, 2007; Omaggio Hadley, 2001; Ur, 1996) and to develop evaluation schemes specially adapted to their contexts.

As suggested in our review of course design principles, continuous NA should serve as a primary data source for instructional planning and materials selection. An account of learner needs and institutional aims is indispensable to an accurate appraisal of the level of difficulty, pedagogical orientation, content, and apparatus of reading textbooks. We must likewise evaluate the suitability of a textbook for use in a given course or institution. For instance, a self-contained, general reading skills or integrated skills textbook might be a wise choice for a low- or intermediate-level reading-and-writing course in an English-language academy or a college-based IEP in an English-speaking setting.[4] The same book, though suitable for learners at similar proficiency levels, might not work so well as a core textbook in a university-based EAP course whose students expect to develop specific academic literacies and university-level reading skills (Hyon, 2001, 2002; Toledo, 2005). Similarly, a literary anthology might match the needs of a pre-mainstream ESL or EAP course in an English-medium university, where students will advance to undergraduate composition courses in which they will read literary and other genres. Adopting a literary anthology in an ESP reading course, however, might be a poor selection, as students' needs and expectations will involve the reading and reproduction of discipline-specific genres (e.g., science, engineering, commerce) (Celce-Murcia & Olshtain, 2000; Dudley-Evans & St. John, 1998; Ferris & Hedgcock, 2005; Grasso, 2005; Hirvela, 2004; Johns, 1997, 2003; Johns & Price-Machado, 2001; Tomlinson, 1998, 2003).

A final word on reading textbooks takes the form of a simple reminder: No literacy course necessarily needs to be based on a published textbook. Many instructors who teach EAP, ESP, and content-based courses manage quite effectively without any textbooks at all, preferring to compile their own anthologies and reading packets to accommodate their students' real needs and expressed preferences. For many courses, textbooks designed for L2 reading instruction may not even exist. If a textbook is required or desired, it is worth recalling that no published textbook or series can fulfill everyone's needs. "One-size-fits-all" textbooks that will work well in any context are rare to nonexistent. Teachers should anticipate the need to supplement and adapt even the very best published materials (Masuhara, 1998).

Planning L2 Literacy Lessons: Principles and Precepts

In this section, we introduce principles of instructional planning as a logical follow-on to our recommendations for syllabus design. Chapter 5 discusses and illustrates lesson-planning procedures in depth, with specific reference to introducing, practicing, and monitoring intensive reading functions.

Specifying Lesson Objectives

As a prelude to considering the mechanics of daily lesson planning, we would like to affirm conventional wisdom, which holds that "one of the most important aspects of planning a daily lesson is to identify the objective(s) that you want to achieve by the end of the class period" (Shrum & Glisan, 2005, p. 84). Productive lesson objectives should identify the observable behaviors that students will demonstrate as a result of instruction and relate in some discernible way to course goals and assessment standards (Cruickshank, Bainer, & Metcalf, 1999; Farris et al., 2004; Jensen, 2001; Nuttall, 2005; Woodward, 2001). Pedagogy experts often recommend cognitive processing and critical reasoning frameworks such as Bloom's (1956) taxonomy, literacy skills hierarchies (see Figure 1.8), or strategy inventories (see Figure 1.9) in setting learning priorities and organizing lessons. Regardless of the models they select, teachers "should be aware of what level of thinking they are requiring students to perform" in designing learning experiences (Shrum & Glisan, 2005 p. 84). Many experienced teachers admittedly plan and deliver excellent lessons without formalizing their objectives in writing, but effective teachers organize classroom tasks with an achievable purpose in mind. "Each activity needs to have a reason," wrote Purgason (1991), and teachers should contemplate "why that activity is important . . . and what [students] will be able to do when they finish it" (p. 423).

To that end, we strongly recommend characterizing lesson aims in performative terms. "Effective objectives are measurable and describe what learners will be able to do" (Shrum & Glisan, 2005, p. 84). Useful and meaningful objectives statements should thus be worded with action verbs (e.g., *identify, compare, describe*), rather than with verbs such as *learn, understand,* and *read,* which are difficult to observe and measure (Ferris & Hedgcock, 2005; Shrum & Glisan, 2005; Skowron, 2006). For instance, building on selected targets from the *National TESOL Standards, English Language Arts—ESL* (see pp. 126–127), a daily lesson plan for an intermediate- or advanced-level EAP course might specify critical reading aims. One such objective might read: "Students will (be able to) distinguish fact from opinion as they analyze, discuss, and write about the article, *Beyond Rivalry* in *Topics for Today*" (Smith & Mare, 2004, pp. 50–53). A strategy-oriented lesson aim for the same course might read, "Students will (be able to) make accurate oral and written predictions about the structure and conclusions of the *Animal–Human Hybrids Spark Controversy* excerpt in *Well Read 4*" (Pasternak & Wrangell, 2007, pp. 174–176). We could classify these statements as *terminal* objectives, which are "final learning outcomes that you will be responsible for assessing," or as *enabling* objectives, which consist of "interim steps" leading to a terminal objective (Brown, 2007b, p. 165). These aims (SWBATs) specify observable learner actions and operations, rather than global cognitive targets (e.g., "Students will learn critical reading skills") or instructional procedures (e.g., "The teacher will present prediction strategies").

Organizing a Daily Lesson Plan

Depending on the teacher's style and work habits, a daily lesson plan can take a number of forms, but a lesson outline or script should ideally provide the teacher with a scheme for presenting materials, interacting with students, and leading them through structured and open-ended tasks. A workable lesson outline should present a chronology of classroom events, as well as a scaffold for addressing student needs as operationalized in course goals and objectives. In this respect, a lesson script functions as a link between curricular targets and intermediate learning benchmarks. Planning and delivering a lesson "is where the known (instructional objectives, texts, and so on) meets the unknown" (student readers and their development processes) (Ferris & Hedgcock, 2005, p. 98).

Research summarized by Freeman (1996), Nunan (1992), and Skowron (2006) demonstrates that effective teachers plan instruction "first by assessing what their students already know or bring to the learning task and then figuring out what they need to teach them to get them to the appropriate objective" (Shrum & Glisan, 2005, p. 85). Through these processes, teachers may construct a formal outline or script, although it is useful to remember that lessons may have an exploratory, experimental dimension. That is, we can't possibly predict everything that might take place during a given class period or ensure that every lesson will succeed. We should consequently prepare for teaching "by expecting the unexpected" and by building flexibility into our lessons (Ferris & Hedgcock, 2005, p. 98). The planning advice offered by Hillocks (1995) is highly valuable in this regard: "The thoughtful teacher, in searching for ways to help students learn more effectively, will plan real trials (what researchers call quasi-experiments), determine what effect they have . . . and consider new options as a result" (p. 125). Seasoned teachers appreciate the necessity of advance planning, which can equip them to depart from their plans when the need arises (Bailey, 1996a; Skowron, 2006). Whether it consists of a simple list of instructional activities or a detailed script describing every procedure, a lesson plan should not only facilitate teaching and learning, but should also enable the teacher to diagnose and correct oversights in lesson planning and execution (Bailey, Curtis, & Nunan, 2001; Crookes, 2003; Richards & Farrell, 2005; Richards & Lockhart, 1994; Skowron, 2006).

Lesson Planning Mechanics

We encourage novice teachers to cultivate their planning skills by preparing lesson scripts, which can be handwritten, word-processed, or constructed digitally using presentation software such as Apple's iWork application, KeyNote, or Microsoft PowerPoint. Such digital tools are especially valuable for those with access to wired teaching environments, where teachers can work directly from laptop or desktop computers and where lesson outlines and materials can be projected for students to see. A low-tech lesson, in contrast, can easily be printed on paper or note cards. Seasoned and self-assured teachers may deliver lessons with no written notes, working from a mental plan developed in writing in preparation for class.

Irrespective of its format, a lesson plan should be systematic, readable, and convenient to refer to during class. As a record of what took place, a written or digital script can be an indispensable tool for reflecting on the lesson's effectiveness after class. An advantage of keeping track of lesson outlines is that they can be adapted and reused if one teaches the same courses multiple times. Rather than proposing a rigid, prescriptive scheme for planning L2 reading lessons, the template and checklist in Figure 4.4 presents practical and procedural aspects of daily lesson planning that can be adapted and individualized. Figure 4.5 more explicitly considers instructional procedures, pedagogical moves, and suggestions for ensuring coherence in the lesson sequence. We refer readers to the sample lesson planning techniques described in Chapter 5, which reflect and exemplify precepts introduced in Figures 4.4 and 4.5.

Figure 4.4 recommends spelling out learning objectives and accounting for outcomes of the prior lesson as part of the daily lesson preparation routine. These steps can remind students of the types of reading, interpretation, problem-solving, and discussion tasks that they should be ready for. This information also enables us to make informed estimates of how much time to allocate to each lesson phase. A list of equipment and materials is useful for getting oneself organized at the start of class, and a checklist of student work to return or collect can likewise save class time. Including a list of announcements and upcoming deadlines in the lesson script can expedite preliminaries and class business. Some teachers habitually write this information on the board or project it on a slide to

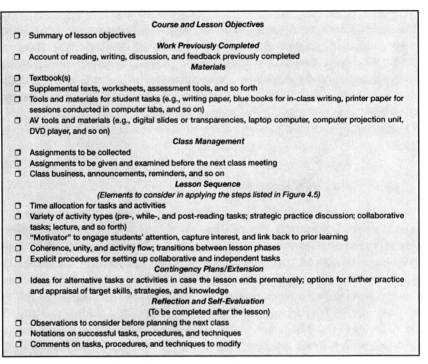

FIGURE 4.4. Lesson Plan Outline and Checklist.
Adapted from Ferris and Hedgcock (2005, p. 100).

avoid consuming class time; others postpone announcements and business matters to the end of class or use an electronic bulletin board for these chores.

A crucial dimension of effective lesson planning entails envisioning how classroom activities will be set in motion by the teacher and carried out by students. A preview or warm-up phase, sometimes called *setting the stage* (Ballman, 1998), should activate learners' formal, content, and cultural schemata, preparing them for lesson input and learning (Figure 4.5). Some researchers urge teachers to use *advance organizers* to capture students' interest and stimulate recall of recent teaching. Ausubel, Novak, and Hanesian (1978) defined advance organizers as "relevant and inclusive introductory materials that are maximally clear and stable." Teachers use advance organizers effectively when they are "used to [establish] a meaningful learning set" as a prelude to core lesson activities (pp. 170–171). Visual aids, graphic organizers (see Chapter 3), and simple pre-reading tasks (see Chapters 3, 5–7) are examples of advance organizers that can effectively orient learners to the work ahead (Shrum & Glisan, 2005; Skowron, 2006).

The lesson core, the gravitational center of the instructional event, may comprise a series of activities and tasks centered on print-based, auditory, and visual input. After the preview phase, learners should be ready to become "actively

Lesson Phase	Teacher Actions	Student Actions
1. Activation of prior learning	• Helps students recall what they have learned or practiced in previous lesson(s) • Invites students to demonstrate new reading skills, strategies, and content knowledge	• Reflect and report on prior learning • Demonstrate new skills, strategies, and knowledge through practice
2. Preview/warm-up	• Previews lesson, connecting new material to material just reviewed or practiced • Checks students' understanding of content and literacy concepts at hand • Guides students in anticipating lesson content by stimulating prediction about topics, texts, and tasks	• Respond to preview • Respond to teacher's prompts • Direct focal attention to lesson aims and tasks
3. Lesson core: instruction, procedures, guided participation	• Communicates lesson objectives • Presents reading strategy, task, activity, lecture • Models strategy, task, or activity; leads students in practicing new skills and strategies • Instructs students to complete task or activity individually or in groups • Provides opportunities for students to practice target skills and strategies independently • Encourages student involvement, participation, and interaction • Checks students' ability to display skills and strategies and their understanding of text content • Introduce transitions from one lesson phase to the next	• Respond to teacher's presentation (e.g., by taking notes, asking questions, and so on) • Observe modeling, ask questions • Undertake task or activity individually or in groups • Elicit teacher's assistance to complete the task, as needed • Complete task or activity independently
4. Closure/gatekeeping	• Informally assesses student participation, performance, and learning • Prompts students to reflect on what they have learned and practiced • Links new skills, strategies, and knowledge to prior learning	• Discuss or describe what they have learned or practiced • Discuss relationship of new learning to prior learning
5. Follow-up, extension, and preparation for future learning	• Presents further tasks or activities to develop new skills, strategies, and content knowledge • Introduces extension tasks and reinforces learning objectives	• Plan or complete further tasks or activities • Take note to prepare for further learning

FIGURE 4.5. Conceptual Framework for Sequencing Literacy Lessons.
Sources: Anderson (1999); Farris et al. (2004); Ferris and Hedgcock (2005); Fitzgerald and Graves (2004); Skowron (2006).

involved in attending to the input and interacting" with the teacher, peers, and texts (Shrum & Glisan, 2005, p. 86). *Guided participation* (Figure 4.5), a notion inspired by Vygotsky (1978, 1986) and developed by Rogoff (1995), refers to "the ways in which people involve [one another] in communicating and coordinating their efforts while taking part in activity that is culturally valued" (Lantolf & Thorne, 2006, p. 158). In guided participation, the teacher and fellow learners offer scaffolded assistance as students perform tasks, solve problems, and interpret texts. Scaffolded assistance does not entail doing learners' work for them, but rather leading them to understand tasks and to discover the linguistic, cognitive, and textual resources for performing the task themselves (Fitzgerald & Graves, 2004). The core processes sketched in Figure 4.5 refer to measuring student performance and progress over the course of a lesson, a vital function in the planning–teaching–assessment cycle (see Chapter 9). Finally, in the closure or gatekeeping phase, the teacher "brings the lesson to a close by asking students to recall what they learned and/or by describing how the current lesson will be used as the basis for the next lesson" (Shrum & Glisan, 2005, p. 86).

The core instructional components in Figure 4.4 reflect strategies for executing the steps sketched in Figure 4.5, which should not be interpreted as linearly prescribed. One core component involves time management, a common challenge for many teachers concerned about fulfilling their lesson aims in a timely manner. Although time management is a skill that may develop over many years of practice, we encourage teachers to anticipate the time required for each lesson activity and then to add several minutes to that estimate. In our experience, it is much easier to pad a lesson with extra time and to end up with a few spare minutes than it is to fall behind and seek ways to make up for it in subsequent class sessions. It can be difficult to estimate time frames accurately, but a useful rule of thumb is that open-ended tasks (e.g., guided and student-led discussions of reading selections, group tasks, conferences, and so forth) will probably take longer than we think they should. Students may have more difficulty understanding a text, need extra time to complete a task, or become engaged in a productive discussion that is worth extending. Building in extra time ("wiggle room") is a good way to apply the "ruthless sense of realism" recommended by Tarvers (1993) and to accommodate Hillocks' (1995) lesson-plan-as-experiment principle.

Related to time management is the precept that classroom lessons should reflect variety in terms of content, task type, and interactional style—a principle long embraced by communicative language teaching proponents, literacy educators, and general education researchers (Anderson, 1999; Brown, 2007b; Farris et al., 2004; Graves, 2000; Jensen, 2001; Skowron, 2006; Smagorinsky, 2008; Weaver, 1998, 2002; Woodward, 2001). It is wholly appropriate for L2 reading lessons to dedicate substantial time to reading processes, skill-building, strategy practice, and progress assessment. Striking an appropriate balance of content and task types, of course, requires the teacher to avoid variety for the sake of variety, a practice that can lead to losing sight of course objectives and student needs. For example, allocating large chunks of class time to practicing bottom-up strategies (e.g., decoding) can lead to under-serving students who also need to cultivate top-down strategies and skills (e.g., reading for global main ideas, gisting) (Birch, 2007; Block & Pressley, 2007; Kuhn & Rasinski, 2007). Similarly, it is important to balance teacher-led activities carefully with student-centered work, such as reading practice, discussions, and collaborative tasks. Furthermore, lesson components should be explicitly linked to one another, as well as to established objectives: Overt links show that lessons are internally coherent and that classroom activities serve both course goals and learner needs (Skowron, 2006; Woodward, 2001). Although building links into lesson plans requires practice and experimentation, making explicit transitions is easier when lesson segments have a discernible purpose and when tasks are framed by transparent, step-by-step instructions.

The final element of daily lesson planning addressed in Figures 4.4 and 4.5 involves post-lesson reflection, which we consider to be an integral aspect of the planning–teaching–assessment cycle (see Figure 4.1). Systematic reflection on a lesson's successes and failures enables teachers to bring subsequent teaching into line with course aims, review and address student needs, and promote professional development (Bailey et al., 2001; Skowron, 2006). We recommend taking a few simple steps during the post-lesson phase to evaluate the content and structure of each lesson and to identify concrete ways to enhance student learning. As Omaggio Hadley (2001) suggested, "Ask yourself how well students responded to the activities you planned and try to diagnose the causes of problems you encountered" (p. 464). To facilitate reflection on the effectiveness of daily lessons, numerous authors advise teachers to maintain an ongoing, written record in the form of a teaching log, which might consist of retrospective field notes or periodic lesson reports (Crookes, 2003; Cruickshank et al., 1999; Murphy, 2001; Richards & Lockhart, 1994). The following lesson elements, paraphrased from Richards and Farrell (2005), can serve as a checklist for reconstructing classroom events systematically:

- ☐ Extent to which tasks, procedures, texts, and other materials succeeded in meeting . . . objectives;
- ☐ Tasks, activities, and procedures that worked especially well;
- ☐ Tasks, activities, and procedures that did not work particularly well;
- ☐ Aspects of the lesson that require changes and improvements;
- ☐ Departures or digressions from the lesson script;
- ☐ Appropriateness and effectiveness of lesson sequence;
- ☐ Challenges that students encountered in working with texts, tasks, directions, and so on;
- ☐ Linguistic structures (words, collocations, grammatical structures, and so forth) that students found difficult. (pp. 38–39)

Prompted by such checklists and reminders, teachers may use their post-lesson reflection exercises as departure points for subsequent planning. As literacy teachers ourselves, we can affirm that this cyclical practice produces a sense of continuity from lesson to lesson and facilitates the process of tracking progress through a course.

Chapter Summary

This chapter has endeavored to facilitate the complex work of literacy course design by exploring principles and procedures designed to answer Grabe's (2004) call for coherent curricular planning. Needs assessment, the starting point for course planning, requires us to understand our L2 students by examining their language and literacy backgrounds, their needs, their strategies and skills, and their preferences and beliefs. We suggested methods for collecting information about learner needs and expectations, a procedure that we believe should be continuous. A key target of needs assessment is the identification of macro-level learning goals, in addition to specific objectives for day-to-day literacy lessons. Recognizing that L2 literacy educators in many contexts may be required to align their teaching with pre-established goals, this chapter suggested ideas for matching course content and instruction with mandated aims and assessment standards, a topic that we examine anew in Chapter 9.

In addressing the "nuts and bolts" of course planning, we argued that the design of a syllabus and outline for an L2 literacy course should be guided by transparent, achievable learning goals shaped by Grabe's (2004) principles for L2 reading instruction. The sample ESL reading syllabus and course outline presented in Appendix 4.2 reflects the criteria outlined in our checklists and discussion. A course description and outline together constitute a macro-level planning device that satisfies the need for structure and coherence, although we stressed the need to balance structure and flexibility in following a syllabus. We then turned our attention to textbook evaluation and adoption, responsibilities often associated (if not synonymous) with course design and materials selection. To assist teachers with these responsibilities, we weighed the benefits and drawbacks of using textbooks, proposing a framework for appraising published course books in the form of an evaluation checklist (Appendix 4.3). The final sections of this chapter then introduced principles of lesson planning, a vital process extending directly from the construction of a coherent syllabus. These principles, along with the implementation steps outlined in Figures 4.4 and 4.5, are intended to serve as flexible tools for designing lessons and materials (see Chapter 5). In concluding our discussion of lesson planning, we proposed simple post-lesson reflection options as tools for closing and reinitiating the planning–teaching–assessment cycle.

Further Reading and Resources

We recommend the sources listed below for further reading on aspects of needs assessment, literacy goals and standards, curriculum and syllabus design, and daily lesson planning.

Resources for needs assessment, curriculum design, and course planning
Brown (1995); Dubin & Olshtain (1986); Graves (2000); Long (2005); Seymour & Walsh (2006); Shanahan & Beck (2006); Shrum & Glisan (2005); Smagorinsky (2008); Verplaetse & Migliacci (2007)
Sample questionnaires and instruments and related instruments
Dörnyei (2001, 2002); Taillefer (2005)
Tools for evaluating and using materials
Brown, H. D. (2007b); Brown, J. D. (1995); Byrd (2001); Epstein & Ormiston (2007); Omaggio Hadley (2001)
Sample lessons, tasks, and exercises for ESL, EFL, and multilingual reading courses
Aebersold & Field (1997); Day (1993); Fang & Schleppegrell (2008); Fitzgerald & Graves (2004); Gambrell et al. (2007); Graves & Graves (2003); Kucer & Silva (2006); Lee & VanPatten (2003); Shrum & Glisan (2005); Silberstein (1994); Turner (2008); Walter (2004)
Task-based instruction
Van den Branden (2006); Willis & Willis (2007)
Survey Monkey
http://www.surveymonkey.com/
Standards
Agor (2001); ACTFL (1998); Shrum & Glisan (2005); Snow (2000)
ACTFL Standards for Foreign Language Learning: Preparing for the 21st Century
http://www.actfl.org/files/public/execsumm.pdf
ACTFL Proficiency Guidelines for Reading
http://www.sil.org/lingualinks/LANGUAGELEARNING/OtherResources/ACTFLProficiencyGuidelines/ACTFLGuidelinesReading.htm
Interagency Language Roundtable Language Skill Level Descriptions for Reading
http://www.govtilr.org/Skills/ILRscale4.htm
IRA/NCTE Standards for English Language Arts
IRA/NCTE (1996)
National TESOL Standards (Pre-K–12)
http://www.gisd.k12.nm.us/standards/esl/
Common European Framework of Reference for Languages: Learning, Teaching, Assessment
http://www.coe.int/t/dg4/linguistic/CADRE_EN.asp
Lesson planning
Brown (2007b); Omaggio Hadley (2001); Shrum & Glisan (2005); Skowron (2006); Woodward (2001)

Reflection and Review

1. How can student background variables (e.g., primary/home language(s), L1 and L2 literacy experiences, prior education, and so on) affect student learning and performance in an L2 literacy course? How can a methodical account of these variables positively affect literacy instruction?

2. How might we distinguish between learner *needs* and *preferences?* Why might this contrast be important in the NA process and in implementing NA results?

3. Identify the distinctions between *goals* and *objectives.* How are the two categories interrelated, and what roles should they play in shaping course syllabi and literacy lessons?

4. Why is specifying goals and objectives in performative terms (e.g., in SWBAT format) useful? Evaluate the following literacy course objectives, decide which most fully meet the criteria presented in this chapter, and explain why:
   - Students will be able to compose useful pre-reading questions as a result of scanning;
   - Teacher will demonstrate prediction strategies;
   - Students will learn about scanning;
   - Students will be able to write a short paraphrase of the author's main arguments;
   - Students will understand expository text structure;
   - Students will use a monolingual dictionary to verify guesses about unfamiliar words.

5. List the ways in which a course description and outline can assist in planning instruction and providing students with varied opportunities for L2 reading practice. Consider how a syllabus can enhance student learning.

6. What are the chief components of an L2 literacy lesson? What cognitive, metacognitive, and affective functions do they serve?

7. Taking into account criteria for selecting and presenting authentic texts introduced in Chapter 3 and our discussion of textbook adoption in this chapter, explain your position concerning the relative benefits of basing a course on a textbook or a selection of other materials.

8. List the short- and long-term benefits of planning methodical lessons and reflecting systematically on their effectiveness.

Application Activities

Application Activity 4.1
L2 Reader Needs Assessment and Profile

Using the background variables listed in Figure 4.2 and relevant items from the Literacy Background Questionnaire in Appendix 4.1, craft an NA survey that you could administer to a prospective cohort of L2 students. Develop a prototype to use in an authentic context, adding or revising items that pertain to your target population. Solicit feedback on your survey from your instructor, colleagues, classmates, or administrators. After revising your survey, administer it in written or digital form (e.g., using an online tool such as Survey Monkey); tally or record frequency results and prepare a profile of your students that captures demographic and relevant language, literacy, and educational data. Analyze your findings and discuss them in a needs assessment report in which you recommend an instructional approach that would be effective for this L2 population.

Application Activity 4.2
Micro-Case Study of an L2 Reader

Develop a set of interview questions based on the demographic and other background variables outlined in Figure 4.2 and Appendix 4.1. Enlist the help of an L2 reader willing to participate in a small-scale case study project. Secure written permission from your student to record one or more interviews that focus on her language learning and literacy history. Take field notes during the interviews or as you listen to the recordings. In compiling and analyzing your data, consider how your student's L1 knowledge, sociocultural background, early educational experiences, immigration status, personal and professional goals, and so forth have helped or hindered her progress as an L2 reader and writer. In addition, consider your volunteer's beliefs about the impact of classroom instruction on his or her development as an L2 learner and reader. Prepare a report of your case-study findings and key insights based on your participant's views of the effectiveness of her L1 and L2 literacy education.

Application Activity 4.3
Using Standards to Develop Goals and Objectives

Locate and consult at least one set of reading or literacy standards geared toward a student population that you are familiar with. The Further Reading and Resources section lists references and Web addresses for a number of such sources; we also encourage you to consult the standards developed for your state, province, local school district, or institution. Some standards (e.g., those developed by TESOL) classify expected learning outcomes by skill area (e.g., reading, listening, speaking, writing, grammar, and so on). In contrast, the

ACTFL Standards cluster outcomes by modality (e.g., listening and reading), making it necessary to examine learning and teaching goals within a theoretical framework. Your task consists of three steps: (1) Carefully review one set of L2 literacy or reading standards with a particular L2 reading course in mind; (2) Evaluate the standards in terms of one of the three classification schemes introduced in this chapter (Genesee & Upshur, 1996; Graves, 2000; or Stern, 1992—see *Establishing Goals and Objectives for Teaching and Learning*); (3) Based on your evaluation and analysis, craft a statement of goals that would be appropriate for inclusion in the official description of your target literacy course.

Application Activity 4.4
Syllabus Evaluation

Collect a syllabus (course description and outline) for an L2 literacy course at a nearby institution. Referring to the checklist in Figure 4.3 and corresponding discussion in this chapter, compare the sample syllabus in Appendix 4.2 to your sample. Prepare a written or oral evaluation of the strengths and weaknesses of the sample syllabus, taking into consideration the educational context, the learner population, and the curriculum. In addition to using the sources above, address the following questions to scaffold your comparative analysis:

a. What are the stated course goals and learning objectives?
b. What theory (or theories) of reading or literacy do these aims suggest?
c. How do course content and organization reflect these goals and objectives?
d. What changes would you make to the syllabus and why?

Application Activity 4.5
Textbook Evaluation

Select a course book designed for use in an L2 literacy or reading course, preferably a book currently in use in a course that you are familiar with. Based on your knowledge of the course, institution, and learner population—and perhaps in consultation with a teacher who has taught with the book—decide which of the criteria in Appendix 4.3 you would apply to construct a manageable textbook evaluation instrument. You may elect to complete the Appendix 4.3 Textbok Evaluation Checklist in its entirety. Use the checklist to evaluate the course book, applying your own weighting system, if you prefer. In a prose commentary of two to three pages, substantiate your evaluation by describing salient features of the book that led to your judgments. In your commentary, discuss the effectiveness of the evaluation checklist, which you should attach as an appendix. As an extension of this task, revise and edit your commentary in the form of a formal book review. Submit your review to the book review editor of a professional or scholarly journal for potential publication.

Application Activity 4.6
Lesson Plan Comparison

Collect a set of lesson plans or scripts from your cooperating teacher, a colleague, or your instructor (anyone who might have taught an L2 reading or literacy course recently). Based on the materials presented in Figures 4.4 and 4.5, analyze and compare your sample lesson scripts, noting the strengths of each in light of what you understand about the course, curriculum, and students. Referring to the criteria and suggestions listed in Figures 4.4 and 4.5, compose a two- to three-page commentary in which you: (1) identify features listed in Figures 4.4 and 4.5 that were present or absent in the scripts; and (2) discuss useful insights gained from examining the sample scripts that might help you as a teacher of reading.

Appendix 4.1
Sample Needs Assessment Questionnaire for a Reading Course

ESL 230—Academic Reading III
Literacy Background Questionnaire

Note to ESL 230 students: This questionnaire asks for information about your English-language skills, your experience as a language learner, your learning goals, and your interests. Your responses will give your instructor information about your needs and expectations for Academic Reading III. Honest, specific responses will help your instructor focus on skills and strategies that will help you succeed as a reader. Thank you for completing this survey!

Background Information

My name: _____	
Number of years I have studied English:	Number of years of primary and secondary school:
Number of years of college or university study:	My major or planned major:
Language(s) (other than English) that I use at home:	
Language(s) (other than English) that I read and write:	
My career goals:	
My favorite pastimes and interests:	
The last book I read for pleasure (in any language):	
One interesting thing that I'd like my teacher to know about me:	

Self-Assessment of English Language Skills

Directions: *For each area listed below, place a check mark (✓) in the column that best describes your skill level.*

5 = Very Strong	4 = Strong	3 = Average	2 = Weak	1 = Very Weak

	5	4	3	2	1
Speaking					
Listening					
Reading					
Writing					
Grammar					
Vocabulary					

Self-Assessment of Native Language and English Literacy Skills

Directions: *In this section, you will describe your opinions of your skills and achievements as a reader. For each statement, place a check mark (✓) in the column that best describes your opinion. Please be honest!*

5 = Strongly Agree	4 = Agree	3 = Not Sure or No Opinion	2 = Disagree	1 = Strongly Disagree

	5	4	3	2	1
1. I am a fast reader in my native language(s).					
2. When I read in my native language(s), I comprehend 90% of what I read.					
3. When I read texts in English, I read quickly.					
4. When I read in English, I comprehend 90–100% of what I read.					

Academic Reading Strategies

Directions: *Think about recent experiences reading texts in English. Place a check mark (✓) in the column that best describes your use of each strategy. If you are unsure about a strategy, ask your instructor. Don't be concerned if you haven't heard of a strategy! This information will help your instructor choose materials and activities to develop your reading strategies.*

O = I often use this strategy	S = I sometimes use this strategy	N = I never use this strategy, but I know what it is	DK = I don't know about this strategy

STRATEGY	O	S	N	DK
1. Before reading, I **identify a purpose** for reading.				
2. Before reading, I **plan the steps** I will take to understand the text.				
3. Before reading, I **preview the text**.				
4. Before reading, I try to **predict what the next part of the text is about**.				
5. As I read, I **check my predictions** by comparing them to what the text says.				
6. As I read, I **ask myself questions** about the text.				
7. As I read, I **find answers** to the questions I've asked.				
8. As I read, I **connect what I already know** to new information in the text.				
9. As I read, I occasionally **summarize** portions of the text.				
10. As I read, I **guess** about main ideas based on what the text says.				
11. As I read, I try to **understand how parts of the text are linked**.				
12. As I read, I notice how the writer **has organized information** in the text.				
13. As I read, I **re-read passages** when I want to be sure to understand them.				
14. As I read, I **guess meanings** when I encounter a new word or phrase.				
15. When necessary, I **look up unfamiliar words** in a dictionary or glossary.				
16. As I read, I **pay attention to words and phrases that signal new ideas**.				
17. I **check my understanding** as I move through a text.				
18. When I don't understand part of a text, I try to **identify my difficulties**.				
19. If I misunderstand a passage, I **identify my mistakes and correct them**.				
20. I **question the author** and sometimes critique him or her.				
21. I **question the text** and sometimes critique it.				
22. After reading, I **check to see if I have met my goals** for reading.				
23. After reading, I **think about what I have learned** from reading.				
24. Other (please describe):				

Reading Experiences, Habits, and Attitudes

Directions: *This section will tell your instructor about your background as a reader. For each statement, place a check mark (✓) in the column that best describes your opinion. Be honest!*

5 = Strongly Agree	4 = Agree	3 = Not Sure or No Opinion	2 = Disagree	1 = Strongly Disagree

	5	4	3	2	1
Think about your past experiences with reading.					
1. I earned high grades (marks) in reading last year.					
2. I like to read texts that make me think.					
3. I visit libraries and bookstores often.					
4. I enjoy reading during my spare time.					
5. Family members would often read to me when I was a child.					
6. I read online sources (websites, blogs, and so on).					
Think about people you know who read.					
7. Members of my family enjoy reading.					
8. My friends like to read.					
9. I know people who can help me with reading when I need it.					
10. I often talk to my friends about the things that I read.					
Think about reading: how useful is it?					
11. I believe I learn a lot from reading.					
12. I have favorite subjects that I enjoy reading about.					
13. I read to learn new information about topics that interest me.					
14. I enjoy reading about new things.					
15. I often use reading to help me in my courses.					

Genre Preferences

Directions: *This section will tell your instructor about the types of text that are familiar to you. For each statement, place a check mark (✓) in the column that best describes your experience.*

O = I read this kind of text often	S = I sometimes read this kind of text	N = I never read this kind of text, but I know what it is	DK = I don't know about this kind of text

How often do you read the following kinds of texts (genres) in English?	O	S	N	DK
College textbooks				
Academic articles and essays				
Fiction (e.g., novels, short stories)				
Non-fiction (e.g., biographies, history, travel, popular science)				
Poetry				
Newspapers and newsmagazines				
Magazines (other than newsmagazines)				
Technical and practical texts (e.g., cookbooks, manuals)				
Comic books				
Websites				
Blogs				
Other (please specify):				

How often do you read the following genres in your native language(s)?	O	S	N	DK
College textbooks				
Academic articles and essays				
Fiction (e.g., novels, short stories)				
Non-fiction (e.g., biographies, history, travel, popular science)				
Poetry				
Newspapers and newsmagazines				
Magazines (other than newsmagazines)				
Technical and practical texts (e.g., cookbooks, manuals)				
Comic books				
Websites				
Blogs				
Other (please specify):				

Content Preferences

Directions: *This section will tell your instructor about familiar topics that appeal to your interests.*

1. Describe three or more subjects related to your studies or your future career that really interest you. For example, if you are a business student, you may be especially interested in marketing or finance. If you are an engineering student, maybe you are interested in "green" technologies.

2. Describe three or more topics, issues, or pastimes not related to your studies that interest you personally. For instance, do you enjoy popular music, movies, or sports? Do you play a musical instrument or enjoy an athletic activity such as surfing or yoga?

Classroom Work Styles

Directions: *Your answers in this section will help your instructor understand how you prefer to work in class. Think about your most recent experiences as a student. For each statement, place a check mark (✓) in the column that best describes your opinion. Please be honest!*

5 = Strongly Agree	4 = Agree	3 = Not Sure or No Opinion	2 = Disagree	1 = Strongly Disagree

	5	4	3	2	1
1. As a student, I have had many opportunities to work with fellow classmates on projects and assignments.					
2. As a student, I have had many opportunities to work with fellow classmates on projects and assignments.					
3. In general, I enjoy working with other students on assignments and projects.					
4. When I work with a partner or small group, I do better work than I do when working alone.					
5. When I work with a partner or small group, I often learn more than I do when working alone.					
6. I am comfortable working with partners who are also learning English.					
7. I prefer working with a partner or with a group when the teacher assigns specific roles to group members.					
8. I hope we will do a lot of pair and group work in ESL 230.					

Sources: Brown (1995); Ferris and Hedgcock (2005); Grabe and Stoller (2002); Graves (2000); Koda (2004); Seymour and Walsh (2006); Taillefer (2005); Weaver (2002); Wigfield and Guthrie (1997).

Appendix 4.2
Sample EAP Reading Course Syllabus

Syllabus and Course Outline
ESL 230 — Academic Reading III
Semester: ____ City College

ESL 230, Section D—4 units	Les Kawada, Instructor
Class Meetings: MWF 9:00–10:20	Office Hours: M 8:00–9:00, Th 9:00–10:00
Classroom: Waltham 318	Tel: 525–9655
Office: Dept. of English and ESL, McNair 242C	e-mail: lkawada@cityc.edu

Course Description, Goals, and Objectives
ESL 230 is an advanced, academically oriented ESL course for resident and international students who have been promoted from ESL 220 or who have achieved the required score on the Language and Critical Skills Test (LCST). The literacy goal for ESL 230 is to develop your reading comprehension skills and strategies using a range of academic and non-academic materials, including fiction, current events articles, opinion pieces, textbook excerpts, and online resources. By successfully completing Academic Reading III, you will be able to:
1. skim and scan academic and literary texts for information
2. read efficiently (i.e., fluently and accurately) for global comprehension and specific details
3. read texts critically and interpret them in multiple ways
4. derive meaning of new vocabulary items and grammatical structures from context
5. evaluate and expand your current vocabulary knowledge and grammatical skills
6. use print and online dictionaries effectively
7. analyze and evaluate your reading skills and strategies.

To achieve these objectives, you will complete reading selections, interpret readings and video segments, post commentaries to the course bulletin board, produce brief formal writing assignments, complete quizzes and tests, and track your progress as an academic reader. Students who complete ESL 230 with a "B–" or higher will be promoted to Freshman Composition I.

Required Course Materials
1. Smith, L. C., & Mare, N. C. (2004). *Topics for today* (3rd ed.). Boston: Thomson/Heinle.
2. *ESL 230 Reading Packet*. Available on E-Reserves.
3. A one-inch, three-ring binder to serve as your ESL 230 Portfolio (see *ESL 230 Portfolio Guidelines* — available on the course bulletin board).
4. A current English dictionary (e.g., *American Heritage Dictionary of the English Language*).
5. An active CCIntranet account and password for the ESL 230D bulletin board.

Classroom Policies
(From the *Department of English and ESL Academic Policies Statement*)
1. **Attendance is mandatory.** An excess of three hours of unexcused absence will result in automatic exclusion from the course. Two late arrivals count as a one-hour absence.
2. **Participation** in class discussions and course bulletin board discussions is expected of all students.
3. **Word processing** is required for most graded assignments and entries in the ESL 230 Portfolio. At the instructor's discretion, students may submit handwritten or word-processed journal entries.
4. **Late work** is not acceptable, except under extenuating circumstances (i.e., illness, personal and family emergencies, and so forth, as defined in the *Student Handbook*).
5. **Mobile phones, pagers, and all electronic devices** must be turned off prior to the start of each class session. Electronic dictionaries may only be used in class at the instructor's discretion.

Assessment and Grading Policies

Your course grade will be calculated according to the following weighted scale:

Reading Journal Entries + Bulletin Board Responses	25%
Reading Exercises	15%
Quizzes	15%
Unit Tests (3)	25%
Literacy Portfolio	20%

1. **Reading Journal + Bulletin Board Entries** will encourage you to practice top-down and bottom-up skills and strategies, draw inferences from texts, and share your interpretations with fellow readers. Journal and Bulletin Board entries may include summaries, paraphrases, commentaries, and brief essays based on assigned and self-selected texts. These assignments will be assessed on the basis of their completeness, critical content, and factual accuracy.
2. **Reading Exercises** will offer practice in developing your academic reading speed and accuracy.
3. **Quizzes** will help assess your factual understanding of content in *Topics for Today* and selections from the *Reading Packet*. Quizzes will also prepare you for the three Unit Tests.
4. **Unit Tests** will cover the thematic units in *Topics for Today* and related outside readings.
5. Your **Literacy Portfolio** will contain a two-page cover letter, three revised Journal Entries or Bulletin Board Responses, two Quizzes, two Unit Tests (including the final Unit Test), and one other entry of your choosing. Directions and options for the Portfolio are explained in the *ESL 230 Portfolio Guidelines*.

Scoring Guide

A = 95–100%	**B+** = 87–90%	**B–** = 80–82%	**C** = 73–76%	**D+** = 67–69%	**D–** = 60–62%
A– = 90–94%	**B** = 83–86%	**C+** = 77–79%	**C–** = 70–72%	**D** = 63–66%	**E** = 0–60%

Course Outline

The course outline (see attached page) lists thematic readings from *Topics for Today* (TT) and selections on the reading process from the *Reading Packet* (RP). Where topics and assignments are listed, please come to class with the relevant work completed. Deadlines for Reading Exercises and Journal/Bulletin Board Entries will be announced in class and on our electronic bulletin board at least a week ahead of time.

ESL 230 Course Outline

Unit	Week	Readings, Tasks, and Assignments
UNIT 1 — *Society: School and Family*	1	• Course Introduction: Review of Literacy Background Questionnaire • Goal-Setting • *TT Chapter 1: Hop, Skip . . . and Software?* • RJ/BB 1
	2	• *TT Chapter 1: Laptop Computers* • *RP Section 1: Reading for Meaning* + Drawing Inferences • Quiz
	3	• *TT Chapter 2: My Husband the Outsider* • *TT Chapter 2: Unwelcome in Chinatown* • RJ/BB 2
	4	• *TT Chapter 3: Beyond Rivalry* • Quiz
	5	• *TT Chapter 3: Middle Children* • Unit 1 Test
UNIT 2 — *Influence on Our Lives: Nature vs. Nurture*	6	• *TT Chapter 4: Who Lives Longer?* • *TT Chapter 4: More Senior Citizens* • RJ/BB 3
	7	• *RP Section 2: Reading for Speed* • *TT Chapter 5: Mindset of Health* • Quiz
	8	• *TT Chapter 5: How to Behave in a Hospital* • *TT Chapter 6: Small Wonders* • RJ/BB 4
	9	• *TT Chapter 6: Reading at 8 Months?* • *RP Section 3: Reading for Details* • Quiz
	10	• Unit 2 Test • *RP Section 4: Note-Taking and Summary Writing* • *Self-Selected Reading*
UNIT 3 — *Technology and Ethical Issues*	11	• *TT Chapter 7: Assisted Suicide* • *TT Chapter 7: Doctors and Terminal Patients* • RJ/BB 5
	12	• *TT Chapter 8: Trading Flesh* • *RP Section 5: Literacy Portfolio Preparation* • Quiz
	13	• *TT Chapter 8: Sales of Kidneys* • *TT Chapter 9: Gift of Life* • Quiz
	14	• *TT Chapter 9: Breath of Life* • Practice Test + Self-Assessment Exercise • RJ/BB 6
	15	• Unit Test 3 • Peer Review: Portfolio Cover Letters
	16	• Final Exam Week—No Class • Submit Literacy Portfolio

TT = Topics for Today; RP = ESL 230 Reading Packet; RJ/BB = Reading Journal or Bulletin Board Entry

Appendix 4.3
Textbook Evaluation Checklist

Textbook Title: _____ Edition: _____ Date: _____

Author: _____ Publisher: _____

RATING SCALE

| NA = Not applicable | 1 = Unsatisfactory | 3 = Good |
| 0 = Totally lacking | 2 = Satisfactory | 4 = Excellent to outstanding |

	Textbook Features and Evaluation Criteria	RATING
Global Features		
1	Authors' record of accomplishment and qualifications to produce a reading textbook for your student population and institution type.	
2	Completeness: How easily can the course be taught using only the student versions and accompanying materials?	
3	Cost-effectiveness: How reasonable is the retail price of the material, given the book's instructional benefits?	
Instructor's Manual and Supplemental Materials		
1	Completeness and explicitness of instructor's manual: Does the manual include a course outline, lesson plans, activities, teaching ideas, assignments, solution keys, and so on?	
2	Flexibility and teachability: Does the manual offer guidance on how to present varied lessons tailored to your educational setting?	
3	Feedback and evaluation tools: Does the manual offer guidance on assessing students' performance and progress as L2 readers?	
4	Usefulness and appropriateness of supplemental materials (e.g., workbook, software, interactive Web support, and so on).	
5	Professional quality, appropriateness, and user-friendliness of student supplements (workbook, software, Website, and so on).	
6	Fit between textbook and supplements: Are the workbook, software, and other resources easy to use alongside the core textbook?	
Goals, Objectives, and Approach		
1	Audience appropriateness: Does the book reflect a good match with your students' cultural backgrounds, educational experiences, L1 literacy, and L2 literacy needs?	
2	Match between textbook and your instructional approach: How well does the book's design and content reflect your theory of reading, teaching practice, and style?	
3	Match between textbook and institutional expectations: Does the textbook accommodate the learning and teaching objectives of your program, department, or institution?	
Content		
1	Appropriateness and potential appeal: Does the book's subject matter include topics, issues, texts, tasks, and processes that will appeal to the interests and needs of your students?	
2	Motivational potential: Do the book's subject matter and apparatus promise to engage and challenge your students, motivating them to develop their literacy skills?	
3	Authenticity: Does the material feature texts and genres that accurately reflect the text sources that students will need to read, comprehend, and reproduce?	
4	Variety: Does the book offer a rich assortment of genres and texts (e.g., academic texts, literary samples, and so forth) to expose students to diverse reading challenges?	
5	Flexibility and potential for adaptation: Is the material varied and flexible enough for you to customize your selection of texts and tasks to student and institutional needs?	
6	Editorial quality and accuracy: Are the texts and apparatus well written, pedagogically sound, stylistically appropriate, and factually accurate?	

Design and Organization		
1	Feasibility: Can the quantity and type of material in the book be covered in the time frame specified in your syllabus?	
2	Sequencing and progression: Do chapters or units present themes, genres, skills, strategies, and tasks clearly and coherently?	
3	Grading: Are texts and tasks graded to accommodate students' L2 proficiency, literacy levels, and content knowledge while promoting development of their reading and vocabulary skills?	
4	Schema-building, review, and recycling: Do the book's content and tasks facilitate development of new knowledge while improving students' existing skills and strategies?	
5	Skills integration and recursion: Is reading practice interwoven with related literacy functions (e.g., writing) so that reading skills and strategies are embedded in purposeful tasks?	
6	Flexibility: How easily can you sequence units, chapters, reading selections, and tasks to fit your syllabus and your students' diverse learning styles and changing needs?	
7	Currency: How recent is the material? Does the book reflect current reading theory and instructional practice?	
Apparatus (explanations, tasks, assignments, exercises, directions, glossaries, indices, etc.)		
1	Potential for engagement and participation: Do tasks and exercises lead to internalization of reading skills and strategies, subject matter, genre knowledge, and vocabulary by encouraging students to participate in reading, discussion, and production tasks?	
2	Promotion of critical thinking: Do pre-, while-, and post-reading tasks encourage students to interpret, apply, analyze, synthesize, and evaluate texts?	
3	Promotion of independent skills: Do tasks enable students to develop autonomous reading skills, strategies, and tactics?	
4	Clarity of presentation: Are the instructions accompanying tasks, exercises, and assignments comprehensible and explicit?	
5	Feedback tools: Does the book offer an effective means of providing feedback on students' skill development and progress?	
Layout and Physical Attributes		
1	Useful front and back matter: Are the table of contents, glossaries, indices, references, and solution keys well located, clearly organized, and easy to use?	
2	Layout and visual appeal: Are text and white space balanced to promote readability? Are margins wide enough to facilitate easy reading and note-taking? Are figures, tables, and illustrations appropriately sized, clearly reproduced, and suitably positioned?	
3	Textual attributes and enhancements: Are the font and font pitch readable and appealing? Does the book include highlighting or boldface type to signal key lexical items?	
4	Physical features: Do your students prefer traditional or spiral binding? Are the format and dimension of the book appropriate for the book's intended uses? Are the paper and binding durable?	

Cumulative Value: Maximum = 136*

Overall quality, suitability, and potential effectiveness: In view of student needs, learning objectives, curricular goals, time constraints, and your theory of reading, to what extent is the book (and its supplemental material) pedagogically sound, appropriate, and cost-effective?

* To calculate a cumulative value, simply sum the ratings for each of the 34 categories. To calculate a percentage value, divide the sum by the maximum score of 136. Use either the raw score or percentage to compare the relative quality of multiple textbooks. Each item can be weighted to reflect specific priorities. Like other tools in this book, this evaluation guide is designed to be adapted, abbreviated, or expanded to suit users' needs.

Sources: Brown (2001); Ferris and Hedgcock (2005); Graves (2000).

Chapter 5
Designing an Intensive Reading Lesson

Questions for Reflection

- When you are about to read a text, what do you do *before* you actually begin to read? Consider different genres encountered in your daily life (e.g., textbook chapters, academic journal articles, newspapers, magazines, novels, Web sources, and so on). Does your approach to reading vary by genre?
- While you are *reading* a text (consider the same range of options as in the previous question), what strategies do you use? How does your approach differ depending on the type of text being considered?
- *After* reading a text, what do you do to ensure your comprehension of the text, to assess what you have read critically, or to connect your reading to other activities (e.g., writing, speaking, research or other practical applications)?

Background: Intensive Reading

Reading courses, as well as language and literacy courses that feature reading as a major component, may utilize *intensive* or *extensive* approaches or a combination of the two. Although we would advocate that, as time and resources permit, most teachers and courses should combine approaches, in this chapter and the next we take up intensive and extensive approaches separately so that the research and practical underpinnings of each can be discussed and considered thoroughly.

An early definition of intensive reading states that its purpose is "to take a text, study it line by line, referring at every moment to our dictionary and our grammar, comparing, analyzing, translating, and retaining every expression that it contains" (Palmer, 1921/1964, cited in Day & Bamford, 1998, p. 5). Nonetheless, most classroom instructors would define intensive reading more broadly, as did Aebersold and Field (1997): "Each text is read carefully and thoroughly for maximum comprehension. Teachers provide direction and help before, sometimes during, and after reading. Students do many exercises that require them to work in depth with various selected aspects of the text" (p. 45).

Characteristics and benefits of intensive reading include the following:

- The texts to be studied are selected by the teacher (perhaps with input from students).
- All students read the same text at the same time and complete in-class or out-of-class exercises and assessments designed or assigned by the teacher.
- The teacher highlights specific linguistic features and content dimensions of the text, introducing and reinforcing selected reading strategies through whole-class instruction and activities.
- Assessment of student comprehension, reading development, and reading efficiency is facilitated by the fact that all students work simultaneously with the same text and activities.

It is worth noting that intensive reading is by far the predominant approach to L2 reading instruction. The vast majority of L2 reading textbooks, as well as books for teachers on how to teach reading, adopt an intensive approach and only occasionally mention extensive, self-selected reading, perhaps as an optional supplement to the reading syllabus (Aebersold & Field, 1997; Anderson, 1999; Dubin et al., 1986; Grabe & Stoller, 2002; Urquhart & Weir, 1998; for a notable exception, see Day, 1993).

To frame the discussion of intensive reading that follows, we make the following assumptions:

1. Intensive reading lessons should in most instances be based on entire texts, not just excerpts (e.g., a newspaper or journal article, a chapter from a textbook or novel, rather than just a few paragraphs).

2. The overall purpose of an intensive reading lesson is only secondarily the comprehension of text content—the overriding goal is to build students' skills and strategies for reading authentic texts beyond the reading classroom.

3. Texts for intensive reading lessons have already been carefully selected by the teacher (either from a textbook or other source) using text selection considerations discussed in Chapters 3 and 4. (Robb, 2001; Shih, 1992)

Stages of Intensive Reading

Although various authors may use slightly different terms, most teachers find it helpful to conceptualize an intensive reading lesson (which may be conducted over a period of days rather than in just one class meeting) in terms of what teacher and students should do *before, during,* and *after* reading (see Aebersold & Field, 1997, Chapter 4–6, and California State University Expository Reading and Writing Task Force, 2008). We will outline goals and strategies for each stage, but it is important to emphasize at the outset that these terms should not be conceptualized as rigid boundaries. Rather, these terms provide an organizational framework for discussing the types of activities that an intensive reading lesson might include. For instance, for a particular text or lesson, an activity labeled as a "during reading" exercise might be more appropriate before or after reading. The reading process and reading lessons are perhaps better characterized as a "tapestry" of interwoven threads than as a taxonomy of skills, strategies, and activities (e.g., Anderson, 1999; Hirvela, 2004; Scarcella & Oxford, 1992; Shrum & Glisan, 2005).

That caveat aside, we will adopt the framework utilized by the California State University Expository Reading and Writing Task Force (2008; see also Ching, 2007) to outline crucial academic reading skills and strategies for intensive reading. Figure 5.1 provides a condensed version of this framework. As we discuss the three stages of intensive reading, their goals, and activity types, we will provide illustrations based on two real-world texts, both reprinted for readers' reference in Appendix 5.1. The first is a short essay, originally printed in the *New York Times,* entitled "The Rewards of Living a Solitary Life" by essayist, poet, and novelist May Sarton (1974). The second is a *New York Times* article (Greenhouse, 2003) entitled "Going for the Look, but Risking Discrimination," which examines the practice of businesses, such as the American retailer Abercrombie and Fitch, hiring sales associates based on a certain "look" (their physical attributes).[1]

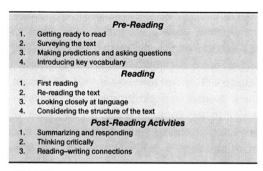

FIGURE 5.1. Intensive Reading Framework.
Adapted from California State University Expository
Reading and Writing Task Force, 2008.

Before Reading

Pre-reading activities are a crucial and often-neglected step in the reading process. Preparing students to read can build their interest, confidence, and motivation for reading the text and can facilitate comprehension when the text is later closely read. Not only do pre-reading exercises help students enjoy and better cope with the task at hand (i.e., reading an assigned selection), but they also provide an excellent opportunity for the teacher to introduce reading strategies that can be extremely helpful for various types of reading students may do in the future. Most pre-reading activities can be accomplished in a relatively small amount of class time (or for homework prior to class), yet they truly provide a large return on the time and effort invested.

1. *Getting Ready to Read.* At least three distinct activity types can be included in this category; the relative proportion of each depends on the text under consideration. The three activity types are *schema activation, schema development* (see Chapters 1 and 2), and *establishing purpose for reading.* Here we will address methods for using schemata to design an intensive reading lesson.

At the *schema activation* point of the pre-reading stage, teachers should ask themselves, "What do students **already know** about the *content, structure,* and *language* of this particular text?" To turn to our illustrative texts, Sarton's (1974) "Rewards of Living a Solitary Life," as one might guess, opines on the virtues and benefits of living alone rather than constantly being around others. To activate students' content schemata prior to reading this selection, the teacher might ask them to freewrite briefly on the question, "Do you enjoy being alone?" or to take a brief Myers-Briggs survey (e.g., Myers & McCaulley, 1985) focusing on the Introversion and Extroversion type indicators. These exercises could be followed by a discussion of introversion and extroversion and how students' preferences might affect their answer to the question about being alone (as well as how they will later react when they read Sarton's essay). Regarding the structure of the text (a personal essay), students could discuss whether they have read other texts in this genre in school or during pleasure reading. A comparative discussion could focus on how the personal essay genre might differ from a news article or a traditional academic essay. As for students' knowledge about the language of the text, the teacher could highlight two key words from the title, *rewards* and *solitary*, soliciting definitions and associations. Students may respond that, whereas *rewards* are positive and pleasurable—something to be achieved and hoped for—*solitary* typically connotes either a punishment (e.g., solitary confinement) or a similarly depressing state of affairs. The discussion of the usual referential and social meanings of the two key words juxtaposed in the title may help them to predict that Sarton is about to make an argument that is surprising or at least somewhat out of the ordinary.

To activate schemata prior to reading "Going for the Look," the teacher could bring in print or video advertisements for retailers in which models illustrate a particular "look" that typifies the merchant. Students can be asked if they can identify characteristics of "the look" from the ads and also be asked to write on the question "Is it fair for companies to only hire people who project their image?" (suggestions adapted from Ching, 2008).

Schema activation exercises can be simplified for students at lower levels of language proficiency (e.g., by showing a picture and asking, "What is the man doing?"), but they fundamentally accomplish the same purpose: To help the teacher and students identify and reflect on what is *already known* about the text—topic, theme(s), key terms and phrases, rhetorical structure, and so forth. In contrast, *schema development* activities recognize that aspects of an assigned text will be new to students. Carrell and Eisterhold (1983) observed that a failure to activate relevant schematic knowledge may result from "the fact that the reader does not possess the appropriate schema anticipated by the author and thus fails to comprehend ... The point is that the appropriate schemata *must exist* and must be activated during text processing" (p. 560, emphasis added). As argued in previous chapters, the fact that a text's content, structure, or language might be unfamiliar is not by itself an argument against utilizing that text in a lesson sequence. Rather, it suggests that the teacher should supply background knowledge that may be lacking so that students can grapple with the text. Such schemata gaps are especially likely with a diverse group of L2 readers (see Chapter 2).

Schema development activities may include background information about: the author (if relevant and available); when and where the text was written; cultural and historical information referenced in the text; and technical or specialized information. For example, it may be interesting for students to learn something about the life of May Sarton; on the other hand, it might not be important for them to know much about the *New York Times* reporter who wrote "Going for the Look." As for cultural and historical information, the fact that Sarton's work mostly emerged in the first half of the twentieth century before the women's movement provides valuable context. That Sarton was a prolific writer in several genres and taught at several prestigious U.S. universities might establish her credibility as an author. Similarly, it may be useful for students to know that the *New York Times* is a highly respected newspaper, trusted by many as a source of information.

For students to comprehend and critically analyze the information and arguments presented in "Going for the Look," it could be helpful to understand that hiring people based on their looks has been standard practice for decades in various industries (e.g., flight attendants), but that federal anti-discrimination laws lead to disagreement and tension about "fairness" versus a company's right to do whatever it takes to be successful. Background information about authors and cultural, historical, technical, or specialized matters can either be provided by the teacher in a mini-lecture or handout; alternatively, students can be instructed to investigate specific questions themselves on the Internet.

In addition to schema activation and schema development, another important component of "preparing to read" is *establishing a purpose for reading*. Students in an academic setting, L2 readers in particular, are often overwhelmed by the volume and complexity of assigned readings. This is especially stressful for students educated in settings where memorization, rehearsal, and recitation are normative learning and assessment practices (Aebersold & Field, 1997; Atkinson, 1997; Bosher & Rowecamp, 1998). Learners may feel that they must understand every word of every text and retrieve detailed information on demand. It is very helpful for them to become aware that different reading situations involve varying demands and expectations (even within the same class) and that their reading strategies can and should be adjusted accordingly.

For example, in our own teacher preparation courses, we may ask students to read hundreds of pages of textbooks and journal articles as background for in-class discussion and lecture. We may ask them to dissect the details and findings of a research study. We may ask them to formulate a critical position relative to the opinions of an author. For the first type of reading, we may only expect students to demonstrate a general understanding of the material through appropriate citations in written assignments or projects and through contributions to class discussion. When that is the established purpose for assigned readings, students can read quickly for global comprehension, perhaps noting a few key quotations as they go along. Such passages can be utilized later in written projects, but readers do not have to absorb, annotate, or memorize every detail of every chapter, as they will never be required to retrieve that information from memory. In contrast, if they must critique an individual research study, they must learn to read it closely and carefully, looking for specific features such as the abstract, the research design, method, findings, and conclusion.

In an intensive reading lesson, the purpose for reading is largely established by the teacher, whose purposes for assigning a particular text will vary. Students may read a text as a springboard for a writing assignment. The teacher may have chosen the text for its content, for its rhetorical structure, for the language to which it will expose students, or for the reading strategies it will lend itself to practicing (or some combination of these factors). The teacher's purpose for assigning a text will likely be realized through the types of during- and post-reading activities the students will complete, whether it is a vocabulary quiz, a summary, an essay, or something more elaborate. To help students understand purposes for reading, the teacher should: (1) articulate several objectives for intensive reading lessons (see Chapter 4); (2) explain objectives and expectations to students prior to reading; and (3) talk with students about the reading strategies most appropriate for achieving these aims (e.g., noticing new vocabulary, scanning for details, skimming for main ideas to use in a summary, and so on).

Examples of purposes for reading for our two illustrative texts include several possibilities. For Sarton's essay, students might write a journal entry summarizing Sarton's views and their reactions, later developing an essay discussing how Sarton's experience is or is not comparable to their own. Although Sarton's brief essay contains some difficult vocabulary, study of that vocabulary is not a major purpose of the lesson sequence; students can focus more generally on the message Sarton is attempting to convey. In "Going for the Look," purposes for reading could include: close examination of the ideas, language, discourse structure, and argumentation; group discussion of the issues raised in the text; an in-class writing assignment in which students analyze a specific quotation; and an out-of-class text-based persuasive essay.

2. Surveying the Text. Previewing a text prior to reading it thoroughly and carefully is a valuable step for any reader but arguably indispensable for inexperienced novice readers for whom academic text comprehension is a challenge. Successful readers employ a variety of *previewing* strategies to survey a text (often unconsciously): Most L2 readers benefit from explicit strategy instruction and practice, as well as discussion of how they can utilize these strategies in other settings (see Chapters 1 and 4). *Surveying* a text involves looking over it prior to reading it in methodical, strategic ways to get a sense of the text's features, including length, sections and divisions (and, if applicable, titles and subheadings), main ideas (thesis, topic sentences, summaries), and any extratextual information that might aid comprehension, such as pictures, graphs, glosses of key or difficult vocabulary, and sidebars or text boxes.

L1 and L2 reading studies and reviews consistently indicate that comprehension is enhanced by gaining an overview of a text prior to reading it (Aebersold & Field, 1997; Chen & Graves, 1995; Dole, Valencia, Gree, & Wardrop, 1991; Eskey & Grabe, 1988; Grabe, 1997; Grabe & Stoller, 2001; Hudson, 2007; Urquhart & Weir, 1998). Eskey and Grabe (1988) argued that, for the L2 reader, "who is often . . . an insecure reader, pre-reading strategies . . . are even more important than they are for the native reader" (p. 229). Aebersold and Field (1997) further pointed out that *previewing* "enables students to establish their own expectations about what information they will find in the text and the way that information will be organized" (p. 73). Chen and Graves (1995) found that, whereas activating background knowledge and previewing a text aided L2 readers' comprehension, the latter was more significant than the former.

Genre can determine the types of previewing activities will be appropriate for a given text. For example, when reading an assigned textbook for a course, it is helpful for students to know that many textbooks include a preview of the chapter's main points or a summary of chapter highlights at the end, much as we have done in the present volume. Learners should also be encouraged to read the author's preface or introduction, even if their instructor does not assign it, as these selections present an overview of the author's goals for the entire text. If students read a research study from an academic journal in the social sciences, they can be taught to look for specific elements such as the abstract, the conclusion, the research questions, and details about methodology. For a novel, they might look at the back cover or the dust jacket for a synopsis of the plot.

Generally speaking, surveying a text involves getting a quick sense of the text's main ideas and macrostructure. Figure 5.2 and Appendix 5.2 present suggestions and activities for helping students engage in productive survey work. For example, Sarton's essay is found in the first two editions of Ruth Spack's (1998) text, *Guidelines*; the selection also includes a photo of Sarton and one of her poems. The teacher might instruct students to look at the title, the photo, the poem, and the first two paragraphs of the essay and then to compose a one-sentence paraphrase of the title ("The Rewards of Living a Solitary Life"). For the article "Going for the Look, but Risking Discrimination," students again might

---

Features to Consider
(as applicable to specific texts and genres)

☐ Title
☐ Information about the author and source of text
☐ Subtitles or subheadings
☐ Photographs, drawings
☐ Graphs, charts, tables
☐ Contrasts in typography (font pitch, boldface and italic type, and so on)

Types of Activities

1. *Examine* the title: identify and define key words; paraphrase title.
2. *Read* the introduction.
3. *Read* the conclusion.
4. *Sample* the first sentence of each body paragraph to get an overview of its information.
5. *Skim* the entire text for overall meaning.
6. *Scan* the text for specific details that could assist overall comprehension.
7. *Outline* the macrostructure of the text (e.g., introduction, body, and conclusion, major divisions within the body).

FIGURE 5.2. Suggestions for Text Surveying.
Sources: Aebersold and Field (1997); Barnett (1989); Day (1993); Grabe and Stoller (2002); Grellet (1981); Jensen (1986; see Appendix 5.3 for sample activities).

examine key words in the title; as it is a longer piece, learners might then read the first five paragraphs and the final paragraph to get a sense of what the article is about (Ching, 2008).

3. Making Predictions and Asking Questions. One of the most well-known and time-honored acronyms in reading instruction is "SQ3R," which stands for *Survey, Question, Read, Recite, Review* (Robinson, 1941; Yorkey, 1982). A number of other overlapping models and acronyms are available (Carrell, 1988a), but the SQ3R process captures the connection between *surveying,* or *previewing,* which are somewhat passive activities, and *questioning* or *predicting,* which are active. At this stage of the pre-reading experience, students take information gathered from schema development and previewing activities and formulate predictions or questions about what they are preparing to read. To the degree that their predictions are later confirmed, such activities can build student confidence both in their own comprehension abilities and in the previewing strategies they have been taught. However, when predictions are contradicted or questions prove to be off-target, the mismatches teach learners that careful reading, not just quick assumptions or guessing, is critical.

Making predictions and asking questions about a text one has not yet read is a relatively more abstract and difficult step than examining actual text and other information on the page. Consequently, learners may first need guidance in how to formulate predictions and then how to turn those predictions into questions. For instance, after previewing Sarton's essay, students might write a sentence predicting what the essay will be about, perhaps using sentence frames such as "I think this essay will be about . . ." and then "Clues that helped me guess this are . . ." Students can then formulate one or two questions that they expect the text to answer (e.g., "Why does Sarton think being alone is so great?"). Several prediction and questioning activities based on the article "Going for the Look" are shown in Figure 5.3. Another technique is to present students with only the opening paragraphs of the text, asking them to predict what will come next and to turn those predictions into questions. An important follow-up once students get to the reading stage is to ask them to revisit their predictions and questions to see what they have discovered. For instance, if students make predictions based on Sarton's transparent title, they are likely to be accurate. However, if they guessed that the title of an essay called "The 'F Word' " (Dumas, 2006) meant that the text was about profanity, they would find on later reading that they were incorrect and that the title was in fact intended to be misleading and even provocative.

4. Introducing Key Vocabulary. A final component of the pre-reading stage is the *introduction of specific lexical items* that might disrupt comprehension as students read the text. There is some debate as to whether pre-teaching vocabulary prior to reading is beneficial or harmful (see Chapter 8). Some would argue that prematurely calling students' attention to certain words distracts them from reading for global meaning; others maintain that, if particular words or phrases in the text are critical to its meaning, unlikely to be part of the students' prior

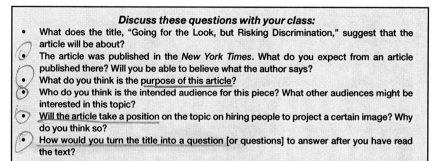

Discuss these questions with your class:
- What does the title, "Going for the Look, but Risking Discrimination," suggest that the article will be about?
- The article was published in the *New York Times*. What do you expect from an article published there? Will you be able to believe what the author says?
- What do you think is the purpose of this article?
- Who do you think is the intended audience for this piece? What other audiences might be interested in this topic?
- Will the article take a position on the topic on hiring people to project a certain image? Why do you think so?
- How would you turn the title into a question [or questions] to answer after you have read the text?

FIGURE 5.3. Prediction/Questioning Activities Based on "Going for the Look."
Text source: Greenhouse (2003); tasks adapted from Ching (2008).

knowledge, and not transparent enough to be guessed at in context, teachers should provide information about those lexical items (Anderson, 1999). As Aebersold and Field (1997) pointed out, "although topic-specific vocabulary is quite useful for short-term comprehension, it may not be frequent enough in the overall L2/FL to be emphasized for students to learn. That is, students need to *recognize* it but may not need to *learn* it" (p. 139, emphases added).

These text-specific items may include culture-specific names, places, or events, as well as slang or jargon. Text-specific lexical items can also include academic or specialized term likely to be unfamiliar to most or all students (Nation, 2001). Such items can be identified by the teacher, by students in a previous class, or by using a corpus-based tool such as Vocabulary Profiler (see Chapter 3). As a brief example, Figure 5.4 shows a Vocabulary Profiler analysis of the first two paragraphs of Sarton's (1974) essay. Several items that could be worth previewing for students emerge from this analysis: *gregarious*, an adjective important to understanding the opening anecdote and occurring in a context that is only minimally helpful; the *Whitney*, the name of a museum in New York (but not as commonly known as, say, the Metropolitan Museum of Art); *solitary bliss*, which to some students would seem to be an oxymoron; and idioms and fixed collocations such as *taken the plunge* and *brink of adventure*.

Several principles for working with vocabulary at the pre-reading stage may be helpful. Aebersold and Field (1997) noted that "the **introduction of a word** and the **learning of a word** are different matters and require different strategies in the classroom" (p. 139). First, teachers should only preview vocabulary that is necessary for overall text comprehension on students' first reading. Other lexical items can be analyzed at later stages of the intensive reading process, along with vocabulary learning strategies (see Chapter 8). Second, as already noted, the best candidates for pre-reading vocabulary work are idiomatic expressions or terms, names or places that could not easily be found in a dictionary (Nation, 2001). A simple principle articulated by Anderson (1999) is that if a teacher thinks she should pre-teach certain vocabulary, she probably should. Third, teachers might consider a separate vocabulary list or glosses provided with the

> The other day an **acquaintance** of mine, a **gregarious** and charming man, told me he had found himself **unexpectedly** alone in New York for an hour or two between appointments. He went to the **Whitney** and spent the "empty" time looking at things in **solitary bliss**. For him it proved to be a shock nearly as great as falling in love to discover that he could enjoy himself so much alone.
>
> What had he been afraid of, I asked myself? That, suddenly alone, he would discover that he **bored** himself, or that there was, quite simply, no self there to meet? But having taken the **plunge**, he is now on the **brink** of adventure; he is about to be **launched** into his own inner space, space as **immense**, **unexplored**, and sometimes frightening as outer space to the **astronaut**. His every *perception* will come to him with a new freshness and, for a time, seem **startlingly** original. For anyone who can see things for himself with a **naked** eye becomes, for a moment or two, something of a **genius**. With another human being present *vision* becomes double *vision, inevitably*. We are busy wondering, what does my companion see or think of this, and what do I think of it? The original *impact* gets lost, or **diffused**.
>
> Note: Words in **bold** were "Off-list" words in the Vocabulary Profiler analysis; Words in *italics* were from the Academic Word List. Source: www.lextutor.ca.

FIGURE 5.4. Vocabulary Profiler Analysis of Sarton's (1974) Essay (first two paragraphs).

text (in the margins or at the beginning or end of the text) rather than a lesson or discussion of the vocabulary. In this way, the information is readily accessible if students stumble over a word or phrase while reading but are reading chiefly for meaning.

If the teacher elects to introduce key vocabulary, this process can be accomplished in several fairly straightforward ways:

- The teacher can provide students with a handout explaining key items or make a brief presentation as part of the "schema development" stage.
- The teacher can elicit meanings or guesses from students.
- The teacher can provide students with the terms and phrases and send them to online dictionaries (if available) to investigate their meanings.
- Students can self-assess their prior knowledge of the key or difficult items using a chart.

It has also been suggested that new vocabulary should be presented in its immediate discursive context, rather than in isolation (Aebersold & Field, 1997;

Jensen, 1986; Nation, 2001). Further vocabulary activities (some of which could be adapted for the pre-reading stage) are discussed later in this chapter, in Chapter 3, and extensively in Chapter 8.

Pre-reading: Summary. As noted earlier, teachers and students often overlook the pre-reading phase. For intensive reading, however, it is critical: Pre-reading can affect not only students' comprehension when they read but also their attitudes and confidence as they approach careful, analytic reading. Newer teachers may wonder how many of the goals and activities discussed in this section are necessary and practical for a given lesson. Clearly, we do not want to spend several weeks on pre-reading, fall into repetitive, mechanical patterns in our lesson design, or tax students' patience. Nonetheless, a judicious combination of pre-reading tasks is vital to the success of an intensive reading lesson. Decisions about these tasks depend on our knowledge of the target text, learners' background knowledge, the time available in and out of class to cover the selection, and the overall goals of the intensive reading lesson sequence.

During Reading

Although reading textbooks and teachers have for decades included post-reading comprehension, discussion, and writing activities as key instructional components, it is only over the past two decades or so that reading specialists have focused more intentionally on what students do (or should do) *during* reading. At least three strands of theory and practice intersect in this consideration of *while-reading* instruction. The first is the increased emphasis over the past 20 years on *interactive* approaches to L2 reading, as we discussed at length in Chapter 1. As teachers have become more aware of the need to assist students with bottom-up, text-based reading strategies (Birch, 2007; Eskey, 1986, 2005), activities focused on text processing have revolved around the reading and post-reading stages, while top-down strategies tend to receive more attention at the pre-reading stage.[2] Second, as secondary and postsecondary institutions have identified and acted on the need to teach study skills, the intentional development of during-reading strategies such as highlighting, annotating, questioning, and reacting has become more common. In ESL/EFL instruction, these procedures are often addressed in the context of English for Specific or Academic Purposes. Finally, attention to *strategic* learning in general and reading strategies in particular among second language professionals has led to the identification of strategies commonly utilized by successful readers and development of materials and techniques for teaching these skills to L2 readers (e.g., Aebersold & Field, 1997; Alderson, 2000; Anderson, 1999; Cohen, 1998; Folse, 2004; Grabe, 2004; Grabe & Stoller, 2001, 2002; Janzen, 1996; Koda, 2004; Oxford, 1990; Shih, 1992; Urquhart & Weir, 1998). The following discussion, again structured by the California State University Task Force Template shown in Figure 5.1, suggests possible instructional activities for an intensive reading lesson (in contrast to what readers "naturally" do while reading—see Chapter 1).

1. First Reading. It could be argued that a *first reading* is part of the pre-reading stage, but we discuss it here to distinguish clearly between the stages of *preparing to read* the text and *actually reading* it. By *first reading*, we refer to a quick read-through of the entire text to develop a sense of its main point(s) and to confirm initial predictions made during pre-reading. Some textbooks suggest that a first reading could be accomplished as a timed reading (Smalzer, 2005). Setting time limits not only works toward the important goal of helping students to read faster (Dubin et al., 1986), but also emphasizes that students need to develop a quick overview of main ideas, not to analyze every sentence in the text or to engage in word attack activities. An alternative approach for the first reading is for the teacher to read the text aloud while students follow along (this technique is more appropriate for brief texts up to about 1,200 words). A well-prepared read-aloud by the teacher appeals to multiple learning styles and modes of processing, allows certain aspects of the texts to be emphasized and "come alive" in ways not possible during a silent reading—and, not unimportantly, it helps the teacher control the amount of class time devoted to the first reading (Brisk & Harrington, 2007; Gambrell et al., 2007; Smith & Elley, 1997). Another option is to ask students to read the text aloud in pairs or small groups.[3] Whether the text is read aloud or students read it silently, the first reading can be followed up with a main idea question (such as the "skimming" questions posed in Appendix 5.2 for Sarton's and Greenhouse's texts). Learners can likewise be asked to revisit their own predictions to see if they were accurate.

2. Re-reading the Text. Having completed pre-reading activities and given the text a quick first reading, students are now ready to read the text intensively through a careful and focused second reading. In line with Grabe's (2004) instructional principles (see Chapter 1), two goals for teacher and students guide the reading process at this point: (1) monitor and ensure student comprehension; and (2) teach and practice effective reading strategies. Taken together, these goals encapsulate the notion of intensive reading.

Facilitating comprehension. Teachers are often more expert at ensuring student comprehension during pre-reading (e.g., through schema development and pre-viewing) and during post-reading (e.g., through comprehension questions) than at guiding the during-reading process. Yet it is during the reading stage that comprehension is most likely to break down, creating frustration and confusion. During-reading activities are especially important if the target text is lengthy, if the content and language are unfamiliar, or if the genre is inherently challenging (Aebersold & Field, 1997; Dubin & Bycina, 1991; Keshavarz et al., 2007).

Several useful strategies can help students at this stage of the process. One strategy is for the teacher to divide the text into sections, enabling students to stop at the end of each section to check comprehension and make predictions about what will come next before moving ahead with their reading (Dubin & Bycina, 1991). In our two sample texts, Sarton's essay could be stopped after the second paragraph, while Greenhouse's "Going for the Look" article could break after the fifth or sixth paragraph. Students can then identify key words, state main ideas, make predictions, or answer specific questions about the target passage, comparing notes with their classmates and instructor before moving on (Grabe & Stoller, 2001, 2002).

In addition to, or instead of, breaking the text into sections (which may not always be necessary if the text is not especially long or complex), students can be given a set of guiding questions to respond to as they are reading. These questions can be completed in class or at home. This technique, called a *guide-o-rama* by Dubin and Bycina (1991), differs from a set of post-reading comprehension questions in that students are specifically asked to work through the questions as they move through the text, rather than after they have finished reading it. See Figure 5.5 for a simple example based on Sarton's essay. Although the questions in this example are interspersed within portions of the text, they could also be provided on a separate handout or overhead slide if that is more convenient.

Another excellent comprehension aid is the *graphic organizer,* a tool used widely by L1 and L2 teachers at all levels of literacy instruction (Dubin & Bycina, 1991; Grabe & Stoller, 2002; Jiang & Grabe, 2007). Although Grabe and Stoller (2002) describe graphic organizers as primarily a way for students to discern text structure, they are also useful in guiding students to pull out key facts and relationships and to record them in a visual format different from (and more easily understandable than) the information contained in potentially dense and lengthy paragraphs. A graphic format may help some visual nonverbal learners to grasp key ideas and connections that they might otherwise miss (see Chapter 2). For all students, graphic organizers facilitate review processes and provide easy reference to key textual components (Kajder, 2006; Shrum & Glisan, 2005).

Graphic organizers can vary widely in form, and the organization and genre of a text can determine which type of organizer is most appropriate. For example, Dubin and Bycina (1991) presented an elaborate flow chart showing how ideas relate to one another. However, for most texts, a simple chart with teacher-provided headings is adequate (and, we might add, within the technological grasp of most instructors to create!). Figure 5.6 shows two sample graphic organizers based on "Going for the Look" (see Chapter 7 for ideas on utilizing graphic organizers with literary texts). In the first, students are directed to particular sections of the text to identify key arguments for and against looks-based hiring. As presenting the two sides of this issue is the main point of the article, this is a critical step both for comprehension and for analysis in the post-reading phase. However, the text presents a lot of information (i.e., names, facts, quotations, and so on); thus, the specific arguments and counterarguments could be overlooked without an exercise that methodically focuses students on them. In the second activity, students chart the quotations. The article contains many quotations from different sources and viewpoints—so many, in fact, that they could distract readers unfamiliar with journalistic style. Understanding the sources and meanings of the quotations is again important for future critical analysis as well as immediate comprehension of the text.

Whatever techniques are chosen to facilitate student comprehension while

1 The other day an acquaintance of mine, a gregarious and charming man, told me he had found himself unexpectedly alone in New York for an hour or two between appointments. He went to the Whitney and spent the "empty" time looking at things in solitary bliss. For him it proved to be a shock nearly as great as falling in love to discover that he could enjoy himself so much alone.

> In ¶ 1, Sarton tells a story about a man she knows. What did her friend discover? Was this discovery a surprise to him? How do you know?

2 What had he been afraid of, I asked myself? That, suddenly alone, he would discover that he bored himself, or that there was, quite simply, no self there to meet? But having taken the plunge, he is now on the brink of adventure; he is about to be launched into his own inner space, space as immense, unexplored, and sometimes frightening as outer space to the astronaut. His every perception will come to him with a new freshness and, for a time, seem startlingly original. For anyone who can see things for himself with a naked eye becomes, for a moment or two, something of a genius. With another human being present vision becomes double vision, inevitably. We are busy wondering, what does my companion see or think of this, and what do I think of it? The original impact gets lost, or diffused.
3 "Music I heard with you was more than music."* Exactly. And therefore music *itself* can only be heard alone. Solitude is the salt of personhood. It brings out the authentic flavor of every experience.

> In ¶s 2–3, Sarton argues that there is a difference between experiencing things with other people and experiencing them alone. What is the difference? Does she think one type of experience is better than the other? What do you think?

4 "Alone one is never lonely: the spirit adventures, walking/In a quiet garden, in a cool house, abiding single there."
5 Loneliness is most acutely felt with other people, for with others, even with a lover sometimes, we suffer from our differences of taste, temperament, mood. Human intercourse often demands that we soften the edge of perception, or withdraw at the very instant of personal truth for fear of hurting, or of being inappropriately present, which is to say naked, in a social situation. Alone we can afford to be wholly whatever we are, and to feel whatever we feel absolutely. That is a great luxury!

> In ¶s 4–5, Sarton contrasts being "alone" and "lonely." What is the difference?

6 For me the most interesting thing about a solitary life, and mine has been that for the last twenty years, is that it becomes increasingly rewarding. When I wake up and watch the sun rise over the ocean, as I do most days, and know that I have an entire day ahead, uninterrupted, in which to write a few pages, take a walk with my dog, lie down in the afternoon for a long think (why does one think better in a horizontal position?), read and listen to music, I am flooded with happiness.
7 I am lonely only when I am overtired, when I have worked too long without a break, when for the time being I feel empty and need filling up. And I am lonely sometimes when I come back home after a lecture trip, when I have seen a lot of people and talked a lot, and am full to the brim with experience that needs to be sorted out.
8 Then for a little while the house feels huge and empty, and I wonder where my self is hiding. It has to be recaptured slowly by watering the plants, perhaps, and looking again at each one as though it were a person, by feeding the two cats, by cooking a meal.
9 It takes a while, as I watch the surf blowing up in fountains at the end of the field, but the moment comes when the world falls away, and the self emerges again from the deep unconscious, bringing back all I have recently experienced to be explored and slowly understood, when I converse again with my hidden powers, and so grow, and so be renewed, till death do us part.

> When does Sarton herself feel "lonely"? How does being "alone" make her feel? What does the final clause "till death do us part" mean? When is that clause typically used? What do you think it refers to in ¶ 9?

FIGURE 5.5. Sample "Guide-o-Rama" for During-Reading Comprehension.

A: Identifying Key Arguments

Section	Arguments for Looks-Based Hiring	Arguments Against Looks-Based Hiring
¶s 1–5	If clerks are good-looking, they will attract customers	None given in this section.
¶s 8–9		
¶ 13		
¶s 14–17		

B: Analyzing quotations

Quotation	Who said it?	What was the point of the Quotation?
"If someone came in with a pretty face, we were told to approach them and ask them if they wanted a job."	Mr. Serrano, a former assistant manager at Abercrombie & Fitch.	To provide evidence to support the anecdote that good-looking customers were offered jobs at Abercrombie & Fitch.

FIGURE 5.6. Sample Graphic Organizers, Based on "Going for the Look" (Greenhouse, 2003).

reading, it is important for teachers to follow up the re-reading phase with in-class discussion and review of students' guide-o-rama questions or graphic organizers to check their accuracy. Teachers should not assume that all students have correctly processed the key ideas and facts in a text.

Developing effective reading strategies. It is widely accepted that perhaps the most important benefit of intensive reading lessons is *strategy instruction*, which may include any or all of the following operations: identifying and making explicit students' current strategies; teaching and practicing new strategies; and helping students become aware of how strategies can and should transfer to other reading contexts (Bernhardt, 2005; Grabe, 2004). Research on and suggestions for strategy instruction and lists of strategies utilized by successful readers abound in the literature (see Chapters 1 and 2), and reading strategy training can occur at all three stages of the intensive reading process (Paris et al., 1991; Pressley & Afflerbach, 1995). The during-reading phase lends itself to helping students develop and practice several key strategies important especially in academic contexts: *highlighting, annotating, questioning and responding,* and *outlining* or *charting* (i.e., teaching students to create their own graphic organizers).

Highlighting is a valuable intensive reading skill, both for comprehension monitoring while reading and for review after reading. Effective highlighting focuses primarily on key ideas in a passage and may identify key quotations that capture the sense of the text in the author's own voice. However, although most students in academic settings know that highlighting is a common technique, many inexperienced learners are unclear about *what* to highlight. Thus, teacher modeling and structured practice can be helpful. Figure 5.7 shows a simple modeling and practice exercise based on Sarton's "Rewards" essay. This strategy-training activity will likely work best at this stage of the process, after students have already read the text a couple of times and understand primary content and main ideas. This awareness will help them to develop an accurate understand of the key ideas and phrases in selected passages. As a follow-up, students can go through and highlight a clean copy of the material; the teacher can collect these copies as an informal assessment of student comprehension and the effectiveness of their highlighting strategies. This follow-up is important for ensuring that students do not indiscriminately highlight entire paragraphs or even pages.

Annotation. Many readers jot notes, comments, and questions in the margins of texts as they read them; such behavior is often considered to be a good indicator of active reading. Again, however, the mere act of annotating does not guarantee that it will be effective or useful (the authors remember from their own

---

Step 1: The teacher explains that highlighting is useful for identifying the most important ideas in a section of text; that such ideas may often (but not always) be found in the introductory or final sentence of a paragraph; and that readers can highlight entire sentences, portions of sentences, or key words. Students can be asked to look at paragraph 5 of Sarton's essay and suggest portions that might be appropriate to highlight. The teacher can then show on an overhead slide a sample highlighted version of the paragraph (see below; highlights are in bold). Teacher and students can discuss what the teacher highlighted and why, and students can pose questions or suggest alternatives.

5 **Loneliness is most acutely felt with other people, for with others, even with a lover sometimes, we suffer from our differences of taste, temperament, mood.** Human intercourse often demands that we soften the edge of perception, or withdraw at the very instant of personal truth for fear of hurting, or of being inappropriately present, which is to say naked, in a social situation. **Alone we can afford to be wholly whatever we are, and to feel whatever we feel absolutely. That is a great luxury!**

Step 2: Students, working individually, are then asked to highlight paragraph 7 of the essay. They can compare their answers with peers in a small group and then the whole class can discuss the exercise with the teacher.

FIGURE 5.7. Highlighting Exercise (Based on Sarton, 1974).

student days looking back on their own annotations of assigned texts and finding them to be incomprehensible after the fact!). It is also important to remind students that annotation strategies can and should vary according to one's purpose(s) for reading, the genre, and individual text. Teachers can help students develop annotation strategies by offering suggestions for the types of information that they might write notes about, by instructing them to annotate a clean copy of a text, by checking students' annotations for their effectiveness, and by showing students their own annotations for a follow-up discussion. Figure 5.8 shows two

---

Annotations Worksheet for Sarton's "Rewards of Living a Solitary Life"
Directions: Write notes about the questions below in the margins of
Sarton's essay or on a separate sheet of paper.

1. What feelings do you have as you read this essay?

2. Does the reading remind you of any personal experiences or memories?

3. Does this reading remind you of anything else you've read, heard (like music) or seen (like a movie or TV show)?

4. What phrases or sentences in the essay do you think are especially important or interesting? Underline or highlight them.

5. Do you have questions about the essay? Write them below.

Annotations Guide for Greenhouse's "Going for the Look"

1. Find and underline the most significant sentence. Why is it the most important sentence in the article?

2. What is the main idea of "Going for the Look"? Write it in the box at the end of the article.

3. Now use highlighters or underline to mark the following parts of the text:
   a. where the introduction ends
   b. where Greenhouse tells you what the issue or problem is that he's writing about
   c. the examples that he gives
   d. the argument of retailers
   e. the advice of the lawyer
   f. the customer's viewpoint
   g. the conclusion.

4. Now exchange your copy of "Going for the Look" with your partner. Read your partner's annotations and then talk about what you chose to mark and how you reacted to the text. Did you agree on what the main idea was?

FIGURE 5.8. Sample Annotations Guides.
Source: Ching (2008).

sample annotations guides. The first, based on Sarton's "Rewards" essay, is fairly generic and could be easily adapted to many different texts. The second, based on "Going for the Look," is designed specifically for that text sample. The teacher should also point out that both highlighting and annotating can be useful for reviewing a text if they will be tested on its content or if they must write a paper using that source.

Questioning and responding. In the previous section on pre-reading, we discussed helping students pose questions that they expect the text will answer. In the during-reading phase, students can ask questions of the text as they read it— in a sense, engaging in a dialogue with the author. They can likewise respond to ideas that surprise them or with which they agree or disagree, either because of personal experience or previously held opinions. Questioning and responding can involve annotation, but it can also take place on a separate sheet of paper or computer file used for notetaking or a double-entry journal. In the typical double-entry journal (Spack, 2006), students take a piece of paper and draw a line down the middle. In the left column, they summarize and paraphrase passages as they go along. In the right column, they write their own questions and reactions to the text content. This exercise can also be completed on the same page as the text if margin space permits. Notes and double-entry journals can be modeled by the teacher (perhaps using a text the class has already read), assigned to students, and informally assessed by the teacher. Double-entry notes can be an excellent indicator of student comprehension and engagement (or lack thereof) as well as a good resource for students later if they are assigned to write a summary, response, or essay based on the text. Figure 5.9 shows a sample double-entry journal based on the first paragraph of Sarton's essay.

Outlining and charting. If a teacher uses graphic organizers to help students with text comprehension, this technique can be taken a step further by showing students how to develop their own outlines or charts for the texts they read. After they have been exposed to several varieties of teacher-provided organizers, students should already have ideas about ways to chart information and ideally should be convinced of their value for text processing and review. Figure 5.10 shows a simple exercise to help students create their own outline or chart for Sarton's "Rewards" essay. Students can be asked individually to develop charts or outlines for a text they have already read as a class and to compare alternatives with their classmates or instructors.

During-reading strategies: Summary. Although the reading strategies described in this section are hardly a comprehensive list, they represent the most commonly used and valuable types of while-reading strategy training activities. They address the primary goal of the during-reading phase, which is to ensure thorough comprehension of the text under consideration, and they address the larger goal of any intensive reading course or lesson, which is to develop effective and transferable reading strategies that students can use for future reading assignments in and beyond reading or language instruction. Several aspects of strategy training should be emphasized before we move on:

Summary	Text: Sarton, "The Rewards of Living a Solitary Life"	Reaction
The author's friend was surprised to find that he enjoyed himself at a museum when he was by himself.	The other day an acquaintance of mine, a gregarious and charming man, told me he had found himself unexpectedly alone in New York for an hour or two between appointments. He went to the Whitney and spent the "empty" time looking at things in solitary bliss. For him it proved to be a shock nearly as great as falling in love to discover that he could enjoy himself so much alone.	Why was he so shocked? Most people can spend an hour or two alone with no problem. I would rather be with other people than by myself, but sometimes being alone is enjoyable.

FIGURE 5.9. Sample Double-Entry Journal (Based on Sarton, 1974). *Outlining* *

Divide the reading into sections and write a heading (title) for each section.

- Section (paragraph #s)___1___   Heading: *A Friend's Surprising Experience*
- Section (paragraph #s)_____   Heading: _____
- Section (paragraph #s)_____   Heading: _____
- Section (paragraph #s)_____   Heading: _____

FIGURE 5.10. Sample Outlining Exercise (Sarton, 1974).

- Teachers should explicitly label and instruct students on the strategy under discussion, modeling its use with sample texts (see Chapter 1 for a strategy inventory).
- Students should be given hands-on opportunities to practice the strategy, perhaps first with a text they have already read and then with the current text being studied.
- Teachers should formally or informally assess students' use of the strategy by observing their in-class responses and by collecting copies of texts or exercises on which students have practiced the strategy (also see Chapter 9).
- Teachers should specifically discuss how students can use this strategy for future reading, including in other courses or professional situations; without explicitly informing them of the strategy's name and purpose, students may well forget it as just another in-class exercise.

- If possible, teachers should help students transfer strategies learned in the reading class to reading of texts for other contexts, perhaps by bringing in texts assigned for other courses (or a training manual or employee handbook for their job), and should encourage (or require) students to keep a notebook of strategies learned, a reflective journal about which strategies they are now using (or not using) in their reading, and should review and reinforce strategies previously discussed in reading lessons later in the course.

Many reading textbooks include a variety of exercises for students to complete before or after reading (and less frequently, during reading), but *completing exercises is not equivalent to, or sufficient for, learning and developing effective, transferable reading strategies.* Instruction must be explicit, intentional, and recursive (i.e., by reviewing and revisiting strategies taught and practiced) if students are to retain the benefits of a particular lesson or activity once the class period is over.

Finally, all of these strategy-building activities can and probably should be adapted for students' online or computer-based reading and writing. Students can use computers for annotations, completing or creating graphic organizers, or responding to guide-o-rama questions (Eagleton & Dobler, 2007). If the text itself is available to them in editable electronic form, they can practice highlighting or annotating on the screen rather than with pen or paper. Teachers might also discuss with their students the differences between reading print copies of texts and reading electronic ones (see Chapter 1). For example, students might read differently or more slowly on a computer screen because less text is immediately visible at any moment. Students who are used to the hands-on aspect of highlighting or annotating a text with an actual highlighter or pen may find their inability to do so distracting, at least at first. Another issue is hyperlinked texts or those with eye-catching or interactive graphic elements (Valmont, 2002). Readers may break their concentration and impair their processing by following a hyperlink while they are reading. In short, the while-reading phase can clearly be affected by the differences between traditional and digital texts, and teachers and students should acknowledge and discuss these differences. As electronic delivery of texts is here to stay and likely to expand exponentially in the coming years, simply complaining about distractions is not an adequate response.

3. Looking closely at language. After students have quickly read through the text once to get an overall sense of the content, a possible next step is for students to spend time, either in class or as a homework assignment, looking carefully at the language of the text. This step could also be undertaken later, after the more thorough re-reading step, or even during post-reading activities. The amount, type, and sequencing of language analysis activities will vary depending on the text, student needs and abilities, and overall lesson and course goals, but they may include the following possibilities.

Vocabulary. At this stage, students can be asked to look again at the vocabulary in the text, but this time from the vantage point of having read the entire text with global comprehension. Two major types of activities can be helpful at this stage (see Chapter 8). The first is to ask students to read through the text again, this time making notes about any new or less familiar words or phrases they encounter in the text. Many experts advocate self-selected vocabulary learning as one approach to both helping students build vocabulary and develop strategies for learning new vocabulary. Words identified in context in this way can facilitate immediate comprehension and can also be entered into vocabulary journals or word cards for future analysis, reference, and review (see Chapter 8).

A second focus of vocabulary work at this stage can be to analyze specialized, technical, or idiomatic lexical items in the text, not necessarily so that students will learn them thoroughly but to enhance their comprehension. These items, if not covered during pre-reading, can be identified as discussed previously through a combination of a computer-based tool such as the Vocabulary Profiler and the teacher's own analysis. For instance, in "Going for the Look," students can be directed to look at examples of advertising jargon, such as *ambassadors to the brand, brand representative, brand enhancer, walking billboard, natural classic American style, social experience for the customer,* and *enticing to the community* (suggestions from Ching's 2008 teaching module). To comprehend the facts, issues, and arguments presented in the article (especially in the direct quotations), students must be able to grapple with "insider-speak" such as this. The instructor and students can discuss the meanings of these terms in their contexts, as well as how they can be used in a manipulative or disingenuous way to justify unfair or illegal practices.

Cohesion. Beyond the analysis of specific lexical items, students can also be shown how to interpret cohesive devices as a map to overall text meaning—its macrostructure as well as relationships within and between individual sentences and sections. Most reading theorists agree that the ability to recognize and interpret cohesion markers accurately is critical to the thorough comprehension of a text (Beck, McKeown, Sinatra, & Loxterman, 1991; Chung, 2000; Cohen et al., 1979; Degand & Sanders, 2002; Hudson, 2007; Irwin, 1986; Moe & Irwin, 1986; Linderholm et al., 2000; McKeown, Beck, Sinatra, & Loxterman, 1992; Roller, 1990; van Dijk, 1977). L2 readers must develop an ability to recognize and use rhetorical devices and structural signposts "as ways to comprehend texts better ... These signals include pronouns, definite articles, repetitions of words and synonyms, words that highlight informational organization (e.g., first, second, third, however, on the other hand, in contrast), and transition words, phrases, and sentences" (Grabe & Stoller, 2002, p. 80).

Because each text exhibits a unique structure and array of cohesive devices, activities appropriate for facilitating student comprehension through under-standing cohesion vary from genre to genre and text to text. For example, in Sarton's "Rewards" essay, her repeated usage of the words *alone, lonely or loneli-ness, solitary* or *solitude* is critical to her argument. Students can be directed to examine each instance of those words and discuss both a working definition particular to Sarton's text as well as how her use of those terms is surprising or provocative. As another example from the same text, students can be asked to examine the use of the word *therefore* in paragraph 3 and discuss how it ties the ideas in the paragraph together (they will have to read the whole paragraph in order to do so). In "Going for the Look," students can be asked why the author begins three consecutive sentences in paragraph 3 with "She looks . . .," the idea being that they will see that *how* "she looks" is central to understanding the introductory anecdote and to the essay as a whole.

Syntactic choices. As discussed in Chapter 3, syntactic complexity can be a factor in comprehension breakdown for L2 readers and it should be a consider-ation in text selection. However, once the text has been selected, possible discus-sion points in the during-reading stage might be either difficult syntactic constructions or unusual syntactic choices that give clues to overall meaning. It is common in academic texts for sentences to be extremely long, to have "heavy" subject noun phrases, to use the passive voice, relative clauses, subordination, adverbials, and so forth (Cohen et al., 1979). To ensure comprehension, teachers can identify potentially challenging syntactic constructions in a given text and plan to discuss them with students, perhaps asking them to paraphrase sentences and/or break them into several shorter units.

In other instances, an author's syntactic choices may provide clues to overall meaning. For example, in Sarton's essay, she makes several unusual stylistic moves through atypical syntax. Paragraph 3, for instance, contains a one-word "sentence": "Exactly." Students can be asked to analyze what that means and why she did that (apparently to respond "conversationally" to the quotation in the previous sentence: "Music I heard with you was more than music"). In Paragraphs 4 and 5, Sarton twice begins sentences with the word "Alone," as in the startling assertion, "Alone one is never lonely" (paragraph 4). The more typical construction would be something like "One is never lonely when one is alone"; students can be shown that Sarton's fronting of the adjective calls atten-tion to it and especially to her strong stance about the difference between being "lonely" and being "alone." It can also be observed that Sarton was an accom-plished poet and that one characteristic of poetry is the violation of the syntactic norms of prose. The important instructional goal is not, however, to discuss poetic license but rather to identify and deconstruct difficult or unusual forms at the sentence level in ways that facilitate text comprehension as students read.

Analyzing stylistic choices. Once students have read a text for meaning, it can also be helpful to point out to students how an author's tone or the mood she sets in a text can affect both how a reader makes meaning and how readers react to it (and, in fact, that the author can manipulate readers into a desired response).

For example, in his essay "The Farce Called Grading," author Arthur E. Lean (1978/1998) uses a number of inflammatory and sarcastic turns of phrase to convey his strong opinion on the topic (*farce, tyrannical, indefensible,* and so forth). Figure 5.11 shows several sample exercises, based on Sarton's and Greenhouse's essays, which direct students toward analyzing stylistic choices made by the authors. Such questions could be incorporated into a guide-o-rama or annotations worksheet; they could also be part of an in-class discussion of the author's stylistic choices and how they convey meaning. It is important to point out that, as a precursor to post-reading critical analysis, a reader does not necessarily have to *agree* with the tone set by the author's use of language, but it is important to be aware of such linguistic choices and how they affect us as we read.

4. *Considering text structure.* Another aspect of text processing that can be explored during the while-reading stage is how texts are structured rhetorically, how their organization conveys the author's purpose and affects comprehension, and whether text structure is a help or a hindrance to the reader. Consideration of text structure can also be included during post-reading reading–writing connections (e.g., analyzing various structural elements of a text as model for students' own writing) (Hirvela, 2004). However, at this stage, the focus of analysis is on how the author conveys meaning and how analyzing a text's macrostructure facilitates the understanding of meaning and how ideas are connected.

The outlining activity in Figure 5.10, discussed in the previous section, is a good basic tool that could be adapted to various texts. Figure 5.12 provides a variety of analysis exercises based on Sarton's and Greenhouse's texts that call students' attention to different aspects of how the texts are structured (such as both texts beginning with opening anecdotes and utilizing quotations to begin many paragraphs). Although some of these exercises imply that students have read both texts and could compare them, they could easily be adapted so that the texts are treated as unrelated entities.

During reading: summary. As noted at the beginning of this section, activities to help students process texts successfully and develop effective reading strategies while they read tend to be overlooked by teachers and materials developers.

- Sarton develops an argument that many readers may find surprising or disagree with. In paragraphs 1 and 2, identify words and phrases (e.g., *solitary bliss*) in which she gives clues about her positive feeling toward "living a solitary life."
- Greenhouse quotes several different people. Read what they say out loud using the tone you think they would use. What kind of person do you think each one is? How much do you think you can trust what they say? Why?
- How formal or informal is "Going for the Look"? How would the text be different if it were intended for a group of retailers? Employment counselors who help people apply for jobs?

FIGURE 5.11. Sample Activities for Analyzing Author's Tone and Mood. Based on Greenhouse (2003) and Sarton (1974); Greenhouse (2003) suggestions adapted from Ching (2008).

- Why do both texts begin with stories?
- Sarton begins talking about "loneliness" in ¶ 5 and returns to it in ¶ 7. What is the purpose of ¶ 6? If you were the author or an editor, would you reorder the paragraphs? Why or why not?
- Both texts use quotations at key spots. What is the purpose of those quotations? Do they improve the texts, or are they distracting? Why do you think so?
- What do you think of the endings of the two texts? Are they "conclusions" in the standard sense? Why or why not?
- How are literary texts (like Sarton's) or newspaper articles (like "Going for the Look") different from academic essays in the ways they may be organized?

FIGURE 5.12. Sample Activities for Analyzing Text Structure (Greenhouse, 2003; Sarton, 1974).

However, they are arguably the centerpiece of intensive reading. After all, if students do not accurately and thoroughly comprehend and interpret a text, then pre-reading activities will be demonstrated to have been inadequate and post-reading activities (which rely on students having carefully analyzed the text) will be unsuccessful. Furthermore, if developing and practicing transferable reading strategies is the primary goal of an intensive reading lesson (and arguably the entire course), attention to strategy training during the reading phase is critically important.

After Reading

After students have read a text several times for main ideas, have comprehended its essential content, and have spent time considering the text's language and structure, the final stage of intensive reading is to help students *evaluate* and *extend* what they have learned about the text and the reading process. The nature and extent of the post-reading phase may vary depending on the type of course and its goals. For example, a reading and composition course may quite intentionally extend the reading process by asking students to write papers about what they have read; a course solely focused on reading may spend less time on writing.[4] We nonetheless encourage all teachers to build substantive post-reading work into their intensive reading lessons rather than simply moving on to the next topic and text. Although it may be tempting to do so—teacher and students may be tired of the text once it has been carefully read and thoroughly understood—students will benefit more from their reading if they are required to evaluate it critically and work with the text in their own language-production activities (speaking and writing) (Hirvela, 2004; Horowitz, 2007; Weissberg, 2006). Post-reading activities also offer the best opportunities for teacher assessment of student progress, as they make the internal reading process and its outcomes more transparent (see Chapter 9). Again following the template in Figure 5.1, we focus here on three general goals of the post-reading stage: (1) summarizing; (2) thinking critically; and (3) making reading–writing connections.

1. Summarizing is both a reading and writing skill. Where reading is concerned, effective summarizing requires an understanding of the key ideas in a text and an ability to distinguish among main points (which belong in a summary) and supporting details (which typically do not). For writing, summarizing requires the writer to express the main points of a text she has read succinctly and in her own words. "The writing of competent summaries in one's second language may be even more difficult than the act of reading needed to make summarizing possible" (Robb, 2001, p. 228) (also see Folse, 2008; Helgesen, 1997; Hirvela, 2004; Schuemann, 2008). Summaries may be as short as one sentence or considerably longer, depending on the purpose for writing a summary (e.g., summaries in a literature review in a journal article tend to be much more succinct than in a literature review in a doctoral dissertation).

Summary-writing is a good review and comprehension check tool. Aebersold and Field (1997) suggest giving students a short period of time, say 10–15 minutes, to write summaries from memory to see how well they can recall main ideas. If the earlier stages of the intensive reading process have been well executed, their knowledge of main ideas, key words, and text structure should aid them in the recall process (Koda, 2004). An extension of this activity is to have students compare summaries (which they themselves have written or which have been prepared for them) in pairs and small groups, decide which summary is most effective, and present it to the class. The brief exercises in Figure 5.13 lead students through summarizing Sarton's essay, which is short and straightforward in its presentation of content (once students have sorted through the potentially challenging language). This sample should provide an easy-to-understand model of the summarization process. These activities could be easily adapted for a wide range of texts. We have found that summarizing is a complex skill to master and that teachers must train students and model the process repeatedly during a course (Ferris & Hedgcock, 2005; Hirvela, 2004). Summarizing is not as easy as we may think (to teach or for students to do), but it is a necessary first step toward responding to and evaluating what we have read. Before discussing what we think about a text, we first need an accurate portrayal of what it *actually says.*

Excellent Summarizing *Scaffolded Summarizing*

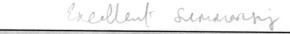

Place an "M" next to sentences that express main ideas. Place a "D" next to sentences that describe supporting details.
_____ 1. May Sarton believes that spending time alone can be an exciting adventure.
_____ 2. Sarton had a friend who visited the Whitney Museum in New York by himself and was surprised to find out how much he enjoyed it.
_____ 3. Sarton often finds that she is exhausted and drained after being around a lot of people.
_____ 4. Sarton makes a distinction between being "alone" and "lonely," and argues that sometimes one can be lonely when around other people.
Now write a brief summary of the essay by following the instructions below. Write your summary as a complete paragraph.
1. What is the author's main idea? State it in one sentence.
2. In 2 or 3 follow-up sentences, briefly state other key points she makes in the essay.

FIGURE 5.13. Summarizing Sarton's (1974) "Rewards" Essay.

Students may overlook this step, inaccurately describing and reacting to texts they have read or inaccurately taking information or quotations out of context.

When students *respond* to a text, they identify their own feelings and reactions to it before moving on to the (somewhat) more objective step of critically evaluating it. Summary and response are often treated as a single step in the post-reading phase (Hirvela, 2004; Spack, 2006), but there is a distinction: Summary focuses on *what the author says* and response on *how the reader feels or experiences* the text. Figure 5.14 presents response questions for students to consider after reading Sarton; these could also be adapted for other texts (Ferris & Hedgcock, 2005; Hirvela, 2004). The questions ask students whether they liked the essay, whether Sarton's text reminded them of similar experiences they might have had, and whether they discovered new ideas about the topic from reading the material. It is important to note that response is not just an impressionistic activity: Response is a necessary precursor to critical evaluation of textual content, as our own emotional responses and prior experiences impact our ability to analyze an author's ideas and arguments objectively. Asking students to articulate these reactions may help them see later if they are evaluating a text fairly or if their own personal responses may cloud their thinking.

2. *Thinking critically* about a text (Atkinson, 1997) may be a new experience for some L2 students who have been educated in systems where they were not expected or encouraged to ever criticize or question the ideas of a published author or authority (Aebersold & Field, 1997; Hirvela, 2004). However, it is also true that critical thinking is not necessarily a strength for adolescents and young adults from *any* cultural or educational background (due to their maturity and cognitive development levels), and helping students to develop good analysis and evaluation skills is a major concern of secondary and postsecondary educators in the United States. It is therefore extremely important that teachers of L2 readers help students to ask the right questions, to pay attention to information in a text and how it is presented, and to express their own opinions about a text in ways that are balanced, objective, and grounded in a thorough and accurate understanding of the text being evaluated.

A variety of in-class and out-of-class activities can induce students to think critically about a text in the post-reading stage. Some examples include debates, which are appropriate when a text presents two sides of an issue, as in "Going for

---

1. Did you like Sarton's essay? Why or why not?
2. Did you discover any new ideas about being alone or "living a solitary life" through reading the essay? If so, what were they?
3. Have you had any experiences similar to Sarton's in which you found that you really enjoyed something that you experienced alone? What was it?
4. Have you ever felt "lonely" when with other people? Explain.

FIGURE 5.14. Responding to Sarton's (1974) "Rewards" Essay.

Sarton ("Rewards of Living a Solitary Life")

1. Sarton writes, "Alone, one is never lonely" and "Loneliness is most acutely felt with other people." Do you agree with these statements? Are they perhaps more true for some people or in some situations than in others?
2. In paragraphs 2 and 3, Sarton claims that we can best enjoy something—music, sunrise—by ourselves rather than with other people. Is this always true, or can we sometimes gain *more* from an experience when we are with others? Explain.

Greenhouse ("Going for the Look, but Risking Discrimination")

1. Why did Greenhouse tell the story of Elizabeth Nill's experience at Abercrombie & Fitch? Is it a good example of the issue being discussed in this article? Why or why not?
2. Who do you think makes the best argument either for or against hiring for the look? Why?
3. Based on what you have read in this article, what is your opinion of the practice of hiring people based on their looks? Is it unfair, or is it a reasonable business choice? Why do you think so?
4. Do you think that Greenhouse represents both sides of the argument objectively or does he appeal to readers' emotions? Give examples of either the way he is objective or the way he slants the arguments. (Adapted from Ching, 2008)

FIGURE 5.15. Sample Critical Thinking Questions (Greenhouse, 2003; Sarton, 1974).

the Look." Students may also respond in writing or in discussion to critical analysis questions about a text (see Figure 5.15 for examples) or compose an essay in which they take a stand on a text's ideas, analyze a key quotation, or compare two contrasting quotations. Students can use questions such as the following to evaluate the information in a persuasive text:

- Does the text present information in an organized way?
- Do arguments follow a step-by-step sequence?
- What information gaps are not addressed?
- Does the text present or affirm any opposing points of view?
- Are the language choices objective in tone?
- Are arguments supported by verifiable evidence, such as statistics or data collected by others not associated with the author?
- Is the credibility of the argument strengthened by references to respected, well-known authorities on the topic?

Questions about the author, if such information is available, might include the following:

- Is the author well-known or highly reputed?
- What are the known biases of the author?
- Is the author affiliated with organizations or groups that have publicly expressed views on the topic?
- What is the author's expertise in the topic area addressed in the text?
- What are the author's views on this topic? (Aebersold & Field, 1997; Dagostino & Carifio, 1994; Silberstein, 1994)

Teaching students to *write* persuasively in response to a particular text is another complex endeavor that is beyond the scope of this chapter (see Ferris & Hedgcock, 2005; Hirvela, 2004; Hyland, 2004a, 2004b; Johns, 1997). However, it seems fair to say that students will be unable to write an effective (or even accurate) text-based argumentative essay if they have not first undertaken the preparatory work of summarizing, responding to, and evaluating the text itself. Obviously, time spent thinking carefully and critically about a text not only promotes deeper comprehension and good reading strategies but should also give students ideas and models for their own writing.

3. Reading–writing connections. Teachers can help students extend their reading of assigned texts to other language development activities in a variety of ways. In-class discussion, formal and informal assessment (e.g., comprehension questions, vocabulary review, and summarizing), speeches, debates, and follow-up research projects (e.g., conducting Web searches for more information related to the text, surveying or interviewing others about ideas in the text) are productive and engaging ways to help students apply what they have learned through reading. In most settings, however, making connections between reading and writing is an important part of the post-reading process. Frequently, reading is taught by itself as a stand-alone skill, but few would argue against the view that reading and writing are inextricably connected: Writing helps students think more deeply about and articulate what they have learned through reading (Ferris & Hedgcock, 2005; Hirvela, 2004; Krashen, 2004; Smith, 2004). Moreover, reading supplies meaningful content for writing, as well as rhetorical and linguistic models for students to follow. As noted in Ferris and Hedgcock (2005), although it is rare for a good writer not to be an effective reader, it is possible for a successful reader to fail to develop good writing skills. Both sides of the literacy coin are essential for academic and professional success in most instances.

Readers interested in further discussion of the reading–writing connection are encouraged to read Chapter 2 of our 2005 book *Teaching ESL Composition* or Hirvela's (2004) excellent treatment of the topic. For the purposes of this chapter on intensive reading, we briefly highlight suggestions for exploiting the reading–writing connection, particularly in the post-reading stage. Perhaps the most common use of reading in a composition (or reading–writing) course is for texts to provide content or serve as inspiration for students' own writing. Figure 5.16 provides two examples of writing assignments based on Sarton's and Greenhouse's texts. Beyond these fairly typical text-based assignments, reading can serve as a model for students to analyze and apply to their own writing. For instance, students could take note of the fact that both Sarton and Greenhouse begin their selections with anecdotes about individuals; students can think about why/how this can be an effective "hook" for a reader and experiment with adding an opening story to an essay on which they are currently working. On a more mechanical level, students could analyze punctuation usage in direct quotations in Greenhouse's essay. They could also be directed to observe that, in the first sentences of paragraphs 12–15 and 17–18, an introductory element is separated from the main body of the sentence by a comma and could make inferences about a rule about comma use in such constructions.

A further post-reading application of the reading–writing connection could involve examining papers (e.g., summaries or essays) previously written by former students based on the text under discussion. Because students have spent a good deal of time at this point studying and analyzing this text, they should be able to do an effective job of assessing whether a peer has accurately and effectively written about it.

Sarton Text
(In-class or out-of-class assignment)
Directions: Write an essay comparing and contrasting your own experience to the ideas in Sarton's essay. To do this, you will have to: (a) explain clearly what Sarton says; (b) describe your own experience; and (c) make connections between what Sarton says and your own experience (adapted from Spack, 2006).

Greenhouse Text
(45-minute in-class writing)
Directions: You will have 45 minutes to plan and write an essay on the topic assigned below. Before you begin writing, read the passage carefully and plan what you will say. Your essay should be as well organized and carefully written as you can make it.

"Retailers defend the approach to hiring based on image as necessary and smart, and industry experts see the point. 'In today's competitive retail environment, the methods have changed for capturing the consumer's awareness of your brand,' said Marshal Cohen, a senior industry analyst with the NPD Group, a market research firm. 'Being able to find a brand enhancer, or what I call a walking billboard, is critical. It's really important to create an environment that's enticing to the community, particularly with the younger, fashionable market. A guy wants to go hang out in a store where he can see good looking gals.' "

Explain Cohen's argument and discuss the extent to which you agree or disagree with his analysis. Support your position, providing reasons and examples from your own experience, observations, or reading.

FIGURE 5.16. Sample Writing Assignments Based on Sarton (1974) and Greenhouse (2003) Texts.
Adapted from Ching (2008).

After reading: Summary. To put it simply, post-reading activities are a critical part of intensive reading because they help to ensure that lessons learned from the text and from earlier stages of the process will not be passed over too quickly and forgotten as the class moves on to a new text and its challenges. As we hope this discussion and the accompanying sample exercises have demonstrated, such activities can and should go far beyond the rather mechanical post-reading comprehension questions of earlier eras (Brown, 2004). Post-reading activities also provide logical contexts for assessment of reading comprehension, although we argue that formal and informal assessment can and should occur throughout intensive reading lesson sequences (see Chapter 9). Finally, if designed thoughtfully, post-reading activities can be creative, interesting, and stimulating for students.

Putting It All Together: Designing an Intensive Reading Lesson

This chapter has presented a number of possible lesson goals and sample activities for all three stages of the intensive reading process. Readers might well wonder how long they should spend working with a single text and whether all of these activities might be excessive. As stated at the outset of this discussion, it was not our intent to suggest that teachers and students should spend weeks on end intensively reading and working with one text, completing all of the activity types suggested. The duration of an intensive reading sequence and the balance within the sequence of the three stages and how much time to spend on each depends on several factors, including: (1) the course itself (e.g., a course dedicated solely to reading, a composition course, an multiple skills language course); (2) the frequency and duration of class meetings; (3) how much homework can reasonably be expected of students; (4) course goals; (5) the text being studied; and (6) the learning aims for the lesson sequence in the larger framework of course design (see Chapter 4).

Suggestions for Intensive Reading Lessons

Clearly, time frames vary depending on the aforementioned factors, but it is probably realistic to think in terms of two to three class meetings, plus preparatory work and homework, to move effectively through the stages of intensive reading. Less time probably means that preparation, comprehension, strategy-building, and extension activities may suffer somewhere; too much more time may mean that the teacher is beating the text to death, not covering enough different kinds of texts in the course, and possibly boring or alienating students.

Limiting the sequence in this way obviously means that teachers and students will be unable to include all of the activity types discussed in this chapter. We have two suggestions along these lines. First, allow the text under consideration to guide your decisions about the activities you will choose, adapt, or develop. For instance, a text may address a familiar topic and require little pre-reading schema development. At the same time, it may include off-list vocabulary items that need to be worked with during the before- and during-reading phases. If a text is short and its syntax and macrostructure are transparent, some techniques for breaking the text into sections or outlining it may not be necessary. Second, it is best to visualize a reading course in its entirety, articulate overall goals, and then fit the goals of a particular intensive reading sequence into the larger framework. Goal-related factors that need to be assessed and prioritized include: (1) how many texts to cover intensively; (2) how to work with vocabulary; (3) specific reading strategies to introduce and reinforce; and (4) what extension activities to use for enrichment and assessment. Naturally, prioritizing and working toward goals take place against the backdrop of other course objectives to be worked on with different texts at various points in the course. In other words, no single text or reading sequence can "do it all" for the students and the course.

Chapter Summary

In this chapter, we attempted to define and describe the intensive reading process. Using a framework from the California State University Expository Reading and Writing Task Force (2008) and two sample reading texts for illustration, we closely examined three major phases of intensive reading—before, during, and after reading—identifying goals for each stage and providing rationales and suggesting tasks to exemplify each goal. The chapter concluded with a discussion of how to apply the information in crafting an intensive reading lesson plan. Specifically, we discussed the following observations and principles:

- *Intensive reading* is the careful, intentional examination of a text for comprehension. Goals beyond immediate comprehension of a text include developing and practicing effective reading strategies, facilitating language development through reading, and building students' confidence in their L2 reading abilities and motivation to read further and more widely.
- *The before-reading stage* is crucial for helping to students *identify* what they might already know about a text's content and language, to *acquire* information about a text that may not be part of their background knowledge, and to *preview* a text to capture its content and structure. It is also valuable for building anticipation and interest prior to close, careful reading.
- *The during-reading stage* is when the teacher facilitates thorough student comprehension and interpretation of the text and guides students to practice reading strategies that may be transferable to other contexts.

- *The after-reading stage* allows students to *summarize, respond to,* and *critically evaluate* what they have read through extension activities that require them to discuss, write about, and investigate what they have learned. The after-reading stage is also where *reading–writing connections* may be intentionally made and where assessment may productively occur.
- *An intensive-reading lesson plan* should be long enough to ensure adequate comprehension and analysis, but not so long that students tire of it and do not read adequate amounts of text during the reading course as a whole.

Not all components of the three intensive reading stages are equally necessary or appropriate for all texts—teachers should be selective about task types and amount of attention given to each of the three stages, depending on the target text and its place in the syllabus.

Intensive reading of expository texts represents but one type of reading instruction and experience available to students, as Chapters 6 and 7 argue. Nonetheless, intensive reading is a fundamental yet highly complex operation for reading teachers and their students. Many textbooks provide reading selections and follow-up activities, but working one's way through a textbook is not the same as knowing *why* such activities are valuable or *how* they may most effectively be implemented. Whether teachers ever design their own materials based on a particular text, it is essential for them to understand the overall goals of the intensive reading process and to develop expertise in addressing those goals.

Further Reading and Resources

Below is a list of selected sources and materials referred to in this chapter. Where applicable, URLs are provided, though we caution readers that these tend to change. Bibliographic information for published sources can be found in the References section at the end of the book.

Intensive reading stages
   Aebersold & Field (1997)
Classic article on schema in L2 reading
   Carrell & Eisterhold (1983)
Study on effects of pre-reading activities
   Chen & Graves (1995)
CSU Task Force template and sample teaching units
   http://www.csupomona.edu/~uwc/pdf/AssignmentTemplatePilotFinal1.pdf

Sarton (1974) text
   http://karrvakarela.blogspot.com/2005/07/rewards-of-living-solitary-life.html
Newhouse (2003) text
   http://www.csupomona.edu/~uwc/pdf/RChingGoingfortheLook-
   numpara2.pdf
Graphic organizer resources
   Grabe & Stoller (2002); Jiang & Grabe (2007)
Strategy training in intensive reading
   Aebersold & Field (1997); Grabe & Stoller (2002); Paris et al. (1991)
Summarizing skills; reading-writing connections
   Ferris & Hedgcock (2005); Hirvela (2004)

Reflection and Review

1. In your own education, have you experienced reading instruction that reflected the emphases or techniques discussed in this chapter? If so, did you find them helpful? Which have you discovered or developed on your own?

2. Look again at the goals and activities suggested for pre-reading. Which of them was a new idea for you? Which one(s) strike you as the most necessary and important, regardless of the specific text being used, and why?

3. Do you think it is possible to spend *too much* time engaged in pre-reading? What are the possible risks or drawbacks?

4. Look carefully at our discussion of approaches to introducing key vocabulary prior to reading. Thinking of your own experiences as a reader of academic text in a first or second language, would you find vocabulary information or activities at this stage helpful or distracting?

5. Which during-reading strategies do you use (or have used) in your own academic reading? Which do you find helpful, and could you have benefited from instruction on how to highlight, annotate, or chart a text?

6. Have you ever been asked by an instructor to complete a graphic organizer for a text you were reading for class? Have you ever created one for your own notetaking or review? For what specific reading–writing tasks might graphic organizers be helpful?

7. Our section on post-reading procedures argues that engaging students in writing about what they have read is a critical part of the learning process. Based on your experience as a student or teacher, do you agree or disagree? Why or why not?

8. If you were designing an intensive reading lesson sequence, how would you sort through the suggestions and activity types presented in this chapter? Assuming you would not try to use all of them in working with a text, what criteria might you use to prioritize activities for each stage of the process?

Application Activities

Note: For the following Application Activities, select appropriate source texts from this chapter or any other.

Application Activity 5.1
Schema Activation and Schema Development

a.   *Schema Activation*

    (1)   Look through the text and identify 2 or 3 major themes or points that are somewhat universal or should elicit prior knowledge (e.g., "friend-ship during hard times"). Brainstorm several discussion questions or freewriting prompts that could help students recall relevant experiences.

    (2)   Look at the organization of the text. What elements should be familiar to students? What aspects might be challenging? How might you help students use their prior knowledge of story structure (formal schemata) to comprehend this text?

    (3)   Should specific words or phrases in the title or in the text be familiar to students? How can you elicit this information from students to enhance their comprehension?

b.   *Schema Development*

Assume a student audience educated primarily in a non-English-speaking environment.

    (1)   What do you know about the author? How could you present the information to the students (or help them find out for themselves)?

    (2)   What historical and cultural information in the text might be unknown to students? How might you develop their awareness of it?

    (3)   What technical or specialized information might help learners under-stand issues developed in the story?

Application Activity 5.2
Surveying the Text

Considering the ideas and examples presented in Figure 5.2 and Appendix 5.2, design a set of questions or tasks that will help students:

- deconstruct the title;
- examine the beginning and ending of the text for clues to overall meaning;
- skim the text for main idea(s);
- scan the text for specific information;
- identify the macrostructure of the text.

Application Activity 5.3
Identifying and Introducing Key Vocabulary Prior to Reading

a. For your selected text, create a list of at least 10 words or phrases that: (1) might be unknown to a student audience educated in a non-English-speaking environment; and (2) are necessary for overall comprehension. Compare your list with a peer; if possible, show the list to an upper-secondary or beginning college-level reader to assess the difficulty of the words you have chosen. Consider cultural and historical terms, as well as specialized vocabulary.
b. Run the text through Vocabulary Profiler (http://www.lextutor.ca). Note especially words that appear on the Academic Word List or as off-list. Are any of the words on the list you generated for the list in (a) above? Examine the words in their context in the essay. What items might be so difficult for L2 learners that they might require preteaching?
c. Considering the lists you have generated in (a) and (b), identify five to ten words or phrases that might be useful at the pre-reading stage. Brainstorm ways to present these words to the students.
d. Using the word list you selected in (c), create a glossary (either on a separate page or as part of the text) with text-specific definitions that will make the items easily accessible to the students as they read.

Application Activity 5.4
Designing "While-Reading" Activities

a. If possible and applicable, break the text into sections and design guide-o-rama questions, as in Figure 5.5.
b. Select two key paragraphs from the text and design a highlighting exercise similar to the one shown in Figure 5.7.
c. Design annotation exercises similar to those shown in Figure 5.8.
d. Create a graphic organizer for the text that will facilitate student comprehension (see Figure 5.6).

If you are completing this activity in a class setting, compare your exercises with your classmates and discuss them with your instructor.

Application Activity 5.5
Designing "After-Reading" Activities

a. Write a one-paragraph summary of your text. Compare your summary with your classmates' and discuss (1) difficulties you encountered; and (2) what you learned about summarizing that you could pass on to future literacy learners.
b. Write three to five reaction and critical-analysis questions that could guide student discussion of your article.

c. Choose a key point or quotation from your article that you might ask students to write about. Discuss the kind of question or prompt that you might provide students.
d. Discuss ideas for an out-of-class essay assignment based on the article.
e. Discuss ideas for an out-of-class research project students could do after reading the article.
f. Identify aspects of the text (structure, mechanics, content, and so forth) that could be used as models for analysis to help students with their own writing.

Appendix 5.1
The Rewards of Living a Solitary Life

May Sarton (1974)

¶1 The other day an acquaintance of mine, a gregarious and charming man, told me he had found himself unexpectedly alone in New York for an hour or two between appointments. He went to the Whitney and spent the "empty" time looking at things in solitary bliss. For him it proved to be a shock nearly as great as falling in love to discover that he could enjoy himself so much alone.

¶2 What had he been afraid of, I asked myself? That, suddenly alone, he would discover that he bored himself, or that there was, quite simply, no self there to meet? But having taken the plunge, he is now on the brink of adventure; he is about to be launched into his own inner space, space as immense, unexplored, and sometimes frightening as outer space to the astronaut. His every perception will come to him with a new freshness and, for a time, seem startlingly original. For anyone who can see things for himself with a naked eye becomes, for a moment or two, something of a genius. With another human being present vision becomes double vision, inevitably. We are busy wondering, what does my companion see or think of this, and what do I think of it? The original impact gets lost, or diffused.

¶3 "Music I heard with you was more than music."* Exactly. And therefore music *itself* can only be heard alone. Solitude is the salt of personhood. It brings out the authentic flavor of every experience.

¶4 "Alone one is never lonely: the spirit adventures, walking/In a quiet garden, in a cool house, abiding single there."

¶5 Loneliness is most acutely felt with other people, for with others, even with a lover sometimes, we suffer from our differences of taste, temperament, mood. Human intercourse often demands that we soften the edge of perception, or withdraw at the very instant of personal truth for fear of hurting, or of being inappropriately present, which is to say naked, in a social situation. Alone we can afford to be wholly whatever we are, and to feel whatever we feel absolutely. That is a great luxury!

¶6 For me the most interesting thing about a solitary life, and mine has been that for the last twenty years, is that it becomes increasingly rewarding. When I wake up and watch the sun rise over the ocean, as I do most days, and know that I have an entire day ahead, uninterrupted, in which to write a few pages, take a walk with my dog, lie down in the afternoon for a long think (why does one think better in a horizontal position?), read and listen to music, I am flooded with happiness.

¶7 I am lonely only when I am overtired, when I have worked too long without a break, when for the time being I feel empty and need filling up. And I am lonely sometimes when I come back home after a lecture trip, when I have seen a lot of people and talked a lot, and am full to the brim with experience that needs to be sorted out.

¶8 Then for a little while the house feels huge and empty, and I wonder where my self is hiding. It has to be recaptured slowly by watering the plants, perhaps, and looking again at each one as though it were a person, by feeding the two cats, by cooking a meal.

¶9 It takes a while, as I watch the surf blowing up in fountains at the end of the field, but the moment comes when the world falls away, and the self emerges again from the deep unconscious, bringing back all I have recently experienced to be explored and slowly understood, when I converse again with my hidden powers, and so grow, and so be renewed, till death do us part.

Going for the Look, but Risking Discrimination

Steven Greenhouse
New York Times, Sunday, July 13, 2003
(http://www.csupomona.edu/~uwc/pdf/RChingGoingfortheLook-
numpara2.pdf)

¶1 A funny thing happens when Elizabeth Nill, a sophomore at Northwestern University, goes shopping at Abercrombie & Fitch.

¶2 At no fewer than three Abercrombie stores, she says, managers have approached her and offered her a job as a clerk.

¶3 "Every time this happens, my little sister says, 'Not again,' " said Ms. Nill, who is 5-foot-6 and has long blond hair. She looks striking. She looks hip. She looks, in fact, as if she belongs in an Abercrombie & Fitch catalog.

¶4 Is this a coincidence? A fluke? No, says Antonio Serrano, a former assistant Abercrombie store manager in Scranton, Pa. It's policy.

¶5 "If someone came in with a pretty face, we were told to approach them and ask them if they wanted a job," Mr. Serrano said. "They thought if we had the best-looking college kids working in our store, everyone will want to shop there."

¶6 Abercrombie's aggressive approach to building a pretty and handsome sales force, an effort that company officials proudly acknowledge, is a leading example of what many industry experts and sociologists describe as a steadily growing trend in American retailing. From Abercrombie to the cosmetics giant L'Oreal, from the sleek W hotel chain to the Gap, businesses are openly seeking workers who are sexy, sleek or simply good-looking.

¶7 Hiring for looks is old news in some industries, as cocktail waitresses, strippers and previous generations of flight attendants know all too well. But many companies have taken that approach to sophisticated new heights in recent years, hiring workers to project an image.

¶8 In doing so, some of those companies have been skirting the edges of antidiscrimination laws and provoking a wave of private and government lawsuits. Hiring attractive people is not necessarily illegal, but discriminating on the basis of age, sex or ethnicity is. That is where things can get confusing and contentious.

¶9 "If you're hiring by looks, then you can run into problems of race discrimination, national origin discrimination, gender discrimination, age discrimination and even disability discrimination," said Olophius Perry, director of the Los Angeles office of the Equal Employment Opportunity Commission, which has accused several companies of practicing race and age discrimination by favoring good-looking young white people in their hiring.

¶10 Some chains, most notably the Gap and Benetton, pride themselves on hiring attractive people from many backgrounds and races. Abercrombie's "classic American" look, pervasive in its store and catalogs and on its Web site, is blond, blue-eyed and preppy. Abercrombie finds such workers and models by concentrating its hiring on certain colleges, fraternities and sororities.

¶11 The company says it does not discriminate. But in a lawsuit filed last month in Federal District Court in San Francisco, some Hispanic, Asian and black job applicants maintained otherwise. Several plaintiffs said in interviews that thwn they applied for jobs, store managers steered them to the stockroom, not to the sales floor.

¶12 In interviews, managers like Mr. Serrano described a recruiting approached used by Abercrombie, which has become one of the most popular retailers among the nation's youth.

¶13 "We were supposed to approach someone in the mall who we think will look attractive in our store," said Mr. Serrano, who said he quit when told he would be promoted only if he accepted a transfer. "If that person said, 'I never worked in retailing before,' we said: 'Who cares? We'll hire you.' But if someone came in who had lots of retail experience and not a pretty face, we were told not to hire them at all."

¶14 Tom Lennox, Abercrombie's communications director, emphatically denied job bias but acknowledged the company likes hiring sales assistants, known as brand representatives, who "look great."

¶15 "Brand representatives are ambassadors to the brand," Mr. Lennox said. "We want to hire brand representatives that will represent the Abercrombie & Fitch brand with natural classic American style, look great while exhibiting individuality, project the brand and themselves with energy and enthusiasm, and make the store a warm, inviting place that provides a social experience for the customer."

¶16 Retailers defend that approach to hiring as necessary and smart, and industry experts see the point.

¶17 "In today's competitive retail environment, the methods have changed for capturing the consumers' awareness of your brand," said Marshal Cohen, a senior industry analyst with the NPD Group, a market research firm. "Being able to find a brand enhancer, or what I call a walking billboard, is critical. It's really important to create an environment that's enticing to the community, particularly with the younger, fashionable market. A guy wants to go hang out in a store where he can see good-looking gals."

¶18 While hiring by looks has a long history, some sociologists and retail consultants agree that the emphasis has increased—not at Wal-Mart and other mass marketers, but at up-scale businesses.

¶19 The federal government has accused some of the businesses of going too far. The hotel entrepreneur Ian Scharger agreed to a $1.08 million settlement three years ago after the Equal Employment Opportunity Commission accused his Mondrian Hotel in West Hollywood of racial discrimination for firing nine valets and bellhops, eight of them nonwhite. Documents filed in court showed that Mr. Schrager had written memos saying that he wanted a trendier group of workers and that the fired employees were "too ethnic."

¶20 Last month the commission reached a $5,00 settlement with 36th Street Food and Drink, a restaurant in St. Joseph, MO, after accusing it of age discrimination against a 47-year-old waitress. The waitress, Michele Cornell, had worked at the restaurant for 23 years, but when it reopened after renovations, it refused to rehire her because, the commission said, she no longer fit the young, trendy look it had adopted.

¶21 "The problem with all this image stuff is it just reeks of marketing for this white-bread, Northern European, thin, wealthy, fashion-model look," said Donna Harper, supervisory attorney in the commission's St. Louis office. "We all can't be Anglo, athletic and young."

¶22 Ms. Harper said an employer who insisted on hiring only athletic-looking people could be viewed as discriminating against a person in a wheelchair. Employers who insisted on hiring only strapping, tall people might be found guilty of discriminating against Mexican-Americans or Asian-Americans, who tend to be shorter, she added.

¶23 Stephen J. Roppolo, a New Orleans lawyer who represents many hotels and restaurants, said: "Hiring someone who is attractive isn't illegal per se. But people's views on what's attractive may be influenced by their race, their religion, their age. If I think Caucasian people are more attractive than African-American people, then I may inadvertently discriminate in some impermissible way. I tell employers that their main focus needs to be hiring somebody who can get the job done. When they want to hire to project a certain image that's where things can get screwy."

¶24 Image seemed very much in evidence the other evening at the Abercrombie & Fitch store in Water Tower Place, one of Chicago's most up-scale malls. Working there was a 6-foot-2 sales clerk with muscles rippling under his Abercrombie T-shirt and a young long-haired blond clerk, her navel showing, who could have been a fashion model.

¶25 "If you see an attractive person working in the store wearing Abercrombie clothes, it makes you want to wear it, too," said Matthew Sheehey, a high school senior from Orland Park, a Chicago suburb.

¶26 Elysa Yanowitz says that when she was a West Coast sales manager for L'Oreal, she felt intense pressure to hire attractive saleswomen, even if they were incompetent. In fact, she says, company officials sought to force her out after she ignored an order to fire a woman a top manager described as not "hot" enough.

¶27 "It was pretty well understood that they had to have magazine-look quality," she said of the sales force. "Everyone is supposed to look like a 110-pound model."

¶28 L'Oreal officials did not respond to a request for comment.

¶29 Melissa Milkie, a sociology professor at the University of Maryland who has written about perceptions of beauty, said: "Good looking people are treated better by others. Maybe companies have noticed that hiring them impacts their bottom line. Whether that's morally proper is a different question."

Appendix 5.2
Sample Text-Surveying Activities
A. Examining the Title

1. "The Rewards of Living a Solitary Life" (Sarton):
    a. Ask students what they think are the two most important words in the title (*rewards* and *solitary*). What do they know about those words (definitions, examples of usage, positive or negative associations)? Is it surprising that those two words are connected in the title?
    b. Ask students to rewrite the title in one sentence in their own words.
2. "Going for the Look, but Risking Discrimination" (Greenhouse): If you have completed schema activation and development exercises, ask learners to paraphrase the first part of the title (*going for the look:* hiring only people who look like the image the company is trying to project for its business). What is the significance of *but* in the title? What does the word *discrimination* mean (definition and positive/negative associations)? What about the word *risking*? (This word suggests that tension or two sides to the issue will be explored, not that the author firmly believes that the practice is discriminatory.)
3. "Friends, Good Friends—and Such Good Friends" (an essay published in *Redbook* by Judith Viorst and included in several reading textbooks, e.g., Spack, 2006; also see Appendix 3.2). Ask students about their reactions to the repetition of the word *friends* and the addition of the words *good* and *such good* the second and third times.
4. "The 'F' Word' " (Dumas, 2006). Ask students if they know what the term "F" *word* typically refers to. What might be the significance of the title? (Note: As it turns out, the title is humorous—the text has nothing to do with profanity.)

B. Looking at the Introduction and Conclusion

1. "Rewards": Ask students to read the first two paragraphs. What happened to the man she describes in the first paragraph? What did he discover? Which sentence in the second paragraph best captures its main idea, and what might it tell you about the rest of the essay? (Note: The sentence to be examined is "But having taken the plunge . . .")

2.   "Look": Ask students to read the first five paragraphs. What are they about? Then have them read the last paragraph. Melissa Milkie asks, "Whether that's morally proper is a different question." What is it that she's wondering about? (from Ching, 2008).

3.   "Friends": Consider the introduction (the first three paragraphs, reprinted below). Why does Viorst repeat the sentence "I once would have said" three times? What sentence in the introduction most likely represents the main idea of the essay? (Note: It is the last sentence of paragraph 3.)

> ¶1 Women are friends, I once would have said, when they totally love and support and trust each other, and bare to each other the secrets of their soul, and run—no questions asked—to help each other, and tell harsh truths to each other (no, you can't wear that dress unless you lose ten pounds first) when harsh truths must be told.
>
> ¶2 Women are friends, I once would have said, when they share the same affection for Ingmar Bergman, plus train rides, cats, warm rain, charades, Camus, and hate with equal ardor Newark and Brussels sprouts and Lawrence Welk and camping.
>
> ¶3 In other words, I once would have said that a friend is a friend all the way, but now I believe that's a narrow point of view. For the friendships I have and the friendships I see are conducted at many levels of intensity, serve many different functions, meet different needs and range from those as all-the-way as the friendship of the soul sisters mentioned above to that of the most nonchalant and casual playmates.

Now ask students to look at the final three paragraphs (reprinted below). Which of the three paragraphs best sums up the ideas of the entire essay? What has Viorst learned about friendship?

> ¶29 There are medium friends, and pretty good friends, and very good friends indeed, and these friendships are defined by their level of intimacy. And what we'll reveal at each of these levels of intimacy is calibrated with care. We might tell a medium friend, for example, that yesterday we had a fight with our husband. And we might tell a pretty good friend that this fight with our husband made us so mad that we slept on the couch. And we might tell a

very good friend that the reason we got so mad in that fight that we slept on the couch had something to do with that girl who works in his office. But it's only to our very best friends that we're willing to tell all, to tell what's going on with that girl in his office.

¶30 The best of friends, I still believe, totally love and support and trust each other, and bare to each other the secrets of their souls, and run—no questions asked—to help each other, and tell harsh truths to each other when they must be told.

¶31 But we needn't agree about everything (only 12-year-old girl-friends agree about everything) to tolerate each other's point of view. To accept without judgment. To give to take without ever keeping score. And to be there, as I am for them and as they are for me, to comfort our sorrows, to celebrate our joys. (Viorst, n.d.)

C. Skimming for Main Ideas

1. "Rewards": Ask students to read Sarton's essay through quickly, looking for the answer to the following question: *What is Sarton's opinion about living alone?*

2. "Going for the Look": Ask students to read the entire essay and then write two sentences that explain the conflict suggested by the title, using the following sentence frames:
   a. Some businesses like to_____.
   b. However, some people argue that_____.

D. Scanning for Specific Information

1. "Rewards": Ask students to look quickly through the text for the words *lonely* and *loneliness*. What claims does Sarton make about those words, and how do they relate to the title of the essay?

2. "Going for the Look": Ask students to look through the article for the words *discriminate* and *discrimination*. What kinds of discrimination are mentioned, and how do they relate to the meaning of the text as a whole?

3. "Friends": Ask students to look for where Viorst discusses "medium friends, pretty good friends, and very good friends." Ask them to read the whole paragraph in which these terms are found and to relate the paragraph to the title of the essay.

E. Understanding the Macrostructure of the Text

1. "Rewards": Ask students to number the paragraphs. Which paragraphs constitute the introduction? The conclusion?
2. "Friends": See Figure 3.9.

Chapter 6
Reading for Quantity
The Benefits and Challenges of Extensive Reading

Given the overwhelming evidence for the importance of extensive reading in learning to read in a second language, why isn't everyone doing it?
William Grabe (1995, cited in Day & Bamford, 1998, p. 41)

Questions for Reflection

- Consider your experiences with intensive reading (close, careful examination of required texts) and extensive reading (reading quantities of self-selected materials for information or pleasure).
  - ➤ How are the two types of experiences distinct?
  - ➤ Which has contributed most to your literacy skills (including reading and writing)?
- What do you see as the possible benefits of extensive reading for L1 and especially L2 readers?
- If you were to adopt an extensive reading approach for all or part of an L2 reading course (or a reading/writing course), what might be some of the risks or potential drawbacks of doing so? Can you think of ways to overcome these drawbacks?

Extensive Reading: Definitions

Because the term *extensive reading* does not always mean exactly the same thing in practice, it is important to begin our discussion with a range of definitions. Day (1993) defined extensive reading in very basic terms: "the teaching of reading *through reading* . . . there is no overt focus on teaching reading. Rather, it is assumed that the best way for students to learn to read is by *reading a great deal of comprehensible material*" (p. xi, emphases added). Day and Bamford (1998) added an early definition from Palmer (1917/1968, 1921/1964), who is credited with being the first to apply the term "extensive reading" to L2 pedagogy, describing it as "rapidly reading book after book." Palmer contrasted it explicitly with intensive reading or "to take a text and study it line by line" (Palmer, 1921/1964, p. 111, cited in Day & Bamford, 1998, p. 5). These definitions focus on *quantity* of materials read, in contrast to the explicit classroom *teaching* of reading.

Another important aspect of the extensive reading definition is connected to *student choice* and *pleasure* in reading. Another early definition cited by Day and Bamford was articulated by Michael West (1931), who saw the purpose of extensive reading as "the development *to the point of enjoyment* of the ability to read in the foreign language" (Day & Bamford, 1998, p. 6, emphasis added). Much later, Krashen (1985, 1989, 2004, n.d.) stressed the importance of Free Voluntary Reading (FVR), meaning "reading because you want to" (Krashen, 2004, p. x). Finally, Aebersold and Field (1997) blend a focus on reading for quantity and overall meaning with student choice in their definition of extensive reading for L2 students: "An extensive approach to teaching reading is based on the belief that when *students read for general comprehension large quantities of text of their own choosing*, their ability to read will consequently improve" (p. 43, emphasis added). Though the "voluntary" and "enjoyment" aspects of the definitions may in practice be a bit idealistic, the common element of all of them is reading for quantity and for general meaning rather than reading shorter texts for close, intensive analysis.

To expand on the definitions a bit further, Aebersold and Field (1997) and Day and Bamford (1998) outlined the characteristics of an extensive reading approach designed for the classroom setting (see Figure 6.1). Two important features distinguish these lists. First, whereas Aebersold and Field stressed the importance of students reading *authentic* texts (i.e., those not written or adapted for language-learning purposes), Day and Bamford encouraged teachers to avoid narrow views of what they called "language-learner literature" (simplified materials for readers at lower L2 proficiency levels). Second, Day and Bamford defined the extensive reading approach as entirely student-directed in terms of choice of reading material), but Aebersold and Field suggested that even teacher-selected readings can be considered part of an extensive reading classroom. We will return to these distinctions later, when we discuss curricular options and assembling materials.

1. Students read as much as possible, perhaps in and definitely out of the classroom.
2. A variety of materials on a wide range of topics is available so as to encourage reading for different reasons and in different ways.
3. Students select what they want to read and have the freedom to stop reading material that fails to interest them.
4. The purposes of reading are generally related to pleasure, information, and general understanding. These purposes are determined by the nature of the material and the interests of the student.
5. Reading is its own reward. There are few or no follow-up exercises after reading.
6. Reading materials are well within the linguistic competence of the students in terms of vocabulary and grammar. Dictionaries are rarely used while reading because the constant stopping to look up words makes fluent reading difficult.
7. Reading is individual and silent, at the student's own pace, and, outside class, done when and where the student chooses.
8. Reading speed is usually faster rather than slower as students read books and material they find easily understandable.
9. Teachers orient students to the goals of the program, explain the methodology, keep track of what each student reads, and guide students in getting the most out of the program.
10. The teacher is a role model of a reader for students—an active member of the classroom reading community, demonstrating what it means to be a reader and the rewards of being a reader.

(Day & Bamford, 1998, pp. 7–8)

- Reading is a means to an end—a summary, book report, discussion, and so on.
- Students are given freedom to choose and responsibility to find materials.
- Reading materials may be entirely self-selected or partially chosen by the teacher.
- Most reading is done outside of class without peer or teacher help.
- The goal of reading is comprehension of main ideas, not every detail or word.
- The quantity of reading required precludes fixating on detail or translating into L1.
- Activities may include reading several texts on the same topic— readers "will bring more background knowledge to each new text they read" (p. 43).
- Extensive reading is not used to teach or practice specific reading strategies or skills.
- All materials are authentic texts, with no accompanying exercises.

(Aebersold & Field, 1997, pp. 43–44)

FIGURE 6.1. Characteristics of Extensive Reading Approaches in L2 Classes.

Perspectives on Extensive Reading

Rarely in language education do we find a teaching approach that is so universally hailed as beneficial, important, and necessary—truly an approach that has *no* detractors and many fervent advocates—yet is so underutilized and even ignored in curricula, course/lesson design, and materials development. As noted by Grabe and Stoller (2002), "*students learn to read by reading a lot, yet reading a lot is not the emphasis of most reading curricula*" (p. 90, emphasis added). This is such a fascinating and glaringly apparent contradiction that we find ourselves speculating on the reasons behind it.

On reflection, we would guess that the issues preventing extensive reading from being widely used are both political and practical. What is termed extensive reading in L2 classrooms derives in part from Whole Language (WL) approaches to L1 elementary literacy education: Children (or L2 readers) are exposed to authentic texts and encouraged to read for meaning (i.e., using "top-down" skills, see Chapter 1) rather than focusing on bottom-up decoding skills such as letter–sound correspondences, spelling, grammar, or punctuation rules, precise definitions of vocabulary words, and so on. The political battle between WL approaches and parts-centered, skills-based approaches rages on to this day, with conservative commentators blaming WL for a host of social ills and liberal pundits claiming that traditional phonics instruction is a means of subjugating linguistic minorities (see Cazden, 1992; Kim & Krashen, 1997; Krashen, 2004; Weaver, 1998, 2002).[1] In the state of California, for example, WL instruction was adopted for elementary education in the mid-1980s and continued as the prescribed (if not preferred) approach until the current state standards for language arts were adopted in 1998. There is a fair amount of anecdotal lamentation among parents, teachers, and political leaders about a "whole generation of California schoolchildren who were 'lost' " during this period of WL "wandering" and who now cannot spell, punctuate, read or write effectively. Scarcella (1996, 2003) indicted both WL approaches to reading and process approaches to writing, arguing that they particularly disadvantaged Generation 1.5 students). Stephen Krashen (2002) called this purported "plummeting" of literacy skills in California as a result of WL an "urban legend." Whether these accusations are reasonable or accurate is an issue that we will explore further; for the moment, it is sufficient to say that any approach to teaching reading that sounds at all like WL is viewed with suspicion by educators from certain contexts (Sweet, 2004). Although extensive reading and WL are not identical or synonymous, the two approaches share enough philosophical and practical similarities that some critics of WL might also be dubious about extensive reading.

Another political reason underlying the neglect of extensive reading in literacy instruction may relate to its most visible proponents, themselves controversial figures. An articulate advocate of top-down, WL-based reading is Frank Smith, whose classic book, *Understanding Reading*, is now in its sixth edition. In the preface to the latest edition, Smith presented a review of the fifth edition:

This volume contains partial truths, contradictions, and cites only references that support the author's view. Either the author is not familiar with the current research literature, or he deliberately avoids citing evidence that is contrary to his point of view . . . This book is no recipe for improving reading skills of children, especially beginning readers and poor readers; it is a recipe for disaster. (Anonymous reviewer, cited in Smith, 2004, p. vii)

Smith quoted another reviewer, whose response to the book was highly favorable, pointing out that both reviewers are education professors who are experts in the field. He described the "head-on clash of attitudes" that permeates all dimensions of reading theory and instruction among teachers, policy-makers, and the general public. This clash "has become a focus of legislation and litigation. One has to turn to religious fundamentalism to find another issue that arouses such bitter controversy" (p. viii). Smith further observed that every edition of *Understanding Reading*, beginning with the first in 1971, has produced similarly polarized reactions and that people who oppose the book's views "anathematize" it (and presumably, him).

As for L2 education, without a doubt the most controversial figure in the field is Professor Emeritus Stephen Krashen of the University of Southern California. Krashen's (1981, 1982, 1985) early work in articulating his five hypotheses of SLA has again been extremely polarizing—widely criticized by other SLA researchers and theorists, yet extremely influential in classroom L2 instruction. Influenced by the pioneering work of Kenneth Goodman and Frank Smith, Krashen (1985, 1988, 1989, 2004) turned his attention to "the power of reading," and the combination of disdain for his SLA theories and general suspicion of WL approaches not only made it difficult for him to get his *Power of Reading* (2004) book published initially but has also led to an unfortunate and counterproductive disregard by many for his important work in literacy education over the past two decades.[2]

In addition to the political furor over WL and the demonizing of its advocates, practical issues have made the widespread adoption of extensive reading for L2 instruction slow and problematic. Aebersold and Field (1997) described extensive reading as "relatively uncommon" (p. 44), and despite the publication of an excellent volume entitled *Extensive Reading in the Second Language Classroom*, the following year by Day and Bamford (1998), we see little evidence that much has changed to date. As we noted in Chapter 1, Smith (2004) gloomily reported that "direct instruction [has] carried the day," with WL being "sidelined rather than vanquished" (p. ix). Practical obstacles to the implementation of extensive reading in L2 contexts (especially at secondary and postsecondary levels) include a lack of resources (i.e., classroom library materials), preestablished curricular objectives, and low student interest (Day & Bamford, 1998; Ferris & Hedgcock, 2005). Further, teachers may not understand how to administer an extensive reading program, which requires organizing a syllabus, planning class sessions, and developing a systematic assessment plan (see Chapters 4 and 9). Even if teachers hear and read about the indisputable benefits of extensive reading for their L2 students and are absolutely convinced of its value, they may not know exactly how to put those insights into practice.

In this chapter, we address the issues outlined above: We will review the case for extensive reading, acknowledging the challenges of utilizing it and suggesting ways to overcome those challenges. We hope that readers will finish this chapter convinced, inspired, empowered, and equipped to help their students take fuller advantage of the power of [extensive] reading.

Benefits of Extensive Reading

As we said previously, extensive reading is an approach to pedagogy with no real detractors. Even those who argue for a balance of intensive and extensive reading acknowledge the importance and indispensability of extensive reading. For example, while warning against "extremes" in reading instruction, Eskey and Grabe (1988) made the following observations:

> Both top-down and bottom-up skills can, in the long run, only be developed by extensive reading over time. Classroom work can point the way but not substitute for the act itself: *People learn to read by reading, not by doing exercises* . . . A reading program that does not involve much reading is clearly a contradiction in terms—and a waste of the teacher's and students' time. (p. 228, emphasis added)

Grabe and Stoller (2002) similarly argued that, "although extensive reading, by itself, is not sufficient for the development of fluent reading comprehension abilities, such abilities cannot be developed without extensive reading" (p. 90).

The benefits of extensive reading in both L1 and L2 are substantial and extremely well documented. Readers interested in comprehensive reviews of the evidence are encouraged especially to examine the first four chapters of Day and Bamford's (1998) book and the first chapter of Krashen (2004). Here we briefly summarize and discuss some of the findings (especially for L2 readers) in six categories (see Figure 6.2).

Extensive Reading Improves Comprehension Skills

As discussed in Chapter 1, reading comprehension is a complex construct that involves the interaction of a number of psycholinguistic processes. It goes far beyond the ability to state the main idea of a text in one sentence, answer questions about details, define vocabulary, accurately read the text aloud, and so forth. Comprehension further involves the simultaneous and largely subconscious application of various types of background knowledge (schemata) and reading skills to particular texts. Extensive reading is fairly rapid and covers quantities of

---

Extensive reading . . .

1. improves comprehension skills;
2. develops automaticity;
3. enhances background knowledge (schemata, both content and formal);
4. builds vocabulary and grammar knowledge (i.e., linguistic schemata);
5. improves production skills (speaking and especially writing);
6. promotes confidence and motivation.

FIGURE 6.2. Benefits of Extensive Reading.

text (compared with other types of reading), and its intent is by definition to *read* rather than to *learn about* reading or to dissect text samples in the ways discussed in Chapter 5. Consequently, extensive reading offers readers crucial practice in applying schemata and strategies. Krashen (2004) summarized a number of studies of the effects of FVR (and other variations of extensive reading, such as *shared reading*) on the reading comprehension of English L1 primary and secondary students as well as English L2 readers (both children and adults). As measured by scores on standardized reading comprehension tests (e.g., Elley, 1991, 1992, 1998; Elley & Mangubhai, 1983) or cloze tests (Mason & Krashen, 1997), readers in all contexts who engaged in in-class extensive reading performed as well as or better than those who received only direct classroom instruction. The studies by Elley and colleagues are especially impressive in that they include large numbers of participants and are longitudinal. See Grabe and Stoller (2002, pp. 144–145) for further discussion of Elley's 1991 study.

Extensive Reading Develops Automaticity

It is widely accepted by L1 reading theorists that fluent reading begins with "the lightning-like, automatic recognition of words" (Day & Bamford, 1998, p. 12). Smith (2004) noted that "fluent readers are able to recognize at least 50,000 words on sight" (p. 126); such "immediate word recognition" then frees up the mind to bring other types of schemata to the reading process, in line with the compensatory model of reading introduced in Chapter 1. The rapid recognition of 50,000 (or more) words is a daunting task even for L1 readers who already have an extensive oral vocabulary. It takes many years of reading exposure for most children to reach that point. Some never reach it, explaining why levels of literacy and reading comprehension ability vary widely across learners, learner populations, and educational settings. For a language learner to become a fluent L2 reader, the task is even more immense, as L2 readers must master unfamiliar vocabulary, morphology, and syntax to recognize words in print automatically (see Chapters 1, 3, and 8). According to Day and Bamford (1998), "the best and easiest way to accomplish this is to read a great deal" (p. 16). Studies showing that vocabulary growth is aided by extensive reading (discussed further below) lend support to the automaticity argument as well (Horst, 2005; Nagy, Anderson, & Herman, 1987; Nagy & Herman, 1987; Nagy, Herman, & Anderson, 1985; Pichette, 2005; Pitts, White, & Krashen, 1989; Saragi, Nation, & Meister, 1978).

Extensive Reading Builds Background Knowledge

As noted in Chapters 2 and 3, L2 readers face challenges that go beyond the formal characteristics of language. Depending on their background, their differing cultural knowledge may cause comprehension gaps (Carrell & Eisterhold, 1983; Eskey, 1986). As an example, the narrative essay "A Mason-Dixon Memory" (Davis, 1997) is included in middle school readers for U.S. schoolchildren. Years of experience in school hearing about historical figures such as Martin Luther King, Jr. and Abraham Lincoln (both of whom have holidays in their honor in the United States) can equip young readers with the content schemata to comprehend such a story. "A Mason-Dixon Memory" presents a straightforward narrative about the Mason-Dixon Line, an indirect reference to what were known as "Jim Crow" laws, which segregated and discriminated against African Americans.

In contrast, students socialized in other cultural settings who have little or no knowledge of U.S. history might not recognize these references. If students come from societies in which ethnic and cultural minorities are routinely and legally discriminated against, they may interpret and react to the stories of Clifton Davis and Dondré Green very differently than do U.S. students living on the other side of the civil rights movement. However, if in their extensive reading they have encountered fiction such as Harper Lee's *To Kill a Mockingbird* or works chronicling the African-American experience, students might approach "A Mason-Dixon Memory" with content and cultural schemata for the turbulent history of African Americans in the mid- to late twentieth century. Similar examples of content knowledge that may be unfamiliar but that could be cultivated through extensive reading might include references to Judeo-Christian traditions (which factor heavily not only in Western literature but in contemporary politics) or sports-related metaphors.

In addition to building content knowledge through reading, L2 readers who are literate and educated in their L1s may have differing formal schemata, or be influenced by what is known as *contrastive* or *intercultural rhetoric* (Connor, 1996, 2002, 2003, 2005; Connor, Nagelhoot, & Rozycki, 2008; Kaplan, 1966). For instance, in some non-Western literary traditions, it is common to embellish descriptions even to the point of what North American readers might consider ineffective digressions (Kaplan, 1966; Liebman, 1992). Students from those backgrounds might not recognize that in many English-language fiction subgenres (e.g., mysteries, thrillers, and tightly scripted works of short fiction), every detail matters, nothing is wasted, and each clue must be noted in order to understand the story. Hinds (1987) described one of the most widely recognized and clearcut examples of how genres may contrast cross-culturally in his analysis of the major distinctions between argumentative writing in Japanese and English. A Japanese L2 reader of English who routinely reads English-language newspapers, including opinion columns and editorials, might over time develop a better understanding of U.S. persuasive style.

It could be argued that classroom teachers can build L2 readers' formal, content, and cultural schemata during the pre-reading phase of intensive reading instruction (see Chapter 5). For instance, a teacher presenting "A Mason-Dixon Memory" to L2 readers educated outside the US could provide historical background about the Civil War, Abraham Lincoln, the Gettysburg Address, the Mason-Dixon Line, Jim Crow laws, and subsequent anti-discrimination legislation. Pre-teaching could help students navigate the somewhat challenging story-within-a-story structure of the Davis narrative by introducing the flashback technique often found in American film and television. Explicit instruction can serve to develop such content and cultural schemata, although such direct approaches can be costly in terms of class time and teacher effort. Moreover, direct instruction may only useful for a single text (and perhaps others closely related to it). In contrast, a student engaged in extensive reading gains background knowledge "for free" (Smith, 1988). That is, she can draw on implicit knowledge for future reading, in the same way that a U.S.-born child, having read *American Girl* novels or *Dear America* journals as a young reader, has developed content schemata that is available when she later studies U.S. history in secondary school.

Finally, Day and Bamford (1998) observed that the background knowledge developed by extensive reading can promote readers' critical thinking skills (e.g., comparing and questioning evidence, evaluating arguments, and so forth). Grabe (1986) noted that discovery and creative reasoning "are emergent processes where the mind, almost of itself, *makes nonobvious connections and relations between independent domains of knowledge* . . . Prior reading experiences are crucial for having the information base to make nonobvious connections" (p. 35, emphasis added). Extensive reading allows students to "read broadly and deeply enough to achieve the mass of background knowledge on which speculative thinking depends" (Day & Bamford, 1998, p. 45). Although Day and Bamford acknowledged that L2 students (particularly academically oriented learners) must master intensive reading skills, they argued that intensive reading alone will not provide this "broad and deep" base of knowledge.

Extensive Reading Builds Vocabulary and Grammar Knowledge

One of the strongest claims made by Krashen, starting with his five hypotheses for SLA (Krashen, 1981, 1982, 1985) and continuing with his "power of reading" work (Krashen, 2004), is that readers (including L2 learners) acquire knowledge about language *incidentally* through reading. He reviewed research specifically for vocabulary, grammar, and spelling knowledge, concluding that students can acquire at least as much linguistic knowledge through FVR as through any type of direct classroom instruction (and, in some studies, significantly more)—and with more enjoyment, less stress, and other attending benefits. L1 research (e.g., Nagy et al., 1985; Saragi et al., 1978; Wigfield & Guthrie, 1997) and reviews of related L1 and L2 studies (e.g., Day & Bamford, 1998; Grabe & Stoller, 2002; Smith, 2004) have drawn similar conclusions.

These claims regarding the ease and efficacy of *incidental learning* of linguistic knowledge through reading have not been without their detractors. For example, Folse (2004) identified "learning new words from context" as a "vocabulary myth," arguing that for L2 readers in particular, the linguistic context itself may be too unfamiliar to be helpful. It is also important to note that being able to use top-down strategies to read a text for meaning, guessing at or skipping over unfamiliar words, does not necessarily mean that readers then acquire those unfamiliar items over the long term. We discuss issues and options surrounding direct vocabulary instruction as well as development of vocabulary learning strategies in Chapter 8.

At this point, however, without adopting an extreme position regarding incidental learning or direct language instruction, research provides fairly incontrovertible evidence that extensive reading can, indeed, promote language development and literacy. In line with Smith (1988, 2004, 2006, 2007), Krashen (2004) noted that "language is too complex to be deliberately and consciously learned one rule or item at a time" (p. 18). This argument seems especially compelling with regard to English syntax, which is characterized by many orthographic and syntactic idiosyncrasies that even the most brilliant linguists struggle to describe and which even literate, well-educated native speakers cannot always understand formally. The English lexicon is also remarkably complex due to its diverse origins and dynamic history (see Chapter 8). There is simply too much complex linguistic information for learners to master consciously or intentionally under the typical time constraints that affect most L2 readers.

Extensive reading naturally exposes readers to naturally-occurring phrasal and clausal patterns, repeated and alternate uses of lexical items and their spellings, and a range of other graphological features such as paragraphing, punctuation, and capitalization conventions. For L2 learners, extensive reading can provide the quantity and exposure to the patterns of language that give native-speaking students such a head start. In fact, beyond arguing that extensive reading can promote language development, we would state the case more strongly (agreeing with Krashen and others). Certain aspects of language can *only* be acquired through extensive and authentic exposure to the L2 (i.e., through reading, listening, and interaction), and once learners arrive at a certain stage of L2 acquisition (intermediate to advanced levels), it is likely that their continued progress in that language will largely result from such natural exposure and not classroom instruction.

Extensive Reading Improves Production Skills (Speaking and Especially Writing)

Having argued that extensive reading promotes various types of schematic development (formal, content, and cultural), it seems fair to assume that having such tools at one's disposal through reading is not only *helpful* to L2 production but *indispensable* to it. As for oral production, whereas reading does not directly address pronunciation, accent, or formal speaking skills, both formal speeches and informal interactions are certainly facilitated by having access to an extensive vocabulary and a grasp of varied syntactic and morphological structures. Where written production is concerned, it has been well established in L1 and L2 research that, although successful readers may not necessarily be effective writers, it is virtually impossible to find successful writers who are not also good readers.[3] For writers, reading provides material to write about, linguistic tools with which to express ideas, and rhetorical models to learn from.

A great deal more that could be said about the reading–writing connection, but we will make two important observations here. First, critical properties distinguish written registers from spoken registers (Biber, 1998, 2006). Residence in an L2 environment, interaction with native speakers, and listening to teachers, radio, and television may improve an L2 learner's comprehension and confidence. These advantages may also promote communicative competence; however, *these forms of input and interaction are not sufficient to help learners become proficient L2 writers (or readers)*. Because written text exhibits unique characteristics, only by reading texts (intensively and extensively) can L2 readers build the necessary schemata. Second, while acknowledging the critical importance of extensive reading for the development of competence in writing, we do not entirely share Krashen's (2004) strong position that "writing style comes from reading, not writing." We would also challenge his assertion that "language acquisition comes from input, not output, from comprehension, not production. Thus, if you write a page a day, your writing style or your command of mechanics will not improve" (p. 136). Krashen conceded that writing *is* good for improving *thinking and problem-solving* skills, but we would also observe that the act of writing can improve one's thinking *about writing* (as well as whatever ideas one is writing about) (Hirvela, 2004). In Krashen's "page-a-day" example, if students think on a daily basis about what to write (ideas), in what order to present those ideas (rhetoric), and what linguistic or extralinguistic tools to utilize (e.g., using new lexical items, applying a punctuation rule learned in class or observed through reading), these regular decision-making processes will surely benefit their long-term development as L2 writers. In other words, as we have argued elsewhere (Ferris & Hedgcock, 2005), we absolutely agree with Krashen and others that extensive reading is a critical foundation of good reading and writing skills, yet we further believe that people *also* "learn to write by writing." That said, we would never argue that writing practice alone should subsume either intensive or extensive reading in L2 literacy instruction.

Extensive Reading Promotes Student Confidence and Motivation

Scholars may disagree about the previous two benefits of extensive reading, but there is unanimous agreement on this final point: Extensive reading (especially FVR) can be extremely enjoyable for students, it can motivate them to take on reading on their own in the future, and it can build confidence in their reading skills and their ability to use the L2 beyond the classroom (Yopp & Yopp, 2005). For example, in a large L1 study, Ivey and Broaddus (2001) reported that over 1700 Grade 6 learners strongly rated "free reading time" and "teacher reading aloud" as their most preferred language arts activities. University L2 students surveyed by McQuillan (1994) strongly favored extensive reading activities over grammar instruction. In a case study by Cho and Krashen (1994), four adult learners reported dramatic changes in attitude toward, and motivation for, reading in English after reading titles from the *Sweet Valley High* or *Sweet Valley Twins* series popular with young U.S. readers. Krashen (2004) reviewed a number of L1 and L2 studies (most involving classroom *sustained silent reading* [SSR]), providing substantial evidence (with only two minor exceptions) that students found in-class free reading very enjoyable and that teachers felt it was very successful both for discipline and for motivating students to read more. Some teachers reported that they had a hard time getting their students to *stop* reading when it was time to move on to some other activity.

A striking example of how FVR can improve student confidence and motivation comes from a longitudinal case study of a Japanese ESL student, Yuko, in a U.S. university (Spack, 2004). In her freshman year, Yuko struggled tremendously with reading for her political science courses, eventually dropping them. However, a remarkable transformation occurred during the summer between Yuko's first and second years: She spent the summer reading novels in English and Japanese (including page-turners such as John Grisham's *The Firm*). "To get through these long books, [Yuko] said she 'just read for the story, the suspense. I didn't use a dictionary because I wasn't paying attention to details' " (Spack, 2004, p. 24). Somewhat surprisingly (even to researcher Spack), this successful and enjoyable FVR experience extended to Yuko's academic reading when she returned to school. Over time, Yuko successfully tackled the courses she had previously given up on and completed her education. Spack (2004) wrote that, when she questioned the leap from reading fiction for pleasure to the reading she would have to do in political science, Yuko responded that "It gave me confidence to read nonfiction too. It's totally different, but I thought I could" (p. 25). Reflecting on the entire four-year process, Spack noted that "Yuko had her first breakthrough after exposure to fiction . . . applying strategies for reading literature to her political science texts, she was able to make immediate strides and overcome her fear of reading" (p. 35). Like many Japanese learners of English, Yuko had had limited experience with reading in English prior to coming to the US to study and found the sheer volume of reading expected of her overwhelming

(Robb, 2001). Extensive reading provided her with the experience and confidence she needed to read larger quantities of material. It can be dangerous to over-generalize from the experience of one L2 reader, though we are reminded of Eskey's (1986) description of the "confidence gap" that L2 readers face: It is not hard to believe that Yuko's experience could be transferable to other L2 readers once they begin to believe they can read a lengthier work in English.

Summary: The Case for Extensive Reading

We have touched only briefly on the potential benefits of extensive reading for L2 students, but it is clear that the case is a powerful one. Extensive reading improves *reading* ability through practice that improves comprehension and efficiency, simultaneously building schematic knowledge, thereby enhancing subsequent reading. Extensive reading also promotes language acquisition, improving productive skills such as writing. Furthermore, it is enjoyable for students and makes them not only *believe* that they can read successfully in their L2 but *want* to do so.

Summing up considerable empirical research, Krashen (2004) concluded that "there is abundant evidence that literacy development can occur without formal instruction. Moreover, this evidence strongly suggests that *reading is potent enough to do the job alone*" (p. 20, emphasis added). Unlike Krashen, we would argue that judicious, thoughtful integration of intensive reading instruction (including vocabulary learning) with extensive reading opportunities provides the best of both worlds (see Chapters 4, 5, and 8; also see Ferris & Hedgcock, 2005). The purpose of this chapter is to explore why L2 teachers should include extensive reading as a key element of the curriculum. The problem, as we have stated, is that most teachers do *not* incorporate extensive reading in L2 literacy instruction. We hope that the foregoing discussion of its benefits will give readers food for thought and a desire to take a first or second look at *how* they might go about implementing and encouraging extensive reading. In short, we believe that Krashen is right to advocate strongly in favor of extensive reading. The power of reading is far too important to be ignored or neglected any longer. Why would we want to deprive our students of its potency?

(Perceived) Problems and Challenges with Extensive Reading

To answer our own question, we doubt that few (or any) teachers would want to "cheat" their students of the obvious benefits that accrue from extensive reading. However, many of us are unclear about how to implement extensive reading effectively in our local instructional contexts. In this section, we turn to the issue of implementation—but first, we will address several of the practical obstacles noted in the introduction to this chapter. Ferris and Hedgcock (2005) offered explanations for the underuse of extensive reading, especially in academic settings beyond the elementary school level; many of the same problems are examined by Day and Bamford (1998). We will discuss several of issues that we consider to be particularly salient: time and competing curricular expectations, limited resources, and student resistance.

Time and Pre-Existing Curricular Requirements

Many studies and procedures for implementing extensive reading examined by Krashen, Day and Bamford, and others were particular to primary and secondary school settings where a single teacher has a great deal of sustained time with a single cohort of students (hours every day for an academic year or even years). In such settings, it is relatively easier to find class time for SSR, for book group discussions, for oral book reports, and for the teacher to read books aloud and take students to the library. It is also easier to make a classroom library available if the same teacher and students spend the entire school day in the same room (in contrast to the typical secondary setting in which students and even teachers move from room to room all day long).[4] Furthermore, at secondary and post-secondary levels, students are often only in English classes for a few hours per week. They may also have a great deal of outside work assigned for all of their courses, potentially limiting the amount of at-home extensive reading that can reasonably be expected. In addition, in many secondary settings, detailed and exhaustive government-imposed standards must be practiced and assessed during a course. Consequently, reading extensively or for pleasure is rarely, if ever, included in such lists of curricular requirements. Similarly, postsecondary language curricula tend to focus on academic literacy skills (i.e., through intensive reading and composition instruction), not on encouraging students to read large quantities of material for meaning and enjoyment or for personal enrichment.

Resources

As we will observe in the final section of this chapter, making appropriate resources available to students (and teaching them how to select materials for their own reading) is absolutely critical to the success of extensive reading programs. For instance, Robb (2001) described an extensive reading course in a Japanese university. This course included structured extensive reading using the popular SRA reading program, as well as self-selected reading from a classroom library of 200–250 books from which students could choose. However, in many settings, the financial means to purchase books, newspapers, and magazines for a classroom or program library are scarce or nonexistent. The students themselves may also be on tight budgets and cannot be expected to purchase materials for themselves. They also may not have ready access to school or public libraries to obtain materials (Krashen, 2007).

Student Resistance

Especially in academic settings, students may not easily see the benefits of exten-sive reading and may resent teachers asking or requiring them to do it. At least two factors may account for such resistance. First, it is no longer a given, even among L1 readers, that students will have much experience with extensive read-ing. As already noted, at all levels of education, classroom activities that promote and encourage FVR or extensive reading have been crowded out of the curric-ulum. In addition, outside of school, students have to manage the distractions of extracurricular activities (sports, music lessons, volunteer work) that are often deemed critical for future college admission, not to mention television, the Internet, and video games.[5] As for L2 readers, some have received their English-language education in settings in which they read very little or in which silent or extensive reading was not a value (see Chapter 2). For example, in a study of Japanese university students in a course for English majors, Robb (1991) reported that "most students enter university studies without ever having read more than two or three pages of English prose at a time" (p. 219)—despite having studied English for five to six years previously. The same was true for Spack's (2004) case-study subject, Yuko, who came from Japan to pursue undergraduate studies in the United States. Even L2 readers mostly or entirely educated in English-speaking environments typically have read relatively less than their native-speaking counterparts, as they face the same classroom constraints and external distractions *and* face the added challenges of a later start in learning English and living in a non- or limited-English-speaking home. In short, for students who have rarely or never read much at all, perhaps in any language, it may be challenging to convince them of the benefits and enjoyment that come from extensive reading.

Even students who have been extensive readers in their L1s may not easily "transfer" those practices to their L2 reading. Although much has been written about the transfer of literacy skills from one language to another (Carson et al., 1990; Cummins, 1981; Hudson, 2007; Koda, 2004; Krashen, 2004; Mohan & Lo, 1985), it also appears to be true that students' lack of ability and confidence in their L2 reading ability can "short-circuit" even fluent L1 reading skills (Clarke, 1980, 1988; Eskey, 1986), causing them to read word-for-word, read too slowly, translate, overuse the dictionary, and so forth. Even highly proficient L2 learners who are avid readers in their L1s may feel that extensive L2 reading seems like work rather than pleasure and, though they know it is good for them, they may not choose to pick up L2 pleasure reading in their spare time (any more than we might "choose" to go to the gym or eat vegetables).[6]

Second, students acquiring academic literacy may be just as aware as their teachers are of the specific literacy skills that they need to master to succeed in their studies and future careers—development of academic and discipline-specific vocabulary and grammar, the ability to read and write effectively across academic genres, coverage of certain types of content, and so on. Learners may not easily see that reading quantities of self-selected material for pleasure will help them to achieve those goals, and they may become frustrated or anxious if their teacher insists on spending class time on FVR or assigns extensive reading as homework.

In summary, legitimate questions and issues should be addressed if teachers are to implement extensive reading successfully in their L2 courses. We do not see any of the above problems as insurmountable, and we will discuss practical options and solutions in the "Implementation" section that follows. It should also be obvious that, given the substantial advantages of extensive reading reviewed here, we believe that teachers have an *obligation* to work toward creative solutions in their contexts, rather than merely dismissing extensive reading as impractical. Before discussing implementation, though, we must outline curricular models in which extensive reading might take place.

Curricular Models for Extensive Reading in L2 Settings

Overall Objective

Regardless of the specific institutional context being considered, we would claim that the primary objective of including an extensive reading component in one's class or curriculum is to *convince students of its value so that they will continue reading extensively on their own once the class is over.* In short, the extensive reading teachers that build into their programs, whatever form it takes, is not an end in itself. Truthfully, the benefits of extensive reading discussed above are mostly for the long-term and would be hard to measure and observe fully within the parameters of one particular course. The various models, discussed in general terms below, are also presented in chart form in Figure 6.3.

Extensive Reading in a Language Program

In self-supporting intensive language programs attached to a college or university, or in a private, independent language school, students typically study the L2 full-time for a relatively brief period (a few weeks to a year in duration depending on the student or program). Most or all of these programs include reading as either a separate course, in a reading–writing course, or in an integrated-skills curriculum. Such programs can be ideal for promoting extensive reading, as they are: (1) usually free from external constraints such as state-mandated or institutional standards; and (2) client-driven, meaning that keeping the students happy and enjoying their language studies is essential to the longevity of the program. Since FVR, SSR, and extensive reading may by all accounts be very pleasurable, they can be an excellent fit for these fairly relaxed settings. Administrators and instructors in intensive language programs can consider dedicating an elective course to extensive reading, incorporate it systematically

Context or setting	Student Goals/needs	Extensive L2 Reading Appropriate?
Intensive language program	Short-term general language development, enjoyment	Yes, for "habit-formation" for lifelong learning and enjoyment of the L2
Foreign-language setting	Complete foreign-language requirements for graduation or college admission	Yes, to provide additional L2 input and exposure outside the classroom
Non-academic setting (e.g., adult or vocational school)	Survival, citizenship, employment	Yes, as a way to speed up language acquisition and assimilation; also to build confidence and enjoyment and reduce stress
Academic setting (secondary)	Complete high school graduation requirements, meet external standards	Yes, as a supplement to teacher/school-selected literary texts to build motivation (reading is not just for English class)
Academic setting (postsecondary)	Build academic literacy skills for further studies	Yes, integrated with intensive reading approaches; student-selected reading as a focus for writing essays, summaries, response papers

FIGURE 6.3. Curricular Models for Extensive Reading in L2 Settings.

into the existing curriculum, or even feature extensive reading as the program's required reading component. Students in such programs may go on to further academic work in L2 institutions: Providing them a low-risk opportunity to read the L2 in quantity can surely build their reading efficiency, confidence, vocabulary size, and schematic knowledge, all of which will serve them well later, even in academic intensive-reading contexts.

Extensive Reading in a Foreign-Language Context

EFL learners typically begin studying English (and other languages) in primary school, continue through high school, and perhaps even through college. Once students have progressed beyond the very beginning levels of L2 instruction, extensive reading may be an extremely good use of their time, whether it comprises an entire reading/language course, supplements other class work or homework, or is simply recommended or offered for extra credit. Students in FL programs in their home countries often suffer from a lack of adequate input in the L2. In addition, their teachers may not be native speakers of the L2, and their classes may be so large that there are few opportunities for interaction or practice. Consequently, learners may have few opportunities to hear, read, or speak the L2 outside of their language courses. Designing an extensive reading component for such students is an excellent way to address this input gap. Further, FL students may never study or use the L2 for academic purposes. After all, only a small fraction of them will study abroad or earn a college degree in an L2-medium institution; therefore, developing academic literacy skills in that language is not necessarily a relevant goal for them. On the other hand, the benefits of extensive reading in the L2 may serve them in a variety of ways in the future, whether they pursue further language study, whether they travel abroad or interact professionally or socially with speakers of the L2, or whether they simply wish to continue developing the L2 for their own enrichment when they are finished with school.

Admittedly, teachers in such settings may need to persuade supervisors, students, and parents of the benefits of an extensive or FVR approach, as opposed to traditional grammar-based approaches. It may appear to observers that teachers committed implementing an extensive reading approach simply have to require students to read instead of "doing their jobs" and that students may not be adequately prepared for required examinations. That said, reports of successful EFL extensive reading programs suggest that institutional resistance can be overcome (Day & Bamford, 1998; Elley, 1991, 1992, 1993; Elley & Mangubhai, 1983; Robb, 2001; Smith & Elley, 1997).

Extensive Reading in Non-Academic Class Settings

Many new immigrants to North America enroll in L2 adult education courses. These may be administered by local K–12 districts, community colleges, or vocational-technical schools, which provide language instruction designed for learners who wish to develop survival language skills, pursue citizenship, or pursue employment prospects. Although students in these courses tend to have fairly low levels of L2 proficiency, it is not necessarily the case that they are uneducated or poor readers in their L1. The primary focus in adult education and vocational programs is (and should be) building "survival" skills and basic literacy skills, but extensive reading can be an excellent and enjoyable supplementary activity both in and out of class. Adult learners often pursue their studies on top of full-time employment and caring for their families; understandably, they may be tired and under stress when they come to class. A few minutes devoted to reading an enjoyable book, magazine, or newspaper may relax them and set them at ease for other class activities. A systematic commitment to building extensive reading habits, FVR, or SSR can facilitate continued language development and learners' socialization into new literacies.

Extensive Reading in Academic Settings

As already noted, most successful models of extensive reading documented in the literature serve primary school children, with fewer examples of FVR and SSR at secondary levels. Even less work on extensive reading at the postsecondary level is available. While recognizing the challenges of implementing extensive reading in academic literacy courses already described (e.g., limited time and resources, student attitudes), teachers nonetheless should find ways to integrate it into instruction and into students' lives. Below we outline several different possibilities for doing so. In addition, Figure 6.4 identifies ideal conditions for making extensive reading work in academic settings.

Extensive reading in secondary L2 instruction. Secondary-level L2 instruction tends to focus primarily on covering selected aspects of the literary canon (often prescribed by official mandate) and secondarily on developing students' composing skills (i.e., literary analysis papers and perhaps a bit of creative or expository writing) (Moon, 2000; Rogers & Soter, 1997; Yancey, 2004). Because students in such courses expect to engage in extensive reading of whole texts (e.g., novels, plays, poems, and so on), it seems natural and practical to incorporate self-selected SSR, perhaps for a few minutes per day several days per week, to make self-selected outside reading a homework assignment, or to award extra credit for extensive reading. Pursuing these options would mean covering a bit less canonical literature over the course of a term or a school year. A word of warning here: Secondary-level educators often enter their profession because of a love of literature and a desire to share it with young students. It can be hard for them to "let go" of their own views of what constitutes "worthwhile" reading to focus instead on the big-picture, long-term goal of encouraging students to develop a lifelong love of reading through self-selection of materials that are interesting and appropriate for them as individuals. For most students, especially L2 readers, this may be a much greater gift than reading yet another Shakespeare play or spending more time on *Huckleberry Finn.*

1. Provide time for extended silent reading in every class session, even if it only involves reading from the textbook.
2. Create opportunities for all types of reading.
3. Find out what students like to read and why.
4. Make interesting, attractive, and level-appropriate reading materials available.
5. Build a well-stocked, diverse class library with clear indications of topic and level of difficulty for each text.
6. Allow students to take books and magazines home to read, and hold students accountable for at-home reading in some simple way.
7. Create incentives for students to read at home.
8. Have students share and recommend reading materials to classmates.
9. Keep records of the amounts of extensive reading completed by students.
10. Seek out class sets of texts (or at least group sets) that everyone can read and discuss.
11. Make use of graded readers, provided that they interest students, are attractive, create sufficient challenge, and offer a good amount of extensive reading practice.
12. Read interesting materials aloud to students on a consistent basis.
13. Visit the school library regularly and set aside time for browsing and reading.
14. Create a reading lab and designate time for lab activities.

FIGURE 6.4. Ideal Conditions for Extensive Reading.
Source: Grabe and Stoller (2001, pp. 198–199).

Extensive reading in college-level L2 courses. For the sake of this discussion, we will assume a target audience of L2 readers in introductory (or even remedial) language and literacy courses offered at the postsecondary level (e.g., college reading, basic writing, college composition, and so on). For reasons that will become clear below, we are not referring to L2 courses designed for language majors or to literature courses, although we recognize that, in some settings, such courses may be required of upper-division undergraduate and even graduate students. We are chiefly concerned with students in the early stages of academic L2 literacy development. We will divide our discussion further between reading courses and reading in composition courses.

In the U.S. context, most community colleges and some four-year institutions offer stand-alone college reading courses, often at multiple proficiency levels. In areas with large L2 learner populations, colleges may also offer separate "sheltered" reading courses for L2 students. Students in such courses need to be prepared for the high-level academic reading demands of later general-education and major courses, which will require both intensive and extensive skills. An intensive-reading approach might seem most appropriate for such students. Even the strongest proponents of extensive reading (Bamford & Day, 2003; Day & Bamford, 1998; Krashen, 2004) acknowledge that academic reading has its own challenges for which FVR will not entirely prepare students. For instance, Krashen (2004) wrote: "I will not claim that FVR is the complete answer. Free readers are not guaranteed admission to Harvard Law School" (p. x). Day and Bamford (1998) similarly acknowledged that "[L2] students in academic preparation programs must certainly master special skills for reading challenging academic texts" (p. 45). We would not argue for an exclusive extensive-reading approach for college-level reading courses, but rather for an integration of intensive and extensive reading components (see Chapters 4 and 5).

Nonetheless, we would maintain that extensive reading has much to offer students even in academic settings. First of all, the confidence and motivation issue is not one to be dismissed lightly for any student, especially L2 readers. Many L1 undergraduates are at least initially taken aback by the amount and difficulty of the reading assigned to them in college.[7] As already noted, some L2 readers have had only minimal experience of reading in the L2, despite years of language study; L2 readers may also come from L1 educational traditions focused only on brief texts that undergo careful analysis (Aebersold & Field, 1997). Spack's (2004) case study of Yuko again shows us that when a student reads even non-academic texts extensively, the experience can produce a "carry-over" effect to more intensive assigned reading. Second, continued experience with the patterns of the language through as much exposure to it as possible builds schemata for various types of language and literacy demands throughout students' academic careers (Smith, 2004; Weaver, 2002).

In a college literacy course focusing on composing and/or reading, extensive reading can be *encouraged* by the teacher, *discussed* in class (through oral presentations by students on self-selected reading or through book groups), and *assigned* as outside homework for the class. Although much class time will and probably should be concerned with intensive reading for academic purposes, it may also be possible to include silent reading as part of each day's lesson.

In a college composition or combined reading-writing course, it can be even more challenging logistically to incorporate extensive reading, especially if the focus of the final course assessment is on students' development in writing, rather than reading. In such courses, reading is seen primarily as a way of providing ideas for students to write about and perhaps secondarily as a source of models for students to analyze and even imitate in their own writing. That said, there is no reason why some of the students' writing assignments cannot be based on topics and readings of the students' own choosing. Students will be more motivated as *both* readers and writers when they are interested in the topic under discussion. Indeed, there is a strong chance that self-selected topics will be more interesting to students than teacher-directed topics.

As noted in Chapter 5, summarizing, reacting to, and thinking critically about texts is an important reading–writing skill. Students can be assigned to complete a certain amount of extensive, self-selected reading per week and to produce summary or reaction papers about what they have read, rather than always writing about readings the teacher has selected for in-class work.[8] Finally, writing teachers aiming to equip students with functional linguistic tools often struggle with how to incorporate grammar and vocabulary instruction effectively into their academic writing courses (Biber, 2006; Hinkel, 2002, 2004). They and their and students can be reminded that extensive reading can provide writers with such tools (linguistic structures, as well as formal, content, and cultural schemata) and with much less effort and much more enjoyment. Again, in all settings or curricular models, teachers need to view themselves as links in a chain of students' language and literacy development—and if they can help students to build lifelong habits of reading extensively, they have given their students a gift that will benefit them long after their course is over.

Practical Matters: Implementation of Extensive Reading

By this point, we hope to have convinced readers that extensive reading is at least worth considering (or taking a second look at) for a wide variety of L2 reading contexts. Yet, as we noted at the outset, "the devil is in the details," meaning that although extensive reading has no real detractors on an abstract level, many teachers are either stopped by the perceived challenges or simply uncertain as to how to go about designing and implementing an extensive reading approach. In this final section, we provide tools and suggestions for appreciating "the power of reading" at work in their classrooms. To do so, we will discuss five specific topics: (1) getting students on board; (2) providing access to reading materials; (3) helping students find and select appropriate materials;

(4) designing in-class activities; and (5) developing accountability or evaluation mechanisms.

Getting Students on Board

As discussed in the "Challenges" section, student resistance to extensive reading may be one of a teacher's biggest obstacles, and this resistance may arise for several reasons and take different forms. As Kim and Krashen (1997) asked in the title of their article, "Why don't language acquirers take advantage of the power of reading?" In a classroom setting, it is probably unrealistic to think that just giving students a pep talk on the power of extensive reading in their L2 is going to convert them into enthusiastic, avid readers. Much as we agree with Krashen and like-minded authorities about the benefits of FVR and SSR, the teacher will most likely need to assign extensive reading and hold students accountable in some way for doing it. Unfortunately, any time we use words like "assign" and "accountable," we have crossed the line from voluntary to required activity, with the attendant and inevitable consequence of the activity becoming less internally motivated and enjoyable for some. That said, it is still possible for even assigned, measured extensive reading to be beneficial and somewhat more pleasurable for students than other types of classroom activity—and to move students toward the larger goal of becoming lifelong readers in their L2s.

We recommend clarifying for students how much they need to read, what kinds of materials they might choose from, how to find materials, and what types of checkpoints will be instituted along the way to make sure they complete the reading. Teachers should likewise attempt to build not only compliance but also enthusiasm for the extensive reading component. As a course gets underway, teachers can prepare a short presentation for students summarizing research on the benefits of extensive reading. Diverse student needs and goals may help determine which benefits the teacher will highlight (see Figure 6.3), although the benefits that may make the most intuitive sense to students are arguments about:

- **quantity** (reading a lot in your L2 helps you cope with challenging, lengthy reading assignments you may get in school or at work);
- **vocabulary** (you need a very large L2 vocabulary to function effectively, and extensive reading will help you learn new words more quickly and easily than simply studying or memorizing them intensively);
- **complexity** (aspects of L2 grammar and spelling are idiomatic and may defy simple rule formulations; in addition, extensive reading exposes you naturally to those language patterns that cannot be learned easily by explicit means).

For adult students who have children or who may have them soon, it can also be motivating to point out that extensive reading may help them read aloud to their children, help children select books, and model good reading habits for them. On the other hand, stressing the "pleasure" aspects of extensive reading might be less productive at the outset of a course—in this case, seeing is believing.

As a course continues, teachers can continue to show students the benefits of extensive reading explicitly and implicitly. An obvious but often neglected way to do this is to model the behaviors of an enthusiastic reader, for example, by talking to students about what they have read, reading along with students during in-class silent reading, recommending books and other materials, reading favorite stories aloud to the class, and so forth. Another approach is to have students share with one another the books and materials they have really enjoyed through small group book discussions, oral presentations, posters, and recommendation forms. As any experienced primary school teacher knows, peer enthusiasm for reading can be quite contagious.[9] By sharing results of standardized assessments administered at the beginning, middle, and end of a course, teachers can also report students' measured progress as readers, even though they may be following what to students seems like an unstructured instructional approach.

Providing Access to Reading Materials

The success of an extensive reading program rises and falls on the availability of varied, appealing reading materials appropriate for students' interests, language proficiency, and literacy skills. Teachers must consider several issues related to extensive reading materials and three general models through which materials can be obtained.

Issues or questions. One question is *how much* extensive reading will be required or expected. As noted above, the answer depends on the type and context of the course (see Figure 6.3), as well as students' ability levels. As for materials acquisition, the more a course is devoted to extensive reading activities, the more materials will be needed. For example, students in a stand-alone extensive reading course in an intensive language program will need many more materials to choose from than students in a university composition course, who may only be asked to read a couple of newspaper articles per week or several self-selected books per term in addition to other teacher-directed reading–writing assignments.

Another important question is *what genres or text types* students should read. Teachers (and their students) may be reluctant to consider the reading of light and popular genres as part of the program, but proponents of extensive reading encourage us to do exactly that. Harris and Sipay (1990) described materials selection for extensive reading as "the lure and the ladder" (p. 674). In other words, easy and accessible materials are the "lure" that draws students into extensive reading, while a varied selection of texts at a range of difficulty levels serve as the "ladder" that students climb as they gain confidence, experience, and efficiency in L2 reading (parallel to the self-regulated learning thought to occur in

Vygotsky's ZPD). With this in mind, teachers are urged to scorn nothing and to consider any type of reading to be valuable. Day and Bamford (1998, Chapter 9 and Appendix) outlined a helpful variety of genre categories to consider:

- language learner literature (simplified versions of literary or other L2 texts);
- children's literature;
- magazines;
- newspapers;
- comic books;
- young adult novels;
- translations of works from students' L1s (e.g., an English L1 reader might choose a Spanish-language version of one of Beverly Cleary's *Ramona* books or *Harry Potter*).

Day and Bamford (1998) and Krashen (2004) also point out the benefits of introducing students to series of books by the same author and with the same characters (series in numerous genres and at various readability levels range from *Ramona* to *Harry Potter* to *Babysitters' Club* to *Hardy Boys* and *Star Wars*, and so forth). Familiarity with the style and plot of the books may help students to read through a number of them fairly quickly. To this list of print options we would add the now-extensive array of options available on the Internet, ranging from online versions of daily newspapers, online books and articles, and weblogs, discussion boards, and websites about an infinite array of topics. With the exception of remote areas of the world in which electricity, computers, and Internet access cannot be assumed, the availability of online materials also addresses one of the major practical concerns about extensive reading, which is cost to a program, teacher, or students of assembling an appropriate array of materials. Finally, we would note that the increasing number of video adaptations of books and audio books or podcasts can provide an excellent supplement to print materials, especially for auditory learners. We would nonetheless caution teachers to remind students that exposure to *written* texts, not simply movies or audio books, is what will help them reap the benefits of extensive reading, and that they should use such materials in conjunction with reading, not instead of it.

Three models for making materials available. In some contexts, it may be possible and appropriate to build a classroom or program library of extensive reading materials that students can browse, read in class or between classes, and check out to take home. Many elementary school classrooms have extensive libraries of age-appropriate reading materials (often accompanied by a comfortable and quiet spot in the classroom set aside for free reading). This can be an excellent model for L2 reading programs for adults, if space is available; if not, space may be available in a student lounge or resource room for a program library, or books can be moved from room to room on a cart or in boxes. As a starting point for a classroom library, Day and Bamford (1998) suggested a formula of one book per student in the class, plus an additional 10 books and an assortment of magazines and newspapers. Funds for materials can be obtained through charging each student a "library fee" (over time, the library can be built up as subsequent students add resources), through fundraising, or through program budgets. Where resources are extremely tight, teachers might again look to what is available online to be read or downloaded, ask friends and relatives to save magazines once they have finished reading them, take advantage of introductory low-cost magazine and newspaper subscriptions (or economical classroom subscription programs available in the US and elsewhere), and investigate used-book stores and online used-books sources (e.g., eBay, Amazon Marketplace, half.com) to purchase books at a fraction of their retail price. Having obtained library materials, teachers should catalogue them by genre and difficulty level and then establish clear checkout procedures for students. Bamford and Day (2003), Day and Bamford (1998), and Nuttall (2005) provide excellent suggestions for setting up classroom libraries.

In other settings, a class library may be neither possible (e.g., due to space constraints) nor necessary (e.g., because students have enough resources to obtain their own materials). In these instances, teachers can set the requirement for the amount of reading expected each week, month, or term, providing students with lists of suggestions for materials (and where to find them). They can also encourage learners to make their own purchases, visit libraries, and conduct online investigations. This approach may be most appropriate for college and university settings.

A final strategy for providing materials is for the teacher to select certain resources and bring them to class for student use. For instance, secondary and postsecondary instructors may choose to adopt a local or national newspaper or magazine (e.g., *USA Today, Newsweek*) as a course text and purchase a classroom subscription. For a low overall cost, a subscription typically includes enough newspapers or magazines for each student in the class, as well as a teacher's guide of activities designed for that issue of the publication. Teachers can require students to pay a small fee as part of their textbook budget for the course.

Further examples of teacher-selected materials can be taken from *literature circle* and *book group* models used in elementary literacy education and now also popular in adult education (Gambrell et al., 2007; Grabe & Stoller, 2001; Keene, 2008; Kucer & Silva, 2006; Popp, 2005; Weaver, 2002). Teachers may select 10–12 short books that might be appropriate and interesting for the class and obtain four or five copies of each one. Every few weeks, students browse the selections and choose which book they would like to read next; they are then placed in a small group with other students who have chosen the same book. Groups set outside reading schedules and then meet occasionally to discuss what they are reading; the cycle repeats every few weeks. Krashen (2004) noted that in one study (McQuillan, 1994), L2 readers actually preferred this option to complete autonomy in materials selection, citing the convenience of having well-chosen books available to them. In both options discussed here, students exercise *some* choice: They may, for example, get to choose which newspaper or magazine articles they are interested in reading, and they get to choose from a range of book options. As we note in the next section, maintaining at least some level of student choice is critical for the success of an extensive reading approach.

Helping Students Find and Select Appropriate Materials

Reading specialists have examined and debated the benefits of FVR, SSR, and extensive reading for several decades now. Convinced by the research showing its benefits, teachers sometimes get on the bandwagon but later end up abandoning the idea due to lack of student cooperation or an overall sense that the program is not working. Problems often lie in making the selection of reading materials *too* wide open, in the name of student choice and autonomy. However, "extensive reading is not just a matter of submerging students in a bath of print" (Day & Bamford, 1998, p. xiii). L2 students new to extensive reading practices definitely need assistance in finding, obtaining, and selecting appropriate free-reading materials. Whether a teacher assembles a classroom library or simply assists students with finding their own reading materials, two principles must be kept in mind: *interest* and *difficulty level*. As for interest, teachers must keep firmly in mind that individuals may enjoy reading about a wide variety of subjects. Some people may adore fantasy; others may loathe it and would prefer a biography of a famous or interesting person. Some enjoy reading texts about immigrants whose experiences are similar to their own, whereas others would rather read something completely different from their own frame of reference or with more universal appeal. Because teachers cannot know what all of their students might enjoy reading about (and students may never have been asked to express their preferences), it can be helpful to design questionnaires on which students can provide information about their interests, as in Figure 6.5.

With respect to difficulty level, some evidence suggests that books and other reading materials that represent a "stretch" for students may have enough intrinsic appeal (e.g., because of the topic or appealing illustrations) for L2 readers to persevere through them (Gambrell et al., 2007). For the purposes of extensive reading, however, a rule of thumb holds that learners should read materials that are at—or even slightly below—their current level of reading proficiency. Day and Bamford (1998) called this guideline $i - 1$ (*i minus one*), where *i* refers to learners' current level of acquisition or skill. The fundamental aim of extensive reading, after all, is for learners to read fluently, in quantity, and with enjoyment. By engaging in fluent reading, L2 readers approximate the experience of *rauding* (see Chapter 1), thereby enhancing both automaticity (Samuels, 1994) and sight vocabulary (see Chapter 8). If texts are too hard for readers, they may not read enough, find the experience stressful, and give up altogether. Over time,

1. **I enjoy movies and television programs about:**
   ☐ science fiction and fantasy
   ☐ romance or love
   ☐ mysteries
   ☐ sports
   ☐ children and family
   ☐ animals
   ☐ comedy
   ☐ other: _____

   Students can be asked to rank-order these choices.

2. **Please provide short answers to the following questions:**
   ➤ What do you like to do in your free time?
   ➤ What kinds of movies do you most enjoy?
   ➤ What are your favorite television programs?
   ➤ Do you play video games? If so, what are some of your favorites?
   ➤ Do you surf the Internet? What are your favorite topics to look up or read about?
   ➤ What do you and your friends talk about?
   ➤ Do you read magazines? Which ones?
   ➤ Do you read newspapers? Which ones, and how frequently?
   ➤ What sorts of books do you read (in your first or second language)?

FIGURE 6.5. Sample Reader Interest Questionnaire Items.
Adapted from Day and Bamford (1998, pp. 110–111).

teachers can encourage readers to take on more challenging texts so that their skills can continue to develop ("the lure and the ladder" principle again), but the most urgent need addressed by extensive reading is to build confidence, motivation, and enjoyment in L2 reading.

Teachers can take several steps toward guiding students in selecting materials of appropriate difficulty levels. If there is a classroom or program library, ideally the materials have already been categorized according to difficulty (e.g., by grade level or advanced- to beginning-level proficiency). The teacher should have a sense of each student's approximate abilities from placement and diagnostic assessments (see Chapter 9). The teacher can also utilize the text analysis tools introduced in Chapter 3 to examine and categorize reading materials by level of difficulty (readability). If teachers are still uncertain about readability of a text, Day and Bamford (1998) suggest asking students read one page of a potential text selection and to identify all unknown words. If students identify more than one or two, the selection may be too difficult to meet the goals of extensive reading (quantity, rapidity, enjoyment). Similarly, if students are assigned to find their own free reading materials (either from a recommended list or on their own), the teacher can ask each student to bring in their book and take a few minutes of class time to ensure that the book is appropriate for them.

Maintaining "choice" in extensive reading. As noted at the outset of this chapter, the term *extensive reading* has been used in a variety of ways by researchers and teacher educators; the FVR advocated so strongly by Krashen is only a subset of how extensive reading is applied. For example, we have known teachers and others in reading–writing courses who claim that they engage students in "extensive reading" by assigning as a novel a course requirement. Similarly, content-based instruction (CBI) has been characterized as a form of "extensive reading" because students read several different texts on the same topic (or the entire course may be structured around a single theme or academic discipline). These types of reading assignments unquestionably offer numerous advantages (see Chapters 3, 4, and 7). However, we would not equate them with extensive reading as we have characterized it here. As worthwhile as assigned texts might be, they are still teacher-selected, and students must read them whether or not they want to or are likely to enjoy them. In short, CBI and literature-based approaches are just like every other course students must take. In contrast, extensive reading approaches should *simulate* what readers do in real life outside of school, and *stimulate* the cultivation of a lifelong reading habit. Like other proponents of extensive reading, we would argue that some element of student choice (including what *not* to read and the freedom to stop reading something if they do not like it) is critical to the primary aims of the approach.

Designing Classroom Activities

Ideas for the *intensive reading* instruction abound (see Chapter 5), but teachers and students may find it hard to envision what an extensive reading class (or component) might look like in practice. Clearly, the teacher's role is quite different in a course that features extensive reading. In addition to the practical principles previously introduced (i.e., explaining the goals and benefits of the program, providing materials, and helping students to select them), teachers can adopt strategies to ensure the success of an extensive reading program.

Giving students advice about extensive reading. Because many L2 students may have little or no experience with extensive reading of any kind in any language, it can be helpful for the teacher, early in the course, to explain to students how they might approach self-selected reading. First, students should be reminded that the purposes for reading vary from one situation to another and that their reading strategies should also vary (Hirvela, 2004; Johns, 1997). Their experience of reading a book or magazine for pleasure should be quite different from the careful reading, annotation, and analysis of a textbook chapter for an examination or writing assignment. In contrast, extensive reading should be rapid, focused on meaning, and enjoyable. Students should be discouraged from using dictionaries as they undertake free reading: If they need dictionaries to get through the text, it is probably too difficult for extensive reading. Indeed, for most readers, consulting a dictionary while reading is slow and tedious, defeating the primary objectives of reading rapidly, in quantity, and for enjoyment (see Chapter 8 for a discussion of dictionary use in intensive reading and vocabulary instruction). Finally, students should be given permission to stop reading something that they do not enjoy and to choose something else. After all, when we select something in a bookstore or library to take on vacation, no one forces us to buy it or check it out if, after reading a few pages, we find we don't like it.

Providing class time for reading. It is tempting for busy instructors simply to assign all extensive reading as homework. Despite the fact that providing class time for reading is costly, we encourage teachers in all contexts to do so anyway, even if it is just a short period of time once or twice a week. In-class reading time (e.g., SSR) can accomplish several important goals. First, it models for students the importance of reading, especially if teachers read along with them. Second, it allows teachers to observe how students are progressing with the free reading process: Do they seem restless? Engaged? Frustrated? SSR time can also provide an opportunity for teachers to consult individually with students about their reading. They can ask students what they are reading, how they like it, how challenging they find the material, whether they need help selecting their next book, and so forth. Third, SSR promotes a classroom *reading community;* students can naturally observe what classmates are reading and perhaps ask them later for reviews or recommendations (Keene, 2008).

Shared reading experiences. The hallmark of an extensive reading approach is individual, self-selected reading, yet classrooms can provide support and motivation for naturally reluctant readers. The popularity of book clubs among many adults demonstrates that, for at least some readers, the experience of reading a good book is heightened when it is shared with others. Students can share reading in class in a variety of ways, starting with the aforementioned literature circle option (Gambrell et al., 2007; Grabe & Stoller, 2001; Keene, 2008; Kucer & Silva, 2006; Popp, 2005; Weaver, 2002). Individual readers can give brief oral or poster presentations about books they have read and enjoyed, write reviews of books that can be posted on a class website, distributed in the classroom, or attached inside the covers of classroom library books for future readers to consider. If technological resources are available, students can also discuss books online through a class message board or in small-group synchronous or asynchronous chats using delivery systems such as WebCT or Moodle. A fun and popular option used in K–12 settings is called *Battle of the Books,* a voluntary program in which teams of students all read the same set of books; they then compete against one another in trivia quizzes about the books. Finally, the teacher can choose books to read aloud to the entire class at regular intervals, a practice that can stimulate interest in a particular book, author, or genre (Popp, 2005; Weaver, 2002). It is important to point out that even in classes where extensive reading is just one component, the suggested in-class activities can be regularly incorporated in a relatively short amount of time.

Developing Accountability and Evaluation Mechanisms

Ideally, an extensive reading, FVR, or SSR program would not require account-ability or check points for students. Nevertheless, while a reading course may *simulate* real-world reading and *stimulate* an interest in FVR, it cannot, in the end, *duplicate* real-world FVR. If we want students to read extensively, we cannot simply hope that they will do so "for their own good." We must require them to do so and verify that they are, in fact, making progress toward meaningful literacy goals. That said, we recommend that accountability mechanisms be as loosely structured and nonintrusive as feasible (Caldwell, 2008; Day & Bamford, 1998).

Requirements. Teachers can set minimum reading requirements for an exten-sive reading program in a number of ways. For instance, in the year-long Japanese university program described by Robb (2001), students were given page requirements, divided up across four grading periods to guard against exces-sive procrastination. Another option is to ask students to read for a minimum period of time each day or week (e.g., 30 minutes per day or three hours per week). Another is to require completion of specific types of materials, such as four books per semester or three newspaper or magazine articles per week. The option selected should depend on the classroom context and students' other out-of-class responsibilities. Crucially, teachers should make the decision at the beginning of the course and communicate expectations clearly to students in a course syllabus, assignment sheet, or classroom announcements (or, ideally, all three).

Accountability options. A most minimally intrusive approach is for students to maintain a simple reading log in which they record the date, titles of what they have read, and the amount of time spent reading or number of pages read. Obviously, this alternative entails a few risks; we therefore suggest pairing the log with some kind of written or oral requirement (a summary, a poster, an oral "book report" given one-on-one to the teacher or presented to the whole class). An accountability tool that is consistent with the spirit and extensive reading program is to ask students to review a book they have read, reporting on what they liked or did not like about it, whether they would recommend it to others, and why. This strategy offers the dual benefit of ensuring that students have read the material and providing ideas for other students.

Evaluation mechanisms. Assessment and grading present logistical dilemmas in an extensive reading program. If students read self-selected material, the teacher cannot be expected to keep up with reading all of it, let alone design individualized assessments for each work read. Methods of avoiding this problem include using commercially available computer reading programs such as *Accelerated Reader* or graded reading programs such as those provided by SRA. Nonetheless, attempting to do so necessarily limits student choice about what to read. Instead, we would recommend a two-pronged approach to evaluation. First, as for assigning course grades based on extensive reading, teachers can assign point values to the amount of material, perhaps as a component of a literacy portfolio (see Chapter 9). Robb

(2001) described such a system, which included additional weighting for the difficulty level of particular materials. Students could earn extra credit for reading more than the minimum requirements or for producing more substantial (or higher-quality) written or oral presentations about what they have read.

Second, if teachers wish to assess overall student progress in reading comprehension and efficiency, vocabulary development, and so forth, they may administer placement, diagnostic, and progress tests (see Chapters 8 and 9). As part of ongoing needs assessment, teachers may also collect data at the beginning and end of a course about student attitudes toward—and enjoyment of—reading by administering questionnaires, interviews, or both (see Chapters 4 and 9; also see Grabe and Stoller (2002, pp. 163–164) for action research guidelines for investigating student engagement in extensive reading). Again, teachers must walk the fine line between structuring the process enough so that students will take it seriously and appreciate its benefits, rather than viewing extensive reading as a burdensome (and potentially unrewarding) course requirement.

Chapter Summary

It should be evident that we strongly favor extensive reading in L2 instruction. In fact, we would like to acknowledge that we have come full-circle during our professional careers on this topic and have had something of a born-again experience, finding new enthusiasm and appreciation for extensive reading that we first gained during our graduate careers in the 1980s at the University of Southern California as students of Stephen Krashen. We find ourselves asking, along with Bill Grabe, "Why isn't everybody doing this?" To summarize, we have covered the following territory:

- We have pointed out that, despite widespread, longstanding enthusiasm for extensive reading and overwhelming research evidence in its favor, its application is still fairly rare in L2 reading courses. We likewise speculated about some of the political and practical reasons for this puzzling paradox.
- We have discussed the six major benefits of extensive reading found in the L1 and L2 reading literature.
- We have outlined three major challenges that may impede the implementation of extensive reading in many settings.
- We have described curricular models of L2 reading instruction, explaining how an extensive reading component could be advantageous in any of them (in different proportions and for varying reasons).
- We have explored practical implementation issues, such as helping students understand the benefits of extensive reading, approaching

the process, making reading materials available, and assessing student participation and progress.

We firmly hold the position that every L2 reading teacher *can and should* utilize extensive reading in some way, yet we also acknowledge the truth of the claim that a successful extensive reading program "takes superior materials, clever teachers who love to read themselves, time and effort to develop the reading habit" (Harris & Sipay, 1990, p. 655). We hope that the ideas in this chapter have provided both inspiration and practical tools for teachers to consider. We also hope to have encouraged educators to add "the power of reading" to their teaching repertoire—and to their students' literate lives.

Further Reading and Resources

The following list points readers to key materials referred to in this chapter. Bibliographic information on published sources can be found in the References. Readers are reminded that URLs may have changed since the time of publication.

Extensive reading resources for L2 instruction
  Bamford & Day (2003); Day & Bamford (1998)
"Yuko" case study
  Spack (1997, 2004)
Reviews of research on extensive reading in L1 and L2
  Day & Bamford (1998, Chapters 1–4); Krashen (2004; also see Krashen's website)
Key studies on incidental vocabulary acquisition through extensive reading
  Nagy et al. (1985); Pitts et al. (1989); Saragi et al. (1978)
Key studies on benefits of extensive reading for L2 students
  Elley (1991, 1992, 1998); Elley & Mangubhai (1983); Mason & Krashen (1997)
Stephen Krashen's website with links to articles
  http://www.sdkrashen.com/
International Reading Association website with links to reading lists
  http://www.reading.org/
National Council of Teachers of English website with links to reading lists
  www.ncte.org
Free online survey design tool
  www.surveymonkey.com

Reflection and Review

1. This chapter argues that one reason for the puzzling neglect of extensive reading may involve biases against WL approaches to reading and their proponents. Do you agree or disagree? Is the neglect of extensive reading more closely related to ignorance or practical constraints that keep teachers from implementing it in L2 literacy curricula? Perform a brief Web search of WL versus phonics debates (see Chapter 1). You might be surprised at the strong opinions expressed!

2. Review the six benefits of extensive reading for L2 students. Referring to your responses to this chapter's Questions for Reflection, does your own experience in L1 and L2 reading illustrate these benefits? Do you believe that extensive reading can, over time, provide the advantages described to L2 students. Is this discussion like weight-loss commercials on cable television—too good to be true?

3. This chapter outlined three major challenges to implementating an extensive reading scheme: time and curricular constraints, limited resources, and learner resistance. Which of these presents the most significant difficulty? Do you think the proposed benefits outweigh the challenge(s)? Explain.

4. Figure 6.3 and the accompanying discussion suggest that any type of L2 reading course could be adapted to include extensive reading. Do you agree, or do you think any part of this discussion is unrealistic?

5. This chapter discussed practical issues to address in implementing extensive reading. Do you feel that you have enough information now to add extensive reading to your teaching repertoire, either now or in the future? If not, what would you still need to learn, and how might you investigate your unanswered questions?

6. As a teacher, would you enjoy teaching an extensive reading course, a reading–writing course, or a multiple-skills course with a significant extensive reading component? What appeals to you the most? What might make you uncomfortable? Explain.

Application Activities

Application Activity 6.1
Investigating Real-World Attitudes toward Extensive Reading

The opening quotation and the first part of this chapter claim that, although extensive reading has many enthusiastic *proponents*, it has surprisingly few *practitioners*. The two small field research projects suggested here allow you to discover for yourself whether this claim is true in your own context.

Option A: Survey of L2 Reading Teachers

Identify a local program (or programs) in which L2 readers are taught by several different teachers. Design a brief questionnaire or interview protocol so that you can ask teachers about their awareness of extensive reading (including FVR and SSR) as an option, about whether they utilize it (or have ever done so), and what they think about it. If they do not use extensive reading, inquire about why. Report your findings to your instructor (and peers) in an oral or written report.

Option B: Survey of L2 Readers

Design a questionnaire or interview protocol through which you can investigate students' prior experiences with extensive L2 reading. Determine if any L2 teacher has ever encouraged or required extensive reading, FVR, or SSR of learners and if the benefits have been explained to them. Ask how they feel (or would feel) about having some kind of extensive reading scheme implemented in one of their courses. Compare your findings with those of other teachers or teachers-in-training.

Having completed one or both of these projects, do you agree that extensive reading has been overlooked as a pedagogical tool in your context?

Application Activity 6.2
Review of Research on the Benefits of Extensive Reading

a. Choose at least one of the six major benefits of extensive reading outlined in Figure 6.2 and discussed in this chapter.

b. Read at least two research studies relevant to this potential benefit. Consult primary sources referenced in this chapter, Krashen (2004), or Day and Bamford (1998), or any other recently published research.

c. From this brief literature survey, determine how persuaded you are that this benefit is potentially important for your present or future students.

d. If you *are* persuaded, write a brief position paper for a real or hypothetical supervisor in which you explain why, from now on, you will incorporate extensive reading as a major component of your reading instruction. In addition, compose a one-page summary of the evidence in terms that your own students could understand, so that you can explain to them why you will be asking them to read extensively.

e. If you are *not* persuaded, write a brief position paper in explaining why the evidence failed to convince you, what it would have taken to persuade you, and why you feel other approaches (alone or in combination) would provide that benefit to students more effectively.

Application Activity 6.3
Examining External or Institutional Reading Standards

a. Examine the California Content Standards for English Language Arts, Grades 9–12 (available at www.sdcoe.k12.ca.us/SCORE/stand/std.html) or other published standards relevant to your context and students (see Chapters 1, 4, and 9 for sample standards and Web links). Review the standards, objectives, or criteria you have chosen with reference to the following questions:

1. Do any of the standards refer explicitly or implicitly to practices or outcomes that relate to extensive reading (including FVR or SSR)? If extensive reading is absent or inadequately represented in these standards, why do you think they have been neglected?
2. Referring to the six major benefits of extensive reading outlined in Figure 6.2 and discussed in this chapter, do you see standards or objectives that could be met (or better satisfied) by incorporating extensive reading into the curriculum?
3. If you could revise these standards in light of what you have learned about extensive reading, how might you change them? Why?

b. Summarize your review of your selected standards in a written report or oral presentation.

Application Activity 6.4
Evaluation of a Reading Course

a. Appendix 4.2 includes a syllabus for a college-level ESL reading course. Examine it carefully, considering the following questions:

1. Do you see direct or implicit evidence that extensive or free voluntary reading is encouraged or is part of the course?
2. Considering our discussion of the goals and needs of students in college language and literacy courses, do you think the goals and emphases of the course (whether explicit or implicit) are appropriate? Would more extensive reading benefit these students? Why or why not?
3. Brainstorm how you might revise the syllabus to include a greater focus on extensive reading. What might you drop or reduce in the course to make room for it?

b. Discuss your evaluation with your peers. Alternatively, outline your responses to the questions and summarize your recommendations in a written reflection.

Application Activity 6.5
Investigating Resources and Materials for an Extensive Reading Library

a. Identify a classroom context familiar to you. Alternatively, use the sample syllabus illustrated in Appendix 4.2 and examined in Application Activity 6.4

as a sample case. Imagine that you are assigned to teach this course and that you will incorporate extensive reading as a major component. Work through the following options for organizing the material resources for your extensive reading scheme.

1. *Classroom library.* Assume that you have the space and resources available to set up a classroom lending library. What books would you obtain to start your library for this class? As a starting point, assume a class size of about 20 students; you would need about 30 books. Refer to the resources listed in Further Reading and Resources as a starting point for your list. Estimate the total cost of assembling this beginning inventory of books. Plan how would you obtain them and minimize costs.

2. *Recommended reading list.* Now imagine instead that your students have enough available outside resources to obtain their own reading materials. What might you add to your classroom library, and where in the community could students go to find books? List brick-and-mortar bookstores and online retailers that sell new and used titles. If students must purchase books or other materials, how much of their textbook budget should they expect to spend?

3. *Additional materials.* In addition to basic lists of books for a classroom library and outside reading, what other materials might you make available or recommend to students? Consider print and online newspapers, magazines and e-zines, websites and weblogs, comic books (including more extensive publications such as *manga* books, and so forth).

b. If you complete this activity as a classroom exercise, compare your lists with those of your classmates and request feedback from your instructor. Merge your lists to create a master list of materials and resources that you could use as a starting point for your own future courses.

c. As an extension of this project, you and your classmates could *annotate* this list by crafting several descriptive sentences for each resource. You need not have read every title on the list to do this. Most books have synopses available online, either as part of professional association reading lists or as part of commercial websites (such as amazon.com).

d. If relevant, assemble supplemental materials. Are there any video adaptations or audio book versions of the titles on your list available? How would you evaluate their quality before recommending them to students? How would you find out about their availability?

Application Activity 6.6
Incorporating Extensive Reading into an Existing Syllabus

a. Refer again to the sample course syllabus provided in Appendix 4.2. Adapt it to include a systematic extensive reading component, considering the suggestions provided in this chapter. Consider the following questions:

1. How much in-class reading time would you provide?

2. What other sorts of in-class reading activities might you include to encourage extensive reading? How would you fit them into the existing syllabus? (*Hint:* You will probably have to drop something.)

3. How would you fit extensive reading into the assessment plan for your course? How would you measure students' compliance and progress? Be specific about how many pages, books, and so on must they read or how much time must they spend. What written or oral accountability tools would you include? What general evaluation measures would you add to the syllabus? Where?

b. Share your adapted syllabus with your peers or your instructor.

Chapter 7
Using Literary Texts in L2 Reading Instruction

Questions for Reflection

- Think of literary texts in any genre (fiction, poetry, drama, memoir) that you have read for school or for pleasure. What texts and experiences reading them were particularly meaningful or enjoyable? Why? Can you recall frustrating or unpleasant moments? What made these encounters frustrating (e.g., dislike of the text itself, the way the teacher presented the material, and so on)?

- Consider the two text excerpts below, one from a first-person essay published in a newspaper in 2001 (Brahm, "Second Chances"; see also Chapter 3) and the other from a poem published in 1916 (Frost, "The Road Not Taken"). What similarities and differences do you notice in theme and language? Which extract communicates its message more clearly? Which evokes more memories and emotions?

Text Excerpt 1: Brahm

Unfortunately, I've come to realize a painful but surprisingly obvious fact of life: We don't get a second chance. Isn't that simple? Once we make a mistake, that's it. No extra tries, bonus chances, or Get Out of Jail Free cards.

Text Excerpt 2: Frost

And both that morning equally lay
In leaves no step had trodden black.
Oh, I kept the first for another day!
Yet knowing how way leads on to way,
I doubted if I should ever come back.

- If you have had significant experience with L2 reading, compare experiences reading literary texts in that language to reading other L2 genres. What are the similarities and differences? Which type of reading was most enjoyable, challenging, or frustrating?
- What do you think are the potential benefits to L2 students of reading literature as part of their language studies? What are potential drawbacks and difficulties? What practical questions would you need to address in selecting and teaching literary works to your L2 students?

Contexts for L2 Literature Teaching

In previous chapters, we considered a range of issues related to readers, texts, curriculum design, and the specific options surrounding teaching intensive and extensive reading. Much of our discussion at least implicitly focused on reading academic texts, with the majority of text extracts from non-literary sources. The ground we covered on all previous topics could be applied equally to any type of reading, including works of literature. For example, an intensive reading lesson could be focused on a short story or poem just as easily as on a newspaper article or academic text (see Chapter 5). As for extensive reading, we assumed that some or most student selections would be literary in nature (novels in particular—see Chapter 6).

In this chapter, we narrow our focus to the selection and teaching of literary texts in L2 literacy education. We feel that this discussion is necessary for several reasons: (1) Literature is ubiquitous across many L2 instructional contexts (Gilroy & Parkinson, 1996; Maley, 2001; Paran, 2006; Rogers & Soter, 1997); (2) Working with literature in L2 instruction results in a number of favorable outcomes (Aebersold & Field, 1997; Carter & Long, 1987, 1991; Collie & Slater, 1987; Gajdusek, 1988; Gajdusek & van Dommelen, 1993; Heath, 1996; Lazar, 1993; Spack, 1985; and (3) Teaching with literary texts in L2 settings poses unique challenges that teachers need to consider and prepare for carefully (Aebersold & Field, 1997; Carter & McRae, 1996; Collie & Slater, 1987; Fecteau, 1999; Gajdusek, 1998; Lazar, 1993). As in the previous chapter on extensive reading, we begin here with a discussion of the benefits of integrating literature into the L2 reading curriculum; we will also look candidly at challenges and strategies for addressing them. We then turn to practical questions such as how much literature to cover, what materials to consider, and instructional approaches that will enable students grapple with literary genres such as fiction, poetry, and drama.

A couple of definitions are in order before we begin. First, we use the term *literature* broadly to include short and full-length works of fiction, poetry, and drama, regardless of a particular work's popularity with readers or stature in the eyes of literary critics and scholars. We agree with Lazar (1993), who argued that, for a definition of literature to be useful for teachers, we must "go beyond the traditional literary canon to include contemporary works [that] recognize that the English language is no longer the preserve of a few nations, but is now used globally" (p. 5). To put these definitions into concrete terms, a *Sherlock Holmes* or *Star Wars* novel is *literary* under our broad definition, and English-language literary works set and written in non-Western, non-Inner Circle societies would also be appropriate choices (Kachru, 1992). For the purposes of discussion here, a given work's critical acclaim or canonical status is secondary to our chief concern with characterizing how *literary texts* differ from other genres typically featured in L2 literacy education, as well as the challenges that these features pose for teachers and learners.[1]

Second, we broadly define the contexts where L2 literature might be incorporated into the curriculum. Our chief target area involves courses that focus on reading and language development, rather than those designed primarily to cover specific literary content. We acknowledge that the settings in which teachers might use literature with L2 readers vary. For example, in secondary English courses in the US, literature is usually a chief focus (Peregoy & Boyle, 2004; Popp, 2005). Where L2 readers are mainstreamed into regular English courses, teachers must know about their unique needs. In postsecondary EFL settings, English majors may study literature as well as language. Even in college composition courses in North American institutions, instructors may include novels and other works of literature, requiring literary analysis assignments in their syllabi (Butler, 2006; Gajdusek & van Dommelen, 1993; Hirvela, 2001, 2004; Spack, 1985). Finally, in postsecondary L2 reading courses, whether in community colleges, universities, or intensive English programs, literary texts present a legitimate curricular option.[2]

Third, we need a working definition of the characteristics of *literary* texts as they contrast with other text genres and subgenres. The quick exercise at the beginning of the chapter (in which we asked readers to compare two text excerpts) should have yielded several observations. The stanza from Frost's poem contains rhyme and meter, repetition (**way** *leads on to* **way**), antiquated language (*trodden*), and metaphor (*way* as a metaphor for the choices one makes in life). Brahm's essay contains idiomatic expressions requiring cultural knowledge (*bonus chances, Get Out of Jail Free cards*), does not rhyme, and is characterized by relatively simple syntax. Both authors express a similar theme—namely, that some of the choices and mistakes made in life cannot be undone later, no matter how badly we might want a *second chance* or *another day*. The linguistic and stylistic choices made to communicate this universal precept are quite unique.

Lazar (1993) observed that literary texts by nature defy easy identification and definition, remarking that "no specialized literary language ... can be isolated and analyzed in the same way as the language of specific fields" such as the law or mass media. A hallmark of literature, she wrote, "is that it feeds creatively on every possible style and register—it has become the one form of discourse in which any use of language is permissible" (p. 6). Nevertheless, aspects of *literary language* can be identified. Although these features can be found in other text types, in literature "they combine to form a highly unified and consistent effect, which strongly reinforces the message of the text" (Lazar, 1993, p. 6; also see Brumfit and Carter [1986] and Carter and McRae [1996]). Figure 7.1 provides definitions and brief literary examples of common features.[3]

In addition to specific *literary devices*, authors have noted that the purposes and structure of literary texts tend to be distinct from those of other text types, although we note overlap across genres, naturally. Lazar (1993) presented a chart that matches general types of language use in literature and their functions (intent of author, effect on reader) (see Figure 7.2, Chart A). Aebersold and Field (1997) provided a chart that compares the content and structure of informational, literary, and poetic texts, suggesting differences in the relative importance of diverse features (see Figure 7.2, Chart B). In short, whereas literary texts share the characteristics of other genres and subgenres, they are unique in their purpose, approach, and use of language. Consequently, this specialized topic deserves separate development in a volume such as this one.

Benefits of Literature for L2 Readers

In the introduction to a much-used and oft-cited book published over 20 years ago, Collie and Slater (1987) noted that at the time, the use of literature with L2 students was "controversial" because: (1) literature embodied "a static, convoluted kind of language, far removed from ... daily communication"; (2) literature was seen as "elitist" and carrying "an undesirable freight of cultural connotations"; and (3) literary analysis took too much time and required too much specialized terminology and knowledge (p. 2). The authors further noted a growing "unease" with keeping literature off the language class syllabus, noting that students "want and love literary texts," and that teachers like incorporating literature because it "provides material with some emotional color" (p. 2).

Over the past several decades (particularly the 1980s and 1990s), books, articles, and chapters have appeared touting the benefits realized by L2 learners who read literature and suggesting approaches to text selection and classroom instruction. It is worth noting, however, that almost no empirical research has examined the hypothesized benefits (or drawbacks) of integrating literature into the

Device	Definition	Literary example
Metaphor	An intentional linkage between two (or more) apparently unrelated subjects using "is" to join the subjects.	"Sharper than a serpent's tooth it is to have a thankless child." (Shakespeare, *King Lear*, Act I, Scene 4)
Simile	Compares two subjects using "like" or "as."	"His bony hand dug its way like a squirrel into his overall pocket . . ." (Steinbeck, *East of Eden*)
Imagery	The use of words or phrases to appeal to the reader's senses so that they can experience what the narrator or character is experiencing.	"Masses of flowers load the cherry branches and color some bushes yellow and some red . . ." (W. C. Williams, "The Widow's Lament in Springtime")
Oxymoron	A phrase that combines two normally contradictory terms.	"Parting is such sweet sorrow." (Shakespeare, *Romeo and Juliet*, Act II, Scene 2)
Alliteration	The matching of repetition of consonant sounds at the beginnings of words or stressed syllables.	"What a tale of terror, now, their turbulency tells!" (Poe, "The Bells")
Assonance	Repetition of vowel sounds within words.	And so, all the night-tide, I lie down by the side Of my darling, my darling, my life and my bride. (Poe, "Annabel Lee")
Repetition of Key Words and Phrases	—	" 'Free! Body and soul free!' she kept whispering." (Chopin, "The Story of an Hour")
Unusual Sentence Structure	—	"Alone, one is never lonely." (Sarton, "The Rewards of Living a Solitary Life")
Double Meanings	The use of multiple word or phrase meanings to convey a message.	"When the doctors came they said she had died of heart disease—of the joy that kills." (Chopin, "The Story of an Hour")
Rhyme and Meter	Specific patterns of rhyming words at the ends of phrases or sentences and the rhythm found in lines of poetry (whether or not they rhyme)	"My little horse must think it queer/ to stop without a farmhouse near." (Frost, "Stopping by Woods on a Snowy Evening")

FIGURE 7.1. Common Literary Devices.*

* For a highly accessible list of literary features, definitions, and examples (including student quizzes) (designed for 11th-grade students), see Mrs. Dowling's Literature Terms: http://www.dowlingcentral.com/MrsD/area/literature/Terms/.html. A similar resource can be found at http://www.uncp.edu/home/canada/work/allam/general/glossary.htm.

Chart A: Language Use and Function in Literary Texts
(Adapted from Lazar, 1993, p. 4)

Type of language	Function
Disciplined technique	Arouses emotions
Charged with meaning	Makes us see differently
Distorts practical language	Raises questions

Chart B: Comparison of Text Type Elements
(Adapted from Aebersold & Field, 1997, p. 160)

Informative text	Literary text	Poetry
Main idea	Plot	Theme
Organization of argument	Character development	Imagery
Credentials of author	Theme or main idea	Special and general vocabulary
Points that support argument	Special and general vocabulary	Sentence structure
Graphs, charts, and so on	Author information, setting, cultural information, tone	Tone, cultural information

FIGURE 7.2. Models of Literary Texts.

language curriculum. Other than a couple of studies on learner perceptions of literature (e.g., Akyel & Yalçin, 1990; Barkhuizin & Gough, 1998), most evidence comes from more general studies on the benefits of extensive reading and FVR among L1 and L2 readers (see Chapter 6). Thus, although the lists of advantages and possible problems discussed below seem to us reasonable and plausible, we caution readers that little research supports or refutes them. Figure 7.3 outlines potential benefits and advantages of literary study for L2 readers.

Cultural Knowledge

More than in any other text type, literary sources embody a wealth of cultural information. Plots and themes may be universal and timeless, but settings, characters, and dialogue tend to be rooted in the time and culture shared or created by the author. Some experts (e.g., Lazar, 1993) portray cross-cultural differences embedded in literary texts as obstacles for teachers to be aware of and to overcome; others approach literature as a window into culture—a strongly positive aspect of utilizing literary texts. As Collie and Slater (1987) noted, literary sources provide "a full and vivid context in which characters from many social backgrounds can be depicted. A reader can discover their thoughts, feelings, customs, possessions, what they buy, believe in, fear, enjoy; how they speak and behave behind closed doors" (p. 4). Readers of Jane Austen or Charlotte or Emily Brontë novels, for instance, can learn about social stratification in early 19th-century

1. Reading literature builds knowledge of culture, values systems, and social structures.
2. Literature provides richer, more complex authentic language exposure than in other types of informational texts.
3. Literature provides input and opportunities for language acquisition.
4. Literature is enjoyable and intrinsically motivating for students.
5. Successful reading of literary texts builds confidence in L2 readers.
6. Literary themes highlight universal human experience and are thus accessible and provide opportunities for reflection and personal growth.
7. Literature provides interesting topics and ideas for students to write about.
8. Literature promotes critical thinking skills.

FIGURE 7.3. Advantages of Literature Study for L2 Readers.
Sources: Aebersold and Field (1997); Carter and Long (1991); Carter and McRae (1996); Collie and Slater (1987); Franklin (1999); Gajdusek (1988); Gajdusek and van Dommelen (1993); Heath (1996); Hirvela (2001, 2004); Kern (2000); Lazar (1993); Peregoy and Boyle (2004); Rogers and Soter (1997); Spack (1985, 2004).

England. Those who read Twain's *Huckleberry Finn* or *Tom Sawyer* are immersed in the regional dialect and cultural practices of the 19th-century antebellum American South. Those who read Harper Lee's *To Kill a Mockingbird* encounter 20th-century racial discrimination faced by African Americans in the Southern US. Readers of Kate Chopin's short story "The Story of an Hour" get a glimpse of the role of women and the state of marriage in 19th-century America. In addition to the general time and place of these works, they are situated with respect to social structures and values systems. Furthermore, literary texts often refer to political leaders and other influential figures, as well as historic events and locations.

Beyond specific cultural awareness, the literature of a particular culture or region may be permeated by prevailing religious views and sociopolitical ideologies. For instance, Western literature is replete with Judeo-Christian allusions and frequently assumes familiarity with biblical texts. Imagine, for example, trying to interpret Milton's *Paradise Lost* without at least a basic understanding of the tenets of Christian doctrine (e.g., salvation by grace, substitutionary atonement, the Trinity). In fact, a recent article in *Research in the Teaching of English* observed that even today's US children of European descent are not uniformly socialized in those traditions; as a result, students encounter problems reading canonical literary works in secondary school, suggesting that perhaps a "Bible as literature" course should be part of the secondary curriculum (Wachlin, 1997). Because cultural awareness and sociolinguistic competence can be the most difficult aspects of second language learning and teaching (de Bot, Lowie, & Verspoor, 2005; Gass & Selinker, 2008; Hall, 2002; McKay & Hornberger, 1996; Mitchell & Myles, 2004; Preston, 1989), providing students a window into the target culture (whether historical or contemporary) through its literature can be an authentic and engaging way for students to cultivate communicative competence: It "can quickly give the foreign reader a feel for . . . a real society" (Collie & Slater, 1987, p. 4).

Rich Language Exposure

A fundamental difference between literary texts and other genres relates to their complex and varied use of language. Literary devices such as inference, metaphor, simile, oxymoron, *double entendre*, unusual or unorthodox syntactic constructions, and so forth must be correctly interpreted to ensure comprehension. These features may make a literary work intrinsically more challenging for L2 readers. Such devices are also found in other text types, although literature "may reveal a higher incidence of certain linguistic features [that] are tightly patterned in the text" (Lazar, 1993, p. 7). As with cultural information, the fact that literary language tends to be more complex can be seen as either a source of difficulty or an opportunity for L2 readers. Reading L2 literature can produce in students "a sharper awareness of the communicative resources of the language being learned" (Widdowson, 1975, p. 83). Exposing readers to these varied uses of language in "tightly patterned" ways, literary language, which has elements of creativity and art, may be more interesting and enjoyable for language students to encounter than the language used in more accessible but less imaginative informational genres (Hirvela, 2001, 2004; Peregoy & Boyle, 2004).

Consider the following opening line from a poem by the 19th-century American poet Emily Dickinson: "My life closed twice before its close . . ." A prosaic paraphrase of this line, which considers the context of the poem in its entirety, might be something like this: "I had two major tragedies in my life that felt like 'deaths' to me." Because most of us have experienced or observed tragedy, this line and its paraphrase are not difficult to understand or empathize with. But the poetic "My life closed twice . . ." is far more imaginative and evocative than a prose paraphrase could be. It uses *closed* as a metaphor for dying, perhaps as an extension of the familiar notions of a door closing or the curtain falling on the final act of a play. We note an oxymoron here: If *closed* means *ended* or *dying*, one cannot die twice before one actually dies (*before its close*). As memorably put by Collie and Slater (1987),

> Literary language is not always that of daily communication . . . but it is special in its way. It is heightened: sometimes elaborate, sometimes marvelously simply yet, somehow, absolutely "right" . . . Figurative language yokes levels of experience that were previously distinct, casting new light on familiar sensations and opening up new dimensions of perception in a way that can be exhilarating but also startling and even unsettling. (p. 5)

In short, the study of literature provides L2 readers with a close-up look at the complexity and potential beauty of the language they are acquiring.

Input for Language Acquisition

As discussed in Chapters 3 and 6, certain aspects of language can *only* be acquired through repeated and varied exposure to them (e.g., anomalous or irregular syntactic and morphological forms, varied lexical meanings and collocations). As noted by Collie and Slater (1987),

> [l]iterature provides a rich context in which individual lexical or syntactical items are made more memorable. Reading a substantial and contextualized body of text, students gain familiarity with sentences, the variety of possible structures, the different ways of connecting ideas . . . The extensive reading required in tackling a novel or a long play develops the students' ability to make inferences from linguistic clues, and to deduce meaning from context, *both useful tools in reading other sorts of material as well*. (p. 5, emphasis added)

Literary texts may be selected and assigned by the teacher (for intensive reading instruction) or self-selected by students (as part of an extensive reading program).

As noted in Chapters 6 and 8, literary sources provide language input and reading practice regardless of the approach to reading instruction emphasized in a course. Studies of *incidental vocabulary acquisition* through the reading of literature illustrate this point (Pitts et al., 1989; Saragi et al., 1978; also see Krashen, 2004, and Koda, 2004 for further discussion). In a clever research design, Saragi et al. (1978) asked adult learners to read the 20th-century novel *A Clockwork Orange*, which contains a specialized slang vocabulary called *nadsat*. Although the novel includes a glossary of these *nadsat* terms with their English equivalents, the glossaries were removed from the copies of the text given to the student participants. Students were told to read for meaning, were given no vocabulary instruction, and were not informed that they would be post-tested on *nadsat* vocabulary. Participants' average post-test score on selected *nadsat* words was 78%.[4] Although incidental learning of specific lexical items and morphosyntactic structures through reading of literature and other text types can be hard to control for and measure, evidence from L1 and L2 research and experience suggests that such learning does occur. As noted above, if literary texts expose readers to less common uses of language, it would appear that reading such texts can facilitate long-term language acquisition at least as well as (and potentially better than) other genres and subgenres of L2 texts. Finally, because the study of literature lends itself well to class discussion, oral presentation, and writing tasks, it can promote language acquisition by providing stimulating, authentic content for these production tasks (Hirvela, 2001, 2004; Peregoy & Boyle, 2004).

Enjoyable and Motivating Material

A strong argument made in favor of using literary texts with L2 students is that learners like reading literature and find it enjoyable (Aebersold & Field, 1997; Carter & McRae, 1996; Collie & Slater, 1987; Heath, 1996; Lazar, 1983; Spack, 2004). Evocative of universal human experience and emotions, the language and content of literature tends to be more interesting than other L2 texts that students might encounter (e.g., textbooks and reading materials created for ESL teaching). Spack's (1997, 2004) case study of Yuko provides a vivid example of how compelling literature can be (see Chapter 6). Yuko enjoyed reading novels both in English and Japanese so much that she not only persevered until she finished them, but she was also motivated to continue reading novels for pleasure. This experience contrasted starkly with her freshman year struggles with reading textbooks for her general education courses at a U.S. university. Ideally, students will enjoy reading literature so much that several things will happen: (1) They will "acquire a great deal of new language almost in passing" (Lazar, 1993, p. 17); (2) They will become so engrossed in plot and characters (in fiction and drama) that they will continue through a text even if the language is difficult; and (3) The experience will be so positive that they will be open to further reading of assigned literary texts, or—even better—will feel motivated to take on self-selected extensive reading for pleasure (Guthrie & Knowles, 2001).

Improved Student Confidence in L2 Reading

A related but separate point is that students feel successful, having accomplished something substantial if they read a complete work with understanding and enjoyment (e.g., a novel, play, or collection of poems or short stories). Several reasons account for this sense of achievement. First, students are aware from prior L1 and L2 literacy instruction that literature is valued in education and that it enjoys higher social status than, say, newspapers, magazines, and even textbooks. Reading and understanding literary works is a substantial accomplishment that can build confidence and generate intrinsic motivation for further reading. Second, the "confidence gap" is a very real problem for academic L2 readers who must cover large quantities of difficult reading material (Eskey, 1986). Students are usually aware of (and anxious about) the fact that literature is more linguistically challenging than other types of reading they may have done. If a teacher leads them through the analysis of a poem or the reading of a novel, and students realize that they can, in fact, read and understand these challenging L2 texts, they may begin to believe that they can succeed in other types of reading tasks as well, as did Yuko. Lazar (1993) further noted that, if students are asked to respond personally to texts, "they will become increasingly confident about expressing their own ideas and emotions in [their L2]. They will feel empowered by their ability to grapple with the text and its language" (p. 19).

A brief personal anecdote may serve to illustrate how such empowerment develops. One of the authors (Ferris)[5] was enrolled in a third-semester college French course (no prior French instruction before this college sequence). To her dismay, the class was assigned Sartre's short novel, *Les Jeux Sont Faits*. The initial homework assignment was to read the first 10 pages or so. It took her an hour to read just the first two pages, dictionary at elbow, stopping frequently to look up the (many) unfamiliar words. She wondered how she was ever going to manage the novel if every day's assignment was going to require five hours! But as the course progressed, an interesting thing happened. She became familiar with the plot, characters, and author's style, and the reading went faster (with many fewer trips to the dictionary). In class, the students and professor would discuss the plot and themes, act out scenes, and write out predictions and possible endings. She did well in the course and ended the experience with a feeling of great satisfaction, and to this day feels fairly confident of her ability to read French. Collie and Slater (1987) noted that "with well-chosen works, the investment of effort can be immensely rewarding, the resulting sense of achievement highly satisfying" (p. 5).

Personal Growth

One of the most appealing aspects of reading literature is that it engages readers on emotional and intellectual levels. Typically, "the process of [language] learning is essentially analytic, piecemeal, and, at the level of the personality, fairly superficial" (Collie & Slater, 1987, p. 5). In contrast, literature "can stimulate the imagination of our students . . . and increase their emotional awareness" (Lazar, 1993, p. 19). Such benefits can be maximized if the reading of literature is paired with opportunities for students to reflect on their reading through journaling, discussion, and formal literary analysis (Hirvela, 2004).

Some might argue that engaging students emotionally and facilitating personal growth is not part of our jobs as language teachers; others would respond that *all* learning necessarily involves "the whole person" (Lazar, 1993, p. 19). It would be a mistake to characterize language acquisition as merely the mechanical mastery of the building blocks of language (Mitchell & Myles, 2004). Given the influential roles of motivation, engagement, and confidence in successful reading experiences, it would be a greater error for reading teachers not to avail themselves of the advantages of personal relevance and emotional engagement especially (if not uniquely) offered by literary texts in particular (Vandrick, 1997).

Stimulating Writing Topics

In contexts in which students engage in both reading and writing, particularly when reading and writing are explicitly connected, the advantages offered by literary works in providing interesting topics for students to write about cannot be underestimated (Hirvela, 2004). As any teacher of L2 writers knows, it can be daunting to find (or help students find) engaging subjects to write about. After all, investment in one's topic is absolutely critical to successful and enjoyable writing experiences (Ferris & Hedgcock, 2005; Johns, 1997). Gajdusek and van Dommelen (1993) emphasized the importance and difficulty of setting successful writing tasks for L2 writers, highlighting several advantages of literary texts in this endeavor. First, literature "allows us to create the level of emotional involvement we have been seeking in more personal, subjective topics . . . without sacrificing the distance and objectivity of reader-based prose" (p. 198). Second, reading literary works requires analysis and reconstruction of meaning that can inform the choices students make as writers as they construct their own texts. Third, because literary analysis involves both the text and personal response to it, a writing task "can no longer be seen as an empty exercise; it becomes a meaningful act of personal exploration and discovery" (Gajdusek & van Dommelen, 1993, p. 199). In other words, not only does literature make *reading* more personal and meaningful to students, but *writing about it* also enhances the individual's investment. Reading–writing interconnections are crucial to L1 and L2 literacy development, and literary texts provide excellent opportunities to take full pedagogical advantage of them (Belcher & Hirvela, 2001; Ferris & Hedgcock, 2005; Hirvela, 2004; also see Chapters 2, 5, and 6).

Critical Thinking Skills

Literary texts lend themselves extremely well to critical analysis and to the development of reading–writing skills useful across a range of text and task types in academic settings. Unlike purely informational texts (e.g., textbook chapters) or news reports (such as "Going for the Look," Chapter 5), literature tends to be organized around central themes, conflicts, character development, or some combination thereof. These themes are frequently timeless and universal, reflecting broad human experience that transcends cultural and historical boundaries. Anyone who has ever faced and struggled with their own weaknesses and temptations can relate to the "Achilles heel" and the Sirens portrayed in the ancient work of the Greek epic poet Homer. A parent with sullen, spoiled teenagers will resonate with Shakespeare's Lear, who describes "a thankless child" as being "sharper than a serpent's tooth." A person in midlife, as Robert Frost was when he wrote "The Road Not Taken," can agree that choices made earlier in life can influence and constrain those made now (an understanding that younger adults, with life before them, may not appreciate yet). People who appreciate quiet time and personal space will understand why Sarton writes of "The Rewards of Living a Solitary Life."

Literary themes and language used by authors can evoke memories or provoke disagreement. For example, an off-the-charts extrovert might think that Sarton's enjoyment of being alone is downright strange or antisocial. Readers of Frost's poem may have bittersweet recollections of choices they made and paths they took—and opinions about whether, in fact, they "traveled" the right "road." Careful readers of *King Lear* will note that it was Lear who was a terrible parent and that his characterization of his daughter Cordelia as a "thankless child" was untrue, unfair, and unkind. Thus, students reading poems, plays, fiction, and literary essays may have strong personal connections with what they read—the author's ideas may remind them of similar experiences, and they may agree or disagree with the author's message depending on how true they find it to their own stories and temperaments. It is also true that students may have a personal reaction to persuasive or informative texts, yet often this reaction has to be fanned into flame by the teacher. For instance, readers of the *New York Times* article "Going for the Look" (Chapter 5) may indeed form opinions about the business practice of hiring employees based on their appearance, once they have been exposed to the issue and thought about it, but the point is that they may never have encountered or considered this issue before.

Literary themes, being based on common human experience, tend to be more immediately accessible and thus available to students for reflection, response, and reaction. Thus, literary texts may promote important critical reasoning skills more quickly, easily, and enjoyably than other types of texts might. Finally,

> if we can use the attitudes and techniques of critical thinking to solve the exciting "problems" of exploring a literary text in the ESL classroom, we can (1) produce genuine, student-centered interaction with the text; (2) model the techniques of critical thinking; and (3) facilitate the transfer of those same techniques to the writing tasks of the composition class-room. (Gajdusek & van Dommelen, 1993, p. 201)

Despite the recent criticisms of "critical thinking" as a construct or pedagogical goal (e.g., Atkinson, 1997), it is nonetheless a highly valued objective among North American educators; to the extent literary analysis can help to develop critical skills, it may well serve students' long-term academic needs.

Benefits: Summary

We have devoted a fair amount of space to reviewing the advantages of using literary texts in L2 literacy instruction. These benefits include language development, improved affect and attitude toward L2 reading, and the development of critical reasoning and writing skills. It is important that these points be enumerated and explained, as many L2 teachers tend to avoid using literature in their courses, for a number of reasons (see Figure 7.4). It is to these challenges and possible drawbacks that we turn next.

Using Literature with L2 Readers: Challenges

Thus far we have cast the notion of integrating literature into the L2 reading curriculum in a positive light, emphasizing the many positive aspects of doing so. However, it is also important and fair to say that not all literary texts are appropriate for all learners in all contexts; in some instances, the selection and study of literature might rarely if ever be appropriate. Many of the benefits

1. *Teacher Discomfort*
   - Lack of experience with or preparation for studying and teaching literature
   - Insufficient resources
2. *Student Resistance*
   - Lack of experience with extended reading in L1 and L2
   - Perceived difficulty of L2 literary texts
   - Concerns about relevance of literature to academic and professional goals
3. *Time Requirements*
   - Out-of-class reading time for students; additional preparation time for the teacher
   - In-class pre-reading and comprehension work
   - Balance with course goals and other priorities
4. *Text Difficulty*
   - Complex language and cultural information
   - Decontextualized nature of literary texts compared with other text types; additional time required to provide ample context to situate literary texts

FIGURE 7.4. Possible Challenges Associated with Using Literature.

discussed in the previous section could also be viewed as challenges under some circumstances. For example, the fact that literature provides a window to culture and models of rich, complex language can make the study of literature so difficult and frustrating for L2 readers that they lose confidence and motivation. In this section we highlight four areas of difficulty that can arise with the use of literature in L2 settings: teacher discomfort, student resistance, time constraints, and text difficulty. We then suggest possible strategies for overcoming these potential problems.

Teacher Discomfort

A potential barrier to working with literature is lack of teacher confidence in their ability to present texts successfully. L2 teachers come from a variety of academic disciplines. A good many may have majored in the literature of English (or another language), whereas others may have backgrounds in linguistics, education, foreign languages, and areas even further afield. For some, their most substantive experience with studying literature in a classroom may date as far back as high school, resulting in differing degrees of comfort with selecting, analyzing, and teaching literary sources in L2 settings.

This concern is legitimate: It *is* intimidating to consider teaching content with which one is not familiar or expert. At the same time, these reservations are not insurmountable. First, teachers who have not studied literature extensively or been trained in teaching it have access to a great many excellent resources to help them develop relevant instructional skills. Such materials include teacher-created websites, teacher resource books, and well-crafted textbooks for students that present carefully selected literary texts as well as ideas and exercises for teacher and student use. Second, as we will discuss later in this chapter, the level of literary analysis required to teach L2 readers is most likely not beyond the abilities of most language teachers, especially if they consult resources such as those mentioned above. Lazar (1993) emphasized the distinction between "the *study* of literature and the *use* of literature as a resource for language teaching" (p. 13). To put it bluntly, discussing Frost's "The Road Not Taken" with freshman ESL students is not as taxing as teaching a graduate literature seminar with sophisticated and well-prepared students.

Student Resistance

Proponents of using literature in L2 instruction cite its popularity with and appeal to students as a primary benefit and advantage. Nonetheless, it is fair to say that not all students respond positively to assigned literary texts and analytic tasks, for a number of reasons. First, some students may have limited experience reading lengthy materials in either L1 or L2, due to home literacy practices and educational background (see Chapters 2 and 6). A student who may never have read an entire novel for pleasure *or* for school is not likely to be excited about being required to do so at the secondary or postsecondary level. For such a student, it may be more appropriate to start with short, high-interest reading selections (e.g., newspaper or magazine selections) than longer, more difficult literary works.

A second reason for student resistance relates to the perceived difficulty of authentic literary texts. Some students may have initially been enthusiastic about reading literature but found that "difficult language, complex cultural issues, and the subtle conventions of various genres of fiction may leave [them] more frustrated than enlightened" (Aebersold & Field, 1997, p. 157). As we have noted throughout this book, reading in an L2 is challenging; many L2 readers lack confidence in their ability to read *any* type of L2 text (Eskey, 1986; Spack, 2004). Even (or especially) if students have read or studied literature in their L1, they may see reading a novel, a short story, a play, or a collection of poems in the L2 as simply far beyond their competence (as Ferris initially did when assigned to read a short novel as an intermediate French student).

Finally, and perhaps most importantly, students may resist studying L2 literature because they do not see it as relevant to their goals. For instance, students in a college composition course may know that the main purpose of the class is to develop their writing abilities; course goals and assessment practices may clearly reflect that aim. Being asked to spend considerable class and outside time reading and writing about literary texts may raise anxiety that students will have insufficient time to focus on what they *really* need to learn. They may also observe that, unless they plan to major in literature, they are never likely to be asked to read or write about literature again, so why should they do so now?

These student concerns are legitimate, and teachers should consider all three seriously. Teachers may need to build inexperienced L2 readers' confidence by working initially with shorter, easier texts and tasks so that they gain positive attitudes toward L2 reading. For students concerned about difficulty level, teachers need to ensure that assigned texts are carefully selected and thoughtfully presented so that students can have a successful and motivating experience with reading literature. For students concerned about relevance, teachers must think through and articulate their course goals, ensuring that the reading and analysis of literature will, in fact, support those objectives rather than undermine them. It is also crucial to convey to students the connections among instructional goals, assigned texts, and literacy tasks (see Chapters 3, 4, 5, and 9).

Time Constraints

Because of the relative length and complexity of some literary works, together with students' developing abilities to read lengthy, challenging texts, it can be time-consuming to emphasize literature in an L2 reading, composition, or language course. For instance, it is not realistic to expect students to read a full-length novel or play outside of class in just a few days; several weeks will likely be required. Nor is it fair to ask them to negotiate a lengthy, challenging reading assignment without appropriate scaffolding, class discussion, and analysis. Although short stories and poetry do not present the same length challenges, in some ways they may be even more difficult for students to understand; these genres may require substantial class time to ensure student comprehension. In most cases it will require more student time and energy to read literature than other types of assigned texts. This drawback alone is often what stops L2 reading teachers from serious consideration of literature as part of the syllabus.

There is no real way to overcome the time barrier, but we can view it in alternative ways. First, it is important to identify one's approach to working with literature. Lazar (1993) identified three distinct models:

1. *Language-based* literature teaching looking at literary texts primarily as language models, as sources of input, and material for analysis;
2. Literature as *content:* The syllabus is constructed around coverage of specific literary texts and perhaps literary criticism, similar to an advanced secondary or postsecondary literature course;
3. Literature for *personal enrichment:* "A useful tool for encouraging students to draw on their own personal experiences, feelings, and opinions . . . helps students to become more actively involved both intellectually and emotionally in learning English and hence aids acquisition" (p. 24).

In models (1) and (3), literature serves as a resource for language teaching, "as one source among many different kinds of texts for promoting interesting language activities" (Lazar, 1993, p. 14). The rest of the discussion in this chapter assumes that literature is utilized as a language development resource rather than the primary content of the L2 literacy syllabus.

Second, in weighing the time issue, teachers need to consider their overall course goals (see Chapter 4) and assess to what extent literary texts help to accomplish those goals. If teachers have determined that including literature (perhaps as a complement to other genres) can help them to meet their objectives, they can feel confident that the time investment required is justified.

Text Difficulty

The linguistic complexity and cultural information embedded in literary texts unquestionably makes them potentially more challenging than other genres for L2 readers (see Chapter 3). In addition to the difficulties posed by unusual vocabulary and sentence structure, as well as the distinctive literary features discussed earlier (see Figures 7.1 and 7.2), literary sources tend to be more decontextualized than texts typically used for academic purposes. Consider the task faced by a fourth-grade L2 student when reading a history textbook. The text probably contains any or all of the following features: (1) chapter preview or highlights of the main concepts at the beginning; (2) key words, phrases, and concepts bolded or glossed in the main text or at the back of the book; (3) visual sidebar material such as maps, illustrations, charts, or graphs; (4) a summary of main points at the end of the chapter; and (5) comprehension questions and activities designed for review and retention. Contrast this experience with reading the first chapter of a novel at the fourth-grade reading level. Other than the book's title, a cover illustration, and maybe a chapter title, the novice reader has none of the redundant aids to comprehension described above. Further, students reading their history text might understand that the course and textbook are about history, establishing a general context for reading. In contrast, the context of a novel (its sociohistorical setting, its plot and theme) is embedded in the novel itself and must be discovered by the reader. In other words, academic texts most often provide rhetorical scaffolding, whereas authentic literary sources lack these explicit metacognitive tools and strategy activators.

Text difficulty is also a significant issue when using literature in L2 reading instruction. Difficulty and readability, of course, relate to the inhibitory factors addressed earlier, namely, student resistance and time constraints. However, again, this obstacle is not insurmountable. Proponents of teaching with literature would respond that the difficulty level of a novel, compared with the history text at the same grade level, is balanced by the premise that the novel will be more enjoyable and motivating for students to read. Furthermore, whereas the *first* chapter of a novel might be difficult for students (as Sartre was for Ferris), it should get progressively easier as students become familiar with the plot, setting, characters, and style, thus creating a "context" for reading. In any case, the text difficulty issue reminds us again of the importance of careful text selection (see Chapters 3, 4, and 8) and especially teacher support in and out of class (e.g., through pre-reading discussions, graphic organizers, comprehension questions, ongoing discussion of assigned texts, and so forth) as students experience reading literature (see Chapter 5).

Possible Drawbacks: Summary

We have highlighted potential problems associated with the use of literary texts. In particular, we find the related issues of time and relevance to be highly compelling, and we would not argue that literature is always appropriate for all students in all contexts. That said, we are also convinced of the benefits of carefully selected literary titles for promoting interest and enjoyment. We are likewise persuaded that using literature in literacy instruction encourages the learners to engage in more of their own self-selected extensive reading for pleasure. To conclude, if teachers feel that incorporating literature is justifiable considering their course goals, devote adequate effort to selecting appropriate literary texts, and provide in- and out-of-class support for students as they read, it is quite possible that the reading experience will be successful for students and yield long-term affective and motivational benefits. In the next section, we turn to practical suggestions for utilizing literature in courses for L2 readers.

Teaching Literature in the L2 Reading Course

In the following discussion, we make several assumptions: (1) The teacher has already articulated clear course goals (Chapter 4); (2) Literature is used as a *resource* for meeting course objectives (rather than primary course *content*); and (3) The teacher has followed the principles for text selection and lesson design discussed in Chapters 3–5. Because approaches to teaching a lesson based on a literary text are so similar to the intensive reading strategies discussed in Chapter 5, we will not reiterate them here. Rather, we will spotlight questions and issues that arise due to the distinctive nature of literary texts. These questions include *how much* literature to use, *what kinds* of texts to select, and *how* to help students comprehend texts and realize the linguistic and affective benefits that reading literary texts can offer them (see Figure 7.5).

How Much Literature?

Teachers have several interconnected decisions to make in response to this question. For example, will literature compose the majority (or even the entirety) of the assigned texts for the course? Will it be combined with other genres in a thematic approach? Will it comprise a separate, stand-alone unit? Will all

1. **How much** literature?
   - Context considerations
   - Time constraints
2. **What kinds** of literary texts?
   - Accessible on linguistic/cultural levels
   - Length of texts
   - Engaging subject matter for students
   - Simplified texts for lower-proficiency students
3. **How** should literary texts be presented?
   - Similarities and differences between intensive reading processes for literary texts and other text types:
     - ➤ Schema activation and development
     - ➤ Graphic organizers
     - ➤ Language analysis
     - ➤ Writing summaries and analyses of literary texts
   - Literature in extensive reading approach
   - Special considerations for teaching literature:
     - ➤ Literary metalanguage
     - ➤ Teaching fiction
     - ➤ Teaching poetry
     - ➤ Teaching drama

FIGURE 7.5. Practical Issues in Teaching Literature.

students read a novel outside of class? Will they read self-selected literature as part of an extensive reading approach or course component (see Chapter 6)?

The answers to these questions depend primarily on the nature of the course and the time available for reading outside of class and working with texts in class. For instance, if a course aims mainly to develop academic literacy skills required for further postsecondary work, students must read and respond to a variety of text types; literary texts may be part of the mix, but they likely should not be the only type selected. Similarly, if the course focuses primarily on composition skills, with reading selections used as input and inspiration for writing, literary texts may well be very useful, but perhaps they should be shorter and not require substantial amounts of class time. However, if the purpose of the course is to promote L2 proficiency through sustained encounters with L2 texts, larger quantities of lengthier texts may be appropriate, provided titles are selected and presented with student interests and language proficiency in mind.

What Kinds of Texts?

Obviously, given the broad way in which we have defined literature for this chapter, the possibilities for text selection are potentially endless. Several general principles should apply in choosing literary texts. First, teachers may wish to avoid literature that is so steeped in unfamiliar culture, history, and unfamiliar language varieties that it will be unreasonably difficult and frustrating for students. Two examples from canonical American literature often mentioned are Mark Twain's *Huckleberry Finn* and J. D. Salinger's *The Catcher in the Rye;* William Faulkner's work, with its extraordinarily lengthy sentence constructions, also comes to mind. Shakespeare's works would also be a stretch for all but the most advanced and experienced L2 readers. After all, many monolingual English speakers struggle to read Shakespeare and would freely admit that they only got through their high school English courses by consulting synopses provided by commercial resources such as *Cliffs Notes* or the online *Sparks Notes*.

Second, teachers may wish to consider shorter works, such as short stories, single-act plays, poetry, short novels or *novelas* (e.g., young adult genres, Steinbeck's *The Pearl*). Some instructors use extracts from longer novels as a way to broaden the textual possibilities while acknowledging time constraints. This approach may nonetheless result in a less authentic, satisfying, and enjoyable reading experience. Third, teachers should consider works with themes, plots, and characters that will be accessible and interesting to student readers. For instance, many U.S. ESL teachers have found success with young adult novels such as *Children of the River* or *A Farewell to Manzanar*, which personalize the immigrant experience (Turner, 2008). In contrast, novels that appeal to middle-aged U.S. teachers for their own pleasure reading may be less interesting and engaging to young adult L2 readers than their teachers might imagine.

Finally, teachers of students at lower L2 proficiency levels may wish to consider simplified, abridged, or adapted versions of literary texts, also referred to as *graded readers* (Bamford & Day, 2003; Day & Bamford, 1998). Appropriately adapted material can introduce students to high-quality L2 literature and expose them to reading in those genres. Day and Bamford (1998) presented an excellent discussion of simplified texts as a "lure" for promoting extensive reading (see Chapter 6). In short, literary text selection is a challenging task for teachers, especially when it involves a major commitment such as an entire novel that students must purchase and spend weeks reading and discussing. Teachers should also keep an eye out for new and unusual literary texts that might be successful for the particular contexts in which they teach.

Where Do Literary Texts Fit in Intensive and Extensive Reading Approaches?

Most of the characteristics of intensive reading lessons discussed in Chapter 5 can and should apply to the presentation of literary texts. For instance, students still benefit from a scaffolded approach that involves *pre-*, *while-*, and *post-reading* tasks, although some of the skills and activities suggested for informational or expository texts may be less relevant for literary texts. Below we briefly outline the similarities and differences between intensive reading lessons with literary texts and other types. We then discuss how literature can be incorporated in an extensive reading approach. Finally, we turn to considerations for teaching in the major literary genres and subgenres (fiction, poetry, drama).

The Intensive Reading Process: Before Reading. Pre-reading activities are crucial for beginning work with literary texts, but not all of the suggestions in Chapter 5 are effective or appropriate. For instance, extensive previewing (e.g., prediction, skimming, scanning) is not likely to be very helpful, as most literary texts have a title but are not divided into sections with headings (or even chapter titles, in many novels) or have other extratextual comprehension aids. However, schema activation (e.g., eliciting students' prior knowledge of and experiences with the themes, plots, and character types in a novel or the theme of a poem) and schema development (providing background knowledge about the author, the time period and setting of the work, and specialized cultural information or vocabulary prior to reading) can be vitally important both to students' initial approach to the text and their ability to read with expectation and resulting comprehension (Gambrell et al., 2007; Irvine, 2007).

During Reading. Students reading fiction and drama can benefit from the advantages offered by graphic organizers, which can help them to identify plot elements, describe characters, and analyze the problem or conflict presented by the story (see Chapters 3 and 5). Teachers should not assume that theme, plot, or character development are obvious or intuitive to all students. In fiction, important plot details are often conveyed indirectly rather than explicitly; students looking for the straightforward cues provided by writers of expository texts may never find them. Further, the language of the text itself may obscure or confuse students about plot details. Figure 7.6 shows several simple graphic organizers developed for a short story entitled "Tito's Goodbye" (see Spack, 2006).

Furthermore, because language use is so critical to understanding and interpreting literature, activities to make students aware of how tone, mode, setting, and character are conveyed through language choices may be more important for teaching literature than for teaching non-literary texts. For instance, in examining Sarton's literary essay "The Rewards of Living a Solitary Life" (see Chapter 5), students can be directed to the first two paragraphs to identify how Sarton telegraphs her positive feelings toward solitude and her awareness that her thesis might startle readers.[6] They could also examine the final stanza of Frost's "The Road Not Taken" to see how Frost communicates whether his decision to "take the road less traveled by" was a good one or a bad one—or whether he feels ambivalent about the question. One could argue that the first line, "I shall be telling this *with a sigh*," suggests that Frost regrets his decision, as a sigh typically signals unhappiness. However, one could argue that the final line, "And that has *made all the difference*," conveys the opposite, as "making a difference" conveys more positive than negative meaning. It could also be observed that Frost's image of "the road less traveled" has evolved in U.S. culture to reference a life choice that is unconventional and even courageous, something to be admired (especially since the publication of M. Scott Peck's book of the same name).

After Reading. In Chapter 5, we outlined post-reading and extension activities, including summary, response, and critical analysis. These tasks are especially appropriate for teaching literature: Among the chief benefits of using literature is

1. Plot

What is happening?
What is the main conflict?
How is the conflict resolved?

2. Setting

Place	Time	Social environment	Physical environment

3. Characters

Tito
Haydée
Inés
Jaime
Beatrice
Other characters not named

FIGURE 7.6. Sample Graphic Organizers: "Tito's Goodbye."
Story found in Spack (2006).

its potential for helping students to respond personally to what they have read, to stimulate interesting ideas and topics to write about, and to think critically about the author's message. However, we would note that the mechanics of writing summaries and analyses of literary works are somewhat different from those that apply to non-literary genres. For example, with expository texts, students are often guided through the summary-writing process through explicit or easily discernible statements of purpose, main ideas, and key supporting evidence. The student summary writer's job is simply to identify main ideas and key supporting points, restating them concisely and accurately. In contrast, summarizing a poem, narrative, or play involves not only understanding the plot or theme but also deciding which plot and character details are essential.

Further, whereas literary analysis essays reflect the rhetorical conventions of other academic essays (e.g., a deductive discursive structure, with an introductory and concluding elements, along with a thesis and supporting evidence), the nature of the thesis and its support is quite distinct. Students identify a thesis particular to the particular work under study, and the evidence used to support the thesis must come directly from the text through quotation, summary, and paraphrase. Writers may also refer to published literary criticism, although integrating critical sources is far less common and practical in L2 reading instruction than in traditional literature courses. Whereas students may include life experience and observation, expert opinion, and other external data sources in non-literary essays, when responding to literature, they must be taught to use the text itself as their primary and perhaps only source of support for their arguments.

To summarize, many of the activity types and suggestions introduced in Chapter 5 will apply to teaching reading through literature. However, given the distinct characteristics of literary works, some activities may be extremely helpful (even critically necessary), while others may be less appropriate. As with other texts, the amount of time given to each stage of the intensive reading process may vary according to the course and lesson goals, time available, and the features of of the text under consideration.

Literature in an Extensive Reading Approach

It should be apparent that literary texts are highly appropriate for the primary goals of extensive reading: to provide students with positive, enjoyable reading experiences that will encourage them to develop and sustain lifelong L2 pleasure reading habits (Chapter 6). Not all extensive reading texts need to be literary: Newspapers, magazines, biographies, and other nonfiction genres may appeal more to some readers for self-selected free reading. Nonetheless, many students enjoy and benefit from exposure to narrative fiction, drama, and poetry.

We will mention here two general strategies for incorporating literature into an extensive reading syllabus or a course that includes assigned extensive reading as a component. First, teachers can assign lengthy literary texts to the whole class. For example, they may require the entire class to read a novel, play, or a set of poems by the same author or on the same theme. Alternatively, the assignment could involve book groups or literature circles in which students select a novel to read together from among teacher-provided alternatives and provide structure and support for one another as they read (see Chapter 6). Teacher-assigned reading cannot properly be characterized as FVR (*free voluntary reading*) in Krashen's (2004) terms, but a successful, pleasurable whole-class or small-group reading experience may give students the confidence and motivation to take on self-selected reading of literary texts on their own. Second, teachers can assign self-selected extensive reading as a course requirement by including literature in a reading list or classroom library. For example, as part of their extensive reading component, students might read at least one complete novel of their one choosing, pushing them beyond short newspaper and magazine articles, although these may also be part of the extensive reading assignment. The teacher's role here is simply to expose students to the possibilities of reading literature for pleasure and to assist them by providing suggestions for narrowing the vast array of possible reading choices.

Specific Considerations for Teaching Literature

In other chapters of this volume, we cover a great deal of ground pertaining to practical aspects of teaching L2 reading, including course and lesson design, text selection, assessment, vocabulary instruction, and approaches to intensive and extensive reading. In the final section of this chapter, we turn our attention to a specialized topic not yet explored: approaches to teaching literary genres. Given space and scope constraints, this discussion will of necessity be general and brief. However, we can recommend several excellent book-length treatments that present a range of teaching suggestions and examples, including Carter and Long (1991), Carter and McRae (1996), Collie and Slater (1987), and Lazar (1993). For brief treatments, we recommend selected chapters in Aebersold and Field (1997), Gajdusek (1988), Gajdusek and van Dommelen (1993), Hirvela (2004), Moon (2000), Popp (2005), and Yancey (2004). In this section, we look first at the topic of *literary metalanguage* and then move in turn through the teaching of fiction, poetry, and drama. We aim to provide teachers with basic tools for incorporating literature into their reading courses if they so desire.

Literary Metalanguage: To Teach or Not to Teach?

As we have already seen, numerous linguistic devices commonly characterize literary texts (see Figure 7.1). The question faced by L2 reading teachers is whether to provide explicit instruction targeting those features and the terminology that labels them.[7] Whether literary metaknowledge is necessary for L2 student readers depends on course goals and the reasons for which literature is included. If students only occasionally examine a short story or poem as part of a thematic unit with other nonliterary genres, a focus on literary metalanguage may not be especially valuable. However, if a substantial portion of the course reading and/or extensive reading component is focused on literature, it may be helpful to take time to present literary terms and concepts to students.

Literary metalanguage is probably best presented via mini-lessons in which the teacher briefly presents the concepts, paired with clear definitions and several straightforward literary examples. Learners then examine several text excerpts to identify for themselves additional instances of the literary device. How many literary terms to present in a mini-lesson (or series of mini-lessons) should be a function of the context and target texts. For instance, if students are to read a poem exemplifying alliteration, assonance, and imagery, it might be worthwhile to present those terms explicitly. However, if they are preparing to read a young adult novel, they may not need such a precise focus on literary language.

Teaching Fiction

Fiction can include full-length novels, short novels (or *novelas*), and short stories. It is important to note distinctions among fictional genres and subgenres. Teachers often gravitate toward short stories because they can be read and discussed in less time, can give students a sense of accomplishment more quickly, and can offer more variety in the syllabus, as students can read a number of different stories in the time that it takes to read a novel (Collie & Slater, 1987;

Hirvela, 2004). However, because of their compact nature and concision, short stories can, ironically, be harder for L2 readers to comprehend than longer texts (Lazar, 1993). Collie and Slater (1987) argued that even greater care must be taken to prepare students to read short stories and to ensure their comprehension than for longer novels; they suggested that multiple readings of the text may be necessary. In contrast, novels enable students to become familiar and comfortable with the plot, characters, setting, and style, building comprehension and confidence as they progress. With short stories, students may have barely acclimated to one story and author before moving on to something completely different. On the other hand, novels require more time and effort to complete, and even if some students do not like a particular assigned novel, they are committed to it for weeks or even months, causing them to lose motivation and feel resentful and frustrated.

Considering the advantages and disadvantages of novels and short stories, a short novel may seem the ideal compromise, and, indeed, many short novels have been successfully utilized in L2 literary instruction. However, relatively fewer appropriate short novels are available, and teachers may grow tired of being restricted to limited genres, such as young adult fiction. These texts tend to appeal to students and are fairly easy for them to read, yet they may lack the compelling content and linguistic and stylistic richness offered by other categories of fiction. In short, all three fiction subgenres entail advantages and disadvantages; teachers should not feel constrained to use one to the exclusion of others. Difficulties can be mitigated with thoughtful text selection (see Chapters 3 and 4) and with preparation of materials to assist student comprehension and maximize their reading enjoyment (see Chapter 5). Effective reading can also be facilitated by careful instructional planning. For example, teachers can break up the reading of a novel so that it neither goes too fast nor drags on too long and so that it is balanced with other genres and literacy tasks.

Far more creative ideas are available for teaching fiction than we have room to include in this text. Essentially, however, students need to understand several things about a work of fiction (see Figure 7.7). Though there are many finer points of literary analysis that could be discussed, for L2 readers, the list in Figure 7.7 is easily understandable, covers the most important information about works of fiction and provides a framework that can be applied to any fictional text. Within that general framework, the teacher can then move students through specific texts, focusing on areas of interpretation for a particular work that could be problematic. For instance, some stories are not sequenced chronologically and utilize alternative time-sequencing (comparable to flashbacks in films). Students may need extra help in identifying elements of plot and setting if the narrative structure is complex. Story maps and graphic organizers can be helpful tools in such instances.

In other works, the language of the text may present challenges. For instance, Kate Chopin's "The Story of an Hour" is short and moves linearly from the beginning to the end of the "hour" in which the story takes place. However, in

- **Global understanding:** What is the *plot*? What actually happens in the story? What is the *conflict, or problem*, being explored in the story? Most works of fiction have some sort of conflict that is presented (and either resolved or not). Conflict may also occur through plot developments, within the internal world of a single character, between characters, or a combination of these.
- **Specific understanding:** What is the *setting*? This includes *time* (both historical time period and even the season of the year), *place* (country/city/house, geographic location, and so on) and *point of view* (who is telling the story—a first-person narrator or omniscient third-person narrator—and through the eyes of which character(s)). Who are the *characters*? What are they like, and how do we know? What is their relationship to one another, and what do we know about the nature and quality of those relationships? How is *language* used to convey information about the plot, conflict, setting, and characters?
- **Interpretation:** What is the *theme*, or the main message or idea that conveyed by the author? (It is important to understand that the plot, conflict, and theme are not identical. The author likely aims to reveal a broader theme by recounting the plot and presenting the conflict.)

FIGURE 7.7. Major Elements in a Work of Fiction.

part because the text is so short, the language is compact, requiring much inferencing on the part of the reader. For example, the story ends thus:

> Some one was opening the front door with a latchkey. It was Brently Mallard who entered, a little travel-stained, composedly carrying his gripsack and umbrella. He had been far from the scene of the accident, and did not even know there had been one. He stood amazed at Josephine's piercing cry; at Richards' quick motion to screen him from the view of his wife.
>
> When the doctors came they said she had died of heart disease—of the joy that kills.

The penultimate paragraph explains that the husband of the protagonist, Mrs. Mallard, had not been killed in a railway accident, as previously thought. This passage is followed by the final sentence, which cryptically reveals that "she" (Mrs. Mallard) had died suddenly from the shock of seeing her very-much-alive husband. However, the text does not say, "When she saw her husband, she was so shocked that she dropped dead of a heart attack." Readers must make that connection for themselves.

Careful readers will note that the layers of meaning in that final sentence are even more complex than that: If Mrs. Mallard died from "heart disease," it was not because she was so overcome with joy that her husband was alive after all, but rather because she was so disappointed that he was not dead. Further, her "heart disease" was not merely literal but metaphorical—her heart had become "diseased" by years in a stifling marriage. In fact, the story is a brief but elegant portrait not just of one hour in one woman's life, but of the repressed state of wives in early 20th-century, upper-class America. However, this is a lot of explicit and implicit information to gather from that final line of such a brief story. It is not impossible for L2 readers to grasp all of these details; on the contrary, the story has been used successfully with ESL students. Nonetheless, they will likely need scaffolded assistance and several re-readings of the story to comprehend the plot accurately and then to decipher the theme (Fitzgerald & Graves, 2004). Figure 7.8 provides a list of activities that a teacher might plan at each stage of the reading process to teach a work of fiction.

Teaching Poetry

Poetry as a genre offers many advantages to the L2 reading teacher. First, many poems are quite short; it is possible to cover one or more poems in a single class session. Second, because poems artistically capture universal experience and elicit emotional responses, students and teachers frequently enjoy reading poetry and find it both moving and satisfying. Third, poetry offers a creative and unique perspective that extends L2 students' awareness and appreciation of the target language (Collie & Slater, 1987; Lazar, 1993). On the other hand, some teachers may feel that "playing around with poetry" is a waste of class time that could be

---

Pre-Reading Activities
1. Help students with cultural and historical background of the author and story.
2. Stimulate interest in the story.
3. Elicit prior knowledge of and experience with the text's thematic content.
4. Pre-teach vocabulary, if appropriate.

While-Reading Activities
1. Help students understand the plot.
2. Help students understand characters, their relationships with one another, and their connections to the plot.
3. Help students understand difficult vocabulary.
4. Help students with style and literary language.

Post-Reading Activities
1. Help students interpret the text.
2. Help students respond to and analyze the text.
3. Lead follow-up oral activities.
4. Guide follow-up writing activities.

FIGURE 7.8. Outline of Activity Types for Feaching Fiction.
Outline adapted from Lazar (1993, pp. 83–84). For a similar outline, see Gajdusek (1988) and Gajdusek and van Dommelen (1993).

devoted to other activities and that poetry is too difficult for L2 readers because the use of language is so idiosyncratic. Teachers may also assume that students likely do not read poetry even in their L1s, and that learners are not always sure they understand poetry. Therefore, how could they possibly lead students through a poem (Lazar, 1993)? Again, of course, the keys to maximizing the benefits of studying poetry and minimizing difficulties lie in text selection and teacher support as students advance through the reading process.

To derive these benefits, we suggest that poetry selected for an L2 reading course be fairly short, contemporary so that students do not struggle with anachronistic and highly literary language, and on themes readily accessible to the student audience. Frost's "The Road Not Taken" (Appendix 7.2) meets all three of these criteria, as the poem is short, less than a hundred years old (and with language somewhat elevated but not impossibly so), and on a discernible theme (decision-making at "crossroads" in life) highly relevant to young adults. In contrast, the famous passage from John Donne's *Devotions for Emergent Occasions* (Meditation XVII), "No Man is an Island," meets two of the three criteria (length and relevance) but not the second (recency, as Donne lived from 1573 to 1621). Given the text's brevity, its two very famous lines ("no man is an island" and "ask not for whom the bell tolls; it tolls for thee"), and its two universal themes (awareness of human interconnectedness and mortality), this selection might still be worth the effort required for students to comprehend it.[8]

Unless poetry is prominently featured in a course, we do not recommend detailed discussion of formal details (e.g., rhythm, meter, scansion, and so forth). Rather, students should focus on understanding the basic information contained in a poem (Figure 7.9). As for moving students through the stages of intensively reading a poem, it may be best to do very little pre-reading work, so that students can encounter the poem without too many preconceived notions. Teachers may offer offer background information about the poet (and perhaps the setting, if relevant), and a brief discussion or writing activity that activates students'

☐ Consider the *speaker* in the poem.
☐ Consider the *subject* of the poem (what the poem is about).
☐ Consider the *setting* (if applicable).
☐ Consider the *characters* in the poem (if applicable).
☐ Consider the *images* (details that engage the senses; non-literal language).

Ask yourself:

- What *ideas* emerge from the details of the poem? (What is the author's main idea or message?)
- What *feeling or emotion* emerges from the details of the poem? (What are the author's emotions? How does it affect the reader?)

FIGURE 7.9. Major Elements in Understanding Poetry.
Adapted from Spack (1998a, pp. 223–225).*
* The second edition of Guidelines (first published in 1996) is the only edition to date to include poetry analysis.

content schemata with respect to the piece's theme. For instance, prior to reading "The Road Not Taken," students could reflect on the theme of major life decisions.

In working with poetry, the while-reading and post-reading stages are more important. The while-reading stage should include a teacher read-aloud(s) of the poem and perhaps choral or individual student readings. It should also include detailed stanza-by-stanza or line-by-line analysis to ensure student comprehension, especially given the unusual syntax and lexical choices found in poetry. The teacher can ask specific questions about sections or lines of the poem, ask students to paraphrase problematic words, phrases, or sections, and provide clarification as needed. Once basic comprehension is achieved, the teacher and students can go back to look at larger issues (subject and theme) and at how specific words, phrases, or verses expressed the theme and conveyed emotions. As for post-reading activities, students can be asked to respond to the message of the poem (through comparison/contrast with their own experiences, agreement or disagreement with the author's perspective), to write a brief analysis about what they think the theme is and why, using specific textual support, to paraphrase the poem, or to write a poem of their own. As a further extension, students can be asked to read and analyze additional poems (either assigned or self-selected) on similar themes or by the same poet.[9]

Teaching Drama

Drama is perhaps the least-utilized literary genre among L2 reading instructors. Like novels, plays can be time-consuming to read and to cover in class. Like short stories and poetry, the language of a play can be challenging for students to grapple with. Further, a unique feature of plays is that they have dual identities: In addition to being texts, plays are intended to be performed by actors on a stage (Lazar, 1993). Thus, in contrast to novels, which provide detailed descriptions of characters and settings and explicit cues to move the plot along, reading a play requires additional imagination and inferencing abilities on the part of the reader: While some information is specifically stated, other aspects of the text are intended to be observed during a performance (e.g., through tone of voice, staging, facial expressions, plot, and so on). For this reason, drama is often seen as more appropriate for a listening–speaking or general language course than for a reading course. Indeed, drama lends itself to excellent opportunities for listening and speaking practice, as students can read plays aloud, act them out, and watch film versions of them (Brauer, 2002; Liu, 2002).

That said, L2 reading teachers might still consider including the reading of a play as an option. Although many universities have separate theater departments, drama is also still considered a major genre to be studied as part of a mainstream literature program. In addition to the advantages of cultivating cross-skill connections and L2 communicative competence, working with plays can engage learners in conversation analysis, as texts are so heavily dependent on dialogue

(Lazar, 1993). Further, many excellent plays (both in the literary canon and outside of it) explore universal themes of life, people, and relationships in engaging and enjoyable ways. Thus, although plays offer unique challenges to teachers and students, they also offer distinct opportunities not as easily found in other literary genres.

Because of the length and time requirements involved in working with drama, it is unlikely that teachers would select more than one for a course unless the course is entirely dedicated to literature or drama. Therefore, teachers must select plays with great care. For L2 readers, because plays make additional demands on their comprehension abilities, it is perhaps best to choose plays written in relatively contemporary language. Although there is much to love about Shakespeare's plays (and many excellent film versions of them are available), they are difficult even for L1 readers to understand; L2 students and their teachers may not have enough time to work through the challenges presented by those texts.[10] Similarly, a staple drama of high school American literature courses is Arthur Miller's fine play *The Crucible*. This work explores compelling themes: a witchhunt, people being persecuted and prosecuted unfairly, mass religious hysteria, and the evolution of a character, John Proctor, as he faces the biggest test (crucible) of his life. *The Crucible* is also linked to real historical events that could be presented as background, but the fact that its language reflects the story's setting in 1692 colonial America may make reading the play an overwhelming challenge for L2 readers and their instructors. On the other hand, if the majority of L2 students have been educated in mainstream English classes at the secondary level in the US, they may have had prior experience with reading dramatic works, including those of Shakespeare.

L2 reading teachers wishing to incorporate drama must consider several options and issues (see Figure 7.10). If the teacher assigns an entire play, as with a novel, the process may take weeks, not days, and the teacher must divide outside reading and in-class work accordingly. Many of the same types of activities for teaching fiction are appropriate with plays—providing cultural and historical background about the author, the play, and its setting (particularly if the play is set in a remote historical period, as with *The Crucible* or Shakespeare's *Julius Caesar* and other historically based dramas). Other information particular to the genre might include previewing the list of characters (usually provided at the beginning of a script) so that students can recognize them and helping students interpret stage directions as they read them. These steps would also include introducing students to script conventions such as character names being listed in all capitals when they are about to deliver a line and stage directions being included in parentheses or italics. Students should also be prepared for the central role of dialogue and extralinguistic information in conveying ideas about the plot, characters, and thematic elements. In some novels, the omniscient narrator sets the scene and fills in the details, and dialogue is part of the story but not all of it. In contrast, in plays, dialogue provides most or all of the exposition, functioning as the chief vehicle for plot development. Except for dramas that include a

Text Background
1. Would a plot summary (provided prior to reading) be helpful or necessary for the students?
2. Will they need specific cultural or historical information to understand the text?
3. Would information about the author's life or other work be useful?
4. Do students need genre information about the play (e.g., drama, comedy, tragedy, and so on) to make sense of it?

The Language of the Text
1. Are there unusual words, phrases, or syntactic constructions? Would it be helpful to pre-teach them?
2. Are there unusual discourse features, such as sudden changes of topic, characters meaning something different from what they are saying, and so on? Does the dialogue follow the norms of conversation, or does it violate them?
3. Is the language outdated or reflective of an unfamiliar historical period? Does it contain colloquial, regional, or nonstandard dialect features?
4. Are there any rhetorical or literary devices that may be hard for students to understand (e.g., absurd or illogical statements or questions, difficult metaphors)?
5. Are there particular features of pronunciation, rhythm, or intonation that the play (or extracts from it) could be used to highlight and practice?

Motivating Students
1. How can the topic or theme be made relevant and interesting to students?
2. In what skills do students need the most practice, and how could the text be used to develop them?
3. What activities would best suit the learning styles, ability levels, and prior experience of the student audience?

FIGURE 7.10. Issues to Consider in Working with Plays.
Adapted from Lazar (1993, pp. 155–156).

narrator, the reader of a script or spectator at a performance must work to understand the story by interpreting dialogue.

Follow-up work once a play's plot and themes are understood can include acting out or rewriting scenes and analyzing scenes for how language reveals meaning, character, and relationships. Figure 7.11 presents an example of such an activity. Finally, building on the performance aspects of a play, extracts can also be used for oral work—to help students (including low-proficiency learners) practice pronunciation, rhythm, and intonation (see Lazar, 1993, pp. 146–154). Finally, if a teacher wishes to introduce students to reading drama or to assign a full-length play, it might be useful to work first with a shorter script (say, from a half-hour television comedy) to familiarize students with reading scripts before tackling a more challenging literary work.

Chapter Summary

Although literary texts pose unique and imposing challenges for L2 readers and their instructors, they also offer many significant benefits. In our view, the two strongest reasons to consider integrating literature into the L2 reading syllabus—and for taking steps to overcome possible obstacles—are, first, that literary texts offer unique opportunities for students to experience the richness of the target

Extract

1. MERRIMAN: Miss Fairfax. (Enter Gwendolen. Exit Merriman.)
2. CECILY: (advancing to meet her) Pray let me introduce myself to you. My name is Cecily Cardew.
3. GWENDOLEN: Cecily Cardew. (moving to her and shaking hands) What a very sweet name! Something tells me we are going to be great friends. I like you already more than I can say. My first impressions of people are never wrong.
4. CECILY: How nice of you to like me so much after we have known each other such a comparatively short time. Pray sit down.
5. GWENDOLEN: (still standing up) I may call you Cecily, may I not?
6. CECILY: With pleasure!
7. GWENDOLEN: And you will always call me Gwendolen, won't you?
8. CECILY: If you wish.
9. GWENDOLEN: Then all is quite settled, is it not?
10. CECILY: I hope so.

(A pause; they both sit down together.)
From Oscar Wilde, *The Importance of Being Earnest.*

Analysis Activity

a. Why does Cecily use the word "pray" (lines 2 and 4)?
b. In her reply to Cecily's introduction (line 3), Gwendolen uses these phrases: "a *very* sweet name"; "*great* friends"; "*more* than I can say." Do these strike you as typical or appropriate for a first meeting? What do they suggest about Gwendolen's attitude toward Cecily?
c. What is suggested by Cecily's reply to Gwendolen in line 4?
d. Cecily asks Gwendolen to sit down, but she does not. Why?
e. Why does Cecily say "If you wish" in line 8? What is implied by saying this?
f. What does Gwendolen mean in line 9 when she says, "Then all is quite settled, is it not?"
g. Why does Cecily reply, "I hope so" (line 10)?
h. How do you think the two women really feel about each other?
i. What do you think is going to happen as their relationship develops further?

FIGURE 7.11. Language/Conversation Analysis of a Play Extract.
Adapted from Lazar (1993, p. 142).

language and, second, that they can be extremely engaging and enjoyable for students. Assigned work with literature can even lead to students to take on more L2 pleasure reading on their own in the future. Our positive orientation toward incorporating literary texts is tempered with caution and a few caveats—unlike our unqualified endorsement of more generalized extensive reading in the previous chapter. Nonetheless, we believe that, in many contexts and under the right circumstances, literature can be a highly valuable addition to a course syllabus. To summarize our previous suggestions, to work effectively with literary texts, L2 reading teachers must:

- understand the purposes for using literary texts in a *language* course (as opposed to a literature course);
- choose texts wisely;
- allow enough time inside and outside of class to cover texts effectively;
- provide background information about the text and the author;

- train students in the basic elements of literary genres and how to recognize and interpret them;
- help students with comprehension checks both in and out of class;
- give students ample opportunity to reflect on, react to, and critically analyze the works they have read.

If teachers follow these guidelines, they and their students can expect successful, motivating, and enjoyable encounters with literary texts in their courses.

Further Reading and Resources

The following list points readers to key materials referred to in this chapter. Bibliographic information on published sources can be found in the References. Readers are reminded that URLs may have changed since the time of publication.

Lists of literary terms and examples
  http://www.dowlingcentral.com/MrsD/area/literature/Terms/.html http://www.uncp.edu/home/canada/work/allam/general/glossary.htm
Reading–writing textbooks with literary selections
  Spack (1998a, 1998b, 2006)
Teacher resources for using literature with English L2 learners
  Aebersold & Field (1997); Bamford & Day (2003); Collie & Slater (1987); Day (1993); Hirvela (2004); Lazar (1993); Paran (2006); Whiteson (1996)
Articles on benefits of literature for L2 students
  Gajdusek (1988); Gajdusek & van Dommelen (1993); Spack (1985, 2004)
Guidelines for graphic organizers
  http://www.wm.ed/TTAC/articles/learning/graphic.htm
Extensive reading information
  http://www.kyoto-su.ac.jp/information/er/
International Reading Association book lists
  http://www.reading.org/resources/tools/choices.html
Free online survey design tool
  http://www.surveymonkey.com

Reflection and Review

1. Now that you have completed this chapter, do you think you would use literary texts in an L2 reading class? Would you *always/frequently* use them, *maybe/sometimes* use them, or *rarely/never* use them? Why?

2. Look again at the list of possible problems with or drawbacks to using literature with L2 readers (see Figure 7.4). Which of these do you find the most compelling or troublesome? Is it a big enough problem for you that you might not seriously consider using literature in some (or all) contexts, or do you feel that the difficulties could be mitigated?

3. This chapter presupposes that in most L2 reading contexts teachers would use literary texts as one among several resources to meet course objectives and student needs. Can you make an argument for a larger role for literature in L2 reading instruction—perhaps even an *exclusive* role? When (or in what contexts) might such an expanded role be appropriate?

4. This chapter has implied that, in most cases, L2 reading teachers should: (a) not teach the metalanguage or technical aspects of literary analysis; and (b) choose texts that are relatively accessible in terms of length, linguistic complexity, and theme. Do you agree or disagree with these viewpoints, or do you feel that students might be cheated by not delving more deeply into literary analysis or by not grappling with more challenging texts?

5. In your own L2 reading course (or a reading–writing or multi-skills course), would you be most likely to incorporate literature for intensive reading purposes (i.e., an assigned text that the whole class studies together) or as an option for an extensive reading component?

6. Considering your own instructional context, which of the three major literary genres (fiction, poetry, drama) interests you the most as a current or future teacher? Which do you find the least interesting or useful, and why?

Application Activities

Application Activity 7.1
Examining Features of Literary Texts

a. Appendices 7.1 and 7.2 contain two short literary texts: Kate Chopin's "The Story of an Hour" (a short story) and Robert Frost's "The Road Not Taken" (a poem). Examine both to identify literary features discussed in this section, using Figure 7.1 and Chart B in Figure 7.2 to guide you. Which samples do you think might pose challenges for L2 readers in a high school or college course?

b. Look back at the general text selection issues discussed in Chapter 3 (e.g., Figures 3.1 and 3.4; Application Activity 3.3). To what extent are the criteria discussed earlier appropriate for examining literary texts? To what extent are further criteria (as in [a] above and Figures 7.1 and 7.2) necessary and helpful?

c. As an optional follow-up, repeat this exercise with a literary sample of your own choosing—a novel (or excerpts), a play (or excerpts), or different short stories or poems. Discuss whether you might choose the text you examined for a reading lesson and why (or why not). If so, for what proficiency levels and context might the text be most appropriate?

Application Activity 7.2
Evaluating Benefits and Challenges of Using Literature

a. Use the two lists of benefits and problems (Figures 7.3 and 7.4) to design a brief questionnaire for teachers or for L2 reading students about their experiences with, and reactions to, the use of literary texts in courses for L2 readers. Administer the questionnaire to 10 or more teachers or to at least one class of L2 reading students.

b. Analyze your findings and synthesize them in an oral or written report. Based on questionnaire responses, would you judge the use of literature with L2 readers to be a good idea? Compare your findings with the discussion in this chapter and with your responses to the Questions for Reflection at the beginning of the chapter. As a prospective or current instructor, describe your evolving opinion on this topic. Has it changed, or have you simply become more convinced about your own initial responses?

Application Activity 7.3
Finding Suitable Literary Texts for L2 Readers

a. As a starting point for this activity, select a student cohort or institution familiar to you. Alternatively, use the course description in Appendix 4.2 as a hypothetical case.

b. Compile a brief list of three to five literary texts that you might consider using in this context. Use your own knowledge of literary texts, check online reading lists (e.g., for young adults, teens, college students, and so forth), or follow the links given in Further Reading and Resources.

c. Develop a text analysis worksheet like the one provided for Application Activity 3.3. In addition, incorporate the distinct characteristics of literary texts (Figures 7.1 and 7.2). For this exercise, skip the Vocabulary Profiler portion of the Application Activity 3.3. Prepare three to five copies of this worksheet.

d. Visit a library or bookstore and look through the texts you had identified as prospective selections. Complete the worksheets for each text. Orally or in writing, discuss why you would use (or not use) these texts with the target student audience you identified in (a).

e. As an extension of this activity, examine one or more additional texts in the library or bookstore that you did not place on your shortlist in (a). Places to look might include junior and young adult sections, new fiction, and literature in English from other parts of the world. Selections might also include work that you have read and enjoyed yourself, but avoid projecting your experiences, ability, and frame of reference onto prospective students. Would you select any of these texts for use with this class? Why or why not?

Application Activity 7.4
Providing Literary Texts for Extensive Reading

a. Choose a course, institution, or group of L2 learners with whom you are familiar. Using the suggestions in Application Activity 7.3, select eight to ten short novels that could be used in a literature circles approach. Selections should be interesting, age-appropriate, graded for student proficiency level, and short enough for students to read easily outside of class over a two- to four-week period.

b. As an extension of (a), develop a handout with guidelines for your book groups. Your guidelines should include instructions for how to set up a group reading schedule, how the group will handle the preparation and leading of discussions of their book, and how to complete required follow-up activities (e.g., group summaries, written or oral book reports, book reviews for future readers, and so on).

c. With the same target audience in mind, develop a reading list of literary texts that would be appropriate for this group as a starting point for their own self-selected reading. Devise a one-page assignment sheet specifying how much self-selected reading must be literary and the types of follow-up activities readers will complete.

Application Activity 7.5
Developing Reading Activities for a Work of Fiction

a. Imagine that you are about to teach "The Story of an Hour" (Appendix 7.1) to intermediate- to advanced-level college L2 readers. Considering the major elements of fiction presented in Figure 7.7 and the outline of activities in Figure 7.8, brainstorm activities for each stage of the reading process.

b. Draw on suggestions given in Chapters 4 and 5, as well as Application Activities 5.1–5.3, 5.5, and 5.6.

c. Now imagine that you will spend about two weeks (four class periods) working with this selection. The instructional period could include work prior to the first class day, homework between class sessions, writing activities after the fourth day, and so on. Using the ideas you generated for (a) and the background information below, complete the lesson-planning template below.

d. As an extension of this activity, imagine that you are going to work with a novel that you have assigned to the class. How might your timeline and activities change if you are working with a longer text?

Background and Template

Background

a. Description of students: You are teaching a high-intermediate to advanced reading course in a college setting. Students are mostly recent immigrants (five years or fewer) or international students.
b. Description of class: You have 30 students whom you see for 75 minutes per day, two days per week over a 15-week semester.
c. Target text: "The Story of an Hour" (Chopin) (Appendix 7.1)

Work Previously Completed

It is about the 12th week of the semester. You have done extensive previous work on reading strategies using non-literary texts. You plan to spend about two weeks (four class periods) on this text, including post-reading follow-up activities.

Lesson Objectives, including SWBATs

Materials Needed

Lesson Sequence
(for each day, with time frames specified)

❑

❑

❑

❑

❑

Homework and Related Future Work
(between meetings and after the sequence is over)

Assessment

Contingency plans

Application Activity 7.6
Developing Reading Activities for a Poem

For this activity, use Frost's "The Road Not Taken" (Appendix 7.2). Considering the elements of poetry (Figure 7.9) and suggestions given in this section, brainstorm activities that you might use for the three stages of reading with this poem.

a. Imagine that you will spend one class period (75 minutes) working through this poem with students (perhaps including pre-class work and homework). Using the same background information as in Application Activity 7.6, complete the lesson-planning template (also found in Application Activity 7.6).
b. For additional practice, look at Donne's "No Man is an Island" passage, below. What words, phrases, and syntax might be difficult for students? How might you go guide students through a purposeful reading? Brainstorm activities you might use to teach this text.

From Meditation XVII: No Man is an Island

No man is an island entire of itself; every man
is a piece of the continent, a part of the main;
if a clod be washed away by the sea, Europe
is the less, as well as if a promontory were, as
well as any manner of thy friends or of thine
own were; any man's death diminishes me,
because I am involved in mankind.
And therefore never send to know for whom
the bell tolls; it tolls for thee.

John Donne (1573–1621), *Devotions On Emergent Occasions*

c. Go to a campus bookstore or library and examine an introductory poetry textbook (e.g., a title used for a lower-division poetry class in an English department). Considering the suggested criteria for poetry selection of length, recency, and relevance, which poems that might be suitable for L2 readers? Which pieces might not be appropriate, and why?

Application Activity 7.7
Working with Scripts

a. Imagine you will instruct students to read a full-length play as a course assignment. Identify a target audience familiar to you, then select an appropriate play for the students and context, bearing in mind the considerations listed in Figure 7.10.
b. Next, imagine that a couple of weeks before assigning the play, you will introduce students to reading scripts using a shorter, simpler text (e.g., a TV

comedy script). If possible, select an episode of the TV show and obtain a copy of the script. What activities focusing on this script might prepare students for the bigger challenge of reading the play you have selected? How could you use this warm-up activity to enhance students' enjoyment of reading scripts and lead them to anticipate the reading of the play?

c.   Now assume that students have read the entire play that you initially selected and successfully understand its plot and theme(s). Select a passage that lends itself to interesting analysis of linguistic features, conversational structure, and design questions such as those in Figure 7.11.

Appendix 7.1
The Story of an Hour
Kate Chopin (1894)

Knowing that Mrs. Mallard was afflicted with a heart trouble, great care was taken to break to her as gently as possible the news of her husband's death.

It was her sister Josephine who told her, in broken sentences; veiled hints that revealed in half concealing. Her husband's friend Richards was there, too, near her. It was he who had been in the newspaper office when intelligence of the railroad disaster was received, with Brently Mallard's name leading the list of "killed." He had only taken the time to assure himself of its truth by a second telegram, and had hastened to forestall any less careful, less tender friend in bearing the sad message.

She did not hear the story as many women have heard the same, with a paralyzed inability to accept its significance. She wept at once, with sudden, wild abandonment, in her sister's arms. When the storm of grief had spent itself she went away to her room alone. She would have no one follow her.

There stood, facing the open window, a comfortable, roomy armchair. Into this she sank, pressed down by a physical exhaustion that haunted her body and seemed to reach into her soul.

She could see in the open square before her house the tops of trees that were all aquiver with the new spring life. The delicious breath of rain was in the air. In the street below a peddler was crying his wares. The notes of a distant song which some one was singing reached her faintly, and countless sparrows were twittering in the eaves.

There were patches of blue sky showing here and there through the clouds that had met and piled one above the other in the west facing her window.

She sat with her head thrown back on the cushion of the chair, quite motionless, except when a sob came up into her throat and shook her, as a child who has cried itself to sleep continues to sob in its dreams.

She was young, with a fair, calm face, whose lines bespoke repression and even a certain strength. But now there was a dull stare in her eyes, whose gaze was fixed away off yonder on one of those patches of blue sky. It was not a glance of reflection, but rather indicated a suspension of intelligent thought.

There was something coming to her and she was waiting for it, fearfully. What was it? She did not know; it was too subtle and elusive to name. But she felt it, creeping out of the sky, reaching toward her through the sounds, the scents, the color that filled the air.

Now her bosom rose and fell tumultuously. She was beginning to recognize this thing that was approaching to possess her, and she was striving to beat it back with her will—as powerless as her two white slender hands would have been. When she abandoned herself a little whispered word escaped her slightly parted lips. She said it over and over under her breath: "free, free, free!" The vacant stare and the look of terror that had followed it went from her eyes. They stayed keen and bright. Her pulses beat fast, and the coursing blood warmed and relaxed every inch of her body.

She did not stop to ask if it were or were not a monstrous joy that held her. A clear and exalted perception enabled her to dismiss the suggestion as trivial. She knew that she would weep again when she saw the kind, tender hands folded in death; the face that had never looked save with love on her, fixed and gray and dead. But she saw beyond that bitter moment a long procession of years to come that would belong to her absolutely. And she opened and spread her arms out to them in welcome.

There would be no one to live for during those coming years; she would live for herself. There would be no powerful will bending hers in that blind persistence with which men and women believe they have a right to impose a private will on a fellow-creature. A kind intention or a cruel intention made the act seem no less a crime as she looked on it in that brief moment of illumination.

And yet she had loved him—sometimes. Often she had not. What did it matter! What could love, the unsolved mystery, count for in the face of this possession of self-assertion which she suddenly recognized as the strongest impulse of her being! "Free! Body and soul free!" she kept whispering.

Josephine was kneeling before the closed door with her lips to the keyhole, imploring for admission. "Louise, open the door! I beg; open the door—you will make yourself ill. What are you doing, Louise? For heaven's sake open the door."

"Go away. I am not making myself ill." No; she was drinking in a very elixir of life through that open window.

Her fancy was running riot along those days ahead of her. Spring days, and summer days, and all sorts of days that would be her own. She breathed a quick prayer that life might be long. It was only yesterday she had thought with a shudder that life might be long.

She arose at length and opened the door to her sister's importunities. There was a feverish triumph in her eyes, and she carried herself unwittingly like a goddess of Victory. She clasped her sister's waist, and together they descended the stairs. Richards stood waiting for them at the bottom.

Some one was opening the front door with a latchkey. It was Brently Mallard who entered, a little travel-stained, composedly carrying his grip-sack and umbrella. He had been far from the scene of the accident, and did not even know there had been one. He stood amazed at Josephine's piercing cry; at Richards' quick motion to screen him from the view of his wife.

When the doctors came they said she had died of heart disease—of the joy that kills.

http://www.vcu.edu/engweb/webtexts/hour/ (Retrieved 25 June 2008)

Appendix 7.2
The Road Not Taken

Robert Frost (1916)

Two roads diverged in a yellow wood,
And sorry I could not travel both
And be one traveler, long I stood
And looked down one as far as I could
To where it bent in the undergrowth;

Then took the other, as just as fair,
And having perhaps the better claim,
Because it was grassy and wanted wear;
Though as for that the passing there
Had worn them really about the same,

And both that morning equally lay
In leaves no step had trodden black.
Oh, I kept the first for another day!
Yet knowing how way leads on to way,
I doubted if I should ever come back.

I shall be telling this with a sigh
Somewhere ages and ages hence:
Two roads diverged in a wood, and I—took the one less traveled by,
And that has made all the difference.

Chapter 8
Vocabulary Learning and Teaching in L2 Reading Instruction

Questions for Reflection

- How many words do you think you use in a typical day? How many words do you have in your L1 vocabulary? When, how, and why did you learn these words?
- If you have learned an L2, what proportion of your language skill relies on the extent of your vocabulary knowledge?
- In what ways are L1 and L2 reading comprehension processes dependent on a sizable and growing vocabulary?
- What are the most effective ways to develop a substantial vocabulary in L1? Are these methods applicable to L2? Why or why not?

If you were to ask a non-specialist to identify the primary means of successful L2 learning, chances are good that he or she would mention vocabulary development as playing a key role. Indeed, the notion that "lexical competence is a central part of communicative competence" (DeCarrico, 2001, p. 285) reflects a commonsense understanding of vocabulary knowledge in L2 learning. Paradoxically, "vocabulary has not always been recognized as a priority" (DeCarrico, 2001, p. 285) and "has failed to receive enough attention" in communicative language teaching (Dubin & Olshtain, 1986, p. 111). Vocabulary development has been neglected partly due to a prevalent but misguided view that most lexical knowledge emerges incidentally, with little or no deliberate effort on the part of the learner or teacher (Folse, 2004; Meara, 1980; Sökmen, 1997). Some L2 educators presuppose that vocabulary knowledge develops on its own as long as learners are supplied with abundant, meaningful L2 input (Krashen, 1981, 1982, 1985). Lexical knowledge can certainly develop incidentally, as discussed in Chapter 6 and in subsequent sections of this chapter. Nonetheless, research in L1 and L2 acquisition, psycholinguistics, and reading development has consistently demonstrated that explicit vocabulary learning contributes positively to language learning, cognitive development, and the emergence of successful reading skills. In fact, "vocabulary has been seen as a primary factor in verbal comprehension throughout much of the history of modern psychological and educational measurement" (Hudson, 2007, p. 227). In recent decades, experts such as Coxhead, Nation, Read, Schmitt, and others have worked tirelessly to make lexical learning a cornerstone of L2 teaching.

Like many of the researchers whose work we review in this chapter, we believe that vocabulary knowledge is a lynchpin of language learning and that it should likewise be a core constituent of the L2 literacy curriculum. In Chapter 1, we introduced Grabe's (2004) call to "emphasize vocabulary learning and create a vocabulary-rich environment" (p. 49). We thus recommend systematically cultivating and monitoring lexical knowledge in L2 literacy courses. However, "language teachers are often unsure about how best to incorporate vocabulary learning into their teaching" (Read, 2004b, p. 146). This uncertainty is understandable: After all, "vocabulary is a big topic area" (Schmitt, 2000, p. xiv). We couldn't agree more, yet we would argue that mindfully integrating vocabulary development into L2 reading instruction and assessment is productive, rewarding, and enjoyable for teachers and learners. In Chapter 3, we explored the importance of vocabulary in selecting and analyzing text samples for use in teaching L2 reading skills and strategies. Chapter 6 presented evidence demonstrating that extensive reading substantially enhances L2 readers' vocabulary knowledge. In this chapter, we examine vocabulary learning more closely by considering the components of lexical knowledge, the contributions of vocabulary acquisition to literacy development, and implications of vocabulary research for L2 teaching reading. The field offers excellent research-based sources on teaching L2 vocabulary: For more extensive and in-depth coverage of this interesting and dynamic vein of research and teaching, we encourage readers to consult the materials listed in the Further Reading and Resources section at the end of the chapter.

Components of Word Knowledge

Chapter 3 explored challenges faced by L2 readers as they encounter novel words, collocations, and idiomatic constructions in L2 texts. In this section, we build on that discussion by examining the structural and conceptual properties that comprise word knowledge. Many people equate word learning with connecting a word's form (its spelling and pronunciation) with its meanings, and then storing these connections in memory. These processes are fundamental to developing a functional mental lexicon, yet form–meaning associations are only part of the picture. Coxhead (2006), Hoey (2005), Nation (2001, 2005), and Read (2004a) proposed more complex models of word knowledge that illustrate the complex, interdependent information sources that constitute the lexical knowledge encoded in our memories, which are highly dynamic. Based on Nation's approach, Figure 8.1 presents a catalogue of linguistic, pragmatic, and cognitive dimensions that considerably broaden traditional views of what it means to "know a word."

By considering the complex components of word knowledge, we can begin to understand that "learning a word" involves processing layers of meaning, a set of syntactic rules and constraints (that is, the word's grammar), as well as the socially constructed patterns governing how, where, and when to use the word appropriately (the word's use patterns, which involve pragmatic and sociolinguistic conventions). In line with Nation's (2001) scheme, Figure 8.1 likewise presents dimensions of lexical knowledge (form, meaning, and use) that specify categories such as communication medium, internal word structure, form–meaning relationships, meaning–meaning relationships, and patterns of occurrence in real language use (Larsen-Freeman, 2003). It is worth noting that this model of word knowledge does not require information about *etymology*, which accounts for the origins and history of a word's form and meaning. Vocabulary expertise is often associated with knowing such historical information, which can certainly be valuable, but which constitutes a kind of metalinguistic information that is not, in fact, essential to functional word knowledge. Figure 8.1 also distinguishes *productive* vocabulary knowledge from *receptive* vocabulary knowledge. For Nation (2001), receptive vocabulary use "involves perceiving the form of a word while listening or reading and retrieving its meaning"; productive vocabulary use entails "wanting to express a meaning through speaking or writing and retrieving and producing the appropriate spoken or written word form" (p. 25). This dichotomy is "not completely suitable because there are productive features in the receptive skills." That is, when we read, we "produce meaning" (Nation, 2001, p. 24). The receptive/productive distinction is often oversimplified and misunderstood. This relationship is perhaps better viewed in scalar, or continuous, terms: Word knowledge is not as absolute as these somewhat arbitrary terms imply, but is more accurately a matter of degree, with the two types of vocabulary knowledge overlapping considerably (Melka Teichroew, 1982).[1]

Before we characterize *word knowledge*, we should first decide how to define *word*, which is not as easy a job as we might think. Linguists and lexicographers use several kinds of unit to identify and count words. One such unit, the *token*, is really an occurrence of a given word form in an oral or written text: If a word form occurs more than once, we count each occurrence (Nation, 2001). The sentence *The prospects of arriving at a mutually acceptable solution to the problem*

Dimension		Knowledge Category	Functions
Form	Spoken	Receptive	Phonology: What does the word sound like?
		Productive	Phonology: How is the word pronounced?
	Written	Receptive	Orthography: What does the word look like?
		Productive	Orthography: How is the word written and spelled?
	Word parts	Receptive	Morphology: What word parts (roots, derivational and inflectional affixes) are recognizable?
		Productive	Morphology: What word parts are needed to express meaning?
Meaning	Form and meaning	Receptive	Semantics: What reference, social, and affective meanings does the word represent?
		Productive	Semantics: What word form can be used to express these meanings?
	Concepts and referents	Receptive	Semantics + Pragmatics: What do the concepts associated with the word represent?
		Productive	Semantics + Pragmatics: To what referents can the concepts be linked?
	Associations (paradigmatic)[a]	Receptive	Synonymy, Polysemy, Hyponymy, + Antonymy: What other words does the word evoke?
		Productive	Synonymy, Polysemy, Hyponymy, + Antonymy: What other words could we use instead of this word?
Use	Grammatical functions	Receptive	Syntax + Morphology: To what grammatical category(-ies) does the word belong?
		Productive	Syntax + Morphology: To what grammatical category(-ies) must this word be confined?
	Co-occurrence (syntagmatic)[b]	Receptive	Collocations: With what words or categories does this word co-occur?
		Productive	Collocations: With what words or categories must we use this word?
	Constraints on use	Receptive	Pragmatics, Register, + Frequency: Where, when, and how often are we likely to encounter this word?
		Productive	Pragmatics, Register, + Frequency: Where, when, and how can/should we use this word?

FIGURE 8.1. Components of Word Knowledge.
Sources: Nation (1990, 2001); Schmitt (2000).

→ superoid.

Notes
[a] *Paradigmatic* refers to relations where two words share a similar meaning (e.g., *renovate* and *refurbish*, which are synonyms whose meanings are not identical) or where one is more general than the other (e.g., the hypernym *change* is broader than its hyponym *improve*).
[b] Syntagmatic refers to collocational relations (e.g., *correct answers, severe weather*, and so on).

aren't very good at this time contains 18 words, although *the* and *at* occur twice each. When we quantify lexical units this way, words are referred to as *tokens* or *running words*. When word-processing applications such as Microsoft Word "count words," they actually quantify *tokens*. Rather than counting tokens, we can count *types*, a method that enables us to measure the size of a student's vocabulary or the number of words needed to comprehend a text. The token count for our sample sentence would thus be 16, as we would count occurrences of *the* and *at* just once (Nation, 2001; Read, 2000; Schmitt, 2000).

The *lemma* is a somewhat more common unit of lexical analysis among lexicographers. The word form listed at the beginning of a dictionary entry is usually a *lemma* (Crystal, 2003), which generally consists of a headword, along with its inflected and reduced forms (e.g., *-n't*). Lemmas also typically include items belonging to the same grammatical category, or part of speech (Francis & Kucera, 1982; Nation, 2001; O'Keeffe, McCarthy, & Carter, 2007). For example, the four-member lemma for the noun *favor* would include both the singular and plural forms (*favors*), the possessive determiner *favor's*, in addition to the variant spelling, *favour*. The lemma for the verb *favor* would similarly entail the following inflected forms: third-person singular present tense *favors*; past simple *favored*; present participle *favoring*; past participle *favored*. Alternative spellings would also be included, yielding a total of ten members for the verb *favor* (or *favour*). Lemmas for adjectives include comparative and superlative inflections (e.g., *nice* becomes *nicer* and *nice* becomes *nicest*, respectively). A significant and encouraging implication of adopting the lemma as a lexical unit is that it considerably reduces the number of units in a text or corpus. In an analysis of the *Brown Corpus*, for example, Bauer and Nation (1993) reported that the total number of tagged types (nearly 62,000) dropped to under 38,000 lemmas, a reduction of nearly 40% of the lexical units! Clearly, approaching L2 vocabulary learning from the standpoint of the lemma offers the potential of reducing the *learning burden* by dramatically shrinking the sheer volume of disparate lexical items that learners must commit to memory. Where an individual lexical item or word cluster is concerned, Nation (1990, 2005) characterized *learning burden* as the degree of effort required to learn (i.e., notice, understand, and permanently store) a word. "[T]he more a word represents patterns and knowledge that learners are already familiar with, the lighter its learning burden" (Nation, 2001, pp. 23–24).

Whereas the lemma is an efficient tool for managing the learning burden, it does not cover as much of the morphological or semantic territory as the *word family* does. The lemma covers inflectional morphology, but the *word family* consists of not only the headword and its inflections but also its derived forms (Coxhead, 2006; Crystal, 2003; Nation, 2001). Thus, the *favor/favour* word family would include of all of the inflectional variants mentioned above, as well as derived alternatives belonging to other grammatical categories, such as *favorable/favourable* and *favorite/favourite* (adjectives), *favorably/favourably* (adverb), and *disfavor/disfavour* (verb + negation). We could easily extend this family by identifying further inflectional and derivational variants, such as *unfavorable*, *unfavorably*, and so forth—a process that can even more dramatically reduce the size of the lexicon and make the learning burden more manageable. A drawback of using word families to quantify words is that we must decide what a word family should include and exclude (O'Keeffe et al., 2007). Moreover, "what might be a sensible word family for one learner may be beyond another learner's present level of proficiency" (Nation, 2001, p. 8).

Characterizing word knowledge in terms of tokens, types, lemmas, and families nonetheless helps us appreciate the depth and breadth of the lexicon, which contains much more than just "words." The lexicon encodes crucial information about grammar, use, and usage. To illustrate the richness and multidimensionality of word knowledge, we will examine the verb *inhibit* from the multiple angles represented in Figure 8.1. We selected *inhibit* owing to its mid-range frequency as determined by Coxhead's (1998, 2000) *Academic Word List* (AWL) (see Chapter 3). *Inhibit* appears in AWL Sublist 6, whose items are slightly less frequent than the mean (Sublist 1 contains the most frequent words; Sublist 10 identifies the least frequent items).

To know the word *inhibit* in the technical senses listed in Figure 8.1 entails a network of knowledge and skills, which Nation (2001, 2005) conveniently enumerated from the perspectives of receptive and productive modalities.[2] Receptive knowledge of *inhibit* would entail:

- Recognizing the word when it is uttered in speech (capturing its phonemic structure and phonetic form);
- Recognizing the word's orthography (written form) when encountering it in print;
- Understanding that *inhibit* comprises two morphemes, *in-* (derivational prefix expressing negation) and -*hibit* (stem, meaning "to hold");
- Retrieving specific meanings associated with *inhibit* (e.g., *to prevent, forbid, prohibit, interdict*);
- Identifying particular meanings in the discursive context where it occurs (these meanings would include reference, social, and affective meanings);
- Retrieving the semantic concepts associated with *inhibit* that will promote understanding of the word when it occurs in other contexts (e.g., understanding that *inhibit* can signal actions such as hindering or restraining another's actions);
- Recognizing that other words can express similar meanings (i.e., that *inhibit* is associated with synonyms such as *restrain, prevent, hinder, slow down, hold back, reduce, forbid*; that *inhibit* may express a weaker action than *forbid*; that words such as *allow* are antonyms);

- Perceiving that *inhibit* is used grammatically and appropriately in its context;
- Knowing that *inhibit* and its variant forms co-occur (*collocate*) with nouns (as in "Poor weather conditions *inhibited* <u>the flow of incoming air traffic</u>") and with the preposition *from* (as in "The subcommittee was *inhibited* <u>from recommending sanctions</u>");
- Recognizing that *inhibit* is not a rare word and that it can convey neutral or negative social and affective meanings; understanding that *inhibit* may be considered more or less formal than its synonyms. (Based on Nation, 2001, pp. 27–28)

Productive knowledge and use, meanwhile, require the following:

- Ability to pronounce the word *inhibit* with appropriate stress and intonation (i.e., application of appropriate phonological rules);
- Capacity to spell the word accurately;
- Ability to construct the word and its morphological constituents by applying the appropriate inflectional and derivational patterns (e.g., affixing the third-person singular agreement marker -*s* to form *inhibits*, nominalizing the verb form by adding the derivational affix -*ion* to form the noun *inhibition*, and so forth);
- Sufficient semantic expertise to produce *inhibit* to express the meanings associated with the word (e.g., *to prevent, forbid, prohibit*, or *interdict*);
- Ability to produce *inhibit* in diverse discourse contexts to convey variable meanings;
- Sufficient knowledge to generate synonyms (e.g., *restrain, hinder*) and antonyms (e.g., *allow, permit*);
- Capacity to use *inhibit* idiomatically in an original sentence string;
- Ability to produce common collocations in speech and writing (e.g., *inhibit* + noun, as in "The noise *inhibited* my ability to concentrate during the interview");
- Sufficient understanding to determine whether to use *inhibit* to match the formality of the speech event or context for writing (e.g., *inhibit* would be a suitably high-register word to use in an academic paper, but it might not be a good word choice during a conversation with a young child). (Based on Nation, 2001, p. 28)

Even if we assume that receptive and productive word knowledge emanate from the same source and originate in the same (or adjacent) modules of the human memory, we can see that "knowledge of vocabulary is multidimensional, encompassing various types of knowledge" (Hudson, 2007, p. 233). Indeed, underlying complete word knowledge is not an inventory of form–meaning associations resembling the unique entries in a dictionary, but rather an intricately interconnected lexicogrammatical system whose contents may shift as learners encounter new vocabulary and whose interconnections develop with practice and use (Coxhead, 2006; Jiang, 2002; Morin, 2003; Vermeer, 2001). The relationships among words in our heads "are connected on different dimensions. Words may be related thematically (*book-journal-manuscript*), phonologically (*rock-sock-wok*), morphologically (*indemnification-notification-intensification*), conceptually (*pan-pot-steamer*), and sociolinguistically (*dude-man-chap*)" (Hudson, 2007, p. 233).

Word meanings and the semantic networks they form not only interact with one another across multiple dimensions, but may also expand and contract over time. For example, word forms can acquire novel meanings and uses, sometimes undergoing functional shifts, such that their grammatical roles spread from one category to another. Consider *Google*, a word that some consider to be a *neologism* (novel word form).[3] *Google* entered the modern English lexicon as a noun, specifically a proper name referring to the popular search engine and, somewhat less frequently, to the high-tech company that developed and popularized it (in this sense, *Google* is an *eponym*, as the word is the label for the entity after which it is named). *Google* continues to express these reference meanings, but it also functions as a verb, as in *John Googled Dana to see what marvelous new books she had written*. This spreading across grammatical categories, from noun to verb (an example of functional shift), likewise involves a subtle change in the semantic representations (meanings) of *Google*. Such shifts illustrate how elements of word knowledge influence one another, highlighting the principle that word knowledge can be fluid, subject to the creative ways in which discourse communities assign meaning to existing words, and construct completely new words, idioms, and collocations (Crystal, 2003; Nattinger & DeCarrico, 1992; Schmitt, 2004; Vermeer, 2001).

Given the complexity and dynamism of word knowledge as characterized by lexicographers, linguists, and psycholinguists, it should be clear why we consider a focus on vocabulary in L2 reading instruction to be not just valuable but essential. Substantial vocabulary knowledge is essential for both L1 and L2 reading development, as we will demonstrate. This information may come as bad news or as good news for L2 reading instructors. One of the authors once heard an MA student express alarm after acquainting herself with research on the interplay between vocabulary knowledge and reading: "Do you mean that, on top of teaching *reading*, I have to teach my students *vocabulary*, too?" Unlike this anxious pre-service teacher, we view research-based insights into vocabulary knowledge and learning to be very good news, indeed. First, instruction designed to enhance receptive and productive vocabulary pays many dividends, as "learning a word" effectively and completely means learning lemmas (if not word families), as well as the lexicogrammatical, pragmatic, and sociolinguistic dimensions of lexical knowledge listed in Figure 8.1. Second, like many literacy educators, we have discovered that teaching L2 vocabulary—or, perhaps more appropriately, integrating vocabulary instruction into teaching and assessment—does not compete with teaching reading, but rather enhances it. Finally, we consider vocabulary instruction to be enjoyable, motivating, and useful.

The Role of Lexical Knowledge in Developing L2 Reading Skills and Strategies

The commonsense notion that reading comprehension and lexical knowledge are interdependent enjoys solid support in reading research.[4] Here and in other sections of this book touching on vocabulary learning, we presuppose a reciprocal, mutually supportive interaction between lexical knowledge and learning to read. In Chapter 6, we considered how extensive reading can promote L2 vocabulary knowledge (that is, more reading → a bigger and better vocabulary). At the same time, "successful comprehension is heavily dependent on knowledge of individual word meanings" (Koda, 2004, p. 48). In other words, vocabulary knowledge undergirds reading skills and promotes literacy development (that is, enhanced vocabulary knowledge → higher reading efficiency). As Nation (2005) observed, "reading can be an opportunity for learning through meaning-focused use, deliberate vocabulary learning, and fluency development" (p. 587).

Interactions between Vocabulary Knowledge and Reading

Summarizing results of a compelling case study, Grabe and Stoller (1997) concluded that "learning to read in a second language generally involves learning words" (p. 119). Empirical evidence favors this hypothesis, provided that we grasp the complexity and multidimensionality of word knowledge as described earlier. In studies of language development and assessment, measurable vocabulary knowledge consistently emerges as a strong correlate of L1 and L2 reading performance, with tests of lexical knowledge consistently and reliably predicting performance on reading comprehension tasks (Anderson & Freebody, 1983; Davis, 1972; Hu & Nation, 2000; Hulstijn, 1997; Koda, 1988; Laufer, 1992, 1996, 1997; Nation, 2002; Nation & Coady, 1988; Qian, 1999; Stahl, 1990; Stanovich, 1986, 2000; Sternberg, 1987; Thorndike, 1973). In fact, research has revealed extraordinarily strong statistical relationships between reading comprehension and lexical knowledge.[5] Carver (2003) claimed that careful studies can generate correlation coefficients of 1.0 (a 100% correlation, signifying a one-to-one relationship). In addition to the strength of the vocabulary–reading connections, the nature and directionality of these relationships is important to understand. Specifically, evidence strongly suggests that "reading and vocabulary are reciprocally causal," with findings routinely supporting the premise that "reading improves vocabulary knowledge and vocabulary knowledge supports reading development" (Grabe & Stoller, 1997, p. 119).

Among the many quasi-experimental and non-interventionist studies of vocabulary–reading interactions in L2 settings is that of Droop and Verhoeven (2003), who measured the lexical knowledge and reading skills of minority-language Grade 3 and 4 pupils in the Netherlands. Parallel to comparable L1 research, Droop and Verhoeven reported powerful statistical relationships between vocabulary knowledge and reading scores. This investigation followed an earlier investigation in the Dutch context: Schoonen, Hulstijn, and Bossers (1998) discovered an extremely high degree of shared variance between the EFL vocabulary and reading scores of junior high school students ($r^2 = .71$). Language testing research has provided similarly robust evidence for vocabulary-reading links. In an early study, Pike (1979) compared the vocabulary and reading sub-scores of ESL and EFL students on the Test of English as a Foreign Language (TOEFL). His analysis revealed correlation coefficients ranging from .84 to .95. Laufer's (1997) review essay examined similar studies yielding more modest but significant correlations between measured L2 reading ability and vocabulary knowledge ($r = .50$ to .75). In a more recent investigation similar to that of Pike (1979), Qian (2002) examined relationships between scores on three vocabulary tests and TOEFL reading subsections. Qian reported impressive correlation co-efficients ranging from .68 to .82, lending further support to the view that reading comprehension and vocabulary knowledge are highly interdependent.

Informed by L1 and L2 findings such as these, which do not actually specify the directionality of the reading–vocabulary relationship, we could posit two general instructional implications. First, as indicated in our review of the benefits of extensive reading (see Chapter 6), reading practice should promote L2 vocabulary development. Second, correlational research suggests that an emphasis on vocabulary development should promote the teaching and learning of L2 reading. After all, "no text comprehension is possible . . . without understanding the text's vocabulary." Nonetheless, "this is not to say that reading comprehension and vocabulary comprehension are the same, or that reading quality is determined by vocabulary alone" (Laufer, 1997, p. 20). We must also ask whether vocabulary instruction will meaningfully "improve reading comprehension abilities in any direct and immediate way" (Grabe, 2004, p. 49). Although questions about the effects of vocabulary instruction on reading development have been raised among L1 literacy researchers (Beck, Perfetti, & McKeown, 1982; McKeown, Beck, Omanson, & Pople, 1985), the relationships have been "difficult to demonstrate," and scant L2 research is currently available (Grabe, 2004, p. 49).

Incidental Vocabulary Learning

Despite the need for more research on vocabulary-reading connections, studies of incidental lexical learning in L1 and L2 point in a fairly consistent direction. Experts generally agree that "much [L2] vocabulary learning occurs incidentally through extensive reading, rather than through explicit vocabulary instruction" (Hudson, 2007, p. 245). Chapter 6 presented evidence favoring incidental vocabulary learning as a consequence of extensive reading, in agreement with arguments advanced by Bamford and Day (2003), Day and Bamford (1998), and Krashen (2004), among others. In an impressive meta-analysis of 20 L1 studies of incidental lexical learning, Swanborn and de Glopper (1999) discovered that participants learned around 15% of the unfamiliar words that they had encountered in novel texts as they engaged in normal reading, or *rauding*.[6] Strong proponents of incidental learning may find this 15% figure to be somewhat discouraging, but Swanborn and de Glopper noted differential effects for factors that may be indirectly related to how reading promotes vocabulary growth. Studies showed differential positive effects for incidental learning depending on variables such as participants' readiness as test takers, grade level, reading proficiency, and their purposes for reading; assessment methods, text density, and frequency of exposure also played important roles.

L1 research on incidental vocabulary learning has produced variable results, but few studies have generated findings suggesting anything but positive effects for incidental learning during reading, however small. For example, Shu, Anderson, and Zhang (1995) measured incidental vocabulary acquisition among L1 readers of English and Chinese in primary grades. Shu et al. discovered that pupils at all levels of reading ability successfully learned new words from context.[7] The Chinese pupils differed from their English-speaking peers in terms of how they used context to infer word meanings, but the authors concluded that incidental vocabulary learning from context during reading may be universal across languages and orthographies, a hypothesis suggesting that incidental learning may be quite natural (Nagy, 1997; Smith, 2004, 2006; Smith & Elley, 1997).

The Shu et al. (1995) study and others like it lend weight to the influential _Levels of Processing_ framework, initially proposed by Craik and Lockhart (1972). The Levels of Processing view holds that information encoded visually, semantically, phonemically, and associatively can become "traced" in memory if it is analyzed in depth, "with deeper levels of analysis associated with more elaborate, longer lasting, and strong traces" (Craik & Lockhart, 1972, p. 675). Applied to word learning during reading, the Levels of Processing perspective (sometimes called _depth of processing_) relies on two assumptions: (1) When successful comprehension requires readers to generate inferences about word meaning, they put forth more cognitive effort than if the matching meaning is supplied for them (e.g., by the text or the teacher); (2) The mental effort involved in processing information through inferencing leads to better, longer-lasting storage of the novel item in memory (Craik & Tulving, 1975). Of course, neither inferencing nor incidental learning automatically occurs when a reader encounters a novel word or lexical chunk (Laufer, 1997; Qian, 2004; Takak, 2008).

A number of L2 studies have shown why the value of incidental learning may be constrained by variables particular to readers and how they interact with text (Huckin & Coady, 1999; Koda, 2004; Read, 2004b). For instance, a study conducted by Zahar, Cobb, and Spada (2001) involving Grade 7 ESL learners in Canada investigated the influence of proficiency level and exposure on incidental vocabulary learning. Noting moderate gains for all participants following normal reading, Zahar et al. determined that word frequency in the experimental text predicted retention levels, but that frequency effects were three to four times greater for the least proficient readers. Nassaji (2003) investigated L2 readers' lexical inferencing strategies during normal reading, reporting that intermediate-level participants produced accurate inferences from context only about 56% of the time. He suggested a need for learners to develop metacognitive inferencing strategies such as repeating the passages surrounding unfamiliar words, comparing guesses to information in surrounding text, and deliberate monitoring of lexical knowledge gaps. Hulstijn's (1992) study showed that L2 readers retain more novel words if they infer meanings from context than if word meanings are given to them before reading. At the same time, his results revealed that L2 readers can make incorrect inferences when they are not given meaning cues, such as L1 glosses, simple sentences reflecting inferable meanings, and multiple-choice options (cf. Laufer, 1997). Rott (1999) examined the relationship between amount of exposure and vocabulary gain among English-speaking learners of German as a foreign language. Not unpredictably, she found that retention of novel words increased with the number of exposures during normal reading. Retention was higher among students who underwent six exposures to target texts than among students who underwent only two or four exposures.

In spite of ongoing interest in incidental vocabulary acquisition, the phenomenon "is still ill understood" (Hudson, 2007, p. 245). Nonetheless, researchers have posited distinct benefits associated with learning vocabulary incidentally: (1) Novel words are embedded in their natural contexts, which help readers draw inferences about rich, subtle meanings; (2) Incidental vocabulary learning occurs simultaneously with reading, making the process efficient; (3) Because readers consciously or unconsciously attend to unfamiliar words, incidental learning is highly individualized (Huckin & Coady, 1999). These advantages, of course, do not necessarily imply that learning lexical items incidentally is either fast or efficient (Koda, 2004; Laufer, 1997; Sternberg, 1987). Learning vocabulary from context alone may take more time than many learners have, as shown by "book flood" studies, which involved treatment periods of 12 to 36 months (Elley, 1991; Elley & Mangubhai, 1981). Evidence suggests that "incidental implicit learning from reading alone may not be an optimal approach in early [L2] reading" (Hudson, 2007, p. 249). Incidental learning for novice L2 readers may be "a bit of a catch-22 in that [they] do not read well enough to make breadth and depth in reading an option. To acquire words requires decoding skills, the ability to recognize an unknown word, and the ability to use context" (Hudson, 2007, p. 249). Low-level and struggling readers cannot easily perform these operations. Consequently, some experts (e.g., Takak, 2008) advise instructional interventions to assist novice L2 readers in developing their lexical knowledge at a reasonable pace and to equip them with strategies for simultaneously cultivating efficient reading skills.

Direct Vocabulary Instruction: Explicit Interventions in Teaching Reading

In Chapters 6 and 7, we advocated extensive reading as a means of promoting incidental learning. Persuaded by research favoring implicit skill and knowledge acquisition, we believe that incidental learning can contribute significantly to building L2 readers' receptive and productive vocabularies. At the same time, creating conditions favoring incidental lexical acquisition in no way precludes explicit, or intentional, instruction as an efficient and lasting method of accelerating vocabulary development (Fukkink, Hulstijn, & Simis, 2005; Hulstijn, 2001; Read, 2004b). Nagy (1997) and colleagues asserted that direct vocabulary instruction and practice are a waste of time, largely because of the complexity of word knowledge and the sheer size of the vocabulary learning effort. We disagree. First, as Nation (2001) pointed out, L2 learners "need to learn the high-frequency words" of their target language, which comprise "a relatively small group of words [that] deserve time and attention." Second, "direct teaching can add to incidental learning of the same words and can raise learners' awareness of particular words so that they notice them" while reading (p. 157). This awareness-raising may not require extensive teaching time, certainly not where individual words are concerned (Coxhead, 2006).

A well-known approach to direct, intentional vocabulary instruction is the *pre-teaching* of unfamiliar lexical items, which involves acquainting readers with the meanings of potentially difficult words before reading begins. Pre-teaching remains a somewhat controversial practice, which some L1 researchers have found to produce little improvement in comprehension (e.g., Stahl, Jacobson, Davis, & Davis, 1989; Tuinman & Brady, 1974). Other investigators (e.g., McKeown et al., 1985) have nonetheless reported positive results for selected pre-teaching activities. In his appraisal of research on pre-teaching effects, Nation (2001) suggested that pre-teaching should feature high-frequency words that will be useful for students' future encounters with other texts, a topic discussed later in this chapter. He further recommended using mixed methods that "provide both contextual and definitional information" (p. 158). Combining contextual and definitional support is thought to produce greater comprehension and vocabulary learning than definitional methods alone (Stahl & Fairbanks, 1986). At the same time, Nation (1990, 2001) cautioned against including low-frequency lexical items in pre-teaching procedures, which can easily misdirect learners in their reading (Stahl, 1990).

The most successful style of lexical pre-teaching appears to be that which involves *rich instruction* (Beck, McKeown, & Omanson, 1987), sometimes called *rich scripting* (McWilliam, 1998). Rich instruction targets high-frequency words that are crucial to text comprehension; it is usually provided after readers have encountered the word a few times, when they are ready to incorporate the item into their active vocabularies. Rich instruction gives "elaborate attention to a word, going beyond the immediate demands of a particular context of occurrence" and can be teacher-fronted or student-led (Nation, 2001, p. 95). Rich instruction procedures can include:

- Efforts to understand the word's meanings;
- Explicitly examining aspects of what it means to know the word (see Figure 8.1);
- Engaging learners actively in methodically processing the word by analyzing its forms and meanings. (Mezynski, 1983; Nation, 2001; Stahl, 1990).

An advantage of pre-teaching and related methods of direct instruction is that explicit attention to lexical items can complement and enhance intensive reading (see Chapter 5). Intensive reading processes such as those that engage readers in systematic inferencing are thought to be valuable because they activate cognitive operations that promote depth of learning. Direct instructional interventions focusing on L2 vocabulary can likewise promote top-down, bottom-up, and integrative skills (see Chapter 1) while increasing the likelihood of deep processing (Craik & Lockhart, 1972). As Hudson (2007) emphasized, "deep processing in which semantic associations are accessed and elaborated leads to longer retention than does shallow processing" (p. 237). Some research (e.g., McKeown et al., 1985) has suggested that considerable class time must be spent on individual lexemes to ensure deep processing. In contrast, McDaniel and Pressley (1989) observed that learners' reading comprehension improved significantly following 30-second interventions, suggesting that deep processing does not always require extended time periods to produce a lasting memory trace.

Lexical Enhancement and L2 Reading: Challenges and Tools

When we consider how emergent vocabulary knowledge contributes to reading skills development—and vice versa—a number of interesting teaching and learning challenges present themselves. Echoing Meara (1980), Folse (2004) observed that L2 learners quickly discover that "their lack of vocabulary knowledge . . . results in serious comprehension problems. Therefore, it should come as no surprise that most L2 learners identify vocabulary deficiencies as their biggest problem in mastering a second language" (p. 110). Knowing that "a large vocabulary can facilitate reading comprehension" (Hudson, 2007, p. 227) is essential for L2 readers and teachers, although it can be difficult to determine what a "large" vocabulary consists of.

As a fundamental component of the learning burden, the size of the target language vocabulary obviously must be taken into account when selecting instructional options. Adding to the learning burden is the complexity of receptive and productive word knowledge itself, as discussed earlier in this chapter (also see Figure 8.1). Nation (2005) further pointed out that a substantial portion of the learning burden "depends on whether these aspects of an L2 word are similar for its L1 translation or are regular and predictable from already known L2 words of similar or related meaning" (p. 584). That is, vocabulary learning may be complicated by the potential influence of L1 knowledge, including L1 orthography (Arabski, 2006). A further aspect of the learning burden involves the time required to build a serviceable base of high-frequency lexemes and a sufficiently large inventory of less-frequent items.

How can L2 reading instruction ease the vocabulary learning burden and integrate vocabulary acquisition into literacy development? Part of the answer to this important practical question involves understanding and addressing the learning burden, a major dimension of which is the size of the lexicon itself. Similarly, teachers and novice readers can benefit from recognizing the essential roles played by word knowledge in reading comprehension, issues briefly addressed below. Building vocabulary knowledge, of course, first requires us to measure learners' existing vocabulary knowledge. Fortunately, valid and reliable diagnostic tools for estimating vocabulary size in many languages are available. For example, thanks to the tireless work of Nation and colleagues, multiple versions of the *Vocabulary Levels Test* for English (Cobb, 2000; Nation, 1983, 1990; Laufer & Nation, 1999) are accessible both online (see Recommended Reading and Resources) and in print (see Nation 2001, Appendices 2–5; Schmitt, 2000, Appendix F). As for pedagogical solutions to the challenge of cultivating vocabulary while teaching reading, we can draw on tools such as word lists to help us determine which lexical items are essential and how to prioritize them. We can likewise consider systematic methods and strategies for working direct vocabulary instruction into L2 literacy courses. In the final section of this chapter, we propose instructional options that reflect the major research findings summarized above.

Vocabulary Size and Reading Development

The *Oxford English Dictionary* contains entries for over 625,000 word forms; *Webster's Third New International Dictionary* claims to contain over 476,000 entries. Adding scientific and technical terms in English adds millions more (Hudson, 2007). If we consider the fact that "native speakers know tens of thousands of word families" (Nation, 2001, p. 95), we can see why L2 readers might view lexical acquisition as an insurmountable task in itself, quite independent of the work of learning to read. Clearly, no one needs to know all the words, lemmas, or word families in a given language. Sternberg (1987) proposed that a mental lexicon containing some tens of thousands of words may be about average for L1 readers, although exceptional adults may accumulate a working vocabulary of 100,000 words or more.

How many words does a reader need? Which words, lemmas, or families do we start with? Fortunately, lexicographers and corpus linguists have compiled tremendously useful *word frequency* lists (e.g., the AWL) containing rank-ordered entries based on frequency of occurrence in corpora of speech and written data. We will consider word banks and their applications in L2 reading instruction below, but first we would like to report a finding that many people—including L2 educators—sometimes find startling, particularly when we consider the conventional wisdom that "good readers" somehow discern the meanings of unfamiliar words "from context" alone. Laufer (1989) postulated that, in order to read and successfully comprehend a text, a reader must know 95% of its words. For a language such as English, she estimated that readers would require a vocabulary of about 5,000 of the most frequent words to comprehend and interpret a majority of the material in a given text sample. In a subsequent investigation of L2 vocabulary and general academic skill, Laufer (1992) argued that readers with a functional vocabulary of under 3,000 frequent word families achieved little or no comprehension (below 70%), irrespective of their general academic competence. Readers with a vocabulary ranging in size from 5,000 to about 6,500 word families successfully achieved a minimally functional level of comprehension (70%), which might or might not be favorably influenced by academic ability. Only readers with a vocabulary containing around 8,000 word families successfully comprehended texts independent of their measured academic abilities, capturing more than 70% of text material. Carver (1994) raised even higher stakes for successful comprehension. In Carver's L1 study, participants who successfully comprehended sample texts and found them easy to read knew 100% of the basic words in the text; participants who found the texts to be relatively difficult still knew 98% of the basic vocabulary items (approximately one unknown word for every 50 to 100 running words). Hu and Nation (2000) compared the effects of *coverage* on L2 readers' comprehension of a fiction text. Coverage (word token) measures refers to the proportion of known words relative to the number of words in a text sample. Hu and Nation (2000) corroborated the 98% threshold posited by Carver.

This small sampling of vocabulary studies demonstrates that we find variable estimates of how many words, lemmas, or word families that readers need to know, in the same way that estimates of the number of words in a given language can vary (O'Keeffe et al., 2007). One such estimate holds that around 200,000 words are in common use in Modern English (Bryson, 1990)—probably a modest approximation. In terms of the size of individual learners' vocabularies, most L1 readers build a lexicon of 40,000 to 50,000 words (20,000 word families) by the end of secondary school (Just & Carpenter, 1987; Nation, 2001, 2005). Interestingly, in commonplace genres such as fiction, news accounts, and academic materials, the 2,000 most frequent words in English may represent 80% of the total words in a given text (Nation, 2001, 2005, 2006). Like Laufer (1992), Hirsh and Nation (1992) calculated that L2 readers require a lexicon of about 5,000 word families to read untreated (unsimplified) novels for pleasure. If that figure seems overwhelming, consider the conclusions of Hazenberg and Hulstijn (1996), who determined that L2 readers in Dutch university studies needed a minimum receptive vocabulary of around 10,000 base words! Fortunately for teachers and learners, vocabulary researchers and theorists (Fukkink et al., 2005; Hirsh & Nation, 1992; Laufer, 1992; Nation, 2001; Nation & Waring, 1997; O'Keeffe et al., 2007) appear to converge on more modest minimum vocabulary size estimates of 3,000 to 5,000 word families for English, although "there is no magic vocabulary size threshold" (Schmitt, 2000, p. 143).

We must remember that these are minimum targets for lexical learning that neither ensure adequate reading comprehension nor guarantee sufficient productive knowledge. Based on our exploration of reading processes, genres, and text features (see Chapters 1–7), it should be clear that the minimum vocabulary size needed to comprehend a given text depends on text features (e.g., genre, topic, length, lexical range, discourse structure, linguistic complexity, propositional density, and so on), the reading task and context for reading, and the reader herself. A 3,000-word lexicon might adequately equip a novice reader to understand a news article or blog entry on a familiar topic. In contrast, a vocabulary of the same size might fall far short if the same reader were to encounter a specialized text on an unfamiliar topic, such as a troubleshooting guide for a new software package, an automotive repair manual, or a specialized academic text. It is also essential to recall that the comprehension threshold for individual texts may be higher than is often believed, especially in courses where top-down skills and strategies are emphasized over bottom-up operations. We noted above that Carver (1994) proposed 98% coverage of running words as a criterion for comprehension. Hu and Nation (2000) arrived at nearly identical results, suggesting the scale of coverages for fictional texts in Table 8.1.

According to Hu and Nation (2000), none of the participants who read texts in the 80% category achieved satisfactory comprehension. Nation (2001) subsequently determined that "the all-or-nothing threshold is around 80% vocabulary coverage for fiction text" (p. 147). In contrast, with the probabilistic threshold of 98%, "almost all learners have a chance of gaining adequate comprehension" (Nation, 2001, p. 147). Taking Laufer's (1992) data into account,

TABLE 8.1 Coverages for Fictional Texts.

Comprehension Level	% Vocabulary Coverage
Unassisted, easy reading (e.g., for pleasure)	98%
Adequate comprehension	95%
Marginal to poor comprehension	90%
Little to no comprehension	80%

Source: Hu and Nation (2000).

Nation suggested that a probabilistic threshold of 95% would represent a "standard of minimally acceptable comprehension" (2001, p. 147).

Word Frequency Lists

As Read (2004b) noted, "the first priority in direct vocabulary teaching is to focus on which words are to be studied" (p. 148). Among the most useful tools for identifying target words, lemmas, and word families are word frequency lists, which reveal several crucial facts about vocabulary in use:

- Some words occur more frequently than others, with function words occurring much more frequently than content words (see Tables 8.2 and 8.3).
- Item frequency initially drops precipitously, then tapers off gradually: "There is a continental shelf of high-frequency, core items, after which the curve takes a nose-dive into the vast depths of tens of thousands of . . . low-frequency words" (O'Keeffe et al., 2007, p. 33).

- Establishing the dividing between high- and low-frequency items is an arbitrary decision (Nation, 2005).
- Word frequency lists and their rankings vary in relation to their lexical benchmarks (i.e., whether analyzers use word form, lemma, or family to calculate frequency) and data sources (whether data are spoken, written, or both).

West's (1953) *General Service List* (GSL), for example, has been used widely since its publication and, though sometimes faulted for its age, is considered a "classic" that "is yet to be superseded" (Read, 2004b, p. 148). Analyses of modern corpora such as the *British National Corpus* (Leech, Rayson, & Wilson, 2001) largely confirm GSL frequencies and rankings (O'Keeffe et al., 2007; Read, 2004b). West's list was a milestone because, in addition to presenting word frequencies, it accounted for the word meanings thought to be most useful for students. Another important feature is that GSL items are listed by word families, which include word stems (*headwords*) in combination with their inflected and derived forms. The GSL also reports the relative frequency of different word meanings. Below is a selective inventory of word frequency lists for Modern English.[8]

- *The Teacher's Word Book of 30,000 Words* (Thorndike & Lorge, 1944) reports word frequencies by occurrence per million; it samples juvenile literature, newspapers, correspondence, the Bible, and factual texts such as farm almanacs and postal regulations.

- The *Computational Analysis of Present-Day American English* (Kucera & Francis, 1967) is a million-word corpus based on U.S. English texts in print in 1961. Text sources include genres ranging from news reporting, editorials, materials on hobbies and crafts, adventure novels, western fiction, and humor to specialized academic texts.

- The *American Heritage Intermediate Corpus* (Carroll, Davies, & Richman, 1971) lists nearly 87,000 word types from about 5.1 million running words from more than 1,000 sources. Geared toward Grade 3–9 learners, this list samples textbooks, workbooks, periodicals, reference materials, and juvenile fiction, with entries classified by grade level and topic.

- A *University Word List* (Xue & Nation, 1984), as its name indicates, targets words and families frequent in university-level texts, drawing from earlier, general, and academic sources (Campion & Elley, 1971; Praninskas, 1972; Thorndike & Lorge, 1944; West, 1953). Aimed at ESL and EFL learners, the final list comprises 737 base words, divided into 10 sublists, all featured in Nation's (1990) *Vocabulary Levels Test.*

- The *Academic Word List* (AWL) (Coxhead, 1998, 2000, 2006) similarly features words from academic genres and disciplines, though it excludes the top 2,000 words in the GSL (West, 1953), as university-level students have presumably mastered these items. When the GSL and AWL are combined, the first 2,000 words of the amalgamated bank account for 86% of the tokens in Coxhead's 3.5-million-word (and growing) corpus (see *AWL* Weblink in Further Reading and Resources).

To illustrate the invaluable information provided by word frequency lists, Table 8.2 lists the 40 most frequent words from the 10-million-word *Cambridge International Corpus* (CIC), which includes both oral and written data sources. Table 8.3, meanwhile, presents 20 items (beginning with the letter "d") from the headwords in the *AWL* (Coxhead, 2000). Corpus-based research and studies involving word frequency lists suggest the following implications for lexical learning and teaching:

- The English lexicon contains 1,500 to 2,000 high-frequency words representing significant vocabulary learning objective. These words are so widely used and so useful "that they deserve all kinds of attention from teachers and learners" (Nation, 2005, p. 582).
- Low-frequency words number in the thousands and must be learned gradually; they may not "deserve teaching time." The most effective way to approach them "is for learners to work on strategies for learning and coping with them" (Nation, 2005, p. 582).

Direct lexical instruction may strike some educators as unfashionable, but the suggestion that early L2 instruction should quickly and efficiently target the most frequent tier of lexical items (i.e., the 2,000 most frequent words in Modern English) enjoys support among leading experts (Coxhead, 2000, 2006; Meara, 1995, 2005; Read, 2004b; Schmitt, 2000). Determining which items to target after reaching the 2,000-word threshold is trickier. To address this challenge, Nation (2001) proposed several frequency-based categories. In addition to high-frequency words (e.g., the first 2,000 in the *GSL*), *specialized vocabularies* such as academic, technical, and other low-frequency words are bounded by the topics and uses of concern to the reader, teacher, or materials developer. We can thus refer to specialized vocabularies "for speaking, for reading academic texts, for reading newspapers, for reading children's stories, or for letter writing" (Nation, 2001, p. 17). Technical vocabularies (e.g., for software development or automotive repair) are specialized, as is academic vocabulary, for which experts recommend Coxhead's (2000, 2006) *AWL*, which covers a breadth of academic disciplines. We should note that academic vocabulary is sometimes considered *sub-technical*, as it contains high-register items, in contrast to technical terms (Nation, 2001; O'Keeffe et al., 2007).

Direct Vocabulary Teaching and L2 Reading Instruction: Practices and Strategies

Equipped with an appreciation for the richness of word knowledge and research-based tools for sorting through a language's lexicon, teachers can deploy numerous strategies for direct vocabulary teaching that complements L2 reading instruction. In this final section, we consider a small array of direct vocabulary teaching practices that reflect top-down, bottom-up, and integrated reading principles (see Chapter 1). Our purposes for introducing explicit approaches to teaching vocabulary align with these guiding precepts:

TABLE 8.2. 40 Most Frequent Words: *Cambridge International Corpus* (10 million words; oral and written data).

Rank	Word	Frequency	Rank	Word	Frequency	Rank	Word	Frequency	Rank	Word	Frequency
1	the	439,723	11	was	107,245	21	with	54,994	31	not	44,977
2	and	256,879	12	yeah	86,092	22	be	52,008	32	no	44,541
3	to	230,431	13	he	78,932	23	it's	50,585	33	what	44,125
4	a	210,178	14	is	75,687	24	so	50,531	34	this	43,024
5	of	194,659	15	on	71,797	25	know	50,307	35	like	42,297
6	I	192,961	16	for	69,392	26	as	49,697	36	all	41,790
7	you	164,021	17	but	64,561	27	at	49,578	37	mm	41,639
8	it	150,707	18	she	61,406	28	we	46,025	38	er	40,923
9	in	142,812	19	they	58,021	29	her	45,574	39	there	39,883
10	that	124,250	20	have	55,892	30	had	45,524	40	do	39,744

Source: O'Keeffe et al. (2007, p. 34).

TABLE 8.3. Sample Set of Headwords of the Word Families in the *Academic Word List*.

Headword[a]	Sublist[b]	Headword[a]	Sublist[b]
data	1	depress	10
debate	4	derive	1
decade	7	design	2
decline	5	despite	4
deduce	3	detect	8
define	1	deviate	8
definite	7	device	9
demonstrate	3	devote	9
denote	8	differentiate	7
deny	7	dimension	4

Source: Coxhead (2000, p. 233).

Notes:
[a] Noun or verb stem.
[b] In the *AWL*, Sublist 1 contains the most frequent words; Sublist 10 contains the least frequent words.

- Connect novel words, lemmas, and clusters with existing knowledge;
- Promote L2 vocabulary strategies, remembering to develop the strategic reader (rather than teaching individual strategies);
- Provide multiple encounters with target words;
- Cultivate deep processing;
- Utilize a variety of text and task types in implementing vocabulary practice.

Spend Time on Words

We propose that vocabulary building and reading instruction go hand in hand. In fact, "there are important vocabulary coping and learning strategies that can be first approached through reading" (Nation, 2005, p. 588). To cultivate such strategies, teachers can work with vocabulary systematically in designing lessons (Blachowicz & Fisher, 2008; Coxhead, 2006; Schmitt, 2000; Zimmerman, 2007). Systematic vocabulary work—"spending time on words" (Nation, 2001, p. 93)—involves two basic questions: (1) Should time be devoted to a given word? (2) If so, how do we handle it pedagogically? In general, it is worthwhile to devote time to a word if the lesson aims to enhance vocabulary and if the target word is a high-frequency item or a valuable technical or topical word. We should also consider dedicating class time to a word if it might provide an occasion for modeling vocabulary learning strategies such as inferencing and word attack (analyzing word parts) (Nation, 2001; Schmitt, 2000).

We recommend the following instructional options for working with new lexical items in the classroom, which are inspired by Nation (2001, pp. 93–94) and informed by other sources:

1. *Pre-teach essential target items.* As we have already noted, pre-teaching works most effectively when it targets high-frequency words and those that are essential for comprehending a target text (Anderson, 1999; Graves & Graves, 2003). Pre-teaching should ideally involve rich instruction and focus on no more than five or six items.

2. *Replace novel lexical items in the text before presenting it to readers.* Texts containing low-frequency words that are not essential to overall comprehension may be worth replacing with higher-frequency words (Nation, 2001; Schmitt, 2000; Shrum & Glisan, 2005). This practice frees the teacher from spending valuable class time on lexical items that may be of marginal value to students.[9]

3. *Selectively gloss unfamiliar items.* High-frequency words that do not merit classroom attention can be glossed in the margin, at the end of a text, or in hyperlinked annotations (in digital texts). Glossing is also appropriate for low-frequency items. Despite the common belief that glosses encourage readers to skip over novel words, judicious glossing can actually promote lexical learning, as it brings words to readers' attention. Glosses induce students to look up target words, see them in a different context, and perhaps return to the original context, thereby activating attentional resources and memory (Al-Seghayer, 2001; Hudson, 2007; Hulstijn, Hollander, & Greidanus, 1996; Schmitt, 2000; Watanabe, 1997).

4. *Include novel words in post-reading tasks.* Lexical items featured in post-reading tasks and exercises should be high-frequency words or words containing useful word parts. Because designing such tasks requires time, the target words should be worth the effort.

5. *Provide concise word meanings.* Low-frequency words that are important for text comprehension but unlikely to be needed later can be defined quickly (Anderson, 1999; Elley, 1989). To avoid using class time on low-impact vocabulary items, the teacher can supply synonyms or brief definitions, produce a picture, or provide an L1 translation (see Nation [2001, pp. 90–93] for detailed procedures for presenting clear, concise definitions).

6. *Do nothing.* Low-frequency items that are not essential for text comprehension may simply not require any attention at all.
7. *Model inferencing (guessing) from context, dictionary use, and word analysis strategies.* Described below, these procedures are appropriate for both high- and low-frequency items. Strategy instruction and practice serve a dual purpose: (a) facilitating comprehension of the target text and (b) cultivating flexible strategies that can be used in the long term (Coxhead, 2006; Folse, 2004; Grabe, 2004; Grabe & Stoller, 2002; Schmitt, 2000; Takak, 2008).
8. *Devote instructional time to examining multiple meanings and collocations.* These rich instruction practices should be directed toward high-frequency words, as well as academic or specialized items that readers are likely to encounter often.

Teach Effective Inferencing Strategies

Perhaps the most commonplace vocabulary-building strategy promoted by instructors and L2 reading textbooks is inferencing, or guessing word meaning from context (see Chapters 3, 5, and 6). Regrettably, excessive zeal for strong top-down approaches to reading has led to a pervasive yet misguided assumption that the optimal approach to vocabulary learning through reading is to encourage students to rely on contextual guessing strategies (see Chapter 1). In line with other critics of this assumption (e.g., Hulstijn, 1993), Laufer (1997) pointed out that "a learner who has been taught guessing strategies will not automatically produce correct guesses" (p. 30). She identified four factors that can inhibit accurate inferencing processes during reading: (1) insufficient textual clues; (2) reader unfamiliarity with clue words; (3) potentially misleading clues in the text; (4) low compatibility between text content and the reader's emergent schematic knowledge. We recommend balancing direct and indirect strategies in the teaching of vocabulary: "Teach context clues, but not at the expense of explicit teaching of vocabulary" (Folse, 2004, p. 122). Bearing in mind constraints on effective lexical inferencing, reading instructors should teach and model contextual guessing strategies systematically, adapting explicit instruction to accommodate learners' proficiency levels. The sequential framework outlined in Figure 8.2 presents a procedure for teaching students how to attack unfamiliar words. We encourage teachers to test and evaluate word attack processes and to consider how they might adapt them in reading lessons.

Teach Effective Dictionary Strategies

One of the final, optional steps included in Figure 8.2 entails consulting a monolingual or bilingual dictionary, a strategy that can promote reader autonomy,

Step	Procedures
1	Determine the word's grammatical category.
2	Examining the clause or sentence where the word occurs, identify the word's functions relative to other constituents. For instance, if the word is a verb, what is its subject? Does it co-occur with any object noun phrases? If the item is an adjective, what noun(s) does it modify?
3	Examine the relationship between the linguistic structure containing the word and surrounding text (e.g., prior and subsequent sentences, paragraphs, and so forth). Whereas some such relationships may be overtly marked by conjunctions (e.g., *and*, *because*) or adverbials (e.g., *nevertheless*, *consequently*), others may be covertly marked (e.g., through exemplification or cause-and-effect rhetorical structures). Co-reference markers such as pronouns (e.g., *this*, *that*) and punctuation can similarly signal relationships providing clues to meaning.
4	Based on information gathered in Steps 1–3, make an educated guess about the word's contextual meaning(s).
5	Test this educated guess for accuracy. a. Verify that the grammatical category of the guess matches that of the target word. If not, review Step 1. b. Replace the unfamiliar word with the word(s) resulting from the guessing process. If the sentence or passage makes sense and is grammatically well-formed, the guess may be correct. c. Analyze the unfamiliar word morphologically: Identify its root(s) and affixes. If the meanings of these word parts match those of the replacement word, the latter may be correct.
(6)	(Optional) Verify the accuracy of the replacement word by checking in a monolingual or bilingual dictionary.
(7)	(Optional) Record the replacement word(s) and other useful information in the margin and/or in a vocabulary log as a means of promoting deep processing.

FIGURE 8.2. Steps for Modeling Contextual Guessing Strategies.
Based on Clarke and Nation (1980); Nation (2001).

build vocabulary, and improve reading comprehension—provided learners deploy efficient dictionary strategies. Dictionary use has unfortunately ignited passions among those who strongly favor or disfavor the practice. Reading research generally shows positive results for dictionary use, provided readers consult dictionaries primarily for unknown words whose meanings cannot be readily inferred from context. Advanced readers are more apt to consult dictionaries selectively, as their lexical knowledge is naturally more extensive. In contrast, novice readers may tend to look up more words, including those that they might know or that they can infer from context. Inexperienced readers often display an over-dependence on dictionaries and consequently do not use them efficiently (Folse, 2004; Hulstijn, 1993; Knight, 1994).

In addition to learner proficiency level, features of lexical items themselves can influence the effectiveness of dictionary use. Luppescu and Day (1993), for example, reported that Japanese EFL readers who consulted dictionaries performed twice as well on a vocabulary test than did students who did not use dictionaries. At the same time, even the high-performing dictionary users experienced difficulty with dictionary entries that offered multiple definitions. This finding suggests that readers need to learn how to use context clues to select from among diverse semantic meanings that dictionaries might provide. Folse (2004) recommended that teachers "teach students how to deal with polysemous words" by practicing bilingual and monolingual dictionary use (p. 124). Such practice can take the form of simple dictionary exercises and work with vocabulary analyzers, as well as tasks that integrate dictionary use with pre-, while-, and post-reading activities (see Chapter 5). As for whether students should use monolingual or bilingual dictionaries, we concur with Folse (2004), who rejected the conventional wisdom that "monolingual dictionaries are better than bilingual dictionaries for understanding and learning L2 vocabulary" (p. 124). We find it counterproductive to discourage (let alone ban) dictionary use, and we urge teachers to avoid such classroom policies. The use of both types of dictionary naturally involves pitfalls (e.g., bilingual dictionaries may supply inappropriate or incorrect translations; monolingual dictionaries may provide overly detailed definitions). Nonetheless, such pitfalls can be overcome when learners are trained to approach dictionary use critically and carefully—and when learners use dictionaries that are geared toward their needs (see Further Reading and Resources).

Consider Working with Graded Readers

Described briefly in Chapter 6, graded readers are single books—typically novels—written with a highly controlled lexical and grammatical range (Schmitt, 2000). Day and Bamford (1998) referred to graded readers as "language learner literature." Oxford University Press's *Bookworms* series, for example, comprises six levels, with titles at the lowest level requiring a vocabulary size of about 400 words. Level two titles add 300 words, requiring a total vocabulary of 700 words, and so on, up to level six, which requires 2,500 cumulative words. Titles include highly abridged and edited versions of familiar titles such as *Mutiny on the Bounty* and *Sherlock Holmes Short Stories*; others are original stories written expressly for the series. Graded readers have traditionally been considered to be an essential tool in literacy and vocabulary development, particularly at beginning and intermediate levels.

The use of graded readers is not uncontroversial: Some educators view them with contempt. Nation (2005) summed up the current status and instructional value of such resources:

> There is . . . prejudice against graded readers, largely by teachers [who] feel that graded readers are not authentic in that they involve controlled or adapted text rather than text intended for native speakers. However, these texts should be seen as authentic in that they provide conditions under which learners at all levels of proficiency can read with a degree of comprehension, ease, and enjoyment that is near that of a native speaker reading unsimplified text. Without graded readers, reading . . . would be one continuous struggle against an overwhelming vocabulary level (Nation & Deweerdt, 2001). Teachers need to be familiar with various series of graded readers . . . (pp. 587–588)

Carefully selected readers offer several advantages. First, the controlled vocabulary ensures early and repeated exposure to the most frequent words. Second, the use of readers can accelerate vocabulary building and the development of basic bottom-up, top-down, and integrated reading skills. Third, students read books where 95% of the lexical content is known to them, minimizing frustration, increasing motivation, and enabling them to experience rauding. Fourth, because the linguistic, lexical, and thematic content of readers is highly controlled, designing courses tends to be less demanding than when working exclusively with authentic texts. Finally, most contemporary reader series include built-in assessment packages.

Ask Questions

Perhaps the most common fall-back reading exercises are those that present readers with comprehension questions (see Chapters 3–7). Although we would caution teachers against over-reliance on this prevalent and often highly predictable exercise type, Nation (2001) recommended developing comprehension prompts that induce readers to use target vocabulary with the goal of strengthening form–meaning links. For example, prompts and questions requiring students to repeat part of the text activate memory retrieval. When learners must use material in the text creatively, they engage in generative use of novel words. Features of well-formulated prompts include "the use of inferential questions to encourage generative use, taking the text away to encourage retrieval, and getting learners to share their answers to get receptive generative use" (Nation, 2001, p. 161). In constructing comprehension questions that simultaneously promote deep text processing and lexical development, we should go beyond stimuli that target discrete, factual textual elements. We likewise encourage teachers to embed comprehension questions in pre-, during-, and post-reading tasks requiring learners to share and compare their responses (Farris et al., 2004; Folse, 2004; Keene, 2008; Nation, 2001; Schmitt, 2000; Shrum & Glisan, 2005). Nation (2001) proposed several criteria for constructing prompts likely to elicit productive responses:

Comprehension questions

- Does the stimulus require readers to incorporate target words in their responses?
- Does the stimulus require readers to use target words generatively (i.e., in a linguistic context that differs from the context in which it occurs in the reading passage)?
- Does the stimulus require readers to recall the target word or search for it in the text?

Match Definitions

Like asking generative questions, definition-matching tasks endeavor to induce readers to connect novel word forms with meanings by activating noticing and retrieval processes (Paribakht & Wesche, 1996). In definition-matching tasks, learners locate target words in a text that match simple definitions provided before or after the text. Whether lists of definitions are presented as pre-reading or post-reading tools, they are often sequenced in the same order as the target words are presented in the original text. In addition to the ordering of definitions, other design features involve the provision of an initial letter cue to trigger easier retrieval, as well as the presentation of definitions on a separate page or screen from the reading text to promote rehearsal (Nation, 2001; Schmitt, 2000). Traditional in design, definition-matching tasks are simple to devise, require minimal class time, can function as individual or group activities, and provide teachers with clues about students' noticing and retrieval skills.

Practice Semantic Mapping

Familiar to many teachers, semantic mapping is a procedure that induces learners "to relate new information to schemata . . . actively integrating new knowledge with the old . . ." (Farris et al., 2004, p. 395). A semantic map, a form of graphic organizer, leads learners to design a visual representation of relationships among words, meanings, images, and propositional content (Blachowicz & Fisher, 2008; Nation, 2001; Yopp & Yopp, 2005). To construct a word map or web such as the sample diagram for *ecology* in Figure 8.3, "students tie new words to previously known words, concepts, or words with similar meanings, [enabling] them to remember the newly acquired word more efficiently" (Farris et al., 2004, p. 395).

A procedure such as the following can be used to construct a semantic map, although many variations are possible:

1. Teacher briefly introduces theme or concept, then writes the target word on the board, a transparency, or chart paper (or displays it on a SmartBoard or in a PowerPoint slide).
2. Teacher instructs students to identify related words and phrases that strike them. As students begin their own lists, they share their recorded words with the teacher.
3. As teacher records students' suggestions on the emerging diagram, students record new additions in their own lists.
4. Teacher elicits synonyms, hyponyms, hypernyms, and so on that students have not suggested, discussing these new contributions.
5. Once satisfied with the list's completeness, teacher guides students in classifying items by category, eliciting discussion of these associations. Teacher and students label categories.

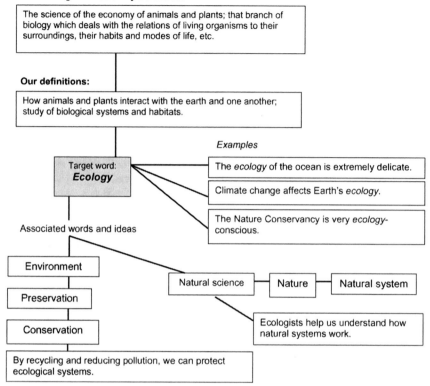

Oxford English Dictionary definition:

The science of the economy of animals and plants; that branch of biology which deals with the relations of living organisms to their surroundings, their habits and modes of life, etc.

Our definitions:

How animals and plants interact with the earth and one another; study of biological systems and habitats.

Examples

Target word: **Ecology**

The *ecology* of the ocean is extremely delicate.

Climate change affects Earth's *ecology*.

The Nature Conservancy is very *ecology*-conscious.

Associated words and ideas

Environment

Preservation

Conservation

Natural science — Nature — Natural system

Ecologists help us understand how natural systems work.

By recycling and reducing pollution, we can protect ecological systems.

FIGURE 8.3. Sample Semantic Map.

6. Teacher or designated student leads class in constructing a semantic map on the board or a slide. Teacher encourages students to add items and categories—or to devise their own, alternative semantic maps.
7. After students read assigned text, teacher leads discussion of the topics, categories, and lexical items discovered (or not discovered) in the text.

Definition-matching and vocabulary-oriented comprehension questions embed vocabulary practice in intensive reading practice (see Chapter 5). Semantic mapping should likewise emerge from, or feed directly into, working with a text, although the technique can sometimes divert attention away from the reading process. As with most vocabulary-building activities, we caution teachers against allowing vocabulary work to overshadow reading practice.

Encourage Use of Word Cards

In addition to the classroom vocabulary task types already discussed, we can encourage readers to undertake independent activities to build their lexical knowledge. Considered unfashionable in some circles, word cards admittedly involve rote learning of L2 items and their L1 equivalents. Nation (2005) nonetheless pointed to a substantial body of research demonstrating that "such learning is very efficient," emphasizing that systematic guidelines can optimize direct learning (p. 590). He noted that learning from word cards quickly boosts vocabulary size, with learners retrieving the meanings of about 70% of the words in a card set after a single run through them. We suspect that such outcomes result from rehearsal and from writing out new words, procedures that aid memory and promote deep processing. Traditional techniques such as word cards should complement and support—not replace—opportunities for readers to comprehend lexical items that they routinely encounter in reading. Judicious use of word cards should also encourage learners to produce new lexical items in their writing and speech (Folse, 2004; Nation, 2001, 2005; Schmitt, 2000; Takak, 2008).

To use word cards effectively, readers require encouragement and training. The word card strategy involves writing useful (e.g., high-frequency) lexical items taken from reading selections, word lists, and other encounters with the L2 (e.g., classroom lessons and lectures) on small cards, with an L1 translation and/or L2 gloss on the other side of the card. The words recorded on cards should be self-selected. Experts advise keeping glosses and examples as simple and concise as possible; card sets should be manageable in size, not to exceed about 50 in number, so that they can be carried and reviewed anywhere. The following guidelines can help learners maximize practice with word cards:

1. Try to retrieve word meaning before looking at the gloss or definition on the other side.

2. Practice with word cards in small intervals, rather than concentrating the rehearsal process in a single time period. The more widely spaced the repetitions, the better.

3. Shuffle cards so that they appear in a different sequence at each practice session.

4. Vocalize each word when looking at it to promote deep processing and long-term storage.

5. Use L1 glosses, at least during early stages of learning; translations are easier to understand.

6. Practice pronouncing difficult words, using mnemonic or word attack strategies to break them into morphological units. Try to use especially difficult words in sentences.

7. Avoid placing related words (synonyms, antonyms, hyponyms, and so on) together.

8. Once items have been learned receptively, advance to productive learning by constructing sentences with new items, using them in writing assignments, and so on. (Adapted from Nation, 2005, pp. 590–591)

Assign Vocabulary Notebooks or Logs

A second independent vocabulary-building task that dovetails with the word card method involves recording novel items in a notebook or log, a process that engages students in ongoing linguistic fieldwork. "Students need to take some responsibility for learning and reviewing words on their own. Some students are natural collectors of words, while others need to be introduced to different [collection] techniques" (Grabe & Stoller, 2002, p. 191). Nation (2005) favors word cards over notebooks, as the notebook format presents target words and meanings together, with entries always appearing in the same sequence. However, some readers prefer notebooks because notebooks assemble lexical information in a single archive and because words and meanings are easy to locate once they have been recorded.

Schmitt and Schmitt (1995) suggested organizing a loose-leaf binder where readers record word pairs and even semantic maps to help them construct associations among word forms, meanings, and existing knowledge. A bound notebook can be practical, but a loose-leaf binder allows the user to arrange pages and entries alphabetically, or by semantic category or theme (Nation, 2001). Some students may prefer to maintain notebooks in electronic format: Word-processing and spreadsheet applications offer great versatility in terms of sequencing and classifying information. The storage capacity of an electronic word file is potentially unlimited, permitting the user to add new items at any time, maintain them in alphabetical order, and conduct easy word searches. As with word cards, vocabulary logs allow readers to select salient lexical items and to generate their own L1 glosses or L2 definitions. DeCarrico (2001) and Grabe and Stoller (2002) further recommended instructing students to maintain a frequency count of their encounters with novel words, study roots and affixes, record stylistic features and collocations, and compose sample sentences. Such strategies heighten reader awareness of subtle lexical features (see Figure 8.1).

Chapter Summary

We have proposed that lexical enhancement methods should be incorporated into the L2 reading curriculum with the aim of complementing reading instruction, improving students' reading efficiency, and mindfully addressing vocabulary in assessment. Given the degree to which L2 reading development depends on building a sizable L2 lexicon, teachers may be tempted to allow vocabulary instruction to focus excessively on discrete words, perhaps at the expense of teaching learners to connect lexical items with their contexts. Rather than calling for a return to mechanical approaches that focus on words in isolation, we would appeal to teachers to view the L2 reading course as an ideal setting for building readers' receptive and productive vocabularies by embracing the dynamic interaction between word knowledge and reading skill.

Steps toward capitalizing on this interaction include understanding the richness of what it means to know a word—and acquainting students with these valuable insights. Research overwhelmingly demonstrates that broad and deep lexical knowledge correlates highly with efficient reading skills. Empirical evidence from lexicology and corpus linguistics has also produced word banks such as the *GSL, AWL*, and others, which tell us which words occur most frequently and thus merit the most careful, sustained attention. The literature on literacy and vocabulary development likewise yields insights into which direct and indirect instructional approaches will promote effective vocabulary learning strategies. This work, in turn, has generated principles and practices for integrating explicit lexical instruction into the L2 literacy curriculum, a sampling of which we introduced here. Because research-based and pedagogical sources on vocabulary learning and teaching are so abundant, we have confined our discussion primarily to those bearing directly on L2 reading instruction. We nonetheless encourage readers to acquaint themselves with this exciting and fast-paced area of research and teaching by consulting the excellent resources listed in Further Reading and Resources.

Further Reading and Resources

We recommend the following sources on vocabulary development, teaching, and assessment as useful supplements for teachers of L2 reading.

Research on L2 vocabulary learning and teaching
    Bogaards & Laufer (2004); Lengyel & Navracsics (2007); Nation (2001); Read (2004b); Schmitt & McCarthy (1997); Takak (2008)
Vocabulary instruction
    Allen (1999); Coxhead (2006); Graves (2006); Hiebert & Kamil (2005); Hoey (2005); Lewis (2002); Morgan & Rinvolucri (2004); Nation (1994, 2001); O'Keeffe et al. (2007); Schmitt (2000); Stahl and Nagy (2006); Zimmerman (2007); Zwier & Bennett (2006)
Vocabulary and teaching reading
    Huckin, Haynes, & Coady (1997); Wagner, Muse, & Tannenbaum (2007)
Vocabulary assessment (also see Chapter 9)
    Daller, Milton, & Treffers-Daller (2008); Read (2000)
Word frequencies for English
    Leech, Rayson, & Wilson (2001)
Academic Word List Online
    http://language.massey.ac.nz/staff/awl/
Academic Word List Exercises
    http://web.uvic.ca/~gluton/awl/
Cambridge International Corpus (CIC)
    http://www.cambridge.org/elt/corpus/international_corpus.htm

Collins Wordbanks Online English Corpus
  http://www.collins.co.uk/Corpus/CorpusSearch.aspx
Word frequency lists included in Leech et al. (2001)
  http://www.comp.lancs.ac.uk/ucrel/bncfreq/flists.html
LexTutor: The Compleat Lexical Tutor
  http://www.lextutor.ca/
Textalyser
  http://textalyser.net/
Vocabulary Acquisition Research Group Archives (VARGA)
  http://www.lognostics.co.uk/varga/
ESL/EFL learner dictionaries
  Collins COBUILD Advanced English Dictionary (Sinclair, 2006); *Longman
  Dictionary of Contemporary English; Oxford Advanced Learner's Dictionary*
  (Hornby & Wehmeier, 2007)
English-language vocabulary tests
  Meara & Jones (1990); Nation (1983)
Receptive Vocabulary Levels Tests, Versions A–C (online) for English
  http://www.er.uqam.ca/nobel/r21270/levels/
Productive Vocabulary Levels Tests, Versions A–C (online) for English
  http://www.lextutor.ca/tests/levels/productive/
Oxford English Dictionary Online
  http://www.oed.com/
Thesaurus.com
  http://thesaurus.reference.com/
Corpus linguistics and L2 teaching
  McEnery et al. (2006); O'Keeffe et al. (2007); Sinclair (2003)

Reflection and Review

1. What does word knowledge consist of? Why is it valuable for educators and learners to appreciate the complexity of this knowledge?

2. How are receptive and productive vocabulary knowledge distinct yet interdependent?

3. What does the vocabulary *learning burden* consist of, and what implications does it offer for text selection, reading instruction, vocabulary building, and assessment?

4. Why do estimates of vocabulary size vary, and how can we settle on reasonable goals for achieving a large enough vocabulary to read efficiently?

5. Some studies show that deep processing is required to ensure long-term storage of novel words; others show gains resulting from incidental learning. How do these contrasting results influence your thinking about direct and indirect approaches to vocabulary instruction?

6. Identify the benefits and drawbacks of direct vocabulary teaching methods (e.g., pre-teaching). Why might the effects of direct teaching be different for L1 and L2 readers?

7. Conventional wisdom in reading pedagogy has held that students should infer word meaning from context, yet some studies reveal that guessing can lead to incorrect inferences. What steps can we take in our teaching to avoid such problems?

8. Despite their recent unpopularity, techniques and tools such as dictionary use, glossing, graded readers, word cards, and so on have been shown to accelerate and enhance vocabulary learning. How can or should we integrate such tools into the L2 literacy syllabus?

Application Activities

Application Activity 8.1
Revisiting the Role of Vocabulary Building

Interest in the lexicon has recently enjoyed a renaissance, though research insights have been slow to influence the thinking and practices of L2 instructors. In this vein, Folse (2004) confronted seven misconceptions about vocabulary learning and teaching. Based on your experience as a learner or teacher, and your understanding of this chapter, respond to these "myths" as they pertain to L2 literacy instruction:

a. In learning another language, vocabulary is not as important as grammar or other areas.

b. Using word lists to learn second language vocabulary is unproductive.

c. Presenting new vocabulary in semantic sets facilitates learning.

d. The use of translations to learn new vocabulary should be discouraged.

e. Guessing words from context is an excellent strategy for learning L2 vocabulary.

f. The best vocabulary learners make use of one or two really good specific vocabulary learning strategies.

g. The best dictionary for L2 learners is a monolingual dictionary.

h. Teachers, textbooks, and curricula cover L2 vocabulary adequately. (Folse, 2004, p. x)

Application Activity 8.2
Reflecting on Incidental Vocabulary Acquisition

Select a text that you have recently read for pleasure and that contained some unfamiliar words (e.g., a novel, a nonfiction book, a magazine). Your reading should have involved *rauding* (normal reading): You should not have stopped to try to learn the unfamiliar words. Respond to the following questions in a discussion with your peers or in a three-page written commentary.

a. Can you recall any of the unfamiliar words without referring to the text? If so, then you have gained some productive knowledge. Can you remember further details about the word and its possible meanings as expressed by the context?
b. If you cannot recall any unfamiliar words, look back at the text to jog your memory, without looking at the surrounding text. How much information can you remember now?
c. Try reading the unfamiliar words anew in context. Do you understand more of the passage now than when you first encountered the word? What receptive knowledge have you gained?
d. How would you convert your receptive knowledge to productive knowledge?

Application Activity 8.3
Analyzing Word Frequencies and Texts

Below is a list of words and their rank-ordered frequencies as indexed in the *General Service List* (West, 1953), which is based on the one-million-word Brown Corpus.

Word	Grammatical category	Rank	Frequency per million words
the	Determiner	1	69,975
be	Copula/auxiliary	2	31,175
of	Preposition	3	36,432
and	Conjunction	4	28,872
a	Determiner	5	26,800
line	Noun	200	522
outside	Adverb	500	221
admit	Verb	1,000	94
wisdom	Noun	1,500	44
scenery	Noun	2,000	15
motherly	Adjective	2,272	1

Select a text from a source of your choosing (a textbook, a novel, a magazine article, an L2 student textbook). Manually or with the aid of a word-processing application or vocabulary profiler such as *LexTutor* or *Textalyser* (see Further

Reading and Resources), perform a frequency count on a two- to three-paragraph extract to determine the frequencies of the words from the *GSL*. Respond to the following questions:

a.   What do your frequencies suggest about the likelihood of learning words of varying frequency from exposure alone (i.e., incidentally)?
b.   Do you think your extract contains enough repetition to learn the target words?
c.   How likely would it be to encounter the same words in a very different text?
d.   At what frequency level would the effort required to teach these words explicitly outweigh the benefit of learning these words?
e.   The *GSL* is based on a one-million-word corpus. Why would a larger corpus (e.g., the CIC [10 million words], the *BNC* [100 million words]) alter word frequencies and rankings?

Application Activity 8.4
Assessing Learners' Receptive and Productive Vocabulary Knowledge

No instrument can provide an exact measure of lexical knowledge, but tools such as the *Vocabulary Levels Test* (*VLT*) (Nation, 2001) can supply useful, reliable estimates to be used for determining threshold levels at which to begin instruction. To familiarize yourself with such tools, select an advanced level of any version of the receptive or productive *VLT* (follow the links provided in Further Reading and Resources). Follow the instructions on the website and complete one or more high-level sections of both the receptive and productive tests. Reflect on your experience by addressing these prompts in writing or in a discussion with peers:

a.   How did you score? Do your scores accurately reflect the size of your receptive and productive vocabularies?
b.   Compare your experience taking the *VLT* to the likely experience of a beginning-, intermediate-, or advanced-level ESL or EFL learner.
c.   In what respects do you think *VLT* results might be useful to you as a teacher and course developer? How might your students benefit from taking the *VLT* diagnostically and subsequently retaking the test (or something similar) as they progress in a course or program?
d.   How might you use the *VLT* or an equivalent instrument in your current or future practice as a reading teacher?

As an extension, administer appropriate sections of the *VLT* to a group of learners, analyze the results, and outline a plan to bring learners to the next-highest threshold level.

Application Activity 8.5
Assessing Vocabulary Treatment in Published Materials

We have asserted that L2 reading instruction should make lexical development a high priority. Paradoxically, L2 textbooks rarely target vocabulary building explicitly, though we note a trend toward more extensive vocabulary treatment in published materials. Select a unit from a recent L2 reading textbook. Based on the principles outlined here and in Chapter 3, evaluate the material from a vocabulary-learning perspective by addressing these questions:

a. What theory of word knowledge or lexical learning do the content and design suggest? On what evidence do you base your inferences?
b. What types of word knowledge do the activities explicitly or implicitly address? What dimensions of lexical expertise are overlooked?
c. How do the texts and apparatus promote receptive and productive vocabulary building? For example, consider, explanations and activities that promote inferencing, dictionary searches, vocabulary-building techniques (e.g., word cards, logs, and so on).
d. What changes to the content and design would you suggest in order to improve the effectiveness of the material?

Prepare a three-page written assessment of your material, attaching a copy of the relevant text pages. Alternatively, share your critique with your peers in a class presentation.

Application Activity 8.6
Diagnosing Reading Fluency and Efficiency

Readers must know 95% or more of the words in a text in order to comprehend it independently. Teachers should therefore determine the proportion of items in assigned materials that might be unfamiliar to students. The *Vocabulary Knowledge Scale* (*VKS*) (Paribakht & Wesche, 1997; Wesche & Paribakht, 1996), developed to measure depth of knowledge in academic settings, ranges from complete unfamiliarity to an ability to use the word fluently. The *VKS* can be used as a self-assessment tool or to measure demonstrated knowledge. The task below, adapted from the original *VKS*, will require you to craft an exercise that makes students aware of their lexical knowledge and provides teachers with valuable diagnostic information.

Procedures

a. Select a reading passage that would be appropriate for learners in an L2 reading course. Readers should not be familiar with the text.
b. Examine the passage and derive a list of potentially unfamiliar words. Grabe and Stoller (2002) recommended including 25 content words (or word

clusters) and 10 or more function words in such checklists. The abbreviated
checklist below is derived from a passage about meeting strangers in *Well
Read 4* (Pasternak & Wrangell, 2007, pp. 36–38), a high-intermediate/low-
advanced ESL/EFL reading textbook.

Pre-Reading Vocabulary Checklist

Name: _____

Directions: Place a check (✓) mark in the column that best describes how
well you know each word. If you select C, D, or E, write your synonym,
translation, or sentence below the chart, as in the first two examples.

How familiar are these words?	A. I don't know this word.	B. I've seen this word, but I don't know its meaning.	C. I've seen this word before, and I think it means _____ (synonym or translation).	D. I know this word. It means _____ (synonym or translation).	E. I can use this word in a sentence.
1. proximity			✓		
2. mutual					✓
3. surroundings					
4. contact					
5. newsworthy					
6. evoke					

1. closeness
2. My roommate and I have no mutual friends.
3.
4.
5.
6.

c. Before administering your checklist, instruct students to judge their word knowledge using the five descriptors in the column headings. Explain and model this step.

d. Collect the questionnaires and tabulate the data. Not all students' responses will be accurate or truthful, but your findings should point toward lexical items that many or most students do not know. Rank-order target words to determine which words to pre-teach.

e. Plan (and, if possible, deliver) a lesson featuring the text sample. To test the value of pre-teaching, pre-teach unfamiliar items as part of your lesson or test the possibility of incidental learning by forgoing pre-teaching.

f. After your lesson, administer the checklist again and perform a follow-up analysis. Compare these results with the pre-reading results.

g. Review and discuss pre- and post-reading questionnaires with students, noting their reactions to the process. Prepare a report summarizing your procedures, results, and implications for learning, teaching, and assessment.

Application Activity 8.7
Teaching Contextual Guessing

Research has challenged the longstanding practice of teaching L2 readers to guess lexical meaning from context (often at the expense of comprehension). However, readers must unquestionably develop semantic inferencing skills. Teachers must therefore introduce, model, and monitor lexical inferencing systematically.

Option 1: Mini-Lesson

Choose a level-appropriate authentic text sample or a passage from a published L2 reading textbook. Guided by the contextual guessing procedures outlined in Figure 8.2, develop an outline for a mini-lesson centered on your text selection: Solicit feedback from your instructor or a classmate before finalizing your outline. If possible, deliver your micro-lesson and write a brief reflective report on the lesson's challenges and successes. Discuss what you learned about students' encounters with novel words, noting changes that you would make to the outline. Include your lesson outline and the reading selection as an appendix.

Option 2: Textbook Evaluation

Based on the contents of this chapter—in particular, the instructional sequence outlined in Figure 8.2—select two recent L2 reading textbooks for a comparative evaluation. Carefully review representative chapters or units from each book, noting how each book's design and apparatus guides (or fails to guide) readers in formulating accurate inferences about unfamiliar lexical items. Considering the persistent danger that students might infer incorrect word meanings, compose a critical commentary of about three pages in which you assess the effectiveness of each textbook's approach to teaching inferencing.

Application Activity 8.8
Harnessing Vocabulary Power

If we account for the multidimensionality of word knowledge (see Figure 8.2), it is easy to understand how learning a few lexical items can trigger a productive multiplier effect. According to Nation (1990), knowing the 14 English words in the list below—including their affixes and roots—can generate knowledge of 14,000 words (e.g., *precept* is made up of the derivational prefix, *pre-* [before], plus its Latinate root, *capere* [take, seize]).

a. Using an online search engine, locate a set of authentic texts containing a subset of these words, roots, and affixes.

b. Determine the root, derivational affixes, and meanings of these word parts for your selected words by consulting a print or online dictionary (e.g., dictionary.com).

c. Analyze two to three of these texts by performing a frequency analysis of the featured items. When compared to the potential benefits of knowing 14,000 words, the cost of memorizing these items seems minimal. Would you consider asking students to memorize such a list? Why or why not? Orally or in writing, reflect on applications of your research to teaching reading.

1. precept	6. monograph	11. reproduction
2. detain	7. epilogue	12. indisposed
3. intermittent	8. aspect	13. oversufficient
4. offer	9. uncomplicated	14. mistranscribe
5. insist	10. nonextended	

(Nation, 1990, p. 171)

Chapter 9
Classroom L2 Reading Assessment

Questions for Reflection

- Reflect on your experience as a classroom learner. What instruments and procedures have your instructors used to evaluate your performance? Do you recall experiences in which your reading skills, progress, or achievement were assessed? Describe your best and worst experiences as a test-taker.

- How have the scores, grades, or other evaluations you have received on your academic performance (including reading) helped you develop your knowledge and skills? How have these marks or evaluations promoted (or inhibited) your learning and mastery?

- If you have teaching experience, describe how you assess students' abilities and performance. What are your greatest assessment challenges? If you are a pre-service teacher, what are your main concerns about assessing students' reading skills? Why?

- What are the appropriate roles of formal assessment in the teaching of reading? Explain.

- Large-scale, high-stakes tests (e.g., SAT, GRE, GMAT, LSAT, TOEFL, TOEIC, IELTS) are used principally for proficiency and placement testing, yet the principles underlying their design can be valuable for classroom teachers. How might the theoretical and conceptual dimensions of such assessments inform routine classroom assessment?

- Are you acquainted with alternative forms of assessment (e.g., self-assessment, portfolios, and so on)? How did you learn about them, and how are they distinct from more traditional assessment types?

Among the many demanding functions performed by educators, measuring and reporting learner performance can be one of the most intimidating. Brown (2004) echoed the sentiments of many students and pre-service teachers: "If you hear the word *test* in any classroom setting, your thoughts are not likely to be positive, pleasant, or affirming" (p. 1). For a quick refresher on how testing situations can influence test-takers, complete the following English vocabulary quizlet.

Directions: Select the definition that best matches the meaning of each word. You have three minutes.

☐ 1. **cholent**   A. Small, edible crustacean endemic to East African rivers   B. Meat and vegetable stew or casserole, typically prepared on Friday and served on the Sabbath   C. Powdered emulsifier used in the manufacture of pharmaceuticals and supplements   D. Wrench-like device designed to adjust orthodontic braces

☐ 2. **excoriate**   A. To remove skin or hide; to flay   B. To strip bark or rind C. To upbraid scathingly, decry, or revile D. All of the above

☐ 3. **glottochronology**   A. Study of the dilation and contraction sequences of the upper portion of the trachea and vocal cords B. Comparative philology   C. Statistical analysis of vocabulary to determine relationships among languages and the sequence of their evolution from a common ancestor   D. None of the above

☐ 4. **humbucker**   A. Scoundrel, rogue, rascal, or villain   B. Small woodfinch native to Northern Europe and the British Isles C. Complex constituent of a cell nucleus that can be readily stained when immersed in a coloring matter   D. Type of stylus, needle, or laser in a gramophone, record deck, or disk player, composed of two coils configured to reduce noise and interference

☐ 5. **pycnodysostosis**   A. Inherited autosomal recessive disorder characterized by excessive bone fragility, short stature, an enlarged skull, small jaw, and abnormality of the fingertips   B. Localized, irregular coagulation of blood in small extremities, chiefly the toes   C. Paralyzing psycho-physiological disorder caused by ingesting certain pycnides (lichens)   D. Mineralization process resulting in columnar aggregations of off-white or yellowish varieties of topaz

Before checking your answers, how well do you think you scored on this exercise?[1] As the words can be found in a standard English dictionary, you should have done pretty well. If not, why wasn't your score higher, and how did you feel about your less-than-stellar result? If you have anxious feelings about tests, quizzes, and other types of educational assessment, you are not alone. In the same way that students are often apprehensive about taking tests, teachers and even test developers can find administering assessments to be disquieting.

One reason for such feelings involves our natural anxiety in the face of the highly complex work of assessing what novice readers know and do. Eliciting fair, meaningful reading performances is not a simple process, and we must carefully select appropriate texts and devise purposeful tasks. Another common source of distress involves interpreting the outcomes of formal and informal assessments, as our interpretations usually lead to important decisions about reporting grades, promoting students, and ensuring that students achieve established standards. Our assessments often have significant consequences for students and institutions; therefore, assessments must be accurate, fair, transparent, and meaningful for all stakeholders.

Understanding the purposes of assessment and approaching the process as a teaching and learning tool can relieve some of this pressure. In line with current trends toward authentic, formative assessment, we embrace the view that appraising students' knowledge and skills is as elemental in the educational process as delivering purposeful instruction (Airasian & Russell, 2008; Bailey, 1998; Brown, 2004; Caldwell, 2008; O'Malley & Valdez Pierce, 1996). In his comprehensive volume on assessing L2 reading, Alderson (2000) emphasized that classroom reading assessment "should be directly and intimately related to the nature of the instruction." Most instruction, he wrote, "is indeed assessment anyway, sometimes quite explicitly so, as when homework assignments are marked and grades are recorded in . . . continuous assessment" (p. 191). Teaching and practice tasks may not always aim directly to elicit a measurable performance, but a good portion of instructional time entails assessment-like activities, such as responding to multiple-choice items after a reading (as in the vocabulary quizlet at the beginning of this chapter), identifying a passage's main ideas, or analyzing a passage's rhetorical structure (Urquhart & Weir, 1998). Thus, the boundaries that divide teaching, learning, and assessment become beneficially blurred, with the difference among these activities becoming "simply one of systematicity and sampling—teachers explicitly record their impressions of pupils' performance, and they seek to sample it in relevant and fair ways" (Alderson, 2000, p. 192). By cyclically engaging students in varied literacy activities that necessitate top-down, bottom-up, and interactive reading, we undertake formative assessment all the time. In other words, the reading processes and procedures introduced throughout this book all constitute potential assessment vehicles. Moreover, the principles and practices of syllabus design and instructional planning (see Chapter 4) go hand in hand with our coverage of approaches to reading assessment.

The premise that assessing reading **is** teaching reading underlies the content and structure of this chapter, which begins by summarizing the chief purposes of assessment in L2 literacy instruction. We then review fundamental constructs in educational measurement as they pertain to the day-to-day processes of gauging reading skills and progress using formal and informal methods. Next, we introduce a framework for designing classroom assessments, highlighting key variables to consider in devising meaningful, practical instruments for measuring reading development and literate knowledge. Working with a sampling of standards for L2 reading instruction, we will then turn our attention to constructing and deploying model tasks. The chapter will culminate by outlining procedures for devising an assessment plan. Throughout our discussion, we emphasize classroom L2 literacy assessment, in contrast to the mechanics of constructing and validating high-stakes, standardized reading assessments. We nonetheless draw extensively on the expertise of language testing specialists and psychometricians: Testing theory and research are indispensable tools for understanding not only the complexity of measuring student performance but also the processes of learning and teaching (Bachman & Cohen, 1998).

The Purposes of L2 Reading Assessment

The aims of classroom and high-stakes assessment may seem obvious to seasoned teachers and language learners. Nonetheless, because assessments differ in terms of what they measure, who uses the results, and how outcomes are used, it is valuable to classify assessments according to their purposes (Airasian & Russell, 2008). Bailey (1998), for example, identified *proficiency* assessments as those that endeavor to measure learners' abilities or place examinees in courses. "We assess proficiency . . . to find out in a broad sense what . . . learners are able to do . . ." (Graves, 2000, 211). Well-known language proficiency assessments include the ACTFL Proficiency Guidelines and TESOL Standards, as well as tests such as TOEFLiBT, TOEIC, and IELTS (see Chapter 1).[2] Universities use TOEFL and IELTS scores as indices of academic English-language ability; scores may determine which applicants are admissible and linguistically prepared to begin studies in an English-medium institution. Proficiency assessments can supply us with a baseline as a student advances through a course and also serve as an index of progress at the end of a course. In proficiency assessments, "it doesn't matter how a . . . learner became proficient" (Bailey, 1998, p. 38). Some institutions use proficiency assessments such as TOEFL and IELTS to assign students to course levels, whereas others may instead (or in addition) administer a *placement* examination, which is designed to characterize a candidate's skills relative to a specific academic program or course. Proficiency and placement assessments may be *criterion-* or *norm-referenced*. Criterion-referenced instruments yield scores that are interpreted relative to a pre-established standard or criterion (Hughes, 2003). In contrast, norm-referenced instruments, associated with the bell-shaped curve, yield scores "based on a comparison of the test-takers to a 'norming group' carefully selected to be representative of those expected to take the test" (Bailey, 1998, p. 246).

In *diagnostic assessments*, we gather evidence for what learners are able or unable to do with reference to a skill, task, or knowledge base as specified in the performative aims of a curriculum or syllabus (Alderson, 2005; Bachman & Palmer, 1996; Graves, 2000). Institutions often administer proficiency tests as pre- or post-course assessments, although diagnostic assessments are typically undertaken at the beginning of a course to evaluate students' readiness to begin working toward specific aims. For instance, in a college EAP course such as the one described in Chapter 4, the teacher might assign early tasks that measure students' reading speed and that require skimming and scanning— two of the seven reading functions explicitly targeted in the syllabus (see Appendix 4.2). These tasks not only form part of the instructor's ongoing assessment plan but also provide a comparative index of how closely students' demonstrated abilities match expected outcomes. Data from diagnostic instruments are part of the needs analysis process (see Chapter 4), and enable the teacher to make key decisions about which skill areas to emphasize as the course progresses.

Progress assessments are perhaps the most familiar form of educational measurement, as all teachers use them—after all, teachers and institutions must continually evaluate and report how successfully their students have mastered course material expanded their skill repertoires. As we noted in Chapter 4, appraisal of learners' developing skills and knowledge is part and parcel of course design and materials selection (Caldwell, 2008). Progress assessments therefore must be "very closely tied to the course content" (Bailey, 1998, p. 39). Progress assessment tools certainly include formal tests, in addition to diverse formal and informal instruments such as quizzes, exercises, reading journals, blog entries, literacy portfolios, individual and collaborative projects, presentations, and classroom discussions. Because progress assessments are typically grounded in local contexts, they offer the highest potential for authenticity in that the instruments can be tailored flexibly to coincide with course aims and literacy needs. Well-designed progress assessment tools usually target and elicit particular literacy skills and strategies (see Figures 1.8–1.10). Both formal instruments (e.g., tests, quizzes) and informal tools (e.g., reading journal entries, classroom discussions) should supply evidence of students' progress toward target criteria as they carry out diverse literacy tasks. This evidence—often described as *formative assessment*—should offer students ongoing feedback on their progress while supplying teachers with information about the effectiveness of their instruction (Afflerbach, 2008; O'Malley & Valdez Pierce, 1996; Urquhart & Weir, 1998).

Like progress assessment, *achievement assessment* is also grounded in the local educational context. We are all familiar with achievement assessments, which may be reported as test scores or as course grades. Although progress and achievement assessment practices may overlap—as well they should—the key distinction between the two categories is that achievement assessments typically report *summative* evaluations, which are "designed to find out what . . . students have mastered with respect to the knowledge and skills that have been taught in the course or unit" (Graves, 2000, p. 212). For teachers, appropriate achievement measurement means devising an *assessment plan* that articulates precisely how grades or marks will be assigned, in line with curricular goals and standards. As in the sample EAP reading course syllabus in Appendix 4.2, this plan may comprise a combination of progress and achievement measures, weighted according to the relative importance of target literacy skills, the representativeness of each assessment, and the effort associated with each component.

Proficiency, diagnostic, progress, and achievement assessments differ not so much with respect to their means and methods, but rather with respect to their purposes. A single evaluation instrument or test (e.g., TOEFL, IELTS, DIALANG) can serve more than one of these aims, as can a combination of measures (e.g., course grades). Nonetheless, teachers and students should understand that assessment results should be carefully interpreted with these complementary but distinct functions in mind. For example, reading subscores on a TOEFLiBT score report can provide valuable information about a candidate's measured English reading skills and abilities, but as a proficiency or achievement metric these subscores can tell us nothing about how the examinee arrived at that skill level. For the reading teacher concerned with assessing student performance in harmony with established curricular goals and content, we summarize the chief reasons for developing effective instruments and a workable assessment plan:

- To determine what students already know and can do as L2 readers;
- To gauge the distance between students' current performance and the criteria they must satisfy at the end of the course;
- To judge students' progress toward completing current assignments and projects;
- To provide learners with continuous feedback on their learning and level of effort so that they can take steps toward meeting performance objectives;
- To appraise the effectiveness of instruction in enhancing students' reading skills and identify better means of achieving goals;
- To generate meaningful evidence of student performance that can be used for purposes beyond the course (e.g., promotion to a higher-level course, university admission).

Principles and Concepts of L2 Reading Assessment

Planning and carrying out effective literacy assessment requires recognition of its multiple purposes as well as an understanding of constructs that undergird conventional practices in educational measurement. The technical complexities of test design, validation procedures, statistical analysis, and so forth are unfortunately beyond the scope of this chapter.[3] The present section reviews fundamental concepts in classroom assessment—language and literacy testing, in particular—which guide the elicitation and evaluation of reading performances from L2 readers. Familiarity with testing constructs and a working knowledge of the field's basic terminology can also make teachers aware of the need for consistent quality control in selecting materials, designing assessment tasks, and interpreting results.

We will operationalize key terms before exploring the more abstract concepts of reliability, validity, washback, and so forth. First, whereas a *test* is always an *assessment* instrument of some kind, an assessment activity is not necessarily a test, per se. We have elected to interpret both terms somewhat broadly while adhering to Brown's (2004) definition of *test*, which "... in simple terms, is a *method for measuring a person's ability, knowledge, or performance in a given domain*" (p. 3). A test should provide the assessor with a method for eliciting a performance from learners (e.g., a task in which readers display comprehension of a text), yielding a measurable outcome (e.g., a score, such as a percentage of correct responses). From these measurable outcomes, we can draw appropriate inferences about examinees' underlying competence as readers (Alderson, 2000). In addition, although administering a literacy test can tell us about the performance or achievement of a group of students, it should also assess and distinguish the "ability, knowledge, or performance" of individual test-takers (Brown, 2004, p. 3). Unless otherwise specified, the term *test* in this chapter will refer exclusively to *direct tests*, in which examinees actually perform target tasks (Brown, 2004). A direct test of reading clearly must engage the examinee in one or more reading subprocess (see Chapter 1). In contrast, *indirect tests* elicit performances that are merely thought to be related to the skill, knowledge base, or underlying competence being measured. For example, instruments that test grammatical knowledge or discrete vocabulary knowledge would be considered *indirect*, even though empirical evidence suggests that grammatical and lexical knowledge are good predictors of reading ability (see Chapters 1 and 8).

Reliability

A deceptively simple criterion, *reliability* is not as easy to achieve as we might think. According to Caldwell (2008), a *reliable* test of reading consistently "yields similar results over time with similar students under similar situations. A reliable test would be scored similarly by all teachers ... and two students of similar ability would receive similar scores" (p. 253). A reliable instrument is thus dependable and stable across comparable groups of examinees, yielding reasonably homogenous results—irrespective of raters, administration conditions, and test format (Brown, H. D., 2004; Brown, J. D., 2005; Hughes, 2003; McNamara, 2000).

Validity

Validity refers to the "extent to which a test measures what it is supposed to measure" (Bailey, 1998, p. 249). Validity relies on "knowing the exact purpose of an assessment and designing an instrument that meets that purpose" (Caldwell, 2008, p. 252). Conventional psychometric wisdom holds that, "in order for a test score to be valid, it must be reliable" (Bachman, 1990, p. 160). Nonetheless, whereas reliability may be a prerequisite to establishing validity, a reliable assessment instrument is useless unless the scores generated are valid (Fulcher & Davidson, 2007). Validity and reliability are thus fundamentally interdependent and should be recognized "as complementary aspects of a common concern in measurement—identifying, estimating, and controlling the factors that affect test scores" (Bachman, 1990, p. 160).

Because numerous criteria can be used to make validity claims, "there is no final, absolute measure of validity" (Brown, 2004, p. 22). Assessment experts routinely invoke several categories of validity, with some arguing that a truly valid instrument must satisfy the requirements of all of the following forms of evidence:

- ☐ *Face validity* cannot be measured empirically, but describes "the degree to which a test *looks* right and *appears* to measure the knowledge or abilities it claims to measure" (Mousavi, 2002, p. 244). A salient dimension of face validity is that test-takers must "view the assessment as fair, relevant, and useful for improving learning" (Gronlund, 1998, p. 210).
- ☐ *Construct validity* asks whether a test truly represents the theoretical construct as defined (Brown, 2004). In L2 literacy assessment, a construct could be any theory or model of reading (e.g., componential; top-down, bottom-up, or integrative) or reading development. Demonstrating construct validity is a chief concern in standardized assessment, but this form of evidence also serves a crucial purpose in classroom evaluation (Chapelle, 1998).
- ☐ *Content validity* is achieved when an instrument "actually samples the subject matter" and requires the examinee "to perform the behavior that is being measured" (Brown, 2004, p. 22). For example, if administered by your instructor as part of a graduate course in teaching L2 reading, the quizlet at the beginning of this chapter would lack content validity, as the material is irrelevant to course content. For Alderson (2000), a crucial aspect of validity in reading assessment is how validity

relates to course content and methods, teacher-student rapport, and the teacher's philosophy.

□ *Criterion validity* refers to "the extent to which the 'criterion' of the test has actually been reached" (Brown, 2004, p. 24). Criterion-referenced assessments measure pre-specified objectives or standards and imply the achievement of established performance levels (e.g., outcomes described in the *National TESOL Standards* or *ACTFL Proficiency Guidelines*—see Chapter 4). "In the case of teacher-made classroom assessments, criterion-related evidence is best demonstrated through a comparison of results of an assessment with results of some other measure of the same criterion" (Brown, 2004, p. 24).

□ *Concurrent validity*, like criterion validity, requires an assessment to generate the same rank order of individual scores as another validated instrument administered under similar conditions at the same time (Bachman & Palmer, 1996; Fulcher & Davidson, 2007; McNamara, 2000). For instance, a high mark on an ESL reading test might exhibit concurrent validity if the examinee can demonstrate L2 reading proficiency beyond the test (Brown, 2004).

□ *Predictive validity*—in a sense, the converse of concurrent validity—can be substantiated if an instrument produces the same results (i.e., test-takers' ranked scores) at a future point in time (Bachman & Palmer, 1996; Hughes, 2003). Predictive validity is essential in developing placement and aptitude measures, whose purpose is to predict candidates' future success.

□ *Consequential validity* "encompasses all the consequences of a test," including "its accuracy in measuring intended criteria, its impact on the preparation of test-takers, its effect on the learner, and the . . . social consequences of a test's interpretation and use" (Brown, 2004, p. 26). Though perhaps more abstract than other criteria, consequential validity is a prime concern for teachers, as we should always consider the positive and negative effects of any assessment on learners (Brindley, 2001; McNamara, 2000; Messick, 1989).

Clearly, these categories overlap and are bound to a complex underlying construct. Nonetheless, we hope that this simplified list of validity criteria will serve teachers as a kind of checklist for ensuring that their reading assessments are theoretically sound, meaningful to learners, and fair.

Authenticity

We have at various junctures alluded to *authenticity*, chiefly with reference to authentic texts (see Chapters 4 and 6). As Urquhart and Weir (1998) urged, literacy tests "should, as far as possible, attempt to activate real-life reading operations performed under appropriate performance conditions," although full replication of reality may not always be practical (p. 119). For the purposes of L2 reading assessment, we find Galloway's description of authenticity to be both practical and appropriate. For Galloway (1998), authentic texts are "those written and oral communications produced by members of a language and culture group for members of the same language group" (p. 133). What distinguishes an authentic text therefore relates to its origin, audience, and purpose, rather than to its genre (Caldwell, 2008; Day & Bamford, 1998; van Lier, 1996). As Villegas and Medley (1988) emphasized, L2 learners benefit from consistent encounters with authentic texts, which are characterized by "naturalness of form and . . . appropriateness of cultural and situational context" (p. 468).

Communicative language teaching and testing have increasingly placed a premium on deploying authenticity in instructional processes and assessment—sometimes in conflict with traditional, psychometrically influenced approaches to performance evaluation, which often involves presenting texts and items in relative isolation (Shrum & Glisan, 2005; Urquhart & Weir, 1998). In addition to considering authenticity of text, we must consider authenticity of *task*. After all, literacy events in the real world "are not undertaken in isolation" (Alderson, 2000, p. 148). For example, a text assigned for a reading course might lead the reader to take notes, draft a paper, and revisit the text anew before revising the draft. Reading a company's website may lead the reader to entering personal data and a credit card number in order to make an online purchase. Brown (2004) defined the role of authenticity in assessment: "When you make a claim for authenticity in a test task, you are saying that this task is likely to be enacted in the 'real world'" (p. 28). In more technical terms, authenticity refers to "the degree of correspondence of the characteristics of a . . . test task to the features of a target language task" (Bachman & Palmer, 1996, p. 23). The following questions, though not exhaustive, can assist test designers in ensuring authenticity of text and task in reading assessment:

☐ Is the language of the text and task natural?

☐ Are tasks, items, and stimuli contextualized, rather than isolated?

☐ Are topics meaningful, relevant, and interesting to examinees?

☐ Are texts, tasks, and items sequenced coherently and cohesively (e.g., organized thematically, chronologically, or hierarchically)?

☐ Do the tasks, items, prompts, and stimuli represent—or at least approximate—real-world literacy tasks or events? (Based on Brown, 2004, p. 28)

Washback

Considering the dynamic interplay between literacy instruction and assessment, we might be tempted to suggest that *washback* constitutes the gravitational center of this chapter. A facet of consequential validity, *washback* commonly describes "the effect of testing on teaching and learning" (Hughes, 2003, p. 1). Washback can obviously produce both positive and negative consequences (Bailey, 1996b). Undesirable washback effects associated with high-stakes standardized tests are "teaching to the test" and cram courses, which prepare learners narrowly for successful test performance but which may slight the teaching of lasting skills. Another common negative washback effect includes test-taker anxiety. Although classroom assessment practices can produce similarly undesirable washback effects, we encourage teachers to develop instruments "that serve as learning devices through which washback is achieved" (Brown, 2004, p. 29). For example, correct responses on an item or task in a reading test can inform the students about content or skills that they have successfully learned, offering insight into how close they are to achieving goals. Correct answers can likewise provide the teacher with an index of his or her teaching effectiveness. By the same token, an analysis of incorrect responses can (and should) lay groundwork for subsequent teaching, including content and skill areas that require further practice, and recycling (Alderson, 2000). This information can similarly guide the teacher in modifying the syllabus, adjusting instructional strategies, introducing alternative text types, and revising assessment methods (Bailey, 1996b, 1998).

The feedback component of positive washback is perhaps its most tangible and productive function. Feedback can serve both *formative* and *summative* purposes. Formative instruments "provide washback in the form of information . . . on progress toward goals" (Brown, 2004, p. 29). Summative assessment usually provides a snapshot of performance (e.g., in the form of a single test score or a course grade). Summative and formative evaluation can (and should) be viewed as complementary, but even summative assessments should provide information on performance and achievement that will help learners continue to learn (Afflerbach, 2008). We believe that effective tests and assessment plans should always "point the way to beneficial washback" (Brown, 2004, p. 37).

An important concept in language testing that is often associated with favorable washback and face validity is *bias for best*, a principle introduced by Swain (1984). In addition to reminding teachers and assessors to devise instruments that serve as learning tools, *bias for best* suggests that teachers and learners should be constructively involved in test preparation, administration, and interpretation. To maximize student performance on classroom measures while gathering accurate appraisals of their learning, biasing for best requires us to:

- Prepare students for test procedures by reviewing content and rehearsing target skills;
- Reveal and model strategies that will benefit students in completing test tasks;
- Select content, sequence tasks, and grade the difficulty of test material to challenge the most skilled students modestly while not overwhelming weaker learners. (Swain, 1984)

Product and Process

As observed in Chapter 1, L1 and L2 reading instruction has shifted from an early emphasis on product (i.e., outcomes on measures of reading comprehension) to approaches that embrace reading as a set of dynamically interrelated (sub)-processes. The product view "presumes that the outcomes of reading are stored in the reader's long-term memory and can be measured by persuading the reader to demonstrate portions of the stored text representation" (Koda, 2004, p. 228). Evidence of the pervasiveness of a product orientation in reading assessment can be found in the continued prevalence of assessment formats such as true–false, multiple-choice, controlled response, and free recall items. Alderson (2000) offered a particularly critical judgment: "All too many [reading] assessment procedures are affected by the use of test methods suitable for high-stakes, large-volume, summative assessment—the ubiquitous use of the multiple-choice test." These methods may nonetheless "be entirely inappropriate for the diagnosis of reading strengths and difficulties and for gaining insights into the reading process" (p. 332). Because of the fundamental role of memory in successfully completing them, controlled response items at some level presuppose an interdependent (if not synonymous) relationship between reading proficiency and memory (Martinez & Johnson, 1982). Strong product views assume that "comprehension occurs only if text information is stored in memory, and content retention is possible only when it is adequately understood" (Koda, 2004, p. 228).

Reading and assessment researchers have understandably questioned the equation of comprehension with memory, noting that readers may perform well on product-oriented reading assessments by retrieving text content but without having *comprehended* the text's meaning (Alderson, 1990; Gambrell et al., 2007; Hudson, 1993, 2005; Kintsch, 1998; Koda, 2004; Perkins et al., 1989; Rott, 2004). A further challenge to the longstanding tradition of treating reading comprehension as a product involves its inattention to how meaning representations are formed and stored (Koda, 2004). The debate between product and process proponents in literacy and assessment circles has ignited passions, frequently leading to fruitful empirical research that is too complex and extensive to summarize here.[4] We believe it is fair to assert that measurement experts increasingly favor literacy assessment procedures designed to monitor reading comprehension processes and strategy use. Emphasizing working memory, process orientations to reading assessment envision comprehension as "the *process* of extracting information from print and integrating it into coherent memory." Process approaches presuppose "a clear distinction between the ability to comprehend and the ability to remember" (Koda, 2004, p. 228). At the same time, we would not exclude a role for data storage as one of the many subprocesses of reading comprehension, which can be seen as multi-componential in nature (see Chapter 1).

A Framework for Designing Classroom L2 Reading Assessments

A key aim of all assessment is to produce performances on the basis of which we can make informed inferences about learners' underlying competence and their progress toward learning goals. Bachman and Palmer (1996) developed a framework specifying "distinguishing characteristics of language use tasks" to be used by assessors to "make inferences that generalize to those specific domains in which . . . test-takers are likely to . . . use language" (p. 44). A macro-level tool for all manner of language tests, the Bachman and Palmer (1996) framework can be readily adapted for the purpose of assessing L2 literacy products and processes. Because the Bachman and Palmer framework provides a level of detail that exceeds our needs in this chapter, we propose the list of task characteristics in Figure 9.1, which bear specifically on the design of use-oriented assessments in L2 reading instruction. Owing to the level of detail provided by Bachman and Palmer (1996), we will restrict ourselves to explaining task characteristics that bear specifically on designing use-oriented assessments.

We have consistently assigned a priority to understanding L2 reading processes and strategies, though certainly not to the exclusion of products that reflect achievement, progress, and proficiency. In keeping with our concern for teaching and monitoring reading processes in the context of authentic use, the Reading Types Matrix in Figure 9.2 presents a sample taxonomy listing specific reading operations around which effective tasks might be devised. We encourage readers to consult more elaborate taxonomies (see Alderson, 2000; Hudson, 2007; Koda, 2004; Urquhart & Weir, 1998), as well as the strategic inventories provided in Chapters 1 and 5, as they outline specifications for developing instruments.

Like similar taxonomies, Figure 9.2 reflects a componential view presupposing that reading is "the product of a complex but decomposable information-processing system" (Carr & Levy, 1990, p. 5). This "reading components" perspective (Grabe, 1991) remains controversial (see Chapter 1). Nonetheless, a systematic inventory of skills, subskills, and strategies is an essential tool for classroom reading assessment, particularly when competencies from quadrants A–D are all sampled proportionately over time (Birch, 2007; Koda, 2004).

Setting and Conditions

☐ Physical setting
☐ Test-takers
☐ Time of task and speededness (time allocation for completing task)

Test or Task Rubrics

☐ Task instructions
  ○ Language of instructions (L1, L2, or combination)
  ○ Delivery channel (written, visual, aural, or combination)
  ○ Procedures for completing task
☐ Test or task structure
  ○ Number and order of parts
  ○ Weighting of parts
  ○ Number of items per part

Scoring

☐ Explicit criteria for accurate responses
☐ Procedures for scoring test-taker responses

Input

☐ Formal characteristics
  ○ Language of text and task (L1, L2, or combination)
  ○ Delivery channel (written, visual, aural, or combination)
  ○ Item type (controlled or constructed response)
  ○ Length (e.g., of reading passages, response tasks)
☐ Linguistic input
  ○ Graphological, lexical, orthographic, morphological, and syntactic features
  ○ Discursive and rhetorical features (text structure, cohesion, coherence)
  ○ Sociolinguistic features (language variety, register, idiomatic and figurative language)
☐ Topical and thematic input
☐ Text and task content (content and cultural schemata required for task completion)

Test-Taker Response

☐ Formal characteristics
  ○ Language of response (L1, L2, or combination)
  ○ Delivery channel (written, visual, oral, or combination)
  ○ Item type (controlled or constructed response)
  ○ Length of desired response
☐ Linguistic characteristics
  ○ Graphological, lexical, orthographic, morphological, and syntactic features
  ○ Discursive and rhetorical features (text structure, cohesion, coherence)
  ○ Sociolinguistic features (language variety, register, idiomatic and figurative language)
☐ Topical, thematic, and schematic content of response

Input–Response Interactions

☐ Directness of interaction between input and response
☐ Scope of interaction between input and response
☐ Reactivity of input-response interaction (reciprocal, non-reciprocal, adaptive)

FIGURE 9.1. Assessment Task Characteristics.
Sources: Alderson (2000); Bachman and Palmer (1996); Brown, H. D. (2004); Brown, J. D. (2005); Read (2000).

	Global Operations	Local Operations
Fluent Reading (Rauding)	***A*** ■ Skim rapidly to identify topic, main ideas, and discursive purpose ■ Search text to locate core information and comprehend material relevant to predetermined needs	***B*** Scan to locate specific information sources (e.g., symbols, names, dates, figures, words, phrases)
Careful Reading	***C*** ■ Read carefully to construct an accurate representation of messages explicitly available in text ■ Make propositional inferences	***D*** ■ Decode syntactic structure of clausal units ■ Understand cohesion as reflected in lexis and grammatical markers ■ Understand lexis by drawing inferences about meaning from morphology and syntactic context

FIGURE 9.2. Matrix of Reading Skills, Subskills, and Strategies for Testing. Sources: Pugh (1978); Urquhart and Weir (1998); Weir (1993).

Reading Assessment Variables: Standards, Readers, and Texts

Top-down, bottom-up, and integrative approaches characterize reading processes and literacy acquisition in ways that enable us to sample measurable performances, although researchers do not universally agree on what behaviors most accurately reflect reading skill.

Standards

Whereas *a priori* literacy standards such as those formalized by ACTFL, CEFR, ILR, IRA, TESOL, and so on (see Chapter 4) implicitly or explicitly adopt a componential view, they usefully delineate expected performance outcomes that align with instructional goals.[5] For example, the *Interagency Language Roundtable Language Skill Level Descriptions* are distributed on a five-point, ten-level scale. The following excerpts exemplify the rubric's L2 reading performance descriptors for the second true score level (R-1—Reading 1 [Elementary Proficiency]:

"Sufficient comprehension to read very simple connected written material in a form equivalent to usual ... typescript ... Able to read and understand known language elements that have been recombined in new ways to achieve different meanings" (Interagency Language Roundtable, 2008). Like the *TESOL Standards* and *CEFR* (see Chapter 4), ILR skill-level descriptors provide crucial benchmarks for assessing reading development.

In addition to explicit performance standards, day-to-day literacy instruction should guide assessment decisions: "A teacher-designed assessment process and associated criteria for evaluation [should] closely reflect what has been taught and how it has been taught" (Alderson, 2000, p. 192). We recommend the following guidelines for devising assessments that authentically link literacy standards and instruction:

- Frequently review course aims and performance standards in designing instruments;
- Ensure content and construct validity by matching instruments to target skills and strategies;
- Monitor for unfavorable bias and variation across instruments, texts, tasks, and learners;
- Design instruments to elicit what students know and have been taught. (Aebersold & Field, 1997; Brantley, 2007; Cohen, 1994; Cooper & Kiger, 2001; Hughes, 2003)

A key step toward developing valid reading assessments includes articulating *test specifications*, which can consist of a simple outline of the instrument. "The level of detail contained in test specifications [may] vary considerably," but specifications for classroom assessments "are likely to be fairly short, with much information implicit in the setting" (Alderson, 2000, p. 171). In contrast, specifications for high-stakes tests must reflect "much more detail and control over what item writers produce" (Alderson, 2000, p. 171). For continuous classroom assessment, Brown (2004) suggested that specifications consist minimally of "(a) a broad outline of the test, (b) what skills you will test, and (c) what the items will look like" (p. 50).[6] Specifications lay groundwork for constructing a meaningful instrument, as does an account of the chief variables that influence reading processes and literacy development. These variables include the *reader*, the *texts* selected for use in assessment activities, the *tasks* that comprise the assessment, and the individual *items* included in these tasks.

Reader Variables

Chapters 2 and 4 examine L2 reader variables and their interaction with L2 literacy development and reading skills. Naturally, the same background characteristics that affect learning to read, needs assessment, and curriculum development are just as germane when it comes to evaluating learner performance and progress. To that list of learner characteristics, we would add test-taking experience and skill, as well as affective variables such as anxiety when reading under speeded conditions (Airasian & Russell, 2008; Alderson, 2000; Brown, 2004).

Text Variables

Chapter 3 directly addresses text-based considerations in teaching L2 reading, and Chapter 8 examines the need to maximize vocabulary development in students' encounters with L2 texts. The textual dimensions that should inform materials selection and reading instruction should likewise inform assessment. Thus, we will not repeat our treatment of guiding principles for selecting appropriate texts, but rather offer a compressed checklist of text components that affect comprehension and, by extension, the effectiveness of assessments:

- ☐ Genre, text type, and rhetorical structure;
- ☐ Topical and thematic range;
- ☐ Propositional content;
- ☐ Text density and linguistic complexity;
- ☐ Lexical range;
- ☐ Channel (i.e., nature and quantity of nonverbal information, such as graphs, charts, illustrations, and so forth);
- ☐ Medium (i.e., paper or digital presentation);
- ☐ Typographical features;
- ☐ Length (Alderson, 2000; Hudson, 2007; Read, 2000; Urquhart & Weir, 1998).

These attributes together influence *text difficulty* or *readability*, which varies by reader and text (see Chapters 3 and 8). Readability measures must account for how "certain text properties—primarily the arrangement of the propositions in the text base . . . word frequency and sentence length—interact with the reader's processing strategies and resources" (Miller & Kintsch, 1980, p. 348). Arcane texts are harder to process, whereas texts on everyday topics situated in familiar settings are "likely to be easier to process than those that are not" (Alderson, 2000, p. 62). Furthermore, "the more concrete, imaginable, and interesting, the more readable the text" (Alderson, 2000). Finally, it is crucial to monitor and vary text length, as excessively short texts do not allow for search reading, skimming, or scanning (Urquhart & Weir, 1998).

Task and Item Development in L2 Reading Assessment: Principles and Procedures

Vital to decision-making about texts is pairing them with appropriate *tasks* for measuring reading comprehension skills, strategy use, and progress. We propose a few general guidelines for constructing instruments of all sorts before delving into controlled and constructed response task types. First, congruent with our recommendations for teaching reading, we encourage teachers to embrace variety as they undertake the work of developing tests. Concentrating on a single method, "say multiple-choice, will encourage teachers and pupils to ignore other exercise/ test types" (Alderson, 2000, p. 199). Second, we concur with Grellet's (1981) reminder that "an exercise should never be imposed on a text." On the contrary, "the text should always be the starting point for determining why one would normally read it, how it would be read, how it might relate to other information before thinking of a particular exercise" (p. 10).

In terms of devising exercises and items, assessment experts offer several directives:

- Questions and prompts should avoid lexical items that are more difficult (less frequent) than those in the target text.[7]
- Controlled response questions and prompts should elicit a single, unequivocal response; constructed response items should generate comparable performances or products that can be fairly measured using a single, *a priori* rubric.
- Questions and prompts should be formulated so that examinees who comprehend the text can provide a reasonable response.
- Distractor items and alternative responses should be as well-formed as the intended solutions (test-takers should not reject incorrect responses on the basis of their ungrammaticality).
- Exercises should not elicit knowledge or skills unrelated to reading (e.g., mathematics).
- Questions and prompts should not focus on incidental or insignificant material in the text.
- Successful item responses should not necessitate stylistic or other subjective judgments.
- The sequence of tasks and items should approximate the manner in which readers would typically process the target text.
- Exercises and items requiring skimming, searching, and so forth should precede prompts requiring careful (bottom-up) skills (Alderson, 2000; Bachman & Palmer, 1996; Brown, 2004; Fillmore & Kay, 1983).

Controlled Response

The preceding guidelines are useful for the two broad task categories examined here, namely, *controlled* and *constructed response* tasks. *Controlled response* items and tasks (sometimes called *directed response, selected response,* and *discrete-point item types*) elicit a particular operation, behavior, or linguistic form as evidence of comprehension (Alderson, 2000; Madsen, 1983). Controlled response exercises offer the significant advantage of requiring a single, unambiguous expected response or solution, making scoring objective and efficient (Bachman & Palmer, 1996). The controlled response format lends itself especially well to implementation via computer software and Web-based educational tools (Chapelle & Douglas, 2006; Douglas & Hegelheimer, 2007). For example, the WebCT suite (Blackboard, 2008)[8] now includes the test authoring program Respondus 3.5, which enables instructors and test writers to construct items using multiple-choice, true–false, matching, jumbled sentence, and short-answer templates (Respondus, 2008). Respondus software also enables test writers to develop an array of constructed response items eliciting paragraph-length output. These advantages assume that test writers follow the guidelines in the preceding section.

Controlled reading comprehension prompts may fall into one of the following categories:

- *Textually explicit questions:* Question or prompt and response are paraphrased or drawn from a single sentence in the text.
- *Textually implicit questions:* Question or prompt and response are neither paraphrased nor located in a single sentence, though they appear in the relevant passage.
- *Scriptally implicit questions:* Passage supplies only partial information needed to respond, requiring examinees to draw on their scripts (formal schemata). (Alderson, 2000; García, 1991; Koda, 2004)

Well-constructed implicit prompts can stimulate deep text processing, but the demands that they place on novice and intermediate-level readers limits their usefulness to assessments designed for more advanced readers. Textually explicit formats (e.g., multiple-choice, gap-filling, matching, and so forth) may nonetheless be appropriate for L2 readers at all proficiency levels. Teachers often reject controlled response tasks because they tend to be mechanical, non-communicative, minimally representative of complex reading (sub)processes, and challenging for teachers to write. Researchers have likewise questioned their construct validity on the grounds that controlled response exercises may provide better measures of memory and recall than of actual text comprehension and interpretation (Britton & Gulgoz, 1991; Hudson, 2007; Koda, 2004; Meyer & Freedle, 1984). On the other hand, controlled response tasks and items are often quite familiar to L2 readers, can reliably measure comprehension, and can provide useful practice—especially when used in combination with constructed response exercises.

Multiple choice. The *multiple-choice* (MC) format, familiar to students around the world, has played a longstanding, though not uncontroversial, role in educational measurement. As Brown (2004) observed, "the traditional 'Read a passage and answer some questions' technique is undoubtedly the oldest and the most common . . . Virtually every proficiency test uses the format, and one would rarely consider assessing reading without some component of the assessment involving impromptu reading and responding to questions" (p. 204). The MC technique offers both reliability and scoring efficiency (Bachman & Palmer, 1996; Fulcher & Davidson, 2007; Weir, 1993). Bailey (1998) succinctly defined MC items as:

> Test items that consist of a stem (the beginning of the item) and either three, four, or five answer options (with four options probably being the most common format). One, and only one, of the options is correct, and this is called the key. The incorrect options are called distractors. (p. 245)

Hughes (2003) described MC items as "notoriously difficult" to construct, and the extent of research on their development, validity, reliability, and washback effects bear out his appraisal. The passage and accompanying MC comprehension items in Figure 9.3 provide a sampling of how we might construct a range of MC items as a function of the text, course goals, and knowledge of our student readers. The 358-word extract from *The Story of English* (McCrum, MacNeil, & Cran, 2002) was selected for a high-intermediate or advanced EAP reading course, given its Flesch-Kincaid Reading Ease score of 42 (Grade 10 equivalent). *Vocabulary Profiler* analysis showed that 71% of the words in the text are among the 1,000 most frequent words in Modern English, 11% are among the second 1,000 most frequent words, and 18% are off-list (see Chapters 3 and 8 for links to these tools).

It should be noted that this task does *not* comprise a string of traditional comprehension questions tracking the linear thread of the passage. Rather, the array of 10 prompts addresses reader comprehension of these dimensions:

- Topic and main idea(s);
- Word forms and collocations in authentic context;
- Vocabulary in context;
- Inference (implied fact and details);
- Grammatical and discursive structure (e.g., co-reference);
- Scanning for specific, explicit detail;

- Excluding unstated facts and details;
- Supporting evidence (facts, details, ideas).

We modeled these items to align with the specifications of the reading subsections of the current-generation TOEFLiBT, which are grounded in research on the skills exhibited by accomplished academic readers (Cohen & Upton, 2006; Educational Testing Service, n.d.; Enright et al., 2000; Rosenfeld, Leung, & Oltman, 2001). Several items elicit effective reading strategies, such as skimming for main ideas, scanning for specific information, deriving meaning from context, inferencing, and so forth. Each item focuses on a single chunk of text or underlying idea, with stems taking the form of either incomplete statements or direct questions (Kehoe, 1995). To write similarly structured tasks based on brief reading passages, teachers can certainly begin with specifications for rigorously validated instruments such as TOEFLiBT and IELTS. In addition to consulting the specifications of established tests, we encourage readers to explore technology-based reading assessments such as TOEFLiBT, which uses interactive functions of the computer interface (Chapelle & Douglas, 2006). In TOEFLiBT reading subtests, candidates not only respond to conventional MC items, but also click and drag to insert missing material into texts, moving their answers into the appropriate location on the screen (see Further Reading and Resources for links to the ETS demonstration site).

Despite their widespread use, MC tasks are not without their critics. Hughes (2003) charged that MC items reflect weaknesses and vulnerabilities that teachers, test writers, and test-takers should consider. First, he asserted that MC prompts elicit only recognition knowledge and promote guessing, both of which can undermine construct validity and generate misleading scores. Similarly, MC questions may place severe constraints on the material covered, potentially generating negative washback. That is, tests that rely heavily on MC items can lead examinees to focus largely, if not exclusively, on test-taking strategies, at the expense of developing more adaptive top-down and interactive literacy skills. Hughes further noted that the MC format makes cheating relatively easy (cf. Bailey, 1998). Finally, he emphasized that constructing valid, reliable MC items is a highly complex challenge for even the most experienced test writers. We do not dispute any of these objections; we readily affirm that designing MC tasks is difficult. Nonetheless, because the MC format is widely used and because MC items can elicit a range of reading behaviors, we encourage teachers to use them judiciously, in combination with other controlled and constructed response exercise types (Fulcher & Davidson, 2007).

Cloze and gap-filling. A second controlled response method for assessing reading involves *gap-filling* tasks, which include *cloze* exercises and their derivatives. For Bachman and Palmer (1996), gap-filling exercises elicit *limited production responses* and therefore contrast with the MC format, as gap-filling requires

Directions: *Preview the questions and statements below before reading the passage. Next, select the option that best answers each question or completes each statement. Write your responses in the boxes at left.*

The Story of English

The computer industry in Silicon Valley is a textbook illustration of the way in which the language coined in California is quickly adopted throughout the English-speaking world. The heartland of America's electronics industry is a super-rich suburb immediately north of San José, about an hour's drive south of San Francisco. It is the home of more than 3,000 companies, including such famous information-technology names as Apple and Hewlett-Packard. Alongside the giants there are dozens of smaller companies spawned from the frustrated talent of other companies and from the computer science graduate programmes of nearby Stanford University at Palo Alto. The streets have names like Semiconductor Drive. The valley is the home of the video game, the VDU, the word processor, the silicon chip and, for the English language, it is a rich jargon factory. Words like *interface, software, input, on-line, data-processing, high tech, computer hacker, to access, diskette* and *modem* are already in most dictionaries of contemporary English.

To be able to use such words easily is to be *computer-literate*. But it is the jargon phrases of Silicon Valley, reapplied to non-computing circumstances to make a kind of high-tech slang, that may eventually prove as influential on the language in the long run. In 1985 John Barry, a columnist on one of Silicon Valley's myriad journals, *Infoworld*, had a list of such usages, plus their slang translations:

He's an *integrated* kind of guy. (He's got his act together.)

He doesn't have *both drives on line.* (He isn't very coordinated.)

She's *high res.* (She's on the ball.)

They're in *emulation mode.* (They're copy cats; they're rip-off artists.)

He's in *beta-test stage.* (He's "wet behind the ears".)

The Silicon Valley story highlights the way in which English permeates the world in which we live through its effortless infiltration of technology and society. In fact, there is evidence that within the last decade or so, this process has evolved to the point where English is no longer wholly dependent on its British and American parents, and is now a global language with a supranational momentum.
(McCrum et al. 2002, pp. 30–31)

☐ 1. What is the main topic of this passage?
   A. Silicon Valley companies
   B. Influences of high-technology industries on language change
   C. Computer literacy
   D. The negative effects of computer jargon

☐ 2. In line 3, the word "heartland" could best be replaced by
   A. territory
   B. soul
   C. substance
   D. center

☐ 3. The passage implies that
   A. employees of small high-tech companies are frustrated
   B. British and American English are no longer different
   C. new words coined by people in California have already been adopted by
      English speakers elsewhere in the world
   D. high-tech slang is now used by parents

☐ 4. The pronoun "it" in line 4 refers to
   A. Silicon Valley
   B. San Francisco
   C. San José
   D. Apple Computer

☐ 5. According to the passage, Silicon Valley
   A. is contaminated by semiconductor waste
   B. is home to only one university
   C. is an affluent community
   D. suffers from high unemployment

☐ 6. Which of the following is *not* mentioned about Silicon Valley?
   A. Hewlett-Packard and Apple Computer operate there
   B. Its high-tech jargon has spread
   C. Some of its streets are named for aspects of the computer industry
   D. It is home to a large number of hackers

☐ 7. The passage indicates that English is becoming a global language because
   A. word processing has become more and more common around the world
   B. it is the primary language of technology and has infiltrated sectors that rely on
      technology
   C. American and British employees enjoy using high-tech slang such as "They're
      in emulation mode"
   D. columnists promote its use in high-tech journals

☐ 8. In the authors' view, it took about _____ years for the global spread of computer
   technology to transform English into a kind of universal language.
   A. ten
   B. twelve
   C. twenty
   D. twenty-five

☐ 9. The word "permeates" in line 28 is closest in meaning to which of the following?
   A. destroys
   B. animates
   C. penetrates
   D. undermines

☐ 10. According to the passage, a chief influence of computer-related jargon on English
   involves
   A. new products released by Hewlett-Packard and Apple Computer
   B. growing numbers of small companies spawned by Stanford University
      computer science graduates
   C. the translation of slang from numerous other languages
   D. the spread of high-tech jargon to non-technology-related uses

KEY: 1. B 2. D 3. C 4. A 5. C 6. D 7. B 8. A 9. C 10. D

FIGURE 9.3. Sample Reading Comprehension Passage and
Multiple-Choice Task.

examinees to generate a word, phrase, or a sentence. Test developers create gap-filling texts by deleting selected elements from texts, a process sometimes called *mutilation* (Bailey, 1998). "Ideally, there should only be one correct answer for each gap" (Alderson, Clapham, & Wall, 1995, p. 54). Because they are indirect, gap-filling approaches remain controversial, as they are thought to measure "only a limited part of our construct of reading proficiency, namely microlinguistic contributory skills." Furthermore, gap-filling tasks may not provide "any evidence on a candidate's ability to extract information expeditiously by search reading or skimming a text or to read it carefully to understand its main ideas" (Urquhart & Weir, 1998, p. 155). Such concerns about the validity of gap-filling methods require the attention of teachers and test writers. At the same time, because measurable grammatical expertise consistently correlates highly with reading comprehension scores (Alderson, 1993; see Chapter 4), gap-filling exercises may be useful, particularly "if the focus of attention . . . is at the microlinguistic level" (Urquhart & Weir, 1998, p. 156). Such might be the case in EAP or ESP contexts where novice readers must develop both a receptive and productive mastery of discipline-specific vocabulary items and their range of meanings (see Chapter 8).

Cloze tasks typically consist of level-appropriate reading passages in which every n^{th} element following the first sentence is replaced with a blank equal in length to that of the missing element (Alderson et al., 1995). Reading passages may be authentic or composed for the purpose of testing. *Cloze*-type exercises, named to capture the Gestalt concept of "closure," are thought to generate valid measures of reading skill, as they require test-takers to activate their *expectancy grammar* (formal, linguistic schemata), background knowledge (content schemata), and strategic ability (Oller, 1979). In filling the evenly spaced gaps, readers must make calculated guesses by drawing on their rhetorical, grammatical, lexical, and content knowledge (Brown, 2004; Horowitz, 2008). The cloze task in Figure 9.4 was constructed by deleting every sixth item, beginning with the first word of the second sentence, from a passage selected from *Reading Matters 4*, an advanced-level ESL textbook (Wholey & Henein, 2002).

Hypnosis

Directions: *Complete the passage by filling in the gaps.*

What is it? Using one of many techniques—like inducing relaxation by asking the subject to count backward—a practitioner brings on a trancelike state. While in it, a patient (1) _____ focus on healing thoughts or (2) ____ letting go of negative habits. (3) _____ one person in ten cannot (4) ____ hypnotized.

    Is it effective? No (5) _____ knows why, but hypnosis does (6) _____ to work for certain conditions. (7) _____ speculate that it acts by (8) _____ the unconscious mind, and putting (9) _____ generally not within our control, (10) _____ as pain perception, under our (11) _____.

KEY: 1. might 2. on 3. About 4. be 5. one 6. seem 7. Scientists 8. touching 9. things 10. such 11. power

---

FIGURE 9.4. Sample Cloze Exercise.
Text source: Wholey and Henein (2002, p. 42).

Testers should avoid drawing broad inferences about comprehension based on cloze tasks, which are essentially word-based. Research suggests that a minimum of 50 deletions is required to produce reliable outcomes and that "quite different cloze tests can be produced on the same text by beginning the ... deletion procedure at a different starting point" (Alderson, 2000, p. 208). A limitation of the nth word, or *fixed-ratio*, deletion technique is that it lacks flexibility: Gaps that examinees find impossible to complete can only be amended by altering the initial deleted word. Finally, as readers might have noticed in examining the sample task in Figure 9.4, scoring cloze tasks can be challenging because test-takers may supply many possible answers for a single gap, thereby comprising scoring consistency (Alderson et al., 1995). Generating a workable response key requires careful pretesting. The *exact word* scoring method awards credit only if test-takers supply the exact word deleted by the tester. In contrast, *appropriate word* scoring credits grammatically correct and contextually appropriate responses (Brown, 2004).

Two variations on the cloze procedure are worth mentioning, although neither has enjoyed widespread popularity. The *C-test* method involves obliterating the second half of every second or third word (based on the number of letters), requiring examinees to restore each word, as in the following sentence, which opened this chapter:

> Among the ma_ _ demanding functions perfo_ _ _ _ by educators, measu_ _ _ _ and reporting lea_ _ _ _ performance can b_ one of t_ _ most intimidating.

Some evidence supports the reliability and validity of C-tests (Dörnyei & Katona, 1992; Klein-Braley, 1985), but they are not widely used, perhaps because "many readers ... find C-tests even more irritating ... than cloze tests" (Alderson, 2000, p. 225). A second variation on the cloze format, the *cloze-elide* procedure, entails inserting intrusive words into a text, as in this familiar excerpt from the beginning of this chapter:

> Among the many some demanding functions performed then by educators, measuring and reporting my learner performance can be have one of the our most intimidating threatening.

Sometimes called the *intrusive word technique,* cloze-elide procedures require test-takers to detect and cross out items that don't belong. This method might more appropriately measure processing speed than reading comprehension (Alderson, 2000; Davies, 1975). A problematic feature of cloze-elide is that "neither the words to insert nor the frequency of insertion [has] any rationale." Furthermore, "fast and efficient readers are not adept at detecting the intrusive words. Good readers naturally weed out such potential interruptions" (Brown, 2004, p. 204).

In *rational deletion* exercises (alternatively known as *modified cloze* tasks), the tester "decides, on some rational basis, which words to delete" (Alderson, 2000, p. 207). Rational deletion tasks might focus on specific lexical items or grammatical structures (Horwitz, 2008). This method allows for some flexibility, but test writers generally avoid leaving fewer than five or six words between gaps, as the lack of intervening text can make it unduly difficult for examinees to restore missing item(s). Figure 9.5 presents two gap-filling exercises based on the same reading passage from *Weaving It Together* (Broukal, 2004), a beginning-level ESL/EFL reading textbook. In Sample A, the deleted items aim to elicit test-takers' abilities to make inferences based on co-reference (items 1–4), entailment (item 4), and collocation (items 5 and 6). In contrast, Sample B requires examinees to supply missing prepositions.

To reduce the scoring difficulties associated with cloze and rational deletion tasks, Brown (2004) suggested presenting gap-filling exercises in MC format to facilitate both manual and computerized scoring procedures. Rather than requir-

---

Sample A: *Birthdays*

Directions: *Complete the passage by filling in the gaps.*

Everybody has a birthday. Many children in other countries celebrate their (1) ____ like children in the United States. They have a birthday (2) ____, gifts, and sometimes a birthday party for friends. Friends and family gather around a table with a birthday cake on it. They sing "Happy Birthday to You." Two American sisters wrote this (3) ____ in 1893, but people still sing this song today! The birthday cake usually has lighted (4) ____ on it, one candle for each year of your life. The birthday child makes a wish and then (5) ____ out all the candles. If the child blows out the candles in one breath, the wish will come (6) ____. Other countries have different customs.

KEY: 1. birthdays   2. cake   3. song   4. candles   5. blows   6. true

Sample B: *Birthdays*

Directions: *Complete the passage by filling in the gaps.*

Everybody has a birthday. Many children (1) ____ other countries celebrate their birthdays like children in the United States. They have a birthday cake, gifts, and sometimes a birthday party (2) ____ friends. Friends and family gather (3) ____ a table with a birthday cake on it. They sing "Happy Birthday (4) ____ You." Two American sisters wrote this song in 1893, but people still sing this song today! The birthday cake usually has lighted candles (5) ____ it, one candle for each year of your life. The birthday child makes a wish and then blows out all the candles. If the child blows out the candles (6) ____ one breath, the wish will come true. Other countries have different customs.

KEY: 1. in   2. for   3. around   4. to   5. on   6. in

FIGURE 9.5. Sample Rational Deletion (Gap-Filling) Exercises.
Text source: Broukal (2004, p. 3).

ing students to supply missing words on their own, MC gap-filling exercises involve selecting one of four or five items for each gap, provided in the instrument itself. Thus, for Sample B in Figure 9.5, the MC options for item 1 might include: A. *of* B. *in* C. *at* D. *on* E. *none of the above*. Such tasks must satisfy criteria for effective MC tasks, including provision of appropriate distractors (see above), a labor-intensive process. A less time-consuming alternative would be to format cloze and rational deletion tasks as shown in Figures 9.4 and 9.5, supplying test-takers with an alphabetized list of missing items, from which they would select appropriate words and insert them in the corresponding gaps.

Matching. Matching tasks, a variation on MC and gap-filling formats, present examinees with two sets of stimuli that must be matched against each other, as in Figure 9.6. If our criterion is reading comprehension, we might well raise questions about the validity of matching tasks: Pure guessing might yield a score that does not reflect the test-taker's reading skill at all. On the other hand, as with gap-filling items, matching tasks embedded in coherent discourse can, in principle, elicit top-down, bottom-up, and interactive reading skills. An alternative to traditional MC and gap-filling formats, matching tasks may be somewhat easier to construct, although they "can become more of a puzzle-solving process than a genuine test of comprehension as examinees struggle with the search for a match" (Brown, 2004, p. 198). Alderson (2000) proposed more sophisticated, discourse-oriented variations in which test-takers match complete utterances (e.g., topic sentences, sentences extracted from within paragraphs) to their corresponding positions in untreated, coherent texts, as in Figure 9.7.

Though still a controlled response exercise, the matching format involves text reconstruction, activating readers' content schemata, formal schemata, and strategic skill (semantic and lexical inferencing, applying knowledge of semantic fields and subset relations). The design derives from the well-known *strip-story* technique in which students reassemble excerpts (strips) of a coherent narrative text. Sequencing and text reconstruction tasks offer potential for positive washback, as these formats require bottom-up, top-down, and interactive subskills. A further advantage is that reconstruction can be easily adapted for computer-based

---

Directions: *Complete the passage by filling each gap with one of the words from the list below.*

Think of your memory as a vast, overgrown jungle. This memory jungle is (1) ____ with wild plants, twisted trees, and creeping (2) ____. It spreads over thousands of square (3) ____. Imagine that the jungle is bounded on all sides by (4) ____ mountains. There is only one entrance to the jungle, a (5) ____ pass through the mountains that opens into a small grassy (6) ____.

Choose from among the following:
area   impassable   miles   narrow   thick   vines   years   desirable

FIGURE 9.6. Sample Matching Exercise.
Text source: Wholey and Henein (2002, p. 86).

Directions: *For items 1–4, choose which of the sentences (A–E) below fit into the numbered gaps in the passage, "Earth's Greenhouse." There is one extra sentence that does not fit into any of the gaps. Indicate your answers at the bottom of the page.*

Earth's Greenhouse

Life on Earth is totally dependent on the greenhouse effect.
Several naturally occurring gases in the atmosphere—such as carbon dioxide, nitrous oxide and methane—act like the glass in a greenhouse and trap some of the heat from the sun as it is radiated back from the surface of the

earth. ⎣1⎦ . . . .

In the 20th century, we created these gases artificially with a massive use of carbon-based fuels—mainly coal and oil. In 1990, humankind artificially pumped about 16 billion metric tons of carbon dioxide into the

atmosphere. ⎣2⎦ . . . . In the last few decades, the

concentration of carbon dioxide in the atmosphere increased by 25%. ⎣3⎦ . . . .

. . . . The director general of the United Nations Environment Program gloomily stated that it would "take a miracle" to save the world's remaining tropical forests.

⎣4⎦ . . . . If today's energy technology is not changed, there

may be an average temperature rise of 5 degrees Celsius in the next 50 years. That may not sound like much, but if we said a river was 5 feet deep, you may find, as you go across, that some parts might be 2 feet deep and others 20 feet deep.

Choose from among the following:

A. By 1999, that figure had risen to 25 billion.
B. If these gases were not there, our planet would be too cold for life as we know it.
C. The insurance industry is preparing itself for "mega-catastrophes," including storms that could do more than $30 billion worth of damage.
D. The artificial increase in greenhouse gases is causing a slow, small rise in the Earth's temperature.
E. Tropical rain forests absorb large amounts of carbon dioxide, but we are cutting them down on a grand scale.

Write your answers here:

1. ___ 2. ___ 3. ___ 4. ___
KEY: 1. B 2. A 3. E 4. D

FIGURE 9.7. Text Reconstruction/Matching Exercise.
Text source: Martin (2006, pp. 103–104).

administration. As mentioned above, TOEFLiBT currently features similar reading subtests, as do comparable large-scale assessments. Chapelle and Douglas (2006) described several technologies designed to administer assessments using this format via interactive software and Web-based tools such as WebCT. Text reconstruction/matching should perhaps be reserved for assessing intermediate- to advanced-level readers, as the procedure requires well-developed L2 reading proficiency. Alderson et al. (1995) also cautioned that such sequencing tasks can be tricky, as we cannot assume that a given text exemplifies a single "logical" order.

Scanning tasks. Scanning refers to reading strategies for locating relevant material in a text (see Chapters 1 and 5). We can assess scanning strategies and skills, comprehension, and efficiency by presenting examinees with a prose text or graphic (e.g., a table, chart, or graph) and instructing them to identify relevant information. Appropriate texts for scanning tests may range from brief samples such as short editorials and essays, news articles, menus, application forms, and charts to short stories, textbook chapters, and technical reports. Objectives for scanning tests might include locating discrete pieces of data in the target text, including:

- Dates, names, and locations in essays, articles, chapters, and the like;
- The setting of a narrative text;
- The chief divisions (headings, subheadings, and so forth) of a book chapter;
- The primary findings or conclusions reported in a research article or technical report;
- A result or quantitative outcome reported in a specified cell in a data table;
- The cost of a dish on a restaurant menu;
- Information needed to complete an application or form. (Brown, 2004; Grellet, 1981)

As controlled response tasks, scanning exercises can be scored objectively and systematically using a simple answer key, provided task directions are specific and transparent (e.g., *How old is the narrator when the story begins? What is the price of the strawberry shortcake on the lunch menu?*). Scoring might also account for test-takers' speed, as a main purpose of scanning is to identify salient elements of a text at a rapid pace.

Editing. A final controlled response format consists of requiring examinees to edit selectively treated passages drawn from authentic sources. Simple in concept and design, *editing* tasks consist of passages in which the test writer has introduced errors or gaps that test-takers must identify. Brown (2004) highlighted several specific advantages associated with editing exercises involving coherent, connected discourse. First, the process is authentic, as students are likely to encounter connected prose in short texts. Second, by stimulating proofreading, this activity promotes grammatical awareness and encourage students to attend to bottom-up skills. Third, editing tasks allow the tester to "draw up specifications for . . . grammatical and rhetorical categories" that match course content, thereby enhancing content validity (Brown, 2004, p. 207). A final advantage is that, because editing exercises revolve around authentic texts, they are easy to construct and adapt to students' proficiency levels. Moreover, we can introduce errors and omissions representative of recurrent malformations in students' production.

As Figure 9.8 indicates, editing tests can present errors and omissions in MC format or can elicit somewhat more open-ended responses (Alderson, 2000). For instance, we can ask candidates to identify a single malformation per line of text and to write the corrected version opposite the line, as in Sample A. A variation on the editing technique can resemble gap-filling or cloze-elide formats. That is, we may delete words from a text without replacing the deleted items with a gap,

---

Sample A

Directions: *Each line of the following passage contains an error. Underline the error, then write each correction on the corresponding line at right. The first one has been done for you.*

A variety of element ^ can positively or negatively affect	1. _____ elements _____
comprehension. Some examples is fatigue, the reader's purpose for	2. _____
reading, the presence or absence of strategies for deal with	3. _____
comprehension roadblocks, the difficulty level on the text, and the	4. _____
reader's interest in the topic. Two other components who play a large	5. _____
role in the comprehension process are the readers background	6. _____
knowledge and the structure of the text. If the topic were familiar, the	7. _____
reader comprehends more easy and more completely. The structure	8. _____
of narrative text makes it easier for comprehend than expository text.	9. _____
Let's examine every of these components.	10. _____

KEY: 1. ~~element~~ elements   2. ~~is~~ are   3. ~~deal~~ dealing   4. ~~on~~ of   5. ~~who~~ that   6. ~~readers~~ reader's   7. ~~were~~ is
8. ~~easy~~ easily   9. ~~for~~ to   10. ~~every~~ each

Sample B

Directions: *Some words have been omitted from the passage below. Indicate the location of the missing word by inserting a caret (^), then write the missing word at right, as in the example.*

A variety ^ elements can positively or negatively affect comprehension.	1. _____ of _____
Some examples are fatigue, the reader's purpose for reading, the	
presence or absence of strategies for dealing comprehension	2. _____
roadblocks, the difficulty level of the text, and reader's interest in	3. _____
the topic. Two other components play a large role in the	4. _____
comprehension process are the reader's background knowledge and	
the structure of the text. The topic is familiar, the reader comprehends	5. _____
more easily and more completely. The structure of narrative text makes	
easier to comprehend than expository text. Let's examine each of	6. _____
components.	7. _____

KEY: 1. variety of elements   2. dealing with comprehension   3. and the reader's   4. components that play
5. . . . . text. If the topic   6. makes it easier   7. of these components

FIGURE 9.8. Sample Editing Tasks.
Text source: Caldwell (2008, p. 176).

as in Sample B. Examinees locate the missing word and write it in the answer column. Test writers select a maximum of one omission per line, leaving some lines intact.

Critics of editing tasks contend that the technique targets a very narrow range of abilities involved in authentic encounters with text (Alderson, 2000). At the same time, editing necessitates careful reading, and, though an indirect index of reading ability, morphosyntactic skill tends to be a robust predictor of reading proficiency. In addition, like MC, gap-filling, and text reconstruction/matching tests, editing exercises lend themselves easily to computer-adapted modes of delivery (Chapelle & Douglas, 2006; Jewett, 2005; Kinzer & Verhoeven, 2007). Materials developers and test writers have developed a much vaster array of controlled response task types than we can introduce here. We encourage readers to consult the L1 and L2 literacy assessment sources listed in Further Reading and Resources.

Constructed Response

As the name suggests, in a *constructed response* task, "the test taker actually has to produce or construct a response" (Bachman & Palmer, 1996, p. 54). In contrast, controlled or discrete-point testing formats aim to test "one 'thing' at a time" (Alderson, 2000, p. 207). By now, we hope it is clear that the relationship between controlled and constructed response formats is complementary. Certain types of gap-filling and even matching tests necessitate production on the part of examinees, as noted above. Bachman and Palmer (1996) distinguished between *limited production* and *extended production response* tasks. An *extended production response* is "longer than a single sentence or utterance, and can range from two sentences or utterances to virtually free composition, either oral or written" (Bachman & Palmer, 1996, p. 54). Extended production often entails text interpretation and/or manipulation, generating variation in examinees' responses. Evaluating constructed responses may therefore involve a degree of subjectivity, which we can reduce by developing clear scoring rubrics (see below). We begin this section with a discussion of *information-transfer* and *short-answer* formats, limited-production types that we believe occupy a middle ground between controlled and constructed response. We then address increasingly integrative approaches to L2 reading assessment, in which "test designers aim to gain a much more general idea of how well students read" (Alderson, 2000, p. 207). The formats that we will sample range from free recall to text reconstruction.

Information transfer. A crucial reading skill entails capturing and interpreting graphemic and other visual information presented in graphic images (e.g., maps, charts, graphs, calendars, diagrams). Such subskills are imperative, given the frequency with which readers encounter texts via computer, a medium that largely favors graphic material—sometimes as a complement to traditional text, sometimes as a substitute for it (Barton, 2007; Chapelle & Douglas, 2006; Eagleton & Dobler, 2007; Jewett, 2005; Kinzer & Verhoeven, 2007; McKenna et al., 2006; Withrow, 2004). *Information transfer* tests require examinees to "identify in the target text the required information and then to transfer it, often in some transposed form, on to a table, map, or whatever" (Alderson, 2000, p. 242). Responses may consist of simple inputs such as names, numbers, and so forth, facilitating objective scoring; on the other hand, information transfer can require constructed responses (e.g., phrases, sentences, and paragraphs). Information transfer can also entail converting verbal input into nonverbal output and vice versa. To comprehend, interpret, and manipulate information across verbal and nonverbal media, readers must:

- Understand conventions of various types of graphic representation;
- Comprehend labels, headings, numbers, and symbols;
- Infer relationships among graphic elements;
- Infer meanings, messages, and relationships that are not presented overtly. (Brown, 2004; McKenna et al., 2006, 2008).

Assessing these abilities and strategies involves a range of tasks that may rely on listening, speaking, and writings, particularly when information transfer tasks are delivered via Web-based electronic media (e.g., Moodle, WebCT). For example, Respondus 3.5 software (Respondus, 2008), described in our discussion of controlled response tests, enables test writers to incorporate images, graphics, and audio and video input into assessment tasks that elicit information transfer from test-takers (see Airasian & Russell, 2008; Eagleton & Dobler, 2007; Valmont, 2002). Figure 9.9 presents suggestions for designing simple information transfer tasks.

We would caution that information transfer tests can introduce cognitive and cultural bias. For instance, a test that requires students to identify statistical data in a factual text and then to transfer those data to empty cells in a table may disadvantage examinees who have not yet developed schemata for tabular presentation. Similarly, information transfer formats can be complicated and therefore confusing for test-takers with little or no experience with multiple modes of information representation. Examinees may "spend so much time understanding what is required and what should go where . . . that performance may be poor on what is linguistically a straightforward task" (Alderson, 2000, p. 248). Test format may thus introduce cognitive difficulties that are not actually present in the text itself. Finally, test writers should avoid materials in which graphics are already associated with a prose text. Deleting data points from a graphic text and then requiring candidates to restore them may pose an unfair challenge: Once the relationship between graphic and verbal material has been disrupted by deletion, "the verbal text becomes harder—if not impossible—to understand" (Alderson, 2000, p. 248).

Short-answer comprehension and recall tasks. The "age old short-answer format," as Brown (2004, p. 207) called it, is a familiar limited production response type that offers a practical alternative to MC and comparably "objective" controlled response tasks (Bachman & Palmer, 1996). The short-answer format presents examinees with a reading passage, followed by questions or prompts eliciting a one- or two-sentence response. Short-answer comprehension questions can reflect the same specifications as MC items, although they should be worded as interrogatives or as imperatives. To illustrate, we can revisit the *Story of English* text sample in Figure 9.3, adjusting the MC items to elicit short-answer responses, such as:

1. What is the topic of this passage?
2. What is meant by the expression, "jargon factory"?
3. According to the passage, how has the high-tech industry in Silicon Valley influenced the English language?
4. Why do you think the authors present computer jargon and slang as examples of the spread of English as a world language?

Match a graphic to a prose text

Read a text, then match the graphic(s) that best complement it, e.g.,

- Passage on the history of eyeglasses: *Click on the photo showing the first bifocal lenses.*
- Article reporting on comparative measurements of greenhouse gases: *Identify the chart showing increases in CO_2 released into the atmosphere over the past decade.*

Short-answer graphic interpretation

Review a graphic, then respond to direct information questions and prompts, e.g.,

- Statistical table: *Are there more dog owners or cat owners in the US?*
- Diagram of a household dishwasher: *Locate and label the vent.*
- Map: *Where is the light rail station?*
- Corporate organizational chart: *Which departments report to the Second Vice President?*

Describe and elaborate on a graphic image or text figure

Review a graphic image and construct a sentence or short paragraph response, e.g.,

- Map: *Measure the distances between Los Angeles, Santa Barbara, and Monterey. Which is the shortest? Which is the longest?*
- Restaurant menu: *What side dishes are served with the vegetarian lasagne?*
- Supermarket advertisements: *Which supermarket offers the lowest price on peaches?*

Short-answer interpretation of a passage and accompanying graphic

Review a passage and its graphic materials; synthesize and interpret the information, e.g.,

- Article on consumer price increases over the last half-century, with data represented in bar graphs: *Describe the main trends you see in consumer pricing, noting the commodities whose prices have increased the most and least.*
- Editorial reporting on the incidence of preventable, communicable diseases in the developing world, with accompanying statistical tables: *In which countries is the incidence of malaria the highest? Lowest? Where have HIV infection rates declined the most? Why?*

Generate inferences and predictions based on a graphic

After reviewing a graphic, report inferences and predictions, e.g.,

- Cake recipe: *How long do you think it would take you to assemble the ingredients, combine them, bake the cake, and frost it?*
- Stock market report: *Based on the company's year-end performance, do you think share values will increase, decrease, or remain stable? Explain your prediction.*
- Article reporting results of medical research: *Considering the frequency of illness relative to the risk factors explored, how vulnerable are you to developing this condition?*

Use graphic artifacts to demonstrate comprehension

Read a text and complete a graphic (a table, figure, or chart) to represent verbal information, e.g.,

- Driving directions from campus to sports arena: *On the map provided, trace the most direct route from campus to the sports arena.*
- Article on the decline of sea otter populations along the Pacific Coast: *Key in the data on sea otter numbers measured over the past 20 years; generate a histogram illustrating population declines.*
- Prose description of a student's class schedule: *Complete the empty scheduling grid with the missing information about Kentoku's current class schedule.*

FIGURE 9.9. Information Transfer Task Suggestions.

Sources: Brown (2004); Hughes (2003); Shrum and Glisan (2005).

Short-answer formats may enjoy reasonably high face validity, as they invite test-takers to compose answers that can provide the teacher with more evidence of comprehension (or comprehension failure) than controlled responses can generate. Test writers can deploy this method to measure a range of skills (e.g., comprehension, interpretation) and strategies (e.g., skimming, scanning, prediction). Brown (2004) pointed out that written responses produce the favorable washback effect of post-test discussion. On the other hand, "short-answer questions are not easy to construct. The question must be worded in such a way that all possible answers are foreseeable" (Alderson, 2000, p. 227). To overcome this threat to reliability and fairness, test writers must develop consistent specifications for accurate responses by asking themselves questions that a reader might reasonably ask. The reliability, fairness, and practicality of scoring short-answer tests depend on a complete solution key that accommodates unanticipated student responses (Airasian & Russell, 2008; Alderson, 2000).

Free recall tests. In *free recall* (or *immediate recall*) tests, examinees read a text that can be read and understood under timed conditions. They then report back everything they can remember, usually in writing (though oral recall tasks are not unknown). In contrast to short-answer, free recall is an extended response technique (Bachman & Palmer, 1996). Recall procedures provide "a purer measure of comprehension, [as] test questions do not intervene between the reader and the text" (Alderson, 2000, p. 230). Free recall tasks can generate positive washback by inducing students to attend to their recall abilities and encouraging them to develop their memory skills. Though simple in design, free recall poses scoring challenges and is perhaps most appropriate for conducting reading research than for L2 literacy assessment, as eliciting production in the L2 may be a fairer test of writing (or oral production) than of L2 reading comprehension (Alderson, 2000; Koda, 2004).

Note-taking and outlining. Further along the constructed response continuum are *note-taking* and *outlining*, informal procedures that can usefully assess L2 readers' comprehension of extensive texts (see Chapter 5). Although controlling administration conditions and speededness can be difficult, outlining and taking notes on an expository text (e.g., a textbook chapter) constitute authentic tasks that enjoy face validity. Note-taking is a common and productive literacy practice observed among many successful academic readers, particularly those who read to learn (Grabe & Stoller, 2002; Hirvela, 2004; Seymour & Walsh, 2006). Such exercises also reflect content, criterion, and consequential validity, as the procedures directly target text content, elicit comprehension processes, and activate text interpretation skills. Incorporating note-taking and outlining into the assessment plan can likewise generate positive washback. "Their utility is in the strategic training that learners gain in retaining information through marginal notes that highlight key information or organizational outlines that put supporting ideas into a visually manageable framework" (Brown, 2004, p. 215). With the help of learner training in note-taking and outlining, as well as a well-constructed

Reading diary.

rubric (see below), raters can evaluate students' notes and outlines as measures of effective reading strategies.

Summary and extended response. Perhaps the most obvious forms of constructed response test of reading comprehension and efficiency are conventional academic genres, such as summaries, compositions, and various types of extended response. In a summary test, examinees read a text and then summarize main ideas (Alderson, 2000). Among the constructs underlying summary exercises are understanding main ideas, distinguishing relevant material from less relevant material, organizing reactions to the text, and synthesizing information (Hirvela, 2004). Constructing summary prompts can be a relatively simple process, and experts tend to agree that simpler prompts are better. Brown (2004) provided the following example, which we have edited:

> Write a summary of the text. Your summary should be about one paragraph in length (100–150 words) and should include your understanding of the main idea and supporting ideas.

In contrast to a summary, which requires an overview or synopsis of a text's key ideas, a response elicits opinions about the material or perhaps comments on a specific proposition or textual element. The following prompt, designed to elicit an extended response to the sample text in Figure 9.3, asks examinees to interpret and react personally to the text:

> In the excerpt from *The Story of English*, the authors imply that English is a global language, partly because of the influence of technology. Write a complete paragraph in which you agree or disagree with the authors' claim. Support your opinion with details from the text and from your own experience.

A principal criterion for a satisfactory response would entail the writing sample's accuracy in capturing factual content, as well as its overt and covert arguments.

The apparent simplicity of prompts for such tasks can be deceiving. For example, scoring examinees' responses to open-ended prompts like the summary and paragraph examples above poses practical dilemmas. Should we rate summaries on the basis of writing quality? After all, a summary test inevitably elicits examinees' writing skills, in addition to their reading skills and critical abilities (Hirvela, 2004). If we are concerned with measuring reading subskills and strategies (e.g., inferencing, synthesizing multiple pieces of information), how can we ensure that a text expresses a single "main idea" or argument, as our prompts imply? Isn't it possible that a text can convey more than a single "main idea"? Alderson (2000) proposed an interesting method of determining a text's main ideas and the criteria for excellent, adequate, and unacceptable summaries: "[G]et the test constructors and summary markers to write their own summaries of the text, and then only to accept as 'main ideas' those that are included by an agreed proportion of respondents (say 100%, or 75%)" (p. 233).

We encourage teachers to utilize constructed response formats in L2 literacy assessment, as we believe that reading–writing connections should be maximized in teaching and evaluating reading (Hirvela, 2004). Nonetheless, we recommend caution, particularly with extended and involved written responses (e.g., summaries, paragraph-length responses, compositions). For instance, summary writing represents a skill set that many, if not most, L2 readers may not have mastered. Learning to summarize documents effectively requires careful scaffolding on the part of the teacher. We cannot simply require students to "write a summary" and expect them to produce meaningful, measurable samples that fairly represent constructs such as reading comprehension. Before using complex academic genres such as summaries or compositions as assessment vehicles, we must first equip learners with attendant writing skills and practice (Belcher & Hirvela, 2001; Ferris & Hedgcock, 2005; Hirvela, 2004; Hyland, 2004b).

Because student-generated summaries vary in structure, substance, length, accuracy, and lexical range, the most likely scoring methods are subjective, necessitating the use of a *scoring rubric*. A "flexible assessment tool," a rubric "allows teachers to make . . . precise and useful measurements" on the basis of "criteria necessary to attain graduated levels of mastery" (Groeber, 2007, p. 28). The following general characteristics, outlined by Shrum and Glisan (2005), typify the rubrics used to assess language and literacy skills:

- A *scale* or range of quantitative values to be assigned in scoring responses along a continuum of quality. Scales often range from 0 to 4, 5, or 6. Test writers may prefer an even number of total points (e.g., 4 or 6) to avoid the natural inclination to assign scores that converge around the middle of the scale.
- *Band descriptors* for each performance level to enhance reliability and prevent bias. The sample rubrics in Figures 9.10 and 9.11 contain four scoring bands; the longitudinal rubric in Figure 9.12 presents three.
- A *holistic* or *analytic design*.[9] *Holistic rubrics* evaluate responses as a whole, assigning a single numeric score to each response, as in Figure 9.10, which could be used to score responses to the summary/response prompts introduced above. *Analytic rubrics* such as the sample in

Figure 9.11 specify multiple rubrics or descriptors corresponding to each criterion or dimension elicited in the test. Figure 9.11 aims to facilitate scoring of oral or written responses to a work of narrative fiction and to justify scores by directly referencing specific performance features.

- Reference to *generic, genre-specific,* or *task-specific* expectations or standards. *Generic* rubrics or scales are "off-the-rack" scoring tools that scorers can use to evaluate a broad performance (as in Figure 9.12) or range of responses (e.g., student essays—see Ferris & Hedgcock, 2005; Glickman-Bond, 2006; Hyland, 2004b; Weigle, 2002). Generic rubrics are also used in standardized tests such as TOEFLiBT, whose integrated reading–writing sub-test is scored on a 0–5 scale (Educational Testing Service, 2004). *Genre-specific* rubrics target specific performance types within a category. *Task-specific* rubrics focus more narrowly on single tests or tasks (though the distinction between genre- and task-specific scales tends to blur in practice). We could classify the sample rubric in Figure 9.10 as genre-specific, as its scoring bands characterize unique features of summary and response genres. The sample rubric in Figure 9.11 could be classified as both genre- and task-specific: It targets both a performance genre (response to a work of fiction) and a specific task or test.

- *Potential for positive washback.* Well-designed rubrics, especially those proven to be reliable and valid, can play a key role in formative assessment by providing students with feedback on their performance and progress. "Rubrics show learners what good performance 'looks like' even before they perform an assessment task" (Shrum & Glisan, 2005, p. 373).

Many teachers use the terms *rubric* and *scoring guide* interchangeably, but it is useful to recall that, strictly speaking, *rubrics*: (1) explicitly measure a stated standard or goal (i.e., a performance, behavior, or quality); (2) spell out a range for rating examinee performance; and (3) define specific performance characteristics arrayed hierarchically so that band descriptors state the degree to which a standard has been achieved (Shrum & Glisan, 2005; San Diego State University, 2001). As *criterion-referenced* scoring tools, rubrics can ensure that scorers evaluate constructed responses with explicit reference to stated learning aims (e.g., SWBATs, course goals, and institutional standards; see Chapters 1, 4, and 5). Systematic use of reliable rubrics enables us to avoid the pitfall of determining "what constitutes a passing score prior to looking at student work samples," an ill-advised approach that, at best, coincides with *norm-referencing.* Instead, scores keyed to rubrics "should alert students to

Score	Descriptor
4	Sample clearly demonstrates complete comprehension of the text's main ideas, supporting evidence, and the links among them. Written in the examinee's own words, with occasional use of wording from the original text, the sample exhibits logical organization and fluent language use.
3	Sample demonstrates comprehension of main ideas and major textual elements, though supporting points and links among them may not be fully represented. Written mainly in the examinee's own words, the sample borrows vocabulary from the original. The sample contains occasional errors, but textual organization and language use are highly comprehensible.
2	Sample suggests only partial comprehension of the original text's main ideas and a weak grasp of supporting evidence. Noticeable borrowing of vocabulary and grammatical constructions from the original indicate marginal interpretation and paraphrasing skill. Organizational, linguistic, and lexical errors compromise the sample's comprehensibility.
1	Sample displays no comprehension or interpretation of the original text, largely or completely imitating the source material. Comprehensible passages may be extracted directly from the original, showing little or no effort to unify them.
0	Not a ratable sample or no response.

FIGURE 9.10. Sample Holistic Rubric for Rating Summaries and Responses.

their real levels of performance," directly serving the purpose of ongoing, formative assessment (Shrum & Glisan, 2005, p. 375). A final advantage of using rubrics in the assessment of constructed responses is that the scoring of individual tests and tasks can be linked to macro-level assessments such as the *longitudinal* rubric in Figure 9.12. Designed for evaluating and placing college-level students into ESL and EAP courses, this scale specifies both a global performance standard and measurable skill level descriptors for three proficiency levels.

Maximizing Controlled and Constructed Response Approaches in L2 Reading Assessment

We have reviewed several controlled and constructed response formats used in L2 reading assessment. Although our survey is far from comprehensive, the range of tools exemplified here should provide L2 literacy educators with options for developing fair, meaningful assessments and practical assessment plans. In the spirit of promoting continuous assessment, we encourage teachers and test writers to apply the principle that meaningful assessment *is* teaching. We further urge educators to build into their assessment plans a variety of formats, task

Task: Students read and respond interpretively to a work of fiction.

Standard: Display critical understanding of narrative fiction in an oral or written response.

Criterion	4	3	2	1	TOTAL
Classification ▪ Identifies story type ▪ Recognizes story mood ▪ Compares with other stories	3 complete elements present	2 complete elements present	1 complete element present	Evidence of 2+ incomplete elements	___ × 3 = ___ points
Plot ▪ Retells in correct order ▪ Distinguishes major events from supporting details ▪ Recognizes subplots	3 complete elements present	2 complete elements present	1 complete element present	Evidence of 2+ incomplete elements	___ × 3 = ___ points
Conflict ▪ Identifies protagonist's struggle or dilemma ▪ Understands nature of protagonist's struggle/dilemma ▪ Identifies type of conflict	3 complete elements present	2 complete elements present	1 complete element present	Evidence of 2+ incomplete elements	___ × 4 = ___ points
Theme(s) ▪ Infers author's underlying message(s) ▪ Synthesizes theme(s) accurately in own words ▪ Identifies passages that convey theme(s)	3 complete elements present	2 complete elements present	1 complete element present	Evidence of 2+ incomplete elements	___ × 5 = ___ points
Comments:					Total score: ___/60 = ___

Scale: 54–60 = A, 48–53 = B, 43–47 = C, 36–42 = D, 30–35 = E

FIGURE 9.11. Sample Analytic Rubric for Rating Responses to a Work of Fiction.

Adapted from Groeber (2007, p. 23).

types, and scoring methods, bearing in mind the following global guiding questions:

1. Are your test procedures and course assessment plan practical?
2. Do your tests and tasks produce reliable results?
3. Do your assessments demonstrate content validity?
4. Do your procedures exhibit face validity, and are the assessments "biased for best"?
5. Do your texts, tasks, and tests reflect as much authenticity as possible?
6. Do individual tests and the overall assessment plan generate beneficial washback? (Airasian & Russell, 2008; Bailey, 1998; Brown, 2004)

Performance Descriptors for College-Level ESL/EAP Readers

Standard for Satisfying the College's ESL Requirement

Students will comprehend university-level texts, interpreting them analytically and efficiently.

NOVICE

At the *Novice* level, students will:

- Correctly decode vocabulary at Grade 13 level;
- Comprehend and accurately summarize the principal arguments and supporting evidence presented in academic texts;
- Acquire specialized vocabulary through reading, incorporating that vocabulary appropriately into writing and speech.

DEVELOPING

At the *Developing* level, students will:

- Develop a framework for organizing texts and relating them to their own frames of reference;
- Accurately decode vocabulary appropriate to the reading material of several disciplines;
- Comprehend, summarize, and apply the major themes or arguments of non-specialized and specialized reading material to intellectual tasks;
- Identify their reading deficiencies and resolve them either independently or by seeking assistance from instructors.

ACCOMPLISHED

At the *Accomplished* level, students will:

- Accurately summarize specialist and non-specialist reading material in multiple disciplines;
- Diagnose most reading deficiencies and resolve them independently;
- Develop a flexible cognitive framework for organizing the meaning of academic texts;
- Summarize the writer's purpose and its connections to the text's chief components;
- Identify surface and implied meanings, recognizing irony, metaphorical language, and intentionally misleading uses of language;
- Recognize the relative importance and relevance of the parts of complex academic texts;
- Locate and evaluate evidence used to support claims.

FIGURE 9.12. Sample Rubric Describing Performance Outcomes.

Alternative L2 Literacy Assessment Options

Literacy educators have proposed a number of "alternative" approaches, which we consider to be creative extensions of—and complements to—conventional assessment procedures (Airasian & Russell, 2008; Caldwell, 2008; Harp, 2000; Kendall & Khuon, 2005; Kucer & Silva, 2006; Smith & Elley, 1997; Weaver, 2002). The array of alternative approaches available exceeds our ability to catalogue them here, but their purposes generally include: (1) engaging students actively in the assessment process; (2) promoting learner autonomy and motivation; (3) enhancing authenticity; and (4) systematically integrating instruction and assessment by maximizing positive washback. The following survey of alternative methods, most of which are informal, provides approaches that can be incorporated into a reading assessment plan and routine classroom teaching:

- *Classroom conversations, interviews, and conferences.* Though not practical for large-scale testing, a "simple conversation between an assessor

... and a reader, or readers in a group, can be used in class" (Alderson, 2000, p. 336). In such conversations, the assessor asks readers what texts they have read, how they liked them, what difficulties they encountered, and so on (Cooper & Kiger, 2001). Prompts can inquire into main ideas or arguments, reading speed, and why students have chosen particular texts. Responses can be recorded in a tracking chart or grid.

- *Miscue analysis.* As explained in Chapter 1, *miscue analysis* involves tracking and examining reader miscues as they read aloud. Miscue analysis procedures are thought to open a window into how readers construct meaning and make sense of unfamiliar text as they read. Because it is time-consuming and labor-intensive, miscue analysis may be most valuable as a supplement to conventional assessments (Alderson, 2000).

- *Technology-enhanced testing methods.* Computer-based technology and Internet access promise to expand the range of tools and materials available for testing L2 reading. Perhaps the most obvious technological contribution to literacy assessment is the inexhaustible inventory of online reading materials now at the fingertips of many teachers. In terms of test design, Web-based tests such as TOEFLiBT and DIALANG can facilitate measurement of test-takers' text processing efficiency, bringing to bear diverse test types (Chapelle & Douglas, 2006). Many computer- and Web-based tests are likewise *adaptive:* Testing software adjusts item difficulty in response to examinees' ongoing performance based on complex algorithms. Technological advances may similarly lead to *learner-adaptive tests,* in which test-takers themselves select easier or more difficult items as they work their way through an instrument (Eagleton & Dobler, 2007; Fulcher & Davidson, 2007). Drawbacks associated with computer- and Web-based assessment include restricted availability of computers with Internet connectivity in many parts of the world, the limited amount of text that can be viewed on screen, fatigue induced by reading on screen, and inhibitory variables that do not affect the processing of paper-based text (e.g., color combinations, variable white space, layout, variable fonts and font pitch, and distracting features such as banners, hyperlinks, animation, audio, and video) (Cummins et al., 2007; Wolf, 2007).

Reading Journals

An informal, free-form variation on summaries, reading responses, and compositions is the *reading journal* (see Chapter 5). Aebersold and Field (1997) described reading journals as a superb way to involve learners in "monitoring comprehension, making comprehension visible, fitting in new knowledge, applying knowledge, and gaining language proficiency" (p. 168). Proponents of reading journals emphasize that journal assignments can be flexible in terms of response type, medium, and assessment scheme (Graves & Graves, 2003; Green & Green, 1993; Mlynarczyk, 1998; Peyton & Reed, 1990). Reading journals, particularly those that involve regular dialogue between teacher and student, work well for readers at all levels of L2 proficiency. Tasks can involve responding to a single question, such as "What did you learn from the reading?" or "What did you like or dislike about the text, and why?" Prompts can engage students in careful, critical reflection. At higher proficiency levels, journal entries might ask students to retell a narrative or to compose responses to their choice of prompts. These might target organizational patterns or ask students to manipulate the text creatively. In writing about fiction, the teacher might invite students to retell the story from the viewpoint of someone other than the narrator. Double-entry journal tasks (see Chapter 5) provide further examples of the how journal writing can encourage students to engage meaningfully with texts while providing the teacher with assessable evidence of comprehension and strategy use.

Though an informal and potentially time-consuming means of assessment, reading journals have proven to be valuable, productive, and inspiring tools in our own teaching. Well-crafted journal tasks capitalize on rich reading–writing connections, encouraging students to use writing to explore texts and reading processes (Ferris & Hedgcock, 2005; Hirvela, 2004). In writing journal entries, learners can monitor the effectiveness of their strategies and recognize the interaction of bottom-up and top-down operations (Sheridan, 1991). We recommend providing learners with a choice of guided but open-ended prompts (Graves & Graves, 2003; Heller, 1999; Hirvela, 2004). We likewise encourage teachers to adopt strategies for easing the workload involved in responding to journals. Aebersold and Field (1997) recommended audio journals as an alternative to written journals, an option that might be practical when students and teachers can efficiently exchange MP3 files. Many teachers elect not to mark or score students' journal entries formally, preferring to respond with handwritten qualitative comments or by inserting notes into electronic files shared via e-mail or a course management system such as WebCT or Moodle. When assigning scores or grades is desired or necessary, a holistic scoring rubric tailored to suit the journal genre would be the appropriate marketing option.

Literacy Portfolios

An "alternative" approach that merits particular attention is the *literacy portfolio*, which can take many forms and can be adapted to contexts ranging from primary and secondary education to postsecondary academic and vocational contexts (Johns, 1997). Widely used in L1 and L2 writing instruction, portfolios represent an "alternative" to conventional testing methods (Ferris & Hedgcock, 2005; Weigle, 2002). In fact, a literacy portfolio can (and probably should) integrate controlled and constructed response tasks and tests, as well as informal student products such as reading journal entries and self-assessment items.

Simply stated, "a portfolio is a collection of student work that spans a grading period or year" (Caldwell, 2008, p. 42). Much more than a "collection" of artifacts, a systematically designed and carefully assessed portfolio is explicitly tied to defined student and teacher goals. "Portfolios can be *formative* or *summative*. A formative portfolio is a collection of work that demonstrates progress. A summative portfolio is a collection of best work and represents a showcase of the student's efforts" (Caldwell, 2008, p. 42). In line with principles of learner autonomy, students should be free to select a portion of samples to include in their portfolios (Airasian & Russell, 2008; Hamp-Lyons & Condon, 2000). Although it is a *product*, a literacy portfolio also represents an iterative *process* that requires teachers and students to invest in reflection and self-appraisal over time. Using portfolios for formative and summative assessment thus commits teachers and students to an ongoing, participatory process integrating authentic literacy events and products. The spread of portfolio assessment from primary and secondary education to postsecondary contexts has led to the discovery of specific advantages accruing to the integration of portfolios in literacy education and other subject areas.

Research points toward several interconnected benefits of literacy portfolios. In particular, portfolio assessment:

- Individualizes instruction and assessment by offering students choices and options;
- Enhances learner autonomy, motivation, and investment by involving students in systematic reflection on—and assessment of—their own products and development;
- Authentically weaves teaching, learning, and assessment;
- Engages learners and teachers in collaborative decision-making around portfolio contents, presentation, and evaluation criteria;
- Promotes authenticity of text and task;
- Generates concrete, longitudinal evidence of student achievement, progress, and proficiency;
- Provides a window into multiple dimensions of language and literacy development;
- Produces favorable washback by giving assessment procedures a coherent purpose beyond isolated tasks and tests;
- Encourages peer collaboration. (Airasian & Russell, 2007; Barrett, 2000; Brown, 2004; Ferris & Hedgcock, 2005; Genesee & Upshur, 1996; Glazer, 2007; Gottlieb, 1995; Hamp-Lyons & Condon, 2000; Johns, 1997; National Capital Language Resource Center, 2004; O'Malley & Valdez Pierce, 1996; Shrum & Glisan, 2005; Weigle, 2002).

A salient feature of portfolios is that they engage students in decision-making about elements of the process, ideally as they progress through a course (Guthrie & Knowles, 2001). "Adults learn best when they actively participate in the learning process, and similarly the best way to assess their progress is to involve them in the process" (Fordham, Holland, & Millican, 1995, p. 106). Thus, a well-constructed portfolio instrument requires students to make choices and assume control over their learning. Among the choices that students and teachers can make in assembling a portfolio is the menu of contents, which may include a combination of any of the instructional tasks introduced in Chapters 3–8 and test products introduced here. Items comprising a diverse L2 literacy portfolio might therefore include a selection of the following artifacts, which can be assembled digitally or in print:

- Self-assessment items such as checklists, strategic inventories, records of extensive reading, reflective commentaries, and cover letters (see below);
- Tests and quizzes;
- Drafts and revised versions of summaries, reading responses, and compositions;
- Reports and projects;
- Homework assignments and practice exercises;
- Reading journals or journal entries;
- Outlines of assigned reading selections and notes taken during or after reading;
- Class notes;
- Audio or video recordings of presentations or demonstrations;
- Creative writing samples, including stories, plays, and poems;
- Drawings and photos related to assigned and self-selected readings.

Traditionally, students assemble these materials in folders or notebooks. Electronic portfolios take the concept a step further by forgoing traditional formats and instead presenting student work in digital formats (e.g., CD-RW) or online (e.g., via *iWebfolio, e-Portfolio*, or *MyPortfolio*). Clearly, the latter options offer the advantage of cultivating students' technological skills and literacies (Eagleton & Dobler, 2007; Egéa-Kuehne, 2004; Withrow, 2004).

The EAP course syllabus in Appendix 4.2 describes artifacts that a literacy portfolio might contain. To guide teachers and students in setting up and working through a portfolio process, the Portfolio Assessment Project (National Capital Language Resource Center, 2004) proposed a series of developmental steps, which we have adapted for L2 literacy instruction:

1. *Articulate the purposes of the assessment:* Specify aspects of literacy and reading development that the portfolio will assess.
2. *Identify instructional aims:* Determine goals for the portfolio and standards for students to work toward.
3. *Match portfolio tasks and components to aims:* Specify what students will do to show progress toward achieving standards over time.
4. *Describe student reflection:* Describe how students will review, assess, and reflect on their work, skills, and strategies.
5. *Articulate criteria:* Set criteria for assessing individual portfolio items and the overall portfolio product (i.e., develop an appropriate rubric).
6. *Determine structure and procedures:* Set forth how the portfolio process will proceed, taking into account its purpose, audience, and presentation requirements (e.g., folder, binder, electronic file/folder, or Web page).
7. *Monitor progress:* Check and oversee the portfolio development process to ensure that artifacts are reliable and valid indexes of target constructs and performance criteria.
8. *Evaluate portfolio processes and products:* Upon completion of each portfolio cycle, appraise its successes and failures to improve procedures, outcomes, and rubrics for the next iteration (i.e., maximize favorable washback).

Self-Assessment

In Chapter 4, we introduced self-assessment as a component of pre-course needs analysis. Learner self-assessment that appraises student performance, progress, and proficiency "is increasingly seen as a useful source of information on learner abilities and processes" (Alderson, 2000, p. 341). Engaging learners in scrutinizing their own developing skills, strategies, and knowledge aligns with principles of learner-centered instruction (e.g., Airasian & Russell, 2008; Cohen, 1994; Gardner, 1996). Furthermore, as indicated above, self-assessment is an essential component of portfolio assessment schemes, which are expressly designed to observe and monitor students' reading and learning processes over time and to promote introspection. Portfolio rubrics typically require students to complete checklists or to compose written appraisals of their processes and progress. Such tasks can engage learners in taking an active role in monitoring and improving their reading skills and strategy use; guided self-assessment likewise encourages students to strengthen their metacognitive awareness (Aebersold & Field, 1997; Brown, 2005; Caldwell, 2008). Empirical research suggests that self-assessments of L2 abilities can fairly reliably predict objective measures of language skills (Alderson, 2000). Ross (1998), for example, reported fairly high correlations ($r \geq .70$) between the two variables.

Level A1	I can understand very short, simple texts, putting together familiar names, words, and basic phrases, by, for example, re-reading parts of the text.
Level B1	I can identify the main conclusions in clearly written argumentative texts. I can recognize the general line of argument in a text but not necessarily in detail.
Level B2	I can read many kinds of texts quite easily, reading different types of text at different speeds and in different ways according to my purpose in reading and the type of text.
Level C1	I can understand in detail a wide range of long, complex texts of different types, provided I can re-read difficult sections.

FIGURE 9.13. Sample Self-Assessment Tool—L2 Reading Strategies.
Source: Alderson (2000, pp. 341–342).

Self-assessment tools can take a wide range of forms, the most common of which consist of surveys and questionnaires that present learners with belief statements, simple rating scales keyed to specific skill domains and task types, and prompts for commenting on their perceived strengths, weaknesses, and goals. The sample self-assessment scale in Figure 9.13, extracted from the DIALANG battery (Alderson, 2000, 2005), presents learners with statements conceived to gather information about their L2 reading strategies.

The self-appraisal questionnaire in Figure 4.2 similarly asks students to rate the effectiveness of their literacy skills, subskills, strategies using Likert-like descriptors. It also elicits information about reading habits and literacy practices. Though designed as a tool for profiling readers at the beginning of a course, this survey could easily serve as an in-progress or end-of-course instrument that could be administered independently or as part of a portfolio scheme.

Alderson (2000), Alderson and Banerjee (2001), and Purpura (1997), among others, have developed self-appraisal inventories of language learning and strategy use—including reading strategies—that can be administered as part of a needs analysis, during performance assessment, or both. We recommend complementing checklists and surveys with qualitatively rich introspective tasks requiring students to reflect critically on their evolving skills, strategy use, and literacy goals in writing (Hirvela, 2004). For instance, the cover letter required for the literacy portfolio described in the EAP syllabus in Appendix 4.2 might ask students to retake the pre-course self-assessment survey and then discuss specific areas of progress made during the term. Students should likewise be reminded of course goals and standards, which should prompt them to recall successes and skill areas where they have made progress. Finally, a cover letter or reflective commentary should invite students to identify specific performance goals to pursue as they advance as L2 readers.

We embrace self-assessment in our own instructional practice and encourage teachers to incorporate it into their own assessment plans, but we recognize its limitations. For example, influential stakeholders (e.g., educational authorities, program directors, supervisors, parents) may view self-assessment procedures with skepticism, questioning their validity, reliability, and fairness. Self-assessment cannot substitute for teacher assessment, but should complement the measurements administered by skilled evaluators. A chief advantage of self-assessment is that learners invest in the assessment process and thus become aware of its benefits (Aebersold & Field, 1997). To maximize that advantage, we recommend adhering to the following general guidelines:

1. Inform students of the aims, benefits, and pitfalls of self-assessment.
2. Define self-assessment tasks and train learners how to use them.
3. Encourage students to avoid subjectivity and inflated self-appraisals by providing them with transparent, unambiguous criteria and anonymous exemplars.
4. Work for beneficial washback by following up on self-assessment tasks (e.g., further self-analysis, reflective journal entries, written teacher feedback, conferencing, and so on). (Airasian & Russell, 2008; Brown, 2004)

Summary: Toward a Coherent Literacy Assessment Plan

Synthesizing theory, research, and practice in an area as complex and as dynamic as reading assessment always incurs risks such as overlooking crucial issues, oversimplifying divergent principles, and providing superficial coverage. We therefore encourage readers interested in exploring assessment theory and research in greater depth to consult primary sources referenced here and in Further Reading and Resources. We nonetheless hope that this chapter has provided an informative overview of key concepts in language and literacy assessment, including reliability and validity. Our overview highlighted the relationships among test-takers, texts, tests, and items in the assessment cycle, which we consider to be inextricable from curricular planning and routine instruction. We likewise described an array of test and item types, ranging from those eliciting controlled responses to those requiring open-ended constructed responses. The chapter closed by examining alternative assessment approaches designed to maximize desirable washback by enhancing learner participation in the process.

If there is a single, overriding message that unifies our treatment of assessment and that loops back to Chapter 4, it could be summarized in Glazer's (2007) precept that "assessment *is* instruction" (p. 227). To highlight this link, we would like to conclude by laying out the following guidelines for developing and implementing a sound plan for carrying out formative and summative assessment in the L2 reading course:

1. Target and repeatedly cycle back to course goals and standards.
2. Understand and revisit the variables at play (students, goals, texts, tests, standards, literacies, and literate contexts).
3. Determine the elements to be featured in the assessment plan (e.g., tests, quizzes, homework, reading journals, portfolios, and so forth).
4. Formalize the plan, include it in the syllabus, and use it as a teaching tool. (Aebersold & Field, 1997; Airasian & Russell, 2008; Graves, 2000)

Further Reading and Resources

Though not exhaustive, the following list provides references to print- and Web-based sources addressing assessment theory, research, and practice that exemplify and elaborate on the major themes and issues introduced in this chapter.

General reference: language assessment
  Bachman (1990); Bachman & Palmer (1996); Bailey (1998); Brown, H. D. (2004); Brown, J. D. (1998, 2005); Brown & Hudson (2002); Cohen (2001); Davies (1990); Davies et al. (1999); Fulcher & Davidson (2007); Graves (2000); Hughes (2003); McNamara (1996, 2000); Norris, Brown, Hudson, & Yoshioka (1998)

Literacy assessment: principles, policy, and practice
  García, McKoon, & August (2006)

L2 reading assessment
  Alderson (2000); Brantley (2007)

L1 reading assessment
  Airasian & Russell (2008); Caldwell (2008); Cooper & Kiger (2001); Harp (2000)

Statistical analyses for language testing
  Bachman (2004)

Educational measurement (general)
  Gronlund (1998)

Technology-based assessment
  Chapelle & Douglas (2006)

National Center for Research on Evaluation, Standards, and Student Testing
  http://www.cse.ucla.edu/index.asp

TOEFLiBT Integrated Reading–Writing Scoring Rubric
  http://www.ets.org/Media/Tests/TOEFL/pdf/Writing_Rubrics.pdf

TOEFLiBT website (with links to iBT Tour)
    http://www.ets.org/toefl/
Sources on the DIALANG Project
    Alderson (2005)
DIALANG Link
    http://www.dialang.org/intro.htm
Test of Reading Comprehension (TORC)
    Brown, Hammill, & Wiederholt (2009)
Rubrics for literacy assessment
    Airasian & Russell (2008); Glickman-Bond (2006); Groeber (2007)
Online rubric design tools
    Rubistar: http://rubistar.4teachers.org/index.php
    teAchnology: http://rubistar.4teachers.org/index.php
    Rubrics 4 Teachers: http://rubrics4teachers.com/
Electronic portfolios
    iWebfolio: http://www.nuventive.com/index.html
    e-Portfolio: http://www.opeus.com/default_e-portfolios.php
    MyPortfolio: http://www.myinternet.com.au/products/myportfolio.html

---

Reflection and Review

1. How are reading assessment, curriculum design, and instruction inter-
    related? What roles does washback play in this relationship?
2. What goals do proficiency, diagnostic, progress, and achievement assess-
    ments share? How are these test types different, and why are the distinctions
    important for reading assessment?
3. How are criterion- and norm-referenced tests distinct? Why are the differ-
    ences important?
4. Define reliability and how we achieve it. What is its relationship to validity?
5. Why do assessors stress the importance of multiple types of validity in read-
    ing assessment?
6. What steps can we take to ensure authenticity in formative and summative
    assessment?
7. How can we integrate process and product in L2 literacy assessment?
8. How are controlled and constructed response tasks complementary? Why
    should we build both categories of exercise into our assessment plans?

Application Activities

Application Activity 9.1
Revisit Your Testing Experiences

Prepare some informal notes about your best and worst test experiences, which may not necessarily have taken place in academic settings. Working with a classmate, share your experiences. Jointly produce a list of aspects that characterized the positive and negative incidents, then construct a composite list of DOs and DON'Ts for test writers based on your insights. As an extension of this task, compose a two- to three-page commentary justifying your list of DOs and DON'Ts for writers of reading tests, referring to this chapter's contents.

Application Activity 9.2
Outline an Assessment Plan

Collect syllabi for one or more L2 literacy courses offered at a local institution. Next, review the Sample EAP Reading Course Syllabus in Appendix 4.2, paying attention to the assessment plan outlined there. Analyze and compare assessment plans, noting common and unique features.

a. Write a critical review of the assessment plans, explicitly considering the following elements: (1) strong points; (2) weak points; and (3) aspects that you would revise.

b. Describe what you learned about planning reading assessment from this evaluative analysis.

c. Apply your new knowledge: Based on your evaluation of these syllabi and the contents of this chapter, outline an assessment plan of your own for an L2 literacy course that you are familiar with. If your assessment plan includes a literacy portfolio, see Application Activity 9.3. You may consider coupling the two assignments.

Application Activity 9.3
Develop a Literacy Portfolio Plan

a. Review the discussion of literacy portfolios in this chapter, then examine the portfolio described in Appendix 4.2.

b. Based on these materials, draft guidelines for a print-based or digital literacy portfolio that would serve as the primary assessment instrument for an L2 literacy course that you are familiar with. Apply the criteria presented in this chapter to your guidelines.

c. Generate a scoring rubric after consulting the sources listed above or adapt an existing rubric (see Further Reading and Resources).

d. In a 500- to 750-word rationale, define the constructs your proposed portfolio will measure, justify its contents and structure, and argue for its validity and reliability.

Application Activity 9.4
Review and Apply a Reading Skills Rubric

a. Consult two or more of the print or online sources for reading rubrics listed above (also see Chapters 1 and 4). Review generic scales (e.g., the CEFR, ACTFL Proficiency Guidelines, TESOL Standards, or ILR Level Descriptions for Reading) or a scoring rubric for the reading subtests of instruments such as TOEFLiBT, IELTS, or DIALANG.
b. Select a scale whose performance descriptors would be a good match for an L2 literacy course familiar to you. Make necessary adjustments.
c. Draft an assessment plan that would bring students from one skill level to the next.
d. Preface your course outline and assessment plan with a 500- to 750-word rationale explaining your choice of rubric and how it helped you organize the material.

Application Activity 9.5
Create a Sample Reading Comprehension Testlet

a. Select an authentic, self-contained reading passage suitable for L2 readers, a passage from a recent L2 reading textbook, or a sample text from this book (see Chapters 3, 5, 6, and 7).
b. Carefully scrutinize your text sample by reviewing the *reader, text,* and relevant *task/item* variables introduced in this chapter and outlined in Figures 9.1 and 9.2.
c. Construct a testlet to be administered under timed conditions. Your instrument should comprise two to three sections representing diverse task/item types. Construct your testlet for presentation either in paper- or Web-based form (e.g., using WebCT, Respondus, Moodle, or a Web tool of your choosing). Include corresponding scoring keys and rubrics.
d. Justify the contents and structure of your testlet in a 500- to 750-word rationale outlining validity and reliability claims. Explicitly characterise the constructs you will measure.

Application Activity 9.6
Develop an L2 Reading Test

Following the procedures in Application Activity 9.5, design a speeded test for a unit of study in an L2 literacy course. Construct an instrument that comprises a variety of controlled and constructed response sections. Develop or adapt suitable instruments, scoring keys, and rubrics.

Application Activity 9.7
Devise a Self-Assessment Tool

a.   Collect at least two self-assessment instruments designed for use with L2 readers (consult Appendix 4.2 and the self-assessment sources listed in this chapter).

b.   Using these tools as starting points, construct and adapt your own survey for an L2 reader population familiar to you. Include a section eliciting qualitative reflection from your students (e.g., prose commentary of some sort). Construct your instrument for presentation in print or digital form (e.g., using WebCT, Respondus, Moodle, or a Web tool of your choice).

c.   Justify the contents and structure of your self-assessment tool in a 500- to 750-word rationale in which you discuss validity, reliability, and the ways in which the self-assessment would complement teacher assessment. Describe how you would score students' responses.

References

Aebersold, J. A., & Field, M. L. (1997). *From reader to reading teacher: Issues and strategies for second language classrooms.* Cambridge, England: Cambridge University Press.

Afflerbach, P. (2008). Best practices in literacy assessment. In L. B. Gambrell, L. M. Morrow, & Pressley, M. (Eds.), *Best practices in literacy instruction* (3rd ed., pp. 264–282). New York: Guilford.

Agor, B. (Ed.). (2001). *Integrating the ESL standards into classroom practice: Grades 9–12.* Alexandria, VA: TESOL.

Airasian, P. W., & Russell, M. K. (2008). *Classroom assessment: Concepts and applications.* New York: McGraw-Hill.

Akamatsu, N. (2003). The effects of first language orthographic features in second language reading in text. *Language Learning, 53,* 207–231.

Akyel, A., & Yalçin, E. (1990). Literature in the EFL class: A study of goal-achievement incongruence. *ELT Journal, 44* (3), 174–180.

Alderson, J. C. (1984). Reading in a foreign language: A reading problem or a language problem? In J. Alderson & A. Urquhart (Eds.), *Reading in a foreign language* (pp. 1–27). New York: Longman.

Alderson, J. C. (1990). Testing reading comprehension skills (part one). *Reading in a Foreign Language, 6,* 425–438.

Alderson, J. C. (1993). The relationship between grammar and reading in an English for academic purposes test battery. In D. Douglas & C. Chapelle (Eds.), *A new decade of language testing research: Selected papers from the 1990 Language Testing Research Colloquium* (pp. 203–219). Alexandria, VA: TESOL.

Alderson, J. C. (2000). *Assessing reading.* Cambridge, England: Cambridge University Press.

Alderson, J. C. (2005). *Diagnosing foreign language proficiency: The interface between learning and assessment.* New York: Continuum.

Alderson, J. C., & Banerjee, J. (2001). Impact and washback research in language testing. In C. Elder, A. Brown, E. Grove, K. Hill, N. Iwashita, T. Lumley, K. McLoughlin, & T.

McNamara (Eds.), *Experimenting with uncertainty: Essays in honor of Alan Davies* (pp. 150–161). Cambridge, England: Cambridge University Press.

Alderson, J. C., Clapham, C., & Wall, D. (1995). *Language test construction and evaluation.* Cambridge, England: Cambridge University Press.

Alderson, J. C., & Lukmani, Y. (1989). Cognition and reading: Cognitive levels as embodied in test questions. *Reading and Writing, 5,* 253–270.

Alexander, P. A., & Jetton, T. L. (2000). Learning from text: A multidimensional and developmental perspective. In M. L. Kamil, P. B. Mosenthal, P. D. Pearson, & R. Barr (Eds.), *Handbook of reading research, Vol. III* (pp. 285–310). Mahwah, NJ: Lawrence Erlbaum.

Allen, E., Bernhardt, E. B., Berry, M. T., & Demel, M. (1988). Comprehension and text genre: An analysis of secondary foreign language readers. *Modern Language Journal, 72,* 63–72.

Allen, J. (1999). *Words, words, words: Teaching vocabulary in grades 4–12.* Portland, ME: Stenhouse.

Allington, R. L. (2006). *What really matters for struggling readers: Designing research-based programs* (2nd ed.). Boston: Allyn & Bacon.

Al-Seghayer, K. (2001). The effect of multimedia annotation modes on L2 vocabulary acquisition: A comparative study. *Language Learning and Technology, 5,* 202–232.

Alvermann, D. E., Hinchman, K. A., Moore, D. W., Phelps, S. F., & Waff, D. R. (Eds.). (2006). *Reconceptualizing the literacies in adolescents' lives.* Mahwah, NJ: Lawrence Erlbaum.

American Council on the Teaching of Foreign Languages. (1998). *ACTFL performance guidelines for K–12 learners.* Yonkers, NY: American Council on the Teaching of Foreign Languages.

American Federation of Teachers. (1999). *Teaching reading is rocket science: What expert teachers of reading should know and be able to do.* Washington, DC: American Federation of Teachers.

Anderson, J. R. (1995). *Cognitive psychology and its implications* (4th ed.). New York: W. H. Freeman.

Anderson, N. J. (1991). Individual differences in strategy use in second language reading and testing. *Modern Language Journal, 75,* 460–472.

Anderson, N. J. (1999). *Exploring second language reading: Issues and strategies.* Boston: Heinle.

Anderson, N. J., & Pearson, P. D. (1988). A schema-theoretic view of basic processes in reading comprehension. In P. Carrell, J. Devine, & D. Eskey (Eds.), *Interactive approaches to second language reading* (pp. 37–55). Cambridge: Cambridge University Press.

Anderson, R. C., & Freebody, P. (1983). Reading comprehension and the assessment and acquisition of word knowledge. In B. Hutson (Ed.), *Advances in reading/language research: A research annual* (pp. 231–256). Greenwich, CT: JAI Press.

Anderson, R. C., Hiebert, E. H., Scott, J. A., & Wilkinson, I. A. G. (1985). *Becoming a nation of readers: The report of the Commission on Reading.* Urbana, IL: Center for the Study of Reading.

Anderson, R. C., & Pearson, P. D. (1984). A schema-theory view of the basic processes in reading. In P. D. Pearson (Ed.), *Handbook of reading research* (pp. 255–291). New York: Longman.

Arabski, J. (Ed.). (2006). *Cross-linguistic influences in the second language lexicon.* Clevedon, England: Multilingual Matters.

Aro, M. (2006). Learning to read: The effect of orthography. In R. Malatesha Joshi &

P. G. Aaron (Eds.), *Handbook of orthography and literacy* (pp. 531–550). Mahwah, NJ: Lawrence Erlbaum.

Atkinson, D. (1997). A critical approach to critical thinking in TESOL. *TESOL Quarterly, 27,* 9–32.

Atkinson, D. (1999). Culture in TESOL. *TESOL Quarterly, 33,* 625–654.

Auerbach, E. R., & Paxton, D. (1997). "It's not the English thing": Bringing reading research into the ESL classroom. *TESOL Quarterly, 31,* 237–261.

August, D., & Shanahan, T. (Eds.). (2006a). *Developing literacy in second-language learners: Report of the National Literacy Panel on Language-Minority Children and Youth.* Mahwah, NJ: Lawrence Erlbaum.

August, D., & Shanahan, T. (Eds.). (2006b). *Executive summary—Developing literacy in second-language learners: Report of the National Literacy Panel on Language-Minority Children and Youth.* Mahwah, NJ: Lawrence Erlbaum. Retrieved January 21, 2008 from http://www.cal.org/projects/archive/nlpreports/Executive_Summary.pdf

August, D., & Shanahan, T. (Eds.). (2007). *Developing reading and writing in second language learners: Lessons from the report of the National Literacy Panel on Language-Minority Children and Youth.* New York: Taylor & Francis.

Ausubel, D. A. (1968). *Educational psychology: A cognitive view.* New York: Holt, Rinehart, & Winston.

Ausubel, D. A., Novak, J. D., & Hanesian, H. (1978). *Educational psychology: A cognitive view.* New York: Holt, Rinehart, & Winston.

Ausubel, D. A., & Robinson, F. G. (1969). *School learning.* New York: Holt, Rinehart, & Winston.

Bachman, L. F. (1990). *Fundamental considerations in language testing.* Oxford, England: Oxford University Press.

Bachman, L. F. (2004). *Statistical analyses for language assessment.* Cambridge, England: Cambridge University Press.

Bachman, L. F., & Cohen, A. D. (Eds.). (1998). *Interfaces between second language acquisition and language testing research.* Cambridge, England: Cambridge University Press.

Bachman, L. F., & Palmer, A. S. (1996). *Language testing in practice: Designing and developing useful language tests.* Oxford: Oxford University Press.

Bailey, K. M. (1996a). The best laid plans: Teachers' in-class decisions to depart from their lesson plans. In K. M. Bailey & D. Nunan (Eds.), *Voices from the language classroom* (pp. 15–40). Cambridge, England: Cambridge University Press.

Bailey, K. M. (1996b). Working for washback. *Language Testing, 13,* 257–277.

Bailey, K. M. (1998). *Learning about language assessment: Dilemmas, decisions, and directions.* Boston: Heinle.

Bailey, K. M., Curtis, A., & Nunan, D. (2001). *Pursuing professional development: The self as source.* Boston: Heinle.

Ballman, T. L. (1998). From teacher-centered to learner-centered: Guidelines for sequencing and presenting the elements of a foreign language class. In J. Harper, M. Lively, & M. Williams (Eds.), *The coming of age of the profession: Issues and emerging ideas for the teaching of foreign languages* (pp. 97–111). Boston: Heinle.

Bamford, J., & Day, R. R. (2003). *Extensive reading activities for teaching language.* Cambridge, England: Cambridge University Press.

Barkhuizen, G. P., & Gough, D. (1998). Language curriculum development in South Africa: What place for English? *TESOL Quarterly, 30,* 453–471.

Barnett, M. A. (1986). Syntactic and lexical/semantic skill in foreign language reading: Importance and interaction. *Modern Language Journal, 70,* 343–349.

Barnett, M. A. (1989). *More than meets the eye: Foreign language reading theory and practice.* Englewood Cliffs, NJ: Prentice-Hall Regents & Center for Applied Linguistics.

Barrett, H. C. (2000). *The electronic portfolio development process.* Retrieved February 1, 2008 from http://www.electronicportfolios.com/portfolios/EPDevProcess.html#epdev

Barton, D. (2007). *Literacy: An introduction to the ecology of written language* (2nd ed.). Malden, MA: Blackwell.

Barton, D., & Hamilton, M. (1998). *Local literacies: Reading and writing in one community.* London: Routledge.

Barton, D., & Tusting, K. (Eds.). (2005). *Beyond communities of practice: Language, power, and social context.* Cambridge, England: Cambridge University Press.

Bauer, L., & Nation, I. S. P. (1993). Word families. *International Journal of Lexicography, 6,* 253–279.

Bauer, T. (1996). Arabic writing. In P. Daniels & W. Bright (Eds.), *The world's writing systems* (pp. 559–564). Oxford, England: Oxford University Press.

Bazerman, C. (Ed.). (2007). *Handbook of research on writing: History, society, school, individual, text.* New York: Taylor & Francis.

Beck, I. L. (2006). *Making sense of phonics: The hows and whys.* New York: Guilford.

Beck, I. L., McKeown, M. G., & Omanson, R. C. (1987). The effects and uses of diverse vocabulary instructional techniques. In M. G. McKeown & M. E. Curtis (Eds.), *The nature of vocabulary acquisition* (pp. 147–163). Hillsdale, NJ: Lawrence Erlbaum.

Beck, I. L., McKeown, M. G., Sinatra, G. M., & Loxterman, J. A. (1991). Revising social studies text from a text-processing perspective: Evidence of improved comprehensibility. *Reading Research Quarterly, 26,* 251–276.

Beck, I., Perfetti, C., & McKeown, M. (1982). The effects of long-term vocabulary instruction on lexical access and reading comprehension. *Journal of Educational Psychology, 74,* 506–521.

Belcher, D., & Hirvela, A. (Eds.). (2001). *Linking literacies: Perspectives on L2 reading–writing connections.* Ann Arbor: University of Michigan Press.

Bell, J., & Burnaby, B. (1984). *A handbook for adult ESL literacy.* Toronto: Ontario Institute for Studies in Education.

Benesch, S. (1996). Needs analysis and curriculum development in EAP: An example of a critical approach. *TESOL Quarterly, 30,* 723–738.

Benesch, S. (2001). *Critical English for academic purposes.* Mahwah, NJ: Lawrence Erlbaum.

Bernhardt, E. B. (1991a). A psycholinguistic perspective on second language literacy. *AILA Review, 8,* 31–44.

Bernhardt, E. B. (1991b). *Reading development in a second language: Theoretical, empirical, and classroom perspectives.* Norwood, NJ: Ablex.

Bernhardt, E. B. (2000). Second-language reading as a case study of reading scholarship in the 20th century. In M. Kamil, P. Mosenthal, P. D. Pearson, & R. Barr (Eds.), *Handbook of reading research: Vol. III* (pp. 791–811). Mahwah, NJ: Lawrence Erlbaum.

Bernhardt, E. B. (2005). Progress and procrastination in second language reading. *Annual Review of Applied Linguistics, 25,* 133–150.

Bernhardt, E. B., & Kamil, M. L. (1995). Interpreting relationships between L1 and L2 reading: Consolidating the linguistic threshold and the linguistic interdependence hypotheses. *Applied Linguistics, 16,* 15–34.

Berwick, R. (1989). Needs assessment in language programming: From theory to practice. In R. K. Johnson (Ed.), *The second language curriculum* (pp. 48–62). Cambridge, England: Cambridge University Press.

Bialystok, E. (2001). *Bilingualism in development: Language, literacy, and cognition.* Cambridge, England: Cambridge University Press.

Biber, D. (1988). *Variation across spoken and written English.* Cambridge, England: Cambridge University Press.

Biber, D. (1995). *Cross-linguistic patterns of register variation: A multi-dimensional comparison of English, Tuvaluan, Korean, and Somali.* Cambridge, England: Cambridge University Press.

Biber, D. (2006). *University language: A corpus-based study of spoken and written registers.* Amsterdam: John Benjamins.

Birch, B. (2007). *English L2 reading: Getting to the bottom* (2nd ed.). Mahwah, NJ: Lawrence Erlbaum.

Blachowicz, C. L. Z., & Fisher, P. J. (2008). Best practices in vocabulary instruction. In L. B. Gambrell, L. M. Morrow, & Pressley, M. (Eds.), *Best practices in literacy instruction* (3rd ed., pp. 178–203). New York: Guilford.

Blackboard. (2008). Blackboard. Retrieved January 24, 2009 from http://www.blackboard.com/Teaching-Learning/Overview.aspx

Blanton, L. L. (1998). *Varied voices: On language and literacy learning.* Mahwah, NJ: Lawrence Erlbaum.

Block, C. C., & Pressley, M. (2007). Best practices in teaching comprehension. In L. B. Gambrell, L. M. Morrow, & Pressley, M. (Eds.), *Best practices in literacy instruction* (3rd ed., pp. 220–242). New York: Guilford.

Bloom, B. S. (1956). *Taxonomy of educational objectives: The classification of educational goals, Handbook 1: Cognitive domain.* New York: David McKay.

Bloome, D., Carter, S. P., Christian, B. M., Otto, S., & Shuart-Faris, N. (2005). *Discourse analysis and the study of classroom language and literacy events: a microethnographic perspective.* Mahwah, NJ: Lawrence Erlbaum.

Boardman, M. (2004). *The language of websites.* London: Routledge.

Bogaards, P., & Laufer, B. (Eds.). (2004). *Vocabulary in a second language.* Amsterdam: John Benjamins.

Bosher. S. & Rowecamp, J. (1998). The refugee/immigrant in higher education: The role of educational background. *College ESL, 8* (1), 23–42.

Bossers, B. (1991). On thresholds, ceilings, and short-circuits: The relation between L1 reading, L2 reading, and L2 knowledge. *AILA Review, 8,* 45–60.

Brahm, J. (2001). Second Chances—If only we could start again. *Sacramento Bee.*

Brandt, D. (1990). *Literacy as involvement: The acts of writers, readers, and texts.* Carbondale, IL: Southern Illinois University Press.

Brantley, D. K. (2007). *Instructional assessment of English language learners in the K–8 classroom.* Boston: Allyn & Bacon.

Brantmeier, C. (2005). Effects of readers' knowledge, text type, and test type on L1 and L2 reading comprehension in Spanish. *Modern Language Journal, 89,* 37–53.

Brauer, G. (Ed.). (2002). *Body and language: Intercultural learning through drama.* Westport, CT: Greenwood.

Breznitz, Z. (2006). *Fluency in reading: Synchronization of processes.* Mahwah, NJ: Lawrence Erlbaum.

Brindley, G. (1989). The role of needs analysis in adult ESL programme design. In R. K. Johnson (Ed.), *The second language curriculum* (pp. 63–78). Cambridge, England: Cambridge University Press.

Brindley, G. (2001). Assessment. In R. Carter & D. Nunan (Eds.), *Cambridge guide to teaching English to speakers of other languages* (pp. 137–143). Cambridge, England: Cambridge University Press.

Brisk, M. E., & Harrington, M. M. (2007). *Literacy and bilingualism: A handbook for ALL teachers* (2nd ed.). New York: Taylor & Francis.

Britton, B. K., & Gulgoz, S. (1991). Using Kintsch's computational model to improve instructional text: Effects of pairing inference calls on recall and cognitive structures. *Journal of Educational Psychology, 83,* 329–345.

Broukal, M. (2004). *Weaving it together: Connecting reading and writing 1* (2nd ed.). Boston: Heinle.

Brown, H. D. (2004). *Language assessment: Principles and classroom practices.* White Plains, NY: Pearson Education.

Brown, H. D. (2007a). *Principles of language learning and teaching* (5th ed.). White Plains, NY: Pearson Education.

Brown, H. D. (2007b). *Teaching by principles: An interactive approach to language pedagogy* (3rd ed.). White Plains, NY: Pearson Education.

Brown, J. D. (1995). *The elements of language curriculum: A systematic approach to program development.* Boston: Heinle.

Brown, J. D. (Ed.). (1998). *New ways of classroom assessment.* Alexandria, VA: TESOL.

Brown, J. D. (2005). *Testing in language programs: A comprehensive guide to English language assessment.* New York: McGraw-Hill.

Brown, J., Goodman, K., & Marek, A. M. (Eds.). (1996). *Studies in miscue analysis.* Newark, DE: International Reading Association.

Brown, J. D., & Hudson, T. (2002). *Criterion-referenced language testing.* New York: Cambridge University Press.

Brown, T. L., & Haynes, M. (1985). Literacy background and reading development in a second language. In T. H. Carr (Ed.), *The development of reading skills: New directions for child development* (pp. 19–34). San Francisco: Jossey-Bass.

Brown, V. L., Hammill, D. D., & Wiederholt, J. L. (2009). *Test of reading comprehension* (4th ed.). Austin, TX: PRO-ED.

Brumfit, C. J., & Carter, R. (Eds.) (1986). *Literature and language teaching.* Oxford: Oxford University Press.

Bryson, B. (1990). *The mother tongue: English and how it got that way.* New York: William Morrow.

Burnaby, B. (1989). Parameters for projects under the settlement language training program. Toronto: TESL Canada Federation. (EDRS No. 318 286). Retrieved December 3, 2008, from http://www.eric.ed.gov/ERICWebPortal/contentdelivery/servlet/ERICServlet?accno=ED318286

Butler, A., & Turbill, J. (1984). *Towards a reading–writing classroom.* Portsmouth, NH: Heinemann.

Butler, I. (2006). A brighter future? Integrating language and literature for first-year university students. In A. Paran (Ed.), *Literature in language teaching and learning* (pp. 11–25). Alexandria, VA: TESOL.

Byrd, P. (2001). Textbooks: Evaluation for selection and analysis for implementation. In M. Celce-Murcia (Ed.), *Teaching English as a second or foreign language* (3rd ed., pp. 415–427). Boston: Heinle.

Byrne, B. (1998). *The foundation of literacy: The child's acquisition of the alphabetic principle.* East Sussex, England: Psychology Press.

Caldwell, J. S. (2008). *Reading assessment: A primer for teachers and coaches* (2nd ed.). New York: Guilford.

California State University Expository Reading and Writing Task Force (2008). *Expository reading and writing course: Semester one and semester two.* Long Beach, CA: California State University.

Campion, M. E., & Elley, W. B. (1971). *An academic vocabulary list.* Wellington, New Zealand: New Zealand Council for Educational Research.

Canale, M. (1983). From communicative competence to communicative language pedagogy. In J. Richards & R. Schmidt (Eds.), *Language and communication* (pp. 2–27). London: Longman.

Canale, M., & Swain, M. (1980). Theoretical bases of communicative approaches to second language teaching and testing. *Applied Linguistics, 1*, 1–47.

Carlo, M. S. (2008). Best practices for literacy instruction for English-language learners. In L. B. Gambrell, L. M. Morrow, & Pressley, M. (Eds.), *Best practices in literacy instruction* (3rd ed., pp. 104–126). New York: Guilford.

Carpenter, P., Miyake, A., & Just, M. (1994). Working memory constraints in comprehension: Evidence from individual differences, aphasia, and aging. In M. A. Gernsbacher (Ed.), *Handbook of psycholinguistics* (pp. 1075–1122). San Diego: Academic Press.

Carr, T. H., Brown, T. L., Vavrus, L. G., & Evans, M. A. (1990). Cognitive skill maps and cognitive skill profiles: Componential analysis of individual differences in children's reading efficiency. In T. H. Carr & B. A. Levy (Eds.), *Reading and its development: Component skills approaches* (pp. 1–55). San Diego: Academic Press.

Carr, T. H., & Levy, B. A. (Eds.). (1990). *Reading and its development: Component skills approaches.* San Diego: Academic Press.

Carrell, P. L. (1983a). Background knowledge in second language comprehension. *Language Learning and Communication, 2*, 25–34.

Carrell, P. L. (1983b). Some issues in studying the role of schemata, or background knowledge, in second language comprehension. *Reading in a Foreign Language, 1*, 81–92.

Carrell, P. L. (1983c). Three components of background knowledge in reading comprehension. *Language Learning, 33*, 183–207.

Carrell, P. L. (1984a). The effects of rhetorical organization on ESL readers. *TESOL Quarterly, 18*, 441–469.

Carrell, P. L. (1984b). Evidence of formal schema in second language comprehension. *Language Learning, 34*, 87–112.

Carrell, P. L. (1984c). Schema theory and ESL reading: Classroom implications and applications. *Modern Language Journal, 68*, 332–343.

Carrell, P. L. (1987a). Content and formal schemata in ESL reading. *TESOL Quarterly, 21*, 461–481.

Carrell, P. L. (1987b). Readability in ESL. *Reading in a Foreign Language, 4*, 21–40.

Carrell, P. L. (1988a). Interactive text processing: Implications for ESL/second language reading classrooms. In P. Carrell, J. Devine, & D. Eskey (Eds.), *Interactive approaches to second language reading* (pp. 239–259). Cambridge: Cambridge University Press.

Carrell, P. L. (1988b). Introduction. In P. L. Carrell, J. Devine, & D. E. Eskey (Eds.), *Interactive approaches to second language reading* (pp. 1–7). Cambridge, England: Cambridge University Press.

Carrell, P. L. (1988c). Some causes of text-boundedness and schema interference in ESL reading. In P. L. Carrell, J. Devine, & D. E. Eskey (Eds.), *Interactive approaches to second language reading* (pp. 101–113). Cambridge, England: Cambridge University Press.

Carrell, P. L. (1991). Second language reading: Reading ability or language proficiency? *Applied Linguistics, 12*, 159–179.

Carrell, P. L., Devine, J., & Eskey, D. (Eds.). (1988). *Interactive approaches to second language reading.* New York: Cambridge University Press.

Carrell, P. L., & Eisterhold, J. (1983). Schema theory and ESL reading pedagogy. *TESOL Quarterly, 17*, 553–573.

Carrell, P. L., Pharis, B. G., & Liberto, J. C. (1989). Metacognitive strategy training for ESL reading. *TESOL Quarterly, 23*, 647–678.

Carroll, J. B. (1964). *Language and thought.* Englewood Cliffs, NJ: Prentice-Hall.

Carroll, J., Davies, P., & Richman, B. (1971). *The American Heritage word frequency book.* New York: American Heritage.

Carson, J., Carrell, P., Silberstein, S., Kroll, B., & Kuehn, P. (1990). Reading–writing relationships in first and second language. *TESOL Quarterly, 24,* 245–266.

Carson, J. G., & Leki, I. (Eds.). (1993). *Reading in the composition classroom: Second language perspectives.* Boston: Heinle & Heinle.

Carter, R., & Long, M. N. (1987). *The web of words: Exploring literature through language.* Cambridge: Cambridge University Press.

Carter, R., & Long, M. N. (1991). *Teaching literature.* Harlow, England: Longman.

Carter, R., & McRae, J. (Eds.). (1996). *Language, literature, and the learner: Creative classroom practice.* London: Longman.

Carver, R. P. (1994). Percentage of unknown vocabulary words in text as a function of the relative difficulty of the text: Implications for instruction. *Journal of Reading Behavior, 26,* 413–437.

Carver, R. P. (1997). Reading for one second, one minute, or one year from the perspective of Rauding theory. *Scientific Studies of Reading, 1,* 3–45.

Carver, R. P. (2000). *The cause of high and low reading achievement.* Mahwah, NJ: Lawrence Erlbaum.

Carver, R. P. (2003). The highly lawful relationships among pseudoword decoding, word identification, spelling, listening, and reading. *Scientific Studies of Reading, 7,* 127–154.

Cassidy, S. (2004). Learning styles: An overview of theories, models, and measures. *Educational psychology, 24,* 419–444.

Cazden, C. (1992). *Whole Language plus.* New York: Teachers College Press.

Celce-Murcia, M., & Olshtain, E. (2000). *Discourse and context in language teaching.* New York: Cambridge University Press.

Chall, J. S. (1958). *Readability: An appraisal of research and application.* Columbus, OH: Ohio State Bureau of Education Research Monographs.

Chamot, A. U., & El-Dinary, P. B. (1999). Children's learning strategies in language immersion classrooms. *Modern Language Journal, 83,* 319–338.

Chamot, A. U., & O'Malley, J. M. (1994a). *The CALLA handbook: Implementing the cognitive academic language learning approach.* Reading, MA: Addison-Wesley.

Chamot, A. U., & O'Malley, J. M. (1994b). Instructional approaches and teaching procedures. In K. Spangenberg-Urbschat & R. Pritchard (Eds.), *Kids come in all languages: Reading instruction for ESL students* (pp. 82–107). Newark, DE: International Reading Association.

Chapelle, C. A. (1998). Construct definition and validity inquiry in SLA research. In L. F. Bachman & A. D. Cohen (Eds.). *Interfaces between second language acquisition and language testing research* (pp. 32–70). Cambridge, England: Cambridge University Press.

Chapelle, C. A., & Douglas, D. (2006). *Assessing language through computer technology.* Cambridge, England: Cambridge University Press.

Chapelle, C., & Green, P. (1992). Field independence/dependence in second language acquisition research. *Language Learning, 42,* 47–83.

Chapelle, C., & Roberts, C. (1986). Ambiguity tolerance and field independence as predictors of proficiency in English as a second language. *Language Learning, 36,* 27–45.

Charrow, V. (1988). Readability vs. comprehensibility: A case study in improving a real document. In A. Davidson & G. M. Green (Eds.), *Linguistic complexity and text comprehension* (pp. 85–114). Hillsdale, NJ: Lawrence Erlbaum.

Chen, H.-C., & Graves, M. (1995). Effects of previewing and providing background knowledge on Taiwanese college students' comprehension of American short stories. *TESOL Quarterly, 29*, 663–686.

Ching, R. J. (2007). Integrating grammar into a high school expository reading and writing course. *CATESOL Journal, 19*, 89–106.

Ching, R. J. (2008). Module 2: "Going for the look." In California State University Expository Reading and Writing Task Force, *Expository reading and writing course: Semester one and semester two*. Long Beach, CA: California State University.

Cho, K.-S., & Krashen, S. D. (1994). Acquisition of vocabulary from the Sweet Valley Kids series: Adult ESL acquisition. *Journal of Reading, 37*, 662–667.

Chung, J. S. L. (2000). Signals and reading comprehension—Theory and practice. *System, 28*, 247–259.

Clapham, C. (1996). *The development of IELTS: A study of the effect of background knowledge on reading comprehension*. Cambridge: Cambridge University Press.

Clarke, D. F., & Nation, I. S. P. (1980). Guessing the meanings of words from context: Strategy and techniques. *System, 8*, 211–220.

Clarke, M. A. (1979). Reading in Spanish and English: Evidence from adult ESL students. *Language Learning, 29*, 121–150.

Clarke, M. A. (1980). The short circuit hypothesis of ESL reading—or when language competence interferes with reading performance. *Modern Language Journal, 64*, 203–209.

Clarke, M. A. (1988). The short circuit hypothesis of ESL reading: Or when language competence interferes with reading performance. In P. L. Carrell, J. Devine, & D. E. Eskey (Eds.), *Interactive approaches to second language reading* (pp. 114–124). New York: Cambridge University Press.

Clarke, M. A., & Silberstein, S. (1979). Toward a realization of psycho-linguistic principles in the ESL reading class. In R. Mackay, B. Barkman, & R. Jordan (Eds.), *Reading in a second language: Hypotheses, organization, and practice* (pp. 48–65). Rowley, MA: Newbury House.

Clay, M. M. (1979). *Reading: The patterning of complex behavior* (2nd ed.). Portsmouth, NH: Heinemann.

Cobb, T. (2000). One size fits all? Francophone learners and English vocabulary tests. *Canadian Modern Language Review, 57*, 295–324.

Cohen, A. D. (1994). *Assessing language ability in the classroom* (2nd ed.). Boston: Heinle.

Cohen, A. D. (1996).Verbal reports as a source of insights into second language learner strategies. *Applied Language Learning, 7*, 5–24.

Cohen, A. D. (1998). *Strategies in learning and using a second language*. London: Longman.

Cohen, A. D. (2001). Second language assessment. In M. Celce-Murcia (Ed.), *Teaching English as a second or foreign language* (3rd ed., pp. 515–534). Boston: Heinle.

Cohen, A. D., Glasman, H., Rosenbaum-Cohen, P. R., Ferrara, J., & Fine, J. (1979). Reading English for specialized purposes: Discourse analysis and the use of student informants. *TESOL Quarterly, 13*, 551–564.

Cohen, A. D., & Upton, T. A. (2006). *Strategies in responding to new TOEFL reading tasks* (TOEFL Monograph No. MS-33). Princeton, NJ: Educational Testing Service.

Collie, J., & Slater, S. (1987). *Literature in the language classroom*. Cambridge: Cambridge University Press.

Collins, J., & Blot, R. (Eds.). (2003). *Literacy and literacies: Texts, power, and identity*. Cambridge, England: Cambridge University Press.

Comber, B., & Simpson, A. (Eds.). (2001). *Negotiating critical literacy in language classrooms*. Mahwah, NJ: Lawrence Erlbaum.

Comings, J., Garner, B., & Smith, C. (Eds.). (2007). *Review of adult learning and literacy: Vol. 7. Connecting research, policy, and practice.* New York: Taylor & Francis.

Comrie, B. (1981). *Language universals and linguistic typology.* Chicago: University of Chicago Press.

Comrie, B. (1989). *Language universals and linguistic typology* (2nd ed.). Cambridge, England: Cambridge University Press.

Connor, U. (1996). *Contrastive rhetoric: Cross-cultural aspects of second-language writing.* New York: Cambridge University Press.

Connor, U. (2002). New directions in contrastive rhetoric. *TESOL Quarterly, 36,* 493–510.

Connor, U. (2003). Changing currents in contrastive rhetoric: Implications for teaching and research. In B. Kroll (Ed.), *Exploring the dynamics of second language writing* (pp. 218–241). Cambridge, England: Cambridge University Press.

Connor, U. (2005). Comment by Ulla Connor. *Journal of Second Language Writing, 14,* 132–136.

Connor, U., Nagelhout, E., & Rozycki, W. (Eds.). (2008). *Contrastive rhetoric: Reaching to intercultural rhetoric.* Amsterdam: John Benjamins.

Cook, V., & Bassetti, B. (Eds.). (2005). *Second language writing systems.* Clevedon, England: Multilingual Matters.

Cooper, J. D., & Kiger, N. D. (2001). *Literacy assessment: Helping teachers plan instruction.* Boston: Houghton Mifflin.

Cope, B., & Kalantzis, M. (Eds.). (2000). *Multiliteracies: Literacy learning and the design of social futures.* London: Routledge.

Corson, D. J. (1995). *Using English words.* Dordrecht, The Netherlands: Kluwer Academic.

Coulmas, F. (1989). *The writing systems of the world.* Malden, MA: Blackwell.

Coxhead, A. (1998). *An academic word list* (Occasional Publication No. 18). Wellington, New Zealand: Victoria University of Wellington, IALS.

Coxhead, A. (2000). A new academic word list. *TESOL Quarterly, 34,* 213–238.

Coxhead, A. (2006). *Essentials of teaching academic vocabulary.* Boston: Houghton Mifflin.

Coxhead, A., & Byrd, P. (2007). Preparing writing teachers to teach the vocabulary and grammar of academic prose. *Journal of Second Language Writing, 16,* 129–147.

Craik, F. I. M., & Lockhart, R. S. (1972). Levels of processing: A framework for memory research. *Journal of Verbal Learning and Verbal Behavior, 11,* 671–684.

Craik, F. I. M., & Tulving, E. (1975). Depth of processing and the retention of words in episodic memory. *Journal of Experimental Psychology: General, 25,* 314–338.

Crandall, J. (1995). The why, what, and how of ESL reading instruction: Some guidelines for writers of ESL reading textbooks. In P. Byrd (Ed.), *Material writer's guide* (pp. 79–94). Boston: Heinle.

Croft, W. (2003). *Typology and universals* (2nd ed.). Cambridge, England: Cambridge University Press.

Crookes, G. (2003). *A practicum in TESOL: Professional development through teaching practice.* New York: Cambridge University Press.

Cruickshank, D. R., Bainer, D. L., & Metcalf, K. K. (1999). *The act of teaching* (2nd ed.). Boston: McGraw-Hill.

Crystal, D. (1997). *Cambridge encyclopedia of language* (2nd ed.). Cambridge, England: Cambridge University Press.

Crystal, D. (2003). *A dictionary of linguistics and phonetics* (5th ed.). Malden, MA: Blackwell.

Csizér, K., & Dörnyei, Z. (2005). Language learners' motivational profiles and their motivated learning behavior. *Language Learning, 55,* 613–659.

Cuddon, J. A. (1991). *Dictionary of literary terms and literary theory* (3rd rev. ed.). Oxford, England: Blackwell.

Cummins, J. (1976). The influence of bilingualism on cognitive growth: A synthesis of research findings and explanatory hypotheses. *Working Papers on Bilingualism, 9,* 1–43.

Cummins, J. (1979). Linguistic interdependence and educational development of bilingual children. *Review of Educational Research, 49,* 222–251.

Cummins, J. (1981). The role of primary language development in promoting educational success for language minority students. In *Schooling and language minority students: A theoretical framework* (pp. 3–49). Los Angeles: California State University Evaluation, Dissemination, and Assessment Center.

Cummins, J., Brown, K., & Sayers, D. (2007). *Literacy, technology, and diversity: Teaching for success in changing times.* Boston: Pearson Education.

Cunningham, P. M. (2000). *Phonics they use: Words for reading and writing* (3rd ed.). Boston: Addison-Wesley.

Cunningham, P. M., & Hall, D. P. (1994). *Making words.* Parsippany, NJ: Good Apple.

Czerniewska, P. (1992). *Learning about writing.* Malden, MA: Blackwell.

Cziko, G. G. (1978). Differences in first- and second-language reading: The use of syntactic, semantic, and discourse constraints. *Canadian Modern Language Review, 34,* 473–489.

Dagostino, L., & Carifio, J. (1994). *Evaluative reading and literacy: A cognitive view.* Boston: Allyn & Bacon.

Dahl, K. L. (2000). *Teaching phonics in context.* Portsmouth, NH: Heinemann.

Dahl, K. L., & Scharer, P. L. (2000). Phonics teaching and learning in Whole Language classrooms: New evidence from research. *The Reading Teacher, 53,* 584–594.

Daller, H., Milton, J., & Treffers-Daller, J. (Eds.). (2008). *Modelling and assessing vocabulary knowledge.* Cambridge, England: Cambridge University Press.

Daniels, P., & Bright, W. (Eds.). (1996). *The world's writing systems.* Oxford, England: Oxford University Press.

Davies, A. (1975). Two tests of speeded reading. In R. L. Jones & B. Spolsky (Eds.), *Testing language proficiency* (pp. 119–130). Arlington, VA: Center for Applied Linguistics.

Davies, A. (1990). *Principles of language testing.* Oxford, England: Blackwell.

Davies, A., Brown, A., Elder, C., Hill, K., Lumley, T., & McNamara, T. (1999). *Dictionary of language testing.* Cambridge, England: Cambridge University Press.

Davis, C. (1997). A Mason–Dixon memory. In J. Canfield, M. V. Hanson, H. McCarty, & M. McCarty, *A 4th course of chicken soup for the soul* (pp. 23–29). Deerfield Beach, FL: Health Communications, Inc.

Davis, F. B. (1972). Psychometric research on comprehension in reading. *Reading Research Quarterly, 7,* 629–678.

Davison, A., Wilson, P., & Herman, G. (1985). *Effects of syntactic connectives and organizing cues on text comprehension.* Champaign, IL: Center for the Study of Reading.

Day, R. R. (Ed.). (1993). *New ways in teaching reading.* Alexandria, VA: TESOL.

Day, R. R., & Bamford, J. (1998). *Extensive reading in the second language classroom.* Cambridge, England: Cambridge University Press.

Day, R. R., Omura, C., & Hiramatsu, M. (1991). Incidental EFL vocabulary learning and reading. *Reading in a Foreign Language, 7,* 541–551.

de Argaez, E. (2006, January). *Internet world stats news, 14.* Retrieved June 11, 2008, from http://www.internetworldstats.com/pr/edi014.htm#3

DeBell, M., & Chapman, C. (2003). *Computer and Internet use by children and adolescents in 2001* (NCES 2004–014). U.S. Department of Education. Washington, DC: National Center for Education Statistics.

de Bot, K., Lowie, W., & Verspoor, M. (2005). *Second language acquisition: An advanced resource book.* London: Routledge.

DeCarrico, J. S. (2001). Vocabulary learning and teaching. In M. Celce-Murcia (Ed.), *Teaching English as a second or foreign language* (3rd ed., pp. 285–299). Boston: Heinle.

Deci, E. (1975). *Intrinsic motivation.* New York: Plenum Press.

Defior, S., Cary, L., & Martos, F. (2002). Differences in reading acquisition development in two shallow orthographies: Portuguese and Spanish. *Applied Psycholinguistics, 23,* 135–148.

Degand, L., & Sanders, T. (2002). The impact of relational markers on expository text comprehension in L1 and L2. *Reading and Writing, 15,* 739–757.

Dole, J., Valencia, S., Gree, E. A., & Wardrop, J. (1991). Effects of two types of prereading instruction on the comprehension of narrative and expository text. *Reading Research Quareterly, 26,* 142–159.

Donin, J., Graves, B., & Goyette, E. (2004). Second language text comprehension: Processing within a multilayered system. *Canadian Modern Language Review, 61,* 53–76.

Dörnyei, Z. (1998). Motivation in second and foreign language learning. *Language Teaching, 31,* 117–135.

Dörnyei, Z. (2001). *Motivational strategies in the language classroom.* Cambridge, England: Cambridge University Press.

Dörnyei, Z. (2002) *Questionnaires in second language research: Construction, administration, and processing.* Mahwah, NJ: Lawrence Erlbaum.

Dörnyei, Z., & Csizér, K. (1998). Ten commandments for motivating language learners: Results of an empirical study. *Language Teaching Research, 2,* 203–229.

Dörnyei, Z., & Katona, L. (1992). Validation of the C-test amongst Hungarian EFL learners. *Language Testing, 9,* 187–206.

Douglas, D., & Hegelheimer, V. (2007). Assessing language using computer technology. *Annual Review of Applied Linguistics, 27,* 115–132.

Dozier, C. (2006). *Responsive literacy coaching: Tools for creating and sustaining purposeful change.* Portland, ME: Stenhouse.

Dressler, C., & Kamil, M. L. (2006). First- and second-language literacy. In D. August & T. Shanahan (Eds.), *Developing literacy in second-language learners: Report of the National Literacy Panel on Language-Minority Children and Youth* (pp. 137–238). Mahwah, NJ: Lawrence Erlbaum.

Droop, M., & Verhoeven, L. (2003). Language proficiency and reading ability in first and second language learners. *Reading Research Quarterly, 38,* 78–103.

Dubin, F. & Bycina, D. (1991). Academic reading and the ESL/EFL teacher. In M. Celce-Murcia (Ed.), *Teaching English as a second or foreign language* (2nd ed., pp. 195–215). Boston: Heinle.

Dubin, F., Eskey, D., & Grabe, W. (Eds.). (1986). *Teaching second language reading for academic purposes.* Reading, MA: Addison-Wesley.

Dubin, F., & Olshtain, E. (1986). *Course design.* Cambridge, England: Cambridge University Press.

Dudley-Evans, T., & St. John, M. J. (1998). *Developments in English for specific purposes: A multidisciplinary approach.* Cambridge, England: Cambridge University Press.

Dumas, F. (2006). The "F Word." In C. G. Latteral (Ed.), *Remix: Reading and composing culture* (pp. 60–63). New York: Bedford/St. Martin's.

Dupuy, B., Tse, L., & Cook, T. (1996, Summer). Bringing books into the classroom: First steps in turning college-level ESL students into readers. *TESOL Journal, 5/4,* 10–15.

Eagleton, M. B., & Dobler, E. (2007). *Reading the web: Strategies for Internet inquiry*. New York: Guilford.

Eagleton, T. (1996). *Literary theory: An introduction* (2nd ed.). Minneapolis: University of Minnesota Press.

Edelsky, C. (2006). *With literacy and justice for all: Rethinking the social in language and education* (3rd ed.). New York: Taylor & Francis.

Educational Testing Service. (n.d.). *Framework for recent TOEFL research*. Retrieved January 15, 2008 from http://www.ets.org/Media/Research/pdf/Framework_Recent_TOEFL_Research.pdf

Educational Testing Service. (2004). *iBT/Next Generation TOEFL Test Integrated Writing Rubrics (Scoring Standards)*. Retrieved February 1, 2008 from http://www.ets.org/Media/Tests/TOEFL/pdf/Writing_Rubrics.pdf

Egéa-Kuehne, D. (2004). Student electronic portfolio assessment. In C. Cherry & L. Bradley (Eds.), *Assessment practices in foreign language education* (pp. 19–28). Valdosta, GA: Southern Conference on Language Teaching.

Eggington, W. G. (1987). Written academic discourse in Korean: Implications for effective communication. In U. Connor & R. B. Kaplan (Eds.), *Writing across languages: Analysis of L2 text* (pp. 153–168). Reading, MA: Addison-Wesley.

Ehri, L. C. (2004). Teaching phonemic awareness and phonics: An explanation of the National Reading Panel meta-analyses. In P. McCardle, & V. Chhabra (Eds.), *The voice of evidence in reading research* (pp. 153–186). Baltimore: Paul H. Brookes.

Ehrman, M. (1996). *Understanding second language learning difficulties*. Thousand Oaks, CA:

Ehrman, M., & Oxford, R. (1990). Adult language learning styles and strategies in an intensive training setting. *Modern Language Journal, 74*, 311–328.

Ehrman, M., & Oxford, R. (1995). Cognition plus: Correlates of language learning success. *Modern Language Journal, 79*, 67–89.

Elley, W. B. (1969). The assessment of readability by noun frequency counts. *Reading Research Quarterly, 4*, 411–427.

Elley, W. B. (1989). Vocabulary acquisition from listening to stories. *Reading Research Quarterly, 24*, 174–187.

Elley, W. B. (1991). Acquiring literacy in a second language: The effect of book-based programs. *Language Learning, 41*, 375–411.

Elley, W. B. (1992). *How in the world do students read? The IEA study of reading/literacy*. The Hague: International Association for the Evaluation of Educational Achievement.

Elley, W. B. (1993). *Reading: Literacy in thirty countries*. Oxford: Pergamon.

Elley, W. B. (1998). *Raising literacy levels in third world countries: A method that works*. Culver City, CA: Language Education Associates.

Elley, W., & Mangubhai, F. (1981). *The impact of a book flood in Fiji primary schools*. Wellington: New Zealand Council for Educational Research.

Elley, W., & Mangubhai, F. (1983). The impact of reading on second language learning. *Reading Research Quarterly, 19*, 53–67.

Ellis, N. (2003). Constructions, chunking, and connectionism: The emergence of second language structure. In C. J. Doughty & M. H. Long (Eds.), *The handbook of second language acquisition* (pp. 63–103). Malden, MA: Blackwell.

Ellis, R. (1997). *Second language acquisition*. Oxford, England: Oxford University Press.

Ellis, R. (2002). The place of grammar instruction in the second/foreign language curriculum. In E. Hinkel & S. Fotos (Eds.), *New perspectives on grammar teaching in second language classrooms* (pp. 17–34). Mahwah, NJ: Lawrence Erlbaum.

Enright, M. K., Grabe, W., Koda, K., Mosenthal, P., Mulcahy-Ernt, P., & Schedl, M. (2000). *TOEFL 2000 reading framework: A working paper* (TOEFL Monograph No. MS-17). Princeton, NJ: Educational Testing Service.

Epstein, R., & Ormiston, M. (2007). *Tools and tips for using ELT materials: A guide for teachers*. Ann Arbor: University of Michigan Press.

Eskey, D. E. (1986). Theoretical foundations. In F. Dubin, D. E. Eskey, & W. Grabe (Eds.), *Teaching second language reading for academic purposes* (pp. 3–23). Reading, MA: Addison-Wesley.

Eskey, D. E. (2005). Reading in a second language. In E. Hinkel (Ed.), *Handbook of research in second language teaching and learning* (pp. 563–579). Mahwah, NJ: Lawrence Erlbaum.

Eskey, D. E., & Grabe, W. (1988). Interactive models for second language reading. In P. Carrell, J. Devine, & D. Eskey (Eds.), *Interactive approaches to second language reading* (pp. 221–238). Cambridge: Cambridge University Press.

Fang, Z., & Schleppegrell, M. J. (2008). *Language and reading in content areas: Toward a linguistically informed second language reading pedagogy*. Ann Arbor: University of Michigan Press.

Farris, P. J., Fuhler, C. J., & Walther, M. P. (2004). *Teaching reading: A balanced approach for today's classrooms*. New York: McGraw-Hill.

Fecteau, M. L. (1999). First- and second-language reading comprehension of literary texts. *Modern Language Journal, 83,* 475–493.

Feiler, A. (2007). *Improving primary literacy: Linking home and school*. London: Routledge.

Felder, R. M., & Henriques, E. R. (1995). Learning and teaching styles in foreign and second language education. *Foreign Language Annals, 28,* 21–31.

Ferris, D. R. (1998). Students' views of academic aural/oral skills: A comparative needs analysis. *TESOL Quarterly, 32,* 289–318.

Ferris, D. R. (2002). *Treatment of error in second language writing classes*. Ann Arbor: University of Michigan Press.

Ferris, D. R. (2009). *Multiple student audiences in L2 writing instruction*. Ann Arbor: University of Michigan Press.

Ferris, D. R., & Hedgcock, J. S. (2005). *Teaching ESL composition: Purpose, process, and practice* (2nd ed.). Mahwah, NJ: Lawrence Erlbaum.

Fillmore, C. J., & Kay, P. (1983). *A text-semantic analysis of reading comprehension tests: Final report*. Berkeley: Institute of Human Learning, University of California. (ERIC Document Reproduction Service No. ED238903.)

Finnegan, R. (1988). *Literacy and orality*. Oxford, England: Blackwell.

Fitzgerald, J., & Graves, M. F. (2004). *Scaffolding reading experiences for English-language learners*. Norwood, MA: Christopher-Gordon.

Flavell, J. H., Miller, P. H., & Miller, S. A. (2002). *Cognitive development* (4th ed.). Upper Saddle River, NJ: Prentice-Hall.

Flippo, R. F. (Ed.). (2001). *Reading researchers in search of common ground*. Mahwah, NJ: Lawrence Erlbaum.

Flower, L., & Hayes, J. R. (1981). A cognitive process theory of writing. *College Composition and Communication, 32,* 365–387.

Flurkey, A. D., Paulson, E. J., & Goodman, K. S. (Eds.). (2007). *Scientific realism in studies of reading*. New York: Taylor & Francis.

Folse, K. (2004). *Vocabulary myths: Applying second language research to classroom teaching*. Ann Arbor: University of Michigan Press.

Folse, K. S. (2008). Myth 1: Teaching vocabulary is not the writing teacher's job. In J. Reid (Ed.), *Writing myths* (pp. 1–17). Ann Arbor: University of Michigan Press.

Fordham, P., Holland, D., & Millican, J. (1995). *Adult literacy: A handbook for development workers*. Oxford, England: Oxfam/Voluntary Service Overseas.

Foster, G. (2005). *What good readers do: Seven steps to better reading*. Portland, ME: Stenhouse.

Fountas, I., & Hannigan, I. (1989). Making sense of Whole Language: The pursuit of informed teaching. *Childhood Education, 65*, 133–137.

Francis, W. N., & Kucera, H. (1982). *Frequency analysis of English usage*. Boston: Houghton Mifflin.

Franklin, E. (Ed.). (1999). *Reading and writing in more than one language: Lessons for teachers*. Alexandria, VA: TESOL.

Frantzen, D. (2003). Factors affecting how second language Spanish students derive meaning from context. *Modern Language Journal, 87*, 168–199.

Fraser, C. (1999). Lexical processing strategy use and vocabulary learning through reading. *Studies in Second Language Acquisition, 21*, 225–241.

Freeman, D. (1996). Redefining the relationship between research and what teachers know. In K. M. Bailey & D. Nunan (Eds.), *Voices from the language classroom* (p. 88–115). Cambridge, England: Cambridge University Press.

Freeman, D., & Freeman, Y. (2000). *Teaching reading in multicultural classrooms*. Portsmouth, NH: Heinemann.

Freeman, Y., & Freeman, D. (1992). *Whole language for second-language learners*. Portsmouth, NH: Heinemann.

Freire, P. (1968). *Pedagogy of the oppressed*. New York: Seabury.

Freire, P., & Macedo, D. (1987). *Literacy: Reading the word and the world*. Cambridge, MA: Bergin & Garvey.

Frodesen, J., & Eyring, J. (2007). *Grammar dimensions: Form, meaning, and use, Book 4* (4th ed.). Boston: Thomson/Heinle.

Fry, E. (1977). *Elementary reading instruction*. New York: McGraw-Hill.

Fukkink, R. G., Hulstijn, J., & Simis, A. (2005). Does training in second-language word recognition skills affect reading comprehension? An experimental study. *Modern Language Journal, 89*, 54–75.

Fulcher, G., & Davidson, F. (2007). *Language testing and assessment: An advanced resource book*. London: Routledge.

Gajdusek, L. (1988). Toward wider use of literature in ESL: Why and how. *TESOL Quarterly, 22*, 227–257.

Gajdusek, L., & van Dommelen, D. (1993). Literature and critical thinking in the composition classroom. In J. G. Carson & I. Leki (Eds.), *Reading in the composition classroom* (pp. 197–218). Boston: Heinle.

Galloway, V. (1998). Constructing cultural realities: "Facts" and frameworks of association. In J. Harper, M. Lively, & M. Williams (Eds.), *The coming of age of the profession* (pp. 129–140). Boston: Heinle.

Gambrell, L. B., Morrow, L. M., & Pressley, M. (2007). *Best practices in literacy instruction* (3rd ed.). New York: Guilford.

García, G. E. (1991). Factors influencing the English reading test performance of Spanish-speaking Hispanic children. *Reading Research Quarterly, 26*, 371–393.

García, G. E., McKoon, G., & August, D. (2006). Synthesis: Language and literacy assessment. In D. August & T. Shanahan (Eds.), *Developing literacy in second-language learners: Report of the National Literacy Panel on Language-Minority Children and Youth* (pp. 583–624). Mahwah, NJ: Lawrence Erlbaum.

Gardner, D. (1996). Self-assessment for self-access learners. *TESOL Journal, 6*, 18–23.

Gardner, R. C., & Lambert, W. (1972). *Attitudes and motivation in second language learning.* Rowley, MA: Newbury House.

Gardner, R. C., & MacIntyre, P. D. (1991). An instrumental motivation in language study: Who says it isn't effective? *Studies in Second Language Acquisition, 13,* 57–72.

Gascoigne, C. (2002). Documenting the initial second language reading experience: The readers speak. *Foreign Language Annals, 35,* 554–560.

Gass, S., & Selinker, L. (2008). *Second language acquisition: An introductory course* (3rd ed.). London: Routledge.

Gaur, A. (1995). Scripts and writing systems: A historical perspective. In I. Taylor & D. R. Olson (Eds.), *Scripts and literacy: Reading and learning to read alphabets, syllabaries, and characters* (pp. 19–30). Dordrecht, The Netherlands: Kluwer Academic.

Gee, J. P. (1988). The legacies of literacy: From Plato to Freire through Harvey Gaff. *Harvard Educational Review, 58,* 195–212.

Gee, J. P. (1991). Socio-cultural approaches to literacy (literacies). *Annual Review of Applied Linguistics, 12,* 31–48.

Gee, J. P. (1996). *Social linguistics and literacies: Ideology in discourses* (2nd ed.). London: Taylor & Francis.

Gee, J. P. (2000). New people in new worlds: Networks, the new capitalism, and schools. In B. Cope & M. Kalantzis (Eds.), *Multiliteracies: Literacy learning and the design of social futures* (pp. 43–68). London: Routledge.

Gee, J. P. (2002). Literacies, identities, and discourses. In M. J. Schleppegrell & M. C. Colombi (Eds.), *Developing advanced literacy in first and second languages: Meaning with power* (pp. 159–175). Mahwah, NJ: Lawrence Erlbaum.

Gee, J. P. (2003). *What video games have to teach us about learning and literacy.* New York: Palgrave Macmillan.

Gee, J. P. (2005). *An introduction to discourse analysis: Theory and method* (2nd ed.). New York: Routledge.

Gee, J. P. (2008). *Social linguistics and literacies: Ideology in discourses* (3rd ed.). New York: Taylor & Francis.

Genesee, F. (1998). Content-based language instruction. In M. Met (Ed.), *Critical issues in early second language learning* (pp. 103–105). Glenview, IL: Scott Foresman-Addison-Wesley.

Genesee, F., & Geva, E. (2006). Cross-linguistic relationships in working memory, phonological processes, and oral language. In D. August & T. Shanahan (Eds.), *Developing literacy in second-language learners: Report of the National Literacy Panel on Language-Minority Children and Youth* (pp. 175–183). Mahwah, NJ: Lawrence Erlbaum.

Genesee, F., Geva, E., Dressler, C., & Kamil, M. L. (2006). Synthesis: Cross-linguistic relationships. In D. August & T. Shanahan (Eds.), *Developing literacy in second-language learners: Report of the National Literacy Panel on Language-Minority Children and Youth* (pp. 153–174). Mahwah, NJ: Lawrence Erlbaum.

Genesee, F., & Upshur, J. (1996). *Classroom-based evaluation in second language education.* Cambridge, England: Cambridge University Press.

Geva, E., & Siegel, L. (2000). Orthographic and cognitive factors in the concurrent development of basic reading skills in two languages. *Reading and Writing, 12,* 1–30.

Gilroy, M., & Parkinson, B. (1996). Teaching literature in a foreign language. *Language Teaching, 29,* 213–225.

Glasgow, N. A., & Farrell, S. C. (2007). *What successful literacy teachers do.* Thousand Oaks, CA: Corwin.

Glazer, S. M. (2007). A classroom portfolio system: Assessment is instruction. In

J. R. Paratore & R. L. McCormack (Eds.), *Classroom literacy assessment: Making sense of what students know and do* (pp. 227–246). New York: Guilford.

Glickman-Bond, J. (2006). *Creating and using rubrics in today's classrooms: A practical guide.* Norwood, MA: Christopher-Gordon.

Goen, S., Porter, P., Swanson, D., & van Dommelen, D. (2002). Working with Generation 1. 5 students and their teachers: ESL meets composition. *CATESOL Journal, 14,* 131–171.

Goldenberg, C., Rueda, R. S., & August, D. (2006). Sociocultural influences on the literacy attainment of language-minority children and youth. In D. August & T. Shanahan (Eds.), *Developing literacy in second-language learners: Report of the National Literacy Panel on Language-Minority Children and Youth* (pp. 269–318). Mahwah, NJ: Lawrence Erlbaum.

Goodman, K. S. (1965). A linguistic study of cues and miscues in reading. *Elementary English, 42,* 639–643.

Goodman, K. S. (1967). Reading: A psycholinguistic guessing game. *Journal of the Reading Specialist, 6,* 126–135.

Goodman, K. S. (1968). The psycholinguistic nature of the reading process. In K. S. Goodman (Ed.), *The psycholinguistic nature of the reading process* (pp. 15–26). Detroit: Wayne State University Press.

Goodman, K. S. (1969). Analysis of oral language miscues: Applied psycholinguistics. *Reading Research Quarterly, 5,* 9–30.

Goodman, K. S. (1976). Reading: A psycholinguistic guessing game. In H. Singer & R. B. Rudell (Eds.), *Theoretical models and processes of reading* (pp. 497–508). Newark, DE: International Reading Association.

Goodman, K. S. (1986). *What's whole in Whole Language.* Portsmouth, NH: Heinemann.

Goodman, K. (1988). The reading process. In P. Carrell, J. Devine, & D. Eskey (Eds.), *Interactive approaches to second language reading* (pp. 11–21). Cambridge: Cambridge University Press.

Goodman, K. S. (1996). *On reading.* Portsmouth, NH: Heinemann.

Goodman, K. S., Shannon, P., Freeman, Y. S., & Murphy, S. (1988). *Report card on basal readers.* Katonah, NY: Richard C. Owen.

Goodman, Y. M. (1989). The roots of Whole Language. *Elementary School Journal, 90,* 113–127.

Goodman, Y. M., & Burke, C. L. (1972). *Reading miscue inventory kit.* New York: MacMillan.

Goodman, Y. M., & Martens, P. (Eds.). (2007). *Critical issues in early literacy: Research and pedagogy.* New York: Taylor & Francis.

Goodman, Y. M., Watson, D. J., & Burke, C. L. (2005). *Reading miscue inventory: From evaluation to instruction* (2nd ed.). Katonah, NY: Richard C. Owen.

Goody, J. (1987). *The interface between the written and the oral.* Cambridge, England: Cambridge University Press.

Gordon, W. M. (1982). *The reading curriculum: A reference guide to criterion-based skill development in grades K–8.* New York: Praeger.

Gottlieb, M. (1995). Nurturing student learning through portfolios. *TESOL Journal, 5,* 12–14.

Gough, P. B. (1972). One second of reading. In F. Kavanaugh & I. G. Mattingly (Eds.), *Language by ear and eye: The relationship between speech and reading* (pp. 331–358). Cambridge, MA: MIT Press.

Gough, P. B., & Wren, S. (1999). Constructing meaning: The role of decoding. In J. Oakhill

& S. Beard (Eds.), *Reading development and the teaching of reading* (pp. 59–78). Malden, MA: Blackwell.

Grabe, W. (1986). The transition from theory to practice in teaching reading. In F. Dubin, D. E. Eskey, & W. Grabe (Eds.), *Teaching second language reading for academic purposes* (pp. 25–48). Reading, MA: Addison-Wesley.

Grabe, W. (1991). Current developments in second language reading research. *TESOL Quarterly, 25*, 375–406.

Grabe, W. (1995, April). *Remarks made at the Colloquium on Research in Reading in a Second Language,* TESOL Conference, Long Beach, CA.

Grabe, W. (1997). Discourse analysis and reading instruction. In T. Miller (Ed.), *Functional approaches to written text: Classroom applications* (pp. 2–15). Washington, DC: United States Information Agency.

Grabe, W. (2004). Research on teaching reading. *Annual Review of Applied Linguistics, 2,* 44–69.

Grabe, W., & Kaplan, R. B. (1996). *Theory and practice of writing: An applied linguistic perspective.* New York: Longman.

Grabe, W., & Stoller, F. (1997). Reading and vocabulary development in a second language: A case study. In J. Coady & T. Huckin (Eds.), *Second language vocabulary acquisition* (pp. 98–122). Cambridge, England: Cambridge University Press.

Grabe, W., & Stoller, F. L. (2001). Reading for academic purposes: Guidelines for the ESL/ EFL teacher. In M. Celce-Murcia (Ed.), *Teaching English as a second or foreign language* (3rd ed., pp. 187–203). Boston: Heinle.

Grabe, W., & Stoller, F. L. (2002). *Teaching and researching reading.* Harlow, England: Longman/Pearson Education.

Grasso, S. (2005). Academic reading: How do we teach it and test it in EAP courses? *Proceedings of the 18th Annual English Australia Education Conference 2005.* Retrieved November 6, 2007 from http://www.elicos.edu.au/index.cgi?E=hcatfuncs&PT=sl&X= getdoc&Lev1=pub_c06_07&Lev2=c05_grasso

Graves, K. (2000). *Designing language courses: A guide for teachers.* Boston: Heinle.

Graves, M. F. (2006). *The vocabulary book: Learning and instruction.* New York: Teachers College Press.

Graves, M., & Graves, B. (2003). *Scaffolding reading experiences: Designs for student success* (2nd ed.). Norwood, MA: Christopher-Gordon.

Green, C., & Green, J. M. (1993). Secret friend journals. *TESOL Journal, 21* (3), 20–23.

Greenhouse, S. (2003). Going for the look, but risking discrimination. *New York Times,* 13 July.

Grellet, F. (1981). *Developing reading skills.* Cambridge, England: Cambridge University Press.

Groeber, J. F. (2007). *Designing and using rubrics for reading and language arts, K–6.* Thousand Oaks, CA: Corwin.

Gronlund, N. (1998). *Assessment of student achievement* (6th ed.). Boston: Allyn & Bacon.

Guthrie, J. T., & Knowles, K. T. (2001). Promoting reading motivation. In L. Verhoeven & C. E. Snow (Eds.), *Literacy and motivation: Reading engagement in individuals and groups* (pp. 159–176). Mahwah, NJ: Lawrence Erlbaum.

Hacquebord, H. (1989). *Reading comprehension of Turkish and Dutch students attending secondary schools.* Groningen: RUG.

Hall, J. K. (2002). *Teaching and researching language and culture.* London: Pearson.

Halliday, M. A. K., & Hasan, R. (1976). *Cohesion in English.* London: Longman.

Hamp-Lyons, L., & Condon, W. (2000). *Assessing the portfolio: Principles for practice, theory, and research.* Cresskill, NJ: Hampton Press.

Harklau, L. (1994). ESL versus mainstream classes: Contrasting L2 learning environments. *TESOL Quarterly, 28,* 241–272.

Harklau, L. (2003). L2 writing by "Generation 1. 5 students": Recent research and pedagogical trends. *Journal of Second Language Writing, 12,* 153–156.

Harklau, L., Losey, K. M., & Siegal, M. (Eds.). (1999). *Generation 1.5 meets college composition.* Mahwah, NJ: Lawrence Erlbaum.

Harp, B. (2000). *Handbook of literacy assessment and evaluation* (2nd ed.). Norwood, MA: Christopher-Gordon Publishers.

Harris, A. J., & Sipay, E. R. (1990). *How to increase reading ability: A guide to developmental and remedial methods* (9th ed.). White Plains, NY: Longman.

Harris, M., & Hatano, G. (Eds.). (1999). *Learning to read and write: A cross-linguistic perspective.* Cambridge, England: Cambridge University Press.

Harris, T. L., & Hodges, R. E. (Eds.). (1981). *Dictionary of reading and related terms.* Newark, DE: International Reading Association.

Hartman, B., & Tarone, E. (1999). Preparation for college writing: Teachers talk about writing instruction for Southeast Asian American students in secondary school. In L. Harklau, K. Losey, & M. Siegal (Eds.), *Generation 1.5 meets college composition: Issues in the teaching of writing to U.S.-educated learners of ESL* (pp. 99–118). Mahwah, NJ: Lawrence Erlbaum.

Hawisher, G. E. (2004). *Literate lives in the information age: Narratives of literacy from the United States.* Mahwah, NJ: Lawrence Erlbaum.

Haynes, M., & Carr, T. H. (1990). Writing system background and second language reading: A component skills analysis of English reading by native-speakers of Chinese. In T. H. Carr & B. A. Levy (Eds.), *Reading and its development: Component skills approaches* (pp. 375–421). San Diego: Academic Press.

Hazenberg, S., & Hulstijn, J. H. (1996). Defining a minimal receptive second-language vocabulary for non-native university students. *Applied Linguistics, 17,* 145–163.

Heath, S. B. (1982). Protean shapes in literacy events: Ever-shifting oral and literate traditions. In D. Tannen (Ed.), *Spoken and written language: Exploring orality and literacy* (pp. 91–118). Norwood, NJ: Ablex.

Heath, S. B. (1983). *Ways with words: Language, life, and work in communities and classrooms.* Cambridge, England: Cambridge University Press.

Heath, S. B. (1996). Re-creating literature in the ESL classroom. *TESOL Quarterly, 30,* 776–779.

Heilman, A. W., Blair, T. R., & Rupley, W. H. (2002). *Principles and practices of teaching reading* (10th ed.). Upper Saddle River, NJ: Prentice-Hall.

Heller, M. F. (1999). *Reading–writing connections: From theory to practice.* Mahwah, NJ: Lawrence Erlbaum.

Helgesen, M. (1997). What one extensive reading program looks like. *Language Teacher, 21,* 31–33.

Hiebert, E. H., & Kamil, M. L. (Eds.). (2005). *Teaching and learning vocabulary: Bringing research to practice.* Mahwah, NJ: Lawrence Erlbaum.

Hill, J. (1972). *The educational sciences.* Detroit: Oakland Community College.

Hilles, S., & Sutton, A. (2001). Teaching adults. In M. Celce-Murcia (Ed.), *Teaching English as a second or foreign language* (3rd ed., pp. 385–399). Boston: Heinle.

Hillocks, G., Jr. (1995). *Teaching writing as reflective practice.* New York: Teachers College Press.

Hinds, J. (1987). Reader versus writer responsibility: A new typology. In U. Connor & R. B. Kaplan (Eds.), *Writing across languages: Analysis of L2 text* (pp. 141–152). Reading, MA: Addison-Wesley.

Hinkel, E. (2002). *Second language writers' text: Linguistic and rhetorical features.* Mahwah, NJ: Lawrence Erlbaum.

Hinkel, E. (2004). *Teaching academic ESL writing: Practical techniques in vocabulary and grammar.* Mahwah, NJ: Lawrence Erlbaum.

Hirsh, D., & Nation, P. (1992). What vocabulary size is needed to read unsimplified texts for pleasure? *Reading in a Foreign Language, 8,* 689–696.

Hirvela, A. (1996). Reader-response theory and ELT. *ELT Journal, 50,* 127–134.

Hirvela, A. (2001). Connecting reading and writing through literature. In D. Belcher & A. Hirvela (Eds.), *Linking literacies: Perspectives on L2 reading–writing connections* (pp. 109–134). Ann Arbor: University of Michigan Press.

Hirvela, A. (2004). *Connecting reading and writing in second language writing instruction.* Ann Arbor: University of Michigan Press.

Hoey, M. (2005). *Lexical priming: A new theory of words and language.* London: Routledge.

Holdaway, D. (1980). *The foundations of literacy.* Portsmouth, NH: Heinemann.

Holman, C. H., & Harmon, W. (1992). *A handbook to literature* (6th ed.). New York: Macmillan.

Hoosain, R. (1995). Getting at the sound and meaning of logographic and alphabetic scripts. In I. Taylor & D. R. Olson (Eds.), *Scripts and literacy: Reading and learning to read alphabets, syllabaries, and characters* (pp. 131–144). Dordrecht, The Netherlands: Kluwer Academic.

Hornby, A. S., & Wehmeier, S. (2007). *Oxford advanced learner's dictionary* (7th rev. ed.). Oxford, England: Oxford University Press.

Horowitz, R. (Ed.). (2007). *Talking texts: How speech and writing interact in school learning.* Mahwah, NJ: Lawrence Erlbaum.

Horst, M. (2005). Learning L2 vocabulary through extensive reading: A measurement study. *Canadian Modern Language Review, 61,* 355–382.

Horwitz, E. (2008). *Becoming a language teacher: A practical guide to second language learning and teaching.* Boston: Pearson Education.

Hu, M. H-C., & Nation, P. (2000). Unknown vocabulary density and reading comprehension. *Reading in a Foreign Language, 13,* 403–430.

Huckin, T. N., & Coady, J. (1999). Incidental vocabulary acquisition in a second language: A review. *Studies in Second Language Acquisition, 21,* 181–193.

Huckin, T. N., Haynes, M., & Coady, J. (Eds.). (1997). *Second language reading and vocabulary learning.* Norwood, NJ: Ablex.

Hudson, T. (1993). Testing the specificity of ESP reading skills. In D. Douglas & C. Chapelle (Eds.), *A new decade of language testing* (pp. 58–82). Alexandria, VA: TESOL.

Hudson, T. (2005). Trends in assessment scales and criterion-referenced language assessment. *Annual Review of Applied Linguistics, 25,* 205–227.

Hudson, T. (2007). *Teaching second language reading.* Oxford, England: Oxford University Press.

Hughes, A. (2003). *Testing for language teachers* (2nd ed.). Cambridge, England: Cambridge University Press.

Hulstijn, J. (1992). Retention of inferred and given word meanings: Experiments in incidental vocabulary learning. In P. J. L. Arnaud & H. Béjoint (Eds.), *Vocabulary and applied linguistics* (pp. 113–125). London: Macmillan.

Hulstijn, J. (1993). When do foreign-language readers look up the meaning of unfamiliar words? The influence of task and learner variables. *Modern Language Journal, 77,* 139–147.

Hulstijn, J. (1997). Mnemonic methods in foreign language vocabulary learning. In J. Coady & T. Huckin (Eds.), *Second language vocabulary acquisition* (pp. 203–224). Cambridge, England: Cambridge University Press.

Hulstijn, J. H. (2001). Intentional and incidental second language vocabulary learning: A reappraisal of elaboration, rehearsal, and automaticity. In P. Robinson (Ed.), *Cognition and second language instruction* (pp. 258–286). Cambridge, England: Cambridge University Press.

Hulstijn, J., Hollander, M., & Greidanus, T. (1996). Incidental vocabulary learning by advanced foreign language students: The influence of marginal glosses, dictionary use, and reoccurrence of unknown words. *Modern Language Journal, 80,* 327–339.

Huss, R. L. (1995). Young children becoming literate in English as a second language. *TESOL Quarterly, 29,* 767–774.

Hutchinson, T., & Waters, A. (1987). *English for specific purposes: A learning-centred approach.* Cambridge, England: Cambridge University Press.

Hyland, K. (2004a). *Disciplinary discourses: Social interactions in academic writing.* Ann Arbor: University of Michigan Press.

Hyland, K. (2004b). *Genre and second language writing.* Ann Arbor: University of Michigan Press.

Hyon, S. (2001). Long-term effects of genre-based instruction: A follow-up study of an EAP reading course. *English for Specific Purposes, 20,* 417–438.

Hyon, S. (2002). Genre in ESL reading: A classroom study. In A. M. Johns (Ed.), *Genre in the classroom: Multiple perspectives* (pp. 121–141). Mahwah, NJ: Lawrence Erlbaum.

Ingraham, B., Levy, P., McKenna, C., & Roberts, G. (2007). Academic literacy in the 21st century. In G. Conole, & M. Oliver (Eds.), *Contemporary perspectives in e-learning research: Themes, methods, and impact on practice* (pp. 160–173). London: Routledge.

Interagency Language Roundtable. (2008). Interagency Language Roundtable Language Skill Level Descriptions. Retrieved July 1, 2008 from: http://www.govtilr.org/Skills/ILRscale4.htm

International Reading Association. (2007). Position statement: Second-language literacy instruction—The role of phonics in reading instruction. Retrieved August 20, 2007 from: http://www.ira.org/resources/issues/positions_phonics.html

International Reading Association/National Council of Teachers of English. (1996). *Standards for the English language arts.* Newark, DE: International Reading Association.

Irvine, C. C. (2007). *Teaching the novel across the curriculum: A handbook for educators.* Westport, CT: Greenwood.

Irwin, J. W. (1986). Cohesion and comprehension: A research review. In J. W. Irwin (Ed.), *Understanding and teaching cohesion comprehension* (pp. 31–43). Newark, DE: International Reading Association.

Iser, W. (1978). *The act of reading: A theory of aesthetic response.* Baltimore: Johns Hopkins University Press.

Israel, S. E., Collins Block, C., Bauserman, K. L., & Kinnucan-Welsch, K. (Eds.). (2005). *Metacognition in literacy learning: Theory, assessment, instruction, and professional development.* Mahwah, NJ: Lawrence Erlbaum.

Ivey, G., & Broaddus, K. (2001). "Just plain reading": A survey of what makes students want to read in middle school classrooms. *Reading Research Quarterly, 36,* 350–377.

Janopoulos, M. (1986). The relationship of pleasure reading and second language writing proficiency. *TESOL Quarterly, 20,* 763–768.

Janzen, J. (1996). Teaching strategic reading. *TESOL Journal, 6* (1), 6–9.

Jensen, L. (1986). Advanced reading skills in a comprehensive course. In F. Dubin, D. E. Eskey, & W. Grabe (Eds.), *Teaching second language reading for academic purposes* (pp. 103–124). Reading, MA: Addison-Wesley.

Jensen, L. (2001). Planning lessons. In M. Celce-Murcia (Ed.), *Teaching English as a second or foreign language* (3rd ed., pp. 403–427). Boston: Heinle.

Jewett, C. (2005). *Technology, literacy, learning: A multimodal approach.* London: Routledge.

Jiang, N. (2002). Form–meaning mapping in vocabulary acquisition in a second language. *Studies in Second Language Acquisition, 24,* 617–638.

Jiang, X., & Grabe, W. (2007). Graphic organizers in reading instruction: Research findings and issues. *Reading in a Foreign Language, 19,* 34–55. Retrieved July 13, 2008 from http://www.nflrc.hawaii.edu/rfl/April2007/jiang/jiang.html

John-Steiner, V. P., & Meehan, T. M. (2000). Creativity and collaboration in knowledge construction. In C. D. Lee & P. Smagorinsky (Eds.), *Vygotskian perspectives on literacy research: Constructing meaning through collaborative inquiry* (pp. 31–48). Cambridge, England: Cambridge University Press.

Johns, A. M. (1997). *Text, role, and context: Developing academic literacies.* Cambridge, England: Cambridge University Press.

Johns, A. M. (2003). Genre and ESL/EFL composition instruction. In B. Kroll (Ed.), *Exploring the dynamics of second language writing* (pp. 195–217). Cambridge, England: Cambridge University Press.

Johns, A. M., & Price-Machado, D. (2001). English for specific purposes: Tailoring courses to student needs—and to the outside world. In M. Celce-Murcia (Ed.), *Teaching English as a second or foreign language* (3rd ed., pp. 43–54). Boston: Heinle.

Johnson, R. K., & Swain, M. (Eds.). (1997). *Immersion education: International perspectives.* Cambridge, England: Cambridge University Press.

Joseph, P. B., Bravmann, S. L., Windschitl, M. A., Mikel, E. R., & Green, N. S. (2000). *Cultures of curriculum.* Mahwah, NJ: Lawrence Erlbaum.

Just, M. A., & Carpenter, P. A. (1980). A theory of reading: From eye fixations to comprehension. *Psychological Review, 87,* 329–354.

Just, M. A., & Carpenter, P. A. (1987). *The psychology of reading and language comprehension.* Boston: Allyn & Bacon.

Kachru, B. B. (Ed.). (1992). *The other tongue: English across cultures* (2nd ed.). Urbana: University of Illinois Press.

Kajder, S. B. (2006). *Bringing the outside in: Visual ways to engage reluctant readers.* Portland, ME: Stenhouse.

Kalantzis, M., & Cope, B. (2000). Changing the role of schools. In B. Cope & M. Kalantzis (Eds.), *Multiliteracies: Literacy learning and the design of social futures* (pp. 121–148). London: Routledge.

Kamil, M. L. (Ed.). (2008). *Handbook of reading research, Vol. IV.* London: Routledge.

Kamil, M. L., Mosenthal, P. B., Pearson, P. D., & Barr, R. (Eds.). (2000). *Handbook of reading research, Vol. III.* Mahwah, NJ: Lawrence Erlbaum.

Kapitzke, C., & Bruce, B. C. (Eds.). (2006). *Libr@ries: Changing information space and practice.* Mahwah, NJ: Lawrence Erlbaum.

Kaplan, R. B. (1966). Cultural thought patterns in intercultural education. *Language learning, 16,* 1–20.

Katz, L., & Frost, R. (1992). Reading in different orthographies: The orthographic depth hypothesis. In L. Katz & R. Frost (Eds.), *Orthography, phonology, morphology, and meaning* (pp. 67–84). Amsterdam: Elsevier.

Keefe, J. W. (1979). *Learning styles: Diagnosing and prescribing programs.* Reston, VA: National Association of Secondary School Principals.

Keene, E. O. (2008). *To understand: New horizons in reading comprehension*. Portsmouth, NH: Heinemann.

Kehoe, J. (1995). Writing multiple-choice test items. *Practical Assessment, Research, & Evaluation, 4* (9). Retrieved July 3, 2008 from http://pareonline.net/getvn.asp?v=4&n=9

Kendall, J., & Khuon, O. (2005). *Making sense: Small-group comprehension lessons for English language learners*. Portland, ME: Stenhouse.

Kern, R. (2000). *Literacy and language teaching*. Oxford, England: Oxford University Press.

Keshavarz, M. H., Atai, M. R., & Ahmadi, H. (2007). Content schemata, linguistic simplification, and EFL readers' comprehension and recall. *Reading in a Foreign Language, 19*, 19–33.

Kim, H., & Krashen, S. (1997). Why don't language acquirers take advantage of the power of reading? *TESOL Journal, 6* (3), 26–29.

Kintsch, W. (1988). The use of knowledge in discourse processing: A construction-integration model. *Psychological Review, 95*, 163–182.

Kintsch, W. (1994). The psychology of discourse processing. In M. A. Gernsbacher (Ed.), *Handbook of psycholinguistics* (pp. 721–739). San Diego: Academic Press.

Kintsch, W. (1998). *Comprehension: A paradigm for cognition*. New York: Cambridge University Press.

Kintsch, W., & van Dijk, T. (1978). Toward a model of text comprehension and production. *Psychological Review, 85*, 363–394.

Kintsch, W., Welsch, D., Schmalhofer, F., & Zimny, S. (1990). Sentence recognition: A theoretical analysis. *Journal of Memory and Language, 29*, 133–159.

Kinzer, C. K., & Verhoeven, L. (2007). *Interactive literacy education: Facilitating literacy environments through technology*. New York: Taylor & Francis.

Klare, G. R. (1963). *The measurement of readability*. Ames: Iowa State University Press.

Klare, G. R. (1974–1975). Assessing readability. *Reading Research Quarterly, 10*, 62–102.

Klein-Braley, C. (1985). A cloze-up on the C-test: A study in the construct validation of authentic tests. *Language Testing, 2*, 76–104.

Knight, S. (1994). Dictionary use while reading: The effects on comprehension and vocabulary acquisition for students of different verbal abilities. *Modern Language Journal, 78*, 285–299.

Koda, K. (1988). Cognitive process in second language reading: Transfer of L1 reading skills and strategies. *Second Language Research, 4*, 133–156.

Koda, K. (1993). Transferred L1 strategies and L2 syntactic structure during L2 sentence comprehension. *Modern Language Journal, 77*, 490–500.

Koda, K. (1995). Cognitive consequences of L1 and L2 orthographies. In I. Taylor & D. R. Olson (Eds.), *Scripts and literacy: Reading and learning to read alphabets, syllabaries, and characters* (pp. 311–326). Dordrecht, The Netherlands: Kluwer Academic.

Koda, K. (1999). Development of L2 intraword orthographic sensitivity and decoding skills. *Modern Language Journal, 83*, 51–64.

Koda, K. (2004). *Insights into second language reading: A cross-linguistic approach*. Cambridge, England: Cambridge University Press.

Koda, K. (2005). Learning to read across writing systems: Transfer, metalinguistic awareness and second-language reading development. In V. Cook & B. Bassetti (Eds.), *Writing systems and second language learning* (pp. 311–334). Clevedon, England: Multilingual Matters.

Koda, K. (Ed.). (2007a). *Reading and language learning*. Malden, MA: Blackwell.

Koda, K. (2007b). Reading and language learning: Crosslinguistic constraints on second language reading development. *Language Learning, 57*, 1–44.

Koda, K., & Zehler, A. M. (Eds.). (2007). *Learning to read across languages: Cross-linguistic relationships in first- and second-language literacy development.* Mahwah, NJ: Lawrence Erlbaum.

Koh, M. Y. (1985). The role of prior knowledge on reading comprehension. *Reading in a Foreign Language, 3,* 375–380.

Konold, T. R., Juel, C., McKinnon, M., & Deffes, R. (2003). A multivariate model of early reading acquisition. *Applied Psycholinguistics, 24,* 89–112.

Krashen, S. D. (1981). *Second language acquisition and second language learning.* Oxford, England: Pergamon.

Krashen, S. D. (1982). *Principles and practice in second language acquisition.* New York: Prentice Hall.

Krashen, S. D. (1984). *Writing: Research, theory, and application.* Oxford, England: Pergamon.

Krashen, S. D. (1985). *Inquiries and insights.* Menlo Park, CA: Alemany Press.

Krashen, S. D. (1988). Do we learn to read by reading? The relationship between free reading and reading ability. In D. Tannen (Ed.), *Linguistics in context: Connecting observation and understanding* (pp. 269–298). Norwood, NJ: Ablex.

Krashen, S. D. (1989). We acquire vocabulary and spelling by reading: Additional evidence for the Input Hypothesis. *Modern Language Journal, 73,* 440–464.

Krashen, S. D. (2004). *The power of reading.* Portsmouth, NH: Heinemann.

Krashen, S. D. (1999). *Three arguments against Whole Language and why they are wrong.* Portsmouth, NH: Heinemann.

Krashen, S. D. (2002). Whole Language and the great plummet of 1987–92: An urban legend from California. *Phi Delta Kappan, 83,* 748–753.

Krashen, S. D. (2004). *The power of reading: Insights from the research* (2nd ed.). Portsmouth, NH: Heinemann.

Krashen, S. D. (2007). Literacy campaigns: Access to books is the first step. *Literacy Network News,* Spring, 7.

Krashen, S. D. (n.d.). *88 generalizations about free voluntary reading.* Handout. Retrieved June 22, 2006 from http://www.sdkrashen.com/handouts/88Generalizations/index.html

Kress, G. R. (2002). *Literacy in the new media age.* London: Routledge.

Kroll, B. (2001). Considerations for teaching an ESL/EFL writing course. In M. Celce-Murcia (Ed.), *Teaching English as a second or foreign language* (3rd ed., pp. 219–232). Boston: Heinle.

Kucer, S. B. (1985). The making of meaning: Reading and writing as parallel processes. *Written Communication, 2,* 317–336.

Kucer, S. B. (2001). *Dimensions of literacy: A conceptual base for teaching reading and writing in school settings.* Mahwah, NJ: Lawrence Erlbaum.

Kucer, S. B., & Silva, C. (2006). *Teaching the dimensions of literacy.* Mahwah, NJ: Lawrence Erlbaum.

Kucera, H., & Francis, W. N. (1967). *Computational analysis of present-day American English.* Providence, RI: Brown University Press.

Kuhn, M. R., & Rasinski, T. (2007). Best practices in fluency instruction. In L. B. Gambrell, L. M. Morrow, & Pressley, M. (Eds.), *Best practices in literacy instruction* (3rd ed., pp. 204–219). New York: Guilford.

Kumaravadivelu, B. (2003). *Macrostrategies for language teaching.* New Haven, CT: Yale University Press.

Kumaravadivelu, B. (2006). *Understanding language teaching: From method to postmethod.* Mahwah, NJ: Lawrence Erlbaum.

Kutz, E. (1997). *Language and literacy: Studying discourse in communities and classrooms.* Portsmouth, NH: Boynton/Cook.

LaBerge, D., & Samuels, S. J. (1974). Toward a theory of automatic information processing in reading. *Cognitive Psychology, 6,* 293–323.

Langer, J. A. (1992). Rethinking literature instruction. In J. A. Langer (Ed.), *Literature instruction: A focus on student responses* (pp. 35–53). Urbana, IL: National Council of Teachers of English.

Lantolf, J. P., & Thorne, S. L. (2006). *Sociocultural theory and the genesis of second language development.* Oxford, England: Oxford University Press.

Lapp, D., Flood, J., Brock, C. H., & Fisher, D. (2007). *Teaching reading to every child* (4th ed.). New York: Taylor & Francis.

Lapp, D., Flood, J., & Farnan, N. (Eds.). (2007). *Content area reading and learning: Instructional strategies* (3rd ed.). New York: Taylor & Francis.

Larsen-Freeman, D. (2003). *Teaching language: From grammar to grammaring.* Boston: Heinle.

Laufer, B. (1989). What percentage of text-lexis is essential for comprehension? In C. Laurén & M. Nordman (Eds.), *Special language: From humans thinking to thinking machines* (pp. 316–323). Clevedon, England: Multilingual Matters.

Laufer, B. (1992). Reading in a foreign language: How does L2 lexical knowledge interact with the reader's general academic ability? *Journal of Research in Reading, 15,* 95–103.

Laufer, B. (1996). The lexical threshold of second language reading comprehension: What it is and how it relates to L1 reading ability. In K. Sajavaara & C. Fairweather (Eds.), *Approaches to second language acquisition* (pp. 55–62). Jyväskylä, Finland: University of Jyväskylä.

Laufer, B. (1997). The lexical plight in second language reading. In J. Coady & T. Huckin (Eds.), *Second language vocabulary acquisition* (pp. 20–34). Cambridge, England: Cambridge University Press.

Laufer, B. (1998). The development of passive and active vocabulary: Same or different? *Applied Linguistics, 19,* 255–271.

Laufer, B., & Nation, I. S. P. (1999). A vocabulary size test of controlled productive ability. *Language Testing, 16,* 33–51.

Lazar, G. (1993). *Literature and language teaching: A guide for teachers and trainers.* Cambridge: Cambridge University Press.

Lazar, G. (1999). *A window on literature.* Cambridge, England: Cambridge University Press.

Lazar, G. (2003). *Meanings and metaphors.* Cambridge, England: Cambridge University Press.

Lean, A. E. (1996). The farce called grading. In R. Spack (1998), *Guidelines: A cross-cultural reading/writing text* (2nd ed., pp. 130–134). New York: St. Martin's Press.

Leaver, B. L., & Stryker, S. B. (1989). Content-based instruction for foreign language classrooms. *Foreign Language Annals, 22,* 269–275.

Lee, C. D. (2000). Signifying in the Zone of Proximal Development. In C. D. Lee & P. Smagorinsky (Eds.), *Vygotskian perspectives on literacy research: Constructing meaning through collaborative inquiry* (pp. 191–225). Cambridge, England: Cambridge University Press.

Lee, C. D., & Smagorinsky, P. (Eds.). (2000). *Vygotskian perspectives on literacy research: Constructing meaning through collaborative inquiry.* Cambridge, England: Cambridge University Press.

Lee, J. F. (1986). Background knowledge and L2 reading. *Modern Language Journal, 70*, 350–354.

Lee, J. F., & Schallert, D. L. (1997). The relative contribution of L2 language proficiency and L1 reading ability to L2 reading performance: A text of the threshold hypothesis in an EFL context. *TESOL Quarterly, 31*, 713–749.

Lee, J. F., & VanPatten, B. (2003). *Making communicative language teaching happen* (2nd ed.). Boston: McGraw-Hill.

Leech, G., Rayson, P., & Wilson, A. (2001). *Word frequencies in spoken and written English.* London: Longman.

Leki, I. (1991). Twenty-five years of contrastive rhetoric. *TESOL Quarterly, 25*, 123–143.

Leki, I. (1999). "Pretty much I screwed up": Ill-served needs of a permanent resident. In L. Harklau, K. Losey, & M. Siegal (Eds.), *Generation 1.5 meets college composition: Issues in the teaching of writing to U.S.-educated learners of ESL* (pp. 17–44). Mahwah, NJ: Lawrence Erlbaum.

Leki, I. (2007). *Undergraduates in a second language: Challenges and complexities of academic literacy development.* New York: Taylor & Francis.

Leki, I., Cumming, A., & Silva, T. (2006). Second-language composition: Teaching and learning. In P. Smagorinsky (Ed.), *Research on composition: Multiple perspectives on two decades of change* (pp. 141–169). New York: Teachers College Press.

Lengyel, Z., & Navracsics, J. (Eds.). (2007). *Second language lexical processes: Applied linguistic and psycholinguistic perspectives.* Clevedon, England: Multilingual Matters.

Leong, C. K. (1995). Orthographic and psycholinguistic considerations in developing literacy in Chinese. In I. Taylor & D. R. Olson (Eds.), *Scripts and literacy: Reading and learning to read alphabets, syllabaries, and characters* (pp. 163–183). Dordrecht, The Netherlands: Kluwer Academic.

Lesaux, N., with Koda, K., Siegel, L., & Shanahan, T. (2006). Development of literacy. In D. August & T. Shanahan (Eds.), *Developing literacy in second-language learners: Report of the National Literacy Panel on Language-Minority Children and Youth* (pp. 75–122). Mahwah, NJ: Lawrence Erlbaum.

Lewis, C. (2001). *Literacy practices as social acts: Power, status, and cultural norms in the classroom.* Mahwah, NJ: Lawrence Erlbaum.

Lewis, C., Enciso, P. E., & Moje, E. B. (Eds.). (2007). *Reframing sociocultural research on literacy: Identity, agency, and power.* New York: Taylor & Francis.

Lewis, M. (2002). *Implementing the lexical approach: Putting theory into practice.* Boston: Thomson/Heinle.

Li, W., Gaffney, J. S., & Packard, J. L. (Eds.). (2002). *Chinese children's reading acquisition: Theoretical and pedagogical issues.* Dordrecht, The Netherlands: Kluwer Academic.

Liebman, J. (1992). Toward a new contrastive rhetoric: Differences between Arabic and Japanese rhetorical instruction. *Journal of Second Language Writing, 1*, 141–165.

Lightbown, P., & Spada, N. (2006). *How languages are learned* (3rd ed.). Oxford, England: Oxford University Press.

Linderholm, T., Everson, M. G., van den Broek, P. W., Mischiniski, M., Crittenden, A., & Samuels, S. J. (2000). Effects of causal text revisions on more- and less-skilled readers' comprehension of easy and difficult texts. *Cognition and Instruction, 18*, 525–556.

Lipson, M. Y. (1983). The influence of religious affiliation on children's memory for text information. *Reading Research Quarterly, 19*, 448–457.

Liu, J. (2002). Process drama in second/foreign language classrooms. In G. Brauer (Ed.), *Body and language: Intercultural learning through drama* (pp. 147–165). Westport, CT: Greenwood.

Long, M. (Ed.). (2005). *Second language needs analysis.* Cambridge, England: Cambridge University Press.

Longman dictionary of contemporary English. London: Pearson ESL.

Lorch, R. F., Jr. (1989). Text signaling devices and their effects on reading and memory processes. *Educational Psychology Review, 1,* 209–234.

Luke, A. (2004). Two takes on the critical. In B. Norton & K. Toohey (Eds.), *Critical pedagogies and language learning* (pp. 21–29). Cambridge, England: Cambridge University Press.

Luke, A., & Elkins, J. (2002). Towards a critical, worldly literacy. *Journal of Adolescent and Adult Literacy, 45,* 668–673.

Lundy, K. G. (2007). *Leap into literacy: Teaching the tough stuff so it sticks.* Portland, ME: Stenhouse.

Lunzer, E., Waite, M., & Dolan, T. (1979). Comprehension and comprehension tests. In E. Lunzer & K. Gardner (Eds.), *The effective use of reading* (pp. 37–71). London: Heinemann Educational Books.

Luppescu, S., & Day, R. R. (1993). Reading, dictionaries, and vocabulary learning. *Language Learning, 43,* 263–287.

Macaro, E. (2006). Strategies for language learning and for language use: Revising the theoretical framework. *Modern Language Journal, 90,* 320–337.

Mackey, M. (2007). *Literacies across media: Playing the text* (2nd ed.). London: Routledge.

Madsen, H. (1983). *Techniques in testing.* New York: Oxford University Press.

Mager, R. R. (1962). *Preparing instructional objectives.* Belmont, CA: Fearon.

Mair, V. (1996). Modern Chinese writing. In P. Daniels & W. Bright (Eds.), *The world's writing systems* (pp. 200–208). Oxford, England: Oxford University Press.

Malatesha Joshi, R., & Aaron, P. G. (Eds.). (2006). *Handbook of orthography and literacy.* Mahwah, NJ: Lawrence Erlbaum.

Maley, A. (2001). Literature in the language classroom. In R. Carter & D. Nunan (Eds.), *The Cambridge guide to teaching English to speakers of other languages* (pp. 180–185). Cambridge, England: Cambridge University Press.

Manguel, A. (1996). *A history of reading.* New York: Penguin.

Martin, J. (2006). *The meaning of the 21st century: A vital blueprint for ensuring our future.* New York: Riverhead Books.

Martinez, J. G. R., & Johnson, P. J. (1982). An analysis of reading proficiency and its relationship to complete and partial report performance. *Reading Research Quarterly, 18,* 105–122.

Mason, B. & Krashen, S. D. (1997). Extensive reading in English as a foreign language. *System, 25,* 91–102.

Masuhara, H. (1998). What do teachers really want from coursebooks? In B. Tomlinson (Ed.), *Materials development in language teaching* (pp. 239–260). Cambridge, England: Cambridge University Press.

Matsuda, P. K. (1997). Contrastive rhetoric in context: A dynamic model of L2 writing. *Journal of Second Language Writing, 6,* 45–60.

Matsuda, P. K. (2001). On the origin of contrastive rhetoric. *International Journal of Applied Linguistics, 11,* 257–260.

Matthewson, G. C. (1994). Model of attitude influence upon reading and learning to read. In R. B. Ruddell, M. P. Ruddell, & H. Singer (Eds.), *Theoretical models and processes of reading* (4th ed.). (pp. 1131–1161). Newark, DE: International Reading Association.

Maxim, H. H. (2002). A study into the feasibility and effects of reading extended authentic discourse in the beginning German language classroom. *Modern Language Journal, 86,* 20–35.

Mayer, R. E., & Massa, L. J. (2003). Three facets of visual and verbal learners: Cognitive ability, cognitive style, and learning preference. *Journal of Educational Psychology, 95,* 833–841.

McCardle, P., & Chhabra, V. (Eds.). (2004). *The voice of evidence in reading research.* Baltimore: Paul H. Brookes.

McCarty, T. (Ed.). (2005). *Language, literacy, and power in schooling.* Mahwah, NJ: Lawrence Erlbaum.

McClelland, J. L., & Rumelhart, D. E. (1985). Distributed memory and the representation of general and specific information. *Journal of Experimental Psychology: General, 114,* 159–188.

McClelland, J. L., Rumelhart, D. E., & Hinton, G. E. (1986). The appeal of parallel distributed processing. In D. E. Rumelhart, J. L. McClelland, & T. P. R. Group (Eds.), *Parallel distributed processing: Explorations in the microstructure of cognition, Vol. I: Foundations* (pp. 3–44). Cambridge, MA: MIT Press.

McCrum, R., MacNeil, R., & Cran, W. (2002). *The story of English* (3rd rev. ed.). New York: Penguin.

McDaniel, M. A., & Pressley, M. (1989). Keyword and context instruction of new vocabulary meanings: Effects on text comprehension and memory. *Journal of Educational Psychology, 81,* 204–213.

McEnery, T., Xiao, R., & Tono, Y. (2006). *Corpus-based language studies: An advanced resource book.* London: Routledge.

McKay, S. L., & Hornberger, N. (Eds.). (1996). *Sociolinguistics and language teaching.* Cambridge, England: Cambridge University Press.

McKay, S. L., & Wong, S. C. (Eds.) (2000). *New immigrants in the United States: Readings for second language educators.* Cambridge: Cambridge University Press.

McKenna, M. C., Labbo, L. D., Kieffer, R. D., & Reinking, D. (Eds.). (2006). *International handbook of literacy and technology, Vol. II.* Mahwah, NJ: Lawrence Erlbaum.

McKenna, M., Labbo, L. D., Reinking, D., & Zucker, T. A. (2008). Effective use of technology in literacy instruction. In L. B. Gambrell, L. M. Morrow, & Pressley, M. (Eds.), *Best practices in literacy instruction* (3rd ed., pp. 344–372). New York: Guilford.

McKeough, A., Phillips, L. M., Timmons, V., & Lupart, J. L. (Eds.). (2006). *Understanding literacy development: A global view.* Mahwah, NJ: Lawrence Erlbaum.

McKeown, M. G., Beck, I. L. Omanson, R., & Pople, M. (1985). Some effects of the nature and frequency of vocabulary instruction on the knowledge and use of words. *Reading Research Quarterly, 20,* 522–535.

McKeown, M. G., Beck, I. L., Sinatra, G. M., & Loxterman, J. A. (1992). The contribution of prior knowledge and coherent text to comprehension. *Reading Research Quarterly, 27,* 79–93.

McNamara, T. (1996). *Measuring second language performance.* London: Longman.

McNamara, T. (2000). *Language testing.* Oxford, England: Oxford University Press.

McQuillan, J. (1994). Reading versus grammar: What students think is pleasurable for language acquisition. *Applied Language Learning, 5,* 95–100.

McQuillan, J. (1998). *The literacy crisis: False claims and real solutions.* Portsmouth, NH: Heinemann.

McWilliam, N. (1998). *What's in a word? Vocabulary development in multilingual classrooms.* Stoke on Trent, England: Trentham Books.

Meara, P. (1980). Vocabulary acquisition: A neglected aspect of language learning. *Language Teaching and Linguistics Abstracts, 13,* 221–246.

Meara, P. (1990). A note on passive vocabulary. *Second Language Research, 6*, 150–154.

Meara, P. (1995). The importance of an early emphasis on L2 vocabulary. *The Language Teacher, 19* (2), 8–10.

Meara, P. (2005). Lexical frequency profiles: A Monte Carlo analysis. *Applied Linguistics, 26*, 1–16.

Meara, P., & Jones, G. (1990). *Eurocentres vocabulary size test 10KA.* Zurich: Eurocentres.

Melka Teichroew, F. J. (1982). Receptive vs. productive vocabulary: A survey. *Interlanguage Studies Bulletin, 6*, 5–33.

Messick, S. (1989). Validity. In R. Linn (Ed.), *Educational measurement* (pp. 13–103). New York: MacMillan.

Met, M. (1999). Making connections. In J. K. Phillips & R. M. Terry (Eds.), *Foreign language standards: Linking research, theories, and practices* (pp. 137–164). Yonkers, NY: American Council on the Teaching of Foreign Languages.

Meyer, B. J. F. (1975). *The organization of prose and its effects on memory.* Amsterdam: North Holland.

Meyer, B. J. F., & Freedle, R. O. (1984). The effects of different discourse types on recall. *American Educational Research Journal, 21*, 121–143.

Meyer, B. J. F., & Rice, G. E. (1982). The interaction of reader strategies and the organization of text. *Text, 2*, 155–192.

Meyer, B. J. F., & Rice, G. E. (1984). The structure of text. In P. D. Pearson (Ed.), *Handbook of reading research, Vol. I* (pp. 319–352). New York: Longman.

Meyer, R. J., & Manning, M. (2007). *Reading and teaching.* New York: Taylor & Francis.

Mezynski, K. (1983). Issues concerning the acquisition of knowledge: Effects of vocabulary training on reading comprehension. *Review of Educational Research, 53*, 253–279.

Miller, J. R., & Kintsch, W. (1980). Readability and recall of short prose passages: A theoretical analysis. *Journal of Experimental Psychology: Human Learning and Memory, 6*, 335–354.

Mitchell, R., & Myles, F. (2004). *Second language learning theories* (2nd ed.). London: Hodder Arnold.

Mlynarczyk, R. W. (1998). *Conversations of the mind: The uses of journal writing for second-language learners.* Mahwah, NJ: Lawrence Erlbaum.

Moe, A. J., & Irwin, J. W. (1986). Cohesion, coherence, and comprehension. In J. W. Irwin (Eds.), *Understanding and teaching cohesion comprehension* (pp. 3–8). Newark, DE: International Reading Association.

Mohan, B., & Lo, W. A-Y. (1985). Academic writing and Chinese students: Transfer and developmental factors. *TESOL Quarterly, 19*, 515–534.

Mokhtari, K., & Sheorey, R. (Eds.). (2008). *Reading strategies of first and second language learners: See how they read.* Norwood, MA: Christopher-Gordon.

Moon, B. (2000). *Studying literature: New approaches to poetry and fiction.* Urbana, IL: National Council of Teachers of English.

Moore, F. (2001). Storage changing so fast it even obsoletes the future. *Computer Technology Review, 21* (1), 1, 28, 34.

Morgan, B., & Ramanathan, V. (2005). Critical literacies and language education: Global and local perspectives. *Annual Review of Applied Linguistics, 25*, 151–169.

Morgan, J., & Rinvolucri, M. (2004). *Vocabulary* (2nd ed.). Oxford, England: Oxford University Press.

Mori, Y. (1998). Effects of first language and phonological accessibility on Kanji recognition. *British Journal of Psychology, 55*, 165–180.

Morin, R. (2003). Derivational morphological analysis as a strategy for vocabulary acquisition in Spanish. *Modern Language Journal, 87*, 200–221.

Morrow, L. M., & Gambrell, L. B. (2000). Literature-based reading instruction. In M. Kamil, P Mosenthal, P. D. Pearson, & R. Barr (Eds.), *Handbook of reading research: Vol. III* (pp. 563–586). Mahwah, NJ: Lawrence Erlbaum.

Morton, J., & Sasanuma, S. (1984). Lexical access in Japanese. In L. Henderson (Ed.), *Orthographies and reading: Perspectives from cognitive psychology, neuropsychology, and linguistics* (pp. 25–42). Hillsdale, NJ: Lawrence Erlbaum.

Mousavi, S. A. (2002). *An encyclopedic dictionary of language testing* (3rd ed.). Taipei: Tung Hua Books.

Muljani, D., Koda, K., & Moates, D. R. (1998). The development of word recognition in a second language. *Applied Psycholinguistics, 19*, 99–113.

Munby, J. (1978). *Communicative syllabus design.* Cambridge, England: Cambridge University Press.

Murphy, J. M. (2001). Reflective teaching in ELT. In M. Celce-Murcia (Ed.), *Teaching English as a second or foreign language* (2nd ed., pp. 499–514). Boston: Heinle.

Murray, D. E., & McPherson, P. (Eds.). (2005). *Navigating to read—Reading to navigate.* Sydney, Australia: National Centre for English Language Teaching and Research.

Myers, I. B., & McCaulley, M. H. (1985). *Manual: A guide to the development and use of the Myers-Briggs Type Indicator.* Palo Alto, CA: Consulting Psychologists Press.

Nagy, W. E. (1997). On the role of context in first- and second-language learning. In N. Schmitt & N. McCarthy (Eds.), *Vocabulary: Description, acquisition, and pedagogy* (pp. 64–83). Cambridge, England: Cambridge University Press.

Nagy, W. E., Anderson, R. C., & Herman, P. A. (1987). Learning word meanings from context during normal reading. *American Educational Research Journal, 24*, 237–270.

Nagy, W. E., & Herman, P. A. (1987). Breadth and depth of vocabulary knowledge: Implications for acquisition and instruction. In M. G. McKeown & M. E. Curtis (Eds.), *The nature of vocabulary acquisition* (pp. 19–35). Hillsdale, NJ: Lawrence Erlbaum.

Nagy, W. E., Herman, P. A., & Anderson, R. C. (1985). Learning words from context. *Reading Research Quarterly, 20*, 233–253.

Nassaji, H. (2003). L2 vocabulary learning from context: Strategies, knowledge sources, and their relationship with success in L2 lexical inferencing. *TESOL Quarterly, 37*, 645–670.

Nation, I. S. P. (1983). Testing and teaching vocabulary. *Guidelines, 5*, 12–25.

Nation, I. S. P. (1990). *Teaching and learning vocabulary.* New York: Newbury House.

Nation, I. S. P. (Ed.). (1994). *New ways in teaching vocabulary.* Alexandria, VA: TESOL.

Nation, I. S. P. (2001). *Learning vocabulary in another language.* Cambridge, England: Cambridge University Press.

Nation, I. S. P. (2002). Vocabulary. In D. Nunan (Ed.), *Practical English language education* (pp. 129–152). New York: McGraw-Hill.

Nation, I. S. P. (2005). Teaching and learning vocabulary. In E. Hinkel (Ed.), *Handbook of research in second language teaching and learning* (pp. 581–595). Mahwah, NJ: Lawrence Erlbaum.

Nation, I. S. P. (2006). How large a vocabulary is needed for reading and listening? *Canadian Modern Language Review, 63*, 59–82.

Nation, I. S. P., & Coady, J. (1988). Vocabulary and reading. In R. Carter & M. McCarthy (Eds.), *Vocabulary and language teaching* (pp. 97–110). London: Longman.

Nation, I. S. P., & Deweerdt, J. (2001). A defence of simplification. *Prospect, 16* (3), 55–67.

Nation, I. S. P., & Waring, R. (1997). Teaching vocabulary. In J. Coady & T. Huckin (Eds.), *Second language vocabulary acquisition* (pp. 238–254). Cambridge, England: Cambridge University Press.

National Capital Language Resource Center. (2004). *Portfolio assessment in the foreign language classroom*. Washington, DC: NCLRC. Retrieved February 1, 2008 from http://www.electronicportfolios.com/portfolios/EPDevProcess.html#epdev

National Reading Panel. (2000). *Report of the National Reading Panel—Teaching children to read: An evidence-based assessment of the scientific research literature on reading and its implications for reading instruction* (National Institute of Health Publication No. 00–4769). Washington: U.S. Government Printing Office.

Nattinger, J. R., & DeCarrico, J. S. (1992). *Lexical phrases and language teaching*. Oxford, England: Oxford University Press.

Norris, J. M., Brown, J. D., Hudson, T., & Yoshioka, J. (1998). *Designing second language performance assessments*. Honolulu: University of Hawai'i Press.

Nunan, D. (1988). *Syllabus design*. Oxford, England: Oxford University Press.

Nunan, D. (1989). *Designing tasks for the communicative classroom*. Cambridge, England: Cambridge University Press.

Nunan, D. (1992). The teacher as decision-maker. In J. Flowerdew, M. Brock, & S. Hsia (Eds.), *Perspectives on second language teacher education* (pp. 135–165). Hong Kong: City Polytechnic of Hong Kong.

Nunan, D. (2001). Syllabus design. In M. Celce-Murcia (Ed.), *Teaching English as a second or foreign language* (3rd ed., pp. 55–65). Boston: Heinle.

Nuttall, C. (2005). *Teaching reading skills in a foreign language* (3rd ed.). Oxford, England: MacMillan ELT.

O'Keeffe, A., McCarthy, M., & Carter, R. (2007). *From corpus to classroom: Language use and language teaching*. Cambridge, England: Cambridge University Press.

Oller, J. W. (1979). *Language tests at school: A pragmatic approach*. London: Longman.

Olsen, L. (1997). *Made in America: Immigrant students in our public schools*. New York: The New York Press.

Olson, D. R. (1994). *The world on paper: The conceptual and cognitive implications of writing and reading*. Cambridge, England: Cambridge University Press.

Olson, D. R., & Cole, M. (Eds.). (2006). *Technology, literacy, and the evolution of society: Implications of the work of Jack Goody*. Mahwah, NJ: Lawrence Erlbaum.

Olson, D. R., & Torrance, N. (Eds.). (1991). *Literacy and orality*. Cambridge, England: Cambridge University Press.

Omaggio Hadley, A. (2001). *Teaching language in context* (3rd ed.). Boston: Heinle.

O'Malley, J. M., & Valdez Pierce, L. (1996). *Authentic assessment for English language learners: Practical approaches for teachers*. White Plains, NY: Addison-Wesley.

Ong, W. (1982). *Orality and literacy: The technologizing of the word*. London: Methuen.

Oxford, R. (1990). *Language learning strategies: What every teacher should know*. Rowley, MA: Newbury House.

Pally, M. (Gen. Ed.). (2000). *Sustained content teaching in academic ESL/EFL: A practical approach*. Boston: Houghton Mifflin.

Palmer, H. E. (1964). *The principles of language-study*. Oxford, England: Oxford University Press. (Original work published 1921.)

Palmer, H. E. (1968). *The scientific study and teaching of languages*. Oxford, England: Oxford University Press. (Original work published 1917.)

Paran, A. (Ed.) (2006). *Literature in language teaching and learning*. Alexandria, VA: TESOL.

Paribakht, T. S., & Wesche, M. B. (1996). Enhancing vocabulary acquisition through reading: A hierarchy of text-related exercise types. *Canadian Modern Language Review, 52*, 155–178.

Paribakht, T. S., & Wesche, M. (1997). Vocabulary enhancement activities and reading for meaning in second language vocabulary assessment. In J. Coady & T. Huckin (Eds.), *Second language vocabulary acquisition* (pp. 174–200). Cambridge, England: Cambridge University Press.

Paribakht, T. S., & Wesche, M. (1999). Reading and "incidental" L2 vocabulary acquisition. *Studies in Second Language Acquisition, 21,* 195–224.

Paris, S. G., Wasik, B. A., & Turner, J. C. (1991). The development of strategic readers. In R. Barr, M. Kamil, P. Mosenthal, & P. D. Pearson (Eds.), *Handbook of reading research, Vol. II* (pp. 609–640). Mahwah, NJ: Lawrence Erlbaum.

Parry, K. (1996). Culture, literacy, and L2 reading. *TESOL Quarterly, 30,* 665–692.

Parsad, B., & Jones, J. (2005). *Internet access in U.S. public schools and classrooms: 1994–2003.* Washington, DC: National Center for Educational Statistics. Retrieved June 11, 2008 from http://nces.ed.gov/pubsearch/pubsinfo.asp?pubid=2005015

Pasternak, M., & Wrangell, E. (2007). *Well read 4: Skills and strategies for reading.* New York: Oxford University Press.

Pearson, P. D. (2000). Reading in the 20th century. In T. L. Good (Ed.), *American education yesterday, today, and tomorrow, Vol. II* (pp. 152–208). Chicago: National Society for the Study of Education.

Pearson, P. D., & Tierney, R. J. (1984). On becoming a thoughtful reader. In A. C. Purves & O. Niles (Eds.), *Becoming readers in a complex society* (pp. 143–173). Chicago: National Society for the Study of Education.

Pennycook, A. (2001). *Critical applied linguistics: A critical introduction.* Mahwah, NJ: Lawrence Erlbaum.

Peregoy, S. F., & Boyle, O. F. (2004). *Reading, writing, and learning in ESL: A resource book for K–12 teachers.* New York: Allyn & Bacon.

Peretz, A. S., & Shoham, M. (1990). Testing reading comprehension in LSP: Does topic familiarity affect assessed difficulty and actual performance? *Reading in a Foreign Language Journal, 7,* 447–454.

Pérez, B. (2004a). Creating a classroom community for literacy. In B. Pérez (Ed.). *Sociocultural contexts of language and literacy* (2nd ed., pp. 309–338). Mahwah, NJ: Lawrence Erlbaum.

Pérez, B. (2004b). Language, literacy, and biliteracy. In B. Pérez (Ed.). *Sociocultural contexts of language and literacy* (2nd ed., pp. 25–56). Mahwah, NJ: Lawrence Erlbaum.

Pérez, B. (2004c). Literacy, curriculum, and language diversity. In B. Pérez (Ed.). *Sociocultural contexts of language and literacy* (2nd ed., pp. 339–375). Mahwah, NJ: Lawrence Erlbaum.

Pérez, B. (Ed.). (2004d). *Sociocultural contexts of language and literacy* (2nd ed.). Mahwah, NJ: Lawrence Erlbaum.

Pérez, B. (2004e). Writing across writing systems. In B. Pérez (Ed.). *Sociocultural contexts of language and literacy* (2nd ed., pp. 57–75). Mahwah, NJ: Lawrence Erlbaum.

Perfetti, C. A. (1985). *Reading ability.* New York: Oxford University Press.

Perfetti, C. A. (1988). Verbal efficiency in reading ability. In M. Daneman, G. E. MacKinnon, & T. G. Waler (Eds.), *Reading research: Advances in theory and practice, Vol. VI* (pp. 109–143). New York: Academic Press.

Perfetti, C. A. (1991). Representations and awareness in the acquisition of reading competence. In L. Rieben & C. A. Perfetti (Eds.), *Learning to read* (pp. 33–44). Hillsdale, NJ: Lawrence Erlbaum.

Perfetti, C. A. (2003). The universal grammar of reading. *Scientific Studies of Reading, 7,* 3–24.

Perkins, K., Brutten, S. R., & Pohlmann, J. T. (1989). First and second language reading comprehension. *RELC Journal, 20,* 1–9.

Peyton, J. K., & Reed, L. (1990). *Dialog journal writing with nonnative English speakers: A handbook for teachers.* Alexandria, VA: TESOL.

Pica, T. (2002). Subject-matter content: How does it assist the interactional and linguistic needs of classroom language learners? *Modern Language Journal, 86,* 1–19.

Pichette, F. (2005). Time spent on reading and reading comprehension in second language learning. *Canadian Modern Language Review, 62,* 243–262.

Pichette, F., Segalowitz, N., & Connors, K. (2003). Impact of maintaining L1 reading skills on L2 reading skill development in adults: Evidence from speakers of Serbo-Croatian learning French. *Modern Language Journal, 87,* 391–403.

Pike, L. (1979). *An evaluation of alternative item formats for testing English as a foreign language.* TOEFL Research Report, No. 2. Princeton, NJ: Educational Testing Service.

Pitts, M., White, H., & Krashen, S. D. (1989). Acquiring second language vocabulary through reading: A replication of the *Clockwork Orange* study using second language acquirers. *Reading in a Foreign Language, 5,* 271–275.

Plaut, D., McClelland, J., Seidenberg, M., & Patterson, K. (1996). Understanding normal and impaired word reading: Computational principles of quasi-regular domains. *Psychological Review, 103,* 56–115.

Popp, M. S. (2005). *Teaching language and literature in elementary classrooms: A resource book for professional development* (2nd ed.). Mahwah, NJ: Lawrence Erlbaum.

Praninskas, J. (1972). *American university word list.* London: Longman.

Pratt, D. (1980). *Curriculum design and development.* New York: Harcourt Brace Jovanovich.

Pressley, M. (1998). *Reading instruction that really works.* New York: Guilford Press.

Pressley, M. (2002). *Reading instruction that works: The case for balanced teaching.* New York: Guilford.

Pressley, M., & Afflerbach, P. (1995). *Verbal protocols of reading: The nature of constructively responsive reading.* Hillsdale, NJ: Lawrence Erlbaum.

Pressley, M., Billman, A. K., Perry, K. H., Reffitt, K. E., & Reynolds, J. M. (Eds.). (2007). *Shaping literacy achievement: Research we have, research we need.* New York: Guilford.

Preston, D. (1989). *Sociolinguistics and second language acquisition.* Malden, MA: Blackwell.

Proctor, R. W., & Dutta, A. (1995). *Skill acquisition and human performance.* Thousand Oaks, CA: Sage.

Pugh, A. K. (1978). *Silent reading.* London: Heinemann.

Pulido, D. (2007). The relationship between text comprehension and second language incidental vocabulary acquisition: A matter of topic familiarity. *Language Learning, 57,* 155–199.

Purcell-Gates, V. (Ed.). (2007). *Cultural practices of literacy: Case studies of language, literacy, social practice, and power.* Mahwah, NJ: Lawrence Erlbaum.

Purcell-Gates, V., Jacobson, E., & Degener, S. (2008). *Print literacy development: Uniting cognitive and social practice theories.* Cambridge, MA: Harvard University Press.

Purgason, K. B. (1991). Planning lessons and units. In M. Celce-Murcia (Ed.), *Teaching English as a second or foreign language* (2nd ed., pp. 419–431). New York: Newbury House.

Purpura, J. (1997). An analysis of the relationships between test takers' cognitive and metacognitive strategy use and second language test performance. *Language Learning, 42,* 289–325.

Qian, D. D. (1999). Assessing the roles of depth and breadth of vocabulary knowledge in reading comprehension. *Canadian Modern Language Review, 56,* 282–307.

Qian, D. D. (2002). Investigating the relationship between vocabulary knowledge and academic reading performance: An assessment perspective. *Language Learning, 52,* 513–536.

Qian, D. D. (2004). Second language lexical inferencing: Preferences, perceptions, and practies. In P. Bogaards & B. Laufer (Eds.), *Vocabulary in a second language* (pp. 155–169). Amsterdam: John Benjamins.

Rae, G. (1998). *Maxnotes guide to literary terms.* Piscataway, NJ: Research & Education Association.

Rasinski, T., Blachowicz, C., & Lems, K. (Eds.). (2006). *Fluency instruction: Research-based best practices.* New York: Guilford.

Rasinski, T. V., & Padak, N. D. (2001). *From phonics to fluency: Effective teaching of decoding and reading fluency in the elementary school.* New York: Longman.

Ravid, D., & Tolchinsky, L. (2002). Developing linguistic literacy: A comprehensive model. *Journal of Child Language, 29,* 417–447.

Rayner, K., & Pollatsek, A. (1989). *The psychology of reading.* Englewood Cliffs, NJ: Prentice Hall.

Read, J. (2000). *Assessing vocabulary.* Cambridge, England: Cambridge University Press.

Read, J. (2004a). Plumbing the depths: How should the construct of vocabulary knowledge be defined? In P. Bogaards & B. Laufer (Eds.), *Vocabulary in a second language* (pp. 209–227). Amsterdam: John Benjamins.

Read, J. (2004b). Research in teaching vocabulary. *Annual Review of Applied Linguistics, 24,* 146–161.

The Reading Matrix. (2004). [Special issue: Generation 1.5 and Academic Language Acquisition], 4 (3). Retrieved December 12, 2008 from http://www.readingmatrix.com/archives/archives_vol4_no3.html

Recht, D. R., & Leslie, L. (1988). Effect of prior knowledge on good and poor readers' memory of text. *Journal of Educational Psychology, 80,* 16–20.

Reder, S., & Davila, E. (2005). Context and literacy practices. *Annual Review of Applied Linguistics, 25,* 170–187.

Reid, J. (1987). The learning style preferences of ESL students. *TESOL Quarterly, 21,* 87–111.

Reid, J. M. (Ed.). (1995). *Learning styles in the ESL/EFL classroom.* Boston: Heinle.

Reid, J. (1998). "Eye" learners and "ear" learners: Identifying the language needs of international students and U.S. resident writers. In P. Byrd & J. M. Reid, *Grammar in the composition classroom: Essays on teaching ESL for college-bound students* (pp. 3–17). Boston: Heinle.

Reid, J. M. (2006). *Essentials of teaching academic writing.* Boston: Houghton Mifflin.

Reid, J. (2008). *Writing myths: Applying second language research to classroom teaching.* Ann Arbor: University of Michigan Press.

Respondus. (2008). Respondus 3.5. Retrieved January 29, 2008 from http://www.respondus.com/

Reynolds, R. E., Taylor, M. A., Steffensen, M. S., Shirey, L. L., & Anderson, R. C. (1982). Cultural schemata and reading comprehension. *Reading Research Quarterly, 17,* 353–366.

Richards, J. C. (2001). *Curriculum development in language teaching.* Cambridge, England: Cambridge University Press.

Richards, J. C., & Farrell, T. S. C. (2005). *Professional development for language teachers: Strategies for teacher learning.* New York: Cambridge University Press.

Richards, J. C., & Lockhart, C. (1994). *Reflective teaching in second language classrooms.* Cambridge, England: Cambridge University Press.

Rigg, P. (1991). Whole Language in TESOL. *TESOL Quarterly, 25,* 521–542.

Rivera, K. M., & Huerta-Macías, A. (Eds.). (2007). *Adult biliteracy: Sociocultural and programmatic responses.* New York: Taylor & Francis.

Robb, T. (2001). "Extensive reading" for Japanese English majors. In J. Murphy &

P. Byrd (Eds.), *Understanding the courses we teach: Local perspectives on English language teaching* (pp. 218–235). Ann Arbor: University of Michigan Press.

Roberge, M. M. (2002). California's Generation 1. 5 immigrants: What experiences, characteristics, and needs do they bring to our English classes? *CATESOL Journal, 14*, 107–129.

Roberge, M. M., Siegal, M., & Harklau, L. (Eds.) (2008). *Generation 1. 5 in college composition.* New York: Taylor & Francis.

Roberts, E. V., & Jacobs, H. E. (2001). *Literature: An introduction to reading and writing.* Upper Saddle River, NJ: Prentice Hall.

Robinson, R. D., McKenna, M. C., & Wedman, J. M. (Eds.). (2007). *Issues and trends in literacy education* (4th ed.). Boston: Allyn & Bacon.

Robinson, R. P. (1941). *Effective study.* New York: Harper and Row.

Rogers, T., & Soter, A. O. (1997). *Reading across cultures: Teaching literature in a diverse society.* New York: Teachers College Press.

Rogoff, B. (1995). Observing sociocultural activity on three planes: Participatory appropriation, guided participation, and apprenticeship. In J. V. Wertsch, P. Del Rio, & A. Alvarez (Eds.), *Sociocultural studies of mind* (pp. 139–164). Cambridge, England: Cambridge University Press.

Roller, C. M. (1990). Commentary: The interaction of knowledge and structure variables in the processing of expository prose. *Reading Research Quarterly, 25* (2), 79–89.

Rosenfeld, M., Leung, S., & Oltman, P. K. (2001). *The reading, writing, speaking, and listening tasks important for academic success at the undergraduate and graduate levels* (TOEFL Monograph No. MS-21). Princeton, NJ: Educational Testing Service.

Rosenshine, B. V. (1980). Skill hierarchies in reading comprehension. In R. J. Spiro, B. C. Bruce, & W. F. Brewer (Eds.), *Theoretical issues in reading comprehension: Perspectives from cognitive psychology, linguistics, artificial intelligence, and education* (pp. 535–554). Hillsdale, NJ: Lawrence Erlbaum.

Ross, S. (1998). Self-assessment in second language testing: A meta-analysis and analysis of experiential factors. *Language Testing, 15*, 1–20.

Rott, S. (1999). The effect of exposure frequency on intermediate language learners' incidental vocabulary acquisition and retention through reading. *Studies in Second Language Acquisition, 21*, 589–619.

Rott, S. (2004). A comparison of output interventions and un-enhanced reading conditions on vocabulary acquisition and text comprehension. *Canadian Modern Language Review, 61*, 169–202.

Rubin, J. (1987). Learner strategies: Theoretical assumptions, research history. In A. Wenden & J. Rubin (Eds.), *Learner strategies in language learning* (pp. 15–30). London: Prentice Hall International.

Rumbaut, R. G., & Ima, K. (1988). *The adaptation of Southeast Asian refugee youth: A comparative study.* Final Report to the U.S. Department of Health and Human Services, Office of Refugee Resettlement, Washington, DC: U.S. Department of Health and Human Services. San Diego: San Diego State University. (ERIC Document Reproduction Service ED 299 372.)

Rumelhart, D. E. (1977). Toward an interactive model of reading. In S. Dornic (Ed.), *Attention and performance Vol. I* (pp. 573–603). Hillsdale, NJ: Lawrence Erlbaum.

Rumelhart, D. E. (1980). Schemata: The building blocks of language. In R. J. Spiro, B. Bruce, & W. Brewer (Eds.), *Theoretical issues on reading comprehension* (pp. 33–58). Hillsdale, NJ: Lawrence Erlbaum.

Rumelhart, D. E., Smolensky, P., McClelland, J. L., & Hinton, G. E. (1986). Schemata and sequential thought processes in PDP models. In J. L. McClelland, D. E. Rumelhart,

& the PDP Research Group (Eds.), *Parallel distributed processing: Explorations in the microstructure of cognition, Vol. II: Psychological and biological models* (pp. 7–57). Cambridge, MA: MIT Press.

Samuels, S. J. (1994). Toward a theory of automatic information processing in reading, revisited. In R. B. Ruddell, M. R. Ruddell, & H. Singer (Eds.), *Theoretical models and processes of reading* (4th ed., pp. 816–837). Newark, DE: International Reading Association.

Samuels, S. J., & Kamil, M. L. (1984). Models of the reading process. In P. D. Pearson, R. Barr, M. Kamil, & P. Mosenthal (Eds.), *Handbook of reading research, Vol. I* (pp. 85–224). New York: Longman.

San Diego State University. (2001). *Rubrics for Web lessons.* Retrieved February 1, 2008 from http://webquest.sdsu.edu/rubrics/weblessons.htm

Saragi, T., Nation, I. S. P., & Meister, G. F. (1978). Vocabulary learning and reading. *System, 6,* 70–78.

Sarton, M. (1974). The rewards of living a solitary life. Retrieved January 22, 2007 from http://karrvakarela. blogspot. com/2005/07/rewards-of-living-solitary-life. html

Scarcella, R. (1996). Secondary education in California and second language research: Instructing ESL students in the 1990s. *CATESOL Journal, 9,* 129–152.

Scarcella, R. (2002). Some key factors affecting English learners' development of advanced literacy. In M. J. Schleppegrell & M. C. Colombi (Eds.), *Developing advanced literacy in first and second languages: Meaning with power* (pp. 209–226). Mahwah, NJ: Lawrence Erlbaum.

Scarcella, R. C. (2003). *Accelerating academic English: A focus on the English learner.* Oakland, CA: Regents of University of California.

Scarcella, R., & Oxford, R. L. (1992). *The tapestry of language learning: The individual in the communicative classroom.* Boston: Heinle.

Schiffrin, D. (1994). *Approaches to discourse.* Oxford, England: Blackwell.

Schleppegrell, M. J., & Colombi, M. C. (Eds.). (2002). *Developing advanced literacy in first and second languages: Meaning with power.* Mahwah, NJ: Lawrence Erlbaum.

Schmitt, N. (2000). *Vocabulary in language teaching.* Cambridge, England: Cambridge University Press.

Schmitt, N. (Ed.). (2004). *Formulaic sequences: Acquisition, processing, and use.* Amsterdam: John Benjamins.

Schmitt, N., & McCarthy, M. (Eds.). (1997). *Vocabulary: Description, acquisition, and pedagogy.* Cambridge, England: Cambridge University Press.

Schmitt, N., & Meara, P. (1997). Researching vocabulary through a word knowledge framework. *Studies in Second Language Acquisition, 19,* 17–36.

Schmitt, N., & Schmitt, D. (1995). Vocabulary notebooks: Theoretical underpinnings and practical suggestions. *English Language Teaching, 49,* 133–143.

Schoonen, R., Hulstijn, J., & Bossers, B. (1998). Metacognitive and language-specific knowledge in native and foreign language reading comprehension: An empirical study among Dutch students in grades 6, 8, and 10. *Language Learning, 48,* 71–106.

Schuemann, C.M. (2008). Myth 2: Teaching citation is someone else's job. In J. Reid (Ed.), *Writing myths* (pp. 18–40). Ann Arbor: University of Michigan Press.

Schunk, D. (2000). *Learning theories: An educational perspective* (3rd ed.). Upper Saddle River, NJ: Merrill.

Schwanenflugel, P. J., Stahl, S. A., & McFalls, E. L. (1997). Partial word knowledge and vocabulary growth during reading comprehension. *Journal of Literacy Research, 29,* 531–553.

Scollon, R. (1997). Contrastive rhetoric, contrastive poetics, or perhaps something else? *TESOL Quarterly, 31,* 352–358.

Scribner, S., & Cole, M. (1981). *The psychology of literacy.* Cambridge, MA: Harvard University Press.

Seymour, S., & Walsh, L. (2006). *Essentials of teaching academic reading.* Boston: Houghton Mifflin.

Shanahan, T. (2006). Developing fluency in the context of effective literacy instruction. In T. Rasinski, C. Blachowicz, & K. Lems (Eds.), *Fluency instruction: Research-based best practices* (pp. 21–38). New York: Guilford.

Shanahan, T., & Beck, I. (2006). Effective literacy teaching for English-language learners. In D. August & T. Shanahan (Eds.), *Developing literacy in second-language learners: Report of the National Literacy Panel on Language-Minority Children and Youth* (pp. 415–488). Mahwah, NJ: Lawrence Erlbaum.

Sheridan, D. (1991). Changing business as usual: Reader response in the classroom. *College English, 53,* 804–814.

Shih, M. (1992). Beyond comprehension exercises in the ESL academic reading class. *TESOL Quarterly, 26,* 289–318.

Shrum, J. L., & Glisan, E. W. (2005). *Teacher's handbook: Contextualized language instruction* (3rd ed.). Boston: Thomson/Heinle.

Shu, H., Anderson, R. C., & Zhang, H. (1995). Incidental learning of word meanings while reading: A Chinese and American cross-cultural study. *Reading Research Quarterly, 30,* 76–95.

Silberstein, S. (1994). *Techniques and resources in teaching reading.* New York: Oxford University Press.

Sinatra, R. (1986). *Visual literacy connections to thinking, reading, and writing.* Springfield, IL: Charles C. Thomas.

Sinclair, J. (2003). *Reading concordances.* London: Pearson ESL

Sinclair, J. (Ed.). (2006). *Collins COBUILD advanced English dictionary* (5th ed.). London: HarperCollins.

Skehan, P. (1991). Individual differences in second language learning. *Studies in Second Language Acquisition, 13,* 275–298.

Skowron, J. (2006). *Powerful lesson planning: Every teacher's guide to effective instruction* (2nd ed.). Thousand Oaks, CA: Corwin Press.

Smagorinsky, P. (2008). *Teaching English by design: How to create and carry out instructional units.* Portsmouth, NH: Heinemann.

Smalzer, W. R. (2005). *Write to be read* (2nd ed.). Cambridge: Cambridge University Press.

Smith, F. (1983). Reading like a writer. *Language Arts, 60,* 558–567.

Smith, F. (1988). *Joining the literacy club: Essays into literacy.* Portsmouth, NH: Heinemann.

Smith, F. (2004). *Understanding reading* (6th ed.). Mahwah, NJ: Lawrence Erlbaum.

Smith, F. (2006). *Reading without nonsense* (4th ed.). New York: Teachers College Press.

Smith, F. (2007). *Reading: FAQ.* New York: Teachers College Press.

Smith, J., & Elley, W. (1997). *How children learn to read.* Katonah, NY: Richard C. Owen.

Smith, L. C., & Mare, N. C. (2004). *Topics for today* (3rd ed.). Boston: Thomson/Heinle.

Snow, C. E. (2004). Foreword. In P. McCardle, & V. Chhabra (Eds.), *The voice of evidence in reading research* (pp. xix–xxv). Baltimore: Paul H. Brookes.

Snow, C. E., Burns, M. S., & Griffin, P. (Eds.). (1998). *Preventing reading difficulties in young children.* Washington: National Academy Press.

Snow, C., Griffin, P., & Burns, M. S. (Eds.). (2007). *Knowledge to support the teaching of reading: Preparing teachers for a changing world.* San Francisco: Jossey-Bass.

Snow, M. A. (Ed.). (2000). *Implementing the ESL standards for pre-K–12 students through teacher education.* Alexandria, VA: TESOL.

Snow, M. A., & Brinton, D. M. (1997). *The content-based classroom: Perspectives on integrating language and content.* New York: Addison-Wesley Longman.

Sökmen, A. J. (1997). Current trends in teaching second language vocabulary. In N. Schmitt & M. McCarthy (Eds.), *Vocabulary: Description, acquisition, and pedagogy* (pp. 237–257). Cambridge, England: Cambridge University Press.

Song, J. J. (2001). *Linguistic typology.* Harlow, England: Pearson.

Soter, A. O. (1988). The second language learner and cultural transfer in narration. In A. C. Purves (Ed.), *Writing across languages and cultures: Issues in contrastive rhetoric* (pp. 177–205). Newbury Park, CA: Sage.

Spack, R. (1985). Literature, reading, writing, and ESL: Bridging the gaps. *TESOL Quarterly, 19,* 703–725,

Spack, R. (1997). The acquisition of academic literacy in a second language. *Written Communication, 14,* 3–62.

Spack, R. (1998a). *Guidelines: A cross-cultural reading/writing text* (2nd ed.). New York: Cambridge University Press.

Spack, R. (1998b). *The international story: An anthology for reading and writing about fiction.* New York: Cambridge University Press.

Spack, R. (2004). The acquisition of academic literacy in a second language: A longitudinal case study, updated. In V. Zamel & R. Spack (Eds.), *Crossing the curriculum: Multilingual learners in college classrooms* (pp. 19–45). Mahwah, NJ: Lawrence Erlbaum.

Spack, R. (2006). *Guidelines: A cross-cultural reading/writing text* (3rd ed.). New York: Cambridge University Press.

Sperber, D., & Wilson, D. (1986). *Relevance: Communication and cognition.* Oxford, England: Blackwell.

Stahl, S. A. (1990). *Beyond the instrumentalist hypothesis: Some relationships between word meanings and comprehension* (Technical Report No. 505). University of Illinois at Urbana-Champaign: Center for the Study of Reading. (ERIC Document Reproduction Service No. ED321242.)

Stahl, S. A., & Fairbanks, M. M. (1986). The effects of vocabulary instruction: A model-based meta-analysis. *Review of Educational Resarch, 56,* 72–110.

Stahl, S. A., & Hayes, D. (1997). *Instructional models in reading.* Mahwah, NJ: Lawrence Erlbaum.

Stahl, S. A., & Murray, B. A. (1994). Defining phonological awareness and its relationship to early reading. *Journal of Educational Psychology, 86,* 221–234.

Stahl, S. A., & Nagy, W. E. (2006). *Teaching word meanings.* Mahwah, NJ: Lawrence Erlbaum.

Stahl, S. A., Duffy-Hester, A. M., & Dougherty Stahl, K. A. (1998). Everything you wanted to know about phonics (but were afraid to ask). *Reading Research Quarterly, 33,* 338–355.

Stahl, S. A., Jacobson, M. G., Davis, C. E., & Davis, R. L. (1989). Prior knowledge and difficult vocabulary in the comprehension of unfamiliar text. *Reading Research Quarterly, 24,* 27–43.

Stanovich, K. E. (1980). Toward an interactive-compensatory model of individual differences in the acquisition of iteracy. *Reading Research Quarterly, 16,* 32–71.

Stanovich, K. E. (1986). Matthew effects in reading: Some consequences of individual differences in the acquisition of literacy. *Reading Research Quarterly, 21,* 360–407.

Stanovich, K. E. (1991). Changing models of reading and acquisition. In L. Rieben & C. A. Perfetti (Eds.), *Learning to read* (pp. 19–32). Hillsdale, NJ: Lawrence Erlbaum.

Stanovich, K. E. (2000). *Progress in understanding reading: Scientific foundations and new frontiers.* New York: Guilford.

Stanovich, K. E., Cunningham, A. E., & Cramer, B. B. (1984). Assessing phonological awareness of kindergarten children: Issues of task comparability. *Journal of Experimental
Psychology, 38,* 175–190.

Stanovich, K. E., & Stanovich, P. (1999). How research might inform the debate about early
reading acquisition. In J. Oakhill & R. Beard (Eds.), *Reading development and the
teaching of reading* (pp. 12–41). Oxford, England: Blackwell.

Steinberg, M. T. (1995). Teaching Japanese toddlers to read *kanji* and *kana*. In I. Taylor
& D. R. Olson (Eds.), *Scripts and literacy: Reading and learning to read alphabets,
syllabaries, and characters* (pp. 199–214). Dordrecht, The Netherlands: Kluwer
Academic.

Stern, H. H. (1992). *Issues and options in language teaching.* Oxford, England: Oxford
University Press.

Sternberg, R. J. (1987). Most vocabulary is learned from context. In M. McKeown &
M. E. Curtis (Eds.), *The nature of vocabulary acquisition* (pp. 89–105). Hillsdale, NJ:
Lawrence Erlbaum.

Stoller, F. L. (2004). Content-based instruction: Perspectives on curriculum planning.
Annual Review of Applied Linguistics, 24, 261–283.

Street, B. V. (1984). *Literacy in theory and practice.* Cambridge, England: Cambridge
University Press.

Street, B. V. (1995). *Social literacies: Critical approaches to literacy in development, eth-
nography, and education.* London: Longman.

Strickland, D. (1998). *Teaching phonics today: A primer for educators.* Newark, DE: International Reading Association.

Stubbs, M. (1980). *Language and literacy: The sociolinguistics of reading and writing.*
London: Routledge.

Sturtevant, E. G., Boyd, F. B., Brozo, W. G., Hinchman, K. A., Moore, D. W., & Alvermann,
D. E. (2006). *Principled practices for adolescent literacy: A framework for instruction and
policy.* Mahwah, NJ: Lawrence Erlbaum.

Sullivan, J. H. (Ed.). (2002). *Research in second language learning, Vol. I: Literacy and the
second language learner.* Greenwich, CT: Information Age.

Swain, M. (1984). Large scale communicative language testing. In S. Savignon & M. Berns
(Eds.), *Initiatives in communicative language teaching* (pp. 185–201). Reading, MA:
Addison-Wesley.

Swanborn, M., & de Glopper, K. (1999). Incidental word learning while reading: A
meta-analysis. *Review of Educational Research, 69,* 261–285.

Sweet, R. W., Jr. (2004). The big picture: Where we are nationally on the reading front and
how we got here. In P. McCardly & V. Chhabra (Eds.), *The voice of evidence in reading
research* (pp. 13–44). Baltimore: Paul H. Brookes.

Taft, M., & Zhu, X. (1995). The representation of bound morphemes in the lexicon: A
Chinese study. In L. Reiben & C. A. Pewrfetti (Eds.), *Learning to read: Basic research
and its implications* (pp. 19–31). Hillsdale, NJ: Lawrence Erlbaum.

Taillefer, G. F. (2005). Foreign language reading and study abroad: Cross-cultural and
cross-linguistic questions. *Modern Language Journal, 89,* 503–528.

Takak, V. P. (2008). *Vocabulary learning strategies and foreign language learning.* Clevedon,
England: Multilingual Matters.

Tarone, E., & Bigelow, M. (2005). Impact of literacy on oral language processing: Implications for second language acquisition research. *Annual Review of Applied Linguistics,
25,* 133–150.

Tarvers, J. K. (1993). *Teaching writing: Theories and practice* (4th ed.). New York:
HarperCollins.

Taylor, I., & Olson, D. R. (Eds.). (1995). *Scripts and literacy: Reading and learning to read alphabets, syllabaries, and characters.* Dordrecht, The Netherlands: Kluwer Academic.

Thorndike, E. L., & Lorge, I. (1944). *The teacher's word book of 30,000 words.* New York: Teachers College Press.

Thorndike, R. L. (1973). *Reading comprehension in fifteen countries.* New York: Wiley.

Thorne, S. L., & Black, R. W. (2007). Language and literacy development in computer-mediated contexts and communities. *Annual Review of Applied Linguistics, 27,* 133–160.

Tierney, R. J., & Pearson, P. D. (1983). Toward a composing model of reading. *Language Arts, 60,* 568–579.

Toledo, P. F. (2005). Genre analysis and reading of English as a foreign language: Genre schemata beyond text typologies. *Journal of Pragmatics, 37,* 1059–1079.

Tomlinson, B. (Ed.). (1998). *Materials development in language teaching.* Cambridge, England: Cambridge University Press.

Tomlinson, B. (Ed.). (2003). *Developing materials for language teaching.* London: Continuum.

Trabasso, T. R., & Bouchard, E. (2002). Teaching readers how to comprehend text strategically. In C. Collins & M. Pressley (Eds.), *Comprehension instruction: Research-based best practices* (pp. 176–200). New York: Guilford.

Trabasso, T. R., Sabatini, J. P., Massaro, D. W., & Calfee, R. (Eds.). (2005). *From orthography to pedagogy: Essays in honor of Richard L. Venezky.* Mahwah, NJ: Lawrence Erlbaum.

Tuinman, J. J., & Brady, M. E. (1974). How does vocabulary account for variance on reading comprehension tests? A preliminary instructional analysis. In P. Nacke (Ed.), *Interaction: Reading and practice for college-adult reading* (pp. 176–184). Clemson, SC: National Reading Conference.

Turner, R. (2008). *Greater expectations: Teaching academic literacy to underrepresented students.* Portland, ME: Stenhouse.

Ulijn, J. M., & Strother, J. B. (1990). The effect of syntactic simplification on reading EST texts as L1 and L2. *Journal of Research in Reading, 13,* 38–54.

Ur, P. (1996). *A course in language teaching.* Cambridge: Cambridge University Press.

Urquhart, S., & Weir, C. (1998). *Reading in a second language: Process, product, and practice.* Harlow, England: Addison-Wesley Longman.

Valmont, W. J. (2002). *Technology for literacy teaching and learning.* Boston: Houghton Mifflin.

Van den Branden, K. (Ed.). (2006). *Task-based language education: From theory to practice.* Cambridge, England: Cambridge University Press.

van Dijk, T. A. (1977). *Text and context.* London: Longman.

van Dijk, T. A., & Kintsch, W. (1983). *Strategies of discourse comprehension.* New York: Academic Press.

van Lier, L. (1996). *Interaction in the language classroom: Awareness, autonomy, and authenticity.* London: Longman.

Vandrick, S. (1997). Diaspora literature: A mirror for ESL students. *College ESL, 7,* 53–69.

Venezky, R. L. (1995). How English is read: Grapheme-phoneme regularity and orthographic structure in word recognition. In I. Taylor & D. R. Olson (Eds.), *Scripts and literacy: Reading and learning to read alphabets, syllabaries, and characters* (pp. 111–130). Dordrecht, The Netherlands: Kluwer Academic.

Verhoeven, L., & Snow, C. E. (Eds.). (2000). *Literacy and motivation: Reading engagement in individuals and groups.* Mahwah, NJ: Lawrence Erlbaum.

Vermeer, A. (2001). Breadth and depth of vocabulary in relation to L1/L2 acquisition and fluency of input. *Applied Psycholinguistics, 22,* 217–234.

Verplaetse, L. S., & Migliacci, N. (Eds.). (2007). *Inclusive pedagogy for English language learners: A handbook of research-informed practices.* New York: Taylor & Francis.

Vigil, V. D. (1987). Authentic text in the college-level Spanish I class as the primary vehicle of instruction. Unpublished doctoral dissertation. Austin, TX: University of Texas.

Villegas, R. C., & Medley, F. W., Jr. (1988). Language with a purpose: Using authentic materials in the foreign language classroom. *Foreign Language Annals, 21,* 467–478.

Viorst, J. (n.d.). Friends, good friends—and such good friends. Retrieved January 30, 2007 from http://www.deil.uiuc.edu/eslservice/units/introtopw/activity2. htm

Vygotsky, L. S. (1978). *Mind in society: The development of higher psychological processes.* Cambridge, MA: Harvard University Press.

Vygotsky, L. S. (1986). *Thought and language.* Cambridge, England: Cambridge University Press.

Wachlin, M. G. (1997). The place of Bible literature in public high school classes. *Research in the Teaching of English, 31,* 7–50.

Wagner, R. K., Muse, A. E., & Tannenbaum, K. R. (Eds.). (2007). *Vocabulary acquisition: Implications for reading comprehension.* New York: Guilford.

Walker, D. F. (2003). *Fundamentals of curriculum: Passion and professionalism.* Mahwah, NJ: Lawrence Erlbaum.

Wallace, C. (1993). *Reading.* Oxford: Oxford University Press.

Walter, T. (2004). *Teaching English language learners: The how-to-handbook.* White Plains, NY: Pearson/Longman.

Wang, M., & Koda, K. (2005). Commonalities and differences in word identification skills among English second language learners. *Language Learning, 55,* 73100.

Wang, M., Koda, K., & Perfetti, C. A. (2003). Alphabetic and non-alphabetic L1 effects in English semantic processing: A comparison of Korean and Chinese English L2 learners. *Cognition, 87,* 129–149.

Warschauer, M. (1999). *Electronic literacies: Language, culture, and power in online education.* Mahwah, NJ: Lawrence Erlbaum.

Watanabe, Y. (1997). Input, intake, and retention: Effects of increased processing on incidental learning of foreign language vocabulary. *Studies in Second Language Acquisition, 19,* 287–307.

Watson, D. (1989). Defining and describing whole language. *Elementary School Journal, 90,* 129–141.

Weaver, C. (Ed.). (1998). *Reconsidering a balanced approach to reading.* Urbana, IL: NCTE.

Weaver, C. (2002). *Reading process and practice: From socio-psycholinguistics to Whole Language* (3rd ed.). Portsmouth, NH: Heinemann.

Weaver, C. A., & Kintsch, W. (1991). Expository text. In R. Barr, M. L. Kamil, P. Mosenthal, & P. D. Pearson (Eds.), *Handbook of reading research, Vol. II* (pp. 230–245). Mahwah, NJ: Lawrence Erlbaum.

Wegman, B., & Knezevic, M. P. (2001). *Mosaic 1 reading* (4th ed.). New York: McGraw-Hill.

Wegman, B., Knezevic, M. P., & Bernstein, M. (2001). *Mosaic 2 reading* (4th ed.). New York: McGraw-Hill.

Weigle, S. (2002). *Assessing writing.* Cambridge, England: Cambridge University Press.

Weir, C. J. (1993). *Understanding and developing language tests.* London: Prentice Hall.

Weissberg, R. (2006). *Connecting speaking and writing in second language writing instruction.* Ann Arbor: University of Michigan Press.

Wells, J., & Lewis, L. (2005). *Internet access in U.S. public schools and classrooms: 1994–2005.* Washington, DC: National Center for Educational Statistics. Retrieved June 11, 2008 from http://nces.ed.gov/pubsearch/pubsinfo.asp?pubid=2007020

Wertsch, J. V. (1985). *Vygotsky and the social formation of mind.* Cambridge, MA: Harvard University Press.

Wesche, M., & Paribakht, T. (1996). Assessing second language vocabulary knowledge: Depth vs. breadth. *Canadian Modern Language Review, 53,* 13–40.

West, M. (1931). *Robinson Crusoe.* London: Longman, Green. (Adapted from the original book by Daniel Defoe.)

West, M. (1953). *A general service list of English words.* London: Longman.

White, R. (1988). *The ELT curriculum.* Oxford, England: Blackwell.

Whiteson, V. (Ed.) (1996). *New ways of using drama and literature in language teaching.* Alexandria, VA: TESOL.

Wholey, M. L., & Henein, N. (2002). *Reading matters 4: An interactive approach to reading.* Boston: Houghton Mifflin.

Widdowson, H. G. (1975). *Stylistic and the teaching of literature.* London: Longman.

Widdowson, H. G. (1992). *Practical stylistics.* Oxford: Oxford University Press.

Wigfield, A., & Guthrie, J. T. (1997). Relations of children's motivation for reading to the amount and breadth of their reading. *Journal of Educational Psychology, 89,* 420–432.

Willis, A. I. (2007). *Reading comprehension research and testing in the US: Undercurrents of race, class, and power in the struggle for meaning.* Mahwah, NJ: Lawrence Erlbaum.

Willis, D., & Willis, J. (2007). *Doing task-based teaching.* Cambridge, England: Cambridge University Press.

Withrow, F. B. (2004). *Literacy in the digital age: Reading, writing, viewing, and computing.* Lanham, MD: Scarecrow Education.

Wixson, K. L. (1979). Miscue analysis: A critical review. *Journal of Behavior, 11,* 163–175.

Wolf, M. (2007). *Proust and the squid: The story and science of the reading brain.* New York: HarperCollins.

Woodward, T. (2001). *Planning lessons and courses: Designing sequences of work for the language classroom.* Cambridge, England: Cambridge University Press.

Wray, D., & Medwell, J. (2007). *Learners' views of literacy.* London: Routledge.

Xue, G.-Y., & Nation, I. S. P. (1984). A university word list. *Language Learning and Communication, 3,* 215–229.

Yamashita, J. (2002). Mutual compensation between L1 reading ability and L2 language proficiency in L2 reading. *Journal of Research in Reading, 25,* 81–95.

Yancey, K. B. (2004). *Teaching literature as reflective practice.* Urbana, IL: National Council of Teachers of English.

Yopp, H. K., & Yopp, R. H. (2005). *Literature-based reading activities* (4th ed.). Boston: Allyn & Bacon.

Yorio, C. A. (1971). Some sources of reading problems for foreign language learners. *Language Learning, 21,* 101–115.

Yorkey, R. C. (1982). *Study skills for students of English* (2nd ed.). New York: McGraw-Hill.

Young, D. J. (1993). Processing strategies of foreign language readers: Authentic and edited input. *Foreign Language Annals, 26,* 451–468.

Young, D. J. (1999). Linguistic simplification of SL reading material: Effective instructional practice? *Modern Language Journal, 83,* 350–366.

Zahar, R., Cobb, T., & Spada, N. (2001). Acquiring vocabulary through reading: Effects of frequency and contextual richness. *Canadian Modern Language Review, 57,* 41–72.

Zimmerman, C. B. (2007). *Word knowledge: The vocabulary teacher's handbook.* Oxford, England: Oxford University Press.

Zwier, L. J., & Bennett, G. R. (2006). *Teaching a lexis-based academic writing course: A guide to building academic vocabulary.* Ann Arbor: University of Michigan Press.

Notes

1 Fundamentals of L1 and L2 Literacy: Reading and Learning to Read

1 For the sake of commonality with comparable sources in the field, we will use the abbreviation "L2" to refer to foreign languages, second languages, and even third and fourth languages. We recognize that many learners around the world develop language and literacy skills in multiple languages from an early age. We believe that the term "L2," though a compromise, is a suitable way of referring to any additional language(s) that is/are not among the learner's *primary* language repertoire, even if we are concerned with multilingual, multiliterate learners.

2 Because the scope of this research is vast, an exhaustive survey would be impractical. The sources recommended in the Further Reading and Resources section at the end of this chapter provide in-depth syntheses and critiques of contemporary L1 and L2 literacy research and theory.

3 It is widely believed that the first writing system emerged in the fourth century BCE in Mesopotamia (modern Iraq and Syria) among the Sumerian and Akkadian peoples. The Egyptians developed a writing system soon thereafter. Written texts dating to the third century BCE have been located in the Indus valley (modern Pakistan and India), and the roots of the Chinese sinographic system can be traced to the same period (Coulmas, 1989; Crystal, 1997; Daniels & Bright, 1996; Gaur, 1995). "Cumulative evidence . . . suggests that writing was invented at least three times in the last part of the fourth millennium BCE, and at least three more times in different parts of the world in later periods" (Wolf, 2007, p. 47).

4 A fair, thorough discussion of critical literacies is unfortunately not possible here. We encourage readers to consult Morgan and Ramanathan (2005), a state-of-the-art review of critical literacy studies. See also Benesch (2001), Comber and Simpson (2001), Kutz (1997), Lewis (2001), Luke (2004), Luke and Elkins (2002), Pennycook (2001), and Schleppegrell and Colombi (2002).

5 Scholars do not agree on the "naturalness" of literacy in comparison to oral language.

For example, Smith (2004) asked: "[W]hy should language written in an alphabetic script be particularly difficult? The answer is that it isn't. Reading print is no more complex than reading faces . . ." (p. 3). He concluded that "reading print is as natural as reading faces" (p. 5) and, by extension, speech. In contrast, a prevailing view among reading researchers holds that the human brain is not actually "wired" to read print (Wolf, 2007).

6 Weaver (2002, Chapter 6) presented a systematic guide for designing and conducting oral reading sessions, as well as for developing and analyzing miscue records in the classroom. See also Goodman et al. (2005) and Chapter 9 of this volume.

7 Although K. Goodman (1986), Y. Goodman (1989), Smith (1988), and Watson (1989) were instrumental in promoting the WL movement in North America, WL originated in Australia and New Zealand with the work of Butler and Turbill (1984), Clay (1979), and Holdaway (1980), among others.

8 Persuasive support for this claim can be found in studies by Alderson (1993), Bossers (1991), Brisbois (1995), Droop and Verhoeven (2003), Hacqueboord (1989), Lee and Schallert (1997), Perkins, Brutten, and Pohlmann (1989), and Yamashita (2002).

9 In contrast, Smith (2004) argued—not uncontroversially—that comprehension "can't be measured in the way that some aspects of information can. Comprehension can't be measured at all, despite constant educational efforts to do so, because it is not a quantity of anything. Comprehension doesn't have dimension or weight . . ." (p. 60).

10 Similar L2 reading taxonomies include: Aebersold and Field (1997), Grabe and Stoller (2001, 2002), Grasso (2005), Grellet (1981), Koda (2004), Urquhart and Weir (1998).

2 L2 Reading: Focus on the Reader

1 Though scholars in recent years have cautioned against the overuse or "reification" of the term "Generation 1.5" (e.g., Harklau, 2003; Roberge, 2002), we use it here because it is descriptive, accessible, and widely used. However, we appreciate and reiterate these experts' concerns that the term "1.5" can imply a "deficit" model of referring to second language students.

2 For in-depth discussion of Generation 1.5 issues, see Harklau et al. (1999), Roberge, Siegal, and Harklau (2008), and Goen et al. (2002).

3 For introductory overviews of SLA research that include discussion of individual (learner) differences, see Brown (2007a), Ellis (1997); Gass and Selinker (2008), Krashen (1982), Lightbown and Spada (2006), and Mitchell and Myles (2004).

4 We assume that none of our readers would consider *stealing* the magazine from the dentist's office, or—even more heinous—tearing the interesting article out of the magazine, leaving the mutilated remnants for future patients!

3 L2 Reading: Focus on the Text

1 See Birch (2007, Chapter 5) and Koda (2004, Chapters 3 and 5) for more detailed and technical discussions of cross-linguistic differences in writing systems and how they impact word-recognition processes.

2 See Koda (2004, Chapter 6) for an up-to-date research review on sentence-processing issues in L2 reading.

3 Websites such as those of Voice of America (VOA: www.voanews.com/english/portal. cfm) and National Public Radio (NPR: www.npr.org) offer both print and audio files of their texts at low cost or for free. These and others are excellent resources for L2 learners and their instructors.

4 It is worth noting that the Flesch RE score is 38.4 and the Flesch-Kincaid grade level is

15.2, both scores indicating that the text is quite difficult. In short, despite its being "short" and "designed for ESL instruction," its readability is problematic.

5   For further discussion of the use of word lists for reading and vocabulary instruction, see Chapter 8. Other useful sources include Coxhead (2006), Coxhead and Byrd (2007), Folse (2004), and Reid (2008).

4 Syllabus Design and Instructional Planning for the L2 Reading Course

1   Further objections to setting *a priori* instructional aims relate to their unfavorable association with behavioral psychology, in particular, the charge that explicit goals can trivialize classroom teaching by requiring teachers to emphasize narrow skill areas and strategies (Ferris & Hedgcock, 2005; Hillocks, 1995). Some critics further maintain that formalized aims can constrain teachers' freedom while perpetuating current (and potentially undesirable) practices (Benesch, 1996; Joseph, Bravmann, Windschitl, Mikel, & Green, 2000).

2   The authors readily admit that their own syllabi sometimes reflect this inclination!

3   As emphasized earlier in this chapter, research evidence contradicts the conventional belief that student readers (particularly low-proficiency learners) require easy or "simplified" texts (see Chapters 3 and 6). Citing numerous studies (e.g., Vigil, 1987; Young, 1993, 1999), Shrum and Glisan (2005) stressed that "the opposite is true." Novice L2 readers display significantly greater comprehension "on texts that are read in their unedited, authentic forms as opposed to versions simplified through lexical changes" (p. 171).

4   Examples include Pasternak and Wrangell (2007), Smith and Mare (2004), Wegman and Knezevic (2001), and Wegman, Knezevic, and Bernstein (2001), to name but a few.

5 Designing an Intensive Reading Lesson

1   An entire reading–writing teaching module developed by Roberta Ching of CSU Sacramento based on "Going for the Look" can also be found in the CSU Expository Reading and Writing Task Force (2008) publication.

2   It is not necessarily our position that top-down and bottom-up strategies *should* be relegated to specific stages of intensive reading. We have simply observed that, in practice, this is how these skills tend to be covered.

3   Some teachers are enthusiastic about student read-alouds as a means of making lessons more student-centered, engaging learners, and assessing reading ability. However, we caution that lengthy reading aloud by L2 students can be stressful for some readers and frustrating (as well as boring) for their classmates. We urge utilizing the read-aloud technique in moderation.

4   We would not suggest that teachers *should* de-emphasize writing in a reading course. Rather, we acknowledge that curricular realities sometimes lead teachers to do so.

6 Reading for Quantity: The Benefits and Challenges of Extensive Reading

1   See Smith (2004) for an articulate summary of the decades-long conflict.

2   For an up-to-date resource, see Krashen's website: http://www.sdkrashen.com/.

3   For reviews of research on reading–writing connections, see: Belcher and Hirvela (2001); Carson et al. (1990); Carson and Leki (1993); Elley and Mangubhai (1983); Ferris and Hedgcock (2005); Hirvela (2004); Hudson (2007); Janopolous (1986); Krashen (1984, 1985, 2004); Kucer (1985, 2001); Spack (2004).

4   It may be hypothetically "easier" for extensive reading activities to take place in elementary and lower secondary settings, but it is only fair to note that teachers in many

contexts are also constrained by the increased emphasis on state and federal standards, as well as frequent high-stakes standardized testing.

5   The 14-year-old daughter of one of the authors will only read a book not required for school if bribed to do so or if trapped for hours in a car or airplane—despite the fact that she is a more-than-competent reader and has been reared in an extremely print-rich environment where reading is highly valued and modeled by all members of her family except for her Labrador retriever.

6   The daughter of one of the authors provides a good case study here. She was educated in a K–6 Spanish Immersion program, completing the entire secondary Spanish program by the 10th grade. She is now in college and has enjoyed studying Spanish literature in classes. She is also an avid reader in English, her L1. She is well aware that her continued progress in the Spanish language will depend in a large part on her extensive reading in Spanish, and she has of her own volition and at her own expense collected a small library of pleasure reading materials in Spanish over the past several years. And yet, when she has spare time, she does not pick up one of her Spanish novels or a Spanish newspaper or read a Spanish-language website or blog. She knows it would be "good for her," she likes to read, she enjoys learning Spanish—still, reading Spanish is not as "pleasurable" or "relaxing" for her as reading in English.

7   One of the authors remembers being assigned to read Thomas Kuhn's *The Structure of Scientific Revolutions* in the very first quarter of the college freshman year and nearly drowning in terms and concepts such as *paradigm shift*—despite a well-established FVR habit!

8   For approaches to summary-writing as a tool in a university extensive-reading course, see Ferris and Hedgcock (2005), Hirvela (2004), and Robb (2001).

9   One of the authors remembers distinctly how page 28 of Mario Puzo's novel *The Godfather* (containing an explicit sex scene) was covertly passed around the sixth-grade classroom. Although we would not necessarily recommend R-rated reading material for underage students, this anecdote illustrates how peers can generate enthusiasm for reading materials!

7 Using Literary Texts in L2 Reading Instruction

1   Several book-length treatments of the topic of literature in L2 instruction are available. For in-depth resources providing practical teaching suggestions, see Bamford and Day (2003), Carter and Long (1991), Carter and McRae (1996), Collie and Slater (1987), Heath (1996), Hirvela (2004), Lazar (1993), Moon (2000), Paran (2006), Popp (2005), Rogers and Soter (1997), and Yancey (2004). For additional information, see Day and Bamford's (1998) book on extensive reading and Spack's (1998, 2006) reading–writing textbooks.

2   We reiterate the point we made in the preface to this volume: We do not believe that stand-alone reading courses that fail to incorporate a writing component are the most effective curricular option. However, we recognize that in many postsecondary ESL and EFL contexts, the separation of reading and writing into different skills and courses is conventional. Our discussion in this chapter and throughout this book acknowledges this reality.

3   An extended discussion of literary language and interpretation is beyond the scope of this book. Interested readers are encouraged to examine work by Widdowson (1975, 1992) for scholarly treatments. See Lazar (1993, 1999, 2003) for classroom applications. Additional sources include Moon (2000), Popp (2005), Rogers and Soter (1997), and Yancey (2004). For comprehensive treatments, see Cuddon (1991), Eagleton (1996), Holman and Harmon (1992), Rae (1998), and Roberts and Jacobs (2001). We

are aware that our discussion is quite elementary for those who have studied literature as undergraduate or graduate students. We provide this introductory material for the many L2 teachers who come from other academic backgrounds.

4 Because *nadsat* terms were created for the novel, there was no chance that the participants would have encountered them through prior exposure or instruction: No pretest was needed.

5 We are careful to specify that it is Ferris in this anecdote, as Hedgcock is actually highly proficient in French!

6 Sarton's piece, an essay, does not neatly fall into the literary categories outlined in this chapter, as Sarton was a poet who even included poetic language in the essay. Nevertheless, we believe the selection exhibits literary qualities that justify its inclusion in this discussion and in Figure 7.1.

7 See Lazar (1993, pp. 43–45) for a discussion of this issue, along with ideas for presenting the material to students.

8 We acknowledge that literary commentators do not consider Donne's passage to be a poem in the strictest sense. However, as it is often included in introductory anthologies on poetry, we add it here as well.

9 For intermediate-to-advanced students, we highly recommend Spack's (1998) second edition of *Guidelines*, which contains an excellent selection of accessible and appealing poems, clear suggestions for students on how to interpret and analyze them, and an outstanding poetry anthology assignment that has proven successful and popular with our students.

10 Collie and Slater (1987) discussed at length how to teach *Romeo and Juliet* in an ESL setting. Given the subject matter (star-crossed young lovers with interfering parents), this story might well appeal to student audiences and might thus be the one Shakespeare play worth considering. Even so, teachers must consider whether the time and effort required for students to read it is a good use of resources and meets course goals.

8 Vocabulary Learning and Teaching in L2 Reading Instruction

1 The relationship between receptive ("passive") and productive vocabulary knowledge has been controversial, as the terms are essentially arbitrary (Melka Teichroew, 1982). Reception and production can be seen as continuously related, but "this is by no means the only way of viewing the distinction" (Nation, 2001, p. 25). For Meara (1990), active and passive lexical knowledge come about by distinct associative means. In contrast, Corson (1995) proposed a continuous model, where passive vocabulary knowledge entails active vocabulary.

2 We consulted the *Oxford English Dictionary Online* for the lexical information presented in our lists (see Further Reading and Resources).

3 The *Oxford English Dictionary Online* reveals that the verb *google* is attested in early 20th-century texts as a back-formation from the noun *googly*, a cricket ball that "breaks from the off." The verb *google* describes how the cricket ball breaks and swerves like a *googly*, as in "That bowler can spin the ball and *google* it" (see Further Reading and Resources).

4 As a matter of fact, second language acquisition (SLA) has cast a spotlight on the essential nature of vocabulary learning in multiple domains of L2 learning and teaching. Meara (1995), for example, suggested that L2 instruction should concentrate from the very beginning on basic L2 vocabulary. Ellis (2002) argued that "if grammar teaching is to accord with how learners learn, then it should not be directed at beginners. Rather, it should await the time when learners have developed a sufficiently

varied lexis to provide a basis for the process of rule extraction." We should therefore postpone grammar instruction, "focusing initially on the development of vocabulary and the activation of the strategies for using lexis in context to make meaning and only later [drawing] learners' attention to the rule-governed nature of language" (p. 23).

5 An important meta-analysis of L1 vocabulary studies by Stahl and Fairbanks (1986) challenged the prevailing assumption that lexical knowledge was the single greatest contributor to L1 reading comprehension. Among the reasons for weak vocabulary-reading interactions cited by Stahl and Fairbanks were the overly simple definitions of word knowledge used by the researchers in their survey, as well as problematic definitions of reading improvement.

6 Carver (1997) described *rauding* as "the type of reading that is most typical; it is normal reading, ordinary reading, natural or simple reading." Rauding occurs when adults read texts that are "relatively easy . . . to comprehend" (pp. 5–6).

7 This finding is consistent with the outcomes of L1 studies (e.g., Nagy et al., 1987; Nagy et al., 1985; Schwanenflugel, Stahl, & McFalls, 1997) and comparable L2 investigations (e.g., Day, Omura, & Hiramatsu, 1991; Frantzen, 2003; Fraser, 1999; Paribakht & Wesche, 1999; Pitts, White, & Krashen, 1989; Pulido, 2007; Saragi, Nation, & Meister, 1978).

8 Excellent resources containing word frequency lists and links to online data banks, text corpora, and concordancing tools include Coxhead (2006), McEnery, Xiao, and Tono (2006), O'Keeffe et al. (2007), Sinclair (2003).

9 We recognize that such substitutions can "simplify" and de-authenticate texts, contradicting our preference for leaving authentic materials intact (see Chapters 2 and 4).

9 Classroom L2 Reading Assessment

1 Solutions: 1. B 2. D 3. C 4. D 5. A.

2 TOEFLiBT = *Test of English as a Foreign Language-Internet-Based Test*; TOEIC = *Test of English for International Communication*; IELTS = *International English Language Testing System.*

3 We encourage readers to consult Alderson's (2000) comprehensive volume on L2 reading assessment. We likewise commend the sources on language assessment, (L1) literacy assessment, and educational measurement included in Further Reading and Resources.

4 Alderson (2000, Chapter 9) presents a thorough survey of process-oriented approaches to assessing L2 reading proficiency and achievement. Further sources include Caldwell (2008), Koda (2004), and Urquhart and Weir (1998).

5 Further Reading and Resources in Chapters 1 and 4 list references and links to scales and standards.

6 See Alderson (2000) for elements to include in specifications for high-stakes measures of L2 reading comprehension and efficiency. General sources on language test specifications can be found in Bachman and Palmer (1996), Brown (2004), and Hughes (2003). Consult the TOEFLiBT website for links to model test specifications for TOEFLiBT reading subtests (see Further Reading and Resources).

7 Consider your experience completing the quizlet at the opening of this chapter.

8 WebCT was merged with Blackboard in early 2007.

9 *Primary-* and *multiple-trait* scoring rubrics represent a third category. Most often used in writing assessment, primary- and multiple-trait scales specify traits or characteristics unique to specific genres and assignments (Ferris & Hedgcock, 2005). *Genre-* and *task-specific* rubrics, described in this section, share similar purposes and features.

Author Index

Subject Index

Lightning Source UK Ltd.
Milton Keynes UK
UKOW020750081211

183417UK00011B/54/P